95. 9.

# CONTEMPORARY COMMUNICATION
# RESEARCH METHODS

# CONTEMPORARY COMMUNICATION RESEARCH METHODS

MARY JOHN SMITH

Wadsworth Publishing Company
Belmont, California
A Division of Wadsworth, Inc.

Communications Editor: **Kris Clerkin**
Editorial Assistant: **Melissa Harris**
Production Editor: **Lisa Danchi**
Print Buyer: **Barbara Britton**
Cover and Interior Designer: **Vargas / Williams / Design**
Copy Editor: **Brenda Griffing**
Compositor: **G & S Typesetters, Inc.**

Printed in the United States of America   34
    3  4  5  6  7  8  9  10—92  91  90

Library of Congress Cataloging-in-Publication Data

Smith, Mary John.
    Contemporary communication research methods.

    Bibliography: p.
    Includes indexes.
    1. Communication—Methodology.  2. Communication—
Research.  I. Title.
P91.S55   1988        001.51′01′8        87-16047
ISBN 0-534-08610-1

For the gingerbread girl

# CONTENTS

# PREFACE

In recent decades, communication research methods have changed remarkably, paralleling our changing views of the nature of communication itself. Moving from an almost exclusive reliance on the experimental paradigm in the 1950s and 1960s, contemporary researchers now employ a rich and varied assortment of methods for unraveling the peculiarities of human communication. Thus, contemporary communication research is characterized by a shift from a monistic to a pluralistic methodology and by the development of distinctively communicative research methods rather than a continued use of general social scientific designs.

*Contemporary Communication Research Methods* reflects this dual methodological movement, emphasizing both "contemporary" and "communication" methods of scholarly inquiry. Given this focus, I have organized the book around three research directions that, taken together, capture the diversity as well as the disciplinary sensitivity of contemporary communication research. First, the materials in the book evidence a burgeoning trend toward naturalistic studies. This trend recognizes communication as an everyday activity enabling people to conduct their affairs and fashion their futures by interacting with others. Although laboratory research is amply treated, I present it as one among many alternatives available to contemporary researchers.

Second, the book reflects an increasing use of research methods whose principal function is the analysis of human communication processes—what people say to one another, how they go about saying it, and what they "do to" each other when exchanging messages. This communication orientation contrasts with more general methodologies that dominated pre-1970s research. Such methods, borrowed from allied disciplines like psychology and sociology, often treated people's individual and shared meanings not as the end product of research but as starting points for deriving conclusions about related antecedents and consequences. The current emphasis on communication processes supports the view that the communication discipline's proper research domain is the meanings and actions inherent in human talk.

Third and finally, this book chronicles the growing popularity of "hybrid" communication methodologies, which blend traditional scientific empiricism with analytical and critical methods derived from the arts and humanities. This union of science and humanism recognizes the essentially "human" nature of communication, yet it injects scientific rigor into the study of meaningful discourse. Moreover, the trend reflects an emerging disciplinary consensus that a pluralistic approach is required to capture the richness and diversity of human communication.

Given this three-part philosophical grounding, the book is partitioned into four parts. In Part I, I devote five chapters to the conceptual foundations of contemporary communication research. Chapter 1 introduces scientific inquiry as a way of knowing, then Chapters 2 and 3 explore basic conceptual and operational issues in communication research. In Chapter 4, I discuss methods of collecting and measuring communication data, and Chapter 5 details the theory and practice of sampling. Part II describes in three chapters the nature of statistical inquiry. Chapter 6, coauthored with mathematician Diane M. Spresser, introduces basic statistical principles and concepts. Chapter 7 treats the statistical analysis of differences and Chapter 8 examines the statistical analysis of relationships. Throughout Part II, I emphasize the logic of statistical inference, supplying the knowledge that students require for understanding computer-assisted numerical analysis.

Part III devotes five chapters to contemporary research designs, including traditional methods as well as more contemporaneous approaches. After reviewing the general nature of research designs in Chapter 9, I discuss experimental research in Chapter 10 and describe survey methods in Chapter 11. Chapter 12 details the theory and practice of conversational analysis, and in Chapter 13, I discuss methods of analyzing narrative discourse, among them content analysis and rhetorical criticism. Finally, Part IV chronicles in two chapters several contemporary issues in communication research. Chapter 14 describes ethical and pragmatic constraints on the research process, and in Chapter 15, I discuss contemporary conceptual directions in the communication discipline. My aim in the last chapter is to evaluate current research practices in the context of the intellectual milieu that gave rise to them. The appendices contain instructions for designing a prospectus and guidelines for writing a research report, as well as the usual statistical tables.

The book features four important teaching and learning aids. First, each chapter is followed by a summary of main points that recaps the major ideas developed in the chapter. Second, I present a set of task-oriented review exercises at the end of each chapter, asking students to "do things" with the chapter's materials. Certain exercises call for library research, some require numerical computations and instrument construction, and others ask students to ponder hypothetical problems illustrating important conceptual issues. Although the exercises may be solved individually, many lend themselves nicely to small study group projects. The final two instructional aids appear at the book's conclusion. A glossary of terms defines each significant concept the book addresses, and all mathematical and statistical conventions are presented in a glossary of symbols.

As the content overview indicates, this book is designed for a first course in communication research and therefore assumes no prior knowledge of research methods or statistical reasoning. Despite their introductory nature, the materials covered in the book are intellectually robust, comprehensive, and reflective of research methods found in the contemporary communication literature.

To the people who contributed to the book's development, I extend my thanks: To Bill Donaghy, my department chair, and to the faculty and staff at the University of Wyoming, who encouraged me to do my work; to Sam Riccillo, who gave a sense of reality to my Western odyssey; to the Wyoming graduate students—Shawn, Susan, Kileen, Steve, Theresa, Becky, Sue, Pat, and all the rest—who made my sojourn there a rewarding experience; to Anne, who still believed in me; to Annabel, who gave continuity to my comings and goings; to my mother, whose courage made me strong; to Judy, whose cheerfulness sustained me; and to Ginger and T. J., whose constancy and love kept the mean-spirited demons at bay. They all taught me much and none of them ever knew it. I owe a considerable debt to Terrance Albrecht, Noreen Carrocci, Glen Clatterbuck, Anne Gabbard-Alley, Annabel Hagood, Sally Jackson, Dennis Klinzing, Gerald Miller, and Peter Monge for reviewing all or part of this manuscript. Their insights influenced substantially my thinking about contemporary communication research, and I appreciate their wise counsel. R. J. Domangue, statistician and assistant professor of mathematics at James Madison University, reviewed the final manuscript for purposes of ensuring both the conceptual and computational correctness of all quantitative materials, and I thank him for this valuable contribution. I am especially indebted to Diane Spresser, professor and head of the Department of Mathematics and Computer Science at James Madison University, for her assistance with this book. Diane collaborated in the writing of Chapter 6 and served as a statistical consultant for the balance of the manuscript. Her analytical precision and creative temperament—in short, her point of view—did much to shape the book's ultimate form. Finally, I am grateful to Kris Clerkin of Wadsworth Publishing Company for her thoughtful advice, generous support, and unfailing belief in the worth of this project. It was good to have her on my side.

MJS
Charlottesville, Virginia

<br />

# PART

# I

# CONCEPTUAL FOUNDATIONS OF CONTEMPORARY COMMUNICATION RESEARCH

<br />

CHAPTER 1
CONTEMPORARY SCIENTIFIC INQUIRY

CHAPTER 2
CONCEPTUALIZING RESEARCH

CHAPTER 3
OPERATIONALIZING RESEARCH

CHAPTER 4
COLLECTING AND MEASURING DATA

CHAPTER 5
SAMPLING METHODS

<br />

<br />

<br />

1

discourse
演讲. 讲话.

# CHAPTER 1

# CONTEMPORARY SCIENTIFIC INQUIRY

This chapter introduces the scientific method of studying human communication. A three-stage model of scientific inquiry is described. At the first stage, the researcher observes patterns of communication, including events like ordinary conversations, public discourse, and mass communication. The second stage involves constructing a theoretical explanation for one's observations. During the final phase, the researcher verifies the reasonableness of the explanation generated during the second stage.

# CHAPTER OUTLINE

During the early twentieth century, scholars regarded human speech as a passive vehicle for transferring thoughts about objects and ideas. From this view, utterances like "I feel depressed" and "You look great today" presumably did nothing but convey "pictures" describing the self and other people.[1] This early perspective ignored the possibility that such statements might be implicit requests for sympathy or attempts to establish friendly relationships.

In the context of this "picture" theory, the social anthropologist Bronislaw Malinowski began studying the conversations of primitive tribes in Melanesia.[2] He observed that the primitive peoples' communication involved three different topics. They discussed tasks, like food gathering, and magic, which was used to ward off evil spirits and supplicate the gods. Oddly, the third type of communication seemed to serve no descriptive purpose. The islanders simply sat around and chatted about nothing in particular, a variety of talk Malinowski called "phatic communion." These findings were puzzling because they contradicted the generally accepted view that communication merely describes objects and ideas. Malinowski explained his findings with a revolutionary new action theory, arguing that human communication is not primarily descriptive; rather, it is a functional tool that people use to create the social reality where they live and work.

Within this novel theoretical framework, phatic communication was understandable, because it created a sense of community among the Melanesian peoples. Likewise, comments that indirectly request others' sympathy or solicit their friendship aim to create positive self concepts and establish satisfying relationships. Replacement of the old "communication as passive description" theory with a "communication as creative action" explanation was a significant advancement in knowledge about human communication.[3]

Malinowski's systematic observations and rational explanations of primitive conversation illustrate well the scientific study of communication. In this chapter, I explore contemporary science as a method of understanding human communication. Next, I examine the basic stages of communication inquiry and describe the uses of theory. The chapter concludes with an illustration of the communication scholar at work, systematically observing and theorizing about human communication.

## THE NATURE OF SCIENTIFIC INQUIRY

Humans are an inquisitive lot, continually engaged in a quest to know themselves and the world around them. To survive emotionally and physically, we must know ourselves and our surroundings. Such knowledge enables us to understand our place in the world, to predict others' reactions to us, and to make decisions about future actions. This desire for predictability in life is a pervasive human motivation.[4] People are able to function effectively in their social world, moving confidently from one day to the next because they "know" what to expect from each new tomorrow.

Within Western culture, scientific inquiry is a dominant way of obtaining reliable knowledge about the self and about the environment, including the individual's communicative interactions with others. The relationship between science and the acquisition of knowledge is fundamental; indeed, the word "science" is derived from the Latin root *scire*, meaning "to know" or "to learn."[5] For the communication scientist, scientific inquiry is directed toward learning about the nature, forms, and functions of human talk. In learning about communication, we come to know how we create and maintain our world, including our self-identities and our relationships with others.

Scientists generate knowledge about human

**6**

PART I
Conceptual
Foundations of
Contemporary
Communica-
tion Research

communication by systematically observing communicative acts and rationally speculating about what they observe. By applying the reasoning capacities of the human mind to observations, we are able to discern relationships among communicative acts and to explain the relationships. Rational observation enabled Malinowski to discover the three-part structure of Melanesian communication, to determine the relationship between primitive talk and its social functions, and to explain tribal conversation in terms of a creative action theory.

Two tools are required for conducting scientific inquiry: the human senses, permitting observation of the empirical world, and the human mind, allowing rational speculation about what we observe. Thus, science is often called a *logical-empirical* system of knowing. Following this characterization, **scientific inquiry** may be defined as a systematic investigation of the relationships among and explanations for the empirical phenomena with which a discipline is concerned.

Scientific inquiry in communication aims to (1) observe and describe the structure of communication, (2) explain the observed structure, and (3) verify the reasonableness of explanations. To accomplish these objectives, the communication scholar must determine what kinds of communication exist in the empirical world, how different varieties of communication are related, and why the relationships are structured as they are. An ultimate objective of science is to construct reliable explanations for related communication patterns.

## Assumptions of Science

A scientific approach to explaining the world is based on three fundamental assumptions. First, scientists assume that all objects of scholarly inquiry are directly or indirectly *observable*. Because scientific phenomena have "empirical referents,"[6] their existence can be either observed or inferred from observation. For example, we can investigate conversational episodes such as verbal conflict or study the content of television entertainment programs because we can directly observe both. Likewise, scientists can explore a communicator's mental states, including reasons for communicating, because these states are manifested indirectly in observable behavior, including self-descriptions of motivations.

Second, the scientific method assumes that phenomena in the empirical world are patterned and *orderly*, not random and chaotic. Whereas people often tolerate the appearance of disorder in their everyday interactions, scientists regard communication as something more than a string of disconnected noises. Science assumes that human talk always means something. It is a coherent system of interrelated utterances directed toward the achievement of important personal and social goals.

Third and finally, science assumes that empirical phenomena can be explained by referring to other natural *antecedent* phenomena. This assumption entails two corollary beliefs. First, scientists assume that all empirical phenomena are explainable. Science abhors the "mystification of residuals,"[7] a commonsense tendency to dismiss particularly puzzling events as being beyond the realm of comprehension. Second, science rejects metaphysical or "other-worldly" explanations, assuming that natural phenomena can be explained by referring to other natural phenomena. Thus, scientists may explain speech acts such as insults or compliments by pointing to a communicator's reasons for making the statements. Likewise, we might account for conditions like communication anxiety by referring to factors in a person's history that led to a fear of speaking. In short, science admits no mysteries that cannot be explained ultimately by rational speculation and creative observation.

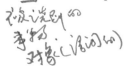

## Distinguishing Features of Science

Science is distinguished from other ways of knowing by the careful methods scientists use to study the world. Five of these features are especially pertinent.

1. *Science is systematic*. Scientists approach the task of observing and explaining the world in a methodical fashion. Scientific inquiry proceeds through two systematic phases called discovery and justification.[8] During **discovery**, scientists derive explanations for observed patterns of behavior. They verify these explanations in the **justification** stage, using stringent criteria agreed upon by members of the scholarly community.

2. *Science is rational*, meaning that scientists employ rigorous rules of logic both in discovering and verifying explanations. Two modes of reasoning are used extensively in science: **induction** and **deduction**.[9] Inductive reasoning begins with observations of particular instances of some phenomenon and proceeds to a generalized conclusion about the *probable* properties of the phenomenon. By contrast, deductive logic begins with a general premise assumed to be true and derives *certain* conclusions about particular instances falling within the general premise.[10] Inductive reasoning is used extensively during the discovery phase of inquiry, whereas deduction predominates when scientists verify general explanations.

3. *Science is self-correcting*. Scientists often begin research by observing empirical data. They then draw general conclusions about the nature of observed phenomena and finally, they return to observations to test the general conclusions. Conclusions are corrected based on the goodness-of-fit between them and empirical data. Scientific inquiry, which turns back upon itself over and over again in a process that matches observed phenomena with general explanations for observations, is inherently self-correcting.

This self-correcting quality gives science a mechanism for altering knowledge in the face of changing circumstances. Science continually generates new ideas that threaten old ways of believing and behaving. For this reason, the world of science can be uncomfortable for "true believers" who "know" all there is to know about the world. However, science is an ideal environment for individuals who seek to challenge old systems of knowing and replace them with new and better approaches to human understanding.

4. *Science is self-reflexive*, meaning that preconceptions influence what scientists observe, how they interpret what they observe, and the explanations they construct for observations. To illustrate, suppose I believe that television advertisements portray women in a demeaning and sexist manner, but you disagree, believing instead that commercials present a favorable image of women. If we both observe the same advertisements, I am more likely than you to "see" examples of sexism because we have approached the observation task with radically different expectations. Because a researcher's attitudes are involved in observation, science relies on the scholarly community's collective judgment to generate knowledge that many different people agree reflects the nature of the world. Thus, "truth" in science is an *intersubjective* rather than an objective phenomenon. When a group of scholars, using the systematic, rational, and self-correcting methods of science, "agree that something exists, we treat the thing as though it had objective existence."[11]

5. *Science is creative*.[12] At first blush, the claim that science is a creative activity seems internally contradictory. Further reflection sug-

FIGURE 1.1
A MODEL OF COMMUNICATION INQUIRY

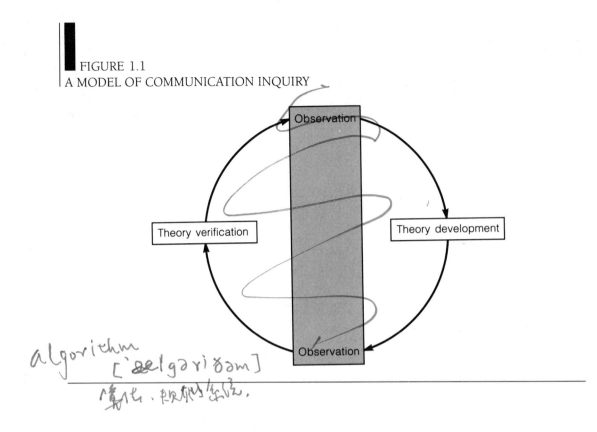

algorithm
[ˈælɡərɪðəm]
变化，程序。

gests this is not the case at all. The scientist is not a camera passively snapping photographs of the world; rather, human imagination is involved in the process of inquiry. Indeed, scientific creativity enables researchers to discover things that were "unseeable" until the time of discovery. For example, physicists described quarks, a subatomic glue holding the universe together, long before instruments were available to permit the observation of these particles. Likewise, Einstein's creative genius led him to conclude that mass is "frozen" energy and energy is "fluid" mass 20 years before the equation $E = Mc^2$ was empirically verified. Finally, it took more than a quarter-century to confirm Malinowski's visionary conception of communication as "creative action."

## A THREE-STAGE MODEL OF COMMUNICATION INQUIRY

Three highly interrelated processes are involved in the quest for scientific knowledge about human communication: observing and describing communication phenomena, developing theoretical explanations for observed phenomena, and verifying the reasonableness of theoretical formulations. As Figure 1.1 indicates, communication inquiry is an algorithmic process, involving recurring movements through the observational and theoretical stages of research. Not only do observations suggest new theories and modifications in old ones, but our theories also structure observations, directing us to observe certain things and shaping our perceptions of what we observe. Communication inquiry, then, is not a linear process that begins with observation and ends

8

with verification. Rather, communication researchers move in a spiraling fashion through the three stages of inquiry, variously pitting observation against theory, and vice versa. This recurring process gives communication inquiry the self-correcting quality that characterizes science itself.

## Stage I: Observing Communication Phenomena

During the observational stage of inquiry, the researcher's task is *to discover the underlying structure of meanings and actions inherent in human communication processes.* Unlike the physical scientist who studies a universe without preexisting meaning, the communication researcher faces a world of communicative acts that already have meaning for the people living in that world. Austin characterized the meaningful world of communication as a body of "institutional facts."[13] Unlike "brute facts," which exist independent of the meanings we assign to them, institutional facts exist only because communicators agree that they exist.

Thus, the utterance "You are a bastard" is an "insult" to those who have agreed on such a meaning. However, Pearce reported that among certain urban youths, statements disparaging another's parentage are not regarded as insults at all, but rather they count as one-upmanship in the street game called "playing the dozens."[14] Because the empirical "facts" of communication are created by people's shared meanings, the researcher must discover the meanings communicators have in mind when they talk with others in particular contexts.

To study communicative meanings and actions, researchers must perform three observational tasks. They must decide what domain of communication to observe, how to interpret observations, and how interpreted observations are related.

## Specifying the observational domain

Human communication represents an "ongoing stream of behavior," both verbal and nonverbal, emanating from the self and others in face-to-face and mass media settings.[15] To conduct meaningful observation, the researcher must select certain units for study from this complex stream. A researcher's practical and conceptual interests will determine the slice of communicative life that he or she selects for observation. Thus, if I am especially interested in the rules governing ordinary conversations, or alternately, in theories explaining the effects of televised soap operas, my observational domain is prestructured by these scholarly concerns. Such interests direct researchers to observe certain aspects of communication and ignore others.

## Selecting interpretive schemes

Once researchers have settled on an observational domain, they must decide how to interpret observations. The process of assigning meaning to observed events is complicated by two factors. First, we have seen that communication behaviors are institutional facts; they have meanings already assigned by communicators themselves. Second, a researcher's interpretations of others' meanings are, in Hanson's words, "inherently theory-laden."[16] Our beliefs and preferred theories profoundly affect what we "see" when we observe human communication.

To illustrate how laden with theory is observation, suppose I advocate a "picture" theory of communication, believing that human talk describes objects and ideas. However, you support the creative action theory, holding that words are actions that people "do to" and "with" one another. Now suppose that we hear a physician tell a patient, "The pathologist's report indicates that your disease is fatal." Although each of us has received the same aural stimulus, we likely will "hear" remarkably dif-

**10**

PART I
Conceptual
Foundations of
Contemporary
Communica-
tion Research

ferent things. I will hear only a description of an illness, but you will hear a death sentence, creating hopelessness in a previously vital human being. Communicative events, then, are subjectively perceived through the unique prism of each researcher's preconceptions. They are not objective "facts" untouched by human perception.

Since communicators pre-create their own meanings for communication events and researchers then recreate meanings for the same events, interpretation is a second-order creative activity. The researcher's aim is to assign meanings to utterances that match as closely as possible the meanings of communicators themselves. To accomplish this task, researchers often follow the empathic tradition of the German sociologist-economist Max Weber, placing themselves in the position of the object of their inquiry and thereby gaining an understanding of the communicator's view of reality.[17] According to the rule of **intersubjectivity**, the "facts" a researcher ultimately assembles are interpretations that are generally agreed upon by the scholarly community.

### Determining relationships

During the final stage of observation, researchers must determine the relationships that exist among interpreted communicative acts and utterances. Utterances are related to one another and collectively they are related to the goals communicators wish to achieve by talking with others. The researcher's task is to discover this underlying structure of meanings and actions.

Discovering communicative structures requires considerable analytical and creative thought, since relationships are not readily apparent. People do not consciously organize their talk into patterns, noting a beginning, an end, and a goal-state toward which their conversation is moving. The Melanesian islanders observed by Malinowski did not deliberately organize their talk into a three-part structure relating to work, magic, and community. Likewise, contemporary communicators do not bundle their communicative behaviors into orderly packages ready to present to the first scientist who wanders by.

The researcher's mission is to construct a descriptive framework that "fits" observed sequences of human communication. Descriptive frameworks are often called **models**, that is, verbal or visual representations of the structural or functional properties of some object or process.[18] Models give order and meaning to observed communication patterns. Moreover, they serve as sources of information for developing theoretical explanations and as data bases for testing new theories.

## Stage II: Discovering Theoretical Explanations

A primary aim of science is to discover explanations for observed phenomena, an activity performed during the second stage of our three-part model. Although observational models describe what exists and how existing phenomena are related, they do not explain why observations take the form they do. To explain communication, the researcher must move from description to a theoretical analysis, seeking to develop theories that offer satisfactory answers to the question "Why?" Thus, a researcher's aim in the discovery phase is *to generate theoretical explanations for observed patterns of human communication*.

To illustrate a theoretical explanation, suppose we observe, as many researchers have, that conversations between physicians and their patients are often one-sided. Many physicians exhibit authoritarian communication styles, controlling topic selection and ignoring patients' questions and comments.[19] A researcher might theorize that this pattern is a function of the greater expertise of medical doctors relative to patients. Yet the researcher could explain the same observations with a personality theory, arguing that individuals who choose a socially prestigious medical career have high control needs and therefore wish to dominate others. Notice that both formulations could be used to explain the same doctor-patient communication pattern, indicating that alternative theories can account for any one phenomenon. The most plausible explanation is determined in the course of justification, the third stage of inquiry where competing theories are tested against observational data.

To successfully construct theoretical explanations, the researcher must understand the nature of theory, the available forms of theoretical explanation, and the logic underlying theory discovery.

## The nature of theory

Theories are generalizations that explain persistent patterns of, for example, communication behaviors. Whereas many explanations are theoretical, the term "theory" typically is reserved for a well-established explanation and "theoretical hypothesis" is used to signify an explanation lacking overwhelming confirmation. A **theory** may be defined formally as a set of statements specifying an explanatory relationship between two or more classes of communication phenomena.

Structurally, most theories have three components: a *generative force* or motivating reason, a pattern of communication *effects*, and *boundary conditions* stipulating how and under what circumstances the generative force is likely to explain its effects. Thus, a communication theory often takes the following form: If $X$ (generative force), then probably $Y$ (effects), under conditions $Z_1, \ldots, Z_n$ (boundary conditions). Placed in this form, a theory discussed earlier is: Physicians' power needs (generative force) explain authoritarian communication styles (effects) when the people with whom they communicate occupy a low-status role (that is, the role of "patient" regardless of how well educated or otherwise important they may be) (boundary condition).

Because theories attempt to explain communication phenomena, they allow us to predict the recurrence of communication patterns and to exercise some control over them. Suppose, for example, I know that certain adult emotional disturbances are the result of dysfunctional family communication during childhood. Given this explanatory relationship, I can predict, upon observing dysfunctional family communication, its likely emotional consequences. Moreover, I can take steps to break dysfunctional sequences, thereby controlling the likelihood of future disturbances.

## Forms of explanation: Causes and reasons

When researchers seek to generate communication theories, they usually are searching for generative forces that explain a pattern of effects. Two kinds of generative forces are said to explain human communication: causes and reasons. A **cause** is an antecedent condition that produces a consequent effect over which communicators have no control. For example, a speech impediment can cause nonfluent communication patterns, just as hearing deficits or language deficiencies can lead to disjointed, often incoherent conversations. A theory that accounts for communication patterns by referring to uncontrollable antecedents employs **causal explanation** and is called a **law** of communication.[20] (Chapter 15 presents an elaborated discussion of communication laws.)

**Reasons**, the second class of generative forces, refer to the preexisting goals, needs, and desires of a communicator that explain patterns of communication. A person's need for dominance may account for authoritarian communication patterns, just as an employee's desire to impress a supervisor often explains a polite and

Conjecture n. 推测. 猜想. 假设.

12

PART I
Conceptual
Foundations of
Contemporary
Communica-
tion Research

cooperative conversational approach. When we explain a person's behavior by referring to subjective reasons for acting, we are employing **teleological explanation**. Teleological explanation implies that communication behaviors are freely performed for reasons, not forced by causes beyond people's control. A theory that explains communication behavior by linking it with human intentions, purposes, or goals is called a communication **rule**.[21] (Rules are described more fully in Chapters 12 and 15.)

## The logic of discovering theories

The way a scientist goes about generating theories has long been a subject of controversy. There are two dominant approaches to theory construction, each employing a unique logic: the **data-to-theory** perspective and the **theory-to-data** method. Related to our model of scientific inquiry, depicted earlier in Figure 1.1, the data-to-theory approach begins with observation and proceeds to theory development. By contrast, a theory-to-data perspective focuses initially on developing an explanatory theory, which is then tested against observational data.

*Data-to-theory: An inductive approach.* The data-to-theory perspective assumes that explanations are derived principally from empirical data, requiring minimal rational speculation or creative imagination. Researchers following this tradition carefully observe patterns of verbal and nonverbal communication, noting regularities as well as generative forces that appear to explain the regularities. To the extent possible, researchers suspend their conceptual biases, allowing explanations to emerge from observations. The logic of data-to-theory discovery is inductive.

The data-to-theory approach is sometimes used in the analysis of people's everyday conversations. Researchers gather transcripts of ordinary discourse and draw theoretical conclusions about the rules of talk that seem to explain observed communication patterns. For such researchers, theory development is tied firmly to observational data that serve both as a source for discovering theory and as an information base for theory verification.

*Theory-to-data: A deductive approach.* The theory-to-data perspective begins with the development of a tentative theory, which is then tested against observational data. The logic of such theory construction is deductive. Thus, for example, a mass communication researcher might speculate that people's economic status affects their choice of media news sources, with wealthier persons relying more on print and less well-to-do individuals preferring television. This tentative theory could be tested by observing the actual news-seeking behaviors of selected groups of upper-, middle-, and lower-income persons.

Whereas data-to-theory researchers are restricted to explanations arising from observable data, the theory-to-data researcher is free to generate explanations from any source of inspiration. Theory-to-data explanations can range from strictly data-based conclusions to explanations Albert Einstein called "free creations of the mind."[22] Some philosophers and scientists argue that all good theories are "conjectures" or "self-made instruments of thought."[23] Einstein agreed when he wrote of his dissatisfaction with "the now fashionable . . . tendency of clinging to what is observable," insisting instead that a worthwhile theory "cannot be fabricated out of the results of observation, but . . . can only be invented."[24]

A theory-to-data discovery process, then, is indifferent to the source of theoretical explanations, whether data-based or purely intuitive. The approach requires only that theories be capable of explaining the empirical phenomena they purport to explain. Whereas observation serves both as the source and the test of data-to-theory explanations, observational data test but do not necessarily give rise to theory-to-data explanations.

*Relative merits of the two approaches.* Both approaches have advantages and drawbacks. Data-to-theory researchers seek to suspend preconceptions about the nature of observed phenomena. This practice reduces the probability that, in discovery, we will tend to "create" what we expect to find in particular settings, thus setting up a self-fulfilling prophecy. However, data-to-theory explanations are limited to phenomena that can be observed with current measuring instruments, presenting disadvantages compared with the theory-to-data approach.

Restricting scholarly inquiry to what we can directly measure places severe limits on the communication behaviors amenable to explanation. Important communication phenomena that are not directly measurable include mental constructs like "meaning" and inferences about the logical, social, and historical implications of human discourse, including ordinary conversations, public rhetoric, and mass communication. In forsaking such phenomena, we abandon many concepts lying at the heart of communication processes. Moreover, we relinquish the uniquely human ability to imagine, to infer the existence of things not yet "seeable" with available measuring instruments.

# Stage III: Verifying Theoretical Explanations

Following the algorithmic model of scientific inquiry, the verification process brings us back full circle to our starting base: observations in the empirical world. During the justification stage of inquiry, the researcher's task is *to verify the theoretical explanations formulated during discovery.* Whether theories are synthesized from data or generated through creative imagination, they must be tested against observations to determine their adequacy.

We may test the adequacy of a single explanation for some phenomenon, or alternately, assess the relative merits of several theoretical accounts of the same phenomenon. Because the observations used to verify theories represent researchers' interpretations, we rely heavily on the rule of intersubjectivity when testing theoretical explanations. Like all aspects of inquiry, verification is a collective activity of a scholarly community. The process entails testing predictions derived from theories and evaluating theories according to criteria agreed upon by the community of scholars.

## Testing theoretical predictions

Researchers verify theories by empirically testing predictions derived from them. Predictions are expectations of consequences that can be observed if the theory that generated them is a valid explanation. To illustrate the verification process, consider Leon Festinger's well-known theory of cognitive dissonance.[25] The theory holds that inconsistency among people's beliefs or cognitions produces an uncomfortable state called dissonance. Dissonance, in turn, prompts individuals to reorganize their beliefs to restore consistency. A principal prediction derived from this theory is that expressing an opinion contrary to one's beliefs will produce discomfort, prompting a change in belief toward the counterattitudinal opinion.

Festinger and Carlsmith tested this prediction in an early experiment requiring participants to perform an extremely boring task. After the task was finished, the experimenters asked some of the participants to falsely tell a group of people waiting to take part in the study that the task was very enjoyable, whereas the other participants were not asked to lie. Consistent with the dissonance prediction, the group that lied to others actually came to believe that the task was quite interesting, but the honest group continued to view the task as exceedingly dull.[26]

Over the years, researchers have proposed numerous alternative theories to explain people's tendency to believe their counterattitudinal statements. One alternative expla-

**14**

PART I
Conceptual
Foundations of
Contemporary
Communica-
tion Research

nation, the impression-management theory, argues that people change their beliefs toward overt statements, not because of internal dissonance, but because they desire to present a consistent public image.[27] To test the relative merits of the two theories, Tedeschi and his colleagues induced one group of people to lie to others in a public setting, whereas other people were asked to lie anonymously. The researchers reasoned that if internal discomfort were responsible for opinion change, the participants in both the public and anonymous conditions would change their attitudes in the direction of their overt lies. However, if the desire to "appear" consistent were the motivating force, only the persons who lied publicly would alter their opinions. Results supported impression-management theory, since only public liars changed beliefs to conform with their false statements.[28]

As these studies illustrate, the ultimate test of a theory is the goodness-of-fit between observed behaviors and the explanations proposed for them. Moreover, the studies indicate that theories usually cannot be tested directly, but researchers must test predictions derived from them.

## Criteria for evaluating theories

Scholars have devised several criteria for testing the adequacy of theoretical explanations. Each criterion bears either directly or indirectly on the theory-data linkage. Thus, the researcher should routinely apply the standards when assessing one or more explanations. Six of these criteria are especially pertinent.[29]

1. *Validity*. The acid test of any theory, *empirical validity*, addresses the question, Is the proposed explanation consistent with the observed "facts" the theory purports to explain? In our discussion of counterattitudinal advocacy, we saw that impression-management theory appeared to fit the observed consequences of deception, whereas dissonance theory failed the validity test. A scholarly community ultimately discards any theory that consistently fails to explain observable patterns of behavior.

2. *Predictability*. The predictability criterion raises the question, Does a theory's generative force *regularly* explain its specified effects? If a generative force only occasionally relates to pertinent effects, the theory in question is an unreliable predictor of communicative behaviors.

3. *Precision*. This criterion asks if the basic components of a theory and the statements linking the components together are clearly and precisely defined. Without clear definitions of key theoretical concepts and their presumed relations, one cannot deduce unambiguous predictions to test against observations. Some early rules theories of communication suffered from conceptual fuzziness, impeding their development as explanations. For example, in a survey of pre-1970s teleological theories, Ganz found 11 different conceptual definitions of a "rule."[30] If theories are to yield verifiable predictions, their conceptual framework must be clear and precise.

4. *Consistency*. The consistency standard addresses the question, Are the components of the theory, including their meanings and implications, congruent with one another? Inconsistent concepts within a single theory lead to divergent, often contradictory, predictions and render a theory untestable against empirical data.

5. *Scope*. The scope criterion asks whether the domain addressed by the theory is sufficiently general. A theoretical domain is the group of communication behaviors to be explained. The domain should be broad enough to provide reliable explanations for some well-defined class of communication phenomena. For example, a theory might explain the effects of several newspaper editorials on readers' attitudes toward selected

political issues; alternately, it might assess the general impact of television on American cultural norms. Whether a theorist chooses to address a relatively small class of phenomena (selected political attitudes) or a very large class (American cultural norms), explanations should be complete within the specified domain.

6. *Utility*. The utility criterion raises issues such as: Does the theory explain previously inexplicable communication phenomena? Does it increase our practical understanding of human communication, adding new insights? Does the theory have heuristic value—that is, does it have the capacity to stimulate further research and theorizing on the issue it addresses?

All these questions point to the conclusion that a theory worth anything is *useful*; it should make a "difference" in our understanding of human communication. If a theory meets all the criteria previously discussed, yet fails the utility test, it is little more than an interesting museum piece. A worthwhile theory is, above all, a practical entity that can point the way toward a richer understanding of communication among humans.

# THE COMMUNICATION RESEARCHER AT WORK: AN APPLICATION OF THE THREE-STAGE MODEL

I shall summarize our discussion of scientific inquiry by reviewing a study that illustrates the three-stage model of communication research.[31] In the early 1980s, Alan Sillars set out to explore patterns of verbal conflict and conflict resolution among college roommates living in dormitories. He aimed to describe, explain, and verify an explanation for the communication strategies that roommates select for resolving their disagreements.

## Stage I: Observing Conflict and Conflict Resolution

Sillars began the observational phase of inquiry by studying the nature and structure of conflict among college roommates and the types of communication strategies used to resolve these differences. To explore the nature of conflict, Sillars asked several dormitory residents to discuss problems they had experienced with their roommates. (In a typical discussion, one person reported that the problem between her and her roommate was one of "simple incompatibility.")

An analysis of conflict situations reported in prior research showed that people often use communication strategies of three types to deal with disagreements: (1) *passive-indirect* strategies, which avoid acknowledging differences and suppress conversation about conflicts; (2) *distributive* strategies such as threats and demands, which promote individual self-interests and generally aggravate rather than reconcile differences; and (3) *integrative* strategies, involving positive discussion, mutual concessions, and honest efforts to resolve disagreements.

Having established the nature of conflict as well as conflict resolution strategies, Sillars was ready to discover a theoretical explanation for the strategies college roommates choose for handling their differences.

## Stage II: Discovering a Theoretical Explanation

Following a theory-to-data discovery pattern, Sillars reasoned that social attribution theory might account for an individual's choice of conflict resolution strategies. According to attribution theory, people base their actions on the motives, intentions, and characteristics they ascribe to themselves and others.[32] Applying this theory to conflict resolution, Sillars developed

**16**

PART I
Conceptual
Foundations of
Contemporary
Communica-
tion Research

a three-part theoretical explanation. First, he argued that people are likely to choose positive integrative strategies over negative passive-indirect and distributive ones if they blame disagreements on themselves instead of others. Conversely, the attribution of responsibility to others should prompt an individual to choose avoidance or disruptive tactics.

Second, Sillars reasoned that attributing conflict to stable factors like personality differences should increase the use of confrontational and avoidance strategies. However, attributing conflict to temporary variables such as stress induced by grade problems should lead to honest efforts to resolve disagreements. Finally, Sillars proposed that attributing a cooperative attitude to a roommate should prompt one to use positive integrative communication, whereas attributions of uncooperativeness ought to promote confrontation or avoidance. These three theoretical hypotheses, Sillars concluded, were sufficient to explain choices of conflict resolution strategies.

## Stage III: Verifying the Theoretical Explanation

To test this theoretical explanation against observational data, Sillars designed and distributed questionnaires to 140 dormitory residents at a large Midwestern university. He asked them to (1) recall a specific interpersonal problem they had encountered with their roommates, (2) describe the communication strategies they had used to deal with the problem, (3) indicate whether they believed that they or their roommates had been responsible for the problem, (4) assess the extent to which the problem was due to stable or temporary factors, and (5) indicate whether they felt that their roommates had been willing to cooperate to solve the problem.

Sillars analyzed the questionnaires by coding all the described communication strategies as either passive-indirect, distributive, or integrative. He then compared people's strategy choices with their attributions of responsibility, stability, and cooperativeness. Results strongly supported the three-part theoretical explanation. Positive integrative strategies were used extensively when individuals attributed more responsibility to themselves than to their roommates, when they attributed instability to conflicts, and when they attributed a flexible and cooperative attitude to their roommates. By contrast, avoidance and confrontational strategies were chosen when individuals felt their roommates were responsible for disagreements, when they believed differences were due to unchangeable factors, and when they regarded their roommates as obstinate and uncooperative.

## INTERFACE: CHAPTERS 1 AND 2

Sillars's study of conflict among college roommates illustrates well the three-stage model of communication inquiry developed in this chapter. Such inquiry begins with observations of communication events, proceeds to develop a theoretical explanation for those events, and finally verifies the reasonableness of the explanation.

In Chapter 2, we begin an examination of the concrete tasks required to develop and verify theories. The chapter describes methods of formulating and defining one's theoretical research problem, a process known as conceptualization. The subsequent chapters of Part One will explore operational procedures for resolving the questions embodied in research problems.

*(handwritten top margin: premises 前提. 'monograph 专题文章. (著作))*

*(handwritten margin: 职位没给.)*

## MAIN POINTS

**1.** The three purposes of scientific inquiry are to describe communication events, explain those events, and verify the explanations.

**2.** Science assumes that communication phenomena are observable, orderly, and explainable.

**3.** The five distinguishing features of science are: (a) science is systematic, (b) science is rational, (c) science is self-correcting, (d) science is self-reflexive, and (e) science is creative.

**4.** Two types of reasoning are used extensively by scientists: (a) inductive reasoning, which draws general conclusions based on specific instances, and (b) deductive reasoning, which derives specific conclusions from general premises.

**5.** The three-stage model of communication inquiry entails (a) observing and describing communication phenomena, (b) developing theoretical explanations for observed phenomena, and (c) verifying the reasonableness of theoretical explanations.

**6.** During the first observational stage of communication inquiry, the researcher's task is to discover the underlying structure of meanings and actions inherent in human communication processes. To accomplish this task, the researcher must decide what to observe, how to interpret observations, and how the interpreted observations are related.

**7.** During the second discovery stage of communication inquiry, the communication researcher aims to generate theoretical explanations for observed patterns of human communication.

**8.** A theory explains persistent patterns of communication behaviors by specifying a generative force, a pattern of effects explained by the generative force, and a set of boundary conditions stipulating the circumstances under which the generative force is likely to explain its effects.

**9.** A causal explanation accounts for communication effects by referring to uncontrollable antecedent conditions and is called a law. A teleological explanation, called a rule, explains communication behaviors by referring to people's reasons for communicating.

**10.** The data-to-theory approach to theory construction begins with observations and then develops a theoretical explanation. By contrast, the theory-to-data perspective focuses initially on an explanatory theory, which is tested against observational data. The logic of the data-to-theory pattern is inductive, whereas deductive logic characterizes the theory-to-data approach.

**11.** During the third, or justification, stage of communication inquiry, the researcher verifies the theoretical explanation that was formulated to account for the initial observations.

**12.** Six criteria aid in testing the adequacy of theoretical explanations: validity, predictability, precision, consistency, scope, and utility.

*(handwritten: n. 范围: The n. of a history book.)*

## REVIEW EXERCISES

**1.** Read a report on the results of a scientific study in communication in a scholarly journal. Journals you might consult include *Human Communication Research*, *Communication Monographs*, and *Journal of Communication*. Describe the author's approach to each of the three stages of communication inquiry, including his or her observational techniques, strategies of theory construction, and methods of theory verification. Did the author use a data-to-theory or a theory-to-data approach to theory construction? Justify your conclusions by citing specific evidence from the article.

*(handwritten: 引用·证. 举例. cite.)*

**18**

PART I
Conceptual
Foundations of
Contemporary
Communica-
tion Research

2. Evaluate one theoretical explanation generated in the article you consulted in Exercise 1, using the criteria of validity, predictability, precision, consistency, scope, and utility. Based on these six tests, is the author's explanation for his or her observations a "good" theory?

# NOTES

1. This view, called the representational theory of meaning, is described in C. K. Ogden and I. A. Richards, *The Meaning of Meaning* (New York: Harcourt, Brace, 1923); and I. A. Richards, *The Philosophy of Rhetoric* (London: Oxford University Press, 1936).

2. Bronislaw Malinowski, "The Problem of Meaning in Primitive Languages," in Ogden and Richards, pp. 296–336.

3. Malinowski's action theory of communication has since been developed into several robust actional theories, including Mead's "symbolic interactionism," Searle's theory of "speech acts," and Pearce's "coordinated management of meaning" theory. See George Herbert Mead, *Mind, Self, and Society* (Chicago: University of Chicago Press, 1953); John R. Searle, *Speech Acts: An Essay in the Philosophy of Language* (Cambridge: Cambridge University Press, 1969); and W. Barnett Pearce and Vernon E. Cronen, *Communication, Action, and Meaning: The Creation of Social Realities* (New York: Frederick A. Praeger, 1980).

4. See Charles R. Berger and James J. Bradac, *Language and Social Knowledge: Uncertainty in Interpersonal Relations* (London: Edward Arnold, 1982).

5. Sir William Cecil Dampier, *A History of Science and its Relations with Philosophy and Religion*, 4th ed. (Cambridge: Cambridge University Press, 1966), p. xiii.

6. Pietro Badia and Richard P. Runyon, *Fundamentals of Behavioral Research* (Reading, MA: Addison-Wesley, 1982), p. 33.

7. Earl Babbie, *The Practice of Social Research*, 3rd ed. (Belmont, CA: Wadsworth, 1983), pp. 15–16.

8. Hans Reichenbach, *Experience and Prediction* (Chicago: University of Chicago Press, 1938), pp. 6–7.

9. See Charles S. Peirce, *Essays in the Philosophy of Science*, ed. Vincent Tomas (Indianapolis: Bobbs-Merrill, 1957), pp. 14–30.

10. See Irving M. Copi, *Introduction to Logic*, 3rd ed. (New York: Macmillan, 1968), pp. 322–72.

11. Babbie, p. 36.

12. For a discussion of the creative qualities of science, see J. Bronowski, *Science and Human Values* (New York: Harper & Row, 1965).

13. John L. Austin, *How to Do Things with Words* (Cambridge, MA: Harvard University Press, 1962).

14. Vernon E. Cronen, W. Barnett Pearce, and Linda M. Harris, "The Coordinated Management of Meaning: A Theory of Communication," in *Human Communication Theory: Comparative Essays*, ed. Frank E. X. Dance (New York: Harper & Row, 1982), pp. 73–74.

15. Darren A. Newtson, "Foundations of Attribution: The Perception of Ongoing Behavior," in *New Directions in Attribution Research*, ed. John H. Harvey, William J. Ickes, and Robert F. Kidd (Hillsdale, NJ: Lawrence Erlbaum, 1976); and Darren A. Newtson, "Attribution and the Unit of Perception of Ongoing Behavior, *Journal of Personality and Social Psychology*, 28 (1973): 28–38.

16. Norwood Russel Hanson, *Patterns of Discovery* (Cambridge: Cambridge University Press, 1958).

17. See Max Weber, *The Theory of Social and Economic Organization*, ed. Talcott Parsons, trans. A. M. Henderson and Talcott Parsons (New York: Oxford University Press, 1947).

18. Leonard C. Hawes, *Pragmatics of Analoguing: Theory and Model Construction in Communication* (Reading, MA: Addison-Wesley, 1975), p. 111.

19. See Peter Tate, "Doctors' Style," in *Doctor-Patient Communication*, ed. David Pendleton and John Hasler (London: Academic Press, 1983), pp. 75–85; and Anne S. Gabbard-Alley, "A Study of the Influence Strategies and Communication Style of Physicians," paper presented to the Speech Communication Association, Denver, 1985.

20. See Charles R. Berger, "The Covering Law Perspective as a Theoretical Basis for the Study of Human Communication," *Communication Quarterly*, 25 (1977): 7–18.

21. See Donald P. Cushman, "The Rules Perspective as a Theoretical Basis for the Study of Human Communication," *Communication Quarterly*,

25 (1977): 30–45; and Donald P. Cushman and Gordon C. Whiting, "An Approach to Communication Theory: Toward a Consensus on Rules," *Journal of Communication*, 22 (1972): 217–38.

**22.** Ernest Nagel, *Technology Revisited and Other Essays in the Philosophy and History of Science* (New York: Columbia University Press, 1979), p. 15.

**23.** Karl Popper, *Conjectures and Refutations: The Growth of Scientific Knowledge*, 2nd ed. (New York: Basic Books, 1965), pp. 115, 117.

**24.** See Karl R. Popper, *The Logic of Scientific Discovery* (New York: Science Editions, 1961), p. 458.

**25.** Leon Festinger, *A Theory of Cognitive Dissonance* (Stanford, CA: Stanford University Press, 1957).

**26.** Leon Festinger and James M. Carlsmith, "Cognitive Consequences of Forced Compliance," *Journal of Abnormal and Social Psychology*, 58 (1959): 203–210.

**27.** See James T. Tedeschi, Barry R. Schlenker, and Thomas V. Bonoma, "Cognitive Dissonance: Private Ratiocination or Public Spectacle?" *American Psychologist*, 26 (1971): 685–95; and Gerald G. Gaes, Robert J. Kalle, and James T. Tedeschi, "Impression Management in the Forced Compliance Situation: Two Studies Using the Bogus Pipeline," *Journal of Experimental Social Psychology*, 14 (1978): 493–510.

**28.** See Gaes, Kalle, and Tedeschi.

**29.** For extensive discussions of criteria for evaluating theories, see W. H. Newton-Smith, *The Rationality of Science* (Boston: Routledge & Kegan Paul, 1981); Thomas S. Kuhn, *The Essential Tension* (Chicago: University of Chicago Press, 1977); Morton Deutsch and Robert M. Krauss, *Theories in Social Psychology* (New York: Basic Books, 1965); and Abraham Kaplan, *The Conduct of Inquiry* (San Francisco: Chandler, 1964).

**30.** Joan Safron Ganz, *Rules: A Systematic Study* (Paris: Mouton, 1971), pp. 128–29.

**31.** Alan Sillars, "Attributions and Communication in Roommate Conflicts," *Communication Monographs*, 47 (1980): 180–200.

**32.** See Fritz Heider, *The Psychology of Interpersonal Relations* (New York: John Wiley, 1958); Harold H. Kelley, "The Process of Causal Attribution," *American Psychologist*, 28 (1973): 107–128; and Daryl J. Bem, "Self-Perception Theory," in *Advances in Experimental Social Psychology*, ed. Leonard Berkowitz (New York: Academic Press, 1972).

# CHAPTER

# 2

# CONCEPTUALIZING RESEARCH

The chapter begins a concrete discussion of the tasks required to conduct communication research. Conceptualization, the process of formulating and defining problems for research, is described. Practical techniques for framing problem statements, including research questions and hypotheses, are presented. The chapter concludes with a discussion of methods of defining the important terms in problem statements.

# CHAPTER OUTLINE

**A WORKING MODEL OF COMMUNICATION RESEARCH**

I. Identifying the research problem

II. Formulating the problem statement

III. Defining the terms in problem statements

IV. Selecting an appropriate methodology

V. Observing relevant empirical data

VI. Analyzing observational data

The six-step model and theory development

**CONCEPTUALIZING PROBLEM STATEMENTS**

Types of problem statements: Questions and hypotheses

Criteria for formulating problem statements

Components of problem statements

**DEFINING THE TERMS IN PROBLEM STATEMENTS**

Conceptual and operational definitions

The nature of conceptual definitions

Although best known for literary works such as *The Autobiography of Alice B. Toklas* and pithy phrases like "A rose is a rose is a rose," Gertrude Stein was an expansive intellect and had a considerable interest in science. In the late 1800s, Miss Stein studied psychology at Radcliffe, published experiments she conducted at Harvard, and came close to getting an M.D. degree at Johns Hopkins University. Her interest in science continued throughout her life, although she devoted most of her creative genius to the arts. When Gertrude Stein died in 1946 at the age of 72, after a long and successful literary career, her scientific spirit apparently was intact. With her last words, she captured one of the most important issues in scholarly inquiry. "What is the answer?" Miss Stein asked of her companion Alice B. Toklas. Getting no reply, she said laughing, "In that case, what is the question?"[1]

For scholars bent on understanding communication's world, the "answer" is usually secondary to the "question" that guides research. Questions tell us what to observe and how to conduct our observations. In the eighteenth century, the philosopher Immanuel Kant said, "Nature does not simply call out to the knower information about her character and content, but answers the questions [one puts]."[2] Similarly, the contemporary methodologist Fred Kerlinger noted that "If one wants to solve a problem, one must generally know what the problem is. It can be said that a large part of the solution lies in knowing what it is one is trying to do."[3] Thus, the nature of our questions largely determines the kinds of answers we can expect from communication inquiry.

This chapter is about "asking questions," about conceptualizing the problem for research. I begin by describing the communication research process, identifying the role of conceptualization in that activity. Next, problem statements, including questions and hypotheses, are explored. Finally, I discuss practical techniques for defining research problems.

Throughout its development, the chapter emphasizes the effects research questions have on the answers we are likely to get from scholarly inquiry.

# A WORKING MODEL OF COMMUNICATION RESEARCH

The two great tools of research are the human senses, which permit observation, and the human mind, which allows speculation about what we observe. Paralleling this dual system of knowing, the research process entails two related levels of inquiry: the *conceptual* level, involving rational speculation about what kinds of communication exist, how different communicative acts are related, and why communication patterns occur as they do; and the *operational* level, also called the empirical level, entailing observations of people's communicative actions and interactions. Recall from Chapter 1 that communication research involves three stages of conceptual and operational inquiry: observing communication events, developing theoretical explanations for observations, and verifying these explanations. This section will extend this general scientific model into a working set of guidelines for conducting research, describing the concrete tasks required for developing and verifying theories.

Six sequential conceptual and operational tasks are required for theory development and verification. The researcher must (1) identify the theoretical research problem, (2) formulate the problem statement, (3) define the terms in the problem statement, (4) select and implement a research methodology, (5) observe empirical data, and (6) analyze observational findings. Conceptual processes occupy the first three tasks, whereas operationalization predominates during the latter three. **Conceptualization**, then, may be defined as the process of formulating and defining the problem at

**24**

PART I
Conceptual
Foundations of
Contemporary
Communica-
tion Research

hand. *Operationalization*, to be discussed in Chapter 3, is the process of observing and measuring communication phenomena relevant to one's research problem. To understand the role of conceptualizing in theory development and verification, it will be useful to briefly describe the six steps comprising this working model of communication research.

## I. Identifying the Research Problem

The starting point for all research is identifying a problem in need of solution. A good research problem usually addresses the relationship between or among classes of communication phenomena, has theoretical import (meaning it is concerned with explanation), and is verifiable by empirical observation. To illustrate these qualities, consider two examples. Suppose first you suspect that the mass media portray stereotyped images of women and that such portrayals have an adverse impact on the self concepts of young female viewers. Second, imagine that every time you visit your parents, you get into quarrels that you believe stem from cross-generational differences in values and life styles.

In each case, you have identified a communication problem worthy of study. The first problem addresses the relationship between media programming and young women's self concepts. The suspected relationship is theoretical, since you believe that media stereotyping may contribute to diminished self-esteem. Finally, the relationship can be tested by observation. Likewise, the second example relates unwanted arguments and conflicting values in a theoretical fashion, since the latter may explain the former. Moreover, empirical investigation can confirm or disconfirm this explanatory relationship.

Some communication research problems, unlike those just described, may not explicitly address relationships between two or more

classes of phenomena. For example, a media survey of viewers' attitudes toward certain television programs and an organizational study of employee job satisfaction appear to describe singular phenomena—media attitudes and worker morale, respectively. Even so, these research problems involve implicit relationships: people's subjective responses are being associated with certain external stimuli, here television programs and work environments. Indeed, researchers often undertake such studies because they believe that particular features of a given external stimulus relate systematically to the nature, direction, or intensity of people's subjective reactions to it. A common objective of this research is to identify and describe heretofore undiscovered relationships. Thus, it is reasonable to regard most research problems not only as theoretical and empirically verifiable inquiries, but as relational propositions as well.

## II. Formulating the Problem Statement

Once a general research problem has been identified, it must be refined into a specific problem statement. Kerlinger refers to a **problem statement** as a precise "interrogative sentence or statement that asks: What relation exists between two or more [classes of communication phenomena]?"[4] Problem statements usually take the form either of research questions or hypotheses. **Research questions** typically ask what kind of relationship, if any, exists between certain classes of communication behaviors. **Hypotheses** are declarative sentences predicting that a particular kind of relationship exists between specified classes of phenomena. "Do stereotyped portrayals of women in television entertainment programs affect the self concepts of young female viewers?" is a research question derived from one of the problems mentioned earlier. A research hypothesis derived from the other problem is "Different value systems of parents and their college-age children are linked to unwanted verbal conflict."

## III. Defining the Terms in Problem Statements

Problem statements contain descriptive terms representing classes of communication phenomena as well as operative terms that clarify the relationship between the specified classes.[5] To understand the difference, consider the hypothesis: "Viewing educational television is related to increased learning among children." Key descriptive terms are "educational television," "learning," and "children," whereas a pertinent operative phrase is "is related to increased." The researcher must provide both conceptual and operational definitions for these terms.

**Conceptual definitions** characterize concepts or classes of phenomena by relating them to other concepts, whereas **operational definitions** specify procedures for observing and measuring concepts. To illustrate, we might give the descriptive term "learning" the following conceptual definition: "the acquisition of information." Operationally, however, we might define it by a test designed to measure the amount of information one acquires from viewing educational programs. To take a second example, the operative phrase, "is related to increased" may be conceptualized as a predictive relationship and operationalized by measuring whether children who view educational television programs acquire more information than children not viewing them.

## IV. Selecting an Appropriate Methodology

With operative and descriptive terms defined, the researcher must choose a research methodology to determine whether the relationship specified in a problem statement actually exists. During this fourth inquiry stage, then, the researcher selects appropriate tests for measuring communication phenomena and chooses procedures for selecting samples of phenomena to measure. The character of the problem statement as it has been conceptually and operationally defined will largely determine the required research methodology.

## V. Observing Relevant Empirical Data

At the fifth phase of inquiry, the researcher observes and measures the classes of communication phenomena specified in problem statements and assesses the nature, direction, and magnitude of the relationship between them.

## VI. Analyzing Observational Data

During the final stage, the researcher analyzes the results just obtained in relation to the problem statement that initiated the research process. Researchers determine whether observational data confirm or disconfirm research questions or hypotheses and they refine their original theoretical frameworks accordingly. Data analysis returns the researcher to the conceptual level of inquiry, where the research process continues with a refined problem statement.

## The Six-Step Model and Theory Development

The six-step working model depicted in Figure 2.1 subsumes each of the three stages of inquiry stipulated in the generalized research paradigm of Chapter 1. Recall that the general model conceptualized scientific inquiry as a process

*algorithmic*

*algorithm [ˈælɡərɪðəm]*
*구조법, 해법계산법*

**FIGURE 2.1**
A SIX-STEP MODEL OF THE RESEARCH PROCESS

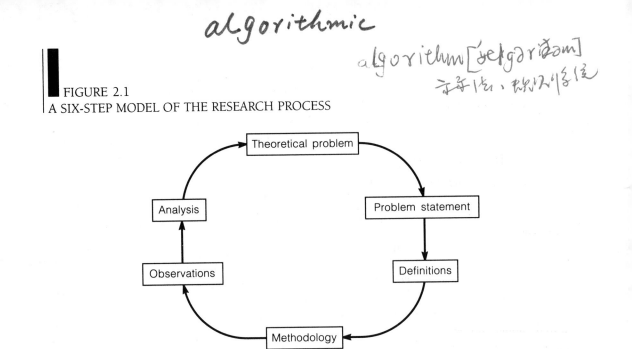

involving observation, theory discovery, and theory verification. In our six-step model, the formulation and refinement of a research question or hypothesis is equivalent to discovering a tentative theory. Such a theory may be derived from observations of communication events, rational speculation about those events, or a combination of the two sources of inspiration. Theory verification is accomplished by selecting a research methodology, observing relevant communication events, and testing one's research question or hypothesis against observational data. Thus, the six-step model represents a set of practical procedures for conducting systematic observations, developing explanations for observations, and verifying these explanations.

The six-step model, like the formulation in Chapter 1, describes an algorithmic process, involving repeated movements between the conceptual and operational levels of inquiry. Not only do our theoretical conceptions structure the observational process, but operational procedures also suggest modifications in old conceptual systems. Thus, researchers move repeatedly through the six phases of inquiry, variously pitting conceptual problems and observations against one another.

Having shown the interplay between conceptual and operational activities in the context of a working research model, I will devote the balance of this chapter to the conceptual tasks of problem identification, problem statement formulation, and term definition. Operationalization is discussed in Chapter 3 and in subsequent chapters on data collection, sampling methods, statistical analysis, and research design selection.

## CONCEPTUALIZING PROBLEM STATEMENTS

Earlier we learned that a problem statement is either an interrogatory or declarative sentence that capsulizes the subject matter of inquiry. Framed as either a research question or a hypothesis, a problem statement often takes the general theoretical form: If $X$, then probably $Y$, under boundary conditions $Z_1, \ldots, Z_n$.

Problem statements are often suggested by two sources of information: a researcher's direct

observations and speculations about communication behaviors, and published reports of
others' observations and the theories they advance to explain these observations. If, for example, I am interested in the connections, if
any, between televised violence and childhood
aggression, I can begin to formulate my research problem by (1) directly observing children who view large quantities of televised violence and those who do not, (2) reading articles
detailing the observations of others who have
studied the problem, and (3) surveying published theories relating symbolic violence to
children's behavior. Identifying a research problem, then, involves considerable library research.[6] Books and scholarly articles relevant to
one's interests should be studied. A thorough
familiarity with the current state of knowledge
on a topic is essential to the framing of an intelligent problem statement. After surveying pertinent materials, the researcher can formulate a
problem statement. Its exact form—that is, a
research question or hypothesis—will depend
on the richness of the information gathered
from direct observation and library research.

## Types of Problem Statements: Questions and Hypotheses

If research fails to point to a clear prediction
about the problem of interest, the researcher
should formulate a **research question**, in either an open-ended or closed form. An **open-
ended question** leaves the nature of the relationship to be investigated as well as its boundary conditions unspecified. It often asks what
kind of relationship, if any, exists between
two or more classes of communication behaviors ($X$ and $Y$) and under what conditions
($Z_1, \ldots, Z_n$). In contrast, a **closed question**
asks whether a specified type of relationship
exists between two or more sets of behaviors
($X$ and $Y$) under a specified set of boundary
conditions ($Z_1, \ldots, Z_n$).

Applied to the possible link between media
violence and children's aggressiveness, an open-
ended question is, "Are heavy viewing of televised violence and childhood aggression ($X$ and
$Y$) related to one another and, if so, under what
conditions ($Z_1, \ldots, Z_n$)?" A parallel closed
question is, "Is heavy viewing of televised violence ($X$) related to increased aggression ($Y$) in
children who are predisposed toward aggressiveness ($Z_1, \ldots, Z_n$)?" A closed question usually is preferable to an open-ended one because
closed questions are more precise, indicating as
they do the nature, direction, and conditions
associated with suspected relationships.

Often the information available from research will be sufficiently detailed to permit
researchers to frame research hypotheses. A **research hypothesis** is a conjectural statement
predicting a specified type of relationship between two or more classes of communication
behaviors under explicitly defined boundary
conditions. Hypotheses often take the form
mentioned earlier: If $X$, then probably $Y$, under
boundary conditions $Z_1, \ldots, Z_n$. A plausible
research hypothesis derived from published
theory and research on media violence and
childhood aggression is "Heavy viewing of televised violence ($X$) is linked to increased aggressiveness ($Y$) among children who already
have latent aggressive tendencies ($Z$)."

Assuming hypotheses are feasible, they are
usually preferable to research questions for two
reasons. First, hypotheses often delineate research problems more fully and precisely than
questions. They specify the nature of suspected
relationships between communication phenomena along with necessary boundary conditions. Second, when problem statements are
empirically tested, the researcher actually tests
what is called the **null hypothesis**, a statement
that no relationship whatsoever exists between
specified classes of phenomena. (Null hypotheses are described fully in Chapter 6.) A research hypothesis, representing an affirmative
statement that some specific relationship exists,

28

PART I
Conceptual
Foundations of
Contemporary
Communica-
tion Research

corresponds directly to the empirically verifiable null hypothesis. Hypotheses, then, are often more exact than questions and usually more suitable to empirical testing procedures.

## Criteria for Formulating Problem Statements

Problem statements must be carefully formulated because they play a pivotal role in the research process, affecting each subsequent stage of inquiry. Well-formulated problem statements should have the following five characteristics.

1. *Problem statements should be specific*, delineating as precisely as possible the classes of phenomena to be investigated and the nature of their relationships. Based on this specificity criterion, research hypotheses are often preferred over research questions, and closed questions are usually superior to open-ended ones.

2. *Problem statements should be empirically verifiable*; that is, we should be able to measure the nature and magnitude of the stated relationships. Problem statements should not contain explicit value judgments about the rightness or wrongness of relationships. Personal values are unprovable assumptions about the "right" and "wrong" ways to study communication. As such, they may influence the selection of problem statements but are not directly incorporated within them.

3. *Problem statements should be phrased affirmatively*. Statements with negative wording are less useful research guides because they do not provide as much information about the nature of expected relationships. Consider the following affirmative hypothesis: "Physical attractiveness (*X*) is linked to increased (or decreased) persuasiveness (*Y*) when the attractive persuader has effective (or ineffective) communication skills (*Z*)." This kind of prediction is far more informative than the negatively phrased null hy-

pothesis, namely, "There is no relationship between physical attractiveness and persuasibility under any conditions." Although data analytic procedures test null hypotheses, the research hypothesis is the practical guide to research activity and should contain the richest and most detailed information possible about the problem at hand.

4. *Problem statements should be phrased simply*, avoiding compound-complex sentence structures. The statement "Physical attractiveness is related to increased credibility and persuasiveness" violates the simplicity criterion because it contains two independent hypotheses. One hypothesis predicts that attractiveness is related to increased source credibility, whereas the other suggests a link between attractiveness and acceptance of a message. A well-formulated question or hypothesis should be a single, simply worded interrogatory or declarative statement.

5. *Problem statements should be clear and unambiguous*. Hypotheses or questions containing obscure or equivocal terms are poor guides for research. Suppose someone hypothesizes that "Television viewing is associated with apathy." What kind or amount of television viewing does the framer have in mind? What type or magnitude of apathy? Based on this statement, we cannot tell. However, the prediction that "Heavy viewing of televised crime drama is linked to apathetic attitudes toward violence among adult male viewers" provides a clearer statement of the nature of descriptive terms, the expected relationship among them, and the conditions under which such a relationship should occur.

## Components of Problem Statements

Earlier I suggested that problem statements contain descriptive terms, which refer to classes of communication phenomena, and operative terms, which stipulate the nature of the relationship among descriptive terms. In the hypothesis "Commercial advertising strategies (X) are related to enhanced social aspirations (Y), among low-income viewers (Z)," the descriptive terms are "commercial advertising strategies," "social aspirations," and "low-income viewers," and the phrase "is related to enhanced" is the pertinent operative term.

## Descriptive terms: Constructs and variables

The descriptive terms in hypotheses and questions are called concepts or **constructs**, defined as "classes or sets of objects or events bound together by the possession of some common characteristic.[7] Constructs are abstract entities formed by generalization from particular instances of some phenomenon.[8] The construct "Southern dialect" is an abstract category representing the idiomatic speech of millions of Americans. As an abstraction, it symbolizes several identifying features of Southern speech but obscures a host of differences among individual speakers. Similarly, constructs such as "commercial advertising strategies," "social aspirations," and "low-income viewers," are general categories that capture some but not all of the phenomena the constructs are meant to represent.

Before moving from a conceptual to an operational inquiry level, researchers must convert the constructs appearing in problem statements to variables, since "it is as variables that our concepts will eventually appear in hypotheses and be tested."[9] The distinction between constructs and variables is reflected in the practice of referring to problem statements containing constructs as "theoretical hypotheses" and those containing variables as "research hypotheses."

The term **variable** is used to refer to any class of communication behaviors that can take on different values. Variables that can assume any ordered value within a specified range are called **continuous variables**. For example,

"communication anxiety" is a continuous variable because it can range from no anxiety to some maximally defined fear of speaking, with all shades of anxiety in between. Similarly, phenomena like "shyness," "conversational coherence," and "socioeconomic status" can vary in degree from very little to a great deal of each. **Discrete variables**, on the other hand, change by distinct steps instead of following a continuously ordered progression. For instance, "gender" has the discrete properties of maleness and femaleness, and "news sources" are often differentiated as newspapers, magazines, television, word of mouth, and so forth.

Research hypotheses usually contain variables of three types: independent variables, dependent variables, and intervening variables. **Independent variables** are input variables that are presumed to predict or explain other variables. **Dependent variables** are the classes of communication behaviors requiring explanation. **Intervening variables**, also called *control variables*, are boundary conditions that affect the relationship between independent and dependent variables. These variable types are often linked together in research hypotheses in the now familiar conditional form: If X (independent variable), then probably Y (dependent variable), under conditions $Z_1, \ldots, Z_n$ (intervening variables). In the hypothesis "Providing patients with information about their illnesses is associated with increased compliance with a doctor's orders among female but not male patients," the independent variable is "information," the dependent variable is "compliance," and the intervening variable is gender. (Independent, dependent, and intervening variables are described in greater detail in Chapter 10.)

## Operative terms: Relationships among variables

**Operative terms** in problem statements stipulate the nature of the expected relationship between or among variables. To illustrate, consider the hypothesis, "Increasing fear appeals in persuasive messages is related to in-

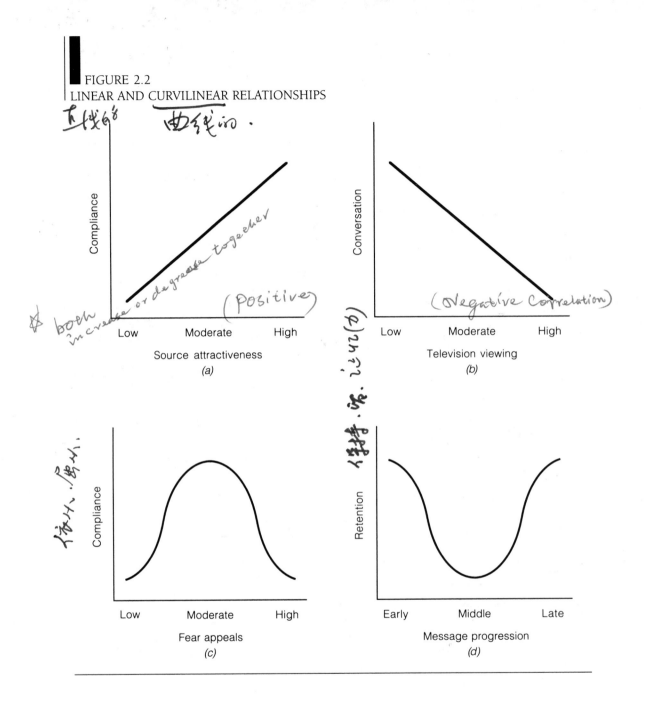

# FIGURE 2.2
## LINEAR AND CURVILINEAR RELATIONSHIPS

直线的          曲线的.

Compliance

both increase or decrease together

(Positive)

Low     Moderate     High

Source attractiveness

(a)

Conversation

(Negative Correlation)

Low     Moderate     High

Television viewing

(b)

Compliance

Low     Moderate     High

Fear appeals

(c)

Retention

Early     Middle     Late

Message progression

(d)

creased message agreement if recipients believe that remedies proposed by the speaker are effective." 治疗(法)药物. 补救[问]

The independent, dependent, and intervening variables, respectively, are "fear appeals,"

"agreement," and "remedies," whereas the operative terms are "increasing," "is related to increased," and "effective." The terms "increasing" and "is related to increased" pinpoint the nature of the relationship between the independent and dependent variables. They tell us that the relationship is a positive one, meaning that as fear appeals increase, agreement should also increase. The term "effective" addresses the magnitude of the relationship, suggesting that we can expect the amount of compliance to depend on whether message recipients believe the recommended actions will alleviate their problems. To empirically test hypotheses, the researcher must clarify through operational definitions the precise meaning of each operative term, as explained in Chapter 3.

Two general types of relationships are often indicated by operative terms: linear and curvilinear relationships, or correlations. A **linear correlation** can be represented by a straight line and may be either direct or inverse. A **direct** or **positive** linear **correlation**, depicted in Figure 2.2a, occurs when two phenomena vary together in the same direction; both increase or decrease at the same time in a systematic fashion. As Figure 2.2a indicates, when a speaker's physical attractiveness increases, so does agreement with his or her message; conversely, as attractiveness declines, we can expect a corresponding decrease in compliance. In contrast, an **inverse** or **negative correlation** exists when one variable systematically increases as another declines. Figure 2.2b suggests that as television viewing increases, conversation among family members diminishes.

A **curvilinear correlation**, or relationship, does not follow a straight-line pattern. Two curvilinear relationships are exceedingly prevalent in communication: the inverted-U and U-shaped types. An **inverted-U correlation**, like that depicted in Figure 2.2c, occurs when two variables initially increase together, after which one continues to increase as the other systematically declines. Fear appeals and compliance with a persuasive message often follow an inverted-U pattern, with compliance increasing from low to moderate levels of fear arousal, then beginning to decrease as fear appeals reach high intensity levels.

The **U-shaped correlation** (Figure 2.2d) occurs when one variable initially increases as the other declines, after which the two increase together. The relation between a listener's recall of message content and the progression of a message frequently follows a U-shaped pattern. Whereas information retention often is quite high for the introductory portions of a public speech, it decreases until near the end of the speech, at which time it increases to levels equivalent to that at the beginning. In other words, listeners tend to remember introductions and conclusions but may forget much of the rest of what they hear. (Linear and curvilinear relationships are discussed more fully in Chapter 8.)

## DEFINING THE TERMS IN PROBLEM STATEMENTS

Defining the descriptive and operative terms in problem statements is an exceedingly important task in the research process. Clear definitions set the stage for selecting research designs that will fully test one's research question or hypothesis.

### Conceptual and Operational Definitions

Researchers must define the key terms in problem statements both conceptually and operationally. As we learned earlier, *conceptual definitions* define constructs or variables by relating them to other constructs. Thus, the construct "learning" might be conceptually defined as the "acquisition of information," with the two concepts "acquisition" and "information" being used to explicate the primary construct "learning."

An *operational definition* "assigns meaning to a construct or variable by specifying the activities or 'operations' necessary to measure it."[10]

FIGURE 2.3
THE ROLE OF CONCEPTUAL DEFINITIONS IN THE RESEARCH PROCESS

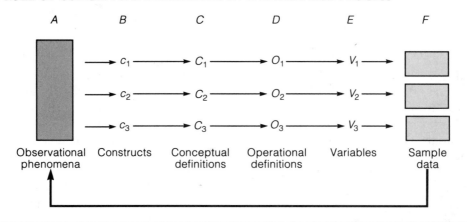

We might operationally define "learning" by giving out a questionnaire that measures the information acquired from some stimulus of interest, say an instructional television program. Conceptual and operational definitions are integrally related. Conceptual definitions structure the operationalization process, spelling out exactly what researchers must measure. In this section, I will describe methods of developing conceptual definitions, reserving for the next chapter a discussion of procedures for framing operational definitions.

## The Nature of Conceptual Definitions

To understand conceptual definitions, it will be useful to illustrate their role in the research process. As Figure 2.3 shows, we begin the research process with a large and undifferentiated mass of *observational phenomena* in the empirical world of communication, point A. We give structure to that world by grouping phenomena into constructs or related classes of behaviors that are pertinent to our research problem, a process denoted by B. Thus, if I am interested in whether animated cartoons enhance children's creativity, I must create the descriptive constructs "cartoons" and "creativity" and the operative class "enhancement."

Once the relevant constructs have been designated, researchers must conceptually define them; this is the research stage denoted by C. Operational definitions are constructed at point D. By specifying ways to measure constructs, operational definitions transform constructs into the variables indicated at point E. The research process finishes one complete cycle when the researcher tests the variables in problem statements against **samples** of relevant observational data at point F. As this model suggests, conceptual definitions play a pivotal role in the research process, setting up the conceptual framework required to proceed to the operational level of inquiry.

### Constructing conceptual definitions

Recall that a researcher creates conceptual definitions by relating the construct to be defined to other constructs. For example, we could conceptually define "communication" as "verbal and nonverbal interactions between two or

Communication
Verbal ⟩ Secondary: interactions
Nonverbal two or more persons

33
CHAPTER 2
Conceptualizing Research

Verbal inter—
└ written or spoken language
Nonverbal inter—
└ gestures & other Non linguistic de - vices.

more persons." This definition relates the primary construct, "communication," to three secondary descriptive constructs, "verbal interaction," "nonverbal interaction," and "persons," and to a single operative phrase, "between two or more." Some secondary constructs need definitions and others do not. To fully define "communication," we need to define both "verbal interaction" and "nonverbal interaction," but not "between two or more" or "persons." "Verbal interaction" might be defined as the use of "written or spoken language" to exchange messages, whereas the "nonverbal" kind could be characterized by the use of "gestures and other nonlinguistic devices" to send reciprocal messages.

This example illustrates the two categories researchers use to generate conceptual definitions: primitive terms and derived terms. A **primitive term** is a concept with a generally agreed upon meaning, a term that "cannot be defined by other concepts."[11] Sense concepts like colors (yellow, red) and tastes (sweet, sour) are classic examples of primitive terms. We usually define them by pointing to examples, as I have done. Definitions that clarify by example or demonstration are called *ostensive definitions*.[12] In our conceptual definition of communication, the concepts "persons" and "between two or more" are generally agreed upon primitive terms requiring no further formal definitions.

**Derived terms**, the second group researchers use to define constructs, are terms "that can be defined by the use of primitive terms."[13] "Verbal" and "nonverbal" are examples of derived terms. Notice that I used the primitive terms "written or spoken language" to define "verbal" and the primitive phrase "gestures and other nonlinguistic devices" to denote "nonverbal" interaction. Conceptual definitions, then, consist of primitive and derived terms, with derived terms being secondarily defined by primitive concepts. A fully developed conceptual definition is reducible to primitive terms whose meanings are shared by members of the same scholarly community.

## Criteria for formulating conceptual definitions

Four criteria are especially useful guidelines for framing conceptual definitions.

1. *Conceptual definitions should denote the essential qualities of constructs and exclude nonessential ones.* Since conceptual definitions abstract some but not all the characteristics of constructs, the researcher must include qualities that are essential to a construct's definition and exclude all others. What is "essential" and "nonessential" depends on the problem statement within which a construct appears. If the construct "communication" appears in a theoretical hypothesis about the effects of interpersonal communication on friendship formation, orally transmitted communication will be pertinent but written messages may be irrelevant. However, if "communication" appears in a problem statement concerned with message transmission in large organizations, both oral and written communication likely will be relevant.

2. *Conceptual definitions should not be circular*: the definition of a construct should not contain any linguistic variant of the construct to be defined. Thus, the researcher should avoid circular definitions like "a female is a person having feminine characteristics," since "feminine" restates rather than defines the primary construct "female."

3. *Conceptual definitions should be clear and precise*, implying that researchers should avoid vague terminology. The best way to ensure clarity and precision is to use only terms that are easily reducible to a set of primitive terms, since primitive terms are understood by members of the same speech community.

Empathic 移情的.

**34**

PART I
Conceptual
Foundations of
Contemporary
Communica-
tion Research

4. *Conceptual definitions should be complete*; that is, the researcher should provide conceptual definitions for all the key terms in problem statements, both descriptive and operative. A common mistake is to define descriptive terms and not operative terms. Thus, in hypotheses like "Role-playing is related to enhanced empathic communication skills," researchers must conceptually define not only the descriptive terms "role-playing" and "empathic communication skills," but also the operative phrase "is related to enhanced" to have a complete set of conceptual definitions.

interrrogatory
疑虑(问 100.
质问 -

## INTERFACE: CHAPTERS 2 AND 3

In this chapter, I began to stipulate the concrete tasks required for conducting research projects. Conceptualization, the process of developing and refining research problems, was explored. Practical techniques for formulating problem statements, including research questions and hypotheses, were presented. The chapter concluded with a discussion of methods of defining and evaluating the terms in problem statements.

实际
实践
的.

Chapter 3 will continue our examination of pragmatic research procedures, describing the process of operationalizing the terms in problem statements. Techniques of measuring communication events will be discussed, and methods of assessing the validity and reliability of measurements are presented.

assess
评估(估)
确定(定)

## MAIN POINTS

1. A research problem usually addresses relationships, has theoretical import, and is empirically verifiable.

2. Conceptualization is the process of formulating and defining a problem in communication research.

3. A working model of communication research involves six tasks: (a) identifying the research problem, (b) framing the problem statement, (c) defining the terms in the problem statement, (d) selecting and implementing a methodology, (e) observing empirical data, and (f) analyzing observational findings.

4. A problem statement is an interrogatory or declarative sentence that capsulizes the subject of research. It is framed as either a research question or a research hypothesis.

5. Research questions ask what kind of relationship, if any, exists between classes of communication behaviors, whereas research hypotheses are statements predicting that a particular kind of relationship exists between classes of communication phenomena.

6. Well-formulated problem statements are specific, empirically verifiable, affirmatively worded, simple, and unambiguous.

7. Problem statements contain descriptive terms, which identify the communication constructs to be investigated, and operative terms, which stipulate the nature of the relationship among the constructs.

8. A construct is an abstract class of communication behaviors, and a variable is the empirical counterpart of a construct.

9. Three types of variables appear in problem statements: independent variables, which predict or explain other variables; dependent variables, which require explanation; and intervening variables, which affect the relationship between independent and dependent variables.

10. The relationship (or correlation) between any two variables may be classified as linear or curvilinear. Linear relationships are either direct (positive) or inverse (negative). Common curvilinear relationships are inverted-U and U-shaped relationships.

11. A conceptual definition defines a construct by relating it to other constructs, whereas an operational definition specifies the activities required to measure a construct.

12. Conceptual definitions are built on primitive terms, which have a generally agreed upon meaning, and derived terms, which are defined by referring to primitive terms.

13. A well-formulated conceptual definition should (a) capture the essential qualities of a construct, (b) contain no circular terms, (c) be clear and precise, and (d) be complete.

## REVIEW EXERCISES

1. Suggest three general topics in communication that would be interesting problems for a research project. Select the one topic you find the most interesting and consult two sources of published information about it. Sources to consult include books as well as articles in scholarly journals like *Journal of Communication, Communication Monographs, Human Communication Research, Journalism Quarterly,* and *Journal of Broadcasting & Electronic Media.* After reading the published materials, frame a problem statement of each of the following types: an open-ended question, a closed question, and a hypothesis. How well does each problem statement conform to the criteria outlined in this chapter for formulating problem statements?

2. Select one of the problem statements you formulated in Exercise 1 and identify all its descriptive terms and operative terms. Construct a conceptual definition for each descriptive term (construct/variable) and each operative term in the problem statement. How well do your definitions conform to the criteria outlined in this chapter for formulating conceptual definitions?

## NOTES

1. F. W. Dupee, "General Introduction," in *Selected Writings of Gertrude Stein,* ed. Carl van Vechten (New York: Modern Library, 1962), pp. ix–xvii.
2. See Marjorie Grene, *The Knower and the Known* (Berkeley: University of California Press, 1974), p. 135.
3. Fred N. Kerlinger, *Foundations of Behavioral Research,* 2nd ed. (New York: Holt, Rinehart & Winston, 1973), p. 17.
4. Kerlinger, p. 17.
5. Leonard C. Hawes, *Pragmatics of Analoguing: Theory and Model Construction in Communication* (Reading, MA: Addison-Wesley, 1975), pp. 29–30.
6. An excellent treatment of library resources is found in Rebecca B. Rubin, Alan M. Rubin, and Linda J. Piele, *Communication Research: Strategies and Sources* (Belmont, CA: Wadsworth, 1986).
7. Fred N. Kerlinger, *Foundations of Behavioral Research* (New York: Holt, Rinehart & Winston, 1964), p. 4.
8. Kerlinger, 1973, p. 28.
9. David Nachmias and Chava Nachmias, *Research Methods in the Social Sciences,* 2nd ed. (New York: St. Martin's Press, 1981), p. 58.
10. Kerlinger, 1973, p. 31.
11. Nachmias and Nachmias, p. 32.
12. Nachmias and Nachmias.
13. Nachmias and Nachmias, p. 33.

# CHAPTER

# 3

# OPERATIONALIZING RESEARCH

This chapter describes principles and procedures for operationalizing or measuring communication behaviors. Measurement is the process of converting constructs into a set of numerals that can be analyzed statistically. Four levels of measurement—nominal, ordinal, interval, and ratio—are discussed, along with guidelines for using each. The chapter concludes by describing reliability and validity in measurement. Procedures for assessing the reliability and validity of a measuring instrument are presented.

# CHAPTER OUTLINE

I n his essay on the "Imperfections of Science," Warren Weaver quoted a passage from a poem by e.e. cummings that challenges the value of this chapter's subject matter. With characteristic wit, cummings wrote:

> while you and i have lips and voices which
> are for kissing and to sing with
> who cares if some oneeyed son of a bitch
> invents an instrument to measure Spring with?[1]

With these few lines, the poet has captured the essence of a major scientific dilemma: How can one reduce to "mere numbers" such rich experiences as the loveliness of springtime or autumn's brilliance without destroying the meaningfulness of these experiences? If operationalizing transforms robust communication activities like "intimate conversation" and "verbal conflict" into barely recognizable shadows, then science is inherently self-defeating, obscuring by its methods what it set out to illuminate.

To escape this dilemma, researchers must find ways to operationalize or to "count and measure" phenomena without sacrificing their essential qualities. If I wish to operationalize a person's "verbal anxiety" or level of "communicative intimacy," I must design instruments that measure the critical features of these variables. Because a direct link between conceptualizing and measuring must be maintained, operationalization is one of the more difficult tasks in communication research.

This chapter and the next two chronicle the problems and the promise of operationalizing research. I begin this chapter by describing operationalization, then explore the theory and practice of measurement. Next, numerical systems are discussed. Finally, I examine principles of assessing the validity and reliability of measurements.

# THE PROCESS OF OPERATIONALIZATION

When researchers operationalize constructs, they specify "the activities or 'operations' necessary to measure [them]."[2] Suppose I am interested in the effects of intelligence on communication competence. The constructs "intelligence" and "communication competence" are neither directly nor fully observable. Each is an internal state whose existence must be inferred from such overt behaviors as oral comments and performance on written examinations.

To operationalize these constructs, the researcher must specify their critical **empirical indicators**, defined as essential properties that can be directly observed and measured. We may decide that a high grade point average (GPA) and a superior intelligence quotient (IQ) are adequate empirical indicators of intelligence. Empirical indicators of communication competence might include effective speech behaviors or high marks on a written test of people's knowledge of communication principles. In either case, we are reducing an unobservable concept to a series of tangible indicators. **Operationalization**, then, may be defined as the process of transforming abstract constructs into a set of concrete indicators that can be observed and measured.

## The Domain of Operationalization

In Figure 3.1, which depicts the full scope of operationalization, including its important relationship to conceptual processes, we see that the three-stage process begins with an **operational definition** of some variable. By operationally defining a variable, say "communication competence" or "empathic conversation," one specifies ways to observe and measure its

*Correlate*

FIGURE 3.1
THE PROCESS OF OPERATIONALIZATION

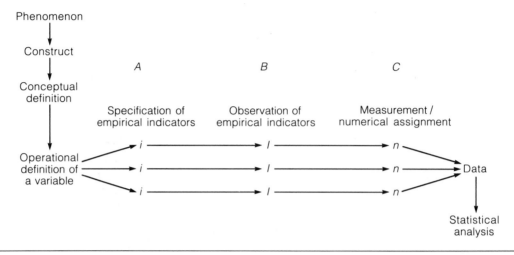

critical empirical indicators, a process denoted by the letter *A* in Figure 3.1. We learned in Chapter 2 that operational definitions are structured by conceptual definitions of constructs that themselves symbolize "real" empirical phenomena.

If "communication competence" is conceptually defined as knowledge of effective speech principles, our operational definition will differ markedly from that based on "communication competence" conceptually defined as, say, the effective use of speech. In the former instance, a mastery of principles will indicate competence, whereas skillful behavior will signify competence in the latter. In any case, operationalization begins when a researcher specifies a variable's empirical indicators based on the properties of its associated construct.

Once a variable's empirical indicators have been stipulated, a researcher may observe them at point *B*, a process to be explored in Chapters 4 and 5. After observation, the researcher moves to the *measurement* stage indicated at point *C* and systematically assigns a set of numerals to observed empirical indicators. If, for example, several speakers have been evaluated

on their knowledge of speech principles using a 50-question test, the researcher might assign each speaker a score of 0 to 50 depending on the number of correctly answered questions. The process of assigning numerals to empirical indicators is called **mapping**, a topic discussed later. (Principles of constructing composite measuring instruments are explored fully in Chapter 4.)

Measurement yields a body of numerical **data**, which the researcher analyzes statistically; this is the subject of Part II. By analyzing data, researchers confirm or disconfirm their research hypotheses. A researcher who originally hypothesized that high intelligence is related to communication competence might statistically correlate each speaker's IQ with his or her score on a communication competence test. If the two sets of scores correlate positively, that is, if high scorers on the first instrument also score well on the second, there is support for the hypothesis. The purpose of statistical analysis, then, is to test the "reasonableness" of research hypotheses and questions.

# Operationalization and Variable Types

The variables appearing in hypotheses and questions influence heavily how a researcher will operationalize them. Any one variable may be classified as manifest or latent, and as discrete or continuous.

## Manifest or latent variables

All variables appearing in problem statements represent phenomena that are not fully observable, yet some variables can be more readily observed than others. **Manifest variables** have direct empirical referents, whereas **latent variables** are only indirectly observable, representing internal states whose existence must be inferred from overt behavior.

In the hypothesis "Instructional television relates to increased verbal learning among children but not among adults," "instructional television" and "age" are manifest variables. Specific television programs and people of different ages can be directly identified. In contrast, "verbal learning" is latent, representing a cognitive state that cannot be directly observed but is only inferred from behavior. Stipulating the empirical indicators of latent variables is often problematic because researchers must choose from a whole range of observable behaviors those most directly relevant to the internal states. In the case of "verbal learning," the researcher might decide that the ability to solve a set of written problems is a key empirical indicator or alternately, that proficiency in oral communication skills is a manifestation of verbal learning.

## Discrete or continuous variables

We learned in Chapter 2 that **discrete variables** change in distinct steps, whereas **continuous variables** take on "an ordered set of values" ranging from low to high.[3] In the hypothesis "High intelligence is linked to increased communication competence among females but not among males," the gender variable is discrete, having the two categorical variations, male and female. However, "intelligence" and "communication competence" are naturally continuous; they can assume any value ranging from very little to a great deal of each.

Operationalizing naturally discrete variables like gender is relatively unproblematic. Relevant empirical indicators of gender are the physical features defining the groups "male" and "female." Far more deliberation may be required for operationalizing naturally continuous variables. If one's research design permits, continuous variables should be operationalized to capture each variable's entire spectrum of values, ranging from none or very little of the variable to all or a great deal of it. For example, if we are using a 50-item skills test to measure "communication competence," we might assign a 0 to the lowest skills level and 50 to the highest, allowing for all shades of proficiency in between. Similarly, "intelligence" could be operationalized by stipulating varying degrees of mental capacity on a scale ranging from low to high IQ.

It is not always feasible to operationalize continuous variables in a continuous manner. Some research designs require researchers to change naturally continuous variables into discrete ones. For example, a researcher studying the continuous variable "televised violence" might be interested in the impact of several distinct types of violent programming. In such a case, the researcher might specify the empirical indicators of three general types of programs: those containing no violence, those with a moderate violence content, and finally programs depicting extremely violent episodes. Next, the researcher would subdivide all television programs into these three categories, permitting measurement of the effects of the three program types. Researchers should try to avoid reducing naturally continuous vari-

Substantive.

**42**

PART I
Conceptual
Foundations of
Contemporary
Communica-
tion Research

ables to arbitrarily created discrete ones, since much information about the entire spectrum of a variable's values is lost in the translation process.

# PRINCIPLES AND TECHNIQUES OF MEASUREMENT

Since operational definitions specify how one should measure a variable's empirical indicators, the researcher needs a thorough understanding of **measurement**. The measurement process yields *data*, defined as "reports of observations" of a variable's empirical indicators.[4] These reports, or data, are then used to test one's research question or hypothesis.

According to the often-quoted definition of S. S. Stevens, "Measurement is the assignment of numerals to objects or events according to rules."[5] The definition contains four key terms: objects or events, numerals, assignment, and rules. *Objects or events* are empirical indicators of the variables appearing in research hypotheses and questions. **Numerals** are symbols, such as 1, 2, 3, that may represent a variable's empirical indicators. Numerals have no intrinsic quantitative meaning, but may be used simply as qualitative labeling devices. The numerals appearing on automobile license plates or sports uniforms serve merely as labels to differentiate individual cars and athletes. In communication research, we often use numerals to designate the different subclasses of discrete variables. For example, "gender" might be differentiated by letting a 1 signify males and 2 represent females.

Numerals that are given quantitative meaning represent **numbers**, which can be manipulated mathematically in operations like addition, subtraction, multiplication, and division. For example, scores on a test measuring respondents' knowledge of communication prin-

ciples are numbers. We can total the correctly answered questions to form a score for each person, combine several people's scores into a group average, and the like. To summarize, when symbols are used to identify and differentiate classes of communication phenomena, they are known as qualitative numerals, whereas those taking on an ordered set of quantitative values are called numbers.

The term *assignment* refers to *mapping*, the systematic matching of a set of substantive concepts (the empirical indicators of variables) with a corresponding set of structural values (numerals).[6] Thus, mapping converts a variable's empirical indicators into a set of numerals. Earlier, we mapped the discrete variable "gender" with its empirical indicators male and female by letting the numeral 1 designate all males and 2 all females. The continuous variable "speech anxiety" could be converted to numerals by constructing a set of descriptions paired with values ranging from 0, indicating no anxiety, to an arbitrarily defined ceiling like 25, signifying maximum anxiety.

The final term in the definition of measurement, *rules*, means guidelines for assigning or mapping one set of objects (empirical indicators of variables) onto another set of objects (numerals). The critical rule used in measurement, a *rule of correspondence*, tells us how to assign "each member of one set" to "some member of another set."[7] If we wish to measure the continuous variable "persuasiveness" on a scale of 1 to 5, an appropriate rule of correspondence might be: Assign a 5 to communicators who are "very persuasive," a 4 to "moderately persuasive" people, a 3 to speakers with "average persuasive" abilities, a 2 to "moderately unpersuasive" communicators, and a 1 to "very unpersuasive" individuals. To take a second example, a proper correspondence rule for mapping the discrete variable "message type" might be: Assign a 1 to designate an "informative" message, a 2 to indicate a "persuasive" message, and a 3 to signify an "entertaining" message.

The distinction between Numbers & Numerals.

*Alluring* 诱惑的.

同型性.

## Reality Isomorphism and Measurement

The concept of reality isomorphism addresses the issue raised at the beginning of this chapter: How can one reduce to numbers such rich communication variables as "intimate conversations" and "argumentativeness" without destroying their meaningfulness? If our measurements have no "empirical correspondence with reality,"[8] scientific research will produce conclusions about phenomena that do not in fact exist. To ensure that numerical data correspond to the actual nature of communication phenomena, measurement procedures must be isomorphic with the phenomena they are designed to measure.

*Isomorphism* means similarity or identity of structure, and the **reality isomorphism principle** implies that one's measurement schemes should be "similar in structure to the structure of the objects or events being measured."[9] We adhere to the principle of reality isomorphism when our measurement scales contain values reflecting the structure of the phenomena we intend to measure. A departure from this principle is exemplified by the common practice mentioned earlier of reducing naturally continuous variables to arbitrarily discrete forms. Since the values of a naturally continuous variable range from low to high, they cannot be adequately measured on an instrument that varies by distinct steps.

计划
方案
组合
考考
後
结构.

## Levels of Measurement

To keep faith with the reality isomorphism principle, the researcher must select a numerical system whose properties correspond to those of the variable to be measured. Four numerical system types, traditionally called *levels of measurement,* are available for measuring a variable's empirical indicators: nominal, ordinal, interval, and ratio measurement levels.

These levels are progressive, ranging from the relatively simple nominal system to ratio measurement, which can be quite complex. Beginning at the ordinal level, each numerical system has all the properties of the former ones plus additional characteristics. This implies that any variable that is measurable at a higher level can also be measured at each lower one. Moreover, as one proceeds from nominal up to ratio measurement, increasingly complicated mathematical operations can be performed on measured data. Despite the alluring qualities of complexity, researchers should choose numerical systems on the basis of their isomorphism (structural similarity) with the variables being measured, not their level of mathematical sophistication.

Categories
TV. Radio
Print .....

gender { F = = M }

### Nominal measurement

At the **nominal measurement** level, researchers use qualitative numerals as labels for categorizing a variable's empirical indicators. Thus, nominal systems are appropriate for measuring discrete variables. We nominally measure discrete variables by assigning a numeral to designate each of a variable's subclasses and to differentiate all subclasses from one another. If the variable "news sources" is operationalized as the categories "television," "radio," "print," and "word of mouth," we could satisfactorily represent the variable by assigning to its four categories or subsets the numerals 1 through 4.

Importantly, a variable's subsets may be equally well represented by any set of numerical labels, and the subsets' labels can be interchanged without altering category meanings. Thus, we could designate the four categories of news sources with 85, 12, 3, 20 instead of 1, 2, 3, 4. Or, we could reorder our original numerals 1, 2, 3, 4 to 4, 3, 2, 1 or 1, 4, 3, 2 without changing the meaning of the four subclasses.

An adequate nominal numerical system has three critical characteristics.[10] First, the subclasses into which a variable is divided should

discrete,
not "degree"

Continuous
/
"degree"

little — great
deal
low — High

**44**

PART I
Conceptual
Foundations of
Contemporary
Communica-
tion Research

be *exhaustive*; that is, the subsets taken together should include all members of the class of phenomena the variable represents. For example, if we divide the variable "physical gender" into the subgroups male and female, we have an exhaustive classification; as a practical matter, all persons fall into one of those two categories. However, if we divide the variable "psychological sex type" into the two categories masculine and feminine, our classification system is not exhaustive. People are known to fall into at least two other subsets of the general class: androgynous persons, that is, those possessing high levels of both masculine and feminine traits, and undifferentiated individuals, who possess few traditional masculine or feminine characteristics.[11]

Second, the subclasses into which a variable is divided should be *mutually exclusive*, with each member of the general class falling into one and only one subclass. If a person could be categorized as both masculine and androgynous (an impossibility in this case), the subclasses of the variable "psychological sex type" would not be mutually exclusive. Third, each of a variable's subclasses should be represented by a different numerical symbol, to differentiate each subset from all other subsets.

## Ordinal measurement

Not only are the empirical indicators of some variables classifiable into exhaustive and mutually exclusive categories, but the categories have a quantitative or mathematical relationship to one another. **Ordinal measurement** is appropriate when the quantitative relationship among a variable's subclasses is *rank-ordered*, with one subclass possessing more of some property than a second subclass, the second having a greater value than the third, and so forth. If, for example, we gave 100 people our list of four categories of news sources (television, radio, print, and word of mouth) and asked them to rank the "importance" of each as

a source of information on current events, our results could be measured ordinally. We might discover that our sample regarded television as the most important news source, print second, radio third, and word of mouth was considered least important.

Unlike nominal measurement, which is indifferent to the numerals designating subclasses, the numbers assigned to rank-ordered subclasses must themselves be a rank-ordered sequence, such as 1, 2, 3 or 3, 2, 1. The sequence must contain one high number, one low number, and any required intermediate value or values between the two extremes. When a variable's subclasses are mapped onto a rank-ordered number sequence, the following correspondence rule should be followed: Assign the subclass with the greatest value the highest (or the lowest) number in a sequence, the next greatest subclass the next highest (or next lowest) number, and so on, until the subclass with the least value is given the last (either the highest or the lowest) number in the series. Following this rule, we could assign the series 1, 2, 3, 4, or alternately 4, 3, 2, 1, to the rank-ordered importance of news sources: television, print, radio, and word of mouth. We often use the symbols $>$, meaning "greater than," and $<$, denoting "less than," to display an ordinal measurement scale. Hence, if we assign a 1 to indicate the perceived importance of television news and a 4 to designate the informational importance of word of mouth, the ordinal scale is $1 > 2 > 3 > 4$.

Ordinal measurement has two distinctive qualities. First, the numbers used to represent a rank-ordered sequence of categories indicate each category's rank in that sequence and nothing more. For example, the number 1 denoting the ranked importance of television in our example does not represent an absolute preference for television. Rather, it signifies television's importance relative to other news sources. Because no fixed value is implied, the other extreme number in the sequence, 4, could represent television's relative importance rank-ing as well as the first number, 1.

Second, the distances between rank-ordered categories are not necessarily equal. Although the first rank is greater than the sec-ond, which in turn is greater than the third, the numerical distance between any two rankings may differ considerably from that separating any two others. Applied to our example, tele-vision may be two or three times more impor-tant than print as a news source, yet print may be only slightly more important than radio. Al-ternately, television could rank just above print, and print might be considerably more important than radio. The distances could be equal, too. The point is that ordinal measure-ment makes no assumptions of equality.

An ordinal numeral system is appropriate for measuring continuous variables when the distance between the different values of the variables either is unknown or is known to be unequal and a rank ordering can be imposed. Thus, if we are measuring a continuous variable like "persuasiveness" and we are not confident that the distance between its varying levels ("very," "moderately," "mildly," and the like) are the same, ordinal measurement may be preferred.

## Interval measurement

Like ordinal scaling, **interval measurement** assumes an ordered quantitative relationship among a variable's subclasses such that their values can be rank-ordered from high to low. However, interval measurement assumes an exact and an equal distance or "interval" be-tween each rank. With interval measurement, we not only know that some category A is greater than category B and that B is greater than C, but we also know that the intervals between A and B and B and C are the same. Moreover, we know the magnitude of the dis-tance between the paired categories. The nu-merals representing each category of a variable

signify not only the category's rank in a se-quence of numbers, but also its relative value within the sequence. Unlike ordinal measure-ment, the sequence of numbers assigned to a set of ordered interval categories cannot be re-versed without altering the meaning of each category. This property suggests the following rule of correspondence for interval measure-ment: Assign equidistant numbers ranging from the highest to the lowest to a variable's categories ranging from the largest to the smallest.

To illustrate interval scaling, suppose I wish to measure the continuous variable "commu-nication competence" with a five-question test assessing people's knowledge of effective speech principles. Suppose further that a per-fect score of 5 indicates "high" competence, 4 out of 5 correct responses signifies "moder-ate" effectiveness, a score of 3 means "average" competence, 2 denotes "below average" profi-ciency, 1 right answer represents "minimal" competence, and a score of 0 indicates a "poor" level of competence.

This hypothetical test is a six-interval scale (0–5) with a constant difference of 1 unit be-tween scores. We can perform mathematical operations on such scores that are impossible with an ordinal scale, such as adding the num-ber of correct responses to derive a total score. Importantly, the zero points on interval scales are arbitrarily chosen; they do not represent the absolute absence of variables like "communica-tion competence." Rather, the zero point on an interval scale typically signifies the smallest measurable quantity of a variable, as when we used a zero to designate "poor" communication competence.

## Ratio measurement

In addition to possessing all the properties of an interval numerical system, **ratio measurement** scales have a natural zero point, signifying a complete absence of the variable being mea-

46

PART I
Conceptual
Foundations of
Contemporary
Communica-
tion Research

sured. Instruments for measuring physical phenomena like weight, length, and speed are ratio scales because their zero points represent absolutely no heaviness, distance, or velocity. Because ratio measures have natural zero points, the numbers representing categories along a scale (for example, pounds, inches, miles per hour) are fixed values for the categories. This contrasts with interval numbers, which represent the relative value of each category in relation to an arbitrary zero point.

In communication research, ratio scales are often used to measure such physiological phenomena as emotional arousal in response to messages. Indices of arousal that are amenable to ratio scaling include heart rate, galvanic skin response (GSR), and pupillary dilation and contraction. Additionally, any counting of communication behaviors, such as the number of statements used in a conversation or the number of occurrences of certain nonverbal behaviors, may be ratio measures as well. On ratio data, we can perform mathematical operations, such as multiplying and dividing scores, that are inappropriate for interval measurements.

# RELIABILITY AND VALIDITY IN MEASUREMENT

The issues of *reliability* and *validity* address the crucial question: To what extent do the data yielded by measurement schemes accurately represent the nature and structure of the phenomenon being measured? We adhere to the principle of reality isomorphism only if our measuring instruments produce reasonably reliable and valid information about the variables we aim to understand.

## Reliability

**Reliability** is equated with a measuring instrument's consistency or stability. If the same scale is administered repeatedly to the same individuals and it yields roughly the same set of responses, the scale is said to be reliable. For example, if you and your classmates were to take one of your course examinations several times and the average class grades were approximately the same each time, the test is probably a reliable measure of the class's mastery of the materials covered by the questions on the examination. However, if the class average varies considerably from one test to another, the examination is probably unreliable.

## Random error and reliability

Unreliable test scores result from *random errors* of measurement, produced by factors such as fatigue or carelessness. Random errors result in responses that do not reflect a person's "true" knowledge or beliefs about the concepts being measured. Applied to a course examination, random errors can occur when students who know the correct answers carelessly select the wrong answers to multiple-choice or true-false questions. Reliability, then, may be thought of as the relative absence of random errors from the data yielded by a measuring instrument.[12] The reliability of any set of data can range from 0, meaning no reliability at all, to 1, signifying perfect reliability. If people's responses contain no random error whatsoever, reliability is a perfect 1. However, if their responses consist completely of random error, reliability is 0.

## Assessing reliability

Several procedures are available for testing the reliability of a measuring instrument. Recall that response consistency is the key to a scale's reliability; if the same people repeatedly respond to the same instrument in virtually the same way, the instrument is considered to be reliable. Three sets of procedures are commonly used to determine response consistency and thereby to estimate reliability: the test-retest method, the alternative-forms technique, and the internal consistency method. Each

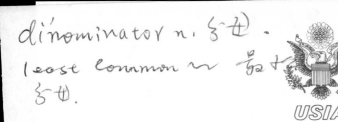

*United States Information Agency*

natural random error and leads to an artificially inflated reliability level. Second, people's views may change between the first administration of an instrument and the retest. In such a case, reliability will be underestimated, since what appear to be random error fluctuations are in reality changes in true scores.

Although potentially damaging, these problems can be alleviated by setting a time period between test administrations that is long enough to diminish the impact of memory, but sufficiently short that people are unlikely to change their views on the concept being measured. Judgments about the ideal waiting period vary depending on the type and complexity of the instrument; some researchers recommend at least one full day but not more than a month between administrations.[13]

*The alternative-forms method.* Designed to overcome the two flaws in the test-retest approach, the alternative-forms method requires two parallel versions of the same instrument. That is, the two instruments use different scale items to measure precisely the same concept. The two versions of the instrument are administered to the same group of people, often reversing the order of presentation for roughly one-half the group members. As with the test-retest method, the scores on the two forms are compared to assess response consistency.

The principal problem with this approach is the difficulty of constructing truly parallel versions of the same instrument. This drawback, along with the lack of an adequate method for determining when one has achieved parallelism, reduces the otherwise important advantages of the alternative-forms approach over the test-retest method.

*Internal consistency methods.* Designed to surmount the problems associated with both the test-retest and alternative-forms approaches, the internal consistency method administers a single instrument to one group of people at the same time. After administration, the researcher divides the original instrument into two or more subsets of questions and assesses the extent to which responses to each separate subset are consistent with one another.

An early version of the internal consistency method, the *split-halves approach*, divides a measuring instrument into two equal parts and correlates the scores derived from each part for response consistency. A later and more sophisticated version of the approach, Cronbach's *alpha coefficient method*, randomly selects multiple pairs of subsets from an instrument, correlates each pair's scores, and then uses the composite correlation between all the paired subsets as an index of the total instrument's internal consistency.[14] Most standard computer software

**48**

PART I
Conceptual
Foundations of
Contemporary
Communica-
tion Research

*Criterion [kɾai'tɪəɾɪən] n. standard of judgement principle by which sth. is measured for value.*

for the social sciences contains subroutines for computing alpha coefficients and other indices of internal consistency.

## Validity

Recall that the measurement process links abstract concepts to numerals representing their empirical indicators. To be useful, a measuring instrument must yield data that faithfully reflect the empirical properties of the constructs we wish to study. A measuring instrument is considered *valid* when it fully and accurately measures the construct it purports to measure.

To illustrate, consider the test administered to applicants for an automobile driver's license. Since the test purports to measure the construct "ability to operate a motor vehicle," it is valid only if people who receive high scores are good drivers. If the test actually measures ability to memorize facts about highway safety rules, it is a valid measure of recall but an invalid measure of driving ability, the construct of interest. As this example indicates, "one validates not the measuring instrument itself but the measuring instrument in relation to the purpose for which it is being used."[15] **Validity**, then, addresses the critical link between our measurement schemes and the precise constructs we wish to measure.

*arrangement ordered system. △ design.*

### Types of validity

Methodologists have described three different types of validity: content validity, criterion validity, and construct validity.[16] Although each conception addresses the relationship between the constructs we wish to study and instruments for measuring them, they confront that relationship from different perspectives.

(1) *Content validity*, sometimes called *face validity*, asks whether a measuring instrument fully reflects a construct's universe of discourse, that is, whether it contains a representative sample of a construct's empirical indicators. When students complain that a final examination was unfair because it did not ask about the material

covered in the course, they are questioning the content validity of the test. Likewise, suppose the construct "communication competence" is composed of two dimensions, knowledge of speech principles and possession of effective speaking skills. If a measuring instrument assesses only one of these components, and hence, taps only half of the construct's universe of discourse, it lacks content validity.

(2) *Criterion validity*, also called *predictive validity*, concerns the extent to which a measuring instrument's scores can accurately predict an important behavioral manifestation of the construct being measured. The behavior we wish to predict is called the *criterion* and the measuring instrument itself is the *predictor*. If the Scholastic Aptitude Test (SAT) can accurately predict academic success in college, it has criterion or predictive validity. Similarly, a measure of a person's attitude toward some behavior has criterion validity if it reliably predicts the behavior in question.

(3) *Construct validity*, a more comprehensive and robust concept than either content or criterion validity, directly confronts the question: Does one's chosen measuring instrument accurately and completely measure the specific theoretical construct to be studied? Construct validity implies "that the measuring instrument is actually measuring the concept in question and not some other concept" and further "that the concept is being measured accurately."[17] Because of its global emphasis on the goodness-of-fit between a measuring instrument and a construct's theoretical properties, construct validity is by far the most important of the three conceptions. Indeed, if an instrument has construct validity, it is considered to be valid from content and criterion perspectives as well. For that reason, when we refer to "validity" in measurement, we usually mean construct validity.

### Assessing validity

Validity assessment is one of the more important topics in measurement. By assessing our measuring instrument's validity, we determine whether we are measuring phenomena relevant to the constructs appearing in problem statements. Four procedures are useful for testing a measuring instrument's validity: the content method, the predictive approach, the known-groups technique, and the convergence method. As their names imply, the first two methods take a content and criterion approach, respectively, whereas the last two procedures focus directly on construct validity.

1. *The content procedure*. This approach is designed to determine whether an instrument measures a representative sample of a construct's empirical indicators. To use the procedure, a researcher must perform four tasks: (1) specify a construct's universe of content, (2) design an instrument believed to measure a representative sample of that content, (3) ask several persons to judge whether the instrument's content is, in fact, representative of the construct's universe of content, and (4) compare all individual judgments to determine the extent of intersubjective agreement. Assuming substantial agreement among judges, the researcher has reasonable evidence that the instrument is measuring the essential qualities of the construct of interest.

Suppose you wish to measure the construct "communication competence," conceptually defined as knowledge of effective speaking principles. Your first task is to compile a list of all the principles relevant to effective speech. These may be taken from textbooks or from your personal knowledge of effective communication. After generating a comprehensive list, you should select a representative sample of principles and construct a test, perhaps a true-false or a multiple-choice instrument, to measure people's knowledge of the selected principles. Now, ask several people to independently judge whether the test is a fair assessment of effective speech principles. If your judges agree that the examination contains a

representative sample of principle-related questions, you have good evidence that the test is, in fact, measuring "communication competence."

2. *The predictive approach*. Predictive validity assessment is a two-stage process: select a behavior that is an important manifestation of the construct being measured, and compare that behavior with a person's scores on an instrument designed to measure the same construct. If the two are similar, we can assume that our instrument is a valid measure of the behavior-relevant construct. Such an assessment is meaningless, of course, if the researcher fails to select a criterion behavior that is truly representative of the construct of interest.

To illustrate the predictive approach, suppose you wish to measure the construct "authoritarianism," a personality trait characterized by a tendency to agree with the opinions of experts or authority figures. Suppose further that you decide to measure the construct by giving a group of your classmates the California F Scale, an instrument designed to assess authoritarianism.[18] To test the validity of the F Scale, you might note the extent to which your classmates overtly agree with the course instructor's opinions. If those who scored high on the F Scale agree with the instructor's opinions far more often than those scoring low, the F Scale is probably a valid measure of authoritarian behaviors.

3. *The known-groups method*. This three-step procedure focuses directly on construct validity. First, administer a measuring instrument to a group of people who are known to possess high levels of a construct's empirical indicators; then administer the same instrument to a group known to possess low levels of the construct's properties. Finally, compare the scores of the two groups. If the instrument clearly differentiates between the groups on the relevant construct, you can assume the instrument's probable validity.

**50**

PART I
Conceptual
Foundations of
Contemporary
Communica-
tion Research

Rokeach used this method to test the construct validity of his instrument for measuring "dogmatism," or closed-mindedness. He began by asking a large group of college professors and graduate students to select friends who, in their judgment, were closed-minded and others whom they believed were open-minded. Rokeach then administered the dogmatism instrument to both groups and found that it clearly differentiated the two, furnishing evidence for its probable validity.[19]

4. *The convergence technique.* This method is based on the *principle of convergence*, according to which if two or more independent instruments produce similar or convergent results, they are measuring the same construct.[20] The convergence validation process involves (1) measuring the construct of interest with at least two different instruments, including the researcher's preferred instrument, and (2) comparing the scores yielded by all the instruments. Following the principle of convergence, a high positive correlation among the different scores supports the probable validity of one's preferred measuring instrument.

To illustrate, suppose I wish to measure the construct "public speaking anxiety" with a written questionnaire asking speakers to report felt apprehension levels when delivering speeches. To assess the validity of this instrument, I administer it to a group of public speakers along with two additional measures of anxiety: a physiological measure of arousal when delivering a speech, and a behavioral measure involving a group of judges who observe and report anxiety symptoms during speech delivery. If the physiological and behavioral measures correlate highly with my written instrument, I can assume that all three measures, including my preferred test, are probably measuring the same construct, "public speaking anxiety."

# INTERFACE: CHAPTERS 3 AND 4

This chapter has explored principles and procedures for operationalizing or measuring communication behaviors. Four levels of measurement—nominal, ordinal, interval, and ratio—were discussed, along with guidelines for using each. Reliability and validity in measurement were described. The chapter concluded by presenting methods of assessing the reliability and validity of measurements.

In the next chapter, we will discuss practical procedures for designing measuring instruments. Several standard measurement schemes are described and techniques for assessing their reliability and validity are explored. Chapter 4, then, is an extension and application of the measurement principles discussed in this chapter.

# MAIN POINTS

**1.** Operationalization is the process of transforming abstract constructs into a set of concrete indicators that can be observed and measured.

**2.** Measurement is the assignment of numerals to objects and events according to rules.

**3.** Numerals are qualitative labeling devices for communication variables, whereas numbers are quantitative symbols that can be mathematically combined with operations like addition and multiplication.

**4.** The principle of reality isomorphism suggests that one's measurement schemes should be similar in structure to the structure of the constructs being measured.

**5.** Four different types of numerical systems, called levels of measurement, are available for measuring a communication variable: nominal measurement, ordinal measurement, interval measurement, and ratio measurement.

**6.** Reliability is equated with a measuring instrument's consistency. Thus, if an instrument that is administered repeatedly to the same individuals consistently yields virtually the same results, the instrument is said to be reliable.

**7.** Three procedures are commonly used to assess reliability: the test-retest method, the alternative forms method, and the internal consistency method.

**8.** A measuring instrument is considered valid when it fully and accurately measures the construct it purports to measure.

**9.** The three types of validity are content validity, criterion validity, and construct validity.

**10.** Four procedures are useful for assessing a measuring instrument's validity: the content method, the predictive approach, the known-groups technique, and the convergence method.

## REVIEW EXERCISES

**1.** Construct a research question or a hypothesis on a communication problem that interests you. Then describe exactly how you would go about measuring each of your variables. Classify each measurement scheme as nominal, ordinal, interval, or ratio. Explain why the level of measurement you chose for each variable is appropriate. How well does each measurement scheme conform to the principle of reality isomorphism?

**2.** Focus on one of the measurement schemes you developed in Exercise 1 and explain how you would assess its reliability using one or more of the procedures outlined in this chapter. Why did you choose the procedure(s) you did? Now explain how you would assess the measure's validity using one or more of the proce-

dures suggested in the chapter. Why did you choose the procedure(s) you did?

## NOTES

**1.** See Warren Weaver, "Imperfections of Science," in *Science: Method and Meaning*, ed. S. Rapport and H. Wright (New York: Washington Square Press, 1964). This quotation was called to my attention in Leonard C. Hawes, *Pragmatics of Analoguing: Theory and Model Construction in Communication* (Reading, MA: Addison-Wesley, 1975), p. vii.

**2.** Fred N. Kerlinger, *Foundations of Behavioral Research*, 2nd ed. (New York: Holt, Rinehart & Winston, 1973), p. 3.

**3.** Kerlinger, p. 39.

**4.** Frederick Williams, *Reasoning with Statistics*, 2nd ed. (New York: Holt, Rinehart & Winston, 1979), p. 5.

**5.** S. S. Stevens, "Mathematics, Measurement and Psychophysics," in *Handbook of Experimental Psychology*, ed. S. S. Stevens (New York: John Wiley, 1951), p. 1.

**6.** See Hawes, p. 112; David Nachmias and Chava Nachmias, *Research Methods in the Social Sciences*, 2nd ed. (New York: St. Martin's Press, 1981), p. 133; and Kerlinger, p. 428.

**7.** Kerlinger, p. 31.

**8.** Nachmias and Nachmias, p. 134.

**9.** Nachmias and Nachmias.

**10.** Nachmias and Nachmias, p. 135.

**11.** See Sandra L. Bem, "On the Utility of Alternative Procedures of Assessing Psychological Androgyny," *Journal of Consulting and Clinical Psychology*, 45 (1977): 196–205.

**12.** Kerlinger, p. 443.

**13.** See Jim C. Nunnally, *Educational Measurement and Evaluation* (New York: McGraw-Hill, 1964), p. 85; and Walter Dick and Nancy Hagerty, *Topics in Measurement: Reliability and Validity* (New York: McGraw-Hill, 1971), pp. 18–19.

**14.** See Lee J. Cronbach, "Coefficient Alpha and the Internal Structure of Tests," *Psychometrika*, 16 (1951): 279–334; and Kerlinger, pp. 451–52.

**15.** Edward G. Carmines and Richard A. Zeller, *Reliability and Validity Assessment* (Beverly Hills, CA: Sage, 1979), p. 17.

**52**

PART I
Conceptual
Foundations of
Contemporary
Communica-
tion Research

**16.** Lee J. Cronbach, "Test Validation," in *Educational Measurement*, 2nd ed., ed. R. Thorndike (Washington, DC: American Council on Education, 1971), pp. 443–507.

**17.** Kenneth D. Bailey, *Methods of Social Research*, 2nd ed. (New York: Free Press, 1982), p. 68.

**18.** See Theodore W. Adorno, Else Frenkel-Brunswik, D. J. Leninson, and R. N. Sanford, *The Authoritarian Personality* (New York: Harper & Row, 1950).

**19.** Milton Rokeach, *The Open and the Closed Mind* (New York: Basic Books, 1960).

**20.** See Donald T. Campbell and Donald W. Fiske, "Convergent and Discriminant Validation by the Multitrait-Multimethod Matrix," *Psychological Bulletin*, 56 (1959): 81–105. The convergent technique is one part of a more complex validation method discussed by Campbell and Fiske.

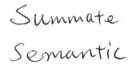
Summate
Semantic

# COLLECTING AND MEASURING DATA

This chapter discusses the instruments researchers use to collect and measure communication data. A measuring instrument is a set of scales that converts the constructs we wish to study into numerals. Three standard instruments that are used extensively by communication researchers are described: Likert's summated rating method, Osgood's semantic differential approach, and free-response scaling. Practical procedures for designing valid and reliable versions of each instrument are presented.

*Legitimacy* [lɪ́dʒɪtɪmosɪ] *Skeletal*
n. 合法性, 正(당)성.

55
CHAPTER 4
Collecting and
Measuring
Data

I began the last chapter with a quotation from e.e. cummings, who derided a nameless "oneeyed son of a bitch" for inventing "an instrument to measure Spring with." The poet was questioning both the legitimacy and the vision of people who design instruments for collecting and measuring data. For cummings, to reduce a phenomenon to data destroys its essential qualities, rendering it at best a skeletal image of itself and at worst a meaningless set of numbers.

This chapter attempts to show that researchers can collect data that capture the essence of important forms of human communication. I expect to demonstrate that careful data collection and measurement enable us to discover things that otherwise would pass unnoticed. I begin by describing sources of communication data, then discuss the nature of measurement scales. Finally, I examine several measuring instruments that are commonly used in contemporary communication research and describe procedures for ensuring their reliability and validity.

## THE DATA COLLECTION AND MEASUREMENT PROCESS

Data collection and measurement involve gathering information about the empirical indicators of constructs, recording the collected information, and converting the data into summary information, typically a set of numerals that can be statistically analyzed. I will first describe information gathering and recording methods, then examine numerical conversion.

### Gathering and Recording Data

Methods of gathering and recording information vary depending on the data source. Three sources of communication information are available: self-report sources, behavioral sources, and physiological sources.

### Self-report sources

When using self-report sources, a researcher gathers data by asking people to report on their communicative activities, either orally or in writing. Survey questionnaires are frequently used to generate written **self-report data**, whereas oral information may be collected in face-to-face and telephone interviews. Researchers often record oral data on audio tape, to be preserved in that form or converted into a written transcript for later analysis.

### Behavioral sources

**Behavioral data** are collected by observing the verbal and nonverbal actions of communicators. Researchers sometimes observe people's communication directly in "live" settings. Alternately, they may study past events by using audio, video, or written records of conversations, public speeches, media programs, and other forms of communication. If observation is direct, the behaviors of interest are usually recorded on audio or video tape for subsequent study. Taped data are often transcribed for detailed analysis. Whether researchers conduct observations themselves or use observations collected by others, the materials they ultimately analyze are written, oral, or visual records of observations.

### Physiological sources

**Physiological data** are derived from physical responses that are not subject to conscious control. As we have noted, involuntary physiological reactions used in communication research include heart rate, pupillary dilation and contraction, and GSR, as well as sweating, blushing, and muscular contractions and relaxations.[1] Specialized equipment is usually required to gather and record physiological

When I communicate with others, I usually feel:

Adequate ___5___ : ___4___ : ___3___ : , ___2___ : ___1___ Inadequate
        Very    Moderately   Unsure   Moderately   Very

data. Although such data are excellent information sources, many important aspects of human communication such as media performances, public discourse, and conversations are not physiological. This probably explains why physiological sources are not used as often as behavioral and self-report methods in communication research.

## Measurement Scales and Data Conversion

To statistically analyze self-report, behavioral, or physiological data, researchers must have appropriate measurement scales allowing them to convert collected information into numerals. Measurement **scales** are schemes for assigning numerals to designate the empirical properties of communication constructs.[2] Thus, scales serve as vehicles for mapping communication phenomena onto a set of numerals according to rules, a process explored in Chapter 3.

To illustrate how scales map data onto numerals, consider the scale in Figure 4.1, which measures self-report data on one dimension of the construct "communication competence." Notice that this scale maps the empirical properties of "felt adequacy" onto the numbers 1–5. The relevant correspondence rule is: Assign a 5 if the communicator reported feeling "very" adequate, a 4 if "moderately" adequate, and so on.

The next scale illustrates an instrument one might construct for measuring behavioral data on "persuasive strategy use." After observing

the interactions of several persuasive communicators, a researcher can convert these observations into numerals using the following scaling instruction:

> Classify the persuasive strategies you observed by assigning a 1 to each utterance that appeared to be "confrontational" and a 2 to all utterances that seemed to be "conciliatory."

Unlike the "competence" scale, this measure classifies utterances into subsets that have no mathematical relationship to each other. Notice that an appropriate rule of correspondence is contained in the instructions for constructing the scale.

These examples indicate that measurement scales may be either qualitative or quantitative. The two scale types are distinguished by the levels of measurement each represents. Recall from Chapter 3 that a scale may take on one of four different measurement levels: nominal, ordinal, interval, and ratio. **Qualitative scales**, often called *typologies* or *taxonomies*, are nominal measures. They differentiate the subclasses associated with constructs, subclasses that are not mathematically related. The classification of persuasive strategies as either "conciliatory" or "confrontational" illustrates a qualitative scale yielding a two-part taxonomy. **Quantitative scales** are either ordinal, interval, or ratio measures, and thus are appropriate for measuring variables whose empirical properties can be related in an ordered mathematical way. Our example in which "communication competence" was converted to the number sequence 1 to 5 illustrates a quantitative scale.

■ FIGURE 4.2

UNIDIMENSIONAL SCALING: ONE-DIMENSIONAL SPACE

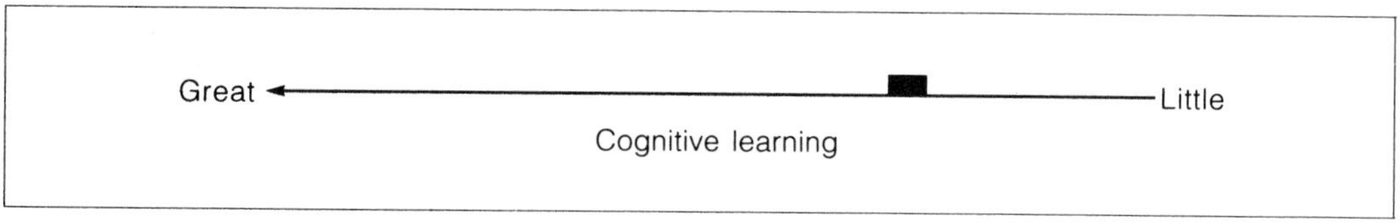

Great ◄————————————————■————————— Little

Cognitive learning

The type of measurement scale to be used is dictated by the principle of reality isomorphism discussed in Chapter 3; that is, measurement scales must be structurally similar to the constructs being measured. Thus, if the variable one wishes to study is discrete, qualitative scales are required. However, variables having a continuous range of values are usually measured quantitatively.

# DESIGNING MEASURING INSTRUMENTS

A **measuring instrument** consists of a set of measurement scales that organize communication information and transform it into numerical data. Such instruments may be either unidimensional or multidimensional. A **unidimensional** instrument is a scale or set of scales that measures a single dimension associated with a construct. These instruments are useful when the construct of interest possesses only one dimension or when only one of several dimensions of a construct is relevant. For instance, a set of scales that measures a communicator's feelings about some conversational topic is unidimensional because "feelings" are an affective construct representing the single dimension: likes and dislikes.

To take a slightly different situation, a researcher studying the effects of television on learning might be interested in the cognitive aspects of learning only, caring little about affective learning or the acquisition of psychomotor skills. In this case, a unidimensional in-

strument would do the job. Figure 4.2 displays the results of such a hypothetical investigation, indicating that television may contribute little to cognitive learning.

**Multidimensional** instruments contain scales for measuring several dimensions associated with a construct, thereby allowing "for the possibility—indeed the great likelihood—that there is more than a single dimension that underlies [most complex communication phenomena]."[3] To pursue the example of "learning" from mass media, a multidimensional instrument might incorporate subsets of scales for measuring each dimension of learning, including cognitive, affective, psychomotor, and the like. As Figure 4.3 shows, a common objective of multidimensional scaling is to locate the position of the measured variable in multidimensional space. These hypothetical results suggest that television contributes little to cognitive and psychomotor learning but is positively linked to affective learning.

A number of standard instruments are available for measuring unidimensional and multidimensional communication constructs, including Thurstone's equal-appearing intervals method,[4] Guttman's scalogram,[5] Likert's method of summated ratings,[6] Osgood's semantic differential approach,[7] and free-response scaling. I limit my discussion to Likert's summated rating scales, Osgood's semantic differentials, and free-response scaling—these approaches are used extensively in contemporary research, whereas the others are rarely employed. Although each of the instruments described can measure unidimensional

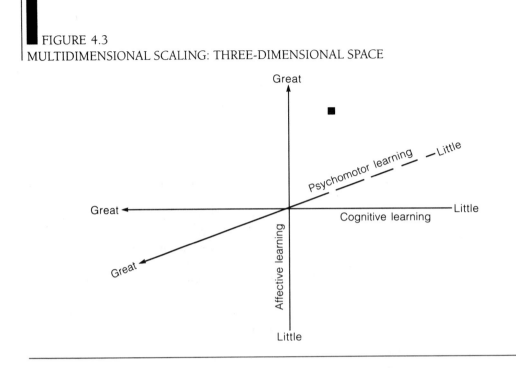

and multidimensional phenomena, the summated rating method is particularly useful as a unidimensional measure, semantic differentials are easily adapted to multidimensional measurement, and free-response scaling is equally comfortable with both measurement tasks.

## Likert's Summated Rating Method

The *summated rating* approach, often known simply as **Likert scales**, is a widely used measuring instrument. Nunnally explained the method's popularity when he noted that the instrument "makes sense and works well in practice."[8]

### The nature of Likert scales

Likert scales consist of a series of positive and negative opinion statements concerning a construct, each accompanied by a five- or seven-point response scale. Research participants typically are asked the extent of their agreement or disagreement with each statement on a scale ranging from "Strongly agree" to "Strongly disagree." Alternately, respondents may be asked whether they believe each of a series of statements is accurate or inaccurate, this time on a measurement scale ranging from "Almost always true" (or "Definitely true") to "Almost never true" (or "Definitely false"). Each person's responses to a set of statements are summed, so that individuals with the most favorable opinions or strongest beliefs have the highest scores and those with the least favorable opinions or weakest beliefs have the lowest scores.

Table 4.1 displays a two-scale Likert instrument extrapolated from Vidmar's and Rokeach's 11-scale instrument for assessing viewers' liking of the 1970s television comedy series "All in the Family."[9] A slightly different two-scale Likert instrument, shown in Table 4.2, was taken from a 10-scale instrument Rosenberg used to measure a person's level of self-esteem.[10] As the tables indicate, standard instructions for completing Likert scales ask respondents to mark the single response option that most

TABLE 4.1
A LIKERT INSTRUMENT MEASURING ATTITUDES TOWARD A TELEVISION COMEDY

**Instructions:** Please check the single response option following each statement that most closely reflects your opinion.

1. On the whole, I find the program enjoyable.

_____Strongly agree

_____Moderately agree

_____Agree somewhat

_____Unsure

_____Disagree somewhat

_____Moderately disagree

_____Strongly disagree

2. The main character's frequent references to various minority groups as "coloreds," "coons," "Chinks," etc. are offensive.

_____Strongly agree

_____Moderately agree

_____Agree somewhat

_____Unsure

_____Disagree somewhat

_____Moderately disagree

_____Strongly disagree

---

■

TABLE 4.2
A LIKERT INSTRUMENT MEASURING SELF-ESTEEM

**Instructions:** Please check the single response option following each statement that most closely reflects your judgment.

1. I feel I have a number of good qualities.

_____Almost always true

_____Often true

_____Sometimes true

_____Seldom true

_____Almost never true

2. I feel I do not have much to be proud of.

_____Almost always true

_____Often true

_____Sometimes true

_____Seldom true

_____Almost never true

---

nearly represents their reactions to each statement. Thus, Likert scales are forced-choice instruments, requiring respondents to select one response from among a fixed set of options provided by the researcher.

Notice that each statement in Table 4.1 is followed by seven response options or scale points. Since the first statement is positively worded, the "Strongly agree" scale position should be scored as 7 and the "Strongly disagree" option should be scored as 1. However, the scale values should be reversed when scoring the second negatively phrased statement, with "Strongly agree" scored as 1 and "Strongly

**60**

PART I
Conceptual
Foundations of
Contemporary
Communica-
tion Research

disagree" as 7. This practice ensures that the higher scores on both scales will represent greater levels of "liking," the construct being measured. In Table 4.2, each statement is followed by five rather than seven response options. However, scoring procedures are similar: the "Almost always true" position on the first scale should be scored as 5, whereas the scoring sequence should be reversed for the second negatively worded statement. These two examples illustrate four important features of summated rating scales.

First, the two instruments highlight a fundamental principle underlying Likert scaling procedures, namely, all scales in any one instrument should be related to a single common factor or dimension. In our examples, these dimensions are attitudes toward a television comedy and self-esteem, respectively. Thus, individual Likert instruments are *unidimensional insofar as the scales as a group measure a single quality or attribute of the construct under investigation.*[11] The principle of unidimensionality is reflected in procedures for scoring a Likert instrument. Because a person's score is the sum of all scale responses, each scale must contribute information to the cumulative score. To obtain a meaningful additive score, of course, the scale values on all negatively phrased statements are reversed, so that higher scores on every scale represent greater levels of the commonly measured dimension. Researchers wishing to measure several dimensions of a construct or several different constructs must develop a separate instrument or set of scales for each dimension or construct.

Second, Likert scales are flexible measuring instruments. The number of response options may vary, although the most typical numbers are five and seven. Moreover, the meaning of the options can be tailored to suit a researcher's special needs. In our first example, levels of attitudinal "agreement" were used, whereas a "truth" dimension was employed in the second. Third, Likert instruments are multiple-scale measures containing approximately the same number of positively and negatively phrased statements. This mixture reduces the probability of **response bias**, a tendency of some respondents to check the same response option for every statement. Fourth, Likert scales are usually treated as interval measures, although Likert himself originally assumed that they achieved only an ordinal level. The assumption of equal distances between response options should be reexamined each time the researcher employs Likert scales.

## Constructing Likert instruments

Because of the flexibility and general usefulness of Likert scales, the researcher must understand how to construct them. Designing a Likert instrument involves four steps: (1) determining the constructs to be measured, (2) compiling a battery of possible scales for measuring each construct, (3) determining each scale's discriminative power, and (4) selecting the final set of scales.

First, researchers must clarify exactly what construct is to be measured and whether the construct is single or multidimensional. Separate instruments (that is, separate sets of Likert scales) must be constructed for each dimension of a multidimensional construct. Once a researcher has isolated the precise dimension of interest—say, attitudes toward news reporting or self-perceptions of speaking competence—it is time to compile a battery of possible scales for measuring the dimension. This task requires a researcher to draft a series of opinion statements that appear to directly measure the pertinent construct, being careful to include approximately equal numbers of positive and negative statements. Then the researcher selects appropriate response options, deciding the number of options to use and the meanings to apply to each option. As I noted earlier, five to seven response options are usually adequate, and the most frequently employed continua of meanings are "agree-disagree" and "true-false."

Once a tentative list of statements and response scales has been compiled, the re-

FIGURE 4.4
THE THREE-DIMENSIONAL EPA SPACE

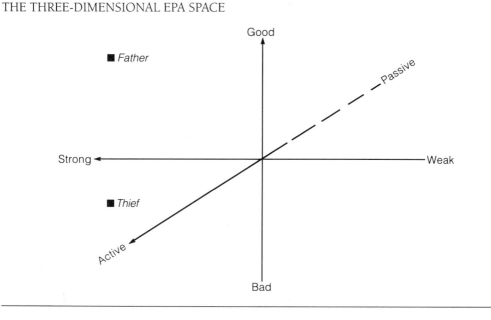

searcher must test each scale's discriminative power. **Discriminative power** refers to a scale's ability to measure only the construct under investigation; thus, it is a test of the unidimensionality as well as the validity of a set of Likert scales. To assess discriminative power, the researcher should first administer the tentative scales to a group of people whose characteristics match those of the individuals for whom the final scale is intended. If I have constructed scales to measure children's learning from mass media, I will administer my tentative instrument to a sample of children who are members of the same general group I plan to test later. Once administered, the researcher computes each respondent's score by summing responses to all scale items. These scores are the data required to assess each scale's discriminative power.

Several methods are available for determining discriminative power. One especially useful approach, the internal consistency method, was discussed as a reliability test in Chapter 3.[12] The approach compares respondents' scores on each individual scale with their total scores on all scales. If any one scale is tapping the same dimension as the other scales, it should have a high positive correlation with the total score. Scales correlating negatively or not at all with total scores should be eliminated.

## Osgood's Semantic Differential Method

Closely rivaling Likert scales in popularity, **semantic differential (SD) scales** measure the multifaceted meaning of constructs. Although not inherently multidimensional, SD scales are particularly useful for measuring multidimensional constructs. Osgood and his associates argued that the meaning of any concept can be represented as a point in semantic space formed by three dimensions: (1) *evaluation* (E), representing a "good-bad" continuum of meaning; (2) *potency* (P), denoting a "weak-strong" dimension; and (3) *activity* (A), signifying an "active-passive" continuum of meaning.[13] Figure 4.4 illustrates the three-dimensional (EPA)

SEMANTIC DIFFERENTIAL INSTRUMENT MEASURING SOURCE CREDIBILITY

**Instructions:** Please give your first impressions of the concept listed below by checking a position on each of the scales following the concept.

**Billy Graham speaking on religion**

1. Experienced \_\_\_\_\_:\_\_\_\_\_:\_\_\_\_\_:\_\_\_\_\_:\_\_\_\_\_:\_\_\_\_\_ Inexperienced

2. Dishonest \_\_\_\_\_:\_\_\_\_\_:\_\_\_\_\_:\_\_\_\_\_:\_\_\_\_\_:\_\_\_\_\_ Honest

3. Open-minded \_\_\_\_\_:\_\_\_\_\_:\_\_\_\_\_:\_\_\_\_\_:\_\_\_\_\_:\_\_\_\_\_ Close-minded

4. Unintelligent \_\_\_\_\_:\_\_\_\_\_:\_\_\_\_\_:\_\_\_\_\_:\_\_\_\_\_:\_\_\_\_\_ Intelligent

5. Aggressive \_\_\_\_\_:\_\_\_\_\_:\_\_\_\_\_:\_\_\_\_\_:\_\_\_\_\_:\_\_\_\_\_ Meek

6. Timid \_\_\_\_\_:\_\_\_\_\_:\_\_\_\_\_:\_\_\_\_\_:\_\_\_\_\_:\_\_\_\_\_ Bold

7. Skilled \_\_\_\_\_:\_\_\_\_\_:\_\_\_\_\_:\_\_\_\_\_:\_\_\_\_\_:\_\_\_\_\_ Unskilled

8. Passive \_\_\_\_\_:\_\_\_\_\_:\_\_\_\_\_:\_\_\_\_\_:\_\_\_\_\_:\_\_\_\_\_ Active

9. Trustworthy \_\_\_\_\_:\_\_\_\_\_:\_\_\_\_\_:\_\_\_\_\_:\_\_\_\_\_:\_\_\_\_\_ Untrustworthy

10. Partial \_\_\_\_\_:\_\_\_\_\_:\_\_\_\_\_:\_\_\_\_\_:\_\_\_\_\_:\_\_\_\_\_ Impartial

11. Right \_\_\_\_\_:\_\_\_\_\_:\_\_\_\_\_:\_\_\_\_\_:\_\_\_\_\_:\_\_\_\_\_ Wrong

12. Subjective \_\_\_\_\_:\_\_\_\_\_:\_\_\_\_\_:\_\_\_\_\_:\_\_\_\_\_:\_\_\_\_\_ Objective

space associated with hypothetical meanings of the concepts "father" and "thief," with the center or origin of the space representing neutrality on each dimension. Notice that both concepts are regarded as active and strong, yet "father" is associated with goodness and "thief" connotes evil or badness.

Although the three-dimensional EPA structure is often associated with semantic differential scales, dimensions of other types can be measured equally well. For instance, we might use SD scales to measure "source credibility" as a two-dimensional construct entailing trustworthiness and expertise. Likewise, "learning" from mass media could be measured on the three dimensions—cognitive, affective, and psychomotor. In short, SD scales are useful instruments for measuring multidimensional communication constructs regardless of their associated dimensions.

Operationally, a semantic differential instrument consists of a construct one wishes to measure followed by a series of response scales, each of which is a seven-point continuum bounded at its extremes by bipolar adjective pairs. The following adjective pairs are commonly used as the end points on evaluative, potency, and activity SD scales:

| *Evaluative* | *Potency* | *Activity* |
|---|---|---|
| Good-bad | Strong-weak | Active-passive |
| Pleasant-unpleasant | Rugged-delicate | Fast-slow |
| Beautiful-ugly | Dominant-submissive | Outgoing-withdrawn |

Table 4.3 displays a sample 12-scale SD instrument drawn from Applbaum's and Anatol's research on listeners' reactions to the preaching of evangelist Billy Graham.[14] Four dimensions or factors of source credibility are measured by

TABLE 4.4
SEMANTIC DIFFERENTIAL INSTRUMENT MEASURING REACTIONS TO MALE AND FEMALE TELEVISION CHARACTERS

**Instructions:** Please complete the sentence below by checking a position on each of the scales following the sentence. Give your first impressions or immediate reactions.

### When compared to females, males are:

1. Aggressive ____:____:____:____:____:____:____Submissive

2. Weak ____:____:____:____:____:____:____Strong

3. Logical ____:____:____:____:____:____:____Illogical

4. Withdrawn ____:____:____:____:____:____:____Outgoing

5. Sturdy ____:____:____:____:____:____:____Fragile

6. Insensitive ____:____:____:____:____:____:____Sensitive

7. Bold ____:____:____:____:____:____:____Timid

8. Dependent ____:____:____:____:____:____:____Self-reliant

9. Realistic ____:____:____:____:____:____:____Unrealistic

this 12-scale instrument: *expertise*, tapped by scales 1, 4, and 7; *trustworthiness*, measured by scales 2, 9, and 11; *dynamism*, gauged by scales 5, 6, and 8; and *objectivity*, measured by scales 3, 10, and 12. Importantly, the positive pole of each scale is scored as 7 and the negative pole as 1. An example of a 9-scale SD instrument that measures the traditional EPA structure is shown in Table 4.4. The instrument was extrapolated from Busby's research on children's reactions to male and female characters in commercial television programs.[15] Notice that scales 1, 4, and 7 are measuring an *activity* factor; *potency* is tapped by scales 2, 5, and 8; and scales 3, 6, and 9 measure an *evaluative* dimension. Again, the positive pole of each scale is scored as 7 and the negative pole as 1.

As the instructions in both tables indicate, respondents are asked for their first impressions or immediate reactions to the construct being measured. They register these impressions by checking one of the seven positions on each scale. SD scales, like Likert scales, are forced-choice instruments. The standard in-structions for responding to SD scales follow Heise's recommendation that respondents be told "that the purpose of the SD is to find out how people feel about things" and that they should use their "first impressions and not try to figure out the 'right answer' or the answer that makes the most sense."[16]

Semantic differential scales are flexible measuring instruments. As our two examples illustrate, they are useful for measuring multidimensional constructs. However, they can measure single dimensions of constructs as well. For example, a researcher interested only in children's "evaluative" reactions to male and female television characters could present respondents with scales 3, 6, and 9 drawn from Busby's research. Similarly, "trustworthiness" as a separate entity could be measured with Applbaum's and Anatol's credibility scales 2, 9, and 11. Thus, SD scales can easily accommodate unidimensional measurement. However, they typically find their greatest usefulness in multidimensional investigation.

SD scales serve two important functions in

**64**

PART I
Conceptual
Foundations of
Contemporary
Communica-
tion Research

multidimensional measurement. First, they are often used to measure constructs whose different dimensions are well known to the researcher, as for example, when we measure a construct like "emotion," which is known to contain the dimensions cognition and affective arousal. Second, SD scales are useful for determining whether a given construct is in fact multidimensional and, if so, what its dimensions are. In this case, the researcher presents respondents with bipolar adjective pairs measuring a large number of potentially relevant dimensions. Responses are used to determine which of the potential dimensions are actually relevant to the construct. In the source credibility study of Applbaum and Anatol referred to earlier, the researchers sought to determine what factors were associated with communicator effectiveness and uncovered a four-dimensional structure. The identification of unknown dimensions of constructs is a common use of SD scaling.

Beyond these multidimensional applications, SD scales have three additional features the researcher should understand. First, like Likert scales, SD scales are treated as interval measures with arbitrary zero points and equal distances between each of the seven points on each scale. Second, SD instruments are multiple-scale measures whose positive-to-negative directionality on alternate scales should be reversed. The reversing practice helps counteract the tendency of some respondents to mark the same point on all scales. Finally, SD scales are scored by summing or averaging responses on all scale items associated with each measured dimension. As I have said, the positive pole of each scale item is scored as 7 and the negative pole is scored as 1.

Three tasks are required to design and implement semantic differential instruments: construct the scales, select an appropriate format for presenting the scales, and analyze the scale scores.

## Constructing semantic differential scales

Constructing semantic differential scales is a three-stage process. It begins when we identify the concepts to be measured, proceeds to a determination of the dimensions associated with each concept, and ends with a selection of appropriate adjective pairs for measuring the dimensions of each concept.

Any concept that is known or suspected of being multidimensional is a prime candidate for SD scaling. Once such concepts have been identified, the researcher must decide whether the dimensions of each are already known or must be determined by SD scaling. If the dimensions are known, the researcher should specify them. On the other hand, if a concept's dimensional features are unclear, all suspected dimensions should be enumerated. In either case, the list of known or suspected dimensions will often include Osgood's evaluation, potency, and activity dimensions. However, it may contain only some of these, or it may include additional dimensions that researchers suspect are associated with the target construct.

Once a concept's actual or tentative dimensional structure has been specified, the researcher is ready to select appropriate sets of bipolar adjective pairs. Selecting appropriate adjective pairs entails two tasks: (1) generating a series of adjective pairs that are relevant to the concept to be measured, and (2) determining the representativeness of the adjective pairs. The *relevance* task requires the researcher to select adjective pairs which "relate meaningfully to the concepts being judged and which make distinctions that are familiar [to respondents]."[17] A useful method of assuring concept relevance and familiarity is to generate a large group of bipolar adjective scales and ask a sample of people drawn from the population who will respond to the final instrument to rate each scale's pertinence to the concept being measured. The researcher should then retain all scales receiving high ratings and eliminate the lower rated scales.[18]

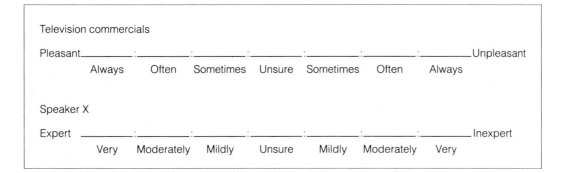

Once a pool of concept-relevant adjective pairs has been established, the researcher must check the retained scales for *representativeness*. That is, the pool of concept-relevant adjective pairs must have within it sets of scales that tap *each* of the actual or suspected dimensions of the concept of interest. There should be at least two but not more than 10 scales per dimension, with four scales being the optimal number.[19]

## The format of semantic differential scales

Format, the proper arrangement of SD scales for presentation to respondents, entails five important considerations. First, each concept ordinarily is presented separately, followed by a list of all the adjective scales. This arrangement facilitates data processing because all information relevant to a single concept is grouped together, making score computation and statistical analysis relatively easy.[20]

Second, the scales for the different dimensions of a construct should be mixed so that, for example, evaluation, potency, and activity scales are alternated rather than presented in blocks. Third, the directionality or polarity of SD scales should be alternated to ensure that the positive extremes are not always on the same side. These two practices help prevent respondents from developing response sets that

might diminish their sensitivity to the individual scales.

Fourth, the seven SD scale positions should be labeled with appropriate adverbial qualifiers as in the single-scale examples in Figure 4.5. Adverbial qualifiers are justified by studies showing that respondents are able to use labeled scales better than unlabeled ones.[21] Fifth and finally, SD scales should usually be planned so that respondents can complete them within a predetermined time limit. Osgood has suggested that 400 scales can be responded to during a one hour session,[22] undoubtedly an upper limit, since it allows only 9 seconds per scale. A more realistic figure might be around 250 scales per hour of response time, giving respondents about 15 seconds to respond to each scale.

## Analyzing semantic differential scores

SD scales are analyzed by computing *dimension scores* for the respondents as a group. A dimension score may be either the sum or the arithmetic average of people's scale responses on each dimension of a construct. Precise methods of analyzing SD scale data vary depending on whether the researcher is measuring a concept's known dimensions or seeking to identify unknown dimensions. If known dimensions are

**66**

PART I
Conceptual
Foundations of
Contemporary
Communica-
tion Research

measured, the researcher computes dimension scores in the straightforward fashion just described. To discover a concept's hidden dimensions, however, the researcher needs special statistical techniques like factor analysis, to be discussed in Chapter 8. **Factor analysis** separates out all factors or dimensions that are pertinent to the construct being measured. When relevant factors have been identified, dimension scores can be computed in the usual manner.

## Free-Response Scaling

Despite the popularity and general usefulness of Likert and SD methods, forced-choice scales have certain drawbacks. By offering a fixed number of categories, regardless of how few or how many, the researcher may inadvertently affect people's reactions, principally by limiting their response options.[23] Information about the full range of respondents' beliefs and behaviors may be lost if researcher-supplied options are not available for expressing the beliefs and behaviors.

**Free-response scaling**, a respondent-based procedure, is designed to overcome this limitation by letting people express unstructured responses with little or no interference from the researcher. The procedure consists of asking individuals to react in a natural, open-ended fashion to some stimulus of interest. For example, a researcher might ask a group of married couples to describe the communication strategies they use when trying to influence each other. Alternately, a researcher might observe a group of employees discussing job performance issues with their supervisors. The researcher typically analyzes such communication behaviors with the aim of developing categories describing how people communicate in their everyday lives.

Free-response scaling often represents a nominal measurement level, as when re-searchers compile taxonomies of utterances based either on self-reports or on transcripts of their actual conversations. However, free-response data may also be scored at other levels of measurement, including ordinal and interval scaling. For instance, an ordinal measure would result if we were to rank a group of employees' self-reported grievances or married couples' communication problems in the order of their importance to these communicators. Whatever its measurement level, free-response scaling has some important advantages over Likert and semantic differential measures. People's responses are not limited to researcher-supplied response options, allowing respondents to report all relevant reactions regardless of whether the researcher had anticipated them. Thus, the procedure eliminates the risk of suppressing or distorting natural communication behaviors, which is a threat to the validity of forced-choice methods.

### Examples of free-response scaling

The potential usefulness of free-response scaling can be understood by reviewing some representative examples in contemporary research. In the first example, Cody, McLaughlin, and Jordan explored the compliance-gaining strategies people use when trying to persuade one another.[24] To generate free responses, the investigators asked a group of college students to write out the strategies they would use in three situations: persuading one's best friend to repay a long overdue $25 loan, persuading one's next door neighbor to keep his dog from barking all night, and persuading the owner of an antique store to lower the price of a chair. The researchers found that all freely generated compliance-gaining strategies fell into one of four principal categories: (1) "direct-rational" strategies, where the communicators offered reasons or supportive arguments justifying their requests; (2) "exchange" strategies, involving offers to compromise or make concessions in exchange for compliance; (3) "manipulation" tactics including guilt inducement, flattery, and deceit as means of gaining compliance; and (4) "threat" strategies spelling out ways the persuaders would punish the persuadees if they didn't comply.

In a second study, Ragan examined people's alignment talk, which she defined as "strategies that communicators use to repair misunderstandings or disruptions in conversation."[25] The researcher generated free responses by videotaping and transcribing 12 job interviews. Six were role-played interviews in which graduate students pretended to apply for health care internships, and six were natural job interviews of undergraduates applying for data processing and personnel management positions.

An analysis of the transcribed interviews uncovered six major communication strategies used by the interviewers and interviewees: (1) "accounts," defined as statements explaining or making excuses for questionable or embarrassing behaviors; (2) "formulations," referring to utterances that summarize or interpret previous utterances; (3) "metatalk," such as requests and clarifying comments; (4) "side sequences," including questions and repetitions of previous comments; (5) "metacommunicative digressions," representing extended talk about personal or job-peripheral matters; and (6) "qualifiers," defined as tentative, uncertain, or nonassertive utterances. Not unexpectedly, Ragan found that job applicants used more accounts and qualifiers than did the interviewers, whereas interviewers engaged in more formulations, metatalk, side sequences, and metacommunicative digressions.[26]

As these examples illustrate, free-response scaling is a useful measurement device. For that reason, researchers need to understand how to design and implement the procedure. To use free-response scaling, the researcher must perform three tasks: construct a response-triggering stimulus, record responses, and analyze responses.

## Designing a stimulus

To elicit free-response data, researchers must prepare a *stimulus activity* that will generate information relevant to the research problem. Three varieties of stimuli are often used. First, the researcher can design *hypothetical scenarios* about particular communication situations and ask respondents to report their probable responses to such situations. The use of fictional persuasive encounters to generate compliance-gaining strategies by Cody and his colleagues exemplifies this procedure.[27]

Second, researchers can record *natural or simulated conversations* among communicators and analyze taped or written transcripts for patterns of free-response data. This approach was nicely illustrated by Ragan's use of transcribed conversations from both role-played and natural employment interviews. Finally, free-response data can be generated by conducting *structured interviews*, which permit the asking of open-ended questions about people's past communication behaviors and their present opinions about communication phenomena.

## Recording responses

Research subjects may transmit their free responses either orally or in written form. When the oral mode is used, responses should be taped and transcribed into a written record for intensive data analysis.

## Analyzing responses

Free response data often are analyzed by grouping units of related information into nominal or ordinal categories, then identifying the categories with appropriate descriptive labels.[28] This task requires several knowledgeable people, usually three to five individuals called judges or raters, who independently categorize or rank-order data and supply category names. When there is substantial agreement among judges regarding the nature and composition of a

**68**

PART I
Conceptual
Foundations of
Contemporary
Communica-
tion Research

nominal or rank-ordered category, it is retained. However, categories lacking high interrater agreement are discarded. The final taxonomy emerging from free-response data
analysis represents the collective wisdom of a
group of independent judges.

# VALIDITY AND RELIABILITY OF MEASURING INSTRUMENTS

Recall from Chapter 3 that a measuring instrument is both valid and reliable if it consistently
measures only the construct under investigation. I shall conclude our treatment of data
collection and measurement by summarizing
some important practices that enhance a measuring instrument's validity and reliability. Two
categories of procedures are especially pertinent: instrument construction guidelines and
instrument administration practices.

## Instrument Construction Guidelines

Instrument construction practices, including
formulating questions and response scales,
affect profoundly an instrument's validity and
reliability. Data-seeking questions may be either closed or open-ended. **Closed questions**,
exemplified by Likert and SD forced-choice instruments, ask people to select their responses
from scale options supplied by the researcher.
**Open-ended questions** encourage respondents to generate free responses to the stimulus
provided.

The two approaches have complementary
advantages and drawbacks. Open-ended methods eliminate any biasing effect that researcher-
supplied scales might exert on people's reactions. At the same time, open-ended questions
call for respondents to put considerable time

and effort into a research project, exceeding the
commitment some are willing to make. In contrast, closed questions are easy to answer, yet
researchers risk suppressing a respondent's true
feelings and beliefs. A choice between these two
methods will hinge on one's research problem.
If a researcher seeks general information from a
large population, closed questions may be
useful. However, when researchers require in-
depth information or wish to explore the reasons underlying a communicative activity, free-
response procedures may be preferable.

Aside from the choice of scaling methods,
the way questions are worded and presented to
respondents affects a measuring instrument's
reliability and validity. Researchers should
phrase all questions, response-triggering stimuli, and response scales very clearly. Ambiguous words and phrases can be interpreted differently by different respondents. This increases
the likelihood that people will react not to a
single response-seeking stimulus but to different interpretations of the same stimulus. The
order of presenting questions can affect responses as well. For example, some researchers
have found that Likert-type opinion statements
that appear early in an instrument are more
likely to generate agreement than those appearing later.[29] This effect compromises validity because it reflects responses not pertinent to the
constructs being measured. Detailed instructions for constructing and ordering questions
are presented in Chapter 11 under the heading
"Designing a Survey Questionnaire." It might
be useful for the reader to refer now to that
discussion.

## Instrument Administration Practices

Three administration practices can enhance validity and reliability of measuring instruments.
First, researchers should provide clear instruc-

tions regarding the nature of measuring instruments and procedures for responding to them. The precise meaning of all points along Likert and SD measurement scales, including the extreme and intermediate positions, should be made known. Moreover, stimuli for triggering free responses should be explained. Giving respondents a sample scale or triggering stimulus before a measurement session begins is an excellent way to explain what the instrument means and what behaviors are expected of respondents.

Second, data ideally should be collected from all respondents under the same conditions. This is not always feasible, however. If a measuring instrument must be administered to different groups of respondents at different times, administration conditions should be relatively constant. The researcher should give all groups identical instructions and administer the scales at approximately the same time of the day and in the same physical environment. This practice decreases the chances that extraneous conditions like administration time (for example, early morning versus late afternoon) or different physical conditions (for instance, a small versus a large room or comfortable versus uncomfortable seating arrangements) will affect responses. If it is impossible to maintain reasonably constant testing conditions, the researcher should note the different circumstances and check later to determine whether the differences seemed to affect people's responses.

Third and finally, people should be assured of the **confidentiality** of their responses, thereby increasing the probability of "true" or honest reactions. Confidentiality is especially important when seeking opinions or observing conversations on socially or politically sensitive issues. If respondents truly believe that their views on such sensitive topics as drug use or sexual behavior will remain confidential, they are less likely to distort responses toward positions they regard as more socially acceptable than their private opinions or actual practices. (Confidentiality requirements are discussed at length in Chapter 14.)

## Formal Reliability and Validity Assessment

A measuring instrument's reliability and validity can be formally assessed using the procedures described in Chapter 3. Recall that reliability can be checked by the test-retest method, the alternative-forms technique, or the internal consistency approach. Validity can be assessed using the content procedure, the predictive method, the known-groups approach, or the convergence technique.

Each of these methods can be applied to a measuring instrument before or during the actual administration of the measuring device. Prior assessment is preferred, whenever feasible. If an instrument is administered to a pilot group of respondents who belong to the same population as the people who ultimately will respond to the stimulus, an initially defective instrument can be revised and corrected before it is used in research.

## INTERFACE: CHAPTERS 4 AND 5

This chapter has described instruments for collecting and measuring communication data. I discussed three measuring devices that are used extensively in contemporary research: Likert's summated rating method, Osgood's semantic differential approach, and free-response scaling. Procedures for assessing each instrument's validity and reliability were presented.

**70**

PART I
Conceptual
Foundations of
Contemporary
Communica-
tion Research

In Chapter 5, we will conclude our discussion of the conceptual foundations of communication research. Methods of selecting samples of communication phenomena to observe and measure are described, along with practical techniques for enhancing the representativeness of selected samples.

## MAIN POINTS

1.   The data collection and measurement process involves gathering information about communication constructs, recording the collected information, and converting the information into a set of numerals that can be statistically analyzed.

2.   Three sources of information that are available to communication researchers are self-report sources, behavioral sources, and physiological sources.

3.   Measurement scales are schemes for assigning numerals to designate the empirical properties of constructs. A measurement scale may be qualitative or quantitative.

4.   A measuring instrument is a set of scales for assigning numerals to a construct's empirical indicators. Measuring instruments may be unidimensional or multidimensional.

5.   Three types of measuring instruments are used extensively in communication research: Likert's summated rating method, Osgood's semantic differential approach, and free-response scaling.

6.   Likert scales consist of a series of positive and negative opinion statements concerning some communication construct, each usually accompanied by five- or seven-point response options. Likert scales are especially useful for measuring unidimensional constructs.

7.   A semantic differential measuring instrument contains the construct to be measured

followed by a series of response scales, each of which is a seven-point continuum bounded at its end points by bipolar adjective pairs. SD scales are especially useful for measuring multidimensional constructs.

8.   Free-response scaling is a measurement procedure that asks people to react in a natural and open-ended fashion to some communication stimulus of interest.

9.   Questions used in a measuring instrument can be closed or open-ended. A closed question asks people to select a response from several fixed options supplied by the researcher, whereas open-ended questions encourage respondents to generate their own unstructured responses.

10.   To enhance a measuring instrument's reliability and validity, researchers should adhere to the following five guidelines when constructing and administering the instrument: (a) select scaling methods, whether closed or open-ended, that are appropriate to the problem statement; (b) formulate clear and unambiguous questions; (c) provide clear instructions to respondents; (d) collect data from all respondents under similar conditions; and (e) assure respondents that their responses will remain confidential.

11.   A measuring instrument's reliability can be formally assessed using the test-retest method, the alternative-forms technique, or the internal consistency approach. Validity can be checked using the content procedure, the predictive method, the known-groups approach, or the convergence technique.

## REVIEW EXERCISES

1.   Select a one-dimensional communication construct or isolate a single dimension of a construct having several dimensions. Now design a Likert summated rating instrument containing

at least two separate scales, each of which appears to measure the communication dimension of interest.

**2.** Select a multidimensional communication construct and specify clearly each dimension. Now draft a series of semantic differential scales that will measure the construct. Be sure to include from two to four scales that measure *each* dimension.

**3.** Formulate a problem statement, either a question or a hypothesis, that can be adequately studied using free-response scaling. Design a stimulus activity (perhaps a hypothetical scenario, a natural or simulated conversation, or an interview) to elicit the kinds of responses necessary to answer your question or test your hypothesis. Explain why you selected the particular stimulus activity you did. What kinds of information do you expect to get from individuals who respond to the stimulus? How will you record (for later analysis) people's responses to the stimulus activity?

# NOTES

**1.** For an example of a persuasion study using physiological measures, see John T. Cacioppo and Richard E. Petty, "Attitudes and Cognitive Responses: An Electrophysiological Approach," *Journal of Personality and Social Psychology*, 37 (1979): 2181–99.

**2.** Frederick Williams, *Reasoning with Statistics*, 2nd ed. (New York: Holt, Rinehart & Winston, 1979), p. 5.

**3.** John P. McIver and Edward G. Carmines, *Unidimensional Scaling* (Beverly Hills, CA: Sage, 1981), p. 13.

**4.** Louis L. Thurstone, "Attitudes Can Be Measured," *American Journal of Sociology*, 33 (1928): 529–54.

**5.** Louis Guttman, "A Basis for Scaling Qualitative Data," *American Sociological Review*, 9 (1944): 139–50.

**6.** Rensis Likert, "A Technique for the Measurement of Attitudes," *Archives of Psychology*, No. 140 (New York: Columbia University Press, 1932).

**7.** Charles E. Osgood, George J. Suci, and Percy H. Tannenbaum, *The Measurement of Meaning* (Urbana: University of Illinois Press, 1957).

**8.** Jim C. Nunnally, *Psychometric Theory* (New York: McGraw-Hill, 1978), p. 84.

**9.** Neil Vidmar and Milton Rokeach, "Archie Bunker's Bigotry: A Study in Selective Perception and Exposure," *Journal of Communication*, 24, No. 1 (1974): 36–47.

**10.** Milton J. Rosenberg, *Society and the Adolescent Self-Image* (Princeton, NJ: Princeton University Press, 1965).

**11.** McIver and Carmines, p. 23.

**12.** Another common method for assessing discriminative power, the item analysis approach, is described in G. Murphy and Rensis Likert, *Public Opinion and the Individual* (New York: Harper & Row, 1937), pp. 289–90.

**13.** Osgood, Suci, and Tannenbaum.

**14.** Ronald L. Applbaum and Karl W. E. Anatol, "Dimensions of Source Credibility: A Test for Reproducibility," *Speech Monographs*, 40 (1973): 231–37.

**15.** Linda J. Busby, "Sex-Role Research on the Mass Media," *Journal of Communication*, 25, No. 4 (1975): 107–31.

**16.** David R. Heise, "The Semantic Differential and Attitude Research," in *Attitude Measurement*, ed. Gene F. Summers (Chicago: Rand McNally, 1970), p. 241.

**17.** Heise, p. 238.

**18.** Heise.

**19.** Heise, p. 239.

**20.** Heise, p. 240.

**21.** W. D. Wells and Georgianna Smith, "Four Semantic Rating Scales Compared," *Journal of Applied Psychology*, 44 (1960): 393–97.

**22.** Osgood, Suci, and Tannenbaum.

**23.** See Milton Lodge, *Magnitude Scaling: Quantitative Measurement of Opinions* (Beverly Hills, CA: Sage, 1981), pp. 5–6.

**24.** Michael J. Cody, Margaret L. McLaughlin, and William J. Jordan, "A Multidimensional Scaling of Three Sets of Compliance-Gaining Strategies," *Communication Quarterly*, 28 (1980): 34–46.

**25.** Sandra L. Ragan, "Alignment and Conversational Coherence," in *Conversational Coherence:*

**72**

PART I
Conceptual
Foundations of
Contemporary
Communica-
tion Research

*Form, Structure, and Strategy*, ed. Robert T. Craig and Karen Tracy (Beverly Hills, CA: Sage, 1983), p. 158.

**26.** Ragan, pp. 157–71.

**27.** The use of hypothetical scenarios is also nicely illustrated in Kileen T. Smyth, "Toward Discourse Categorization of Compliance-Gaining Strategies in Lieu of Influential Context Variables," unpublished master's thesis, University of Wyoming, 1986.

**28.** Free-response data can be scored at any level of measurement in principle, including interval measurement. However, the beginning researcher will likely find nominal and ordinal scaling suitable for most research purposes.

**29.** See William A. Belson, "The Effects of Reversing the Presentation Order on Verbal Rating Scales," *Journal of Advertising Research*, 6, No. 4 (1966): 30–37.

CHAPTER

5

# SAMPLING METHODS

This chapter describes methods of selecting samples of communication phenomena to observe and measure. A sample is a group selected from a larger population, and it should represent the population from which it came. Several probability methods of selecting representative samples are discussed, including simple random sampling, systematic sampling, stratified sampling, and multistage cluster sampling. Some special nonprobability sampling procedures are presented, including purposive, convenience, and quota sampling. Practical techniques for reducing sampling errors are emphasized throughout the chapter.

I n November 1984 Ronald Reagan was reelected President of the United States, garnering 59% of the popular vote to Democrat Walter Mondale's 41%. Numerous preelection opinion polls had predicted such an outcome. For example, a *Washington Post*–ABC News poll sampled 8969 registered voters a few days before the election and concluded that Reagan would win with 57% of the vote, compared to 39% for Mondale (and 4% undecided). Similarly, a CBS News–*New York Times* poll sampled slightly more than 1000 likely voters and predicted a 58% Reagan victory, with 37% for Mondale and 5% undecided. Gallup's final preelection poll correctly predicted that the popular vote would split 59/41 in favor of Mr. Reagan. These results were stunningly accurate considering that all three polling agencies based their estimates on the voting intentions of a tiny fraction—0.01% or less—of the 92.5 million people who voted in the 1984 election.[1]

This chapter will examine sampling methods, illustrating procedures for drawing conclusions about a large population based on the responses of a relatively small group. I begin by discussing basic sampling concepts and principles. Next, several probability sampling methods are detailed. Finally, I describe some nonprobability sampling techniques used in communication research.

## PRINCIPLES OF SAMPLING

Once a measuring instrument has been designed, researchers must decide how to administer it and to whom. Suppose, for example, that one person wishes to measure the violence content of television programming, another wants to analyze the conversations of married couples, and yet a third proposes to study communication anxiety in public speakers. Clearly, it is infeasible for our three hypothetical researchers to gather data about all television programs, all married couples, and all public speakers. Rather, they must collect data from samples or subsets of the three larger populations. Each sample must be representative of its parent group, however, or else any general conclusions drawn about television violence, marital communication, and public speaking anxiety will not be valid.

Sampling methodology provides guidelines for choosing from a population some smaller group that represents the population's important characteristics. Sampling procedures affect profoundly the **validity** of research results. Applied to sampling methods, the concept of validity raises the question, To what extent can conclusions about a sample be generalized to the population from which the sample was drawn? If I use a sample of 50 public speakers to study the construct "public speaking anxiety," my results will be valid only if the sample happens to be representative of all public speakers. In most cases, a researcher's aim is to generate data that not only describe a sample accurately but also allow generalization of the results to the parent population.

There are two general approaches to selecting samples: probability and nonprobability sampling. **Probability sampling** is a scientific method of selecting a representative sample from a population, whereas **nonprobability sampling** does not ensure a representative sample. Since the validity criterion requires sample representativeness, I shall devote the bulk of my discussion to probability methods, reserving space toward the end of the chapter to describe some special uses of nonprobability sampling.

### Basic Sampling Concepts

Eight concepts are fundamental to an understanding of sampling procedures: element, sampling unit, observation unit, population,

76

PART I
Conceptual
Foundations of
Contemporary
Communica-
tion Research

sampling frame, sample, statistics and parameters, and sampling error.[2]

## Element

An **element** is the basic unit or "thing" about which information is collected.[3] Two categories of elements are prevalent in communication research: communicators themselves, studied either as individuals or groups, and the communicative outputs of individual and group communicators. *Communicators* are the basic elements of research when we ask people to report subjective perceptions, feelings, or beliefs about their own communicative activities. For example, we focus on communicators when we collect data about people's self-perceptions of their speaking abilities or when we seek viewers' attitudes toward television news reporting. When our hypotheses require information about people's collective cognitions, groups of two or more persons are relevant elements. For instance, the coordinated beliefs of dyads and small groups are often relevant research elements in studies of family communication and in many organizational studies.

Researchers often are interested in the objective content of people's communication, caring little about their subjective perceptions and beliefs. In such cases, the *communicative outputs* of individuals and groups are elements of interest. Communicative outputs include verbal utterances such as formal speeches or informal conversations, nonverbal displays such as facial expressions or gestures, and mass media broadcasts, including both commercial advertisements and entertainment programming. In many media studies, individual television programs or perhaps separate episodes within a group of programs are pertinent research elements. Conversational units such as speech acts and speaking turns are relevant elements in many studies of ordinary discourse. Finally, facial displays—smiles and frowns, or eye behav-

ior, including direct or downward gaze—are often elements in studies of nonverbal communication. In each of these examples, the objective content of individual or group communicative outputs is analyzed with little regard for the communicators' subjective perceptions, feelings, and beliefs. This quality differentiates the second category of elements from the first.

## Sampling unit

A **sampling unit** is "that element or set of elements considered for selection in some stage of sampling."[4] Although the precise element about which we seek information is always a sampling unit, sampling units may include elements other than those forming the basis of our study. To illustrate this distinction, suppose I wish to gather data about students enrolled in public speaking courses in the United States (the elements of interest). As a first step, I might select a sample of colleges and universities, after which I would pick a sample of public speaking classes from those colleges and universities. Finally, I might choose a sample of students from the selected public speaking classes. In this three-stage sampling process, colleges and universities are the initial or *primary sampling units* (PSUs), public speaking classes are *secondary sampling units* (SSUs), and the *final sampling units* (FSUs) are public speaking students, the target elements in my hypothetical study. The FSU is always a study's target element.

## Observation unit

An **observation unit** is the person or persons from whom we collect information about a target element. Observation units and elements are often identical. We frequently ask individuals who are the elements of interest to report information about themselves. However, observation units and elements are not always the same, especially when communicative outputs such as verbal utterances or nonverbal displays are pertinent research elements.

Suppose I wish to collect information about competence in public speaking or, alternately, want to study the erotic content of television programming. I might ask a group of observers to rate individual speakers and television programs on competence and eroticism scales, respectively. In these two instances, the outside judges serve as observation units reporting information about my target elements.

## Population

A **population** is a comprehensive and well-defined group (a universal set) of the elements pertinent to a given research question or hypothesis. A researcher interested in voting preferences might define the pertinent population as all registered voters in the United States. In studies of racist or sexist television programming, all commercial television shows could be the population. As a practical matter, however, it is useful to distinguish between two types of populations: target and survey. A **target population** is an aggregation of all the elements pertinent to a study; it is an idealized group representing the totality of target elements that interest a researcher. In contrast, a **survey population** is an aggregation of all the elements from which a researcher's sample will actually be taken. It is the realistic group of elements available to a researcher after practical constraints have been taken into account.[5]

To illustrate these differences, consider a hypothetical study of televised portrayals of elderly persons. It is obviously impossible to sample from among all television programs, past and present, produced by all networks including commercial, public, and cable outlets. Hence, the researcher must place some practical limits on the target population, perhaps by sampling only from commercial network programs shown during prime time viewing hours over a six-month period. Similarly, public opin-

ion pollsters usually do not sample from among all registered voters; rather, they often eliminate those who live abroad, those serving in the armed forces, those who are in hospitals, and other groups particularly difficult to identify or locate. A survey population should match its target population as closely as possible, yet the two are rarely identical. Since the survey population is the group with which a researcher actually works, sample findings must never be generalized beyond it.

## Sampling frame

A **sampling frame** is an actual list of the sampling units—usually target elements—from which a sample is selected. For example, a list of all students enrolled in a certain university, perhaps obtained from the registrar's office, is a sampling frame for the population of students attending that institution, just as a voter registration roll is a sampling frame for the population of registered voters in a given geographic area. A sampling frame, then, is the concrete embodiment of one's survey population, providing a roster of population members.

The validity of sample data depends in part on how accurately and completely a researcher's sampling frame represents the population of interest. The larger the discrepancy between a sampling frame and the composition of a survey population, the greater the likelihood that sample results will not reflect population characteristics. Indeed, some of the greatest political polling debacles in American history were largely due to the use of sampling frames that were unrepresentative of the survey population.

Perhaps the most famous instance occurred in 1936 when the *Literary Digest* predicted that Republican Alf Landon would defeat the incumbent Democratic President Franklin Roosevelt 57% to 43%. However, Roosevelt was returned to office by the largest landslide in history, capturing 61% of the popular vote and

**78**

PART I
Conceptual
Foundations of
Contemporary
Communica-
tion Research

523 electoral votes versus only 8 for Landon. A principal reason for the *Digest's* erroneous prediction lay in its sampling frame, which consisted of listings of telephone subscribers and automobile owners. Since, in 1936 (roughly the midpoint of the Great Depression), ownership of cars and telephones was by no means the norm, the *Digest's* sampling frame had contained a disproportionately large quantity of relatively wealthy voters. Yet, great numbers of people who were excluded from the sampling frame voted for Roosevelt and his New Deal programs in 1936, handing political pollsters one of their great embarrassments of all time. A researcher's sample results, then, are no better than the sampling frame used to represent the population of interest.

## Sample

A **sample** is a subset of a population. As a practical matter, a sample usually consists of a proportionately small number of sampling units—usually target elements—selected from one's sampling frame. To yield valid results, a sample must be representative of the population embodied by the sampling frame. This means that a sampling frame itself must represent well its survey population and, furthermore, that the survey population must closely approximate its target population.

Given these successive criteria, we may define a **representative sample** as a sample selected in such a way that it reflects well the characteristics of its parent population. Researchers can secure a representative sample by selecting samples at random from the parent population. A **random sample** may be defined as a sample of fixed size *n* that is selected in such a way that every other same-sized sample that could be drawn from the parent population has an equal chance of being selected.[6] When one's sample size (*n*) is 1, each element in the population has an equal chance of being selected.[7] If the elements in a given population

do not have equal selection probabilities, a sample drawn from that population might contain a disproportionately large number of elements whose chances of selection are greater than those of other population members.

A sample selected in such a way that other samples of elements do not have an equal chance of being selected might be called a *biased sample*. Examples of biased sampling include interviews on street corners or in shopping malls and certain popular radio and television call-in shows. All individuals who are not shopping at the time the interview is conducted and people who are not tuned in to the call-in programs have no chance of selection. In the case of some call-in shows, only certain types of people, perhaps more opinionated individuals, may watch or listen, and an even smaller proportion of this special group is likely to call in opinions.

Two factors often contribute to biased samples: (1) the samples are not selected at random even though the sampling frame may be representative of the target population, and (2) samples are selected at random but from a sampling frame that is unrepresentative of its target population. In either case, samples are not selected randomly from the parent population itself. Since random sampling is an important means of achieving a representative sample, we shall have occasion to return often to the subject as we proceed through this chapter.

## Statistics and parameters

A **statistic** is a numerical characteristic of a sample, whereas a **parameter** is a numerical feature of the population from which a sample is drawn. A statistic may take the form of a percentage or a sample's average score on some measurement scale. For example, we may discover that 52% of a sample of 100 public speakers reported feeling nervous when delivering messages. Alternately, we might calculate that a sample of 100 television viewers gave prime time programs an average entertainment rating of 4.2, signifying a judgment of "moderately entertaining" on a scale of 1 to 5.

If we were able to question the entire populations from which these two hypothetical samples came, the percentage of those reporting nervousness and the average entertainment rating would represent parameters. Of course, we can rarely question entire populations and therefore, we usually do not know the exact values of population parameters. Herein lies the reason for sampling: we use statistics or sample values to estimate population parameters. Public opinion pollsters can estimate the voting behavior of millions of people based on a relatively small sample of potential voters. Similarly, communication researchers can estimate communication parameters based on relatively small samples of communicators or communicative outputs. The accuracy of our estimates depends on the extent to which our samples are representative of their parent populations.

## Sampling error

**Sampling error** is defined as the extent to which population parameters deviate from sample statistics. Regardless of how carefully we choose our sampling frame or how scrupulously we select a representative sample from it, sample values are only approximations of population parameters. Fortunately, probability theory enables us to estimate how far our sample statistics are likely to diverge from population values, using two key indices called confidence levels and confidence intervals.

A **confidence level** specifies how confident we can be that our statistics are reliable estimates of population parameters, whereas a **confidence interval** stipulates how far we can expect population parameters to deviate from sample values. To illustrate, recall the *Washington Post*–ABC News poll referred to in connection with the 1984 presidential election:

57% and 39% represent statistics or the self-reported intentions of a sample of 8969 registered voters to vote for Mr. Reagan and Mr. Mondale, respectively. The *Post*-ABC poll had a confidence level of 95% and its confidence interval was plus or minus three percentage points (±3%). This means that pollsters could be 95% confident that Mr. Reagan's share of the 92.5 million popular votes would range between 54 and 60%, whereas Mr. Mondale's vote should vary between 36 and 42%. (The assumptions on which this statement is based, as well as mathematical procedures for calculating sampling error, are presented in Chapter 6.) As it turned out, these sampling error estimates were on target. The actual population parameters emerging on November 6, 1984, were a 59% total for the incumbent president and a 41% vote for the challenger Mondale.

I will now explore how pollsters work such "wizardry" by briefly examining probability theory. We shall see that sampling error estimates depend on the size of our selected samples as well as the character of the populations from which samples are drawn.

## Sampling and Probability Theory

In a completely *homogeneous* population—that is, one in which all members are identical—there would be no need for careful sampling. A sample of one would adequately reflect population parameters. Unfortunately, human communication phenomena, including communicators and their verbal and nonverbal outputs, differ in multiple ways. Samples from such *heterogeneous* populations should be randomly selected so that they contain essentially the same mixture of variations as the parent populations.

Probability theory is based on random selection procedures and it assumes that (1) each

**80**

PART I
Conceptual
Foundations of
Contemporary
Communica-
tion Research

random sample drawn from a population provides an estimate of the true population parameter, (2) multiple random samples drawn from the same population will yield statistics that cluster around the true population value in a predictable way, and (3) we can calculate the sampling error associated with any one sample. A sampling error estimates how far a given statistic will probably deviate from its population parameter.

The magnitude of sampling error associated with any random sample is a function of two primary variables: the homogeneity of the population from which the random sample was drawn and the sample's size. The more homogeneous a parent population, the smaller the sampling error associated with a given random sample. Moreover, sampling error declines as the size of one's random sample increases, since larger samples are more likely than smaller ones to capture a representative portion of the parent population. We shall see in the next section and in later chapters (see Chapter 11 on survey research) that researchers can take advantage of the homogeneity and sample size principles to reduce the sampling error associated with any randomly selected sample.

# PROBABILITY SAMPLING DESIGNS

Probability sampling designs use random selection methods to ensure a sample's representativeness, although different designs approach the random selection process from different angles. Four types of probability sampling designs are especially useful: simple random sampling, systematic sampling with a random start, stratified sampling, and multistage cluster sampling. Except for cluster methods, each design assumes that the researcher has a sampling frame listing the elements in the population of interest. Design choices will depend on one's research problem and a number of practical constraints that render certain designs more feasible than others.

## Simple Random Sampling

A **simple random sample** may be generated by (1) assigning consecutive numbers to the elements in a sampling frame, (2) generating a list of random numbers equal to one's desired sample size, and (3) selecting from the sampling frame all elements having assigned numbers that correspond to one's list of random numbers. A table of random numbers like the one in Appendix C is often used to generate the numbers required for selecting a simple random sample. The following six steps are involved in generating a simple random sample using a random numbers table:

1. *Assign consecutive numbers beginning with 1 to each population element listed in the sampling frame.* If, for example, the frame contains 1500 elements, the first element should be numbered 1 and the last 1500. (The number of digits in the last number, in this case four, represents the portion of each of the table's random number sequences that we must select to generate a usable sample of random numbers.)

2. *Determine the desired sample size.* The total number of random sequences a researcher requires from a random numbers table is equal to the desired sample size. If, for example, we want a sample of 150 elements from a 1500-element frame, then 150 four-digit numbers must be selected from the random numbers table.

3. *Adopt a systematic pattern for creating numbers having the required number of digits from each entry in the random numbers table.* To continue our example, we require a four-digit number from each of the five-digit entries in the table shown in Appendix C. We can select either the four left-most digits or the four right-most ones. (Notice that if we required numbers with fewer than four

Con'secutive an(连续(表)的。
interseet 接触, 和--交叉

digits, the alternative blocks we might select from a five-digit sequence increase beyond two.) The particular alternative we choose is irrelevant; it is important only that we adopt one and follow it consistently until we have accumulated our required 150 four-digit numbers.

**4.** *Select a plan for progressing through the random numbers table.* In amassing our required set of random numbers, we can proceed across table rows from left to right or right to left. Alternatively, we can move up or down table columns or we may progress along the table's diagonals. Any one of these plans is acceptable as long as we stick with it.

**5.** *Decide where to select the first number from the table.* The starting point in the table should be chosen randomly by, for example, closing your eyes, pointing to a spot on the table, and beginning there—or making up a column number and a row number, such as the sixth column and the fourth row, and starting your selection process where the randomly chosen column and row intersect.

**6.** *Systematically select the required number of random number sequences.* Proceed through the table according to your chosen plans until you accumulate 150 numbers. Skip all selected numbers that exceed the upper limit of the sampling frame—for example, 2000 or 1550—and eliminate duplicate numbers.

When this six-stage process is complete, the researcher gathers the required sample by selecting from the sampling frame all the elements having numbers corresponding to the random numbers set.

## Systematic Sampling with a Random Start

As our discussion of simple random sampling indicates, the method is often cumbersome and inefficient. For that reason, researchers some-

times prefer systematic sampling, an approach that, under appropriate circumstances, can generate equally representative samples with relative ease. A **systematic sample** *with a random start* is generated by selecting every *k*th element (for example, every fifth or fiftieth element) listed in a sampling frame, with the first element being picked at random. Thus, a systematic sample of 100 can be derived from a 1000-element sampling frame by selecting every tenth element in the frame, beginning with a randomly chosen initial element.

Two interrelated concepts are associated with systematic sampling: sampling ratio and sampling interval. A **sampling ratio** is the proportion of elements in the desired sample relative to the total number of elements in the sampling frame. With a projected sample size of 100 and a sampling frame of 1000, the sampling ratio is 1/10, whereas if the desired sample is 100 and the sampling frame contains 5000 elements, the sampling ratio is 1/50.

A **sampling interval**, representing the constant distance between selected elements, is derived from the sampling ratio. With a 1/10 sampling ratio, the sampling interval is 10, meaning that the researcher selects every tenth element in a given sampling frame. Similarly, a 1/50 sampling ratio requires the researcher to select every fiftieth frame element. The first element in a systematic sample must be randomly selected from among the elements in the first sampling interval. With a sampling interval of 10, the first element should be a number randomly selected from the series 1, . . . ,10. After this initial selection, we choose every tenth element until we come back full circle to the initiation point in the sampling frame.

Systematic sampling with a random start is a relatively uncomplicated method, yet it yields samples that are highly representative of the populations from which they are drawn. Although systematic samples are not, strictly speaking, "random samples," they often are sufficiently representative of parent populations to

*periodicity*

**82**

PART I
Conceptual
Foundations of
Contemporary
Communica-
tion Research

permit us to treat them as if they were randomly selected. Even so, the researcher should be alert to the potential systematic sampling problem called *sampling frame periodicity*, which does not affect simple random methods.[8]

A sampling frame is periodical if its elements are arranged in a cyclical pattern that coincides with one's sampling interval. Babbie has described a study of soldiers that illustrates how sampling frame periodicity can produce seriously unrepresentative systematic samples. Babbie reports that the researchers used unit rosters as sampling frames and selected every tenth soldier for their final sample. As it turned out, the rosters were arranged by squads containing 10 members each, and squad members were listed by rank, with sergeants first, followed by corporals and privates. Because this cyclical arrangement coincided with the 10-element sampling interval, the resulting sample contained only sergeants.[9]

To avoid this potential hazard, researchers should carefully study their sampling frame for evidence of periodicity. Periodicity can be corrected either by randomizing the entire list before sampling from it or, alternately, by drawing a simple random sample from within each cyclical portion of the frame.

## Stratified Sampling

Stratified sampling is not an alternative to systematic sampling with a random start or to simple random sampling. Rather, it represents a modified framework within which the two methods are used. As we shall see, the modification introduced by stratified sampling can generate a sample that is more representative of a population of interest than we might have obtained using either simple random or systematic procedures alone. Instead of sampling from a total population as simple and systematic methods do, the **stratified sampling** approach organizes a population into homogeneous subsets and selects elements from each

subset, using either systematic or simple random procedures. This approach assures that all pertinent subgroups within a target population are represented in the final sample.

To generate a **stratified sample**, the researcher begins by specifying the population subgroups or *stratification variables* that are to be represented in a sample. For example, if one is sampling from the population of all students enrolled at a particular university, characteristics such as gender and class year are likely to be important stratification variables. After stipulating these variables, the researcher divides all sampling frame elements into homogeneous subsets representing a saturated mix of relevant stratification characteristics. For example, in Table 5.1, which depicts the 10 subgroups resulting from stratifying a college student population by gender and class year, freshman males are in subgroup 1, junior females are in subgroup 6, and so on. Once the population has been stratified, a researcher uses either simple random sampling or systematic sampling with a random start to generate a representative sample from the elements falling within each subgroup.

Elements from each subgroup of a stratified population typically are selected according to a method called *probability proportionate to size* (PPS) sampling, in which the size of the sample taken from each subset is proportionate to the subset's size relative to the total population.[10] Thus, if the student population referred to in Table 5.1 contains 60% females and 40% males, the final sample should reflect this 60/40 population ratio. Similarly, if freshmen, sophomores, juniors, seniors, and graduate students constitute 35, 25, 20, 15, and 5% of the student body, respectively, the samples of each subset should reflect these population proportions. Combining the two stratification variables, the freshmen sample should contain about 35% of the total sample, and 60% of this subsample should be female. The other class years should be apportioned in a similar fashion.

**TABLE 5.1**
STUDENT POPULATION STRATIFIED BY GENDER AND CLASS YEAR

|  | Male | Female |
|---|---|---|
| Freshmen | Subgroup 1 | Subgroup 2 |
| Sophomores | Subgroup 3 | Subgroup 4 |
| Juniors | Subgroup 5 | Subgroup 6 |
| Seniors | Subgroup 7 | Subgroup 8 |
| Graduate students | Subgroup 9 | Subgroup 10 |

## Stratified Sampling and Representativeness

Stratified sampling methods can generate a highly useful sample of any well-defined population. A stratified sample may, under certain circumstances, have a smaller sampling error than either simple random or systematic samples of comparable size. To understand this potential advantage, recall that sampling error is reduced in two ways: by increasing sample size or by augmenting the homogeneity of the population from which a given sample is selected.

Stratified sampling takes advantage of the homogeneity factor. Samples are selected by simple random or systematic methods from within population subsets that themselves are more homogeneous than the population at large. For example, freshman males are more similar to one another than to the total population of college students. Sampling error may decline due to greater homogeneity in the subsets from which samples are randomly or systematically selected. In any case, stratified sampling ensures that all pertinent population subgroups are proportionately represented in a sample.

## Multistage Cluster Sampling

If one wishes to sample from a very large population, say, all college students or all registered voters in the United States, a comprehensive sampling frame may not be available. In such cases, a modified sampling method called cluster sampling is appropriate. **Multistage cluster sampling** begins with the systematic or simple random selection of subgroups or *clusters* within a population, followed by a systematic or simple random selection of elements within each selected cluster.

Although the two-stage process described in this definition is a common cluster sampling design, additional stages may be included. For instance, a researcher might initially select very large groups, then choose smaller groups from within the large groups, and finally select elements from each of the small groups. Because the number of stages varies, the general method

84

PART I
Conceptual
Foundations of
Contemporary
Communica-
tion Research

is referred to as "multistage" cluster sampling. Regardless of the number of stages, the clusters are labeled according to the convention introduced in our discussion of sampling units: the first set of clusters selected is called primary sampling units (PSUs), the second clusters (if any) are secondary sampling units (SSUs), and the elements selected during the last phase are known as final sampling units (FSUs).

To illustrate, suppose I wish to select a representative sample of all college faculty members in the United States. Although a comprehensive list of faculty may not be available, a list of all colleges and universities is easily obtained. Taking individual institutions as my PSUs, I will begin the cluster sampling process by selecting a representative group of colleges and universities, using either systematic or simple random methods. Once this group has been selected, I can either directly select a representative sample of faculty members (FSUs) from each selected school or select a representative sample of academic departments (or schools) within each selected college (SSUs), followed by a systematic or simple random selection of faculty members (FSUs) within the selected departments (or schools).

If I elect the first option, I will need a complete roster of all faculty members at each selected college or university. The second option requires sampling frames of each selected institution's academic departments (or schools) followed by rosters of faculty members in the selected departments (or schools) only.

## Sampling Error and Multistage Sampling

Multistage sampling is a highly efficient method of selecting samples from large populations. However, the samples it produces generally are not as representative as those yielded by stratified, systematic, and simple random sampling. These latter methods are subject to a single sampling error, whereas multistage sampling incurs a sampling error at each separate sampling stage. Put another way, we run the risk of selecting unrepresentative sampling units at every stage of the sampling process. Because of the increased probability of generating an unrepresentative sample, we need to consider methods of minimizing the sampling errors associated with cluster sampling.

Recall that sampling error can be reduced either by increasing sample sizes or by increasing the homogeneity of the populations from which samples are selected. Because clusters within a population are relatively homogeneous subsets, we can minimize sampling errors by selecting a large number of homogeneous clusters and by selecting a large number of elements from within each cluster. However, the practical need to keep one's sample size reasonably small creates a dilemma. If we increase the number of selected clusters, the number of elements chosen from each cluster must decline, and vice versa. Fortunately, the principle of homogeneity provides a satisfactory solution for this problem.

The elements within a cluster are more homogeneous than are all the elements comprising the total population. For this reason, the number of elements needed to represent adequately a given cluster is relatively small, whereas relatively large numbers of clusters are required to reflect the diversity of a population. Thus, "the general guideline for cluster design . . . is to maximize the number of clusters selected while decreasing the number of elements within each cluster."[11] In addition to following this rule, a researcher can often increase the representativeness of a multistage cluster sample by using stratification methods at each sampling stage. Initial clusters can be stratified by size, geographic location, and the like. The elements within each cluster can also be stratified by variables such as age and ethnic origin. As stratification increases at each stage of the sampling process, homogeneity and sample representativeness should increase proportionately.

## NONPROBABILITY SAMPLING METHODS

Probability sampling uses some variant of random selection, so that each selected sample of a fixed size has a chance of selection roughly equal to that of other samples of the same size. This approach ensures that selected samples will likely reflect population parameters. By contrast, *nonprobability* methods employ nonrandom selection methods and usually do not claim to generate representative samples. Moreover, many nonprobability sampling procedures do not require sampling frames of parent populations to generate relevant samples.

As a general rule, researchers should avoid nonprobability methods. In special circumstances, however, these approaches may be the only feasible methods available, or alternately, they may be preferred for testing certain research hypotheses. Three nonprobability sampling methods may be useful to communication researchers: purposive sampling, convenience sampling, and quota sampling.

### Purposive Sampling

Often researchers are interested in studying the behaviors of particular groups, for example, the communication strategies of a local religious sect, the language patterns of an identifiable minority group, or the news reporting of a given television network. In such cases, individual research objectives require the investigators to intentionally focus on the target group to the exclusion of other similar groups. Findings from a random sample of all religious sects, minority groups, or television networks will not accomplish the stated research purposes. Rather, the researcher requires a *case*

*study* of the group of interest and does not seek to generalize findings beyond the target group. When case study data are required, **purposive sampling** is the preferred method of collecting information.

### Convenience Sampling

When researchers employ **convenience sampling**, also called *availability sampling*, they nonrandomly select samples from populations that are easily accessible. Minimal consideration is given to sample representativeness. The use of an available group of college students as research subjects is a common example of convenience sampling. Because convenience samples usually do not reflect well their parent populations, findings should not be generalized beyond the selected sample. Convenience sampling, then, is justified when a researcher is not concerned about the generality of results, but wishes only to examine some phenomenon within a selected sample.

### Quota Sampling

Unlike purposive and convenience sampling methods, **quota sampling** aims to generate a representative sample but in a different manner from probability sampling procedures. Quota sampling, which was used extensively before the development of probability methods, calls for a complex sampling frame called a *quota matrix* to divide a target population into all its relevant subclasses. In constructing such a matrix, researchers must stratify a given population by gender, educational level, income, age, ethnic origin, race, geographic region, political orientation, and a host of other demographic variables. Moreover, they must accurately determine the proportion of population members falling into each relevant subclass or cell of the quota matrix.

Once a quota matrix has been constructed,

**86**

PART I
Conceptual
Foundations of
Contemporary
Communica-
tion Research

data are collected from persons having all the characteristics of each matrix cell, and all cells are weighted to reflect their proportionate sizes in the total population. Importantly, samples from each matrix cell are not randomly selected; rather, all available individuals falling into each cell are selected until researchers reach the predetermined number or "quota" of people they wish to include in the final sample. Quota sampling is a cumbersome sampling method that is defective on a number of counts. First, it is quite difficult to construct a complete quota matrix because doing so requires the researcher to know and account for every potentially relevant characteristic of a given population. Second, the nonrandom selection of samples from each cell decreases the likelihood of generating a representative sample. Third, unlike probability methods, quota sampling has no reliable procedures for estimating sampling error. Finally, even if an adequate matrix could be constructed and a highly representative quota sample could be generated, probability sampling would still be preferred, because the latter procedure is easier to execute than quota sampling methods.

# INTERFACE:
# CHAPTER 5 AND PART II

In this chapter, we have examined methods of selecting samples of communication phenomena. Several probability procedures for generating representative samples were described, including simple random sampling, systematic sampling with a random start, stratified sampling, and multistage cluster sampling. The chapter presented some special nonprobability sampling designs, including purposive, convenience, and quota sampling. Finally, techniques for reducing sampling error were discussed.

This chapter concludes our exploration of the conceptual foundations of contemporary communication research. In Part II, methods for statistically analyzing sample data are examined. Chapter 6 discusses basic statistical concepts and principles. In Chapter 7, procedures for statistically analyzing population differences are described, and Chapter 8 presents methods for the statistical analysis of population relationships.

# MAIN POINTS

**1.** When a researcher has achieved sampling validity, conclusions about a sample can be generalized to the population from which the sample was selected.

**2.** Probability sampling is a scientific method of selecting representative samples from populations, whereas nonprobability sampling does not ensure the representativeness of selected samples.

**3.** Eight concepts are fundamental to an understanding of sampling: element, sampling unit, observation unit, population, sampling frame, sample, statistics and parameters, and sampling error.

**4.** An element is the basic unit about which information is sought. Two categories of elements are prevalent in communication research: communicators themselves, studied either as individuals or as groups; and the communicative outputs of individuals and groups.

**5.** A population is a well-defined group or universal set containing all the elements of interest in a given research project, whereas a sample is a subset of a population.

**6.** A sampling frame is a list of the elements in a population.

**7.** A random sample is a sample of fixed size

*n*, selected in such a way that every other sample of size *n* in the population has an equal chance of selection. A biased sample is selected in such a way that other samples do not have an equal chance of selection.

**8.** A statistic is a numerical characteristic of a sample, and a parameter is a numerical characteristic of a population.

**9.** Sampling error estimates the extent to which population parameters probably deviate from sample statistics. The magnitude of sampling error associated with any random sample is a function of the homogeneity of the parent population and the sample's size.

**10.** There are four principal types of probability sampling designs: simple random sampling, systematic sampling with a random start, stratified sampling, and multistage cluster sampling.

**11.** A simple random sample is selected in such a way that each element in the population has an equal chance of selection. It is generated by selecting from a sampling frame all elements having assigned numbers that correspond to a set of randomly generated digits.

**12.** A systematic sample with a random start is generated by selecting every *k*th element listed in a sampling frame, with the first element being picked at random.

**13.** A stratified sample is generated by organizing a population into homogeneous subsets and selecting elements from within each subset, using either systematic or simple random sampling. Usually, the size of the sample taken from each subset should be proportionate to the subset's relative size in the population.

**14.** Multistage cluster sampling begins with the systematic or simple random selection of clusters within a population, followed by a systematic or simple random selection of elements within each cluster.

**15.** There are three primary nonprobability sampling methods: purposive sampling, convenience sampling, and quota sampling.

# REVIEW EXERCISES

**1.** Secure a recent telephone directory of your college or university. Treat the faculty listings in the directory as a sampling frame for conducting a study of faculty members' satisfaction with task-oriented communication patterns within the university hierarchy. Now generate a sample of 50 faculty members using each of the following sampling methods: simple random sampling, systematic sampling with a random start, stratified sampling, multistage cluster sampling, and purposive sampling.

**2.** Suppose you wish to study the persuasive strategies used in television advertisements aired during prime time. Describe precisely the following dimensions of your study: the elements of interest, the population (including both the target and survey populations), and the sampling frame. What probability sampling method would be most likely to yield a representative sample of the elements that interest you? Why?

# NOTES

**1.** See *Washington Post*, November 4, 1984, p. A16; *Denver Post*, November 5, 1984, p. 3A; and *Denver Post*, November 11, 1984, p. 6I.

**2.** The following discussion of basic sampling concepts draws heavily on Leslie Kish, *Survey Sampling* (New York: John Wiley, 1965).

**3.** Earl Babbie, *Survey Research Methods* (Belmont, CA: Wadsworth, 1973), p. 79.

**4.** Earl Babbie, *The Practice of Social Research*, 4th ed. (Belmont, CA: Wadsworth, 1986), p. 142.

**5.** See Graham Kalton, *Introduction to Survey Sampling* (Beverly Hills, CA: Sage, 1983), p. 6.

PART I
Conceptual
Foundations of
Contemporary
Communica-
tion Research

6. Robert Johnson, *Elementary Statistics*, 4th ed. (Boston: Duxbury Press, 1984), p. 16; and John E. Freund, *Modern Elementary Statistics*, 6th ed. (Englewood Cliffs, NJ: Prentice-Hall, 1984), p. 235.

7. Johnson.

8. See Freund, p. 239; and Babbie, 1986, p. 159.

9. Babbie, 1986, pp. 159–60.

10. Under certain circumstances, researchers use *disproportionate* sampling procedures; that is, they select samples that are larger or smaller than proportionate population sizes. For a discussion of circumstances that may warrant disproportionate sampling, see Babbie, 1986, pp. 169–71.

11. Babbie, 1986, p. 159.

PART

II

# STATISTICAL ANALYSIS IN CONTEMPORARY COMMUNICATION RESEARCH

['indisi:z]

indices
pl. of index
Sth. that points
to or indicates;
pointer showing
measurements.

Frequency distribution
Indices of Central Ten
-dency
Indices of dispersion

# CHAPTER
# 6

descriptive Statistics
inferential Statistics
Sampling
distributions

# STATISTICAL INQUIRY

MARY JOHN SMITH AND DIANE M. SPRESSER

This chapter describes basic concepts and methods of descriptive and inferential statistics. Descriptive statistics involves procedures for describing sample data, whereas inferential statistics is a logical system for drawing conclusions about population characteristics based on sample descriptions. Descriptive tools like frequency distributions, indices of central tendency, and indices of dispersion are presented. Sampling distributions that provide a bridge between descriptive and inferential statistics are explained. The chapter concludes with a discussion of principles and procedures for testing hypotheses.

dispersal

Note: Diane M. Spresser is professor and head of the Department of Mathematics and Computer Science, James Madison University, Harrisonburg, Virginia.

CHAPTER
OUTLINE

*Statistics:
facts shown
in numbers.

*Statistics: is
the science of
describing &
reasoning from
numerial data.

Trepidation n. 发抖. 惶惶.

dual: of two, double, divided in two.

# THE NATURE OF STATISTICAL INQUIRY

Like the patient suffering from a multiple personality disorder, statistics leads at least three separate lives. The first is capsulized in clichés like "There are lies, damn lies, and then there's statistics," and "A politician uses statistics the way a drunk uses a lamppost—more for support than illumination." From the mid-seventeenth century when probability principles were first employed to calculate gambling odds to the use of probabilities by some contemporary politicians and advertisers to advance narrow self-interests, statistics' first persona has been shaped by the unsavory company it sometimes keeps. At times, however, statistics is viewed as an unexciting field of scholarship, especially by students outside the field, who often approach its study with trepidation, expecting to meet the second "face" of statistical inquiry.

Given this dual image problem, it is not surprising that statistics' third and most important "face"—that of a powerful tool for generating reliable knowledge about the empirical world—is sometimes underemphasized. Statistics is a mechanism for understanding data and inferring conclusions that transcend the data themselves. Without statistics, our knowledge of human communication would be meager indeed. Thus, anyone who aspires to become a communication researcher must master the mechanics of statistical analysis.

In this chapter, we outline the fundamentals of statistical inquiry, covering two major topics. First, statistical procedures for describing sample data are discussed. We examine key sample characteristics, including indices of central tendency and dispersion. Second, methods of inferring conclusions about populations based on sample data are presented. We describe the nature of statistical reasoning and explain the logic of hypothesis testing.

dispersion

**Statistics**, a singular noun designating a field of scholarly inquiry, is defined as the science of describing and reasoning from numerical data.[1] To perform statistical analysis, a researcher requires a set of data and a system for assigning numerals to represent the data.

We learned in Chapter 5 that data are often derived from samples, including communicators themselves and their verbal and nonverbal outputs. Statistical analysis allows us to perform two tasks with data. First, statistics provides a mechanism for systematically describing the characteristics of a sample. Recall that sample characteristics are themselves called **statistics**, a plural noun denoting the empirical features of a sample. Second, statistics as a field of inquiry enables researchers to generalize sample statistics to the **parameters** of a sample's parent population.

These dual functions parallel two branches of statistics: descriptive and inferential statistics. **Descriptive statistics** involves procedures for summarizing the characteristics of sample data, whereas **inferential statistics** is a logical system for estimating population characteristics based on sample descriptions.

# DESCRIPTIVE STATISTICS

Once researchers have gathered data according to some sampling scheme, it is often helpful to compile and present the data in pictorial form. This gives a useful summary of the data, allowing us to visualize patterns exhibited by the variable under study. Graphic presentations are especially helpful when the sample is a large one.

savory
适宜的.
任务的.
名声的.

parameters [pə'ræmitə]
(数) 参(变)
数.

meager
贫乏的.

FREQUENCY DISTRIBUTION: PERSUASIVE STRATEGIES USED TO INFLUENCE
CLOSE FRIENDS

| Persuasive strategy | Number of students using strategy |
|---|---|
| Reasoning | 578 |
| Manipulation | 465 |
| Bargaining | 121 |
| Threats | 49 |
| | 1213 |

■ FIGURE 6.1
BAR GRAPH: PERSUASIVE STRATEGIES USED TO INFLUENCE CLOSE FRIENDS

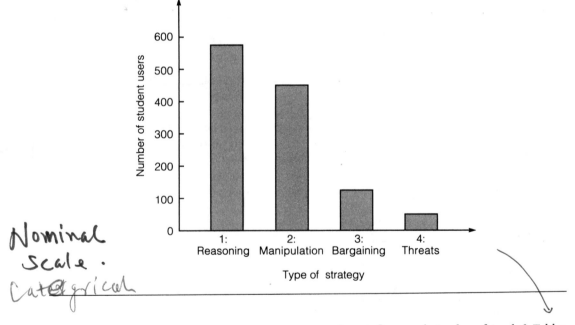

*Nominal scale. Categorical* (handwritten)

## Frequency Distributions and their Graphic Presentations

The data displayed in Table 6.1 were derived from a large sample of college students who described the persuasive strategies they often used to influence their close friends.[2] Tables like this are termed **frequency distributions** or simply **distributions**. The same data may be displayed on a **bar graph**, as in Figure 6.1. All the persuasive strategies the sample reported using fell into one of four discrete categories: reasoning was the most frequently used technique, followed by manipulative ploys, bar-

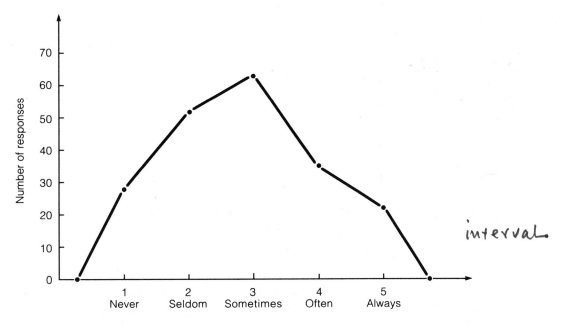

*interval*

Frequency with which strategies are motivated by desire for acceptance and respect

FIGURE 6.3
FIVE-POINT LIKERT SCALE

| How often are your choices of communication strategies motivated by a desire to achieve acceptance and respect in the community where you live and work? | | | | |
|---|---|---|---|---|
| 29 : | 52 : | 64 : | 38 : | 26 |
| Never | Seldom | Sometimes | Often | Always |

gaining attempts, and threatening strategies. Notice that the horizontal axis in Figure 6.1 represents the four-category nominal scale, whereas the number, the frequency, of respondent strategies falling into each category is registered on the vertical axis.

Another form of graphical presentation is the **frequency polygon**. The frequency polygon in Figure 6.2, for example, displays a distribution of interval data gathered in a study of college students' motives for communicating.[3] The data represent the responses of a sample of 209 students to the five-point Likert scale in Figure 6.3. The frequency polygon shows that

FIGURE 6.4
HISTOGRAM 直视图 矩形图

Norm 标准
规范 准则

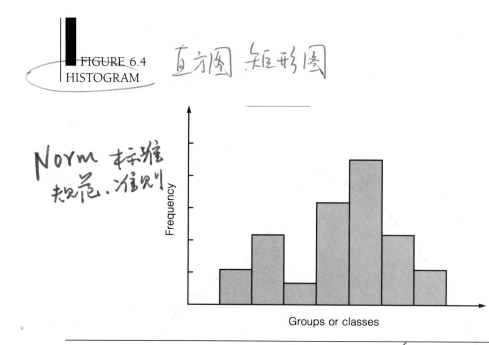

Groups or classes

most respondents held a moderate position on the issue, indicating that social norms were important motivators only some of the time. This distribution, like the nominal one displayed earlier (Figure 6.1), contains both a measurement scale and a frequency count. The five-point scale appears along the graph's baseline, whereas the vertical coordinate registers the frequency of responses to each of the five scale options. Notice that lines have been extended from each end of the polygon to anchor the polygon to its horizontal axis.

A **histogram**, shown in Figure 6.4, is similar to a bar graph in that the heights of the rectangles correspond to frequencies. The horizontal scale, however, is a continuous one. The histogram is an extremely useful display mechanism. Assuming that a sample is representative, the general shape of the sample's histogram should be similar to that of the parent population. The shape of one's distribution summarizes many important features of the collected data.

If we were to graphically depict the number of adults viewing television on a scale representing the evening hours of 6 P.M. until 12 midnight, a *bell-shaped* or *normal* distribution would likely emerge with the greatest frequency of viewers clustered around the hours of 8–10 P.M. and considerably fewer tuned in between 6 and 8 and 10 until 12. The histogram for this distribution would resemble that in Figure 6.5.

Figure 6.6 illustrates a *uniform* or *flat* distribution, indicating that the data are scattered quite evenly along a measurement scale. If a college or university with 10,000 undergraduates had approximately equal numbers of freshman, sophomore, junior, and senior students, then the distribution of students who earned credit hours would be approximately uniform or flat, with about 2500 students in each of the four classes.

Other distributions may be *skewed*, either to the right or left, with the distribution taking its name from the end of the scale toward which its sloping tail points. Figure 6.7 displays a distribution skewed to the right: that is, the tail, representing declining numbers of responses, slopes toward the scale's right extreme. In a distribution skewed to the left (Figure 6.8), the tail points toward the left end of the scale.

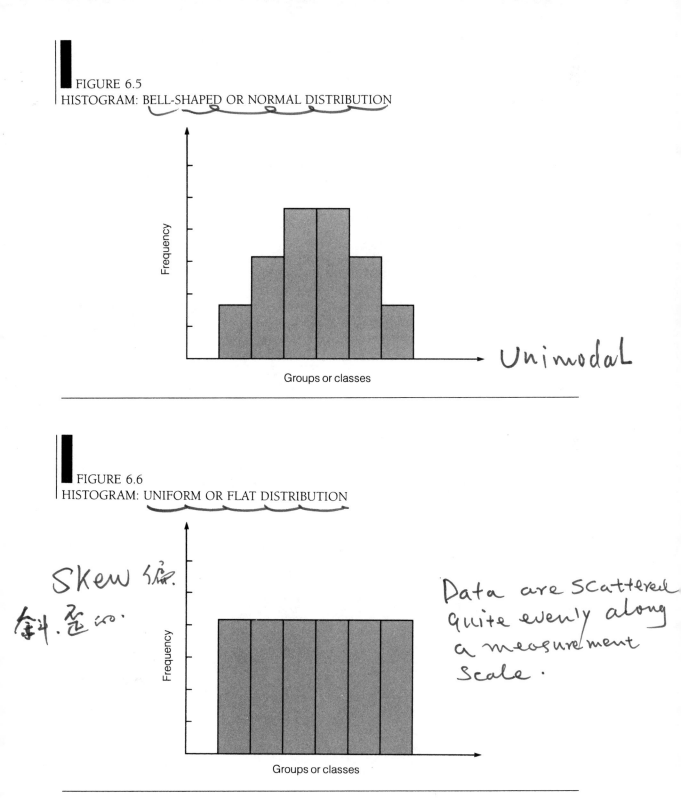

■ FIGURE 6.5
HISTOGRAM: BELL-SHAPED OR NORMAL DISTRIBUTION

Frequency

Groups or classes

*Unimodal*

■ FIGURE 6.6
HISTOGRAM: UNIFORM OR FLAT DISTRIBUTION

Skew 偏.
斜.歪的.

Frequency

Groups or classes

Data are scattered quite evenly along a measurement scale.

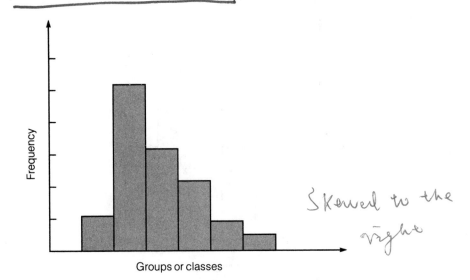

*Skewed to the right*

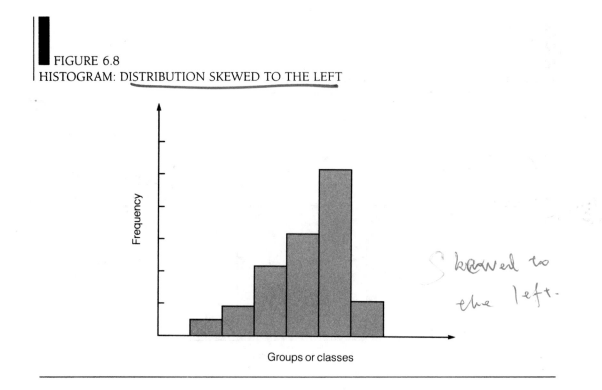

*Skewed to the left*

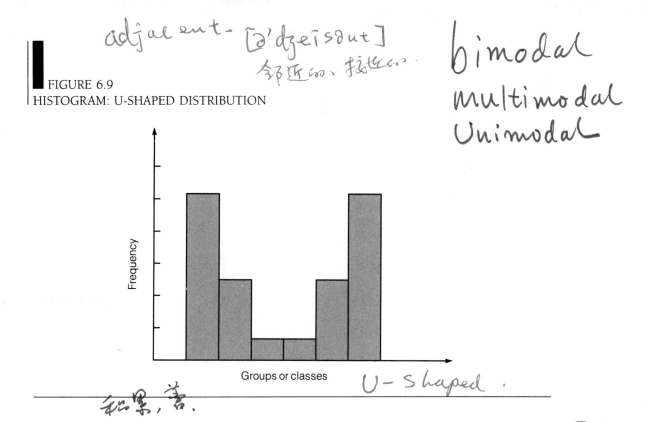

**FIGURE 6.9**
HISTOGRAM: U-SHAPED DISTRIBUTION

A *U-shaped* distribution depicted in Figure 6.9 is characterized by high response frequencies, which cluster at both the left and right extremes of the measurement scale, with few responses in the middle. When the two classes or groups garnering the most responses are separated by at least one other class, as in Figure 6.10, the distribution is *bimodal*. When this characteristic is generalized to more than two classes, as in Figure 6.11, the distribution is said to be *multimodal*. A distribution with a single highest frequency class is *unimodal*. The bell-shaped or normal distribution of Figure 6.5 is also unimodal, since its two highest frequency classes are adjacent. The mode will be discussed further in a later section of this chapter.

## Statistical Indices Describing Distributions

Thus far, we have discussed the characteristics of distributions by referring to pictorial representations of measurement scales and their as-sociated frequencies. Each of the histogram shapes we have examined reflects two inter-related features of a distribution: the *cluster* of scores at certain points along a measurement scale, and the *scatter* of scores along the scale. These two features are important building blocks of statistical inquiry. Indeed, researchers can nicely describe any body of data if they have reliable information about its cluster and scatter along some measurement scale.

Pictorial representations are conceptually useful, yet they provide only generalized information about cluster and scatter. Fortunately, there are statistical procedures for calculating precise indices of these two qualities: indices of *central tendency* refer to statistical measures of the clustering features of data, and indices of *dispersion* represent mathematical measures of the scatter of data along its measurement scale.

### Indices of central tendency

Three indices of central tendency are commonly used in communication research: mode, median, and mean.

99

FIGURE 6.10
HISTOGRAM: BIMODAL DISTRIBUTION

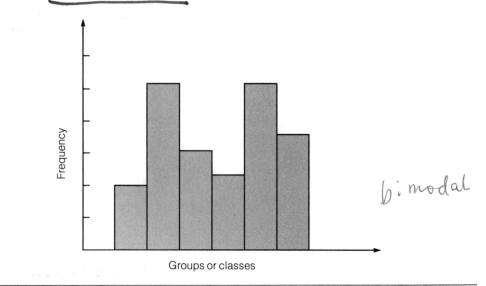

bi·modal

FIGURE 6.11
HISTOGRAM: MULTIMODAL DISTRIBUTION

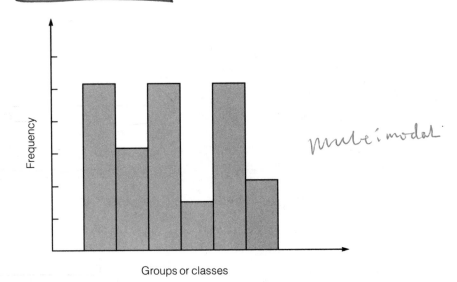

multi·modal

**Mode** The **mode** is the most frequently occurring score or scores in a distribution. Given a distribution containing the 10 scores 1, 2, 2, 3, 4, 4, 4, 5, 6, and 7, the mode is 4. The distribution is unimodal because it has a single most frequently occurring score. Some distributions contain more than one mode. For instance, if the score 1 in the foregoing distribution were instead a 2, the data would be bimodal, since the numbers 2 and 4 would occur with equal frequency. The mode does not exist for a uniform or flat distribution, where all scores appear with equal frequency. For example, the distribution 1, 1, 2, 2, 3, 3, 4, 4, 5, 5, 6, 6 has no mode.

The mode can generally be determined for all four levels of measurement, that is, nominal, ordinal, interval, and ratio data. However, it is the preferred index for representing the central tendency of nominal data. For other measurement levels, the mode is seldom very useful. The mode's insensitivity to all scores permits highly dissimilar ordered distributions such as 1, 2, 3, 3, 3, and 3, 3, 3, 9, 10 to be indexed by an identical mode, in this case 3. This characteristic, together with other liabilities (for example, there may be no distribution mode, or the distribution may contain more than one modal value), suggests that the mode may be of little value as a measure of central tendency for noncategorical data.

**Median** The **median** is the midpoint in a distribution or that position above and below which half the scores fall. As a middle value, the median is a computed value or a point rather than an actual sample score: the point may coincide with an actual score or it may be some value falling between two actual scores. In the 11-score ascending distribution 1, 2, 2, 3, 4, **5**, 6, 6, 6, 7, 7, the boldfaced number 5 coincides with the distribution's median because exactly half the other scores fall above it and half fall below it.

To calculate a distribution's median, the researcher should first place all scores in an ordered array from lowest to highest, or vice versa. Then, assuming that the distribution contains an odd number of scores as shown, the median position in the array can be determined by dividing the total number of scores in the distribution plus one by the number 2, that is, $(n + 1)/2$. Our example, $(11 + 1)/2 = 6$, indicates that the sixth position in the ordered array coincides with the distribution's median. If a distribution contains an even number of scores, the median point falls between two distribution scores and a small calculation adjustment is required. To illustrate the computational adjustment, consider the distribution 5, 10, 10, **20**, **25**, 28, 30, 40. To isolate the two boldfaced middle positions, the researcher performs the usual procedure $(8 + 1)/2 = 4.5$, then divides the sum of the scores in the fourth and fifth positions $(20 + 25)$ by 2 to derive the median of 22.5.[4]

To speak of the midpoint of a distribution implies the existence of an arithmetic order. Thus, the median can be computed for ordinal, interval, and ratio data, but not for nominal measurements. The median is usually the preferred central tendency index for ordinal data, and it is sometimes used for badly skewed distributions or for interval and ratio measures containing extreme or outlying data.

**Mean** The arithmetic average or **mean** is the sum of all the scores in a distribution divided by the total number of scores. It is designated by the symbol $\bar{x}$ (stated as "x-bar") when applied to a sample and by the lowercase Greek letter mu $(\mu)$ when referring to a population. The sample mean is calculated with the formula:

$$\bar{x} = \frac{\Sigma x}{n},$$

where $x$ signifies each individual score, $n$ refers to the total number of scores in the sample, and the symbol $\Sigma$ means "the sum of." Thus, the

*[handwritten: denote v. 指示、表示]*

*[handwritten top right: A central tendency represents the typical or "average" score in a distribution. Indices of dispersion tell us about the variations among distribution scores]*

# TABLE 6.2
## THE MEAN AS A DISTRIBUTION'S BALANCE POINT

| Individual scores, $x$ | Deviations, $d$<br>($d = x - \bar{x}$) |
|:---:|:---:|
| 2 — 6.5 | −4.5 |
| 3 | −3.5 |
| 4 | −2.5 |
| 5 | −1.5 |
| 7 | +0.5 |
| 9 | +2.5 |
| 10 | +3.5 |
| 12 | +5.5 |
| $\Sigma x = 52$ | $\Sigma d = 0$ |

*[handwritten bracket grouping first four deviations: −12; last four: +12]*

$$\text{Mean: } \bar{x} = \frac{\Sigma x}{n} = \frac{52}{8} = 6.5$$

*[handwritten left: Sum of individual scores. $\frac{\Sigma x}{8} = 6.5$   $\bar{X}$   No of Scores in the sample.]*

*[handwritten: $\mu$: population mean]*

*[handwritten: gravity 重心.]*

mean of the sample data 2, 3, 4, 5, 7, 9, 10, and 12 is 52/8 = 6.5. A sample's mean ($\bar{x}$) also represents the best estimate of the mean ($\mu$) of the population from which the sample was selected.

The mean is sensitive to all the scores in a sample, representing what we might call a distribution's center of gravity. To illustrate the mean's balancing function, imagine that the scores in an interval or ratio distribution were weights placed along a balance bar. Given this imaginary arrangement, the mean of the distribution designates the bar's balance point, since the sum of the negative deviations from the mean of all the scores equals the sum of all positive deviations. Put another way, the sum of all positive and negative deviations is zero. Table 6.2 illustrates the balancing qualities of the mean, where each score's deviation from the sample mean is denoted by $d$, so that $d = x - \bar{x}$.

Because the mean is sensitive to all scores in a sample, extreme or outlying data in the sample can greatly affect this index of central tendency. Suppose, for example, that the annual household incomes of five families are $25,000, $30,000, $20,000, $35,000, and $300,000, respectively. The mean household income of this sample is $82,000. The one extreme or outlying income of $300,000 has influenced greatly the calculation of the mean. In this instance, the median value of $30,000 may offer a more meaningful reflection of the data's central tendency than the mean.

The mean can be computed for all numerical data. It is usually the preferred index of central tendency for data measured at the interval and ratio levels.

*[handwritten: 分散、差异. (高低差异趋势)]*

## Indices of dispersion   *[handwritten: [indisi:z]]*

Whereas a central tendency represents the typical or "average" score in a distribution, indices of *dispersion* tell us about the variations among distribution scores—specifically, how a distribution's scores scatter about the "average" score. Three common measures of dispersion are range, variance, and standard deviation.

*Range* The **range**, representing the difference between the highest and lowest scores in a distribution, is the simplest of all dispersion indices to calculate. The range is not sensitive to all scores in a distribution; rather, it indexes only two. For instance, given the data 1, 3, 4, 8, and 12, the range is 12 − 1 = 11. However, the same range value applies to the radically differ-

**102**

*deviations* *→ from the mean.*

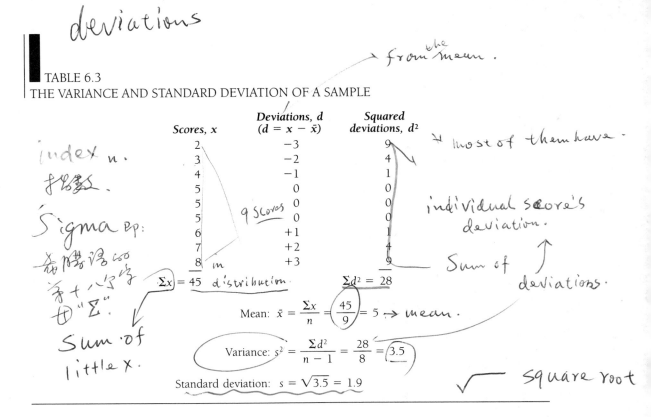

TABLE 6.3
THE VARIANCE AND STANDARD DEVIATION OF A SAMPLE

*index n.*

*frees.*

*Sigma Pp:*

*⊕ "Σ".*

*Sum of little x.*

*# most of them have.*

*individual score's deviation.*

*Sum of deviations.*

*square root*

| Scores, x | Deviations, d (d = x − x̄) | Squared deviations, d² |
|---|---|---|
| 2 | −3 | 9 |
| 3 | −2 | 4 |
| 4 | −1 | 1 |
| 5 | 0 | 0 |
| 5 | 0 | 0 |
| 5 | 0 | 0 |
| 6 | +1 | 1 |
| 7 | +2 | 4 |
| 8 | +3 | 9 |
| $\Sigma x = 45$ | | $\Sigma d^2 = 28$ |

*9 scores* *distribution. m*

$$\text{Mean: } \bar{x} = \frac{\Sigma x}{n} = \frac{45}{9} = 5 \rightarrow \text{mean.}$$

$$\text{Variance: } s^2 = \frac{\Sigma d^2}{n-1} = \frac{28}{8} = 3.5$$

$$\text{Standard deviation: } s = \sqrt{3.5} = 1.9$$

ent distribution 1, 9, 10, 10, 12, illustrating the weakness of the range as a dispersion index. Although the range can be computed for ordinal, interval, and ratio data, it is seldom meaningful as a sole dispersion index. However, it is frequently useful in combination with other measures of dispersion.

*Variance* Like the mean index of central tendency, the **variance** is sensitive to all distribution scores. Often denoted by the symbol $s^2$ when applied to samples and the lowercase Greek sigma squared ($\sigma^2$) when referring to populations, variance is derived from the sum of the squared deviations of all scores in a distribution about the mean.

The variance of a sample is calculated by:

$$s^2 = \frac{\Sigma d^2}{n-1},$$

where d signifies the deviation of each score from the sample mean $(x - \bar{x})$ and n is the total number of scores in the sample. More generally, the numerator is the sum of squared deviations

and is often referred to as a **sum of squares**. To calculate the sample variance using this formula, one must:

1. Compute the sample mean $\bar{x}$.
2. Compute the deviation $d = x - \bar{x}$ of each score from the mean.
3. Square each value of d.
4. Sum all the values of $d^2$.
5. Divide that sum by $n - 1$.

Table 6.3 illustrates these procedures for calculating a sample variance $s^2$.

The formula for the variance of a population is given by:

$$\sigma^2 = \frac{\Sigma D^2}{N},$$

*total population*

where $D = x - \mu$ signifies the deviation of each score (x) from the population mean ($\mu$) and N is the total number of scores in the population. Notice the similarity between the formulas for $\sigma^2$ and $s^2$. If in the formula for $s^2$ one replaces d by D and n by N, and modifies the computation of $d = x - \bar{x}$ so that $D = x - \mu$,

103

*di'nominator n. 分母.*

*histogram*
*(统计学300)直方图，矩形图*

one gets the formula for $\sigma^2$—almost! The difference in the denominators is based on theoretical results indicating that if a denominator of $n$ were used instead of $n - 1$ in the computation of $s^2$, the computation of $s^2$ would be a *biased* estimator of $\sigma^2$. An estimator is *unbiased* when its values on the average equal the quantity it purports to estimate, whereas an estimator is biased when its values on the average are too high or too low. It can be shown theoretically that the sample variance $s^2$, with its denominator of $n - 1$, is an unbiased estimator of the population variance $\sigma^2$, but an analogous $s^2$ with a denominator of $n$ produces biased results. It is therefore quite usual nowadays to compute the sample variance $s^2$ by dividing by $n - 1$, instead of $n$.

*Standard deviation* The **standard deviation**, typically denoted by a lowercase $s$ in samples and lowercase Greek sigma ($\sigma$) in populations, is perhaps the most commonly used index of dispersion. Table 6.3 shows that a standard deviation represents the square root of a distribution's variance. More particularly, a sample's standard deviation is computed with the formula:

$$s = \sqrt{\frac{\Sigma d^2}{n - 1}},$$

and a population's standard deviation is computed by:

$$\sigma = \sqrt{\frac{\Sigma D^2}{N}}.$$

Like the variance from which it is derived, a standard deviation is sensitive to all the scores in a distribution and therefore represents an exceedingly good index of dispersion.

## The Normal Distribution

*α,两个界限点*

The symmetrical, bell-shaped histogram in Figure 6.5 represents a **normal distribution**.[6] If we considered the parent population from which the sample data in Figure 6.5 were selected, we would probably find a distribution corresponding to the theoretical probability curve shown in Figure 6.12. The histogram of the sample has a shape that, when subjected to "smoothing" techniques, is very similar to the theoretical curve of the parent population. See Figure 6.13.

The normal distribution is called "normal" because many phenomena, including, for example, communication anxiety, opinions about communication topics, and personal traits such as intelligence, can be represented as being distributed along a gently sloping bell curve. On an intelligence index, most people are neither geniuses nor idiots, but rather have average intellectual abilities. Likewise, only a few people adopt extreme or radical opinions; instead, most hold middle-of-the-road views. Similarly,

# FIGURE 6.13
## NORMAL DISTRIBUTION CURVE SUPERIMPOSED OVER CORRESPONDING HISTOGRAM

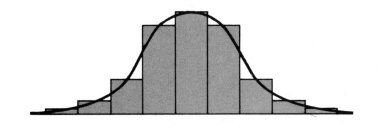

# FIGURE 6.14
## DISTRIBUTION OF DATA UNDER A NORMAL CURVE

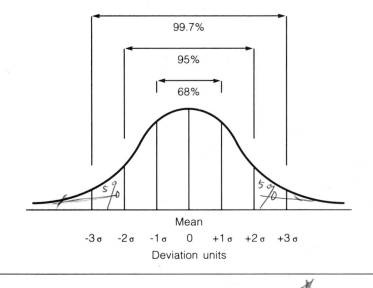

most communicators show moderate levels of anxiety when speaking in a public setting: they are neither extremely nervous nor totally free of anxiety. Because many naturally occurring populations approach the shape of the normal distribution, the latter often can be taken as an idealized reflection of the former.

Assuming that a distribution is approximately normal, the standard deviation provides a basis for estimating where the scores in the distribution are likely to fall along a measurement scale. Approximately 68% of all scores will fall within plus or minus (±) one standard deviation of the distribution's mean, roughly 95% will be within ± 2 standard deviations of the mean, and more than 99% will fall within ± 3 standard deviations of the distribution mean.[7] This predictive quality of a normal distribution, as reflected in Figure 6.14, is exceedingly important for inferring population

**106**

PART II
Statistical
Analysis in
Contemporary
Commu-
nication
Research

parameters from sample data, the issue to which we now turn.

# INFERENTIAL STATISTICS: REASONING FROM SAMPLES TO POPULATIONS

Thus far, we have described sample character-istics, including their shapes, central ten-dencies, and dispersion qualities. Recall that sample characteristics such as means and stan-dard deviations are called *statistics*. In this sec-tion, we shall explore procedures for estimating population *parameters* based on our knowledge of sample statistics, a reasoning process called statistical inference.[8]

Inferential statistics is based on at least four assumptions: (1) all sample data are to be se-lected randomly, insofar as possible, from some well-defined population; (2) the characteristics of each random sample drawn from a popula-tion are related to the true population parame-ters; (3) multiple random samples drawn from the same population yield statistics that cluster around true population parameters in predict-able ways; and (4) we can calculate the sam-pling error associated with a sample statistic, estimating how far a population parameter is likely to deviate from a given sample statistic.

Inferential statistics, then, allows a re-searcher to use the statistics derived from a randomly selected sample to estimate popula-tion parameters. The essential bridge allowing us to make the inferential leap from known statistics to reliable estimates of unknown pa-rameters is a distribution we have yet to ex-plore: a sampling distribution.

## Sampling Distributions

Although sampling distributions can be de-rived theoretically, their nature is easily under-stood by imagining how we might empirically construct one. Suppose we have a well-defined population, say, all public speakers, and we randomly select from it a sample of 30 indi-viduals. Suppose further that we administer to our sample an anxiety scale ranging from 1 (not anxious) to 5 (very anxious) and calculate the sample mean ($\bar{x}$). We repeat this process for a second sample, a third, and so on. If we selected from the population containing all public speakers 100 random samples, each containing 30 public speakers, and if we computed the mean of each sample, we would undoubtedly notice differences in the mean anxiety scores. For example, one sample might report a mean score of 3.0, another 3.2, yet another 3.4, and so forth. However, we might also begin to no-tice numerous duplicate means, such that sev-eral different samples might have the same mean scores: 3.0, 3.2, 3.4, and the like. Once we have collected all 100 samples and noted their means, we have the groundwork for constructing a *sampling distribution of sample means.*

Table 6.4 displays our empirical data, in-cluding all means and the number of samples exhibiting each mean. Figure 6.15 depicts the histogram associated with the data, thereby il-lustrating the nature of an empirically derived **sampling distribution**, in this case a sampling distribution of sample means. Sampling distri-butions are not limited to sample means but can represent the distributed values of other sample statistics: median scores, percentages, and so forth. Importantly, if *all* possible ran-dom samples of size $n$ are selected from a given population, we have the basis for a theoretical sampling distribution of sample means. A sam-pling distribution of sample means:

1. Has a mean equal to the mean of the parent population
2. Has a standard deviation that is related to that of the parent population and is calcu-lated by $\sigma/\sqrt{n}$
3. Is normally distributed when the parent population is normally distributed and is

# TABLE 6.4
## FREQUENCY DISTRIBUTION: MEANS FROM 100 SAMPLES

| Mean score | Frequency or number of samples |
|---|---|
| 1.8 | 1 |
| 2.0 | 1 |
| 2.2 | 3 |
| 2.4 | 4 |
| 2.6 | 6 |
| 2.8 | 7 |
| 3.0 | 17 |
| 3.2 | 20 |
| 3.4 | 16 |
| 3.6 | 8 |
| 3.8 | 7 |
| 4.0 | 4 |
| 4.2 | 3 |
| 4.4 | 2 |
| 4.6 | 1 |

*[Handwritten annotations in margins:]*

*Theorem*

*Consonant*

$\bar{x} = \dfrac{\Sigma x}{n} = \dfrac{48}{15} = 3.2$

$S = \sqrt{\dfrac{\Sigma d^2}{n-1}} = \sqrt{\dfrac{87.6}{15-1}} = 2.5$

$S_{\bar{x}} = \dfrac{2.5}{\sqrt{15}} = .6$

$48 \div 15 = 3.2$ Sample mean.

(all samples)

*Squared deviations $d^2$: 4.2, 3.6, 3, 2.4, 1.8, 1.2, 0.6, 6, 12, 18, 24, 3.6, 4.2; $\Sigma d^2 = 81.6$*

approximately normal even when the parent population is not normally distributed if the samples are large (size $n = 30$ or more).

Recall that $\sigma$ denotes the population standard deviation and that $n$ denotes the sample size. The foregoing list gives the essence of an important result about the theoretical sampling distribution of sample means, a result known in statistics as the central limit theorem.[9]

We can see from observing the histogram of our sampling distribution in Figure 6.15 that its mean is around 3.2 and that the sample means appear to be normally distributed around this mean. We can, in fact, estimate the expected deviation of a sample mean from the sampling distribution mean using a statistic called a **standard error**, defined as the standard deviation of a sampling distribution. Standard errors can be computed for all types of sampling distributions. Since we are concerned with a sampling distribution of sample means, the appropriate standard error is called the **standard error of the mean.** When the standard deviation of the parent population $\sigma$ is known and we are referring to the standard

error of a theoretical distribution, we use the symbol $\sigma_{\bar{x}}$ and calculate:

$$\sigma_{\bar{x}} = \frac{\sigma}{\sqrt{n}}.$$

When the standard deviation of the parent population is not known, as is often the case, we use the sample standard deviation $s$ to estimate $\sigma$.

Let us consider further the example of 100 random samples. If the parent population containing all public speakers were known to have a mean $\mu$ of 3.2 and a standard deviation $\sigma$ of 2.7, one would expect the sampling distribution displayed in Table 6.4 to have a mean of approximately 3.2 and a standard deviation (standard error of the mean) of approximately:

$$\frac{2.7}{\sqrt{30}} = .5.$$

*[Handwritten: $\dfrac{\sigma}{\sqrt{n}} = \sigma_{\bar{x}}$ standard error of the mean]*

As mentioned earlier, our observations of the histogram in Figure 6.15 are consistent with a mean value of 3.2. As we shall see shortly, a standard error (of the mean) equal to .5 will also be consonant with that histogram. To

107

*[Handwritten: [kɔnsɔnənt] (with or to)]*

*The true population mean: μ
Individual sample mean (x̄)*

FIGURE 6.15

HISTOGRAM: SAMPLING DISTRIBUTION OF 100 SAMPLE MEANS

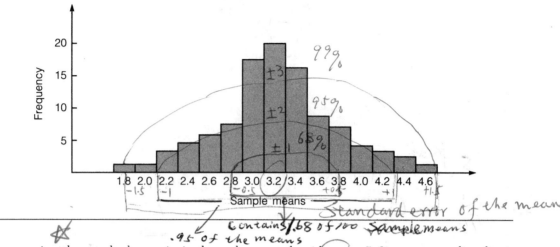

*Contains .68 of 100 sample means*
*.95 of the means*
*Standard error of the mean*

summarize, the standard error is, in the end, a standard deviation (of a sampling distribution of sample means), and it estimates the **sampling error** of the distribution.

## Confidence intervals and confidence levels

Sampling error has two interrelated conceptual properties: a confidence level and a confidence interval. In our example of 100 random samples, each sample has a sample mean. The average of all 100 sample means is a value that is very close to the true population mean ($\mu$). Each individual sample mean ($\bar{x}$), however, will not equal $\mu$. All we can say is that $\mu$ should be "fairly close" to $\bar{x}$, or equivalently, that $\mu$ should be in some interval around $\bar{x}$. We therefore estimate $\mu$ by an interval in which we believe it resides, rather than by a specific number. We also state our "level of confidence" that this interval actually contains $\mu$. Such an interval is a **confidence interval**, and it has an accompanying **confidence level**, which indicates the degree of "assurance" that the interval does indeed contain $\mu$.

These conceptual properties may be illustrated by reconsidering our public speaker ex-

ample with $\sigma_{\bar{x}} = .5$. Since our sampling distribution is approximately normal, a standard error of .5 means that about 68% of the sample means lie within $\pm 1$ standard error (.5) of 3.2, about 95% of the means fall within $\pm 2$ standard errors (1.0) of 3.2, and more than 99% of the means fall within $\pm 3$ standard errors (1.5) of the mean. The data reported in Table 6.4 and Figure 6.15 are consonant with these expected percentages. The interval formed by 3.2 $\pm .5$, which is the interval from 2.7 to 3.7, contains about .68 of the 100 sample means. The interval from 2.2 to 4.2 contains about .95 of the means, and the interval from 1.7 to 4.7 contains more than .99 of the means.

To view these concepts from a slightly different angle, imagine that intervals of width .5 (one standard error) are placed around each of the 100 sample means of Table 6.4. For a sample mean of 3.0, such an interval would have limits of 2.5 and 3.5. We can expect about 68 of the 100 intervals so formed to contain the mean value of 3.2. If one formed intervals of width 1.0 (two standard errors) around each of the 100 sample means, one could expect about 95 of these intervals to contain the mean value of 3.2. The term "95% confidence" or a confidence level of .95 means that we expect 95% of the confidence intervals we have formed about the various sample means to contain the true population mean $\mu$.

Researchers are especially interested in intervals for which the levels of confidence are .95 and .99. The more accurate confidence intervals about the mean ($\mu$) of a normally distributed **population** are:

$$\bar{x} \pm 1.96\,\sigma_{\bar{x}} \quad \text{for a confidence level of .95}$$

and

$$\bar{x} \pm 2.58\,\sigma_{\bar{x}} \quad \text{for a confidence level of .99.}$$

*[handwritten: Standard error of the mean]*

Applied to our public speakers example for a sample with $\bar{x} = 3.0$, the 95% confidence interval for $\mu$ is:

*[handwritten: 2 SD]*

$$\bar{x} \pm 1.96\,\sigma_{\bar{x}} = \bar{x} \pm 1.96\frac{\sigma}{\sqrt{n}}$$

$$= 3.0 \pm 1.96\frac{2.7}{\sqrt{30}}$$

$$= 3.0 \pm 1.96(.5) \quad \text{[handwritten: } 1.96 \times 5 = 0.98 \text{]}$$

$$= 3.0 \pm 1.0.$$

Thus, for $\bar{x} = 3.0$, the confidence interval at the 95% confidence level ranges from approximately 2.0 to 4.0. We can say with .95 confidence, then, that the interval between 2.0 and 4.0 contains the true population mean of all public speakers.

## Calculating sampling error from sample data

As we have seen, a sampling error (also called a standard error) can be used to specify confidence intervals and to estimate the value of a population parameter. Sampling error estimates are derived from sample data, and their calculation procedures depend on the particular kind of sample statistic that interests a researcher. One of the most useful estimates of sampling error, the *standard error of the mean*, was referred to in our treatment of sampling

distributions. The standard error of the mean is the standard deviation of a sampling distribution of sample means, and it estimates the sampling error associated with mean sample scores. For a theoretical distribution, the standard error of the mean $\sigma_{\bar{x}}$ is calculated with the formula:

$$\sigma_{\bar{x}} = \frac{\sigma}{\sqrt{n}}$$

where $\sigma$ is the standard deviation of the parent population and $n$ represents the number of scores in each sample. As we said earlier, when the standard deviation of the parent population is not known, we use the sample standard deviation ($s$) to estimate $\sigma$ in calculating the standard error. The formula for calculating a standard error of the mean (sampling error), denoted by $s_{\bar{x}}$ from sample data is:

*[handwritten: Very important]*

$$s_{\bar{x}} = \frac{s}{\sqrt{n}}$$

*[handwritten: Standard deviation / sample size]*

*[handwritten: Two Standard errors: 1. the standard error of the mean. 2. Standard error of proportion]*

Table 6.5 illustrates the computational procedures required to derive a standard error of the mean using a sample of 10 items of data. The standard error of the mean is useful only when a researcher is estimating population parameters from sample *means*. When one is concerned, as survey researchers often are, with sample *percentages* rather than means, sampling error is estimated using a statistic called the **standard error of proportions** ($\sigma_{\bar{p}}$), which is calculated as follows:

$$\sigma_{\bar{p}} = \sqrt{\frac{pq}{n}},$$

where $n$ refers to the number of sample members;[10] $p$ is the true proportion or percentage of population members who respond in a given way (for example, those reporting they prefer candidate X); and $q$ represents the true proportion of the same population who register an opposing response (in this case, people who do not prefer candidate X).[11] Thus, $q$ is $1 - p$.

homogeneity [hɔmoʊdʒɛ'niti]

**TABLE 6.5**
**CALCULATING A STANDARD ERROR OF THE MEAN**

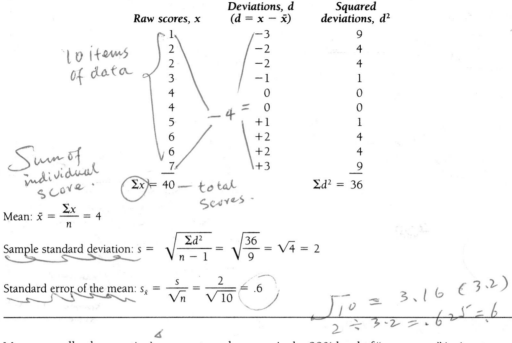

| Raw scores, x | Deviations, d (d = x − x̄) | Squared deviations, d² |
|---|---|---|
| 1 | −3 | 9 |
| 2 | −2 | 4 |
| 2 | −2 | 4 |
| 3 | −1 | 1 |
| 4 | 0 | 0 |
| 4 | 0 | 0 |
| 5 | +1 | 1 |
| 6 | +2 | 4 |
| 6 | +2 | 4 |
| 7 | +3 | 9 |
| $\Sigma x = 40$ | | $\Sigma d^2 = 36$ |

*10 items of data*

*Sum of individual score.*

*$\Sigma x = 40$ — total scores.*

Mean: $\bar{x} = \dfrac{\Sigma x}{n} = 4$

Sample standard deviation: $s = \sqrt{\dfrac{\Sigma d^2}{n-1}} = \sqrt{\dfrac{36}{9}} = \sqrt{4} = 2$

Standard error of the mean: $s_{\bar{x}} = \dfrac{s}{\sqrt{n}} = \dfrac{2}{\sqrt{10}} = .6$

*$\sqrt{10} = 3.16 \; (3.2)$*
*$2 \div 3.2 = .625 = .6$*

---

More generally, the equation's numerator calculates the dispersion of responses in the sample, whereas the denominator refers to sample size.

The use of this error estimate of an empirically derived distribution can be understood by supposing that 60% of a sample of 500 people drawn from a population express a preference for candidate X. In such a case, the sampling error for the empirical distribution, denoted by the symbol $s_{\bar{p}}$, is:

*proportion*

$$s_{\bar{p}} = \sqrt{\dfrac{(.60)(.40)}{500}} = .022,$$

*.08 × .6*

or about ±2 percentage points at the 68% level of confidence, meaning that we can be 68% confident that the proportion of people who prefer candidate X lies between 58% and 62% ($\pm 1 s_{\bar{p}}$). At the 95% confidence level, the sampling error increases to around ±4 percentage points:

*($\pm 2 s_{\bar{p}}$)*

$$\pm 1.96 \; s_{\bar{p}} = \pm 1.96 \, (.022) = \pm .043.$$

*95%*

At the 99% level of "assurance," it rises to more than ±5%:

*($\pm 3 s_{\bar{p}}$)*

$$\pm 2.58 \; s_{\bar{p}} = \pm 2.58 \, (.022) = .057.$$

*99%*

## The Magnitude of Sampling Error

The formulas for computing both the standard error of the mean and the standard error of proportions indicate that the magnitude of sampling error associated with any random sample is a function of two variables: the *homogeneity* of the population from which the random sample was drawn and *sample size*. Each equation's numerator estimates population homogeneity. An $s_{\bar{x}}$ accomplishes this by calculating how close a random sample's scores are to the sample mean. The $s_{\bar{p}}$ gauges the extent to which all members of a random sample report the same responses. In general, the greater the

*s² estimates population homogeneity.*

110

heterogeneous.

[ˌhetərouˈdʒiːnjəs] a. different
made of different kinds.

[pəˈræmitə] 參(變)數
parameter n. 參項
different, unlike.

mean deviations or the more evenly divided the proportional responses in a given sample, the more heterogeneous the parent population, and therefore, the larger the sampling error. The second variable, sample size, is assessed in each equation's denominator. Sampling error declines as the size of the sample increases, since larger samples improve the probability that a researcher will capture a representative portion of the parent population.

To illustrate the effects of greater homogeneity as well as sample size on sampling error, suppose that 80% of a given sample rather than the 60% used in our example hold the same opinion regarding some issue. Applying the $s_{\bar{p}}$ estimate, sampling error declines from .022 to:

$$s_{\bar{p}} = \sqrt{\frac{(.80)(.20)}{500}} = .018,$$

or less than 2 percentage points at the 68% level of confidence. By doubling the sample size to 1000, sampling error declines even further to:

$$s_{\bar{p}} = \sqrt{\frac{(.80)(.20)}{1000}} = .013,$$

or a little more than 1 percentage point at the 68% confidence level. Thus, sampling error may be reduced by increasing the homogeneity of a sample or by increasing the amount of data in a sample.

## THE LOGIC OF HYPOTHESIS TESTING

In the preceding section, we discussed inferential statistics as a tool for estimating unknown population characteristics based on a knowledge of sample statistics. We will now explore a slightly different use of inferential statistics: testing "predictions" about a population using sample data. Our "predictions" or conjectures about population characteristics or relationships are called **hypotheses**; thus, this application of inferential statistics is known as hy-

pothesis testing. Hypothesis testing differs from estimation in at least one critical respect. Estimation begins with the selection of a sample whose statistics are then used to project unknown population parameters. In contrast, when testing hypotheses, we initially formulate "assumptions" about population parameters and then generate sample data to confirm or disconfirm our a priori assumptions. The assumptions we generate often predict that some kind of relationship exists between two or more population parameters.[12]

The logic of hypothesis testing entails five basic steps: (1) formulating appropriate hypotheses about population characteristics or relationships, (2) specifying the probability of error, (3) framing a decision rule for hypothesis testing, based on the sampling distribution for the statistic of interest, (4) gathering the relevant sample statistics, and (5) making decisions about the hypotheses. We examine the first two steps in this chapter. The completion of step 3, plus the last two steps, are discussed in Chapters 7 and 8.

## Formulating Hypotheses

Two kinds of hypotheses are critical to hypothesis testing: research hypotheses (also termed alternative hypotheses) and null hypotheses.

### The research hypothesis

We learned in Chapter 2 that **research hypotheses** (often designated by the symbols $H_1$, . . . , $H_n$) "predict" or conjecture that important relationships exist between populations of communication phenomena. Although the projected relationships can take many forms, research hypotheses often predict that two or more populations are different in one or more respects. For example, we might suspect that males and females differ on the variable "verbal assertiveness." The exact nature of our hypothesis will depend on how much we know

[ˌinfəˈrenʃəl]
推理的.

assertive a. 過信言的. 肯定的.
过分自信的. 武断的.

**112**

PART II
Statistical
Analysis in
Contemporary
Commu-
nication
Research

about suspected differences. If we believe that the mean assertiveness levels of males and females differ yet cannot specify the difference, our research hypothesis should take the *non-directional* form:

$$H_1: \mu_m \neq \mu_f,$$

where $\mu_m$ and $\mu_f$ denote male and female population means, respectively, and $\neq$ indicates simply that the two means are not equal.

Often, we can make more precise "predictions" than this. For instance, we might have reason to suspect that populations of males are more verbally assertive than females. In this case, our research hypothesis will take the *directional* form:

$$H_2: \mu_m > \mu_f,$$

indicating that the mean assertiveness of males is substantially greater than ($>$) female assertiveness. Both hypotheses call for a test of *significance of difference* between the means of populations. Thus, the projected relationship is one of difference or inequality.

## The Null Hypothesis

A **null hypothesis**, generally denoted by the symbol $H_0$, is the antithesis of a research hypothesis. Applied to the nondirectional research hypothesis, $\mu_1 \neq \mu_2$, the null hypothesis takes the form:

$$H_0: \mu_1 = \mu_2,$$

meaning that the two population means are equal and that any observed sample differences are due to chance. The null hypothesis associated with the directional research hypothesis $\mu_1 > \mu_2$ is:

$$H_0: \mu_1 \leqq \mu_2,$$

indicating that the first population mean is less than or equal to ($\leqq$) the second population mean.

Our hypothesis testing proceeds under the assumption that the null hypothesis as stated is indeed true. In that sense, we treat the null hypothesis as if it were a statement about the status quo. The null hypothesis makes a statement, assumed to be true, about population parameters. For this reason, null hypotheses are widely stated using only the equality sign. The null hypothesis associated with the directional research hypothesis $\mu_1 > \mu_2$ would then be written:

$$H_0: \mu_1 = \mu_2 \ (\leqq).$$

We will include the symbol ($\leqq$) to remind us that we have grouped $<$ and $=$ together in $H_0$.

Null hypotheses play a crucial role in hypothesis testing because all statistical procedures test the null hypothesis. Thus, researchers confirm or disconfirm their research hypotheses by assessing the "truth" of the null hypothesis: one may reject the null hypothesis or fail to reject it. By rejecting the null hypothesis, one accepts the research hypothesis as a default option.

Some researchers prefer the term "accept $H_0$" to "fail to reject $H_0$." In some ways, "fail to reject $H_0$" is a more accurate way of phrasing the outcome, however. The situation is somewhat analogous to criminal proceedings, where failure to convict is not the same as proving innocence. The whole process of hypothesis testing is, in many ways, analogous to a criminal trial. The accused is presumed innocent ($H_0$ is assumed true) unless sufficient evidence exists to convict (reject $H_0$). In the absence of that sufficient evidence, one fails to convict or, equivalently, one acquits (fails to reject $H_0$ or, as sometimes stated, "accepts $H_0$").

## Further Framework for Hypothesis Testing

Suppose we formulate the research hypothesis, "Physically attractive speakers are more persuasive than unattractive ones." The null and research hypotheses, respectively, would take the forms:

$$H_0: \mu_a = \mu_u \; (\mu_a \leqq \mu_u)$$

and

$$H_1: \mu_a > \mu_u,$$

where $\mu_a$ and $\mu_u$ symbolize mean reactions of two populations who listen to attractive and unattractive speakers, respectively. Note that the research hypothesis $H_1$ takes a directional form.

Suppose further that we measure the reactions to the same message of two samples of 100 individuals, one exposed to an attractive persuader and the other to an unattractive speaker. Suppose finally that the sample hearing the attractive persuader has a mean ($\bar{x}_a$) agreement score of 5.20, whereas the sample exposed to the unattractive speaker shows a 4.00 mean ($\bar{x}_u$). Although the attractive speaker produced greater agreement than the unattractive one in the two samples, the pertinent question is: Are these sample means sufficiently different to permit us to say that they probably reflect real population differences, or are these sample differences likely to be attributable to chance?

To answer this question satisfactorily, we need an estimate of the sampling error associated with 1.20, the mean difference between our two samples, as well as an appropriate sampling distribution. The required sampling distribution is a sampling distribution of mean differences, and the pertinent sampling error is called a standard error of the difference between means. The **standard error of difference between means**, often denoted by the symbol $\sigma_{\bar{x}_1 - \bar{x}_2}$, is the standard deviation of a theoretical sampling distribution of mean differences. Recall that standard (sampling) error can provide an estimate of how far population values are likely to deviate from sample statistics at specified confidence levels.

## Sampling distributions of mean differences and sampling error

In our earlier illustration of an empirically derived sampling distribution in which we selected several samples from a population, we noted the mean of each and ultimately constructed a frequency distribution of sample means (see Table 6.4). Similarly, we can construct an empirically derived sampling distribution of mean differences. Specifically, we could select some number of independent samples of size $n_1$ at random from one population and an equal number of independent samples of size $n_2$ at random from another population and note the differences between the means of each selected pair (one sample from each population). Note that such a distribution is empirically derived and includes differences in means only for the samples actually selected.

If *all* possible samples are randomly selected from the two populations and all possible mean differences are computed, we have the basis for a theoretical sampling distribution of mean differences. More specifically, if $\bar{x}_1$ and $\bar{x}_2$ denote the means of two independent, randomly selected samples of large sizes $n_1$ and $n_2$, respectively, the sampling distribution of the statistic $\bar{x}_1 - \bar{x}_2$ is approximately normal, with a mean:

$$\mu_{\bar{x}_1 - \bar{x}_2} = \mu_1 - \mu_2$$

and a standard deviation (standard error of mean differences):

$$\sigma_{\bar{x}_1 - \bar{x}_2} = \sqrt{\frac{\sigma_1^2}{n_1} + \frac{\sigma_2^2}{n_2}},$$

where $\mu_1$, $\mu_2$, $\sigma_1^2$, and $\sigma_2^2$ are the means and variances of the two parent populations.[13]

With this information, let us return to our example about attractive and unattractive speakers. Recall that the samples, each of size 100, had mean agreement scores of 5.20 and 4.00, yielding a mean difference of 1.20. Suppose further that we calculate the variances $s_a^2$ (for the sample hearing the attractive persuader) and $s_u^2$ (for the sample exposed to the unattractive speaker). If we place these calculated values into the formula for computing a standard error for mean differences, we might derive a value of, say, .60:

**114**

PART II
Statistical
Analysis in
Contemporary
Commu-
nication
Research

*Threshold ['θreʃhould] n. stone or plank under a door way in a dwelling-house.*

$$\sigma_{\bar{x}_a - \bar{x}_u} \approx s_{\bar{x}_a - \bar{x}_u} = \sqrt{\frac{s_a^2}{n_a} + \frac{s_u^2}{n_u}}$$

$$= \sqrt{\frac{s_a^2}{100} + \frac{s_u^2}{100}} = .60,$$

where ≈ stands for "is approximately equal to." Furthermore, if there really are no differences between samples exposed to attractive speakers and those exposed to unattractive ones, the mean difference is zero.

Since the sampling distribution of mean differences is approximately normal, we can expect about 68% of the data to fall within $\pm 1$ $s_{\bar{x}_a - \bar{x}_u}$ of the mean difference of zero; that is, within $\pm.60$ of the mean difference of zero. We could expect to pick up about 95% of the data within: *(2 SD)*

$$\pm 1.96 \, s_{\bar{x}_a - \bar{x}_u} = \pm(1.96)(.60) = \pm 1.18.$$
*(1.176)*

Finally, we would expect about 99% of the data to be within:

$$\pm 2.58 \, s_{\bar{x}_a - \bar{x}_u} = \pm(2.58)(.60) = \pm 1.55.$$
*(1.548)*

The observed mean difference of 1.20 between our two samples is slightly greater than 1.18. This implies that there is about a .95 probability that the observed mean difference is a reflection of true population differences. Note, however, that there is still about a .05 probability that the mean difference of 1.20 is due to chance or sampling error. Although these observations intuitively support the "reasonableness" of our original research hypothesis, we need a clear procedure for actually testing its "truth."

### Choosing a significance level

What we require is a numerical value for rejecting the null hypothesis. Social scientists have traditionally regarded a probability level of .05 as a suitable cutoff point for rejecting the null hypothesis; that is, even though the null hypothesis may in fact be true, there is a 95% or better chance that the research hypothesis is the

acceptable alternative. This probability for rejecting a null hypothesis when it is true is often called the **significance level** or **alpha ($\alpha$) level**. If support for the null hypothesis is less than 5%, researchers say that their research results are *statistically significant*. This means they are justified in accepting the research hypothesis. We often express this 5% rule using the notation $p < .05$ where $p$ is "probability" and the symbol < means "less than."

Although the 5% rule is conventional for rejecting a null hypothesis, other significance levels are justified in certain special circumstances. For example, in a preliminary study seeking general trend data, a researcher may set the significance level as high as .10. This defines a 90% chance that a research hypothesis is the acceptable alternative. On the other hand, when researchers want more confidence in the acceptability of a given research hypothesis, a .01 significance level is often selected, yielding a probability of .99 that the research hypothesis is the correct alternative. There is a price to pay, however, for this increased confidence. Stronger evidence is required for the same research hypothesis to be the acceptable alternative at a level of .01 than at .05.

In theory, the selection of a significance level is arbitrary. In practice, levels of .05, .10, and .01 are used almost exclusively, with .05 being the conventional choice. The .05 level is generally an acceptable threshold for the scholarly journals in communication. *limit*

### Applying the significance level to hypotheses

Some research hypotheses predict that two or more population means differ significantly, without specifying the direction of the difference. We frame nondirectional hypotheses like $\mu_1 \neq \mu_2$ when we are unsure which population mean is greater than the other. If $\mu_1$ actually turns out to be greater than $\mu_2$, the difference between means ($\mu_1 - \mu_2$) will be a positive value. However, the difference between means

*Significance level: alpha ($\alpha$) level*

*0.95*
*0.05*
*1.00*

*0.5 level is the Conventional Choice & an acceptable threshold for the Scholarly Journals in Comm.*

FIGURE 6.16

REJECTION REGION (SHADED) FOR NONDIRECTIONAL NULL HYPOTHESIS $H_0: \mu_1 = \mu_2$

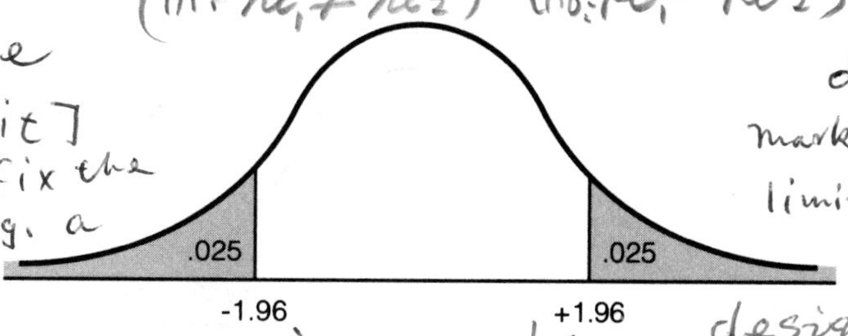

.025   .025

-1.96   +1.96

will be negative if the second population mean is, in fact, greater than the first. When testing such nondirectional hypotheses, Figure 6.16 shows that the conventional 5% required to reject the null hypothesis ($\mu_1 = \mu_2$) is taken from both the negative and the positive tails of our sampling distribution. This practice allows for the equal probability that $\bar{x}_1 - \bar{x}_2$ will be positive or negative. A nondirectional hypothesis test is called a **two-tailed test**, defined as a statistical procedure that takes the probability level required to reject a null hypothesis from the areas under both tails of a sampling distribution's curve.

Researchers often formulate directional research hypotheses, stating that one population mean is greater than the other (for example, $\mu_1 > \mu_2$). In this circumstance, the null hypothesis becomes $H_0: \mu_1 = \mu_2$ ($\mu_1 \leq \mu_2$), meaning that the first population mean is less than or equal to the second. When testing directional research hypotheses, researchers use a **one-tailed test**, defined as a statistical test that takes the probability level required to reject the null hypothesis (typically 5%) from the area under only one tail of the sampling distribution. The hypothesis symbolized by $\mu_1 > \mu_2$ indicates that the researcher believes the first population mean to be greater than the second. In other words, the researcher expects the difference between the two means ($\mu_1 - \mu_2$) to be a positive value. When this is so, the area for

rejecting the null hypothesis is taken from the positive end of the distribution, as indicated in Figure 6.17. However, when the difference between means is expected to be a negative value ($\mu_1 < \mu_2$), the area for rejecting the null hypothesis is taken from the distribution's negative extreme (Figure 6.18). Figures 6.16, 6.17, and 6.18 show that the 95% demarcation points along a normally distributed sampling distribution's baseline are $\pm 1.65 \, \sigma_{\bar{x}_1 - \bar{x}_2}$ for one-tailed tests and $\pm 1.96 \, \sigma_{\bar{x}_1 - \bar{x}_2}$ for two-tailed tests. Use a one-tailed test when your research hypothesis is directional and a two-tailed test when "predictions" are non-directional.

## Decision Errors in Hypothesis Testing

A researcher's significance level, typically $p < .05$, is an important element of the decision structure for rejecting null hypotheses and accepting research hypotheses by default. Two kinds of errors associated with this decision are designated Type I and Type II.

A **Type I error**, sometimes called an alpha ($\alpha$) error, results from rejecting a null hypothesis when it is true. Given the $p < .05$ significance level, researchers accept their research hypotheses when the probability supporting the null hypothesis is less than .05. Notice that

**115**

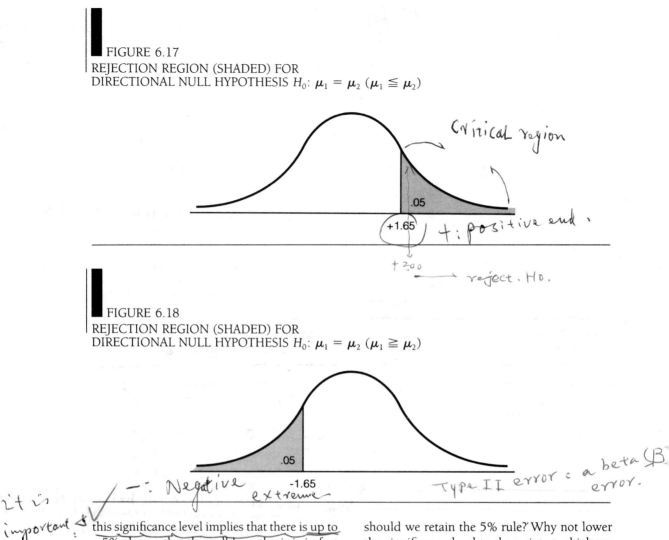

**FIGURE 6.17**
REJECTION REGION (SHADED) FOR
DIRECTIONAL NULL HYPOTHESIS $H_0$: $\mu_1 = \mu_2$ ($\mu_1 \leqq \mu_2$)

*Critical region*

.05

+1.65   *+: positive end.*

*+ 2.00   → reject. H0.*

**FIGURE 6.18**
REJECTION REGION (SHADED) FOR
DIRECTIONAL NULL HYPOTHESIS $H_0$: $\mu_1 = \mu_2$ ($\mu_1 \geqq \mu_2$)

.05

*−: Negative   -1.65   extreme*

*it is important*

*Type II error = a beta $\beta$ error.*

this significance level implies that there is up to a 5% chance that the null hypothesis is in fact correct. Thus, the use of the 5% rule means that over the long run researchers commit Type I errors about 5% of the time.

The probability of committing Type I errors can be reduced directly by lowering the significance level required to reject null hypotheses. With a $p < .01$ level, for example, the chance of committing a Type I error is reduced to less than 1%. An even more conservative significance level such as $p < .001$ diminishes the probability of a Type I error to less than 0.1% or almost 1 chance in 1000 of rejecting a true null hypothesis. Since the likelihood of committing Type I errors can be reduced so easily, why

should we retain the 5% rule? Why not lower the significance level to the point at which we virtually eliminate the probability of a Type I error?

The reason for retaining the more liberal 5% rule can be clarified by examining Type II errors and their relationship to the first error type. A **Type II error**, sometimes called a **beta** ($\beta$) error, results from failing to reject the null hypothesis when it is in fact false. Statisticians often use the term statistical **power** $(1 - \beta)$ to refer to the probability of *not* committing a Type II error. Thus, power indexes the probability of correctly rejecting a false null hypothesis.

Table 6.6 summarizes the four outcomes

**116**

*reject*: put aside, throw away, refuse to accept.

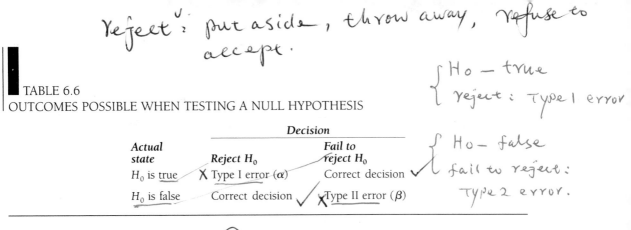

$\{$ $H_0$ — true
reject: Type 1 error

$\{$ $H_0$ — false
fail to reject:
Type 2 error.

**TABLE 6.6**

**OUTCOMES POSSIBLE WHEN TESTING A NULL HYPOTHESIS**

| *Actual state* | **Decision** | |
| --- | --- | --- |
| | **Reject $H_0$** | **Fail to reject $H_0$** |
| $H_0$ is true | Type I error ($\alpha$) | Correct decision |
| $H_0$ is false | Correct decision | Type II error ($\beta$) |

possible when testing a null hypothesis ($H_0$). If $H_0$ is actually true and the decision is made not to reject (that is, to accept) it, then the decision is correct. A similarly correct decision is made when $H_0$ is actually false and we reject it. If, on the other hand, $H_0$ is actually false and we fail to reject it, we have made a Type II error in our decision. A Type I error results when $H_0$ is actually true and we reject it.

Although the association is inexact, there is an inverse or negative relationship between the probabilities of committing Type I and Type II errors. As the probability of making a Type I error declines, the chance of committing a Type II error increases. Similarly, as the probability of a Type II error increases, the probability of a Type I error is diminished. Thus, we need to strike a reasonable balance between the probabilities of committing both error types.

A principal way to simultaneously decrease the probability of committing both Type I and Type II errors is to increase the size of the samples we use to test hypotheses. Since greater sample sizes increase the stability of the statistics derived from them, the entire decision-making process, both in terms of correctly rejecting false null hypotheses and correctly accepting true ones, becomes more trustworthy.[14]

## The Hypothesis Test: A Step-by-Step Procedure

We return to our earlier research hypothesis: "Physically attractive speakers are more persuasive than unattractive ones." The five steps

required for testing this hypothesis apply to all hypothesis tests.

*Step 1.*
*Formulate the research and null hypotheses.*

$$H_0: \mu_a = \mu_u \ (\mu_a \leqq \mu_u)$$
$$H_1: \mu_a > \mu_u$$

*Step 2.*
*Specify the probability (p) of a Type I error (level of significance).*
We specify $p < .05$, or equivalently, we set the level of significance as $\alpha = .05$.

*Step 3.*
*Frame the decision rule or criterion for rejecting $H_0$, based on the sampling distribution of the statistic of interest.*
Two actions are required to implement this step: determine the appropriate test statistic, and define the critical region. Since the research hypothesis in this example is a directional one, we will use a one-tailed test. The dividing line or **critical value** for rejecting $H_0$ is 1.65 (refer to Figure 6.17). The **critical region** is the shaded area of the curve to the right of 1.65. If the value of the appropriate **test statistic** lies in the critical region, we will reject the null hypothesis; otherwise, we will fail to reject $H_0$. Appropriate test statistics (in this example it is the $z$ statistic) will be discussed in Chapter 7.

*Step 4.*
*Calculate the value of the test statistic.*
The value of the $z$ statistic in this example is derived with the formula:

(1) one-tailed
or
two-tailed test

(2) $\pm 1.65$
or
$\pm 1.96$

**117**

**118**

PART II
Statistical
Analysis in
Contemporary
Commu-
nication
Research

$$z = \frac{(\bar{x}_a - \bar{x}_u) - 0}{s_{\bar{x}_a - \bar{x}_u}}$$

$$= \frac{1.20}{.60} = 2.00.$$

*Step 5.*

*Decide whether to reject $H_0$ or fail to reject it, and interpret the decision.*

Since 2.00 is greater than 1.65, it falls in the critical region. Thus we can reject $H_0$ and conclude that physically attractive speakers are more persuasive than unattractive ones.

Steps 4 and 5 will be discussed further in the two chapters that follow. To summarize, hypothesis testing involves five distinct steps:

1. State the research and null *hypotheses*.
2. State the *probability of error*.
3. Determine the *criterion* or decision rule.
4. Perform *calculations* on the test statistic.
5. Make the *decision*.

## INTERFACE: CHAPTERS 6, 7, AND 8

In describing basic concepts and principles of descriptive and inferential statistics, this chapter has presented descriptive tools like frequency distributions, indices of central tendency, and indices of dispersion. Methods for inferring population parameters based on sample descriptions were examined. The chapter concluded with a discussion of principles and procedures for testing hypotheses.

Chapters 7 and 8 will extend our treatment of the theory and practice of hypothesis testing, examining specific test statistics for making decisions about the probable truth or falsity of null hypotheses. Chapter 7 describes statistical procedures for testing hypotheses about popu-

lation differences, whereas Chapter 8 focuses on hypothesis testing of population relationships. By the conclusion of Part II, you will have acquired the skills necessary to proceed through the five stages of hypothesis testing, making confident and informed decisions about whether to reject or fail to reject null hypotheses about important problems in human communication.

## MAIN POINTS

1. Descriptive statistics involves procedures for summarizing sample data, whereas inferential statistics is a logical system for estimating population characteristics from sample descriptions.

2. A frequency distribution summarizes data by listing scores or values ($x$) together with their frequencies. Each value of $x$ may be listed alone in the distribution, or else the values of $x$ may be categorized or grouped.

3. Data may be displayed in a pictorial form on a bar graph, in a frequency polygon, or with a histogram. The scores or values ($x$) appear on the horizontal axis and their frequencies on the vertical axis.

4. The shape of a sample's histogram generally resembles that of the parent population if the sample is representative. Shapes a histogram may take include bell-shaped or normal, uniform or flat, skewed, U-shaped, unimodal, bimodal, and multimodal.

5. Three key indices of a distribution's central tendency are mode, median, and mean. The mode is the most frequently occurring score or scores in a distribution. The median is the midpoint of a distribution. The mean is the sum of all scores in a distribution divided by the total number of scores.

6. Three common indices of the dispersion of

*Three key indices of a distribution's central tendency are: (1) mode, (2) median, and (3) mean.*

*Three common indices of dispersion of scores in a distribution are: (1) range, (2) variance, and (3) standard deviation*

scores in a distribution are range, variance, and standard deviation. The range represents the difference between the highest and lowest scores in a distribution. The variance of a sample is the sum of the squared deviations of all scores, divided by one less than the total number of scores. A standard deviation is the square root of a distribution's variance.

7. A normal curve is a theoretical probability curve that is symmetrical and bell-shaped. Approximately 68% of all scores are within $\pm 1$ standard deviation of the distribution's mean, roughly 95% are within $\pm 2$ standard deviations, and more than 99% are within $\pm 3$ standard deviations.

8. A statistic is a numerical characteristic of a sample, whereas a parameter is a numerical characteristic of a population.

9. A sampling distribution for a particular sample statistic is a distribution of values obtained from all possible samples of a given size $n$, randomly selected from a well-defined population.

10. A sampling distribution of sample means: (a) has a mean equal to that of the parent population; (b) has a standard deviation that is related to that of the parent population and is calculated by $\sigma/\sqrt{n}$; and (c) is normally distributed when the parent population is normally distributed and is approximately normal even when the parent population is not normally distributed if the samples are large (size $n = 30$ or more). The symbol $\sigma$ denotes population standard deviation and $n$ signifies sample size.

11. Sampling error (also called a standard error) estimates probable deviations of population parameters from sample statistics at some specified level of confidence. The magnitude of sampling error is a function of the homogeneity of the population from which the random sample was drawn and the sample size.

12. A research hypothesis conjectures that a

particular kind of relationship exists between or among populations, whereas a null hypothesis conjectures that no such relationship exists.

13. A researcher's level of significance, typically $p < .05$, is an important element of the hypothesis testing structure for rejecting null hypotheses and accepting research hypotheses. The use of the 5% rule means that over the long run, researchers will reject a null hypothesis when it is actually true about 5% of the time.

14. A two-tailed test is a statistical procedure for testing a nondirectional research hypothesis, whereas a one-tailed test assesses the acceptability of directional research hypotheses.

15. A Type I error (alpha error) results from rejecting a true null hypothesis. A Type II error (beta error) results from accepting a false null hypothesis.

16. Statistical power refers to the probability of *not* committing a Type II error.

*what is power ?*

17. Hypothesis testing involves five steps: (a) state the research and null hypotheses, (b) state the probability of a Type I error or the level of significance, (c) determine the criterion or decision rule, (d) perform calculations on the appropriate test statistic, and (e) make the decision. Two actions required to determine the criterion or decision rule are determining the appropriate test statistic and defining the critical region.

## REVIEW EXERCISES

1. In a study of credibility or believability of television news versus printed news, a sample of 35 adults was selected from residents of an urban area in the Northeast. Each person was asked to express his or her opinion regarding the statement: "Television news is more trustworthy than corresponding news reported in the printed media." Responses were measured

120

PART II
Statistical
Analysis in
Contemporary
Commu-
nication
Research

on a five-point scale from "Strongly agree" (1) to "Strongly disagree" (5), and were reported as follows:

| | | | |
|---|---|---|---|
| 5 | 5 | 5 | 2 |
| 5 | 4 | 5 | 5 |
| 4 | 1 | 4 | 1 |
| 1 | 5 | 3 | 4 |
| 5 | 5 | 5 | 5 |
| 5 | 4 | 4 | 3 |
| 2 | 5 | 1 | 5 |
| 4 | 4 | 4 | 5 |
| 5 | 5 | 5 | |

Construct a frequency distribution that corresponds to these data and draw a bar graph of the distribution.

**2.** For the 35 responses in Exercise 1, calculate: the mean, the median, the mode, the range, and the standard deviation.

[**Answers:** mean $\bar{x} = 4$; median $= 5$; mode $= 5$; range $= 4$; standard deviation $s = 1.4$.]

**3.** Which of the three "averages" computed in Exercise 1 do you think best characterizes the data? Why?

**4.** In a study similar to that described in Exercise 1, a sample of 35 adults was selected from among the residents of a rural area in the Midwest. The responses of these individuals were reported as follows:

| | | | |
|---|---|---|---|
| 2 | 2 | 1 | 1 |
| 2 | 2 | 3 | 4 |
| 3 | 3 | 2 | 2 |
| 3 | 4 | 2 | 3 |
| 3 | 1 | 1 | 1 |
| 1 | 2 | 2 | 2 |
| 3 | 2 | 3 | 2 |
| 2 | 2 | 2 | 3 |
| 3 | 1 | 2 | |

Construct a frequency distribution that corresponds to these data and draw a bar graph of the distribution.

**5.** For the 35 responses in Exercise 4, determine: the mean, the median, the mode, the range, and the standard deviation.

[**Answers:** mean $\bar{x} = 2.2$; median $= 2$; mode $= 2$; range $= 3$; standard deviation $s = 0.8$.]

**6.** Which of the three "averages" computed in Exercise 5 do you think best characterizes the data? Why?

**7.** What do the measurements of dispersion calculated in Exercises 1 and 4 tell you about the two samples? Which sample appears to be more homogeneous in its opinions? What reason(s) might contribute to this greater homogeneity?

**8.** What do the measurements of central tendency tell you about the opinions of the two samples regarding the believability of television news versus printed news? Can you suggest some explanation(s) for the differences in "average" responses between the two samples?

**9.** Earphones and Earplugs, Inc., a manufacturer of stereo equipment, wanted to focus its marketing for a new compact disc player on young, affluent professionals. The marketing department identified two magazines, *Condo Living* and *Quiche and Volvo*, which were especially popular with the target population. The advertising department of *Quiche and Volvo* claimed that its average subscriber was younger than the average subscriber of *Condo Living*. Formulate the research and null hypotheses to test this claim. Then determine the critical region for a level of significance $\alpha = .05$ (probability of Type I error).

**10.** The advertising department of *Condo Living* countered that, in fact, there were no differences in the average ages of subscribers to the two magazines. Formulate the research and null hypotheses to test this counterclaim. Then determine the critical region for a level of significance $\alpha = .05$ (probability of a Type I error).

**11.** A random sample of size 30 was selected from individual subscribers to *Condo Living*. The ages (in years) of these subscribers were reported as follows:

| | | | |
|---|---|---|---|
| 25 | 28 | 48 | 25 |
| 60 | 35 | 37 | 26 |
| 45 | 48 | 26 | 53 |
| 32 | 50 | 55 | 55 |
| 40 | 43 | 61 | 27 |
| 35 | 70 | 69 | 50 |
| 62 | 22 | 32 | |
| 51 | 65 | 75 | |

Calculate the mean and the standard deviation.

[**Answers:** $\bar{x} = 45$; $s = 15.5$.]

**12.** A random sample of size 40 was selected from individual subscribers to *Quiche and Volvo*. The ages (in years) of the subscribers were reported as follows:

| | | | |
|---|---|---|---|
| 36 | 30 | 26 | 40 |
| 40 | 37 | 35 | 35 |
| 22 | 48 | 58 | 48 |
| 31 | 32 | 57 | 41 |
| 50 | 24 | 57 | 56 |
| 23 | 28 | 49 | 44 |
| 52 | 55 | 48 | 52 |
| 38 | 38 | 55 | 39 |
| 40 | 23 | 31 | 42 |
| 52 | 59 | 59 | 50 |

Calculate the mean and the standard deviation.

[**Answers:** $\bar{x} = 42$; $s = 11.3$.]

**13.** For the data reported in Exercise 12, calculate the .95 confidence interval about the mean and the .99 confidence interval about the mean.

**14.** Which of the two intervals in Exercise 13 is larger? Interpret the difference in the widths of the two intervals.

**15. a.** Estimate the standard error of the mean $\sigma_{\bar{x}}$ for the population sampled in Exercise 11.

    **b.** Do the same for Exercise 12.

    **c.** Discuss the magnitude of sampling error in terms of your answers to parts a and b. How do homogeneity (as measured by standard deviation) and sample size influence sampling error?

# NOTES

**1.** For further discussion, see Patrick Brockett and Arnold Levine, *Statistics and Probability and Their Applications* (Philadelphia: Saunders, 1984), p. 3.

**2.** Mary John Smith, unpublished data, University of Wyoming, Laramie, 1985.

**3.** Smith, 1985.

**4.** This procedure for determining a distribution's median is taken from Gene V Glass and Julian C. Stanley, *Statistical Methods in Psychology and Education* (Englewood Cliffs, NJ: Prentice-Hall, 1970), pp. 59–60. Glass and Stanley also discuss procedures for calculating the median in grouped frequency distributions.

**5.** See John E. Freund, *Modern Elementary Statistics*, 6th ed. (Englewood Cliffs, NJ: Prentice-Hall, 1984), pp. 55–56.

**6.** Glass and Stanley, p. 98.

**7.** These predictions are stated in a property sometimes termed the "empirical rule." See Robert Johnson, *Elementary Statistics*, 4th ed. (Boston: Duxbury Press, 1984), p. 64; and Freund, pp. 59–60.

**8.** For detailed treatments of inferential statistics, see Brockett and Levine; Freund; and Johnson.

**9.** See Johnson, pp. 240–41; and Brockett and Levine, p. 164.

**10.** This formula assumes the following conditions are met: $n > 20$, $np > 5$, and $nq > 5$. See Johnson, p. 312.

**11.** The appropriate sampling distribution for dichotomized variables like these is called a binomial sampling distribution. See Gene M. Lutz, *Understanding Social Statistics* (New York: Macmillan, 1983), pp. 236–41.

**12.** See David Nachmias and Chava Nachmias, *Research Methods in the Social Sciences*, 2nd ed. (New York: St. Martin's Press, 1981), p. 447.

**13.** For further discussion, see Johnson, p. 338.

**14.** See Lutz, p. 278.

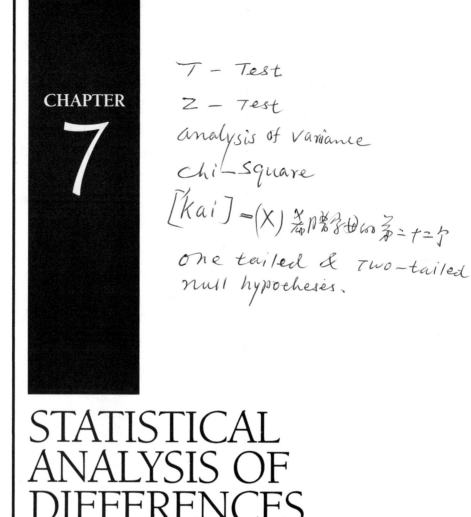

# CHAPTER 7

# STATISTICAL ANALYSIS OF DIFFERENCES

This chapter examines statistical procedures for testing hypotheses about differences between and among populations. Two categories of test statistics are described. First, tests for differences between or among group means are presented: the t test, the z test for mean differences, and analysis of variance. Second, the chapter discusses test statistics for assessing frequency differences. A z test for proportional differences and the chi-square statistic are described. Throughout its development, the chapter focuses on decision rules for testing hypotheses about population differences, including determining critical values and critical regions for rejecting for both one-tailed and two-tailed null hypotheses.

# CHAPTER OUTLINE

*Variance: a mean of square.*

R esearch <u>hypotheses</u> typically predict that either significant differences or significant relationships exist among population parameters. For example, we may suspect that males generally are more talkative than females. Or, we might hypothesize that people's voting preferences are positively related to the number of political advertisements they see. In the first case, we wish to test for <u>population differences</u> and in the second, <u>population relationships</u> are our focus.

This chapter discusses statistical procedures for testing hypotheses about significant population differences. I begin by describing the concept of variance, a notion central to statistical difference analysis. The balance of the chapter explores specific procedures for testing hypotheses about population differences, including tests for differences among sample means and frequencies, Then, in Chapter 8, I examine relationship testing.

## THE CONCEPT OF VARIANCE

Recall from Chapter 6 that a sample (**variance,** also called a **mean square**, measures the dispersion of scores about the sample mean and is calculated with the formula:

*The variance of a sample*
$$s^2 = \frac{\Sigma d^2}{n-1},$$

where $\Sigma d^2$ represents the sum of the squared deviations of all scores from a sample's mean (typically called the **sum of squares**) and $n$ refers to the total number of sample scores. Since <u>variance measures how scores differ from one another</u>, it is a critical index for estimating <u>differences among populations from which samples are drawn.</u>

## Components of Variance

The **total variance** ($s_t^2$) associated with any set of sample scores is partitioned into two components: systematic or true variance and random error variance. **Systematic variance** is the variation among scores that is due to some influence that "pushes" scores in one direction or another.[1] For example, the communication skills of students who have taken a public speaking course are likely to be systematically greater than the skills of people with no speech training. The training itself is presumed to "weight" students' skills toward greater communication competence compared to untrained individuals. Observed differences between such groups are often called **between-groups variance** ($s_b^2$).

Contrasted with systematic variance, **error variance** represents fluctuations in group scores that are due to random or chance factors. Often called **within-groups variance** ($s_w^2$), error variations are completely unsystematic: scores fluctuate both up and down in a random-like fashion. Variables such as carelessness, fatigue, and situational distractions contribute to error variance when researchers collect data from individuals.

To illustrate within-groups or error variance, consider the communication skills of public speaking students. Although their performance should be systematically better than untrained students, we can expect error variations in our measures of both groups' skills. For instance, some trained speakers may perform poorly on the day measures are taken, perhaps because of carelessness, illness, or distraction by personal problems. On some other day, the same speakers might perform significantly better than expected due to facilitating rather than inhibiting random variables. Similarly, some of our untrained speakers are likely to do better and others worse than expected because of personal and situational facilitators and inhibitors. In

**126**

PART II
Statistical
Analysis in
Contemporary
Commu-
nication
Research

*foreuitous a. ... ...*
*foreuity. n.*

short, we can expect upward and downward fluctuations in the performance of both groups for reasons quite unrelated to the presence or absence of prior speech training. These fortuitous fluctuations constitute random error or within-groups variance.

## Variance and Hypothesis Testing

Estimates of between-groups variance ($s_b^2$) and within-groups variance ($s_w^2$) allow us to test hypotheses that significant differences exist between the populations yielding sample groups. In our example, we might test for skill level differences between trained and untrained speakers. Specifically, we compare between-groups variance to within-groups or error variance, treating the two as the ratio $s_b^2/s_w^2$.

In general, the greater the magnitude of $s_b^2$ relative to $s_w^2$, the more confident we could be that real population differences exist between, for instance, the speaking skills of individuals with and without formal speech training. All specific statistical procedures examined in the rest of this chapter test hypotheses of significant population differences by comparing observed group differences registered by indices like between-groups variance with estimates of error variance such as within-groups variance.

## STATISTICAL TESTS FOR SIGNIFICANCE OF DIFFERENCE

Recall from Chapter 6 that five steps are required for testing hypotheses: (1) formulate the research and null hypotheses; (2) state the significance level or probability of Type I error, typically $p < .05$ or $p < .01$; (3) determine the criterion or decision rule for rejecting the null hypothesis, including the stipulation of an appropriate test statistic along with its critical

value and critical region for rejecting null hypotheses; (4) calculate the test statistic and determine whether its value exceeds the critical value and therefore falls into the critical rejection region; and (5) decide whether to reject or fail to reject the null hypothesis.

We are now ready to examine specific **test statistics** (and their associated critical values and rejection regions) for assessing hypotheses of significant differences. Since computer software is available for performing tedious test statistic calculations, I will focus on the tests' conceptual properties, referring to computations as required to illustrate underlying logics. This will provide students with the knowledge required to use the results of computer-assisted computations to make decisions about whether to reject or fail to reject null hypotheses.[2]

Two groups of test statistics for assessing population differences are examined: tests for differences between and among group *means*, and tests for differences between and among groups of *frequencies*. Test statistics of both types examine samples to determine whether significant differences probably exist in the populations from which the samples were drawn. Certain tests, including those assessing mean differences, assume that either the parent population or an associated sampling distribution is normally distributed. Procedures that incorporate assumptions about the population being sampled are called **parametric** tests. Other procedures, including certain tests for differences in frequency data, make no assumptions about either population or sampling distribution shapes. Thus, they are referred to as **nonparametric** or distribution-free tests.

Whether parametric or nonparametric, any significance of difference test can be applied to two types of sample groups: independent groups and related groups. **Independent groups** are samples whose members are unrelated. For example, suppose we use simple random methods to select a sample of people and randomly assign each person to hear either a highly credible speaker or a low-credibility source. These two groups—the one exposed to high credibility and the other to low—represent independent samples that we might test for differences in their agreement with the respective speakers' recommendations.

In contrast, **related groups** are correlated or associated in some fashion. To illustrate a common source of group relatedness, suppose we expose a group of individuals first to a violent motion picture and then to a nonviolent one. These groups are related because they consist of the same people who saw different films on two separate occasions. Groups may be related for reasons other than repeated exposure to the same stimulus. In general, any time two groups of scores tend to rise and fall together or are contrasting so that one set of scores rises as the other falls, the groups are said to be related.[3]

## TEST STATISTICS
## FOR MEAN DIFFERENCES

All tests for significant differences between independent as well as related group means compare two statistical indices: an index of observed differences between two or more sample means (a measure analogous to between-groups variance), and an estimate of the amount of the observed difference that is due to chance, sampling error, or what we referred to earlier as error or within-groups variance. The two indices are presented as the ratio:

$$\frac{\text{Observed group mean differences}}{\text{Error or chance mean differences}}.$$

The outcome of this sample ratio is used to estimate the probability that real differences exist in the populations from which the samples were drawn. The greater the magnitude of actual differences relative to chance fluctuations, the greater the probability that sample values fall into critical rejection re-

gions and therefore reflect true population differences.

Three parametric test statistics are widely used to test for significant mean differences in populations: the $t$ test, the $z$ test for mean differences, and several techniques known cumulatively as analysis of variance.

## The $t$ Test

The **$t$ test** is a test for assessing the significance of difference between two population means ($\mu_1 - \mu_2$) based on data derived from two samples, of which at least one sample is small, typically containing fewer than 30 scores.[4] Like other difference procedures, the $t$ test takes the form of a ratio, with the observed mean difference between two groups representing the numerator and an estimate of sampling error serving as the denominator. The formula for computing a $t$ score for two independent samples randomly selected from approximately normal populations and with roughly equal within-groups variances is:

$$t = \frac{\bar{x}_1 - \bar{x}_2}{\sqrt{\left(\frac{\Sigma d_1^2 + \Sigma d_2^2}{n_1 + n_2 - 2}\right)\left(\frac{n_1 + n_2}{n_1 n_2}\right)}},$$

where $\bar{x}_1$ and $\bar{x}_2$ are the means of two sample groups, the term $\Sigma d_1^2 + \Sigma d_2^2$ is the summed squared deviations of the two samples of scores from their respective sample means, and $n_1$ and $n_2$ are the number of scores in the two sample groups, respectively.[5] More generally, the formula's denominator represents an estimate of sampling error, specifically, the standard error of difference between the two sample means.

Table 7.1 illustrates $t$ test calculations for testing the following nondirectional (two-tailed) research hypothesis: "The mean compliance rate of audiences hearing high-credibility sources will differ from that of audiences exposed to low-credibility sources ($\mu_1 \neq \mu_2$)." The null hypothesis ($H_0$) is $\mu_1 = \mu_2$, and we

TABLE 7.1
CALCULATION OF A $t$ TEST

**Raw Scores, Deviations, Squared Deviations, and Group Means**

| High credibility | | | Low credibility | | |
|---|---|---|---|---|---|
| $x_1$ | $d_1$ | $d_1^2$ | $x_2$ | $d_2$ | $d_2^2$ |
| 3 | $-2$ | 4 | 1 | $-1$ | 1 |
| 4 | $-1$ | 1 | 2 | 0 | 0 |
| 5 | 0 | 0 | 2 | 0 | 0 |
| 6 | $+1$ | 1 | 2 | 0 | 0 |
| 7 | $+2$ | 4 | 3 | $+1$ | 1 |

$$\Sigma x_1 = 25 \qquad \Sigma d_1^2 = 10 \qquad\qquad \Sigma x_2 = 10 \qquad \Sigma d_2^2 = 2$$
$$\bar{x}_1 = 5 \qquad\qquad\qquad\qquad\qquad \bar{x}_2 = 2$$

**Calculation of $t$**

$$t = \frac{\bar{x}_1 - \bar{x}_2}{\sqrt{\left(\frac{\Sigma d_1^2 + \Sigma d_2^2}{n_1 + n_2 - 2}\right)\left(\frac{n_1 + n_2}{n_1 n_2}\right)}}$$

$$= \frac{5 - 2}{\sqrt{\left(\frac{10 + 2}{5 + 5 - 2}\right)\left(\frac{5 + 5}{5 \times 5}\right)}} = 3.87 \qquad T \ value -$$

might set the significance level for rejecting $H_0$ at $p < .05$. Table 7.1 shows hypothetical message compliance scores of the two five-member sample groups, one hearing a message delivered by a highly credible speaker (group 1) and the other who listened to a low-credibility source present the same message (group 2). The high-credibility sample had a mean compliance score of 5, whereas the low-credibility group's mean was 2. A $t$ test for significance of difference between these two means yields a $t$ value of 3.87. We use this value to estimate whether the difference observed between our two sample means reflect differences we could expect in their parent populations were they exposed to high- and low-credibility speakers.

To determine whether the observed mean differences reflect population values, we must refer to the sampling distribution of $t$ scores appearing in Appendix D. The $t$ sampling distribution lists the **critical values** of $t$ required

to reject the null hypothesis that no population differences exist between two groups. To apply our obtained $t$ score to the $t$ distribution, we must take sample sizes into account using a concept called **degrees of freedom** (df). The magnitude of $t$ required to reject null hypotheses declines as sample sizes, reflected by degrees of freedom, increase. This occurs because sampling errors or chance fluctuations decrease with increasing sample sizes. Put another way, the larger our sample size, the greater our chances of selecting samples that reflect well all the important characteristics of their parent populations.

For a $t$ test between two independent samples, degrees of freedom equal the sum of the scores in each sample group minus 1:

$$\mathrm{df}_t = (n_1 - 1) + (n_2 - 1), \qquad \text{or} \qquad n_1 + n_2 - 2.$$

Applied to our hypothetical samples of five people each, $\mathrm{df}_t$ is 8. Referring to the $t$ distri-

magnitude 量值. 程. 大小

**129**

CHAPTER 7
Statistical
Analysis of
Differences

bution in Appendix D, you will see that with 8 df and using two-tailed values, we require a critical $t$ value of a magnitude greater than 2.30 to conclude that observed mean differences are significant at $p < .05$, our chosen significance level. (A $t$ score of more than 3.35 would have been required if we had selected the $p < .01$ significance level. Moreover, if we had framed a one-tailed hypothesis, critical $t$ values of better than 1.85 and 2.89 would have been needed to reject the null hypothesis at $p < .05$ and $p < .01$, respectively.) Our derived $t$ value of 3.87 exceeds the critical value of 2.30 and therefore falls into the **critical region** of rejection associated with $p < .05$. (Indeed, the $t$ value exceeds the critical value of 3.35 required for significance $p < .01$.) Thus, we can conclude that populations of listeners will probably exhibit significantly different message acceptance rates as a function of source credibility.

## The $z$ Test for Mean Differences

Whereas a $t$ test is appropriate for estimating significance of difference between small samples, the $z$ test is used with large samples. Specifically, a **$z$ test for mean differences** assesses differences between two population means based on data derived from large independent random samples, typically groups containing at least 30 scores each.[6] (Recall that a $z$ test was recommended as the test statistic for assessing differences between two 100-member samples at the conclusion of Chapter 6.) Like other significance-of-difference tests, the $z$ test takes the form of a ratio, with observed mean differences in the numerator and estimated chance differences in the denominator. Thus, the general formula for $z$ is:

$$z = \frac{\bar{x}_1 - \bar{x}_2}{s_{\bar{x}_1 - \bar{x}_2}}.$$

The numerator terms $\bar{x}_1$ and $\bar{x}_2$ represent the mean scores of samples 1 and 2, respectively,

whereas the denominator is an estimate of sampling error called the **standard error of difference between means** ($s_{\bar{x}_1 - \bar{x}_2}$). Recall from Chapter 6 that $s_{\bar{x}_1 - \bar{x}_2}$ is computed with the formula:

$$s_{\bar{x}_1 - \bar{x}_2} = \sqrt{\frac{s_1^2}{n_1} + \frac{s_2^2}{n_2}}.$$

Table 7.2 illustrates procedures for computing a $z$ test based on a hypothetical study of 50 males (group 1) and 50 females (group 2) who were asked to judge the entertainment value of prime time commercial television. The research hypothesis we wish to test is a directional (one-tailed) prediction that males generally enjoy prime time television more than females ($\mu_1 > \mu_2$). The corresponding null hypothesis is $\mu_1 = \mu_2$ ($\mu_1 \leq \mu_2$), and we might set our significance level at the conventional $p < .05$. Table 7.2 presents summary data for testing this hypothesis, omitting the raw scores for each group. Notice that our sample of male viewers gave prime time shows a mean rating of 5.1 compared to a 4.0 rating given by females. Employing the three steps shown in Table 7.2 for computing a $z$ test, we derive a $z$ value of 3.79.

To determine whether this $z$ value reflects genuine population differences, we must refer to a $z$ sampling distribution, which is the normal distribution described in Chapter 6. A $z$ distribution, unlike $t$ distributions, does not take sample size ($df$) into account when reporting critical values required to reject null hypotheses. This is because a $z$ test assumes sample sizes sufficiently large that random error does not fluctuate widely. A $z$ sampling distribution will show that a critical $z$ value of more than 1.65 is required to reject a one-tailed null hypothesis at $p < .05$. (A one-tailed critical $z$ score of greater than 2.32 would be needed had our significance level been set at $p < .01$. Furthermore, if our hypothesis had required a two-tailed analysis, critical $z$ values of better than $\pm 1.96$ and $\pm 2.58$ would be needed at $p < .05$ and $p < .01$, respectively.) Our obtained

*Z not take sample size (df) into account for it assumes a large sample size used.*

TABLE 7.2
PROCEDURES FOR COMPUTING A $z$ SCORE

**Summary Data for Two Large Groups**

| | Group 1 (males) | Group 2 (females) |
|---|---|---|
| Means: | $\bar{x}_1 = 5.1$ | $\bar{x}_2 = 4.0$ |
| Sample sizes: | $n_1 = 50$ | $n_2 = 50$ |
| Sums of squared mean deviations: | $\Sigma d_1^2 = 125$ | $\Sigma d_2^2 = 85$ |

**Formulas Required for Computing $z$**

$$1.\ z = \frac{\bar{x}_1 - \bar{x}_2}{s_{\bar{x}_1 - \bar{x}_2}}$$

$$2.\ s_{\bar{x}_1 - \bar{x}_2} = \sqrt{\left(\frac{s_1^2}{n_1}\right) + \left(\frac{s_2^2}{n_2}\right)}$$

$$3.\ s^2 = \frac{\Sigma d^2}{(n-1)}$$

**Steps Required to Compute $z$**

1. Compute the variance ($s^2$) associated with each sample.

$$s_1^2 = \frac{\Sigma d_1^2}{(n_1 - 1)} = \frac{125}{49} = 2.55$$

$$s_2^2 = \frac{\Sigma d_2^2}{(n_2 - 1)} = \frac{85}{49} = 1.73$$

*Variances.*

2. Compute the standard error of the difference between the sample means ($s_{\bar{x}_1 - \bar{x}_2}$).

$$s_{\bar{x}_1 - \bar{x}_2} = \sqrt{\left(\frac{s_1^2}{n_1}\right) + \left(\frac{s_2^2}{n_2}\right)} = \sqrt{\frac{2.55}{50} + \frac{1.73}{50}} = .29$$

3. Compute the $z$ score.

$$z = \frac{\bar{x}_1 - \bar{x}_2}{s_{\bar{x}_1 - \bar{x}_2}} = \frac{5.1 - 4.0}{.29} = 3.79$$

ANOVA = F Tests

one-tailed $z$ score of 3.79 exceeds the required critical value, falling into the critical region for rejecting the null hypothesis at $p < .05$ (and $p < .01$ as well). Thus, we can conclude that males probably enjoy prime time television more than their female counterparts.

## Analysis of Variance

**Analysis of variance** procedures, also called ANOVA methods and F tests, allow us to test for significance of difference among two or more independent as well as related group means.

*grand mean = the mean of the scores in all groups.*

The logic of ANOVA resembles $t$ and $z$ procedures in that observed differences among groups are compared to error differences or fluctuations attributable to chance. More particularly, ANOVA takes the form of a ratio discussed earlier that compares between-groups variance with within-groups (error) variance. This comparison yields an **F ratio**, with $F$ referring to Sir Ronald A. Fisher, the English statistician who developed analysis of variance techniques.

The general formula for computing an analysis of variance or $F$ test is:

$$F = \frac{s_b^2}{s_w^2}, \quad \left\{ \begin{array}{l} between\text{-}groups \\ within\text{-}groups \end{array} \right.$$

where $s_b^2$ refers to between-groups variance, that is, the observed deviations of each group's mean from the grand mean (the mean of the scores in all groups) and $s_w^2$ represents within-groups variance as measured by fluctuations of individual scores around their group's mean score. The greater the value of $F$, the more likely it is that observed group differences reflect real differences in the populations from which the sample groups were selected.

Of the several varieties of analysis of variance used in contemporary research, I shall discuss the single-factor and multiple-factor types.

## Single-factor analysis of variance

**Single-factor analysis of variance**, often called one-way ANOVA, tests group differences that are attributable to a single independent variable, called a **factor**. Recall from Chapter 2 that an independent variable (a factor) is an input variable that relates to an output or dependent effect. In the hypothesis "Fear appeals in a persuasive message relate to increased message acceptance," "fear appeals" is an independent factor related to the output effect, "message acceptance."

To illustrate the use of single-factor ANOVA, suppose we decide to test this hypothesis by exposing a group of 10 individuals to a message containing high fear appeals (group 1), a second group of 10 to a message using moderate levels of fear arousal (group 2), and yet a third 10-person group to a message with no fear appeals (group 3). The null hypothesis is that the three population means do not differ from one another ($\mu_1 = \mu_2 = \mu_3$), whereas our research hypothesis states that at least two of the population means are significantly different. We will set our significance level for rejecting the null hypothesis at $p < .01$. Suppose that upon measuring postexposure reactions, we find that the mean acceptance scores of our three groups are 12, 20, and 10, respectively. Suppose further that we determine that the $s_b^2$ reflecting our three groups' mean deviations from the grand mean of 14 is 18.67, whereas the $s_w^2$ or error variance is 3.00.

Based on these values, we can derive the following $F$ ratio:

$$F = \frac{18.67}{3.00} = 6.22 \quad \text{F value}$$

Similar to $t$ and $z$ procedures, we use this $F$ value to estimate whether the mean acceptance differences observed among our three samples reflect differences we could expect if their parent populations were exposed to the three message types. To resolve this issue, we must refer to the $F$ sampling distribution appearing in Appendix E. An $F$ distribution lists the critical values of $F$ required to reject the null hypothesis that no population differences exist among our three groups. Importantly, we normally use only the area under the right-hand tail of an $F$ distribution as a critical region for rejecting nondirectional as well as directional hypotheses about three or more population means.[7] The larger an $F$ value, the greater the probability that directional and nondirectional differences among sample means cannot be attributed to chance.

To apply our obtained $F$ score of 6.22 to an $F$ distribution, we need the concept of degrees of

*F's characteristics.*

*attributable a.* 方法 图 方法 的 …… 方法 方法 的

**132**

PART II
Statistical
Analysis in
Contemporary
Commu-
nication
Research

freedom (df), reflecting the size of our samples. The F ratio has degrees of freedom associated with both its numerator (between-groups variance) and its denominator (within-groups or error variance). Numerator degrees of freedom ($df_n$) are equal to the total number of sample groups ($k$) minus 1, whereas denominator degrees of freedom ($df_d$) equal the combined number of scores in all groups ($N$) minus the number of groups ($k$). With three groups of 10 scores each in our example, we obtain $df_n = 2$ and $df_d = 27$ as follows:

$$df_n = k - 1 = 3 - 1 = 2$$

$$df_d = N - k = 30 - 3 = 27.$$

To find the critical F value required to reject our nondirectional null hypothesis at $p < .01$, refer to the F distribution in Appendix E and locate the values where the row number 2 representing $df_n$ and the column number 27 signifying $df_d$ intersect. As the 2/27 intersection point shows, a critical F value of better than 5.48 is required for statistical significance at the $p < .01$ level. Our obtained F value of 6.22, which exceeds 5.48, falls into the F distribution's critical rejection region. Thus, we can reject the null hypothesis and conclude that populations of message receivers probably will exhibit significantly different acceptance levels after hearing fear-arousing messages of different types. Notice that, like t scores, the critical values of F required for statistical significance decline as sample size increases due to decreasing sampling error.

When ANOVA is applied to three or more group means, a statistically significant F value does not imply that all groups differ significantly from one another. Rather, it means that there are significant differences between at least two groups. Moreover, a statistically significant F does not identify exactly which groups differ from one another. To isolate specific group differences, we must compute **pairwise comparisons** among our groups, so that in our example, the means of groups 1 and 2, 1 and 3,

and 2 and 3 are systematically analyzed for significant differences. Pairwise comparison tests are modified t procedures and include such tests as Duncan's multiple range test, Scheffé's test, and the Student Newman–Keuls test.[8]

## Multiple-factor analysis of variance

**Multiple-factor analysis of variance**, also called multiway ANOVA, analyzes group differences that are attributable to more than one independent variable or factor. To illustrate the use of multiway ANOVA, consider the following research problem.[9] Suppose we asked a sample of 10 boys and 10 girls to view two kinds of television programs, one depicting explicit violence and the second containing no violence. Suppose further that we measure the aggressive behaviors of all 20 children after they have viewed one of these two program types. As Table 7.3 shows, this research problem creates what is called a 2 × 2 factorial design, so named because it includes two independent factors with two categories associated with each. The first factor, "gender," is comprised of males and females whereas the second, "program type," consists of the categories of violence and nonviolence. As Table 7.3 indicates, this 2 × 2 arrangement generates four groups of five people each whose postviewing behaviors we are interested in comparing for significance of difference.

This research design raises three separate questions:

1. Does gender affect children's aggressive behavior, regardless of the type of program viewed?
2. Does exposure to violent television programs affect aggression levels in children, regardless of the viewer's gender?
3. Do gender and program type act together to influence a young viewer's aggressiveness?

The first two questions pertain to what we call **main effects**, defined as the impact of a single independent variable on some dependent mea-

TABLE 7.3

A 2 × 2 FACTORIAL DESIGN

|  | Violent program | Nonviolent program |  |
|---|---|---|---|
| Males | **Group 1**<br>$n = 5$<br>$\bar{x} = 20$ | **Group 2**<br>$n = 5$<br>$\bar{x} = 14$ | Male $\bar{x} = 17$ |
| Females | **Group 3**<br>$n = 5$<br>$\bar{x} = 10$ | **Group 4**<br>$n = 5$<br>$\bar{x} = 8$ | Female $\bar{x} = 9$ |

Violence $\bar{x} = 15$   Nonviolence $\bar{x} = 11$  *mean of*

Grand $\bar{X} = 13$

sure. By contrast, the third question concerns an **interaction effect**, defined as the unique effect of two or more independent variables operating together on an outcome measure. These three questions can be stated as the following research hypotheses that we might test at the $p < .05$ significance level:

1. Males will exhibit greater mean aggression levels than females ($\mu_m > \mu_f$).
2. Violent television programs will lead to greater mean aggression levels than nonviolent programs ($\mu_v > \mu_n$).
3. Different program types will produce different mean aggression levels in male and female viewers ($\mu_{m-v} - \mu_{m-n} \neq \mu_{f-v} - \mu_{f-n}$).

Stated more directly, our interaction hypothesis is predicting that violent programs, compared to nonviolent ones, will have different aggression effects on males as compared to female viewers.

Analysis of variance (ANOVA) procedures can reliably test all three hypotheses. Table 7.4 displays the calculations required to test for gender and program main effects (hypotheses 1 and 2) as well as any interaction effect produced by gender and programming operating in tandem (hypothesis 3). Despite the

table's forbidding appearance, all three effects are tested by calculating the now familiar between-groups/within-groups variance ratio or *F* test.

## Assessing main effects: Hypotheses 1 and 2

To test for main effects of gender and program type (hypotheses 1 and 2), we must compute a between-groups variance ($s_b^2$) for each of the two independent variables along with an estimate of within-groups or error variance ($s_w^2$). With these values, an *F* ratio ($s_b^2/s_w^2$) can then be calculated for each main effect. The Between-Groups portion of Table 7.4 shows that between-groups variances are computed first by deriving a sum of squares ($SS_b$) for each separate independent variable. Notice that $SS_b$ is the sum of the squared deviations ($D^2$) of each group mean from the grand mean ($\bar{X}$) multiplied by the number of scores in each group ($n$). In the Summary Table portion of Table 7.4, the two sums of squares are reduced to *mean squares* (MS) or variances by dividing them by their appropriate degrees of freedom (df's). The Within-Groups segment of the table indicates that a within-groups or error sum of squares ($SS_w$) is computed for all 20 scores by summing each score's squared deviation ($d^2$) from its

**133**

# TABLE 7.4
## MULTIPLE-FACTOR ANALYSIS OF VARIANCE

### Computation of Means Required for Analysis of Variance

| Group 1 (M − V): $\bar{x}_1 = 20$ | Group 2 (M − N): $\bar{x}_2 = 14$ | Group 3 (F − V): $\bar{x}_3 = 10$ | Group 4 (F − N): $\bar{x}_4 = 8$ |
|---|---|---|---|
| 18 | 11 | 8 | 6 |
| 18 | 13 | 9 | 7 |
| 20 | 15 | 10 | 8 |
| 22 | 15 | 11 | 9 |
| 22 | 16 | 12 | 10 |
| $\Sigma x_1 = 100$ | $\Sigma x_2 = 70$ | $\Sigma x_3 = 50$ | $\Sigma x_4 = 40$ |

$\bar{x}$ for males (M): $\dfrac{100 + 70}{10} = 17$

$\bar{x}$ for females (F): $\dfrac{50 + 40}{10} = 9$

$\bar{x}$ for violent programs (V): $\dfrac{100 + 50}{10} = 15$

$\bar{x}$ for nonviolent programs (N): $\dfrac{70 + 40}{10} = 11$

Grand $\bar{X}$: $(100 + 70 + 50 + 40) = 13$

*[handwritten: $\geq (5 + 5 + 5 + 5)$]*

### Between-Groups Sum of Squares ($SS_b$)

| | Gender main effect | | | Program main effect | |
|---|---|---|---|---|---|
| | Male (M) | Female (F) | | Violent (V) | Nonviolent (N) |
| $n$ | 10 | 10 | $n$ | 10 | 10 |
| $\bar{x}$ | 17 | 9 | $\bar{x}$ | 15 | 11 |
| $D$ | +4 | −4 | $D$ | +2 | −2 |
| $D^2$ | 16 | 16 | $D^2$ | 4 | 4 |
| $nD^2$ | 160 | 160 | $nD^2$ | 40 | 40 |

*[handwritten left margin: deviation of a subgroup mean from the grand mean]*

*[handwritten right margin: individual deviation]*

$SS_b$ for gender: $\Sigma nD^2 = (160 + 160) = 320$

$SS_b$ for program: $\Sigma nD^2 = (40 + 40) = 80$

Where $D =$ deviation of each group mean from the grand $\bar{X}$ (13)

### Within-Groups Sum of Squares ($SS_w$)

| Group 1 (M − V): $\bar{x} = 20$ | | | Group 2 (M − N): $\bar{x} = 14$ | | |
|---|---|---|---|---|---|
| $x_1$ | $d_1$ | $d_1^2$ | $x_2$ | $d_2$ | $d_2^2$ |
| 18 | −2 | 4 | 11 | −3 | 9 |
| 18 | −2 | 4 | 13 | −1 | 1 |
| 20 | 0 | 0 | 15 | +1 | 1 |
| 22 | +2 | 4 | 15 | +1 | 1 |
| 22 | +2 | 4 | 16 | +2 | 4 |
| | | $\Sigma d_1^2 = 16$ | | | $\Sigma d_2^2 = 16$ |

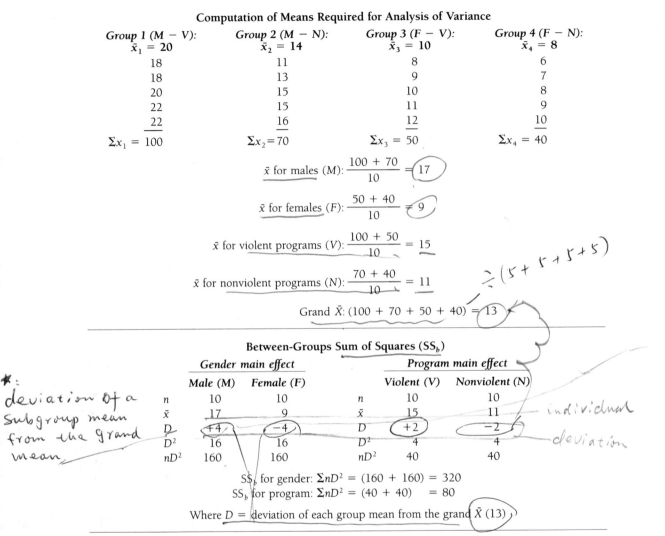

TABLE 7.4
Continued

| Group 3 (F − V): $\bar{x} = 10$ | | | | Group 4 (F − N): $\bar{x} = 8$ | | |
|---|---|---|---|---|---|---|
| $x_3$ | $d_3$ | $d_3^2$ | | $x_4$ | $d_4$ | $d_4^2$ |
| 8 | −2 | 4 | | 6 | −2 | 4 |
| 9 | −1 | 1 | | 7 | −1 | 1 |
| 10 | 0 | 0 | | 8 | 0 | 0 |
| 11 | +1 | 1 | | 9 | +1 | 1 |
| 12 | +2 | 4 | | 10 | +2 | 4 |
| | | $\Sigma d_3^2 = 10$ | | | | $\Sigma d_4^2 = 10$ |

$$SS_w = \Sigma d^2 = (16 + 16 + 10 + 10) = 52$$

### Interaction Sum of Squares ($SS_b$)

*Take the effect away.*

| | Group 1 (M − V) | Group 2 (M − N) | Group 3 (F − V) | Group 4 (F − N) | |
|---|---|---|---|---|---|
| Group means | 20 | 14 | 10 | 8 | |
| Gender effect removed | −4 | −4 | +4 | +4 | |
| Program effect removed | −2 | +2 | −2 | +2 | |
| Group means minus effects | 14 | 12 | 12 | 14 | *Sum* |
| D from grand $\bar{X}$ (13) | +1 | −1 | −1 | +1 | |
| $D^2$ | 1 | 1 | 1 | 1 | |
| $nD^2$ (n = 5) | 5 | 5 | 5 | 5 | |

$$SS_b = \Sigma nD^2 = (5 + 5 + 5 + 5) = 20$$

Where $D$ = deviation of group means after removal of main effects from the grand mean (13)

$$SS_b \ (320 + 80 + 20) + SS_w \ (52) = SS_t \ (472)$$

### Summary Table: Calculating F

*mean square*

*between group*

| Source of variance | SS | df | MS (variance) | F |
|---|---|---|---|---|
| Gender | 320 | 1 | 320 | 98.46* |
| Programming | 80 | 1 | 80 | 24.62* |
| Gender × program | 20 | 1 | 20 | 6.15** |
| Error | 52 | 16 | 3.25 | |

$$df_n/df_d = 1/16$$

*Sum of Square.*

*$p < .01$.
**$p < .05$.

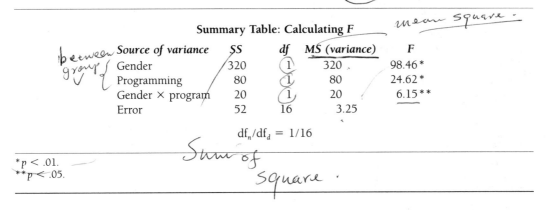

**136**

PART II
Statistical
Analysis in
Contemporary
Commu-
nication
Research

group mean ($\bar{x}$). Then, in the Summary Table, $SS_w$ is reduced to a variance (MS) by dividing by its appropriate degrees of freedom (df).

Recall that the between-groups or numerator df equals the number of groups minus one ($k - 1$), whereas a within-groups or denominator df represents the combined number of scores in all groups minus the total number of groups ($N - k$). With 20 scores and four groups, $df_d = 16$. The $df_n$ for gender is 1 and the $df_n$ for program type is 1, since two groups are associated with each of the two variables. The Summary Table in Table 7.4 displays F values of 98.46 for gender effects and 24.62 for program effects. These F scores are derived by computing an F ratio ($s_b^2/s_w^2$) for each independent variable.

The F distribution in Appendix E shows that, with a 1/16 $df_n/df_d$ ratio, a critical F value of greater than 4.49 is required to reject the null hypothesis at our chosen $p < .05$ level of significance. (A critical F value of more than 8.53 justifies rejecting the null hypothesis at $p < .01$.) Our very large F values for gender (male and female) and programming (violent and nonviolent) fall into the $p < .05$ critical rejection region (and into the $p < .01$ region as well). Thus, we can conclude that (1) boys probably exhibit greater aggression than girls, regardless of the type of television programs they view, and (2) children who watch violent television programs probably are more aggressive than their counterparts who view nonviolent programming, regardless of gender.

Notice that we have used overall F values to interpret the main effects of gender and programming. Such an approach is justified in this problem because only two sample groups are associated with each of our two independent variables. If one or both variables had contained more than two sample groups (for example, if there had been three rather than two program types), we would have needed additional computations to identify the group differences accounting for significant F values.

Recall from our discussion of single-factor ANOVA that a significant F value for three or more groups means only that at least two groups differ from each other. Pairwise comparisons are required to isolate specific group differences. When, as here, only two groups are associated with each significant F score, no further analysis is required to interpret main effects.

## Assessing interaction effects: Hypothesis 3

Our third hypothesis predicted that gender and program type interact to produce different mean aggression levels among young viewers. The computation of an F value for the interaction between gender and programming is slightly more difficult to conceptualize than are main effects. As the Interaction section of Table 7.4 shows, a between-groups sum of squares ($SS_b$) for interaction effects is derived by removing from all four group means the portion of each that is attributable to the main effects of the two independent variables.

To understand this removal operation, notice from the Between-Groups segment of Table 7.4 that the mean aggression score for all males was 17, or 4 points above the grand aggression mean of 13, whereas the females' mean score of 9 was 4 points below the grand mean. To remove this gender main effect from each group mean, the Interaction section of Table 7.4 shows that we add 4 points to the two female groups and subtract 4 points from the two male groups. Moveover, Table 7.4 indicates that the mean aggression score of children viewing the violent program was 15, or 2 points above the grand mean, whereas the nonviolent program viewers' mean score of 11 was 2 points below the grand mean. This program effect is removed by adding 2 points to the means of the nonviolent program viewers and subtracting 2 points from the scores of the two groups viewing violent programs.

Once these two main effects have been re-

residual [riˈzidjuəl] a. 剩余的. 残留的
residual value 余值.  residual error 残差

moved from each group's mean score, we can calculate a between-groups variance ($s_b^2$) for the remaining interaction scores by dividing the residual sum of squares by its appropriate df. Importantly, an interaction df$_n$ is the product of the df$_n$'s associated with the independent variables contributing to the interaction. In our example, the interaction df$_n$ is $(1) \times (1) = 1$, since each variable involved in the interaction has a df$_n$ of 1. (The denominator df$_d$ remains constant at $20 - 4 = 16$.) Once an interaction between-groups variance has been derived, we can compute an $F$ ratio ($s_b^2/s_w^2$) to assess differences among our four groups that are attributable to interaction variance. If two or more individual group means are significantly different after main effects have been removed, we have a significant interaction.

The Summary Table section in Table 7.4 shows the obtained interaction $F$ value 6.15, which is greater than the critical value of 4.49 required for statistical significance at the $p <$ .05 level of confidence. Therefore, we can conclude that gender and violent program viewing probably interact to produce significant differences in children's aggressive behavior. The exact nature of the difference is not clarified by a significant $F$ ratio; rather, it must be discovered through careful inspection and pairwise comparisons like those used in conjunction with single-factor ANOVA.

A close examination of the four group means, displayed in Table 7.3, suggests that the interaction probably means that boys who view violent programs are significantly more aggressive than boys watching nonviolent programs, whereas girls' aggression levels are unaffected by their television viewing habits. We can confirm or disconfirm this speculation by computing pairwise comparisons among all four group means. This indicates a need to check for statistically significant differences between groups 1 and 2, 1 and 3, 1 and 4, 2 and 3, 2 and 4, and 3 and 4, for a total of six pairwise comparisons.

If our pairwise comparisons show that the mean score of boys who viewed violent programs (group 1) differs significantly from that of boys who watched nonviolent programming (group 2), whereas the two female group means (groups 3 and 4) are not significantly different, then the foregoing speculation would be supported. In Chapter 10's discussion of experimental research designs, I will explore at length methods of interpreting the nature of significant interaction effects.

## TEST STATISTICS FOR FREQUENCY DIFFERENCES

For certain types of communication data, mean scores are not appropriate indices of central tendency. Rather, many contemporary researchers use nominal measures that classify data into descriptive categories. For example, much current persuasion research seeks to categorize the compliance-gaining strategies people use in their everyday interactions.[10] Similarly, many conversational analysts study naturalistic communication by classifying ordinary talk according to the functions it serves in interpersonal and organizational contexts.[11] Finally, mass communication researchers often use nominal measurement to categorize media programs and to analyze the composition of mass audiences.

Such research yields frequency data, or information about the number or percentage of communication events that fall into each category of a measurement scale. Often, researchers want to know whether the frequencies assigned to various categories differ significantly. For example, a persuasion researcher might wish to compare the frequency with which males and females use threatening compliance-gaining strategies, suspecting that men rely more heavily on coercion to get their way than females do. Alternately, an organizational researcher might analyze the transcripts of several employment

Coercion [kou'ə:ʃən] n. 强迫, 压制

**138**

PART II
Statistical
Analysis in
Contemporary
Commu-
nication
Research

interviews to test the hypothesis that the conversational tactics of interviewers and applicants differ in kind and in quantity.

Both hypotheses call for procedures to test for significance of difference between or among frequencies. Such test statistics employ a logic similar to that underlying tests for mean differences. Like mean difference methods, frequency difference tests compare two statistical indices: an index of the frequency differences observed between two or more sample categories, and an estimate of frequency differences that are due to chance or sampling error. These two indices are presented as the ratio:

$$\frac{\text{Observed frequency differences}}{\text{Error or chance differences}}$$

The outcome of this ratio is related to an appropriate sampling distribution to determine the probability of real frequency differences occurring in the populations from which the sample frequencies were drawn.

Two different test statistics are widely used to assess frequency differences: a parametric $z$ test for assessing significance of difference between proportions and the chi-square ($\chi^2$) test, a nonparametric statistic for analyzing contingency table data. The $z$ test is limited to two large samples, whereas $\chi^2$ can process two or more frequency samples including those of moderately small size.

## The $z$ Test for Proportional Differences

Although the **$z$ test for proportional differences** is conceptually identical to the $z$ test for mean differences, the calculation formula is modified to accommodate frequency data. Analogous to the $z$ test for means, the $z$ test for proportions is designed to assess differences between two independent frequencies derived from large samples, typically groups containing 30 or more observations. Like other significance tests, a $z$ test takes the form of a ratio, with observed frequency differences in the numerator and estimated chance differences in the denominator. Thus, the general formula for $z$ is:

$$z = \frac{\bar{p}_1 - \bar{p}_2}{s_{\bar{p}_1 - \bar{p}_2}}$$

The numerator terms $\bar{p}_1$ and $\bar{p}_2$ represent the proportions of some observed frequency in sample groups 1 and 2, respectively, whereas the denominator is an estimate of sampling error called the **standard error of difference between proportions**. The precise calculation formula for the proportional $z$ appears in Table 7.5, where $\bar{p}_e$ and $\bar{q}_e$ denote estimated population proportions.

Table 7.5 displays procedures for computing $z$ based on a hypothetical survey of 100 female and 80 male employees of several large industrial plants. The survey asked employees whether they have difficulties communicating effectively with their immediate supervisors. The data were collected to test the nondirectional (two-tailed) research hypothesis that proportions of communication problems differ for male and female employees ($p_m \neq p_f$). The significance level is set at $p < .05$. Notice that 70 of the female employees reported difficulties communicating with their bosses, whereas only 40 males perceived substantial communication problems. With samples of 100 females and 80 males, the proportions reporting problems are .70 and .50 for women and men, respectively. Using the procedure described in Table 7.5, the $s_{\bar{p}_1 - \bar{p}_2}$, reflecting proportional sampling error, is around .07, or 7%. Based on this information, we derive a $z$ score of 2.73.

To estimate whether this $z$ value reflects population differences, we must refer to a $z$ sampling distribution or normal curve. Recall that a $z$ distribution does not consider sample size (df) when reporting critical values required to reject null hypotheses. Recall further that a critical $z$ value of better than ±1.96 is

*Proportion 66.66⅔%.* (handwritten)

## TABLE 7.5
## CALCULATION OF THE PROPORTIONAL $z$ TEST

**Raw Frequency Data**

|  | Group 1 | Group 2 |
|---|---|---|
| Number in group | 100 | 80 |
| Number reporting communication problems | 70 | 40 |
| Proportion reporting communication problems | .70 | .50 |

**Formulas Required to Compute $z$**

$$z = \frac{\bar{p}_1 - \bar{p}_2}{\sqrt{(\bar{p}_e \bar{q}_e)\,[(n_1 + n_2)/(n_1 n_2)]}}$$

$$\bar{p}_e = \frac{(n_1 \bar{p}_1) + (n_2 \bar{p}_2)}{(n_1 + n_2)}$$

$$\bar{q}_e = 1 - \bar{p}_e$$

**Steps Required to Compute $z$**

1. Compute estimates of population parameters ($\bar{p}_e$ and $\bar{q}_e$).

$$\bar{p}_e = \frac{(n_1 \bar{p}_1) + (n_2 \bar{p}_2)}{n_1 + n_2}$$

$$= \frac{(100 \times .70) + (80 \times .50)}{(100 + 80)}$$

$$= .61$$

$$\bar{q}_e = 1 - \bar{p}_e$$

$$= 1 - .61$$

$$= .39$$

2. Compute $z$.

$$z = \frac{\bar{p}_1 - \bar{p}_2}{\sqrt{(\bar{p}_e \bar{q}_e)\,[(n_1 + n_2)/(n_1 n_2)]}}$$

$$= \frac{.70 - .50}{\sqrt{(.61 \times .39)\,[(100 + 80)/(100 \times 80)]}}$$

$$= \frac{.20}{.0732}$$

$$= 2.73 \quad (2.7322404)$$

(handwritten calculations: $\sqrt{.2379}$  $180 \div 8000 = 0.0225$  $.2379 \times .0225 = 0.0731621$  $0.0732.$)

139

**140**

PART II
Statistical
Analysis in
Contemporary
Commu-
nication
Research

*Versatile ...* (handwritten note in top margin)

required to reject a two-tailed null hypothesis at our preferred $p < .05$ significance level. (A $z$ value greater than $\pm 2.58$ is needed at $p < .01$.) The obtained $z$ score of 2.73 exceeds the required critical value, falling into the rejection region at $p < .05$ (and $p < .01$ as well). Thus, we can assume that male and female employees in large industrial firms probably experience different levels of difficulty when communicating with their immediate supervisors.

## Chi-Square and Contingency Table Analysis

*$\chi^2$ is Nonparametric.* (handwritten note in left margin)

The nonparametric **chi-square test** ($\chi^2$) is more versatile than a $z$ test. Chi-square can assess differences between two or more independent groups with frequencies ranging from moderately small to very large. Moreover, chi-square can perform operations with frequency data that are analogous in function and complexity to single-factor as well as multiple-factor analysis of variance. Because of its versatility and general usefulness, chi-square is a commonly employed test statistic for frequency differences.

Like other significance of difference tests, chi-square takes the form of a ratio between observed frequency differences and random error differences. Its computing formula is:

$$\chi^2 = \Sigma \left[ \frac{(O - E)^2}{E} \right],$$

*Cate-gories* (handwritten note)

where $O$ represents the observed frequency in some particular group or category on a nominal scale and $E$ refers to the expected frequency in the same group, meaning the frequency that could result from chance. Thus, for any one group, $\chi^2$ represents observed minus expected frequencies squared divided by expected (error) frequencies. The summation sign ($\Sigma$) appearing in the formula indicates that we can use $\chi^2$ to assess significant differences among as many different groups or categories as we wish

simply by adding the $(O - E)^2/E$ ratio associated with each group.

Several different chi-square procedures are used in contemporary research and we shall now consider two of the more common ones: single-sample chi-square and multiple-sample chi-square, also called contingency table analysis. *Categories of $\chi^2$.* (handwritten note)

### Single-sample chi-square

Quite often researchers wish to examine how a single group of frequencies distribute into the categories associated with some nominal scale. For example, a conversational analyst might classify the communication behaviors of a single sample of romantic partners along a nominal scale containing categories such as supportive and defensive utterances. Alternately, a mass communication researcher might content analyze a sample of prime time television commercials, categorizing them according to the roles assumed in the advertisements by minority characters. **Single-sample chi-square** enables researchers to test for significance of difference among the categories derived from such samples.

To illustrate the use of single-sample chi-square, suppose a researcher has asked a sample of 30 elementary school teachers to evaluate three different versions of a television program (A, B, and C), each designed to teach reading skills to children. The research hypothesis is that teachers will give different effectiveness ratings to the three programs (A $\neq$ B $\neq$ C). The significance level for testing the corresponding null hypothesis (A = B = C) is $p < .05$. The hypothetical data in Table 7.6 show that 13 of the 30 teachers felt version A was most effective, 15 of them selected version B, and 2 rated version C as the best teaching tool. These totals constitute observed frequencies. In such single-sample designs, expected frequencies (those we could expect by chance) often represent all observed frequencies di-

TABLE 7.6
SINGLE-SAMPLE CHI-SQUARE

|  | Categories of programs | | |
|---|---|---|---|
|  | Version A | Version B | Version C |
| Observed frequencies, $O$ | 13 | 15 | 2 |
| Expected frequencies, $E$ | 10 | 10 | 10 |

**Overall Calculation**

$$\chi^2 = \sum \left[ \frac{(O - E)^2}{E} \right] = \frac{(13 - 10)^2}{10} + \frac{(15 - 10)^2}{10} + \frac{(2 - 10)^2}{10}$$

$$= \left( \frac{9}{10} \right) + \left( \frac{25}{10} \right) + \left( \frac{64}{10} \right)$$

$$= .9 + 2.5 + 6.4$$

$$= 9.8$$

**Pairwise Comparison**

*Groups A and B*

$$\chi^2 = \sum \left[ \frac{(O - E)^2}{E} \right] = \frac{(13 - 10)^2}{10} + \frac{(15 - 10)^2}{10} = 3.40$$

*Groups A and C*

$$\chi^2 = \sum \left[ \frac{(O - E)^2}{E} \right] = \frac{(13 - 10)^2}{10} + \frac{(2 - 10)^2}{10} = 7.30$$

*Groups B and C*

$$\chi^2 = \sum \left[ \frac{(O - E)^2}{E} \right] = \frac{(15 - 10)^2}{10} + \frac{(2 - 10)^2}{10} = 8.90$$

vided by the number of categories into which these frequencies fall. Thus, if all three versions of the program were equally effective, we might expect roughly equal observed frequencies in our three categories, that is, around 10 teachers (30/3) should evaluate each program as the most effective of the three. No. of Cates The calculations displayed in Table 7.6 yield a three-group $\chi^2$ of 9.8. To determine whether this value reflects systematic differences in the way teachers rate the programs, we need to consult the chi-square sampling distribution in Appendix F. Importantly, we typically use only the upper tail of a chi-square distribution as the critical region for rejecting both nondirectional and directional hypotheses about differences among three or more samples. The more an obtained $\chi^2$ value exceeds zero, the greater the probability that directional and nondirectional differences cannot be attributed to chance.[12]

A chi-square distribution, unlike the $z$ distribution, takes degrees of freedom into account when reporting the critical values required for rejecting null hypotheses. For a

**142**

PART II
Statistical
Analysis in
Contemporary
Commu-
nication
Research

*asserliveness.*

single-factor chi-square, df equals the number of groups or categories associated with a nominal scale minus one ($k - 1$). Thus, the df associated with our example in Table 7.6 is $3 - 1$ or 2. Given 2 df, the chi-square sampling distribution indicates that a critical $\chi^2$ value of more than 5.99 is required to conclude that sample differences reflect real population parameters at the $p < .05$ level. (A $\chi^2$ greater than 9.21 indicates statistical significance at $p < .01$.) Since we obtained $\chi^2 = 9.8$, we can assume that significant differences probably exist among our three groups of frequencies.

Notice that, like an $F$ ratio, the chi-square value for three or more groups does not imply that all groups differ from one another, but only that at least two group differences exist. To isolate which groups actually differ, we must conduct pairwise comparisons among our three groups. Appendix F shows that a $\chi^2$ of better than 3.84 is required at $p < .05$ for significant two-group differences (df = 1). Given this critical value, Table 7.6 shows that groups A and B do not differ significantly ($\chi^2 = 3.40$), whereas groups A and C as well as groups B and C are significantly different ($\chi^2 = 7.30$ and 8.90, respectively).

## Multiple-sample chi-square: Contingency table analysis

**Multiple-sample chi-square** is commonly called **contingency table analysis** and it tests for significance of difference among frequencies of two or more independent samples. Multiple-sample chi-square is analogous to multiple-factor analysis of variance. Chi-square samples represent factors (independent variables) whose associated frequencies we wish to test for differences.

To illustrate, suppose an organizational researcher wishes to test (at $p < .05$) the hypothesis that job applicants and interviewers use communication strategies of different types during employment interviews. Suppose further that the researcher has analyzed the tran-

scripts of a group of employment interviews, classifying the utterances of both parties into the following categories: (1) "accounts," referring to comments that defend or justify inappropriate behaviors; (2) "formulations," meaning verbal strategies that exercise control over the interview conversation; (3) "digressions," representing talk about non-job-related issues; and (4) "qualifiers," referring to comments that manifest uncertainty, tentativeness, or non-assertiveness.[13] Using this four-part taxonomy, suppose that our hypothetical researcher classifies a sample of 100 utterances contributed by interviewers and 70 performed by applicants.

Table 7.7 presents the resulting two-factor contingency table along with the observed and expected frequencies associated with each combination of the two factors. The first factor is "communication strategy type" (accounts, formulations, digressions, and qualifiers) and the second is "communicator role" (interviewer and applicant). This two-factor arrangement is called a $4 \times 2$ contingency table because the first independent variable contains four categories, whereas the second has two. When analyzing frequency data associated with two or more factors, Table 7.7 shows that we compute expected frequencies by multiplying the appropriate row sum of observed frequencies by the column sum of observed frequencies and dividing that product by the grand sum representing the total observed frequency count in the contingency table.

Once expected frequencies have been derived, the researcher computes $\chi^2$ values in the manner already described. The calculations shown in Table 7.7 indicate that the overall $\chi^2$ for our $4 \times 2$ contingency table is 45.54. Degrees of freedom are the product of the number of categories associated with each factor minus one ($k - 1$). In our example, df is ($k - 1$) $\times$ ($k - 1$) or $(4 - 1) \times (2 - 1) = 3$. The chi-square distribution appearing in Appendix F shows that with 3 df, a critical $\chi^2$ value greater than 7.81 is required for statistical significance

taxonomy [tæk'sɔnɔmi] 分類學.

4 × 2

TABLE 7.7
A TWO-FACTOR CONTINGENCY TABLE AND $\chi^2$ CALCULATIONS

| Communication strategy type | Interviewers | Applicants | Row sums (O) |
|---|---|---|---|
| Accounts | | | |
| Observed (O) | 5 | 25 | 30 |
| Expected (E) | 18 | 12 | |
| Formulations | | | |
| Observed (O) | 50 | 15 | 65 |
| Expected (E) | 38 | 27 | |
| Digressions | | | |
| Observed (O) | 35 | 10 | 45 |
| Expected (E) | 26 | 19 | |
| Qualifiers | | | |
| Observed (O) | 10 | 20 | 30 |
| Expected (E) | 18 | 12 | |
| Column sums (O) | 100 | 70 | Grand sum (O) = 170 |

Expected Frequencies: $\dfrac{\text{Row sum} \times \text{column sum}}{\text{Grand sum}}$

$$\frac{30 \times 100}{170} = 17.65 \qquad \frac{30 \times 70}{170} = 12.35$$

$$\frac{65 \times 100}{170} = 38.24 \qquad \frac{65 \times 70}{170} = 26.76$$

$$\frac{45 \times 100}{170} = 26.47 \qquad \frac{45 \times 70}{170} = 18.53$$

$$\frac{30 \times 100}{170} = 17.65 \qquad \frac{30 \times 70}{170} = 12.35$$

Chi-Square Calculation:

$$\chi^2 = \Sigma \left[ \frac{(O-E)^2}{E} \right] = \frac{(5-17.65)^2}{17.65} + \frac{(25-12.35)^2}{12.35}$$

$$+ \frac{(50-38.24)^2}{38.24} + \frac{(15-26.76)^2}{26.76}$$

$$+ \frac{(35-26.47)^2}{26.47} + \frac{(10-18.53)^2}{18.53}$$

$$+ \frac{(10-17.65)^2}{17.65} + \frac{(20-12.35)^2}{12.35}$$

$$= 45.54$$

$$df = (2-1) \times (4-1) = 3$$

Second factor    first factor

**144**

PART II
Statistical
Analysis in
Contemporary
Commu-
nication
Research

at the $p < .05$ level. (At $p < .01$, more than 11.34 is needed.) Thus, we can conclude that significant differences probably exist between at least two of the eight separate frequencies in our contingency table. To determine where specific differences lie, we can compute systematic chi-square comparisons between or among any of the table frequencies.

Two general types of frequency difference can be assessed. First, we can directly compute the *main effects* of each separate factor using procedures already described for the calculation of single-sample chi-square. For example, to determine whether the total number of utterances contributed by interviewers is significantly greater than the applicants' total contributions, expected frequencies might be calculated by dividing the total number of observed utterances (170) by the number of categories (2), yielding the number of utterances we could expect by chance from both interviewers and applicants (85). We can compute a chi-square value for interviewer–applicant differences as follows:

$$\chi^2 = \sum \left[ \frac{(O - E)^2}{E} \right]$$

$$= \frac{(100 - 85)^2}{85} + \frac{(70 - 85)^2}{85}$$

$$= 5.29.$$

Since a critical $\chi^2$ of better than 3.84 is required for statistical significance at $p < .05$ with 1 df, we can conclude that interviewers probably talk more during employment interviews than applicants. A similar analysis can check for significant differences among the four types of utterances regardless of the source.

In addition to testing for main effects, a researcher may be interested in interactions or frequency differences that result from the two principal factors operating in tandem. Unfortunately, we cannot directly compute an interaction value using traditional chi-square procedures. However, researchers might indirectly assess interaction effects by computing pairwise chi-square comparisons between any of the eight different frequencies appearing in the contingency table. For example, we could assess the significance of difference between interviewers and applicants in their use of accounts by computing a $\chi^2$ value for the two frequencies appearing in the first row of the contingency table. Similar analyses can check interviewers' and applicants' comparative use of formulations, digressions, and qualifiers. Alternately, a test for differences in the frequency with which formulations versus digressions, accounts versus qualifiers, and so forth, are employed by either interviewers or applicants can be computed. As these examples suggest, extensive pairwise checks might give researchers a general (albeit imprecise) impression of the effects on frequency data of two or more factors working together.

# INTERFACE: CHAPTERS 7 AND 8

This chapter has examined statistical procedures for testing hypotheses about population differences. Two categories of test statistics were described. First, tests for differences between or among group means were presented: the $t$ test, the $z$ test for mean differences, and analysis of variance. Second, the chapter described test statistics for assessing frequency differences. A $z$ test for proportional differences and the chi-square procedure were discussed.

In the next chapter, we will conclude our treatment of statistical inquiry by examining methods for testing hypotheses about population relationships. Bivariate as well as multivariate correlation procedures will be examined.

digression [dai 'greʃən] n. 离题，枝节话。
digressive.
partition n. 5开。区分

TWO tests for frequency differences: Z/χ².

## MAIN POINTS

1. The variance associated with any set of sample scores is partitioned into two components: systematic or between-groups variance and error or within-groups variance.

2. The greater the magnitude of between-groups variance to within-groups variance ($s_b^2/s_w^2$), the greater the chance that real differences exist between or among the populations from which samples are selected.

3. Five steps are required for testing hypotheses about population differences: state the research and null hypotheses; choose a significance level; formulate decision rules for rejecting the null hypothesis, including selecting an appropriate test statistic; calculate the test statistic; and decide whether to reject or fail to reject the null hypothesis.

4. Two general categories of test statistics are tests for differences between or among sample means and tests for differences between or among sample frequencies.

5. Three parametric test statistics are widely used to test for population mean differences: the $t$ test for two samples, of which at least one is small; the $z$ test for mean differences between two large samples; and analysis of variance procedures for assessing differences among two or more samples of varying sizes.

6. Single-factor analysis of variance tests for mean differences that are attributable to a single independent variable or factor, whereas multiple-factor analysis of variance assesses mean differences that are attributable to more than one independent variable.

7. Multiple-factor analysis of variance can assess main effects of separate independent variables as well as interaction effects resulting from the joint operation of two or more independent variables.

8. Two test statistics are widely used to assess frequency differences: a parametric $z$ test for proportional differences between two large samples of frequencies and a nonparametric chi-square ($\chi^2$) test for analyzing differences among two or more frequency samples of moderately small to large sizes.

9. Single-sample chi-square assesses differences among categories of frequencies derived from one sample. Multiple-sample chi-square, commonly called contingency table analysis, tests for differences among the frequency categories of two or more independent samples.

Three parametric Tests: T. Z. ANOVA (Analysis Of variance)

## REVIEW EXERCISES

1. Suppose you wish to test the general hypothesis that populations of males and females differ in their enjoyment of televised crime drama. Suppose further that you have selected random samples of 10 males and 10 females and have measured their attitudes on a scale ranging from 1 ("enjoy very little") to 5 ("enjoy very much"). The raw data follow:

| Males | | Females | |
|---|---|---|---|
| 5 | 4 | 3 | 4 |
| 5 | 4 | 4 | 5 |
| 4 | 4 | 1 | 2 |
| 3 | 5 | 1 | 2 |
| 4 | 2 | 2 | 1 |

State precise two-tailed (nondirectional) research and null hypotheses and select a significance level for rejecting the null hypothesis. Calculate a $t$ test for significance of difference between the mean scores of these two groups. Why is $t$ an appropriate test statistic? What is the critical $t$ value required for rejecting the null hypothesis at your chosen significance level? (Remember that critical $t$ values depend on sample size as indexed by degrees of freedom.) Does your obtained $t$ value exceed this critical value, thereby falling into the critical rejection

Two Tests: test for differences between or among Sample means & Test for differences between or among Sample frequencies.

**146**

PART II
Statistical
Analysis in
Contemporary
Commu-
nication
Research

region of the $t$ sampling distribution? Can you reject the null hypothesis?

[**Answer:** $t = 2.76$; with 18 df, critical $t$ values of better than 2.10 and 2.88 are required for rejecting the null hypothesis at $p < .05$ and $p < .01$, respectively.]

**2.** Refer to the samples of data in Exercises 11 and 12 of Chapter 6. Formulate precise one-tailed (directional) research and null hypotheses about mean differences that might be tested using these two samples of data. Now compute a $z$ test for mean differences between the sample data in Exercise 11 and the sample data in Exercise 12. Why is $z$ an appropriate test statistic? Does your obtained $z$ value exceed the critical normal distribution value of 1.65 required for rejecting a null hypothesis at $p < .05$?

[**Answer:** $z = .90$.]

**3.** Suppose you wish to test the general hypothesis that low-, middle-, and upper-income families have different television viewing habits. Suppose further that you have sampled 10 families from each of these three groups ($N = 30$, $k = 3$). Assume that the calculated between-groups sum of squares ($SS_b$) for the three groups on a viewing habits measure is 20.5, whereas the within-groups sum of squares ($SS_w$) is 44.0. State your precise research and null hypotheses and then compute an $F$ value ($s_b^2/s_w^2$) using the given information. (Remember that variance or $s^2$ represents a sum of squares divided by the appropriate degrees of freedom.) Does your obtained $F$ score exceed the critical $F$ value required to reject the null hypothesis at $p < .05$?

[**Answer:** $F = 6.29$; with a $df_n/df_d$ of 2/27, a critical $F$ value of greater than 3.35 is required to reject the null hypothesis at $p < .05$.]

**4.** Suppose I have conducted a field study at a local shopping mall to investigate how a requester's dress and grooming affect the extent to which people will comply with requests to sign a petition opposing the use of nuclear energy. Suppose I made requests of 100 persons when dressed and groomed neatly and asked an additional 100 persons to sign the petition when my appearance was sloppy. Suppose finally that 60 people signed the petition when I made a neat appearance, whereas 35 signed it when I did not. State precise two-tailed research and null hypotheses that you believe I might test with these data. Compute a $z$ test for significance of difference between proportions using the data. Why is $z$ an appropriate test statistic? Does your obtained $z$ value exceed the critical value of 1.96 required for rejecting a null hypothesis at $p < .05$? Is it equal to or greater than the critical value of 2.58 required at the $p < .01$ level?

[**Answer:** $z = 3.54$.]

**5.** Suppose you wish to know whether the extent to which people subscribe to daily newspapers depends in part on their gender (male versus female) and their living arrangements (lives alone versus lives with others). Suppose further that you have conducted a survey and gathered the accompanying contingency table data (the symbol $O$ means observed frequency of persons who subscribe to daily newspapers).

|  | Male | Female |
|---|---|---|
| Lives alone | Group 1 $O = 30$ | Group 2 $O = 40$ |
| Lives with others | Group 3 $O = 20$ | Group 4 $O = 10$ |

Compute a chi-square value to assess whether there are significant differences in newspaper subscription rates among any of these four subgroups. Does your obtained chi-square value exceed the critical value required for rejecting the null hypothesis at $p < .05$? What about the

$p < .01$ significance level? (Remember that critical chi-square values depend on the degrees of freedom associated with the problem.) [**Answer:** $\chi^2 = 4.76$; with 1 df, critical $\chi^2$ values of better than 3.84 and 6.63 are required at $p < .05$ and $p < .01$, respectively.]

# NOTES

**1.** Fred N. Kerlinger, *Foundations of Behavioral Research*, 2nd ed. (New York: Holt, Rinehart & Winston, 1973), p. 74.

**2.** Two especially useful software packages are SPSS$^x$ (Statistical Package for the Social Sciences) and BMDP. See *SPSS$^x$ User's Guide* (New York: McGraw-Hill, 1983); and W. J. Dixon (ed.), *BMDP Statistical Software* (Berkeley, CA: University of California Press, 1983).

**3.** J. P. Guilford and Benjamin Fruchter, *Fundamental Statistics in Psychology and Education*, 5th ed. (New York: McGraw-Hill, 1973), p. 154.

**4.** See John E. Freund, *Modern Elementary Statistics*, 6th ed. (Englewood Cliffs, NJ: Prentice-Hall, 1984), p. 295.

**5.** For the formula for related groups, see Guilford and Fruchter, p. 161.

**6.** See Freund, pp. 291–95.

**7.** This conclusion, although adequate for our purposes, does not fully state the problem of testing nondirectional hypotheses using an $F$ distribution. For details, see Freund, pp. 319, 368.

**8.** For a discussion of pairwise comparison tests, see C. Mitchell Dayton, *The Design of Educational Experiments* (New York: McGraw-Hill, 1970), pp. 37–44.

**9.** The research problem used here to illustrate multiway ANOVA is patterned after a sample study discussed in Frederick Williams, *Reasoning with Statistics*, 2nd ed. (New York: Holt, Rinehart & Winston, 1979), pp. 90–103.

**10.** See Karen Tracy, Robert T. Craig, Martin Smith, and Frances Spisak, "The Discourse of Requests: Assessment of a Compliance-Gaining Approach," *Human Communication Research*, 10 (1984): 513–38; and Michael J. Cody, Margaret L. McLaughlin, and William J. Jordan, "A Multidimensional Scaling of Three Sets of Compliance-Gaining Strategies," *Communication Quarterly*, 28 (1980): 34–46.

**11.** See William A. Donahue, Mary E. Diez, and Mark Hamilton, "Coding Naturalistic Negotiation Interaction," *Human Communication Research*, 10 (1984): 403–25; and Scott Jacobs and Sally Jackson, "Speech Act Structure in Conversation: Rational Aspects of Pragmatic Coherence," in *Conversational Coherence: Form, Structure, and Strategy*, ed. Robert T. Craig and Karen Tracy (Beverly Hills, CA: Sage, 1983), pp. 47–66.

**12.** See Freund, pp. 341–42; and Gene M. Lutz, *Understanding Social Statistics* (New York: Macmillan, 1983), p. 325.

**13.** These categories were taken from a more extensive taxonomy generated by Sandra L. Ragan, "Alignment and Conversational Coherence," in *Conversational Coherence: Form, Structure, and Strategy*, ed. Robert T. Craig and Karen Tracy (Beverly Hills, CA: Sage, 1983), pp. 157–71.

# CHAPTER

# 8

# STATISTICAL ANALYSIS OF RELATIONSHIPS

This chapter explores statistical methods both for measuring relationships between and among variables and for assessing the statistical significance of such relationships. Two sets of procedures are described. First, bivariate correlation, involving measures of association between two variables, is examined. Specific bivariate tests include Pearson's r, Pearson's phi, and Cramer's V coefficient. Second, the chapter describes multivariate procedures that measure the relationship among three or more variables, presenting multivariate dependence models like multiple correlation and regression analysis and multivariate interdependence methods such as factor analysis and cluster analysis.

# CHAPTER OUTLINE

*[handwritten margin notes at top: "Covary", "Coefficient of correlation", "{ r ~ Sample", "{ P ~ population."]*

*[handwritten margin notes right side: "r & p", "r²" (circled), ".94 X .94 = 0.8836"]*

**M**any research hypotheses focus not on differences, but rather on important population relationships. For example, we may suspect that persuasive message acceptance is positively related to source credibility, meaning that as credibility increases, acceptance goes up proportionately. Alternately, we might hypothesize that television viewing is negatively related to children's creativity, implying that as children watch increasing amounts of television their creativity systematically declines. Although population differences are implicit in both hypotheses, each emphasizes how two or more parameters covary. As we shall see, a statistical analysis of covariation yields information about communicative relationships that is either obscured or ignored in difference analysis.

This chapter explores procedures both for measuring relationships and for assessing their statistical significance. I begin by discussing the concepts of covariance and correlation, central notions in relationship analysis. Next, I examine bivariate correlation, involving measures of association between two variables. Finally, I discuss multivariate procedures that measure the relationship among three or more variables. Test statistics for assessing the significance of both bivariate and multivariate associations are presented.

## COVARIANCE
## AND CORRELATION

Hypotheses predicting that significant relationships exist between population variables are tested by estimating the amount of systematic variance the variables share. Variance that is common to two or more variables is known as **covariance** (see Figure 8.1). In the first case displayed in Figure 8.1, the shaded area represents the common variance (covariance) between the variables "communication competence" and "intelligence." The substantial quantity of shared variance suggests that high intelligence is associated with effective communication skills. In the second case, the absence of common variance means that the variables "gender" and "communication competence" are independent of each other, with maleness and femaleness having no measurable bearing on one's ability to communicate effectively.

The strength of covariation between two variables is indexed by a statistic called a **coefficient of correlation**, symbolized by the lowercase $r$ in samples and by the Greek letter rho ($\rho$) for corresponding population parameters. A coefficient of correlation ranges from $-1$ through 0 to $+1$. A coefficient of $-1$ indicates that a perfect negative relationship exists between two variables (as the value of one variable increases, the value of the other declines systematically). Zero signifies that two variables are not linearly related and $+1$ indicates a perfect positive relationship (as the value of one variable increases, the value of the other increases proportionately).

To understand the meaning of a correlation coefficient, imagine that we correlated the variables "intelligence" and "communication competence" and derived a coefficient of $+.94$. This value indicates that the two variables are strongly related in a positive direction. The more intelligent a person, the more effective he or she is likely to be as a communicator. Importantly, the variance shared by these variables can be expressed as a percentage by squaring their coefficient of correlation to produce an $r^2$. Known as a **coefficient of determination**, an $r^2$ registers the percentage of the combined variability associated with two variables that is common to them. Given our hypothetical $r$ of $+.94$ between intelligence and competence, the corresponding $r^2$ is .88. This index means that the two variables share 88% of their combined variance.[1] The coefficient of determination is an extremely useful index of covariance and, for that reason, it is used extensively in contemporary communication research.

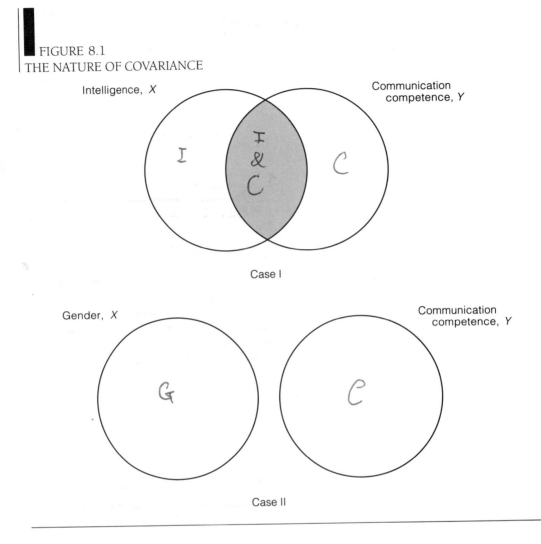

FIGURE 8.1
THE NATURE OF COVARIANCE

Intelligence, *X*                    Communication
                                     competence, *Y*

I        I
         &
         C

                    C

Case I

Gender, *X*                          Communication
                                     competence, *Y*

G                                    C

Case II

## The Practical Meaning of Correlation Coefficients

As we have seen, the closer a given correlation coefficient is to 1 (either $+1$ or $-1$), the greater the strength of association between the correlated variables. Thus, an *r* of $+.94$ indicates an especially strong positive relationship. But what if we derive a coefficient of $+.60$ between two variables? Is this a weak positive relationship? A fairly strong one? And, how about $-.72$? Does this indicate a moderately strong negative relationship or a very strong one? Although specific tests for assessing the statistical significance of correlation coefficients will be explored later, Lutz[2] has suggested the following practical guidelines for interpreting magnitudes of correlation:

| | |
|---|---|
| 0: | No relationship |
| $\pm.01-.25$: | A weak relationship |
| $\pm.26-.55$: | A moderate relationship |
| $\pm.56-.75$: | A strong relationship |
| $\pm.76-.99$: | A very strong relationship |
| $\pm1$: | A perfect relationship. |

*Guidelines for accessing values*

152

## Types of Correlations

Correlations among variables ranging from weak to very strong can be classified in two important ways: linear and curvilinear relationships, and bivariate and multivariate relationships.

### Linear and curvilinear relationships

A **linear correlation** is a straight line relationship between two variables. We learned in Chapter 2 that linear relationships may be either direct (positive) or inverse (negative). A **direct relation**, indicated by a positive (+) correlation coefficient ($r$), occurs when two variables rise or fall together in a systematic fashion. The example in Figure 8.2$a$ indicates that when a speaker's credibility increases, so does compliance with his or her message; conversely, as credibility declines we can expect a corresponding decrease in compliance. An **inverse relation**, signified by a negative (−) correlation coefficient, exists when one variable systematically increases as another declines. Figure 8.2$b$ suggests that as television viewing increases, creativity in children goes down.

Contrasted with these two relationships, a **curvilinear relation** does not follow a straight-line pattern. Two common examples are depicted in Figure 8.2. The **inverted-U correlation**, which is prevalent in communication research, occurs when two variables initially increase together, after which one continues to increase as the other systematically declines. Figure 8.2$c$ illustrates such a relationship: as a commercial advertisement is repeated, acceptance increases with the first few repetitions, then begins to decrease as listeners become tired or bored with the same message.

The **U-shaped correlation** (Figure 8.2$d$) occurs when one variable initially increases as the other declines, after which the two increase together. As noted in Chapter 2, the relationship between listener attention and the time required for a speaker to deliver a message frequently follows a U-shaped pattern. Attention often is quite high during the first few minutes of a public speech or lecture, then it declines until near the end of the message at which time it increases to levels near those at the beginning of the speech.

### Bivariate and multivariate relationships

A **bivariate correlation** is a relationship between two and only two variables. Each of the examples in Figure 8.2 represents a bivariate correlation; both the linear and the nonlinear variety are shown. **Multivariate correlations** are linear or curvilinear relationships among three or more variables. Two general types of multivariate relationships interest researchers: dependence and interdependence correlations.[3]

A **dependence relationship** describes how a correlated set of two or more independent variables affects one or more dependent variables. For example, suppose we were to analyze the intercorrelations among source credibility, receiver ego involvement, and persuasive compliance rates. We might discover that the three variables are associated in such a way that increasing source credibility and decreasing ego involvement together relate to greater compliance with a persuader's recommendations. To take a second small group example, an increasingly authoritarian leadership style coupled with declining task difficulty might relate to increased productivity and decreased morale.

An **interdependence relationship** is a multivariate correlation among three or more variables without regard to independent–dependent connections. For example, we might examine people's perceptions of a speaker's credibility and find they evaluate him or her on the following six dimensions: honesty, intelligence, trustworthiness, expertise, skill, and goodness. Upon assessing the correlations

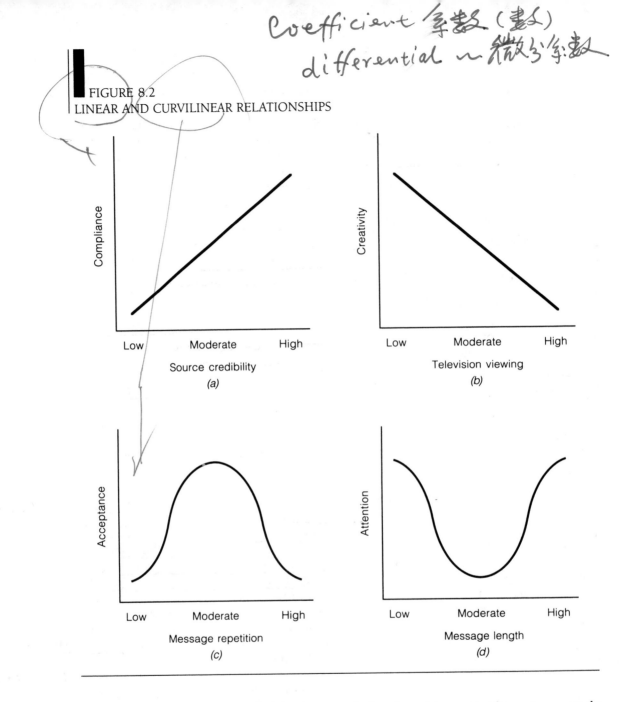

FIGURE 8.2
LINEAR AND CURVILINEAR RELATIONSHIPS

among these variables, we might find that honesty, trustworthiness, and goodness are highly interrelated, whereas intelligence, expertise, and skill form a separate intercorrelated set. Based on this analysis, we might conjecture that our audience has judged the speaker on two (rather than six) separate dimensions, namely "trustworthiness" and "competence." Interdependence analysis allows us to reduce a large number of variables to a smaller set that taps the same construct measured by the larger group.

154

# STATISTICAL TESTS
# OF RELATIONSHIPS

We are now ready to examine several tests for assessing the strength and significance of relationships. The calculations involved in many of these procedures are quite cumbersome. Thus, I recommend that you use the computer software available at your university's computing center to perform the required computations. My principal purpose is to provide students with the knowledge needed to understand the results of computer-assisted calculations.[4]

Two sets of relationship tests are examined: bivariate methods for assessing relationships between two variables and multivariate procedures, including dependence and interdependence methods, which assess intercorrelations among three or more variables.

# BIVARIATE CORRELATION

Research hypotheses predicting a significant correlation between two population variables take the form $\rho \neq 0$, where $\rho$ (rho) denotes the population correlation coefficient corresponding to the sample coefficient $r$. The null hypothesis, $\rho = 0$, states that no linear relationship exists between the population parameters. To test null hypotheses, two steps are required. First, researchers must compute indices of sample covariance—for instance, a coefficient of correlation ($r$) or its corresponding coefficient of determination ($r^2$). Second, to estimate whether sample covariation reflects population relationships, researchers must compare indices of sample covariance ($r$ or $r^2$) to an estimate of error covariance. Error covariance represents shared sample variance that could occur by chance. The greater the magnitude of observed relative-to-error covariance, the greater the likelihood that a systematic bivariate relationship exists in the population.

Methods of computing coefficients of correlation vary depending on one's sample data. I shall now examine methods of deriving correlation coefficients for data measured at interval and ratio levels and for frequency or nominal data.

## Correlating Interval
## and Ratio Data: Pearson's $r$

Suppose we have hypothesized that source credibility and compliance are systematically related to one another ($\rho \neq 0$). Suppose further that we have chosen a $p < .01$ significance level. If these two variables are measured at either interval or ratio levels, a procedure called the *Pearson product–moment coefficient of correlation* (or more simply, **Pearson's $r$**) can be used to test the null hypothesis that $\rho = 0$. Table 8.1 applies Pearson's $r$ to the hypothetical scores of five individuals who evaluated a speaker's credibility on a seven-point interval scale and registered their compliance on a five-point "Agree–Disagree" measure. Because Pearson's formula assumes a linear relationship between two variables, the researcher should test the raw scores appearing in the table for linearity before computing a correlation coefficient.

Although a special procedure called the $F$ test for linearity is available to verify straight line relationships,[5] constructing a *scatter diagram* (scattergram) that plots the two variables' values one against the other is a useful way to assess linearity. The scattergram displayed in Figure 8.3 shows that the relationship between the sample credibility and compliance data shown in Table 8.1 generally follows a positive linear pattern. The ascending diagonal in the Figure represents the straight line that best fits the data's scattering pattern.

Once linearity has been confirmed, the researcher can compute a coefficient of correlation. As Table 8.1 indicates, Pearson's $r$, like all correlation procedures, is a ratio between the

# TABLE 8.1
## PEARSON'S PRODUCT–MOMENT CORRELATION PROCEDURE

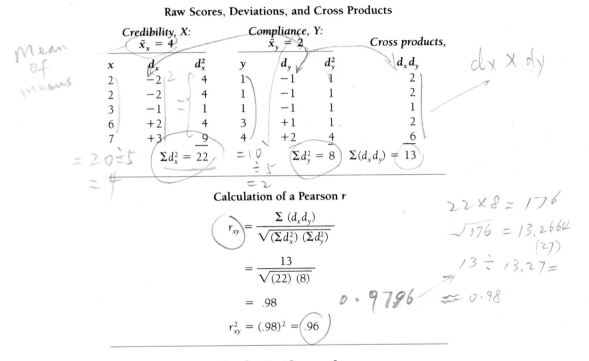

### Raw Scores, Deviations, and Cross Products

| Credibility, X: $\bar{x}_x = 4$ | | | Compliance, Y: $\bar{x}_y = 2$ | | | Cross products, |
|---|---|---|---|---|---|---|
| $x$ | $d_x$ | $d_x^2$ | $y$ | $d_y$ | $d_y^2$ | $d_x d_y$ |
| 2 | −2 | 4 | 1 | −1 | 1 | 2 |
| 2 | −2 | 4 | 1 | −1 | 1 | 2 |
| 3 | −1 | 1 | 1 | −1 | 1 | 1 |
| 6 | +2 | 4 | 3 | +1 | 1 | 2 |
| 7 | +3 | 9 | 4 | +2 | 4 | 6 |
| | | $\Sigma d_x^2 = 22$ | | | $\Sigma d_y^2 = 8$ | $\Sigma(d_x d_y) = 13$ |

*(Handwritten annotations: "Mean of means", "$d_x \times d_y$", "$=20 \div 5 = 4$", "$=10 \div 5 = 2$")*

### Calculation of a Pearson r

$$r_{xy} = \frac{\Sigma(d_x d_y)}{\sqrt{(\Sigma d_x^2)(\Sigma d_y^2)}}$$

$$= \frac{13}{\sqrt{(22)(8)}}$$

$$= .98$$

$$r_{xy}^2 = (.98)^2 = .96$$

*(Handwritten: $22 \times 8 = 176$; $\sqrt{176} = 13.2664$ (27); $13 \div 13.27 = 0.9796 \approx 0.98$)*

### Test for Significance of r

$$t = \frac{r}{\sqrt{(1 - r^2)/(n - 2)}} = \frac{r\sqrt{n - 2}}{\sqrt{1 - r^2}}$$

$$= \frac{.98\sqrt{3}}{\sqrt{1 - .96}} = 8.49$$

$$df = n - 2 = 3$$

*(Handwritten: $\sqrt{3} = 1.7320508 \times .98 = 1.697409$; $1 - .96 = 0.04$ $\sqrt{0.04} = 0.2$; $1.69 \div 0.2 \approx 8.49$)*

two variables' observed covariance and their combined variance. Thus, a Pearson $r$ and its derivative $r^2$ register the amount of total variance that two variables actually share. Given an $r$ of +.98 in our example, we can conclude that source credibility and compliance are positively related, sharing 96% of their combined sample variance ($r^2 = .96$).

To test our hypothesis that this sample relationship can be inferred to its parent population, we use the specialized $t$ test shown in Table 8.1.[6] The formula's numerator represents the sample correlation and its denominator provides an estimate of error covariation. We can determine whether our obtained $t$ value reaches an acceptable significance level by examining the $t$ sampling distribution in Appendix D. Since our original research hypothesis was nondirectional ($\rho \neq 0$), we must refer to two-tailed values of $t$. With 3 df, the distribution shows that a critical $t$ value of better than 5.84 is required for significance at our

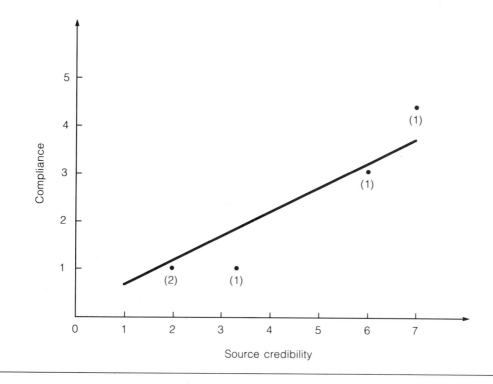

Source credibility

---

selected $p < .01$ significance level. Given a $t$ value of 8.49, we can be confident that the positive correlation observed in our sample probably reflects a positive linear relationship in the population from which the sample came.

## Curvilinearity and Correlation Assessment

Suppose our initial test for linearity had indicated that the relationship between source credibility and compliance actually follows the inverted-U pattern shown in Figure 8.4, suggesting that compliance is greatest at moderate levels of source credibility. Two options are available for assessing the magnitude of curvilinear relationships. First, we can split the

curvilinear pattern into halves and compute two linear coefficients of correlation. With an inverted-U relationship, the first coefficient will register the magnitude of the positive correlation in the first segment of the curve, whereas the second coefficient will assess the negative relationship in the curve's second half.

Although this two-part analysis provides useful information, it does not measure the full strength of the relationship since the curved portions of the correlation are ignored. A better approach is to compute a nonlinear correlation index such as the **eta coefficient**.[7] An eta ($\eta$) coefficient is a positive number that registers the magnitude but not the direction of a curvilinear relationship. The relationship's direction (for example, inverted-U or U-shaped) can be determined by constructing scattergrams like the ones in Figures 8.3 and 8.4.

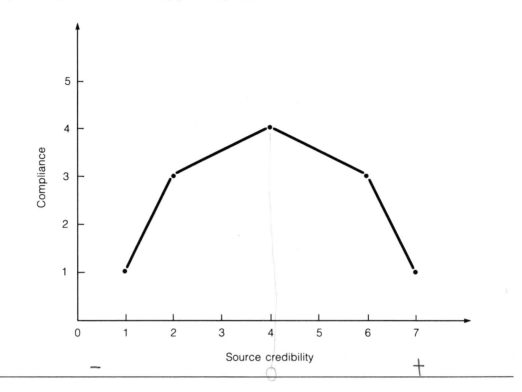

FIGURE 8.4
A CURVILINEAR INVERTED-U SCATTERGRAM

## Bivariate Correlation of Frequency Data

Quite often communication researchers wish to assess relationships between frequency data. For example, a persuasion researcher might want to know if a speaker's gender relates to the use of certain persuasive strategies—for instance, threats versus promises. Alternately, a mass communication specialist might be interested in the relationship between preferred news source (print, radio, or television) and educational level (college graduate or non-college graduate).

A group of procedures called *chi-square methods* assess correlations between nominal variables. Two related methods are especially useful: Pearson's phi coefficient (φ) and Cram-

er's V coefficient. Both φ and V are based on a simple two-stage logic. First, a chi-square value is computed in the manner described in Chapter 7. This procedure establishes whether a statistically significant relationship exists between two categorical variables. Second, the obtained value, called the *observed* $\chi^2$, is compared to the *maximum* $\chi^2$ the two variables are capable of producing, as computed with the general formula:

$$\max \chi^2 = N(k-1),$$

where $N$ refers to the total frequencies (the grand sum) associated with the two variables and $k$ is the number of categories associated with the variable containing the fewest categories.

Each of the two procedures yields an analogue of a correlation coefficient, registering re-

**TABLE 8.2**
**CHI-SQUARE-BASED COEFFICIENTS**

*傷 犯性*

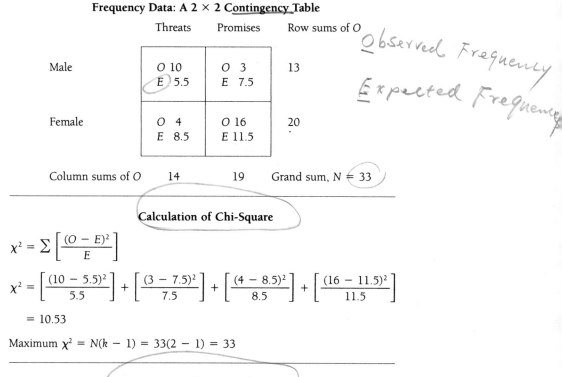

**Frequency Data: A 2 × 2 Contingency Table**

|  | Threats | Promises | Row sums of O |
|---|---|---|---|
| Male | O 10<br>E 5.5 | O 3<br>E 7.5 | 13 |
| Female | O 4<br>E 8.5 | O 16<br>E 11.5 | 20 |
| Column sums of O | 14 | 19 | Grand sum, N = 33 |

*Observed Frequency*
*Expected Frequency*

**Calculation of Chi-Square**

$$\chi^2 = \Sigma \left[ \frac{(O-E)^2}{E} \right]$$

$$\chi^2 = \left[ \frac{(10-5.5)^2}{5.5} \right] + \left[ \frac{(3-7.5)^2}{7.5} \right] + \left[ \frac{(4-8.5)^2}{8.5} \right] + \left[ \frac{(16-11.5)^2}{11.5} \right]$$

$$= 10.53$$

Maximum $\chi^2 = N(k-1) = 33(2-1) = 33$

**Calculation of Two Coefficients**

*Pearson's phi coefficient*

$$\phi = \sqrt{\frac{\chi^2}{N}} = \sqrt{\frac{10.53}{33}} = .56$$

*Cramer's V coefficient*

$$V = \sqrt{\chi^2/N(k-1)} = \sqrt{\frac{10.53}{33(2-1)}} = .56$$

Where $N$ = grand sum of observed frequencies ($O$) associated with the contingency table
$k$ = number of categories associated with the variable having the fewest categories

lationship strength based on the ratio between observed $\chi^2$ and maximum $\chi^2$. This operation is analogous to Pearson's $r$, which compares observed covariance with the total variance associated with two variables. Table 8.2 illustrates this logical process, demonstrating procedures for testing the research hypothesis that gender and persuasive strategy choice are systematically related at $p < .05$. Using the information displayed in the table, let us examine first the

*dichotomous* ...

**160**

PART II
Statistical
Analysis in
Contemporary
Communica-
tion Research

general chi-square logic and then discuss the specialized uses of each coefficient.

As Table 8.2 indicates, a $\chi^2$ of 10.53 is associated with the $2 \times 2$ contingency table created by our two variables. The chi-square sampling distribution in Appendix F, however, shows that with 1 df the critical $\chi^2$ value of 3.84 is all that is required for statistical significance at $p < .05$. Thus, we can be better than 95% confident that gender and strategy choice share a significant relationship in their parent populations ($\rho \neq 0$). If we had obtained a $\chi^2$ of less than 3.84, we would be forced to accept the null hypothesis, namely that the two population variables are probably unrelated ($\rho = 0$). Thus, the function of the initial chi-square test is to ascertain the existence or nonexistence of a significant population relationship.

Having found a population relationship, we can use either Pearson's phi or Cramer's $V$ to assess the magnitude and direction of the relationship between gender and strategy choice. Each procedure accomplishes this task by comparing 10.53, the obtained $\chi^2$, with 33, the maximum $\chi^2$ the two variables are capable of producing. Notice that each formula's numerator contains the observed $\chi^2$, whereas the maximum $\chi^2$ is registered in the denominator. Aside from this fundamental similarity, the two procedures differ in several respects that render them applicable to different kinds of bivariate problems.

### Pearson's phi coefficient ($\phi$)

**Pearson's phi coefficient ($\phi$)** is applicable only to $2 \times 2$ contingency tables; that is, it computes meaningful correlation coefficients between variables having two and only two frequency categories each. When applied to dichotomous variables, the phi method produces a coefficient whose values range from 0 to $+1$. Thus, the closer an obtained $\phi$ is to $+1$, the greater the strength of the relationship. Moreover, a phi coefficient like Pearson's $r$ can be squared to produce a coefficient of determination estima-

ting the percentage of variance shared by two variables.[8]

Since the two variables displayed in Table 8.2 contain two categories each, Pearson's phi is well suited to their analysis and the resulting coefficient of $+.56$ is a meaningful relationship index. Using the practical guidelines discussed earlier, we can conclude that gender and strategy choice have a "strong" positive association in their parent populations. When the phi coefficient is applied to variables having more than two categories each—for example, a $2 \times 3$ or a $3 \times 3$ contingency table—its maximum values exceed 1 and therefore may become uninterpretable. For this reason, Pearson's phi should be used only when dealing with dichotomous variables. *why apply ($\phi$)*

### Cramer's V Coefficient

**Cramer's V coefficient** is a more versatile measure of association between two nominal variables than phi. It overcomes phi's contingency table size restrictions, and therefore, can process variables having more than two frequency categories. A $V$ coefficient, then, is applicable to tables such as $2 \times 2$s, $3 \times 3$s, $2 \times 3$s, and $3 \times 4$s. Of course, as Table 8.2 shows, Cramer's $V$ produces the same correlation coefficient as phi when applied to $2 \times 2$ tables. Like phi, $V$ values have a range of 0 to $+1$. The closer a $V$ coefficient is to $+1$, the greater the strength of association between two variables.

# MULTIVARIATE CORRELATION

Multivariate correlation assesses relationships among three or more variables. Its usefulness can be illustrated by considering the following research problem. Suppose we suspect that people's self-esteem ($X$), their intelligence level ($Y$), and their communication effectiveness ($Z$) are systematically related. Although we could

**FIGURE 8.5**
MULTIPLE CORRELATION

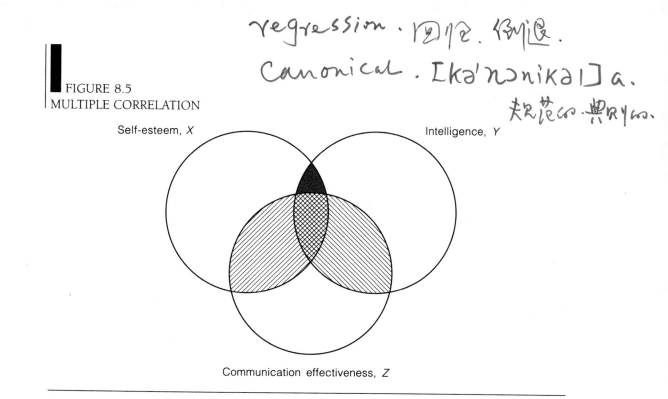

Communication effectiveness, *Z*

learn something of the three variables' relatedness by computing pairwise bivariate correlations (that is, *XY*, *XZ*, and *YZ*), a far more meaningful way to test our speculation is to compute a single intercorrelation index summarizing the magnitude of the three-way association. Figure 8.5 graphically displays the outcome of such an analysis. Notice that the two diagonally lined areas represent the shared variance between *X* and *Z* on the one hand and *Y* and *Z* on the other. The darkly shaded portion depicts the variance that *X* and *Y* share, and the cross-hatched area represents the variability that is common to all three variables.

Recall that multivariate correlation takes one of two forms: dependence analysis or interdependence analysis. Dependence procedures assess the ability of a set of independent variables to predict one or more dependent variables. Interdependence methods examine the intercorrelations among a large number of variables for purposes of reducing them to a smaller set. I will now describe prototypes of each of these two models.

## Multivariate Dependence Analysis

Multivariate dependence analysis focuses on the relationship between two or more independent variables and one or more dependent variables. Numerous multiple dependence models, all designed to assess linear relationships, are useful in communication research, including multiple correlation and regression, canonical correlation, path analysis, and log–linear modeling.[9] I will limit my discussion to multiple correlation and regression analysis, a multivariate approach that illustrates the fundamental logic of the balance of the models.

## Multiple Correlation and Regression Analysis

Multiple correlation and multiple regression are two facets of a statistical model whose purpose is to assess the power of two or more independent variables to predict a single dependent

161

**162**

PART II
Statistical
Analysis in
Contemporary
Communica-
tion Research

variable. The independent variables are called **predictor variables**, whereas the dependent measure is referred to as a **criterion variable**. The correlation component of the model measures the strength of association between known values of criterion and predictor variables, whereas the regression element allows us to predict the probable (unknown) values of a criterion variable based on known values of its predictors.[10] I will first examine multiple correlation procedures and then discuss the predictive qualities of regression analysis.

## Multiple correlation

**Multiple correlation** estimates the amount of variance in a criterion measure that is explained or accounted for by its linear relationship with predictors. Analogous to bivariate methods, multiple correlation yields two general relationship indices: a **coefficient of multiple correlation** signified by an uppercase $R$ (often called a multiple $R$) and a **coefficient of multiple determination** denoted by $R^2$ (referred to as a multiple $R^2$). A multiple $R$ registers the strength of association between criterion and predictor variables, and $R^2$ indicates the percentage of variability in a criterion that is explained by the predictor variables. (Strictly speaking, an $R^2$ registers the percentage of a criterion's sum of squares that is explained by its predictors. As a matter of practice, we often refer to the $R^2$ index as a measure of explained "variance." See Note 1 for a related comment.)

To illustrate multiple correlation, suppose we wish to test the directional hypothesis that initial receiver attitudes and source credibility are important predictors of compliance with a persuasive message. Suppose further that we set our significance level at $p < .01$. Table 8.3 displays 10 people's hypothetical scores on the three variables:

1. Compliance with a message ($Y$), the criterion variable

2. The receivers' initial attitudes toward the message ($X$), one predictor variable
3. Source credibility ($Z$), a second predictor

To compute multiple correlation and determination coefficients, Table 8.3 shows that we first compute bivariate correlation coefficients between each pair of variables. Then, using the formula displayed in the table, we can derive a coefficient of multiple determination ($R^2_{y.xz} = .88$) and its associated coefficient of multiple correlation ($R_{y.xz} = .94$). (Notice that the subscripts $y.xz$ associated with $R^2$ and $R$ signify that $Y$ is the criterion variable and $X$ and $Z$ are the predictors. Similarly, if $X$ were the criterion and $Y$ and $Z$ were predictors, the subscript would read $x.yz$ whereas the notation $z.yx$ would designate $Z$ as the criterion variable and $Y$ and $X$ as predictors).

Given the calculations displayed in Table 8.3, we can conclude that receiver attitudes and source credibility together account for about 88% of the variation in our sample's compliance behavior, leaving only 12% unexplained. If this sample value ($R^2_{y.xz} = .88$) reflects a systematic relationship in the parent population, we can reject the null hypothesis that the multiple coefficient of determination is 0. The $F$ test described in Chapter 7 is an appropriate statistic for testing our nondirectional hypothesis that receiver attitudes and source credibility are important predictors of compliance. Remember that an $F$ value is the ratio of observed variance to error variance. Applied to multiple correlation, the $F$ ratio compares the variance contributed by the predictors to the criterion variable, with the remaining variance not explained by the predictors. Thus, unexplained variance is an estimate of error variance.

In the Test of Significance of $R^2_{y.xz}$ section of Table 8.3, $F$ is the ratio of explained variance ($R^2$ divided by $df_n$) to unexplained variance ($1-R^2$ divided by $df_d$). Degrees of freedom in the numerator ($df_n$) are the number of predictors

TABLE 8.3
## MULTIPLE CORRELATION AND SIGNIFICANCE TEST

*1. & 2. Predictors.*

### Raw Data and Summary Statistics

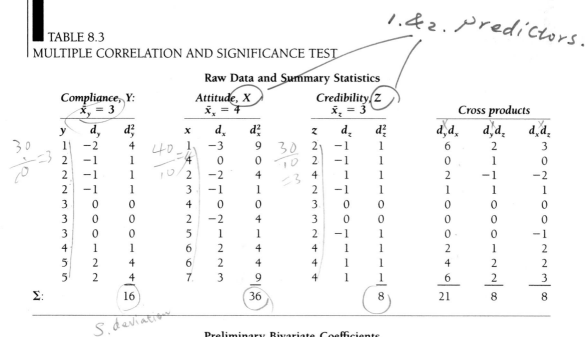

| Compliance, Y: $\bar{x}_y = 3$ | | | Attitude, X $\bar{x}_x = 4$ | | | Credibility, Z $\bar{x}_z = 3$ | | | Cross products | | |
|---|---|---|---|---|---|---|---|---|---|---|---|
| y | $d_y$ | $d_y^2$ | x | $d_x$ | $d_x^2$ | z | $d_z$ | $d_z^2$ | $d_y d_x$ | $d_y d_z$ | $d_x d_z$ |
| 1 | −2 | 4 | 1 | −3 | 9 | 2 | −1 | 1 | 6 | 2 | 3 |
| 2 | −1 | 1 | 4 | 0 | 0 | 2 | −1 | 1 | 0 | 1 | 0 |
| 2 | −1 | 1 | 2 | −2 | 4 | 4 | 1 | 1 | 2 | −1 | −2 |
| 2 | −1 | 1 | 3 | −1 | 1 | 2 | −1 | 1 | 1 | 1 | 1 |
| 3 | 0 | 0 | 4 | 0 | 0 | 3 | 0 | 0 | 0 | 0 | 0 |
| 3 | 0 | 0 | 2 | −2 | 4 | 3 | 0 | 0 | 0 | 0 | 0 |
| 3 | 0 | 0 | 5 | 1 | 1 | 2 | −1 | 1 | 0 | 0 | −1 |
| 4 | 1 | 1 | 6 | 2 | 4 | 4 | 1 | 1 | 2 | 1 | 2 |
| 5 | 2 | 4 | 6 | 2 | 4 | 4 | 1 | 1 | 4 | 2 | 2 |
| 5 | 2 | 4 | 7 | 3 | 9 | 4 | 1 | 1 | 6 | 2 | 3 |
| Σ: | | 16 | | | 36 | | | 8 | 21 | 8 | 8 |

*S. deviation*

*(handwritten, left margin)* 30 ÷ 10 = 3   40 = 4 / 10   30 / 10 = 3

### Preliminary Bivariate Coefficients

$$r_{yx} = \frac{\Sigma(d_y d_x)}{\sqrt{(\Sigma d_y^2)(\Sigma d_x^2)}}$$

$$= \frac{21}{\sqrt{(16)(36)}} = .88$$

$$r_{yx}^2 = (.88)^2 = .77$$

$$r_{yz} = \frac{\Sigma(d_y d_z)}{\sqrt{(\Sigma d_y^2)(\Sigma d_z^2)}}$$

$$= \frac{8}{\sqrt{(16)(8)}} = .71$$

$$r_{yz}^2 = (.71)^2 = .50$$

$$r_{xz} = \frac{\Sigma(d_x d_z)}{\sqrt{(\Sigma d_x^2)(\Sigma d_z^2)}}$$

$$= \frac{8}{\sqrt{(36)(8)}} = .47$$

$$r_{xz}^2 = (.47)^2 = .22$$

*(handwritten, right)*
$16 \times 36 = 576$ $\sqrt{576} = 24$
$21 \div 24 \approx .88 \ (0.875)$
$.88 \times .88 \approx .77 \ (0.7744)$

$16 \times 8 = \sqrt{128} = 11.313708$
$8 \div 11.31 \approx .71 \ (0.7073...)$
$.71 \times .71 = 0.5041$

$36 \times 8 = \sqrt{288} = 16.97$
$8 \div 16.97 = 0.47.14...$
$.47 \times .47 = 0.22(09)$

*Continued*

**Multiple Coefficients of Determination and Correlation**

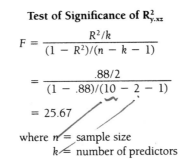

$$R^2_{y.xz} = \frac{r^2_{yx} + r^2_{yz} - [(2)\,(r_{yx})\,(r_{yz})\,(r_{xz})]}{1 - r^2_{xz}}$$

*1,27 =*

$$= \frac{.77 + .50 - [(2)(.88)(.71)(.47)]}{1 - .22 \; = \; .78}$$   *= .5873*

*1.27 − .5873 = .6827)*

$$= .88 \quad = .8752564 \approx .88$$

$$R_{y.xz} = \sqrt{.88} = .94 \quad = .938 \approx .94$$

---

**Test of Significance of $R^2_{y.xz}$**

$$F = \frac{R^2/k}{(1 - R^2)/(n - k - 1)}$$

$$= \frac{.88/2}{(1 - .88)/(10 - 2 - 1)}$$

$$= 25.67$$

where $n$ = sample size
$k$ = number of predictors

---

($k$), whereas $df_d$ represents sample size minus the number of predictors minus 1 ($n - k - 1$). As the calculations show, an $R^2_{y.xz}$ of .88 yields an $F$ value of 25.67.

To determine whether this value reflects a real population relationship, we must refer to the $F$ sampling distribution in Appendix E. With a $df_n/df_d$ of 2/7, the distribution shows that we require a critical $F$ value of more than 9.54 for statistical significance at $p < .01$. With an $F$ of 25.67, we can reject the null hypothesis and conclude that receiver attitudes and source credibility probably are related to compliance behaviors in the population from which our sample was drawn.

The example just presented is useful for illustrating two important principles of multiple correlation: (1) the amount of explained variance in a criterion variable increases as the size of the correlation between the predictors and the criterion goes up, and (2) the amount of explained variance in a criterion variable declines as the size of the correlation between predictor variables increases.[11] The latter effect occurs because highly correlated predictors do not make wholly independent contributions to criterion variance. Rather, some portion of any correlated predictor's contribution is conjoined with the contributions of the other predictors to which it is related.

These dual principles admonish researchers to select predictors that correlate strongly with the criterion variable, but relatively poorly with one another. Table 8.3 shows that receiver attitudes and compliance have a very strong association ($r_{yx} = .88$, $r^2_{yx} = .77$). Moreover, source credibility and compliance are highly related ($r_{yz} = .71$, $r^2_{yz} = .50$). The two predictor variables corrrelate less well ($r_{xz} = .47$, $r^2_{xz} = .22$), although their association is greater than one ideally might prefer. The two predictors' moderate correlation probably explains why re-

admoish 告诫, 力劝.

**165**

CHAPTER 8
Statistical
Analysis of
Relationships

ceiver attitudes and source credibility together account for only 11% more of the variance in compliance behaviors than do receiver attitudes alone ($R^2_{y \cdot xz} = .88$ and $r^2_{yx} = .77$). Had the correlation between the two predictors been .30 instead of .47, for example, and assuming that our predictor–criterion correlations had remained the same, explained criterion variance would have slightly exceeded 98%.

With this result, receiver attitudes and source credibility would have accounted for about 21% more compliance variance than could be explained by receiver attitudes alone. Furthermore, we have already seen that the two predictors could have accounted for around 98% rather than 88% of the total variance associated with compliance behaviors. Even so, source credibility's 11% independent contribution represents a substantial addition to explained criterion variance, making that second predictor a useful component of our correlation analysis. Moreover, 88% is itself an exceptionally large proportion of explained criterion variance, suggesting that our two-predictor model in its present configuration is a highly efficient explanatory device.

## Regression analysis and prediction

As we have seen, multiple correlation measures the strength of association between the known values of predictor and criterion variables. **Regression analysis** has a somewhat different focus, allowing us to predict the probable (unknown) values of a criterion variable based on known values of one or more of its predictors. Suppose, for instance, that we have measured the attitudes of a sample audience toward some speech topic along with its perceptions of a given speaker's credibility. We can use regression analysis to make predictions about the audience's probable reactions to the speaker's topic-related appeals. Thus, regression is an exceedingly useful tool for projecting the likely values of an unknown criterion measure based on our knowledge of its associated predictors.

At its simplest, a regression equation takes the form:

$$Y = a + bX,$$

where $Y$ is the criterion, $X$ is a predictor, and $a$ and $b$ are values called *regression weights* (also known as *regression coefficients*). To understand these two weights, refer to the scattergram in Figure 8.6, which plots the values of compliance rates ($Y$) against receiver attitudes ($X$) appearing in Table 8.3. Notice that the ascending diagonal represents the best fitting straight line or that line best describing the two variable's linear relationship.

The regression coefficient $a$ is a constant value called the *intercept*, and it represents the point at which a best fitting line intersects the vertical criterion axis, in our example, the $Y$ axis. Thus, an $a$ coefficient registers the value of the criterion variable ($Y$) when the predictor ($X$) is zero. More generally, we can assume that the criterion $Y$ will always be "$a$" units greater than the value of the predictor $X$. The coefficient $b$ is called the *slope*, and it tells us how many units a criterion variable $Y$ increases with each unit increase in the predictor $X$. Given any value of $a$, the steeper the best fitting regression line, the greater the magnitude of $b$. For any two variables ($Y$ and $X$), we can compute the values of $a$ and $b$ using the following equations:

$$a = \frac{[(\Sigma y)(\Sigma x^2)] - [(\Sigma x)(\Sigma xy)]}{[n(\Sigma x^2)] - (\Sigma x)^2}$$

$$b = \frac{[n(\Sigma xy)] - [(\Sigma x)(\Sigma y)]}{[n(\Sigma x^2)] - (\Sigma x)^2}.$$

In both equations, $x$ and $y$ refer to raw sample scores and $n$ denotes sample size. Based on the raw data appearing in Table 8.3, these equations yield the following solutions:

$$a = \frac{[(30)(196)] - [(40)(141)]}{[10(196)] - (1600)} = .67$$

$$b = \frac{[10(141)] - [(40)(30)]}{[10(196)] - (1600)} = .58.$$

FIGURE 8.6
SCATTERGRAM OF RECEIVER ATTITUDE AND COMPLIANCE DATA

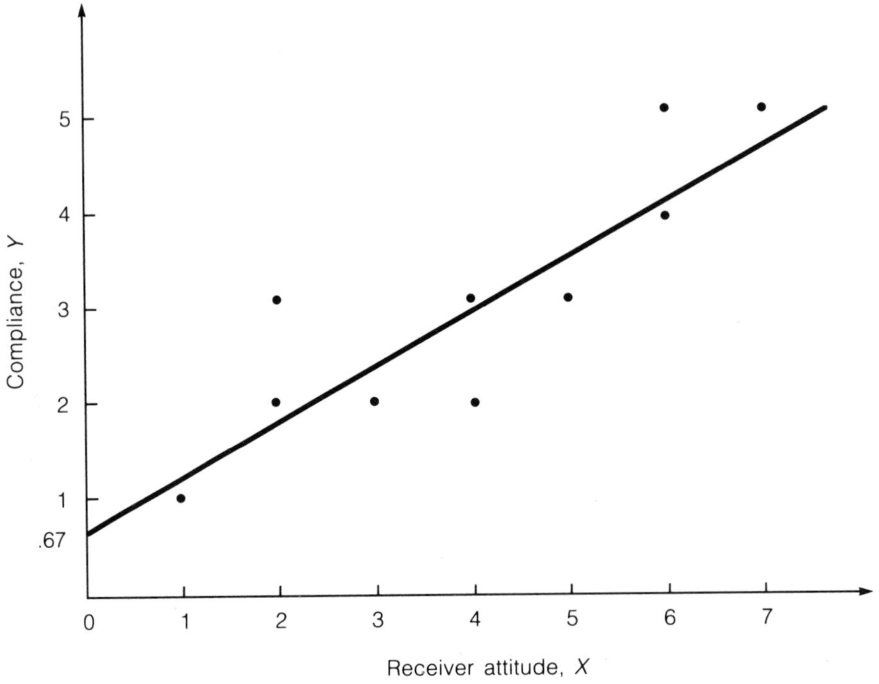

By inserting these two values into our $Y = a + bX$ form, we derive the equation $Y = .67 + .58X$.

Thus, if we know that $X$ is 7, we can predict that $Y$ will be about 4.73. Similarly, if $X$ is 3, then $Y$ should be around 2.41. Since Figure 8.6 indicates that the best fitting line is imperfect (that is, the values of $Y$ and $X$ do not connect in an unbroken straight line but scatter closely around the line), our predictions are subject to error. We can estimate the accuracy of our predictions by calculating a **standard error of estimate** $(s_e)$ for the $Y$ and $X$ scores appearing in Table 8.3 using the following formula:

$$s_{e(yx)} = s_y \sqrt{(1 - r_{yx}^2)\left(\frac{n}{n-2}\right)},$$

where $s_y$ is the standard deviation of our sample of criterion $(Y)$ scores $[s_y = \sqrt{d_y^2/(n-1)} =$

1.33], $r_{yx}^2$ is the coefficient of determination for the variables $Y$ and $X$ (.77), and $n$ is the sample size (10). Inserting these values into the equation, we find that the $s_{e(yx)}$ is .71.

Based on this error estimate, we can be 95% confident that if $X$ is 7, the population value of $Y$ should be no less than 3.34 and no greater than 6.12 ($\pm 1.96 \times .71 = \pm 1.39$ of 4.73). At the 99% confidence level, the population $Y$ value should range from 2.90 to 6.56 ($\pm 2.58 \times .71 = \pm 1.83$ of 4.73). (Notice in Table 8.3 that when $X$ is 7, the sample value of $Y$ is 5.)

Applying these predictive notions to a full regression analysis relating receiver attitudes $X$ and source credibility $Z$ to compliance behaviors $Y$, we derive the following multiple regression form:

$$Y = a + b_1X + b_2Z.$$

166

The term $b_1$ is a standardized regression weight indicating how many units $Y$ should increase for every unit increase in $X$ when the effects of $Z$ are held constant; $b_2$ signifies the unit increase in $Y$ for every unit increase in $Z$ with the effects of $X$ held constant; and $a$ is the constant value by which $Y$ is expected to exceed the zero values of the two predictors.

We can illustrate the use of this multiple regression equation by supposing that $a = 1.00$, $b_1 = .45$, and $b_2 = .20$. With this contrived information, we are able to predict the probable values of $Y$ given certain known values of $X$ and $Z$. For example, if $X = 7$ and $Z = 4$, we can write:

$$Y = 1.00 + .45(7) + .20(4) = 4.95.$$

The accuracy of such predictions can be estimated by computing a standard error of the estimate ($s_{e(y \cdot xz)}$) using the formula described previously.

## Multivariate Interdependence Analysis

Whereas multivariate dependence models examine relationships between independent and dependent variables, multivariate interdependence analysis has a different focus: assessing intercorrelations among a large number of variables for the purpose of reducing them to a smaller, more parsimonious set. Although there are numerous interdependence models,[12] I will restrict my discussion to two procedures that illustrate the logic of much interdependence analysis: factor analysis and cluster analysis. Because interdependence computations are exceedingly complex, computer assistance is needed to perform even the simpler routines. For this reason, I will describe the general nature and functions of factor and cluster analyses without probing their intricate computational procedures.

## Factor analysis

**Factor analysis** assesses the interrelations among a rather large set of variables for purposes of reducing the large array to a smaller, more basic set of hypothetical variables called factors. Thus, factor analysis assumes that observable variables often are related in such a way that they reflect some underlying dimension or factor that is only indirectly observable.[13]

To illustrate factor analysis, suppose we wish to study audience evaluations of the credibility of a speaker who opposed abortion in a public debate. To pursue our investigation, we might distribute a questionnaire at the debate's conclusion asking the audience to rate the speaker on the following 10 attributes: honesty, intelligence, trustworthiness, expertise, dynamism, goodness, experience, knowledge, assertiveness, and competence. Considering the content of these 10 variables, we might reasonably hypothesize that certain items (for example, expertise, knowledge, and competence on the one hand, and honesty and trustworthiness on the other) overlap considerably in denotative meaning. In other words, some variables appear to be so similar that they actually may be measuring the same basic source credibility dimension. We can test this general hypothesis by conducting a factor analysis of our hypothetical survey responses, the results of which appear in Table 8.4.

Two indices displayed in the table are especially important for interpreting factor analytic findings. First, **factor loadings** are coefficients that register the magnitude and direction of the relationship between a variable such as honesty or expertise and its underlying hypothetical factor. The closer a factor loading is to 1.00, the stronger the variable–factor relationship, or to use factor analytic jargon, the more "highly loaded" the variable is said to be. Although specific tests for significance of correlation are available, it is customary to intuitively regard a variable as "highly loaded" if its factor loading is .50 or more. (In Table 8.4, all loadings greater

TABLE 8.4
FACTOR ANALYSIS

| Observed variables | Hypothetical factors | | |
|---|---|---|---|
| | I | II | III |
| | Factor loadings | | |
| Honesty | .07 | **.62** | −.13 |
| Intelligence | **.78** | .10 | .06 |
| Trustworthiness | .20 | **.75** | .15 |
| Expertise | **.80** | .31 | −.02 |
| Dynamism | −.05 | .17 | **.83** |
| Goodness | .29 | **.69** | −.16 |
| Experience | **.70** | .26 | .09 |
| Knowledge | **.65** | −.28 | .18 |
| Assertiveness | −.12 | −.18 | **.90** |
| Competence | **.86** | .06 | .10 |
| Eigenvalues | 3.05 | 1.74 | 1.62 |
| Factor labels | Competence | Trustworthiness | Dynamism |

than .50 are boldfaced.) The second important index appearing in the table, an **eigenvalue**, is defined as the sum of the squared loadings associated with each factor. Many statisticians regard a factor as statistically meaningful if it has an eigenvalue of 1.00 or greater.

Based on these two indices, we are prepared to interpret the meaning of our factor study summarized in Table 8.4. Notice that the five variables—intelligence, expertise, experience, knowledge, and competence—all load very highly on factor I, whereas honesty, trustworthiness, and goodness load strongly on the second factor. Finally, dynamism and assertiveness correlate highly with factor III. Since each of the three emergent factors has an eigenvalue exceeding 1.00, we can assume that our 10 original variables actually reflect only three hypothetical dimensions of source credibility. These three factors may be independent of one another or they may be correlated. If independent, they are called **orthogonal** factors, whereas correlated factors are referred to as **oblique** factors. Based on the denotative meanings of the grouped variables, the researcher

assigns an appropriate label to each hypothetical factor. In our example, the names "competence," "trustworthiness," and "dynamism" are given to factors I, II, and III, respectively.

## Cluster analysis

**Cluster analysis** examines the intercorrelations among a set of measurements for the purpose of grouping the measurements into related subsets (clusters) that themselves are independent of or orthogonal to one another.[14] Thus, the procedure is useful for testing hypotheses about the underlying structure of large sets of data. Although cluster analysis and factor analysis are similar, they differ in two important respects. First, unlike factor analysis, which correlates observed variables with hypothetical (theoretical) factors, cluster analysis assesses the empirical relationships among observed cases. Cluster analysis, then, represents measurement-to-measurement correlations, whereas factor analysis involves measurement-to-theoretical factor associations. Second, most cluster analytic procedures are

TABLE 8.5
CLUSTER ANALYSIS

## Compliance-Gaining Strategies

| Strategy | | Definition |
|---|---|---|
| SI | Self-identity | Appeals to another's private self concept |
| IM | Image maintenance | Appeals to another's self-presentational needs |
| EC | Environmental contingency | Offers of reward for compliance and punishment for noncompliance |
| IR | Interpersonal relationship | Appeals to another's friendship |
| SN | Social normative | Appeals to another to comply for reasons of social acceptability |
| DR | Direct-rational | Appeals that present arguments for compliance |
| EX | Exchange | Offers of concessions in exchange for compliance |
| MP | Manipulation | Indirect, often deceitful persuasive appeals |
| TH | Threats | Invoking of sanctions or negative reinforcement for noncompliance |

### Correlation Matrix

| | SI | IM | EC | IR | SN | DR | EX | MP | TH |
|---|---|---|---|---|---|---|---|---|---|
| SI | — | .95 | .07 | .13 | .20 | .11 | .18 | .90 | .05 |
| IM | .95 | — | .10 | .23 | .30 | .02 | .20 | .90 | .03 |
| EC | .07 | .10 | — | .19 | .28 | .92 | .06 | .13 | .85 |
| IR | .13 | .23 | .19 | — | .75 | .12 | .78 | .06 | .01 |
| SN | .20 | .30 | .28 | .75 | — | .19 | .74 | .07 | .06 |
| DR | .11 | .02 | .92 | .12 | .19 | — | .20 | .02 | .80 |
| EX | .18 | .20 | .06 | .78 | .74 | .20 | — | .04 | .01 |
| MP | .90 | .90 | .13 | .06 | .07 | .02 | .04 | — | .20 |
| TH | .05 | .03 | .85 | .01 | .06 | .80 | .01 | .20 | — |

### Resulting Clusters

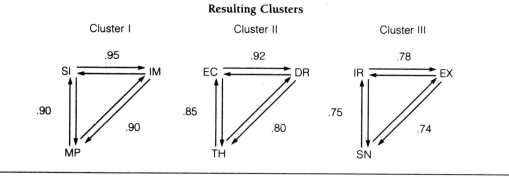

Cluster I     Cluster II     Cluster III

applicable to frequency as well as interval and ratio data. By contrast, factor analysis is most useful for interval or ratio data analysis.

Table 8.5 illustrates a common cluster analytic method called **elementary linkage analysis**.[15] The correlation matrix displays a set of bivariate correlation coefficients between nine different compliance-gaining techniques reportedly used in everyday interactions with close friends by a large sample of people.[16] As Table 8.5 shows, related clusters are created by grouping strategies that correlate highly with one another but poorly with all other strategies. In our example, three such clusters containing

Conciliation 调解. 和.

170

PART II
Statistical
Analysis in
Contemporary
Communica-
tion Research

three strategies each emerged, suggesting that the original nine persuasive tactics fall into three general types of compliance-gaining strategies.

## Uses of interdependence analysis

Multivariate interdependence analysis has two principal uses. First, it is helpful for testing specific hypotheses about the structure of a large set of data. For example, we might suspect that populations of conflict resolution strategies fall into three separate classes called conciliation, confrontation, and avoidance. This hypothesis could be tested by analyzing large samples of behaviors that people exhibit in conflict situations. If our data group themselves into the three predicted classes, the original hypothesis is supported. The use of interdependence analysis as a hypothesis testing device is called *confirmatory* analysis.

A second function of interdependence analysis is *exploratory*.[1] Researchers often have no clear predictions about the structure of a given set of data. Rather, they have research questions about the hidden dimensions of the data, or they simply wish to reduce a large body of data to a smaller, more manageable set. For instance, suppose I have collected data on viewers' reactions to public television and have no explicit assumptions about those reactions. Interdependence analysis can determine whether data fall into meaningful groups of related responses. Such exploratory analysis often sets the stage for developing specific hypotheses that later can be tested with confirmatory analytic techniques.

## INTERFACE:
## CHAPTER 8 AND PART III

This chapter has explored statistical methods for measuring relationships among variables and for assessing their statistical significance.

Two sets of procedures were described: bivariate correlation, involving measures of association between two variables; and multivariate methods for measuring relationships among three or more variables. Multivariate dependence and interdependence models were discussed.

This chapter concludes our treatment of statistical tools for analyzing data. In Part III, I will survey several communication research designs, including the experimental method, survey research, conversational analysis, content analysis, and rhetorical criticism. Most of these designs yield data requiring a statistical analysis of population differences or relationships. Thus, you will have ample opportunity to apply the skills acquired in Part II to a variety of communication research problems.

## MAIN POINTS

**1.** Variance that is common to two or more variables is called covariance.

**2.** A coefficient of correlation ($r$) indexes the strength of a linear relationship between two variables, whereas a coefficient of determination ($r^2$) registers the percentage of variability that is common to two variables.

**3.** A linear correlation between two variables is a straight line relationship that may either be direct (positive) or inverse (negative). A curvilinear correlation does not follow a straight line and is exemplified by inverted-U and U-shaped relationships.

**4.** A bivariate relationship describes a correlation between two and only two variables, whereas a multivariate relationship represents a correlation among three or more variables.

**5.** A multivariate dependence relationship describes how a set of two or more independent variables (predictors) affects one or more dependent (criterion) variables. A multivariate interdependence relationship describes rela-

*dependent V — criterion*
*independent V — predictors*

tionships among three or more variables without regard to independent–dependent connections.

**6.** A Pearson product–moment coefficient of correlation (a Pearson $r$) measures the linear relationship between two variables measured at interval or ratio levels.

**7.** An eta ($\eta$) coefficient measures the nonlinear correlation between two variables.

**8.** Two chi-square procedures, Pearson's phi ($\phi$) and Cramer's $V$ coefficient, measure the linear correlation between two variables measured at the nominal (frequency) level.

**9.** Multiple correlation and regression are two facets of a statistical model whose purpose is to assess the ability of a set of independent variables to predict a single dependent variable. The dependent variable is referred to as the criterion variable, and the independent variables are called predictors. The correlation component measures the strength of association between known values of criterion and predictor variables, whereas the regression element allows us to predict the probable (unknown) values of a criterion variable based on known values of its predictors.

**10.** Factor analysis assesses the interrelation among a large set of variables for purposes of reducing the large array to a smaller set of hypothetical variables called factors.

**11.** Cluster analysis examines the intercorrelations among a set of measurements for purposes of grouping the measurements into classes called clusters.

**12.** Multivariate interdependence analysis may be either exploratory or confirmatory. Exploratory analysis is intended to answer research questions, whereas confirmatory analysis is designed to test hypotheses.

## REVIEW EXERCISES

**1.** Suppose you wish to test the hypothesis that the number of print media (newspapers, magazines, and so forth) that people subscribe to is related to subscribers' education levels ($\rho \neq 0$). Test the corresponding null hypothesis ($\rho = 0$) by computing a Pearson $r$ and testing its statistical significance using a modified $t$ statistic. Use the following hypothetical data gathered from five people:

| Number of subscriptions, X | Education level, Y (years) |
|---|---|
| 4 | 16 |
| 5 | 20 |
| 1 | 8 |
| 2 | 9 |
| 3 | 12 |

Can you reject the null hypothesis that $\rho = 0$ at the $p < .05$ level of significance?

[**Answer:** $r_{xy} = .98$; $t = 8.49$; with 3 df and a two-tailed test, a critical $t$ value of greater than 3.18 is required for rejecting the null hypothesis at $p < .05$.]

**2.** Suppose you wish to test the hypothesis that gender (male or female) and choice of major news source (television or newspaper) are related. Using chi-square procedures, compute Cramer's $V$ coefficient and assess its statistical significance. The data you require were derived from a hypothetical survey of 10 males and 10 females and they appear in the following contingency table, where $O$ denotes observed frequencies of males and females preferring each news source:

|  | Male | Female |
|---|---|---|
| Television | $O = 8$ | $O = 3$ |
| Newspaper | $O = 2$ | $O = 7$ |

Can you reject the null hypothesis that $\rho = 0$ at the $p < .05$ level of significance? (Remember

172

PART II
Statistical
Analysis in
Contemporary
Communica-
tion Research

that the statistical significance of a $V$ coefficient is assessed by referring to the chi-square distribution.)

[**Answer:** $\chi^2 = 5.05$; $V = .50$; with 1 df, a $\chi^2$ of better than 3.84 is required for rejecting the null hypothesis at $p < .05$).]

**3.** Formulate research and null hypotheses that can be tested adequately using multiple correlation and regression procedures. Clearly identify the criterion variable as well as each predictor variable. What statistic might be used to test a multiple $R^2$ for statistical significance?

**4.** You have been given two sets of hypothetical scores, a $Y$ set of criterion scores and an $X$ set of predictor scores. Assume that you know that the $Y$ intercept $(a)$ of $X$ is 1.40 and the slope $(b)$ of the best fitting line associated with $Y$ and $X$ is .50. If $X$ is 10, what is the probable value of $Y$?

[**Answer:** $Y = 6.40$.]

**5.** Describe a research problem that can be explored thoroughly using factor analysis. Why is factor analysis more appropriate than cluster analysis? Does your problem lend itself to an exploratory or a confirmatory analysis? Explain.

## NOTES

**1.** Technically, $r^2$ registers the proportion of the total sum of squares ($SS_t$) that is common to two variables rather than shared variance. (Variance is a sum of squares divided by the appropriate degrees of freedom.) The term "variance" is used here in a nontechnical sense to signify "variability" or "variation" in a set of scores.

**2.** Gene M. Lutz, *Understanding Social Statistics* (New York: Macmillan, 1983), p. 156.

**3.** See Peter R. Monge and Patrick D. Day, "Multivariate Analysis in Communication Research," *Human Communication Research*, 2 (1976): 207–20.

**4.** Computer programs for computing all the statistics discussed in this chapter are available in many popular packages including SPSS$^x$ and BMDP. See *SPSS$^x$ User's Guide* (New York: McGraw-Hill, 1983); and W. J. Dixon (ed.), *BMDP Statistical Software* (Berkeley, CA: University of California Press, 1983).

**5.** The $F$ test for linearity is described in J. P. Guilford and Benjamin Fruchter, *Fundamental Statistics in Psychology and Education*, 5th ed. (New York: McGraw-Hill, 1973), pp. 290–91.

**6.** A $t$ test is appropriate for assessing the statistical significance of bivariate relationships when the null hypothesis is $\rho = 0$. (It is also appropriate when the null hypothesis is either $\rho < 0$ or $\rho > 0$.) However, the $t$ test is inappropriate for testing null hypotheses predicting that a bivariate population relationship is a specified nonzero value, for example, $\rho = .20$ or $\rho = .80$. In such cases, a $z$ test is the suitable statistic. For further discussion, see Patrick Brockett and Arnold Levine, *Statistics and Probability and Their Applications* (Philadelphia: Saunders, 1984), pp. 318–23.

**7.** The eta coefficient is described in Guilford and Fruchter, pp. 285–93.

**8.** See Lutz, p. 436.

**9.** For discussions of multiple correlation and regression methods, see Christopher H. Achen, *Interpreting and Using Regression* (Beverly Hills, CA: Sage, 1982); Michael S. Lewis-Beck, *Applied Regression: An Introduction* (Beverly Hills, CA: Sage, 1980); and Peter R. Monge, "Multivariate Multiple Regression," in *Multivariate Techniques in Human Communication Research*, ed. Peter R. Monge and Joseph N. Cappella (New York: Academic Press, 1980), pp. 14–56. For discussions of canonical correlation, see Raymond K. Tucker and Lawrence J. Chase, "Canonical Correlation," in *Multivariate Techniques in Human Communication Research*, pp. 205–28; and Mark S. Levine, *Canonical Analysis and Factor Comparison* (Beverly Hills, CA: Sage, 1977), pp. 11–36. Path analysis is described in Herbert B. Asher, *Causal Modeling*, 2nd ed. (Beverly Hills: CA: Sage, 1983). For excellent treatments of log–linear modeling, see John J. Kennedy, *Analyzing Qualitative Data: Introductory Log–Linear Analysis for Behavioral Research* (New York: Praeger, 1983); David Knoke and Peter J. Burke, *Log–Linear Models* (Beverly Hills, CA: Sage, 1980); and H. T. Reynolds, *Analysis of Nominal Data* (Beverly Hills, CA: Sage, 1977), pp. 52–82.

**10.** Gerald L. Ericksen, *Scientific Inquiry in the Behavioral Sciences: An Introduction to Statistics* (Glenview, IL: Scott, Foresman, 1970), p. 219.

11.  See Guilford and Fruchter, p. 369.

12.  Useful interdependence models not discussed here include two related procedures called multidimensional scaling and smallest space analysis. For communication applications of these two methods, see Joseph Woelfel and Jeffrey E. Danes, "Multidimensional Scaling Models for Communication Research," in *Multivariate Techniques in Human Communication Research*, ed. Peter R. Monge and Joseph N. Cappella (New York: Academic Press, 1980), pp. 333–64; and Robert W. Norton, "Nonmetric Multidimensional Scaling in Communication Research: Smallest Space Analysis," in *Multivariate Techniques in Human Communication Research*, pp. 309–31.

13.  For detailed discussions of factor analysis, see John E. Hunter, "Factor Analysis," in *Multivariate Techniques in Human Communication Research*, ed. Peter R. Monge and Joseph N. Cappella (New York: Academic Press, 1980), pp. 229–57; Jae-On Kim and Charles W. Mueller, *Introduction to Factor Analysis: What It Is and How To Do It* (Beverly Hills, CA: Sage, 1978); and Jae-On Kim and Charles W. Mueller, *Factor Analysis: Statistical Methods and Practical Issues* (Beverly Hills, CA: Sage, 1978).

14.  For in-depth discussions of cluster analysis, see Mark S. Aldenderfer and Roger K. Blashfield, *Cluster Analysis* (Beverly Hills, CA.: 1984); Kenneth D. Bailey, *Methods of Social Research*, 2nd ed. (New York: Free Press, 1982), pp. 384–85; and Klaus Krippendorff, "Clustering," in *Multivariate Techniques in Human Communication Research*, ed. Peter R. Monge and Joseph N. Cappella (New York: Academic Press, 1980), pp. 259–308.

15.  See Bailey, pp. 384–85.

16.  Although the data are hypothetical, the nine compliance-gaining strategies are drawn from Mary John Smith, "Contingency Rules Theory, Context, and Compliance Behaviors," *Human Communication Research*, 10 (1984): 489–512; and Michael J. Cody, Margaret L. McLaughlin, and William J. Jordan, "A Multidimensional Scaling of Three Sets of Compliance-Gaining Strategies," *Communication Quarterly*, 28 (1980): 34–46.

17.  The distinction between exploratory and confirmatory procedures is more closely associated with factor analysis than with cluster analysis. For a discussion of differences between the two approaches to factor analysis, see J. Scott Long, *Confirmatory Factor Analysis* (Beverly Hills, CA: Sage, 1983), pp. 11–15.

# CONTEMPORARY RESEARCH DESIGNS IN COMMUNICATION

# CHAPTER 9

# CONTEMPORARY RESEARCH DESIGNS

This chapter describes the research designs available to communication researchers. A research design is a comprehensive data collection plan for answering research questions and testing hypotheses. Factors threatening the validity of research designs are discussed, including research progression effects, reactivity effects, and sampling deficiency effects. Practical suggestions are presented for alleviating the problems posed by these sources of invalidity.

177

*hybrid a Po方法*

**179**

CHAPTER 9
Contemporary
Research
Designs

S everal years ago, the editors of the *Journal of Communication* published a special issue called *Ferment in the Field* that addressed contemporary research directions in communication.[1] The issue chronicled the increasing use of hybrid methodologies that blend traditional scientific empiricism with analytical and critical methods of the arts and humanities. Elihu Katz summarized this trend, noting that "if communications research is now in ferment, that ferment can be attributed to its invasion by a broader set of multidisciplinary concerns and particularly to a reunion of the social sciences with the humanities. Perhaps," said Katz, "we will be in a better position to answer [many previously unanswered questions about human communication] with the multidisciplinary armamentarium now at our disposal."[2]

Katz's observations capture the flavor of many contemporary communication research designs. Part III examines several hybrid methodologies that blend science and humanism along with some traditional scientific perspectives. Chapters 10 and 11 present scientific designs, whereas Chapters 12 and 13 focus on hybrid methodologies as well as some purely humanistic approaches. This chapter sets the stage for understanding the designs that consume the balance of Part III. I begin by describing characteristics that are common to all research designs, then discuss designs of specific types. Next, I examine criteria for selecting appropriate research plans and, finally, explore validity problems common to many contemporary designs.

## THE NATURE OF RESEARCH DESIGNS

A **research design** is a comprehensive data collection plan whose purpose is to answer research questions and test research hypotheses.[3]

Thus, designs are detailed prescriptions for solving problems. Problem-solving in communication may assume either a scientific or a humanistic orientation. **Scientific inquiry** emphasizes the counting and measuring of data, whereas **humanism** often uses reasoned argument to unravel the peculiarities of human communication processes. Whether scientific or humanistic, all research designs accomplish two objectives: they specify the elements or units of analysis to be explored and they delineate the observational conditions under which the elements will be studied.

Recall from Chapter 5 that elements are the data required to resolve a research problem; elements may be individual and group communicators or they may consist of the communicative outputs of individuals and groups. The term "observational conditions" covers all the activities researchers must perform to answer research questions and test hypotheses. For example, the researcher must decide whether a given research problem can best be resolved by traditional empiricism or by a design that blends scientific and humanistic perspectives. Additionally, researchers must determine whether their data should be gathered in a structured laboratory environment or in a naturalistic field setting. In general, the specifying of observational conditions means deciding in advance of a study exactly what data collection plan is needed to respond to the research problem.

## Types of Research Designs

Any one research design can be characterized in numerous ways, but the following eight pairs of classification schemes are particularly important: (1) quantitative or qualitative research, (2) interpretive or functional research, (3) experimental or naturalistic research, (4) laboratory or field research, (5) participant or nonparticipant research, (6) overt or unobtrusive

**180**
PART III
Contemporary
Research
Designs in
Communi-
cation

*Longitudinal 经历的了.*
*Longitude 经度*
*Prominent. 突出的. 显著的.*

research, (7) cross-sectional or longitudinal research, and (8) basic or applied research. When fashioning a comprehensive research plan, the researcher should put together a "package" design combining in a consistent way the characteristics of one of the two alternatives posed by *each* of these contrasting approaches. Thus, one's final research design can be classified on all eight dimensions.

## Quantitative or qualitative research

**Quantitative research**, involving the counting and measuring of communication events, is often equated with scientific empiricism. The approach yields a body of numerical data, which the researcher analyzes statistically. Many of the materials we have examined so far in this book, including measurement techniques, sampling methods, and statistical tests, are geared toward quantitative research. Importantly, quantitative analyses may be conducted in naturalistic or laboratory research settings and may be applied to a vast array of communication phenomena, including mass media, organizational communication, and interpersonal interaction. The approach is distinguished only by its use of numerical data as a means of understanding the nature of human communication.

Although statistical analysis is prominent in communication research, much contemporary inquiry is qualitative. Often equated with humanistic studies, **qualitative research** rejects numerical measures in favor of narrative data, meaning that qualitative data "appear in *words* rather than in numbers."[4] Examples of qualitative data may include transcripts of naturalistic conversations, communication documents such as public speeches, and media artifacts like printed editorials and videotapes of television programs. Qualitative analysis involves the critical analysis and synthesis of narrative information to derive verbal rather than statistical conclusions about the content and functions of human talk.

## Interpretive or functional research

**Interpretive research** focuses "on the study of meanings, that is, the way individuals make sense of their world through their communicative behaviors."[5] Studies of people's ordinary conversations, including the meanings and actions associated with talk, are interpretive. Likewise, content analysis of public speeches, television programs, and motion pictures explores the meaning of these communication artifacts.

**Functional research** often treats people's meanings as baseline data for inferring conclusions about related communication behaviors and effects. Methodologies that assess the behavioral and attitudinal effects of various communication forms, including media programs and public discourse, are functional. Unlike interpretive studies, which treat meanings as the end product of research, functional designs typically regard meanings as the starting point for drawing conclusions about the antecedents and consequences of human communication.

## Experimental or naturalistic research

**Experimental research** involves the prestructuring or manipulation of the research environment and the observation of people's reactions to such manipulations. For example, a researcher interested in the effects of leadership style on small group communication might bring several randomly selected groups together, assign an identical problem-solving task to each group, and then "plant" a democratic leader in half of the groups and an autocrat in the other half. Afterward, the researcher would analyze the groups' responses to the different leadership styles. Experimental research usually is functional; it is often quantitative, and it exemplifies traditional scientific research.

**Naturalistic research** involves observing and recording ongoing communication behaviors during the course of "normal life activity" without experimentally manipulating the observational environment.[6] For instance, a researcher interested in family communication might visit several families in their homes and observe the conversational episodes that unfold during a typical day. Alternately, a small group researcher concerned with leadership styles might observe the communicative effects of naturally occurring autocratic and democratic leadership in intact or preexisting business, social, or therapeutic groups. Naturalistic research is often interpretive rather than functional. It may take either a quantitative or qualitative approach to data analysis. Many naturalistic research designs are hybrid methodologies, nicely blending scientific and humanistic traditions in communication research.

## Laboratory or field research

Laboratory and field research are characterized by the respective settings in which observations take place. In **laboratory research**, researchers bring communicators into a controlled environment to observe their verbal and nonverbal behaviors. Although much laboratory research is experimental, it need not be. A researcher interested in people's initial interactions might simply observe the unstructured communicative exchanges of pairs of strangers brought into the laboratory. Whether experimental or naturalistic, all laboratory research takes place in an artificial setting that is not a part of the communicators' normal environment.

**Field research**, on the other hand, takes place in the communicators' natural environment. Much field research is naturalistic, involving observations of people's unstructured interactions, yet experimental research is frequently conducted in field settings as well. For example, a researcher interested in the effects of window displays on buying behavior might arrange with a local store owner to vary the displays on alternate days and attempt to correlate customer purchases with the different displays. Regardless of its manipulative or naturalistic

qualities, field research takes place in an environment where people conduct their ordinary life activities.

## Participant or nonparticipant research

Participant and nonparticipant research designs are distinguished by the role researchers play in the data collection process. When conducting **participant research**, the investigator contributes actively to the communication processes being observed. The communicators may or may not be aware that a "participant observer" is actually a researcher studying their communicative behaviors. In an early example of one type of participatory research, Festinger and his colleagues studied the behaviors of a small, nontraditional religious sect that believed, among other things, that the destruction of the world was imminent. The researchers posed as people interested in this idea, became full-fledged group members, and as Festinger put it, tried to be "nondirective, sympathetic listeners, passive participants who were inquisitive and eager to learn whatever others might want to tell us."[7]

A **nonparticipant researcher** is an outside spectator who does not enter into the target communicative interactions in any way. As in the case of participatory research, the observed communicators may or may not be aware that their behavior is the object of study.[8] Although both forms are used in laboratory and field settings as well as in experimental and naturalistic research, nonparticipant observation often takes place in the laboratory and involves experimental manipulations, whereas participant observation is a fairly common data collection method in naturalistic field studies.

## Overt or unobtrusive research

Differences between overt and unobtrusive research turn on whether communicators know that they are being observed. **Overt research**

**182**

PART III
Contemporary
Research
Designs in
Communi-
cation

may be defined as observation that affects in some manner the communication processes being studied. To observe communicative activities overtly, one must be physically present in the observational environment; hence, the subjects are aware of the researcher's presence.

By contrast, **unobtrusive research** is "any method of data collection that directly removes the researcher from the set of interactions, events, or behavior being investigated."[9] Because the researcher is not physically present in the interaction environment, people are "not aware of being tested, and there is little danger that the act of measurement will itself serve as a force for change in behavior or elicit role-playing that confounds the data."[10] Much mass communication research is unobtrusive; the researcher collects data from tapes of television and radio broadcasts and draws conclusions about their content and consequences. Other unobtrusive observational methods may include content analysis of printed communication documents such as public speeches, investigations of filmed nonverbal behavior, and discourse analysis of the transcripts of conversations.

## Cross-sectional or longitudinal research

**Cross-sectional research** examines communication events at a single point in time, focusing on present conditions and de-emphasizing past history and projected future conditions. Surveys of viewers' reactions to certain television programs or to different news reporting formats are often cross-sectional. Such studies, for example, may profile public opinion at the time the research is conducted, registering little about shifting viewpoints as a function of the passage of time. Similarly, much experimental research is cross-sectional, gauging reactions to a researcher's manipulations at a fixed point in time. Cross-sectional research, then, is the analogue of still photography, providing snapshots of the "here and now" but telling little about the

past or probable future of the "photographed" material.

**Longitudinal research**, often called *time series analysis*, examines communication phenomena as they shift and change over time. Much naturalistic research is longitudinal, as when we study the natural progression of family communication processes or investigate changes in communicative interactions between friends and lovers. Likewise, organizational research is often longitudinal, involving assessments of the extended effects of new marketing techniques, novel management policies, and so forth. Longitudinal research is analogous to motion picture photography, providing a chronicle of changes in "photographed" materials.

## Basic or applied research

Research designs may be classified by purpose as either basic or applied. **Basic research**, often exemplified by the experimental paradigm, explores theoretical relationships with little regard for the practical implications of research findings. Given this focus, basic scientific research is typically conducted in the laboratory, where minimal attention may be paid to generalizing results to real-life settings. Likewise, basic humanistic research may give short shrift to the practical import of the analytical conclusions it derives from studies of human discourse.

Contrasted with this emphasis, **applied research** is concerned with the practical and theoretical sides of communicative life. It explores theoretical relationships for the purpose of understanding and solving problems related to everyday communicative actions and interactions. Survey research, including political polls and analyses of people's media preferences, often has an applied orientation. Public speaking studies that generate prescriptive rules of effective speech may be applied as well. Because of its pragmatic posture, applied research usually takes place in field settings.

## Selecting an Appropriate Research Design

We have reviewed eight sets of contrasting research models. As I indicated earlier, any one research design can be classified as one of the two alternatives posed by *each* of the models. The choice of a composite design involves the systematic selection of one of the alternate perspectives presented by each model. When selecting a comprehensive design, the researcher should be guided by a single criterion: *the nature of the research question or hypothesis to be resolved.*

For example, suppose you wish to answer the following research question: What kinds of persuasive strategies do romantic partners use at different stages in their relationship? Given the nature of the question, a naturalistic field study is a reasonable design choice and a longitudinal analysis clearly is required. Moreover, the problem lends itself nicely to an interpretive analysis of the meanings of the partners' persuasive utterances.

Once these initial decisions have been made, several additional design issues present themselves. For instance, whether you collect data overtly or unobtrusively will depend on whether records of relevant data are already available or must be compiled. In many studies of interpersonal communication, original data collection is required, whereas audio, video, and print records frequently are available to mass communication researchers. Moreover, whether researchers adopt participatory or nonparticipatory roles may depend on whether they wish to distance themselves from the object of their study. Finally, the choice between quantitative and qualitative data analysis will hinge on the extent to which the data are amenable to statistical analysis. Given your research problem, some quantitative data analysis, perhaps a tabulation of the frequency with which romantic partners use different persuasive strategies, is probably in order.

As this extended example indicates, the dominant criterion for all design decisions is the nature of the research question or hypothesis. Research problems differing from the one just discussed, of course, will lead to quite different design choices.

## THE VALIDITY OF RESEARCH DESIGNS

Recall from Chapter 3 that a valid measuring instrument is one that fully and accurately measures the construct it purports to measure. Analogously, the **validity** of a given research design concerns the extent to which it provides a complete and accurate test of the hypothesis or research question it purports to test. Two kinds of validity are pertinent to research designs: internal and external validity.

**Internal validity** asks whether a given research design provides a complete and accurate test of research hypotheses within the sample of elements selected for hypothesis testing. That is, does the design measure the precise sample effects that interest a researcher and no other effects? To illustrate, suppose we wish to test the hypothesis that messages containing fear appeals lead to more attitude change than those having no fear-arousing content. To assess this prediction, we might expose one sample of listeners to a fearful message and another to a speech with no fear appeals and measure their respective attitudes. If attitudinal differences between the two samples can be attributed solely to the experimental fear manipulation (fear appeals versus no fear appeals), our design is internally valid. It is a clean test of the hypothesis of interest, measuring only the effects we wish to measure.

But, what if our samples' attitudinal scores might reasonably be suspected to reflect responses not only to the fear manipulation but to other influences as well? What if the sample hearing the fearful message was more anxious

**184**

PART III
Contemporary
Research
Designs in
Communi-
cation

than the other sample prior to the manipulation, and therefore, was more naturally susceptible to fear arousal? If this were so, our research design would have internal validity problems. We would not have tested the attitudinal effects of fear arousal alone; rather, our results would represent the combined effects of fear arousal and preexisting anxiety. When a design suffers from such internal invalidity, it produces **confounded effects**, meaning the researcher cannot be certain that sample results are pertinent to the specific variables to be studied and to those alone.

Research findings that are generalizable beyond the confines of sample data are said to have **external validity**. This question of generalizability entails two subissues. The first, a *sample-to-population* validity problem, concerns the extent to which sample findings can be generalized to the population from which the sample was drawn. Related to our hypothetical study of fear-arousing messages, the pertinent question is whether the attitude change scores derived from our sample are applicable to the parent population. As we learned in Chapter 5, a research design has sample-to-population validity only if the researcher has selected by probability methods a sample that is representative of its parent population.

The second external validity issue, sometimes called a *setting-to-setting* problem, reflects a practical awareness that data collected in a research environment may not represent the responses people would give in more natural social situations. In other words, is a research environment, involving the scrutiny of communication behaviors in the laboratory or field, a social situation so peculiar that it elicits responses the same communicators would not normally exhibit? Because of its focus on research environment generalizability, this second issue is often called a question of **ecological validity**.

To ensure that a given research design will adequately test the specific hypothesis we wish

to test, researchers must understand and control the effects of numerous factors that threaten internal and external validity. Three general categories of factors can seriously jeopardize a research design's validity: research progression effects, reactivity effects, and sampling deficiency effects. The first category applies principally to internal validity issues, the second threatens both internal and external validity, and the third category primarily addresses external validity concerns.

## Research Progression Effects

From the start of a research project until its completion, numerous changes not related to the project itself can affect the responses of research participants. Such changes, called **research progression effects**, occur as a function of time passage and they threaten the internal validity of research designs. Four progression effects are especially important: history, maturation, mortality, and statistical regression.[11]

### History
The term **history** refers to incidental environmental events occurring during data collection that alter the beliefs and behaviors a research participant ordinarily would exhibit. To illustrate, suppose I design an experiment to investigate the effects of message organization on compliance and comprehension. To test these effects, I decide to manipulate the order of presenting materials in a message advocating increased reliance on nuclear energy.

What if, over the course of my study, a large nuclear power plant in the vicinity leaks radiation? My compliance and comprehension measures will likely be affected not only by the experimental manipulation, but also by media coverage of the nuclear mishap. Thus, my study will not provide a true test of the effects of presentational order and therefore will produce uninterpretable or confounded effects.

Volitional [vou'liʃən] 意志上.
volition, volitive.

185
CHAPTER 9
Contemporary
Research
Designs

## Maturation

**Maturation** refers to changing physiological and psychological processes that affect the beliefs and behaviors of research participants during the course of a study. For example, people frequently become fatigued or bored as data collection progresses. As a consequence, they may begin to respond in ways not related primarily to the study's central focus, thereby confounding the research results. In our hypothetical message organization experiment, boredom and fatigue could lower message comprehension and perhaps compliance rates as well. If this occurred, our final research results would reflect not only the organizational manipulation but also lack of interest and fatigue on the part of the respondents. Obviously, maturation effects become major threats to validity in longitudinal studies.

## Mortality

**Mortality**, referring to the loss of research participants as a study moves toward completion, is a major validity problem in longitudinal studies. For a variety of reasons, some people who participated in early phases of a research project will drop out before the study's conclusion. If a researcher suffers a substantial dropout rate, such that the final sample of participants does not match the original one, it becomes extremely difficult to assess effects as a function of time passage.

## Statistical regression

In any data collection process, some research participants will respond in an extreme fashion at the start of the research project. For example, in a study designed to test the effects of high and low anxiety levels on conversational coherence, certain individuals will initially be very anxious, whereas others will show little if any anxiety. As the study progresses, extremely high and extremely low anxiety scores tend to regress toward the mean anxiety score of all research participants: highly anxious people will become somewhat less anxious and low-anxiety individuals will experience some increase in apprehension due to natural changes over time.

This "settling" effect is called **statistical regression** toward the mean. The resulting variations in participants' responses are quite unrelated to a researcher's hypothesis-testing activities. Thus, research results will be confounded, reflecting regression effects as well as the influence of factors that are pertinent to the problem of interest.

## Controlling research progression effects

In many respects, research progression effects are uncontrollable because they involve fortuitous environmental, physiological, psychological, and statistical factors outside the researcher's volitional powers. However, the researcher can minimize their impact on a design's internal validity by taking certain precautions. First, a full awareness of research progression effects allows the researcher to correct for their potential influence when interpreting research findings. Second, the researcher can take steps to maximize participant interest in a given research project, thereby lowering the chances of substantial boredom effects as well as high dropout rates. Third and finally, the researcher should select research topics and materials that are unlikely to be affected by environmental influences such as prominent media coverage over the course of data collection.

## Reactivity Effects

Suppose I wish to study the communication strategies family members employ to resolve conflicts among themselves. Suppose further that I select 10 families and videotape their interactions in the home over a two-week period. To the extent that family members alter their communication patterns to "play to the

**186**

PART III
Contemporary
Research
Designs in
Communi-
cation

camera," I will get artificial results; that is, my findings will be biased by the phenomenon called **reactivity**.

Reactivity is a serious threat to a study's internal as well as external validity. A researcher is "creating" through observation a set of atypical communication behaviors. Four specialized types of reactivity can jeopardize a research design's internal and external validity: demand characteristics, evaluation apprehension, researcher effects, and test sensitization.

## Demand characteristics

Quite often, researchers (especially experimenters) do not directly inform research participants of the true nature of their hypothesis, since such knowledge can encourage people to give hypothesis-confirming responses, whereupon the research becomes a self-fulfilling prophecy. "Playing to the hypothesis" necessarily evokes at least some non-natural responses.

To reduce the chances for hypothesis-generated reactivity, researchers often give participants misleading information (called **cover stories**), hoping to obtain a purer test of their hypotheses. Considerable evidence suggests, however, that even with the cleverest of cover stories, many research participants are able to guess the hypothesis. We often use the term **demand characteristics** to refer to all the situational cues that implicitly convey this information to participants. Situational cues that help to reveal hypotheses include rumors, past experience as a research participant, the research setting itself, the behavior of the researcher, and the research procedures.

Once a research participant has learned the hypothesis, he or she may adopt one of three roles. Orne calls the first of these the "good subject" role, in which participants give responses they believe will confirm the hypothesis.[12] By contrast, a research participant may elect a "negativistic" role and try to disprove the hypothesis by giving either irrelevant or oppos-

ing responses.[13] Fillenbaum terms the third participant role the "faithful subject."[14] Faithful participants scrupulously follow the researcher's instructions and avoid acting on the basis of any suspicions they have about the study's true purpose. Faithful participants produce reasonably valid responses. Indeed, valid results are possible only if participants are faithful after learning the hypothesis or they are "naive," that is, they do not learn the research hypothesis at all.

To evaluate demand characteristics' threats to internal and external validity, we need to determine the usual proportion of research participants who never learn the hypothesis as well as the number expected to behave faithfully after guessing it. Considerable research suggests that anywhere from 60 to 80% of participants in social scientific research are either naive or faithful and thus present few validity problems.[15]

But what of the 20 to 40% who are aware of the hypothesis? Substantial evidence suggests that bias in social research typically leans in the direction of confirming research hypotheses, meaning that participants often play the "good subject" role.[16] As a result, effect sizes in communication studies may be somewhat greater than we could expect in "real-life" settings, thereby diminishing to some degree internal and external validity. However, the fact that a majority of research participants apparently behave naively or faithfully suggests that most communication research retains acceptable validity levels. Researchers can sometimes augment validity by constructing highly believable cover stories that direct research participants away from a study's true purposes.[17]

## Evaluation apprehension

**Evaluation apprehension**, a second factor thought to bias research participants' responses, is defined as the participant's desire to present a positive self-image to the researcher or at least to provide no grounds for a negative one.[18] Generally, the apprehensive person wishes to give socially acceptable responses when participating in research. If aware of the research hypothesis, apprehensive individuals may try to confirm or disconfirm it depending on which behavior they think will make them look better in the eyes of the researcher and fellow research participants.

There is considerable evidence that evaluation apprehension is widespread. Indeed, when a person's desire to present a positive self-image conflicts with "good subject" demand effects, the desire to present a favorable image usually prevails.[19] In other words, many people who are aware of a research hypothesis will confirm it only when doing so places them in a favorable light. Thus, evaluation apprehension may, in certain cases, offset the validity problems associated with "good subject" demand characteristics.

Although evaluation apprehension can affect participants' behaviors, it probably is not a major threat to validity, especially external validity. Whether in a research setting or in our everyday comings and goings, all of us wish to present positive self-images. Unlike demand characteristics that are peculiar to the research setting, evaluation apprehension is a pervasive force in all social settings and therefore is probably not a serious validity concern in the research context.

## Researcher effects

The third category of reactivity factors bearing on internal and external validity relates to the physical, social, and psychological characteristics of researchers themselves. Two sets of qualities are especially important. First, a researcher's *biosocial* characteristics such as gender and race can affect research participants' behaviors. For example, it has been suggested that because male researchers sometimes are perceived as friendlier than females, they elicit more hypothesis-confirming responses.[20]

Second, a researcher's *psychosocial* charac-teristics can bias responses. These characteristics include the researcher's apparent need for social approval, his or her perceived level of anxiety or warmth, and the researcher's status vis-à-vis participants. For instance, researchers with high social approval needs tend to elicit more positive responses from participants than those with lower approval needs. Similarly, "warmer" researchers frequently get more hypothesis-confirming responses than "cooler" investigators.[21]

If participants' responses relate not only to the research problem at hand, but also to a researcher's personal characteristics, such biasing effects may compromise a study's internal validity. The problem cannot be completely eliminated, but it can be moderated if the researcher strives to assume a relatively neutral psychosocial role. Using a **double-blind paradigm**, in which researchers and respondents alike are unaware of the hypothesis being tested, might help investigators to assume neutral psychosocial postures. Additionally, a researcher might ask both males and females and people of differing racial backgrounds to conduct different aspects of a research project if these variables are likely to affect people's responses.

Contrasted with internal validity problems, a researcher's personal characteristics are likely to have only a minimal impact on a study's external validity. We are all influenced by the biological, psychological, and social characteristics we perceive in other people, whether in a research setting or in more natural environments. Thus, responses to a researcher's biosocial and psychosocial traits may actually enhance the naturalness of the research setting.

## Test sensitization

Test sensitization, the final reactivity effect, is pertinent to studies that ask research subjects to complete written questionnaires or respond to oral interviews. Such test instruments can heighten intrapersonal awareness and prompt

**188**

PART III
Contemporary
Research
Designs in
Communi-
cation

respondents to deliberate more carefully about the problems at issue than they ordinarily would. This heightened awareness is called **test sensitization** and it sometimes produces responses that research participants would not normally exhibit. For example, suppose I wish to interview a group of employers and employees about their work-related communication problems. The act of probing for answers can sometimes "create" problems that respondents have not previously identified in their day-to-day interactions with one another.

A slightly different type of test sensitization occurs in experimental studies when researchers initially ask questions of research participants (a procedure called *pretesting*), then expose them to an experimental manipulation, and finally ask participants *posttest* questions to assess the manipulation's effects. Because people often can recall the pretest questions, the pretest itself can influence their responses to posttest questions, thereby confounding the effects of the experimental manipulation.

For example, an experimenter who wishes to examine the persuasive effects of high and low source credibility might pretest research participants to determine their initial attitudes on a message topic. Afterward, the experimenter will expose the participants to messages delivered by a source either high or low in credibility and administer a postmanipulation test to see whether the credibility variable differentially affected their attitudes toward the message topic. Since the pretest and posttest will contain many of the same attitude assessment questions, any recall of pretest questions will affect responses to posttest items. As a result, reported attitude change will be confounded, reflecting reactions to the credibility manipulation as well as pretest recall effects.

Unobtrusive measurement techniques can control many of the validity problems associated with test sensitization. When unobtrusive measures are infeasible, some test sensitization is likely. A researcher can compensate for these

effects by interpreting final research results in light of their potential contaminating influences. Additionally, the researcher should be careful never to probe for responses beyond the point at which people are attempting to be "good subjects" and are simply providing answers for their own sake.

## Sampling Deficiency Effects

Two general types of **sampling deficiency effects** are pertinent to communication research: sample selection problems and sample assignment problems. Sample selection problems have little impact on a study's internal validity, but they can seriously impair a researcher's ability to generalize research findings to parent populations. By contrast, sample assignment problems have implications for both internal and external validity.

### Sample selection problems

Sample selection problems result from using samples of research participants who are unrepresentative of their parent populations. As we learned in Chapter 5, the key to generating representative samples is to select them by one of several probability methods, including simple random sampling and systematic sampling with a random start. Researchers generate unrepresentative samples when they employ nonprobability methods such as convenience sampling, a procedure involving the use of research participants who are readily accessible to researchers. Convenience sampling often takes one of two forms: using captive college students as research participants and soliciting volunteers (self-selected samples) as research subjects.

Available samples of college students are used in many communication studies. The use of student samples led McNemar to conclude more than 40 years ago that social scientific research may largely be a "science of the behavior of sophomores,"[22] meaning the practice raises generalizability questions. Aside from age differences, college students as a whole are probably more intelligent, better educated, and of a higher social class than the general public. Moreover, their communication behaviors may differ from those of the average adult. Such differences lead one to question whether student sample responses parallel those that other populations might exhibit in similar circumstances. At a more basic level, a convenience sample of college students may not reflect the population of all college students. This is so because convenience samples, by definition, are not selected at random from parent populations.

The practical significance of this validity problem is unclear. Some studies have found that convenience samples of college students generalize quite well to all students and to more general populations. In a series of classic studies on obedience to authority, Milgram used multiple samples of college students, adult professionals, white collar workers, unemployed persons, and industrial workers. He conducted studies in the United States, Germany, Italy, South Africa, and Australia. Milgram reported that the results obtained from these diverse samples were virtually identical.[23] Whether these findings are applicable to a wide range of communication studies is not clear. More research is needed, and until it has been conducted, researchers should be alert to potential external validity problems associated with the use of convenience samples of college students.

If researchers choose not to rely on a captive student sample, they may solicit volunteers or self-selected subjects who willingly agree to participate. A number of writers argue that volunteers threaten the external validity of social scientific studies. For example, Rosenthal and Rosnow contend that volunteers differ radically from the general population because they have higher needs for social approval, higher occupational and educational levels, higher intel-

ligence, and are less responsive to authority figures. As a result, the two methodologists argue that volunteers are unrepresentative of the population from which they are selected.[24]

Other writers contend that self-selected subjects are in fact a rather heterogeneous group representing well their parent populations. For example, Kruglanski argues that people volunteer for a variety of reasons—some have a strong interest in the subject under investigation, others agree to participate after intense appeals from researchers, and so forth. Given "the diversity in bases for volunteering," Kruglanski notes, "it would not seem very plausible to expect subjects volunteering for one reason to resemble in their psychological characteristics those volunteering for quite a disparate reason."[25] Kruglanski then cites several studies that found no significant response differences between volunteers and nonvolunteers. The issue of volunteerism and invalidity is far from settled. However, researchers should be aware that volunteer samples introduce potential validity problems since, by definition, they are not selected at random from their parent populations.

## Sample assignment problems

The second category of sampling deficiencies occurs most often in experimental studies in which researchers expose two or more groups of research participants to some manipulation and measure the manipulation's differential effects. To illustrate the nature of sample assignment problems, suppose I wish to assess children's aggression levels as a function of three types of television programs: nonviolent programs, rewarded violent programs, and punished violent programs.

I might explore this issue by selecting a random sample of children, exposing one-third of the sample to each of the three program types, and measuring the three groups' aggression levels. If my postmanipulation assessment is to be internally and externally valid, the three groups

Confound. vt. 130 1面

190
PART III
Contemporary
Research
Designs in
Communi-
cation

of children must be similar in all respects save exposure to the programs. If the three groups differ before the experimental manipulation (say, one group contains more older children than another, or the three groups differ in terms of latent aggressiveness), my results will be confounded. As a consequence, it will be impossible to say whether observed differences are attributable to the experimental manipulation or to underlying group differences that were present before the programs were viewed.

To avoid these confounded effects, the researcher must assign the original random sample of children to the three groups in ways that ensure their preexperimental similarity. In the preferred approach, **random assignment**, research participants are put into groups using either the simple or systematic random methods described in Chapter 5. Researchers often employ a systematic approach with a random start and sequentially assign each research participant a number from 1 to the maximum number of groups needed for an experiment—in our example, we would use 1, 2, and 3. The first participant to be assigned a number should be picked at random. Then, all participants receiving the number 1 are assigned to the first group, all those getting the number 2 go to the second group, and so on.

If simple random rather than systematic assignment is chosen, the researcher will: (1) assign consecutive numbers (1 through *n*) to all members of the random sample of participants; (2) generate separate sets of random numbers equal to the total number of experimental groups (three in our example); and (3) assign to a first group all sample members with numbers corresponding to those in one set of random numbers, place in a second group all members whose assigned numbers correspond to a second random numbers set, and so forth. Both the simple random approach and the systematic method with a random start ensure that groups of sufficient size drawn from the same

random sample will be comparable before an experimental manipulation is begun.

For certain experimental studies, particularly those conducted in field settings, random subject assignment may not be entirely feasible. In such cases, researchers may use either matched subject assignment or intact groups assignment (sometimes called the quasi-experimental approach). The two procedures are related, since each typically uses a combination of purposive (matching) and random sampling techniques. They differ in their choice of assignment units, with the matched subject approach assigning "individual" research participants to experimental groups, whereas the intact groups perspective assigns aggregate sample "groups" to experimental conditions.

Assuming one's research design includes two experimental groups, the **matched subject assignment** procedure involves the following four steps: (1) measure the pertinent characteristics of all available sample members, that is, test each subject for characteristics relevant to the research hypothesis; (2) rank-order the subjects from highest to lowest (or lowest to highest), based on their possession of the measured characteristics; (3) form subject pairs that are approximately equivalent on the measured characteristics, so that the highest (or lowest) two subjects form a first matched pair, the next two highest (or lowest) subjects constitute a second matched pair, and so forth; and (4) randomly assign individual members of each matched pair to one of the two experimental groups. (For a research design that contains more than two experimental groups—for example, three or four groups—matched clusters of three or four subjects each would be formed for random assignment to the three or four experimental groups, respectively.) If matched subject pairs (or clusters) are approximately equal on the characteristics of interest, the resulting groups should be roughly comparable prior to an experimental manipulation.[26]

The second alternative procedure, **intact groups** (or quasi-experimental) **assignment**, assigns aggregate sample groups rather than individual subjects to different experimental conditions.[27] To illustrate, suppose a researcher wishes to study the impact of a new managerial style on worker productivity in a small business organization (an intact group). After measuring pertinent characteristics of this first group, the researcher purposively selects a second intact business group with characteristics comparable to those of the first sample. One of the groups is then selected at random for exposure to the managerial manipulation (assuming the research problem permits random selection). The second group is exposed either to an alternative managerial manipulation or to no manipulation at all. The two intact groups are then compared for postmanipulation differences in productivity levels. (When the research design contains more than two experimental conditions, more than two intact groups should be selected, randomly assigned, and tested for postmanipulation differences.) Importantly, intact groups must be comparable on all characteristics relevant to the experimental manipulation. In our example, the two business organizations should be similar in size and function and their employees should have similar work histories and habits. Without careful group matching, comparative results will be meaningless, since observed postmanipulation differences might easily be due to preexisting intact group discrepancies.

It should be emphasized that these two sample assignment alternatives are secondary or default options, to be used only when pure random assignment is infeasible. Thus, random assignment from a randomly selected pool of subjects is the preferred approach, since it alone ensures that samples of sufficient size will be comparable before an experimental manipulation is begun.

# INTERFACE: CHAPTER 9 AND PART III

This chapter has explored the general nature of communication research designs. Factors threatening the internal and external validity of designs were described, including research progression effects, reactivity effects, and sampling deficiency effects. Practical suggestions were presented for alleviating the problems posed by these sources of invalidity.

For the rest of Part III, I will examine specific research designs. Chapter 10 focuses on experimental research and Chapter 11 describes survey methods. Conversational analysis is explored in Chapter 12, and Chapter 13 treats content analysis and rhetorical criticism. The principles and procedures outlined in Chapter 9 provide an essential foundation for understanding these particularized research methodologies.

# MAIN POINTS

**1.** A research design is a comprehensive data collection plan whose purpose is to answer research questions and test hypotheses.

**2.** A research design can be classified in eight ways: quantitative or qualitative research, interpretive or functional research, experimental or naturalistic research, laboratory or field research, participant or nonparticipant research, overt or unobtrusive research, cross-sectional or longitudinal research, and basic or applied research.

**3.** Quantitative research involves an analysis of numerical data, whereas qualitative research focuses on narrative information.

**4.** Interpretive research examines the meanings of messages, whereas functional research often regards meanings as baseline data for

**192**

PART III
Contemporary
Research
Designs in
Communi-
cation

inferring conclusions about related behaviors and effects.

**5.** Experimental researchers introduce manipulations into a research environment and observe people's reactions to the manipulations. Naturalistic researchers observe and record people's normal communication behaviors without injecting a manipulation into the research environment.

**6.** Laboratory research takes place in a controlled environment and field research is conducted in a natural setting.

**7.** Participant researchers contribute to the communication processes they observe, whereas nonparticipant researchers assume the role of an outside spectator of observed communication.

**8.** Differences between overt and unobtrusive research turn on whether communicators are aware they are being observed. When research is overt, people are aware of the researcher's presence in the research environment. When research is unobtrusive, the researcher is physically absent from the field of observations.

**9.** Cross-sectional research examines communication events at a single point in time, whereas longitudinal research examines events as they change over time.

**10.** Basic research explores theoretical relationships with little regard for their practical implications. Applied research has a pragmatic orientation, examining theoretical relationships for the purpose of understanding and solving practical problems.

**11.** One's choice of research design is guided by a single criterion: the nature of the research question or hypothesis.

**12.** To possess internal validity, a research design must provide an accurate test of a research hypothesis within the sample selected for hypothesis testing. Externally valid sample findings are generalizable to the populations from which samples are selected.

**13.** Research progression effects, which represent changes occurring during data collection, can threaten the validity of a research design. Four types of progression effects are especially pertinent: (a) history, referring to incidental environmental occurrences that can influence results; (b) maturation, meaning physiological and psychological changes in research participants that may affect responses; (c) mortality, signifying the loss of research participants during a study; and (d) statistical regression, the tendency of initially high and low scores to move toward the mean score of all research participants as a study progresses.

**14.** Reactivity occurs when research participants' behaviors differ from their normal patterns because they are aware of being observed and tested. Four sources of reactivity can threaten a research design's validity: demand characteristics, evaluation apprehension, researcher effects, and test sensitization.

**15.** Demand characteristics refer to situational cues that convey a researcher's hypothesis to research participants. Once participants have learned the hypothesis, they may become "good" subjects, who try to confirm the hypothesis; "negativistic" subjects, who wish to disconfirm the hypothesis; or "faithful" subjects, who try to respond in an unbiased fashion. Participants who do not learn the hypothesis are referred to as "naive" subjects. Demand characteristics can threaten a study's validity.

**16.** Evaluation apprehension, a potential reactivity problem, refers to research participants' desire to give responses that will present themselves in a favorable light.

**17.** Researcher effects are a potential reactivity problem. They refer to the physical, social, and psychological characteristics of researchers that may affect research participants' responses.

**18.** Test sensitization, another reactivity effect, refers to a heightened awareness in research participants that results from questioning and interviewing procedures. Increased awareness can produce responses that participants would not normally exhibit in their everyday interactions.

**19.** Two kinds of sampling deficiencies can affect a research design's validity: sample selection problems and sample assignment problems.

**20.** Sample selection problems result from using research participants who are not representative of their parent populations. Two common sample selection problems are the use of convenience samples consisting of college students and the use of volunteers.

**21.** Sample assignment refers to the distribution of a sample of research participants to different groups of an experimental research design. To validly assess group differences, the groups must be comparable to one another before an experimental manipulation is undertaken. Random assignment methods ensure comparability among groups of sufficient size.

**22.** Two common methods of randomly assigning samples to different groups of an experimental design are simple random assignment and systematic assignment with a random start. Matched subject and intact groups assignment may be used as default options if random assignment is infeasible.

## REVIEW EXERCISES

**1.** Describe a research design that would be appropriate for exploring each of the following research problems:

**a.** What conflict resolution strategies do families use to settle disagreements among members?

**b.** Heavy viewing of televised crime drama promotes fears of falling victim to crimes.

Characterize each of your two designs on the eight dimensions for classifying research de-

signs discussed in the chapter. Explain the bases for your characterizations.

**2.** Suppose you wished to conduct a longitudinal study of the communication problems encountered by married couples during their first year of marriage. Describe any research progression and reactivity effects that might seriously jeopardize the internal and external validity of your study. What single effect is likely to create the greatest threat to internal validity? Which effect will probably present the greatest threat to external validity? Explain your answers.

**3.** Suppose you wished to do an experimental study of the effects of afternoon television soap operas on viewers' self concepts. Describe a research design that you think would satisfactorily answer this research question. Describe one random method you might use to select a sample of viewers and to assign the sample to different experimental groups to ensure the experiment's validity.

## NOTES

**1.** *Ferment in the Field*, Special Issue, *Journal of Communication*, 33, No. 3 (1983).

**2.** Elihu Katz, "The Return of the Humanities and Sociology," *Journal of Communication*, 33, No. 3 (1983): 51–52.

**3.** For a detailed discussion of the nature of research designs, see Paul E. Spector, *Research Designs* (Beverly Hills, CA.: Sage, 1981).

**4.** Matthew B. Miles and A. Michael Huberman, *Qualitative Data Analysis: A Sourcebook of New Methods* (Beverly Hills, CA: Sage, 1984), p. 21. Also see Thomas D. Cook and Charles S. Reichardt, *Qualitative and Quantitative Methods in Evaluation Research* (Beverly Hills, CA: Sage, 1979).

**5.** Linda L. Putnam, "The Interpretive Perspective: An Alternative to Functionalism," in *Communication and Organizations: An Interpretive Approach*, ed. Linda L. Putnam and Michael E. Pacanowsky (Beverly Hills, CA: Sage, 1983), p. 31.

**194**

PART III
Contemporary
Research
Designs in
Communi-
cation

**6.** Gerry Philipsen, "Linearity of Research Design in Ethnographic Studies of Speaking," *Communication Quarterly*, 25 (1977): 43.

**7.** Leon Festinger, Henry Riecken, and Stanley Schachter, *When Prophecy Fails* (Minneapolis: University of Minnesota Press, 1956), p. 237.

**8.** Raymond L. Gold, "Roles in Sociological Field Observation," in *Issues in Participant Observation*, ed. George J. McCall and J. L. Simmons (Reading, MA: Addison-Wesley, 1969), pp. 30–39.

**9.** David Nachmias and Chava Nachmias, *Research Methods in the Social Sciences*, 2nd ed. (New York: St. Martin's Press, 1981), p. 245.

**10.** Eugene J. Webb, Donald T. Campbell, Richard D. Schwartz, and Lee Sechrest, *Unobtrusive Measures: Nonreactive Research in the Social Sciences* (Chicago: Rand McNally, 1966), p. 175.

**11.** Donald T. Campbell and Julian C. Stanley, *Experimental and Quasi-Experimental Designs for Research* (Chicago: Rand McNally, 1963), pp. 5–6.

**12.** Martin T. Orne, "On the Social Psychology of the Psychological Experiment: With Particular Reference to Demand Characteristics and Their Implications," *American Psychologist*, 17 (1962): 776–83.

**13.** Joseph Masling, "Role-Related Behavior of the Subject and Psychologist and Its Effects upon Psychological Data," *Nebraska Symposium on Motivation*, ed. David Levine (Lincoln: University of Nebraska Press, 1966), pp. 67–103.

**14.** Samuel Fillenbaum, "Prior Deception and Subsequent Experimental Performance: The 'Faithful' Subject," *Journal of Personality and Social Psychology*, 4 (1966): 532–37.

**15.** Fillenbaum; Samuel Fillenbaum, and Robert Frey, "More on the 'Faithful' Behavior of Suspicious Subjects," *Journal of Personality*, 38 (1970): 43–51; and Barry Spinner, John G. Adair, and Gordon E. Barnes, "A Reexamination of the Faithful Subject Role," *Journal of Experimental Social Psychology*, 13 (1977): 543–51.

**16.** For a summary of research supporting this conclusion, see Stephen J. Weber and Thomas D. Cook, "Subject Effects in Laboratory Research: An Examination of Subject Roles, Demand Characteristics, and Valid Inference," *Psychological Bulletin*, 77 (1972): 273–95.

**17.** The ethical implications of deception are discussed in Chapter 14.

**18.** Milton J. Rosenberg, "The Conditions and Consequences of Evaluation Apprehension," in *Artifact in Behavioral Research*, ed. Robert Rosenthal and Ralph L. Rosnow (New York: Academic Press, 1969), p. 281.

**19.** See John G. Adair and Brenda S. Schachter, "To Cooperate or to Look Good?: The Subjects' and Experimenters' Perceptions of Each Other's Intentions," *Journal of Experimental Social Psychology*, 8 (1972): 75–85.

**20.** See Robert Rosenthal, "Interpersonal Expectations: Effects of the Experimenter's Hypothesis," in *Artifact in Behavioral Research*, ed. Robert Rosenthal and Ralph L. Rosnow (New York: Academic Press, 1969), pp. 181–277.

**21.** Rosenthal.

**22.** Quinn McNemar, "Opinion-Attitude Methodology," *Psychological Bulletin*, 43 (1946): 333.

**23.** Stanley Milgram, *Obedience to Authority: An Experimental View* (New York: Harper & Row, 1974), pp. 170–71.

**24.** Robert Rosenthal and Ralph L. Rosnow, "The Volunteer Subject," in *Artifact in Behavioral Research*, ed. Robert Rosenthal and Ralph L. Rosnow (New York: Academic Press, 1969), pp. 59–118.

**25.** Arie W. Kruglanski, "Much Ado About the 'Volunteer Artifacts,'" *Journal of Personality and Social Psychology*, 28 (1973): 350.

**26.** This subject assignment method, which Cozby calls "matched random assignment," is described in Paul C. Cozby, *Methods in Behavioral Research*, 3rd ed. (Palo Alto, CA: Mayfield, 1985), pp. 66–67.

**27.** The intact groups method was first elaborated by Campbell in Donald T. Campbell, "Reforms as Experiments," *American Psychologist*, 24 (1969): 409–29.

# EXPERIMENTAL RESEARCH

This chapter examines the nature and uses of experimental research. An experiment is a research design whose purpose is to explain the impact exerted by certain input variables, called independent variables, on other outcome variables known as dependent variables. Procedures for operationalizing and validating independent and dependent variables are discussed. The chapter describes several simple experimental designs along with some important complex designs. Practical guidelines for conducting an experiment are presented.

# CHAPTER OUTLINE

During the late nineteenth century, an obscure French veterinarian named Louvrier invented a vaccine for anthrax, a virulent bacterial disease responsible for the deaths of thousands of cattle, sheep, and other domestic livestock. Although Louvrier claimed to have cured hundreds of afflicted animals, most prominent veterinarians questioned the vaccine's effectiveness, arguing that infected animals often recovered with or without Louvrier's treatment. In the spring of 1881, the eminent scientist Louis Pasteur entered the controversy, offering to test the new vaccine. Pasteur gave the serum to several head of sheep and cattle, leaving an equal number of animals unvaccinated. Afterward, he gave both the vaccinated and unvaccinated livestock lethal doses of anthrax bacteria. Pasteur inspected all the animals two days later. He found the vaccinated ones alive and well, whereas the unvaccinated animals were either dead or dying from anthrax, a result that validated Louvrier's new treatment.[1]

This classic study illustrates well the experiment as a scientific tool for solving complex empirical problems. The experiment has been used extensively in communication research since our discipline embraced the methods of science in the 1930s and 1940s. Indeed, until the early 1970s, communication research was mostly experimental. Since that time, naturalistic designs have attracted considerable interest. Nevertheless, the experiment remains a staple in the arsenal of contemporary research methods.

This chapter will describe the nature and uses of experimental research. I examine laboratory and field experiments and discuss methods of testing their validity. Then, several simple experimental designs are explored, followed by an examination of more complex methods. Finally, I present practical guidelines for conducting experimental research.

# THE NATURE OF EXPERIMENTS

An **experiment** is a functional research design whose purpose is to explain the impact of certain input variables on other outcome variables. The input variables, called **independent variables**, consist either of manipulations constructed by the experimenter or naturally occurring differences among communicators. Outcome or output variables are known as **dependent variables**. Importantly, experiments do not necessarily establish causal relationships between independent and dependent variables. Rather, an experiment assesses the extent to which independent variables are related to or are predictive of dependent measurements. Thus, the basic function of an experiment is to assess the relationship between one or more independent variables and one or more dependent measures.

To illustrate the essential qualities of a traditional experiment, suppose I am interested in the impact of a source's physical attractiveness on the compliance behaviors of male and female listeners. An experiment is an ideal vehicle for resolving this research problem. It allows me to measure the effects that the two independent variables, source attractiveness and receiver gender, exert on the dependent variable, compliance.

Table 10.1 depicts an experimental design involving a two-part manipulation of source attractiveness (attractive and unattractive) and including naturally occurring differences in receiver gender (male and female). It displays some hypothetical mean scores representing listeners' compliance rates. The divisions associated with each independent variable are called **treatment levels**; thus, source attractiveness has two treatment levels (attractive and unattractive), as does receiver gender (male and female).[2] The four groups created by the two independent variables are called **cells** of an experiment. The overall research plan is

TABLE 10.1
A 2 × 2 EXPERIMENTAL DESIGN

|  | Attractive | Unattractive | Row means |
|---|---|---|---|
| Male | **Cell 1** $\bar{x} = 3.5$ | **Cell 2** $\bar{x} = 3.5$ | 3.5 |
| Female | **Cell 3** $\bar{x} = 6.5$ | **Cell 4** $\bar{x} = 2.5$ | 4.5 |
| Column means | 5.0 | 3.0 | |

referred to as a 2 × 2 ("two by two") design, meaning that the experiment contains two independent variables, each with two treatment levels. This multiplicative identification system indexes the structure of a traditional experiment including the number of cells it contains. In our hypothetical study, for example, the multiplicative notation 2 × 2 identifies a four-cell experimental design.

## Operationalizing Independent Variables

As we have seen, independent variables are input variables that the experimenter assumes will explain a set of measurable effects called dependent variables. Researchers typically *operationalize* independent variables by specifying exactly how they will present them to research participants, thereby producing clearly defined treatment levels. Independent variables are often classified as continuous or discrete and as stimulus or organismic; each classification has important implications for operationalization.

### Continuous or discrete variables

A naturally **continuous** independent **variable** contains values that vary along a spectrum

from low to high, whereas a naturally **discrete variable** changes in distinct steps. For example, the variable "physical attractiveness" is naturally continuous, ranging from extremely unattractive to extremely attractive, whereas "gender" is naturally discrete, containing the fixed categories of male and female. Naturally discrete independent variables are relatively easy to operationalize: their naturally occurring categories can become treatment levels. This operationalization is isomorphic with the true nature of the phenomena the variables represent.

Schemes for operationalizing naturally continuous variables are not always consistent with the variables' true character. Indeed, the nature of the traditional experiment often forces researchers to transform naturally continuous variables into artificially discrete ones, thus violating the principle of reality isomorphism discussed in Chapter 3. For example, source attractiveness is naturally continuous, yet we changed it to a two-category discrete variable in our hypothetical compliance-gaining experiment. Similarly, if we were interested in the persuasive effects of fear appeals or language intensity, we might arbitrarily split these naturally continuous variables into categories such as low, moderate, and high fear or intensity to be able to include either in a traditional experiment.

*Contiguous* a. 相接的. 接壤的.

*adjacent* [ə'dʒeisənt] 毗邻的.

a.

Researchers often render naturally continuous variables discrete in one of two ways: (1) by grouping their adjacent or contiguous values into categories—for example, all very high values of fear arousal, language intensity, and the like could be combined into the general category "high," whereas very low values would become the broad category "low," or (2) by dichotomizing variables according to their complete presence and absence, as when we operationalized "physical attractiveness" in our hypothetical study as either "attractive" or "unattractive." Similarly, we could operationalize the variable "fear arousal" by creating the two categories "messages containing fear appeals" and "messages containing no fear appeals."

Importantly, naturally continuous variables can be tested experimentally without being rendered discrete. Researchers can use statistical procedures like multiple regression, discussed in Chapter 8, to assess the predictive effects of continuous independent variables on a dependent or criterion variable. Recall that multiple correlation and regression analysis measures the amount of variability in a criterion that is accounted for by its predictor variables. Naturally continuous independent variables must be transformed into arbitrarily discrete ones only when a researcher employs what we call a "traditional" experimental paradigm. A **traditional experiment** is characterized by the use of discrete independent variables, whereas a **nontraditional experiment** accommodates discrete and continuous independent variables equally well. Because the traditional paradigm serves many important functions in communication research, I will devote much of my discussion to this model. However, the student should be aware that the traditional perspective is not the only approach to experimentation, nor is it necessarily the preferred method, particularly in cases where independent variables are naturally continuous. Continuous independent variables ordinarily should be left in their natural states and re-

searchers should measure their effects with statistical procedures that accommodate their entire spectrum of values.

## Stimulus or organismic variables

Continuous and discrete variables can be either stimulus or organismic. A **stimulus** independent **variable** is external to research participants who are exposed to its treatment levels, whereas an **organismic** independent **variable** is an internal characteristic of research participants.[3] In our hypothetical compliance-gaining experiment, "source attractiveness" is a stimulus variable. It is external to listeners and imposed upon them by the experimenter. However, "receiver gender" is organismic, representing a natural characteristic of research participants. Thus, an organismic variable is not directly "created" by experimenters, but rather is discovered and used by them.

Operationalization procedures vary depending on a variable's stimulus or organismic character. Researchers operationalize stimulus variables by manipulating them: that is, they construct the variables and design appropriate ways to expose them to research participants. Suppose a researcher wishes to examine the impact of message organization on listener comprehension. If the planned experiment is traditional, the continuous stimulus variable, organization, can be rendered discrete by conceptually grouping messages into "well organized" and "poorly organized" units. Then, actual messages having one of these two sets of conceptual properties must be written and delivered to samples of listeners. Finally, all factors save the stimulus, message organization, should be controlled to avoid the confounding effects of intervening variables. As we learned in Chapter 2, an **intervening variable** is any variable, other than an independent one, having the capacity to influence dependent measures.

We can control potential intervening variables in our hypothetical study by ensuring that

*dichotomize* vt. 将…一分为二. 成…两部分. 分. 对分. 二岐.

*reader* 反映. 表示.

**200**

PART III
Contemporary
Research
Designs in
Communi-
cation

well organized and poorly organized messages (1) are identical in content, (2) are delivered by the same speaker, (3) are presented in identical physical and social environments, and (4) are presented to comparable samples of listeners. Comparability is achieved by selecting a large representative sample and randomly assigning each sample member to one of our two experimental conditions, using the procedures described in Chapter 9. If these precautions are taken, any observed differences in comprehension should result from the organization manipulation, not from one or more intervening variables operating singly or in tandem with the independent variable.

When an independent variable is organismic, the researcher does not construct a manipulation, but rather takes advantage of preexisting differences among research participants. An experiment employing organismic variables assesses whether different populations of people respond differently to some fixed external stimulus. For example, a mass communication researcher might wish to know whether boys and girls respond differently to the same instructional television program. In such a study, the researcher should select random samples of children who are comparable except for physical gender, then expose them to identical television programs and measure their reactions. All intervening variables, including the fixed program stimulus, must be held as constant as possible to provide a clear test of gender effects.

Miller has identified three types of experimental designs based on stimulus-organismic characteristics: an all-stimulus paradigm, an all-organismic paradigm, and a mixed model paradigm.[4] An **all-stimulus paradigm** employs only stimulus-independent variables. A study examining the impact of group leadership style (autocratic and democratic) and task difficulty (simple and complex) on the problem-solving behavior of small groups is an all-stimulus paradigm. The **all-organismic**

**paradigm** uses only organismic variables and is exemplified by a study testing the effects of dogmatism (closed-mindedness and open-mindedness) and chronic anxiety (high and low) on susceptibility to persuasion. Finally, a **mixed model paradigm** includes at least one stimulus and one organismic variable. Our earlier example of an experiment examining the persuasive effects of receiver gender and source attractiveness is a mixed model study.

## Sample assignment and design types

I emphasized earlier that to achieve a valid test of an independent variable's effects, the participants in different experimental cells must be comparable. Moreover, I suggested in Chapter 9 that comparability is achieved by first, selecting a reasonably large representative sample of participants, and then randomly assigning the participants to experimental cells. At this juncture, it is important to note that subject assignment methods vary depending on the stimulus-organismic features of one's research design.

In an all-stimulus design, the participants constituting a representative sample should be randomly distributed across experimental cells using procedures like simple random assignment or systematic assignment with a random start. Using the systematic approach with a four-cell stimulus design, the participants in a representative sample would be sequentially assigned the numbers 1, 2, 3, and 4, with the first participant being picked at random. Then, all individuals receiving the number 1 are placed in a first cell, all people getting the number 2 go to a second cell, and so forth, until all participants have been assigned to one of the four cells.

No random cell assignment is required for an all-organismic design. Rather, samples drawn randomly from the different populations of interest are purposively placed in appropriate cells. To illustrate, suppose I am examining persuasibility as a function of gender (male and female) and authoritarianism (high and low). With this all-organismic design, a random sample of highly authoritarian males is purposively assigned to one cell, a low authoritarian male sample goes to a second cell, and authoritarian and nonauthoritarian female samples occupy the third and fourth cells, respectively. Only purposive assignment permits researchers to isolate the effects of organismic variables of interest.

A mixed model paradigm combines these two assignment procedures. Suppose I wish to study small group productivity as a function of gender and task difficulty (simple and complex). I would purposively assign a random sample of males to two of my four cells and allow a female sample to occupy each of the remaining two. However, both males and females would be assigned randomly to one of the two task difficulty conditions, perhaps by systematically giving the members of both groups either the number 1 or 2.

## Validating independent variables

Once stimulus and organismic variables have been operationalized, the researcher must assess their validity. An independent variable is usually considered valid if researchers have actually created the stimulus variable or isolated the organismic variable that they intended to create and isolate, respectively.

Experimenters validate stimulus variables before using them in an actual study by asking samples of individuals to report their perceptions of the intended manipulations. To illustrate the procedure, imagine that a researcher has constructed two messages: one is designed to be well organized and the other shows poor organization. This two-level manipulation might be validated by presenting one of the messages to a random sample drawn from the population from which later research participants will come, and exposing the other message to a different random sample selected from the same population. After hearing the messages, the two samples are asked whether they perceived differences in the organizational features of the messages.

Semantic differential scales like the one appearing in the box below are often used to assess validity perceptions.

The mean scale responses of the different samples are tested for significance of difference using statistical procedures like a $t$ test or analysis of variance. If the message designed to be "well organized" is in fact perceived as significantly better organized than the "poorly organized" message, the manipulation is probably valid.

In addition to these *prior validity checks*, researchers often perform *concurrent validity checks*; that is, they reexamine the validity of stimulus variables during the course of the actual experiment. All research participants are asked to respond to the same validity assessment scales that were completed by the pre-experimental sample. If both samples perceive the existence of the intended manipulation, the experimenter has strong support for the validity of the chosen stimulus variables. As these test methods suggest, a stimulus variable is assumed to be valid if research participants perceive the manipulations as the researcher conceived them.

Procedures for validating organismic variables differ depending on whether the variable in question is a manifest or latent characteristic of research participants. (Manifest and latent

---

The message I heard was:

Well Organized _____:_____:_____:_____:_____ Poorly Organized

Semantic 語意（字）500

202
PART III
Contemporary
Research
Designs in
Communi-
cation

variables were described in Chapter 3.) **Manifest variables** such as physical gender and age are directly observable. They usually can be validated by visually inspecting participants, by consulting available biographical records, and by soliciting participant self-reports. **Latent** organismic **variables** like self-esteem, anxiety, dogmatism, and other internal states are not directly observable. They are often validated by giving research participants written questionnaires or through physiological assessments to establish the existence of relevant internal states. Standardized measures—for example, self-esteem tests and dogmatism scales—are available to validate the presence of many latent variables.

## Assessing Experimental Effects

As we have learned, the measurable effects of independent variables are called dependent variables. Many dependent measures are naturally continuous and are measured continuously. For example, we can measure continuous variables like message compliance on interval scales such as semantic differentials and Likert instruments discussed in Chapter 4. When dependent variables are naturally discrete, we measure them on appropriate nominal scales, noting the frequency of responses falling into each scale category. Suppose we are interested in people's buying behaviors as a function of exposure to either televised or printed advertisements. In such a case, we might use a two-category nominal scale, tabulating the number of purchases among television viewers versus newspaper and magazine readers.

### Main and interaction effects

Independent variables are capable of explaining two kinds of dependent effects: main and interaction. A **main effect** refers to the unique impact of each independent variable on a dependent measure, whereas an **interaction effect**

reflects the joint impact of two or more independent variables operating in tandem.

Main effects can be understood by examining Table 10.1 (see page 198), which illustrates the impact of the two independent variables, "receiver gender" and "source attractiveness," on people's compliance with persuasive recommendations. Notice that the mean compliance scores of men and women are 3.5 and 4.5, respectively (row means), whereas both males and females hearing a physically attractive persuader have a mean compliance score of 5.0 compared to 3.0 for men and women exposed to an unattractive source (column means).

The main effect of the variable, "gender," is indexed by the 1.0 mean difference between male and female compliance rates. If this difference is statistically significant, we can assume that gender had a main effect on compliance. The main effect of the second independent variable, "source attractiveness," is reflected by the 2.0 difference between individuals hearing the attractive versus the unattractive speaker. Assuming that this mean difference is statistically reliable, we can conclude that source attractiveness had a main effect on compliance with persuasive requests. If either of these two differences is statistically insignificant, the independent variable associated with the unreliable difference probably had no main effect on compliance.

The interaction effect jointly produced by these two independent variables is illustrated in Figure 10.1. The interaction between attractiveness and gender indicates that females complied with the attractive speaker's recommendations substantially more than males, whereas in the unattractive source condition, males were more compliant than females. Thus, when the effects of an independent variable at one treatment level of a second independent variable differ from the effects of the first variable at another level of the second variable, an interaction has occurred.

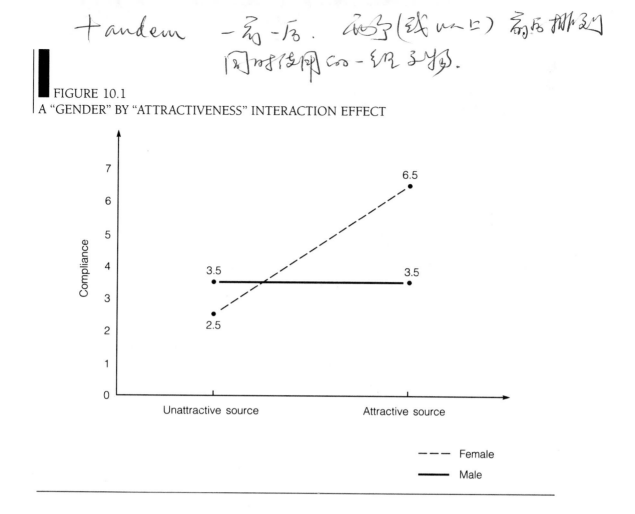

## Types of interaction effects

Many types of interactions are possible, and experimenters must carefully scrutinize the results in each cell of an experimental design to ascertain an interaction's meaning. Any one interaction can be classified on two dimensions: ordinal or disordinal interactions, and symmetrical or nonsymmetrical.[5]

When one obtains an **ordinal interaction**, one independent variable produces significant differences at one treatment level of a second variable, but not at another level of the same variable. By contrast, in a **disordinal interaction**, a first independent variable produces significant effects at all levels of a second independent variable. Regarding the second classification, a **symmetrical interaction** signifies a reversal of one independent variable's effects at all the treatment levels associated with a second independent variable. Put another way, one independent variable's treatment levels produce opposing effects at the treatment levels of a second variable. A **nonsymmetrical interaction** signifies that the effects of one independent variable are not reversed at the second variable's treatment levels.

To unravel the meaning of these classifications, refer to Figure 10.2, which displays four patterns of effects that might be obtained in testing the effects of the two independent variables, "television programs (violent and nonviolent) and "gender" on aggression among children (the dependent variable). Notice that in case 1 there are no interaction effects. The differences between male and female aggression scores at both levels of the independent

FIGURE 10.2
PATTERNS OF INTERACTIONS IN A 2 × 2 DESIGN

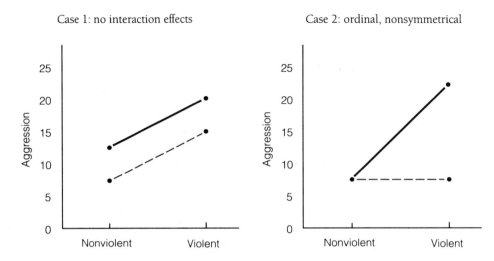

Case 1: no interaction effects

Case 2: ordinal, nonsymmetrical

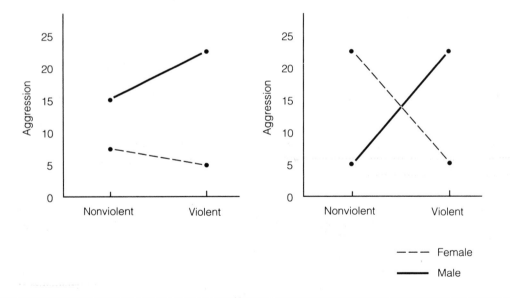

Case 3: disordinal, nonsymmetrical

Case 4: disordinal, symmetrical

- - - - Female
⎯⎯⎯ Male

variable, television programs, are identical. Whenever the effects associated with two or more independent variables either coincide or follow parallel lines, no interaction exists between the variables.

Case 2 in Figure 10.2 depicts an ordinal and nonsymmetrical interaction. The interaction is ordinal because gender produces a significant difference in children's aggression in the violence treatment level, but males and females respond identically to nonviolent programs. Because the gender effects at the two programming levels are not polar opposites, the interaction is nonsymmetrical. Case 3's interaction pattern is nonsymmetrical as well, but the effects are disordinal; that is, male and female responses differ significantly at both levels of the programming variable. However, the difference is substantially greater in the violent as opposed to the nonviolent condition.

Finally, case 4 illustrates a disordinal and symmetrical interaction. Significant differences between males and females occur at both program treatment levels, producing disordinality. Moreover, the pattern of effects is symmetrical because male and female responses are reversed at the two levels of television programs: males aggress significantly more than females in response to violent episodes, whereas females aggress significantly more than males when exposed to nonviolent programs. The case 4 pattern is identical to the compliance interaction shown in Figure 10.1.

## Laboratory and Field Experiments

Studies assessing the main and interaction effects of independent variables may be conducted either in a laboratory or in a field setting. When conducting a field experiment, the researcher goes into real-life settings and exposes people to experimental treatments. For example, a field experimenter interested in the effects of dress and grooming on compliance behaviors might make two visits to a shopping mall—once neatly dressed and the second time sloppily groomed. In each guise, the experimenter might ask for donations to a charity or solicit volunteers for service work. If significantly more people comply when the researcher is well groomed, we can assume that a neat appearance probably exerts a main effect on public compliance.

Contrasted with field research, laboratory experimenters bring subjects into a setting that is not a normal living environment. Two principal features distinguish a laboratory from a field experiment.[6] First, the laboratory experimenter rigorously structures the physical and social environment in which the research is conducted. The size of the experimental room, the color and arrangement of furnishings, the lighting, and the like, can be controlled. Moreover, laboratory researchers carefully control experimental variables. Intervening variables that might confound results are monitored. The laboratory experimenter can make sure that there are few, if any, preexisting differences among subjects to confound results. In the field, such control is difficult because many naturally occurring events can confound experimental findings.

Second, laboratory experimenters often deceive subjects in an effort to obscure their hypotheses. We saw in Chapter 9 that research participants who are aware of the research hypothesis often do not behave naturally. Rather, they try to confirm or disconfirm a suspected hypothesis based on attitudes toward the experimenter and the experiment itself. To prevent participants from learning the hypothesis, laboratory experimenters often devise **cover stories** that initially mislead participants about the nature of the experiment. After the experiment has been completed, participants are fully debriefed, that is, they are told of the experiment's true nature. Field researchers, although sometimes engaging in explicit deception and

**206**

PART III
Contemporary
Research
Designs in
Communi-
cation

subsequent **debriefing**, use these techniques less often than laboratory experimenters. The artificiality of laboratory settings frequently makes the deception and debriefing routine essential to a study's success.

## The Validity of Experiments

The differences between laboratory and field studies raise the issue of internal and external validity. Applied to an experiment, **internal validity** asks whether sample main and interaction effects are attributable solely to the independent variables selected. **External validity** addresses the question of whether sample experimental effects can be generalized to parent populations and to everyday social settings.

Laboratory experiments generally achieve a higher degree of internal validity than do field studies because intervening variables can be controlled better in the laboratory than in the field. However, the field experiment often has more external validity because field researchers operate in natural social settings. Beyond these environmental effects, the internal and external validity of any experiment is threatened by all the factors we discussed in Chapter 9, including research progression effects, reactivity, and sampling deficiencies. The impact of these validity threats on specific experimental designs is discussed in the next section.

## TYPES OF EXPERIMENTAL DESIGNS

I will now examine several experimental designs and describe statistical procedures appropriate to each. Three simple designs that assess the effects of a single independent variable are discussed, followed by an analysis of three complex designs entailing more than one independent variable, each with multiple treatment levels.

## Simple Experimental Designs

Three designs for assessing a single independent variable's effects are especially useful: the pretest-posttest control group design, the posttest-only control group design, and the Solomon four-group design.[7] All three designs use random methods to assign research participants to different experimental cells or treatment levels.

### Pretest-posttest control group design

Table 10.2 illustrates the **pretest-posttest control group design** in its simplest form—that is, a representative sample of research participants (subjects) is randomly assigned to an **experimental group** or to a **control group**. All subjects are given a pretest to assess pertinent pre-experimental characteristics. Then, one of the two groups is exposed to an experimental manipulation, whereas the second group, which receives no experimental manipulation, constitutes a control. Afterward, both groups' responses are assessed with a posttest. Finally, to isolate the impact of the experimental manipulation, a significance of difference test is applied to changes in the two groups' pretest-to-posttest responses. A $t$ test or $z$ test for mean differences is often used when pretest-posttest responses represent mean scores, whereas either a $z$ test for proportional differences or a chi-square statistic is employed if responses are frequency data.

To illustrate this simple design, suppose a researcher wishes to assess the effectiveness of a new method of advertising a certain commercial product. To begin the research, the experimenter will pretest a random sample of consumers to determine relevant attitudes and buying behaviors. Then, half of the sample will be randomly assigned to hear the new advertisement and the other half will receive no manipulation. Pertinent attitudes and buying behaviors will be posttested and any differences

**Pretest-Posttest Control Group Design**

| | | | | |
|---|---|---|---|---|
| R | *Experimental group:* | Pretest | Manipulation | Posttest |
| R | *Control group:* | Pretest | No manipulation | Posttest |

**Posttest-Only Control Group Design**

| | | | |
|---|---|---|---|
| R | *Experimental group:* | Manipulation | Posttest |
| R | *Control group:* | No manipulation | Posttest |

**Solomon Four-Group Design**

| | | | | |
|---|---|---|---|---|
| R | *Experimental group 1:* | Pretest | Manipulation | Posttest |
| R | *Control group 1:* | Pretest | No manipulation | Posttest |
| R | *Experimental group 2:* | | Manipulation | Posttest |
| R | *Control group 2:* | | No manipulation | Posttest |

*The symbol R denotes that subjects are randomly assigned to each group constituting these designs.

will be statistically analyzed. If the experimental group reports significantly more positive reactions to the advertised product than the control group, the researcher can conclude that the new advertising strategy is probably an effective means of promoting the commercial product.

Importantly, this simple two-group design can be extended to assess the impact of an independent variable having more than the two treatment levels (manipulation, no manipulation) exemplified by the design displayed in Table 10.2. For example, a researcher might wish to assess the effectiveness of three different types of commercial advertisements on consumer purchases. The design will include three experimental groups and a single control group. To assess postexperimental differences among the four groups, the researcher might employ a single-factor analysis of variance for mean responses and a single-sample chi-square for frequency reactions.

In addition to the usual sources of invalidity associated with experimentation, the pretest-posttest design is especially vulnerable to the

reactivity problem called test sensitization. As explained in Chapter 9, **test sensitization** results from the probability that experimental subjects will recall pretest items. Recall alone or recall in combination with the experimental manipulation can affect posttest responses and jeopardize a study's internal validity. The next two simple experiments are designed to negate this validity problem partially or completely.

## Posttest-only control group design

As Table 10.2 shows, the **posttest-only control group design** is identical to a pretest-posttest control group arrangement except that pretesting is eliminated. As a consequence, significance of difference tests are computed on postmanipulation scores only.

Although reliance on posttest-only measures alleviates the interaction between test sensitization and the experimental manipulation, it introduces a second potentially troublesome internal invalidity problem. If control and experimental groups are not pretested, the experimenter cannot be sure that the two groups are comparable, especially if sample sizes are

**208**

PART III
Contemporary
Research
Designs in
Communi-
cation

small. Noncomparable groups, of course, destroy an experiment's internal validity. For this reason, a posttest only, control group design should be used only when a researcher is confident that experimental and control groups are in fact comparable on variables of interest. Careful random assignment of a large randomly selected sample to experimental and control groups should ensure that the two groups are comparable.

### Solomon four-group design

As Table 10.2 indicates, the **Solomon four-group design** combines the first two designs into a single experimental paradigm. Assuming that a large representative sample of research participants is randomly assigned to the four groups, the combination design ensures group comparability. At the same time, the design accounts for the main effects of pretest sensitization as well as any effects resulting from an interaction between pretest recall and the experimental manipulation. Since neither of the two control groups is exposed to a manipulation, any observed differences in their posttest responses represent a main effect of pretest sensitization. Any observed differences between the two experimental groups' pretest to posttest scores reflect the interaction effects of pretesting and the experimental manipulation. To isolate the unconfounded main effect of the experimental manipulation, a researcher subtracts control group differences from experimental group differences.

The Solomon four-group design is perhaps the most internally valid simple design available to communication researchers. Pretesting two of the four groups serves to verify experimental and control group comparability; yet by eliminating pretests in the second pair of groups the researcher can isolate the uncontaminated effects of a given experimental manipulation.

## Complex Factorial Designs

Complex experimental designs assess the main and interaction effects of two or more independent variables each having two or more treatment levels. These research paradigms are called **factorial designs** and are often identified with multiplicative labels ($2 \times 2$, $2 \times 4$, $2 \times 2 \times 3$, and so forth). As we learned earlier, a $2 \times 2$ design has two independent variables with two treatment levels each, a $2 \times 4$ has two independent variables with two and four treatment levels respectively, and a $2 \times 2 \times 3$ design has three independent variables with two, two, and three treatments respectively.

Three factorial designs are used frequently in communication research: an independent groups design, a repeated measures design, and a mixed independent groups/repeated measures design.[8] These three designs differ regarding methods of assigning research subjects to experimental cells.

### Independent groups design

An **independent groups design** is characterized by the random assignment of different research subjects to each separate cell of an experiment. Case 1 in Table 10.3 depicts a $2 \times 2$ independent groups arrangement designed to test the effects on learning of live versus videotaped classroom lectures delivered in small versus large classrooms. Notice that 10 subjects (Ss) have been randomly assigned to each of the four experimental cells and that no subject is assigned to more than one cell. Thus, the first 10 subjects ($S_1, \ldots, S_{10}$) of the total random sample of 40 are assigned to one cell, 10 different subjects ($S_{11}, \ldots, S_{20}$) constitute a second cell, and so forth. Each cell contains an independent group of research participants who are exposed to one and only one combination of the design's independent variables; hence the name.

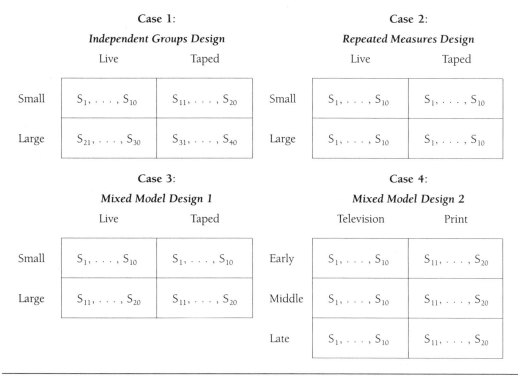

**Case 1:**

*Independent Groups Design*

|  | Live | Taped |
|---|---|---|
| Small | $S_1, \ldots, S_{10}$ | $S_{11}, \ldots, S_{20}$ |
| Large | $S_{21}, \ldots, S_{30}$ | $S_{31}, \ldots, S_{40}$ |

**Case 2:**

*Repeated Measures Design*

|  | Live | Taped |
|---|---|---|
| Small | $S_1, \ldots, S_{10}$ | $S_1, \ldots, S_{10}$ |
| Large | $S_1, \ldots, S_{10}$ | $S_1, \ldots, S_{10}$ |

**Case 3:**

*Mixed Model Design 1*

|  | Live | Taped |
|---|---|---|
| Small | $S_1, \ldots, S_{10}$ | $S_1, \ldots, S_{10}$ |
| Large | $S_{11}, \ldots, S_{20}$ | $S_{11}, \ldots, S_{20}$ |

**Case 4:**

*Mixed Model Design 2*

|  | Television | Print |
|---|---|---|
| Early | $S_1, \ldots, S_{10}$ | $S_{11}, \ldots, S_{20}$ |
| Middle | $S_1, \ldots, S_{10}$ | $S_{11}, \ldots, S_{20}$ |
| Late | $S_1, \ldots, S_{10}$ | $S_{11}, \ldots, S_{20}$ |

## Repeated measures design

Case 2 in Table 10.3 shows that in a **repeated measures design**, the same group of 10 randomly selected experimental subjects participates in every cell of the experiment. Aside from this critical feature, repeated measures and independent groups designs are identical.

## Mixed independent groups/repeated measures design

In a **mixed independent groups/repeated measures design**, different subjects are randomly assigned to the treatment levels associated with at least one independent variable, whereas the same subjects participate in the treatments associated with a second independent variable.

Case 3 of Table 10.3 illustrates this mixed model design. Notice that different subjects participate in the small-classroom versus the large-classroom conditions. However, everyone in the small classroom hears both the live and videotaped lectures as does everyone in the large classroom. Thus, an independent groups perspective is associated with the variable "classroom size," whereas repeated measures apply to the independent variable "lecture type."

## Selecting an appropriate factorial design

Since the same research problem can be investigated using any of these three designs, it will be useful to examine the relative merits of each. A

**210**

PART III
Contemporary
Research
Designs in
Communi-
cation

repeated measures approach, employed separately or in combination with independent groups, is said to have three principal advantages. First, from a theoretical perspective, a repeated measures design offers the researcher perfectly comparable experimental groups (since all cells contain the same people). As a practical matter, this advantage is compromised by sensitization effects resulting from repeated exposures to different independent treatments and to pretesting and posttesting instruments.

Second, a repeated measures design requires fewer research participants than an independent groups design. Thus, if one's pool of experimental subjects is severely limited, a repeated measures design may be the only feasible alternative. Finally, when one independent variable is the passage of time (that is, when the study is longitudinal), a repeated measures approach may be a wise choice. To explain, suppose I were interested in the attitudinal effects of televised versus printed political advertisements during the early, middle, and late stages of an election campaign. Case 4 in Table 10.3 displays a mixed model for investigating this problem. Although independent groups are exposed to the two types of political advertisements, the same groups are tested at three stages of the political campaign.

Clearly, a repeated measures design should be used only in special cases, most particularly when time passage is an independent variable, or alternately, in those rare instances of limited availability of experimental subjects. Otherwise, an independent groups design with random subject assignment is the preferred option. The independent groups approach avoids test sensitization, which may threaten the internal validity of a repeated measures design, yet it assures comparable experimental groups through random sample selection and random subject assignment.

## Statistical analysis of factorial designs

Multiple-factor analysis of variance, discussed in Chapter 7, is a commonly used statistical tool for assessing the main and interaction effects of traditional factorial designs. Within the family of ANOVA methods, specialized procedures are available for exploring repeated measures effects, independent groups effects, and mixed model effects.[9] When independent variables are continuous rather than discrete, multiple correlation and regression analysis, described in Chapter 8, is often used to assess a design's main and interaction effects.

Whether one uses analysis of variance or regression methods, interaction effects are often analyzed and interpreted by computing systematic pairwise comparisons between experimental cells results. Recall from Chapter 7 that pairwise comparison procedures are modified $t$ tests that assess significance differences between all possible pairs of cells in an experimental design. Frequently used pairwise comparison methods include the Student Newman-Keuls test, Duncan's multiple range test, and Scheffé's procedure.[10] A researcher clarifies the meaning of an interaction effect only by isolating exactly which individual cell findings differ significantly from others.

## PROCEDURES FOR CONDUCTING AN EXPERIMENT

Regardless of the nature of one's design, five steps are required to conduct an experiment: select an experimental setting, operationalize and validate the independent and dependent variables, select a sample of subjects and assign sample members to the experimental cells, administer the experiment, and analyze the experimental results. Strategic choices at each stage of research are guided by the nature of the research hypothesis to be tested.

## Selecting an Experimental Setting

Selecting an experimental setting involves determining whether a given research hypothesis can best be tested in a laboratory or a field environment. The relative importance of internal versus external validity is an important criterion for making this decision. If an experimenter seeks to isolate precise predictive connections between independent and dependent variables—that is, if internal validity is an overriding concern—the laboratory is preferred. However, a field experiment may be preferable when a researcher is primarily interested in generalizing findings to more natural social situations.

## Operationalizing and Validating Variables

As we have seen, operationalization procedures differ depending on an independent variable's stimulus or organismic character. For stimulus variables, researchers must physically construct manipulations or treatment levels, whereas organismic variables can simply be isolated. Additionally, a variable's continuous versus discrete character bears on operationalization. If a variable is discrete, its natural subdivisions can become experimental treatment levels. Operationalizing naturally continuous variables requires more deliberation. The researcher may allow them to remain continuous or decide to render them discrete. Once an independent variable has been operationalized, the researcher should check its validity by assessing the match between subjects' perceptions of the manipulations and the researcher's conception of them.

Dependent variables are operationalized by constructing scales—either nominal, ordinal, interval, or ratio—for measuring them. Discrete dependent variables are measured nominally, whereas continuous variables may be measured on ordinal, interval, or ratio scales. All the scale construction techniques discussed in Chapter 4 are applicable to measuring dependent variables. Recall that some of the more common instruments for measuring dependent variables are Likert scales, semantic differentials, and free-response scales. Once a measuring instrument has been constructed, it should be assessed for validity and reliability using procedures detailed in Chapter 3. Recall that validity assessment strategies include the content procedure, the predictive approach, the known groups method, and the convergence technique. Frequently used reliability tests are the test-retest method, the alternative forms approach, and the internal consistency procedure.

## Selecting and Assigning Subjects to Experimental Cells

Regardless of the nature of a design, one's total sample of experimental subjects must be representative of the parent population of interest. Recall from Chapter 5 that representative samples may be selected using one of several probability methods, including simple random sampling and systematic sampling with a random start. Methods of assigning members of a representative sample to experimental cells vary depending on the research design. With an independent groups design and all simple experiments, subjects are randomly assigned to different experimental cells, whereas a repeated measures approach uses the same subjects in each cell.

The stimulus-organismic characteristics of a design likewise influence subject assignment methods. All-stimulus designs employ random

**212**

PART III
Contemporary
Research
Designs in
Communi-
cation

assignment, whereas all-organismic studies require the researcher to purposively place different random samples in their appropriate experimental cells. In general, random cell assignment is the standard subject distribution procedure. We depart from this approach in special circumstances, as when we employ a repeated measures design or include only organismic variables in a study. If random assignment is infeasible, we learned in Chapter 9 that matched subject and intact groups methods may be used as default options.

## Administering the Experiment

The experimental methodology is especially vulnerable to reactivity effects like demand characteristics, evaluation apprehension, and researcher effects. For example, experimental subjects who learn the research hypothesis often deliberately try to confirm or disconfirm it depending on their reactions to the experimenter and the experiment itself.

As explained in Chapter 9, administering an experiment usually entails providing clear instructions about experimental activities, devising and presenting credible cover stories, and fully debriefing subjects regarding an experiment's true nature. Chapter 14 deals fully with the ethical aspects of experimental deception.

## Analyzing Experimental Results

Analyzing results involves selecting appropriate statistical tools for assessing the main and interaction effects of independent variables. Available statistical methods were detailed in Chapters 7 and 8 and reviewed earlier in this chapter. Because of the complex numerical calculations associated with many experiments, computer-assisted computation is a useful adjunct to a full analysis of experimental findings.

## THE EXPERIMENT AND CONTEMPORARY RESEARCH

The popularity of the traditional experiment has declined somewhat in recent years for two reasons. First, many communication researchers consider the experiment an unduly artificial research methodology. "Artificial" qualities include the distorting effects of the traditional experiment on continuous independent variables and its capacity to handle only a small number of variables at a time. Second, a number of communication scholars have criticized the "functional" nature of both traditional and nontraditional experiments, arguing that experimental procedures ignore the meanings inherent in human talk, focusing instead on peripheral causes and effects.

Despite these criticisms, the experiment remains a powerful tool in the communication researcher's methodological arsenal. When researchers wish to establish internally valid explanatory relationships, a well-constructed and well-conducted experiment is often superior to the more naturalistic and "interpretive" research designs that we shall investigate in the remaining chapters of Part III.

## INTERFACE: CHAPTERS 10 AND 11

In this chapter, we have explored the nature and uses of experimental research. Procedures for operationalizing and validating independent and dependent variables were discussed. I examined several simple experimental designs as well as some complex factorial designs. The nature of main and interaction effects was described, and guidelines for conducting an experiment were presented.

The next chapter will discuss survey research. Unlike much experimental research, survey research often has an applied orientation. Thus, it is a useful methodology for researchers who wish to explore practical as well as theoretical problems in human communication.

## MAIN POINTS

**1.** An experiment is a functional research design whose purpose is to explain the impact that certain input variables, called independent variables, exert on outcome variables known as dependent variables.

**2.** Independent variables may be continuous or discrete and stimulus or organismic. A continuous variable contains values that vary along a spectrum from low to high, whereas a discrete variable changes in distinct steps. A stimulus variable is an external manipulation; an organismic variable is an internal characteristic of research participants.

**3.** Independent variables are operationalized by specifying exactly how they will be presented to research participants, resulting in clearly defined treatment levels.

**4.** The continuous-discrete and stimulus-organismic qualities of independent variables influence operationalizing procedures. Naturally continuous variables may remain continuous or may be rendered discrete by splitting them into categorical values. The natural categories of discrete variables usually become experimental treatment levels. A stimulus variable must be constructed by researchers, whereas researchers simply discover and use organismic variables.

**5.** There are three general types of experimental designs based on the stimulus-organismic character of the independent variables: an all-stimulus paradigm, an all-organismic

paradigm, and a mixed model paradigm that includes at least one stimulus variable and at least one organismic variable. Subjects are randomly assigned to experimental cells of the all-stimulus design, but purposive assignment is required in all-organismic paradigms. The mixed model paradigm combines these two assignment procedures.

**6.** Independent variables are validated using both prior and concurrent validity checks. A stimulus variable is assumed to be valid if research participants perceive its manipulations as the researcher conceived them. An organismic variable is validated by direct observation for manifest variables. Latent organismic variables are often validated by means of written questionnaires or physiological assessments of research participants to establish the existence of relevant internal states.

**7.** A main effect refers to the unique impact of each independent variable on a dependent measure, whereas an interaction effect reflects the joint impact of two or more independent variables on a dependent measure.

**8.** Interaction effects may be classified as ordinal or disordinal and as symmetrical or nonsymmetrical.

**9.** An ordinal interaction signifies that one independent variable exhibits significant differences at one treatment level of a second variable, but not at another level. A disordinal interaction means that a first independent variable produces significant effects at all levels of a second variable. A symmetrical interaction represents a reversal of one independent variable's effects at a second variable's treatment levels, whereas a nonsymmetrical interaction means that an independent variable's effects are not reversed at a second variable's treatment levels.

**10.** A field experiment is conducted in a natural setting; a laboratory experiment is conducted in a controlled environment.

**11.** A cover story is an instruction that mis-

**214**

PART III
Contemporary
Research
Designs in
Communi-
cation

leads participants about the nature of an experiment; debriefings inform participants of a study's true purpose.

**12.** In trying to establish internal validity, we ask whether sample main and interaction effects are attributable solely to the independent variables, whereas to ascertain external validity we must determine whether sample results are generalizable to parent populations.

**13.** Simple experiments assess a single independent variable's effects. Three simple designs are: the pretest-posttest control group design; the posttest-only control group design; and the Solomon four-group design.

**14.** A pretest-posttest control group experiment randomly assigns subjects to either an experimental group or a control group and then pretests both groups. After the experimental group has received a manipulation, both groups are posttested to assess the manipulation's effects. The posttest only, control group design is identical except that pretesting is eliminated. The Solomon four-group design combines these two designs into a single experimental paradigm. The Solomon design is probably the most internally valid simple experimental design.

**15.** Complex factorial designs assess the main and interaction effects of two or more independent variables, each having two or more treatment levels. Three types of factorial designs are an independent groups design, a repeated measures design, and a mixed independent groups/repeated measures design.

**16.** An independent groups design is characterized by the random assignment of different research subjects to each experimental cell, whereas a repeated measures design assigns the same sample of subjects to every cell. A mixed design assigns different subjects to one independent variable's treatment cells, but the same subjects to the treatments of a second independent variable. Unless there are special circum-

stances, an independent groups design is the preferred option.

**17.** Five steps are required to conduct an experiment: select an experimental setting, operationalize and validate the independent and dependent variables, select the subjects and assign them to experimental cells, administer the experiment, and analyze the experimental results. Strategic choices at each stage are guided by the nature of the research question or hypothesis.

# REVIEW EXERCISES

**1.** Consider the following hypothesis: Fear appeals in persuasive messages lead to different compliance rates among old and young listeners. Explain how you might operationalize and validate the two independent variables: "fear appeals" and "age." How might you measure the dependent variable "compliance rates"?

**2.** Design an experiment to test the hypothesis presented in Exercise 1. How many cells does the experiment have? Describe how you would select a representative sample of subjects and assign the subjects to the experimental cells. How does the stimulus-organismic nature of your independent variables affect subject assignment methods?

**3.** Suppose you wish to study the impact of a particular Saturday morning instructional television program on children's learning. Design the following three simple experiments to investigate the problem: a pretest-posttest control group design, a posttest-only control group design, and a Solomon four-group design. Which of the three should provide the most valid results? Why?

**4.** Consider the hypothesis: The medium for transmitting musical performances (audio versus video) and the time of transmission (morning versus evening) affect listeners' emotional responses to the music. Design the following three experiments for testing this hypothesis: an independent groups design, a repeated measures design, and a mixed independent groups/repeated measures design.

**5.** Make up some results for a four-cell experiment required to test the hypothesis in Exercise 4 that will illustrate effects of the following kinds: (a) a main effect for the independent variable "medium of transmission," (b) no main effect for the independent variable "time of transmission," (c) no interaction between the two independent variables, (d) an ordinal and nonsymmetrical interaction effect, (e) a disordinal and nonsymmetrical interaction effect, and (f) a disordinal and symmetrical interaction effect.

**6.** Construct a cover story and debriefing information for one of the experiments you described in Exercise 4.

# NOTES

**1.** See Paul de Kruif, *Microbe Hunters* (New York: Harcourt, Brace, 1926).

**2.** Naturally occurring differences such as gender, race, and age are not "treatment" levels in the strictest sense of the term. However, my usage follows the lead of many writers who, as a matter of convenience, refer to both natural and artificially created distinctions as "experimental treatments." See C. Mitchell Dayton, *The Design of Educational Experiments* (New York: McGraw-Hill, 1970), p. 3.

**3.** This distinction is taken from Gerald R. Miller, "Research Setting: Laboratory Studies," in *Methods of Research in Communication*, eds. Philip Emmert and William D. Brooks (Boston: Houghton Mifflin, 1970), pp. 77–104.

**4.** Miller, pp. 85–93. Miller uses the labels "experimental paradigm" and "investigational paradigm" for what I call "all-stimulus" and "all-organismic" designs, respectively.

**5.** These classifications are discussed in Fred N. Kerlinger, *Foundations of Behavioral Research*, 2nd ed. (New York: Holt, Rinehart & Winston, 1973), pp. 265–267.

**6.** The following discussion draws heavily on Miller, pp. 77–85.

**7.** These three simple designs are discussed extensively by Donald T. Campbell and Julian C. Stanley, *Experimental and Quasi-Experimental Designs for Research* (Chicago: Rand McNally, 1963), pp. 13–27.

**8.** These and other factorial designs are detailed in Dayton; and Paul C. Cozby, *Methods in Behavioral Research*, 3rd ed. (Palo Alto, CA.: Mayfield, 1985), pp. 65–91.

**9.** See *SPSS* *User's Guide* (New York: McGraw-Hill, 1983), pp. 465–539; and W. J. Dixon (ed.), *BMDP Statistical Software* (Berkeley, CA: University of California Press, 1983), pp. 347–412.

**10.** For a discussion of pairwise comparison tests, see Dayton, pp. 37–56.

# 11

# SURVEY RESEARCH

This chapter discusses the nature and functions of survey research, which is a process of examining samples of communication behavior for purposes of inferring conclusions about the populations from which the samples were selected. Detailed instructions for conducting survey research are presented. Methods of selecting representative survey samples are described, as are practical guidelines for designing survey questionnaires. The chapter concludes with a discussion of techniques of administering surveys and analyzing survey results.

# CHAPTER OUTLINE

urvey research has a long and distinguished history. Its origins can be traced to ancient Egyptian monarchs, who gathered information about their subjects for the apparent purpose of devising efficient methods of governance.[1] Our own Bureau of the Census continues this tradition, collecting detailed economic and demographic data that are used, for example, in congressional redistricting and socioeconomic planning. In the communication discipline, survey research has long been a standard research method. Lazarsfeld and Merton conducted surveys in the 1940s and 1950s to assess mass media's impact on voting behaviors and American social norms.[2] Contemporary researchers continue this practice, surveying the social and cultural effects of mass communication, including media violence, sexism, and racism.[3]

This chapter examines survey research as a scientific method of communication inquiry. I begin by describing functions of surveys and their types. Then, methods of conducting survey research are presented. Pertinent topics include selecting a survey sample, designing the survey questionnaire, administering a survey, and analyzing survey results. Many of the practical guidelines presented in the chapter are applicable not only to survey research but also to various forms of communication research.

## THE NATURE OF SURVEY RESEARCH

**Survey research** usually examines a single sample for the purpose of inferring conclusions about the population from which the sample was drawn. Since its utility depends on sample representativeness, survey research carefully applies the principles of probability sampling discussed in Chapter 5. Survey methods can serve both basic and applied research purposes. Recall from Chapter 9 that basic research explores theoretical relationships with little regard for their practical implications and typically is conducted in laboratory settings. Applied research is concerned with both the theoretical and practical sides of communicative life; it explores theoretical relationships for the purpose of understanding and solving problems. Because of its pragmatic posture, applied research usually takes place in field settings.

Survey research often has an applied orientation, yet it is not inherently pragmatic. It frequently is used to generate basic theoretical information with little practical application. However, survey research is particularly well suited to applied data analysis. For that reason, it is a useful research tool for scholars who wish to explore theoretical as well as practical communication problems.

## Functions of Survey Research

Surveys serve two principal functions: description and explanation. *Description* is a common function that produces a profile of pertinent characteristics of populations from which samples are drawn. For example, mass communication researchers often conduct surveys to determine the demographic characteristics, attitudes, and preferences of television viewers. Alternately, organizational researchers may survey employees to ascertain their perceptions of work-related communication problems. Researchers often use such data to adjust the content and schedule of media programming and to alleviate organizational difficulties.

Surveys that generate *explanations* build on descriptive data and explore the underlying theoretical reasons for descriptions. For instance, our hypothetical mass communication researcher might go beyond describing viewers' attitudes and preferences to examine the reasons for the opinions. Likewise, an organizational researcher could search for theoretical

**220**

PART III
Contemporary
Research
Designs in
Communi-
cation

factors that explain employees' self-described communication problems. Explanatory information is often used to evaluate previously described communication problems and to suggest solutions for them.

Many communication surveys serve both functions, although some will emphasize one more than the other. Decisions about which functions are appropriate depend on the research question or on the hypothesis itself.

# Types of Surveys

There are two basic survey research designs: cross-sectional and longitudinal. I discuss these in turn.

## Cross-sectional surveys

A **cross-sectional survey** collects information from a sample at a single point in time. Polls of election preferences are classic examples of cross-sectional surveys, telling us about people's voting intentions on the day the research is conducted. Surveys of viewers' reactions to mass media often capture only "here and now" attitudes, implying little about a viewer's past or probable future opinions. Similarly, many communication audits of business organizations emphasize employers' and employees' current perceptions of communication patterns and problems.

## Longitudinal surveys

**Longitudinal surveys**, which collect several samples of data at different points in time and therefore focus on changes in descriptions and explanations, can be trend or panel studies. A **trend study** selects different representative samples from the same population at different times, whereas a **panel study** follows the same sample across time, tapping its evolving characteristics at each test point. To illustrate, suppose I wish to study the changing attitudes of tele-

vision viewers toward minority characters portrayed during prime time. To conduct a trend study, I might survey viewers at four-month intervals for one year, selecting different random samples at each of the three test points. By contrast, a panel study would survey the same sample of viewers at every test period.

The choice between these two approaches depends on three factors: the size of the population, the nature of the research question, and the validity problems posed by the two methods. First, a trend study is feasible only if the target population is quite large. For example, a researcher might wish to study the communication problems of a business employing fewer than 50 people. However, this employee population is so small that multiple random samples could not be drawn from it; thus a panel study of either a single random sample or the entire population would be necessary. Second, some research problems require a purposive rather than a representative sample. If the researcher is interested in studying a particular population subset—for example, a specific business organization or a designated group of families—a panel study is the only design capable of yielding pertinent information.

Third, the comparative validity problems posed by the two methods may affect one's decision. The validity of a panel study depends on a researcher's ability to follow the same people over time without suffering high mortality or attrition rates. As defined in Chapter 9, **mortality** refers to the loss of original sample members: perhaps due to death or illness, to the unwillingness of some to participate in all phases of a study, or to a researcher's inability to locate all sample members at each test period. The lengthier the panel study, the greater the chance of high mortality. For this reason, a trend approach may achieve greater validity when a researcher plans a very long term study, say, one lasting a year or more. For shorter research periods, the panel study is a more feasible option.

### A design variation: Multiple-sample surveys

Although cross-sectional and longitudinal surveys typically examine a single sample drawn from one population, they may simultaneously study two or more samples. These **multiple-sample surveys** aim to describe and explain relationships among two or more populations. For example, we might survey men and women to determine whether their attitudes toward television news differ. Alternately, we could sample single- and dual-parent families to compare patterns of verbal conflict. Since multiple sample surveys allow researchers to compare and contrast different populations, they are akin to naturalistic experiments using all organismic variables.

## Conducting Survey Research

Whether one's design is cross-sectional or longitudinal, survey research entails the following four procedures: selecting a representative survey sample, designing a survey questionnaire, administering the survey questionnaire, and analyzing the survey results. Strategic choices at each procedural stage are guided by the nature of the research problem, which therefore should be well thought out in advance of actual data collection. I will devote the balance of this chapter to an analysis of these critical research stages.

## SELECTING A REPRESENTATIVE SURVEY SAMPLE

Five tasks are required for selecting a representative survey sample: defining the population, specifying sampling elements, securing an adequate sampling frame, selecting a probability sampling method, and determining the required sample size.

## Defining the Population

Survey researchers study samples to be able to infer conclusions about parent populations, the well-defined groups or universal sets pertinent to individual research problems. The researcher must carefully define the population of interest. In a study of political attitudes, the population might be all registered voters. Alternately, it could be defined as registered voters who have voted in at least one national election over the past four years. The exact contours of a population are dictated by the requirements of particular research questions or hypotheses.

## Specifying Sampling Elements

Recall from Chapter 5 that sampling **elements** are the "things" under study in a given population.[4] In many surveys, the elements are individual communicators whose demographic characteristics, attitudes, and behaviors interest a researcher. However, other entities may serve as elements as well. For example, groups of two or more people are often elements in organizational and small group surveys. Additionally, a person's environment or communication context can serve as an element.

To illustrate context elements, suppose I wish to study situational variables that influence people's choice of news sources. This research problem lends itself to a *context study*, that is, a survey designed to gather information about respondents' physical and social environments (family size, neighborhoods, friendship circles, and so forth). Although elements other than individuals can be surveyed, it is important to understand that people—called *observation units* in Chapter 5—must always be selected to report on the elements of interest.

**222**

PART III
Contemporary
Research
Designs in
Communi-
cation

## Securing an Adequate Sampling Frame

To infer sample results to populations, a researcher must secure a **representative sample** of elements, one that reflects well the characteristics of its parent population. A prerequisite to securing a representative sample is the availability of a **sampling frame**, defined earlier as a list of the elements in a population. Telephone directories often serve as sampling frames for the residents of a city, just as voter registration rolls are sampling frames for populations of registered voters.

Since sampling frames are concrete representations of populations, they should be as complete and accurate as possible. Indeed, the ideal sampling frame lists "each population element once and only once" and contains "no other listings."[5] We rarely have access to ideal sampling frames, but instead must rely on the best population list available. However, if the best available frame is seriously defective, our results will be unrepresentative, a conclusion underscored by several early political polling disasters. We learned in Chapter 5 that the *Literary Digest*'s erroneous prediction of Franklin Roosevelt's defeat in the 1936 presidential election was due largely to a flawed sampling frame. Similarly, George Gallup used 1940 census data as a frame for projecting the outcome of the 1948 presidential contest between incumbent Harry S Truman and Republican challenger Thomas E. Dewey. Because substantial segments of the American population had migrated from rural to urban areas between 1940 and 1948, Gallup's sample seriously underrepresented urban dwellers who favored Truman's reelection. Among other factors, this unrepresentative sampling frame led Gallup to wrongly predict that Dewey would defeat the incumbent President.

As these examples emphasize, if a sampling frame does not represent its parent population reasonably well, survey results will not accurately reflect population parameters. Three sampling frame deficiencies seriously threaten the validity of survey findings: missing elements, foreign elements, and duplicate elements.[6] If a sampling frame is found to contain a high incidence of one or more of these defects, the researcher must either correct the frame with supplementary data or discard it in favor of a more representative list of population elements.

### Missing elements

**Missing elements** are legitimate members of a population that are not listed in a sampling frame. Examples of missing elements include the low-income individuals excluded from the *Literary Digest*'s 1936 poll and urban dwellers missing from Gallup's 1948 sampling frame. Common reasons for missing elements are dated frames, as illustrated by the use of 1940 census data in a 1948 poll, and by frames that exclude large and well-defined segments of the population, like the 1936 roster.

If a researcher's sampling frame has missing elements, two corrective actions are available. The preferred method is to acquire supplementary frames that allow the insertion of the missing elements. If supplemental information is unavailable, the researcher must redefine the population to exclude missing elements. Thus, if a researcher who wishes to collect a sample of all college students discovers that graduate and professional students are missing from the only available sampling frame, the population must be redefined as undergraduate students instead of all college students.

### Foreign elements

**Foreign elements** are "listings for elements that no longer exist in the population,"[7] for example, people who have died or have moved out of the population. The only effective correction, deletion of the inappropriate elements, requires supplemental information allowing the survey researcher to identify individuals who no longer belong in the population. Such information usually can be acquired from updated frames or separate rosters of lost population members.

### Duplicate elements

**Duplicate elements** are population members who are listed more than once in a sampling frame. Multiple listings create difficulties because the chance of selecting such elements is greater than their incidence in the population warrants. The problem usually can be eliminated by carefully inspecting the frame for identical names coupled with supplemental listings of recently departed population members.

## Selecting a Sampling Method

Once researchers have secured an adequate sampling frame, they must choose an appropriate strategy for drawing a representative sample from the population embodied by the frame. Except for specialized surveys that require purposive sampling techniques, the researcher should use one of the probability sampling methods discussed in Chapter 5. These options include simple random sampling, systematic sampling with a random start, stratified sampling incorporating simple or systematic random methods, and multistage cluster sampling combined with simple or systematic procedures.

If the researcher has a reasonably complete and accurate sampling frame, a stratified sampling design using systematic selection with a random start might be a good choice. Recall that stratified sampling divides one's frame elements into homogeneous subsets, such as males and females, whites and nonwhites, young and old. Then, the researcher systematically selects every *k*th element from within each homogeneous subset, picking the first element at random. Alternately, researchers can select a simple random sample from each subset.

When an adequate listing of all population elements is unavailable or the population itself is exceptionally large, a multistage cluster method using systematic or simple random selection procedures is a reasonable choice. Recall that a multistage cluster approach begins by randomly selecting homogeneous groups from a large population, after which elements within these groups are randomly selected. Although the multistage procedure typically has a greater sampling error than a single-stage approach, it is often the only feasible alternative when researchers are interested in very large populations that lack comprehensive sampling frames.

## Determining the Required Sample Size

I emphasized in Chapter 5 that sampling error is reduced either by increasing population homogeneity or by increasing one's sample size. In this section, I shall describe a method for determining the minimum sample size needed to ensure adequate population representativeness. As we shall see, required sample sizes depend on the relative homogeneity as well as the size of the parent population.

To determine a minimally adequate sample size, a researcher begins by specifying some desired **confidence level** along with a desired **confidence interval**; in other words, the amount of sampling error the researcher is willing to tolerate must be stipulated at some preferred probability level. To illustrate, suppose we want to be 95% confident (confidence level) that a population parameter will deviate from a sample statistic by no more than $\pm 3$ percentage points (confidence interval). Recall from Chapter 6 that this decision implies that: $\pm 1.96 \times s_{\bar{p}} = \pm 3\%$, where $s_{\bar{p}}$ represents the standard error of proportions and $\pm 1.96$ is the point on either side of a normal sampling distribution's mean that delimits 95% of the area under the distribution curve.

**224**

PART III
Contemporary
Research
Designs in
Communi-
cation

Recall also that the formula for calculating a standard error of proportions at the 95% level of confidence is:

$$s_{\bar{p}(.95)} = \pm 1.96 \sqrt{\frac{pq}{n}},$$

where $\pm 1.96$ is the interval delimiting 95% of the area under a normal distribution's curve, $p$ estimates the proportion of the survey population responding in a specified way, $q$ is $1 - p$, and $n$ is the sample size. More generally, $pq$ is an estimate of population homogeneity. For purposes of calculating projected sample sizes at the 95% confidence level, this formula can be transformed into the equation:

$$n = \frac{(\pm 1.96)^2(pq)}{s_{\bar{p}(.95)}^2},$$

where $n$ is an estimate of required sample size when a 95% confidence level is desired.

By carefully inspecting this formula, the reader will recognize that the higher the value of $p$ relative to $q$ (or alternately, $q$ relative to $p$), the smaller the required sample size. This is so because higher values of $p$ (or $q$) indicate greater population homogeneity. As we learned in Chapter 5, smaller samples are required to adequately represent homogeneous populations than are needed to reflect the characteristics of heterogeneous groups.

## Calculating initial
## sample size estimates

To employ our sample size formula, we must estimate population homogeneity by determining the probable value of $p$. This means we must estimate what proportion of our parent population can be expected to respond in some specified way on a given survey research measure. To illustrate, suppose we are studying the attitudes of a university's student body toward a proposed tuition hike. Based on such information as letters to the campus newspaper and word-of-mouth sources, suppose we estimate

that at least 70% of all students are opposed to increased tuition ($p$). Since this is only an educated guess, we should settle on a conservative or safe final estimate of population homogeneity. A good rule of thumb is to lower one's best estimate of $p$ by about 10 percentage points— in this case to 60%. (An even more conservative approach would assume that $p = q$; that is, that both $p$ and $q$ are 50%.) By lowering our best guess of a population parameter, we can be reasonably sure that our final estimate will be within the expected population response range.

Once we have settled on an estimate for $p$ (in this case, we will use 60%), the required sample size can be computed as follows:

$$n = \frac{(\pm 1.96)^2(.60 \times .40)}{\pm .03^2} = 1024,$$

indicating the need for at least 1024 elements if we want a sampling error of no more than $\pm 3$ percentage points at a 95% confidence level ($\pm 1.96$ delimits 95% of the sampling distribution's curve). Notice that we would require a smaller sample if our population were extremely homogeneous. For instance, if there were strong evidence that 80% of the student population opposed the projected tuition hike ($p$), we would need a sample of only 683 students.

## Calculating final
## sample size estimates

Required sample size depends not only on population homogeneity, but also on the size of the parent population relative to the sample. The smaller the population relative to the sample, the fewer the required number of sample elements. Thus, we need some means of correcting our estimated sample size of 1024 based on its relationship to the size of the parent population. The following formula provides such a correction:

$$n' = \frac{Nn}{N + n},$$

where $n'$ is our final sample size estimate, $N$ denotes the population size, and $n$ is our initial sample size estimate. If the total student body at our hypothetical university numbers 10,000, the final required sample size is:

$$n' = \frac{10,000 \times 1024}{10,000 + 1024} = 929.$$

Given a moderately heterogeneous (60/40) population of 10,000, we require a random sample of at least 929 students to generate findings that should reflect well the parent population's characteristics. When population size is unknown, the researcher must estimate sample size solely on the basis of the projected population's homogeneity.

# DESIGNING A SURVEY QUESTIONNAIRE

To gather sample information pertinent to a given research problem, the researcher must design a data collection instrument similar to one of those described in Chapter 4. Instruments for collecting survey data are called **questionnaires**. Designing a survey questionnaire entails five tasks: (1) determine the types of questions required, (2) construct questions that will elicit the desired information from respondents, (3) organize the questions in patterns that maximize chances of getting the required information, (4) develop appropriate instructions for responding to questions, and (5) design an attractive presentational format. Standards for completing all these tasks are geared toward collecting the kind and quality of information needed to respond adequately to the research question or hypothesis. Importantly, the guidelines presented in this section are applicable not only to survey questionnaires, but to the construction of measuring instruments of many kinds, including those used in experimental research.

# Types of Survey Questions

Any one survey question can be classified by content and by structure. A question's content refers to the kind of information it solicits from respondents; and its structure indicates the way in which response options are organized. Questions are often categorized by content as fact or opinion and by structure as closed or open-ended. Additionally, a special technique that calls for the use of contingency and filter questioning may be superimposed on the four varieties of questions.

## Factual and opinion questions

**Factual questions** solicit information about a respondent's background and his or her communication behaviors or habits. Background information includes demographic data like gender, age, marital status, education level, and income. Behavioral data are elicited by questions such as "How many times during the average week do you read a daily newspaper?" and "How often do you watch afternoon television programs?"

**Opinion questions** seek information about a respondent's inner motives, intentions, and likes and dislikes. Such questions may ask people to express their level of agreement or disagreement with statements like: "Television news is more believable than corresponding news reported in a daily newspaper" and "My primary reason for talking with others is to get what I want from them." Other opinion questions ask respondents to rank communication events like television entertainment programs in the order of their preferences. In sum, any question seeking a verbal expression of a respondent's internal inclinations and attitudes is an opinion question.

Most problems that interest survey researchers require both factual and opinion questions, with the proportionate mix depending on the precise nature of the research question or hypothesis. For example, a survey

**226**

PART III
Contemporary
Research
Designs in
Communi-
cation

seeking to describe people's television viewing habits will likely require many factual questions. However, a study designed to explain the reasons for media preference patterns will include numerous opinion questions. As a general rule, descriptive surveys emphasize factual issues, whereas explanatory research requires more opinion-seeking questions.

### Closed and open-ended questions

As we learned in Chapter 4, a **closed question** is a forced-choice, information-seeking device asking respondents to choose their responses from a list supplied by the researcher. Rating questions, ranking questions, and inventory questions are closed questions often used in survey research. Typical **rating questions** are Likert scales and semantic differentials described fully in Chapter 4. Recall that a Likert scale is an opinion statement accompanied by a five-point or seven-point response scale. Respondents typically are asked the extent of their agreement or disagreement with the statement, or alternately, to indicate whether they believe the statement is accurate or inaccurate. Semantic differential scales measure the meaning of a communication construct on a series of seven-point bipolar adjective scales.

Contrasted with these two rating scales, a **ranking question** asks respondents to rank order a set of communication events according to some evaluative standard. An example is:

> Please rank the following four media in terms of their importance to you as a source of current events information. Give the medium you regard as most important a rank of "1" and the least important a rank of "4."
> ____Radio
> ____Newspapers
> ____Television
> ____Magazines

Finally, an **inventory question** provides respondents with a list and asks them to check all items on the list that apply to them. An example is:

> From which of the following media have you learned an important piece of national news over the last month? (Check all that apply.)
> ____Newspapers
> ____Magazines
> ____Word-of-mouth
> ____Radio
> ____Television
> ____Other

An **open-ended question** is a free-response scaling technique like that described in Chapter 4. It invites respondents to supply unstructured answers to questions or to discuss the subject(s) named. Examples of open-ended questions include: "What kinds of communication problems do you encounter most often when talking with your parents?" and "Describe the types of television programs you prefer."

Closed and open-ended questions have complementary advantages and drawbacks. Closed questions are easy to answer, yet researchers risk suppressing respondents' true beliefs and behaviors if they inadvertently exclude these responses from the available options. Open-ended questions eliminate this biasing effect, yet they ask respondents to expend considerable time and effort completing a questionnaire. The choice between the two approaches will depend on the nature of the research problem. If a researcher seeks mostly descriptive information, including considerable factual data, closed questions may be preferred. However, if explanatory information is required, open-ended questions will be useful. A common approach is to mix the two kinds, combining a series of closed questions with several follow-up free-response probes.

### Contingency and filter questions

A special kind of question that often appears in surveys is called a contingency question. **Contingency questions**, which may be either closed or open-ended, apply to a single subgroup of the total sample of respondents. This subset is identified by a closed question called a **filter question**. An example of a filter-contingency set is:

1. Do you own a videocassette recorder?
   ___Yes
   ___No
   If you answered "Yes," respond to questions 2–4.
   If you responded "No," skip to question 5.

Questions 2–4 will be contingency questions for the subset of persons owning videocassette recorders. They might include questions about brand preferences, the uses owners make of the equipment, and the like.

## Criteria for Constructing Questions

Survey questions should be constructed to yield the precise information a researcher needs to respond to a research problem. Moreover, they should allow respondents to complete them with as little effort as possible. The following five guidelines should help researchers achieve this dual objective. (Certain of these guidelines were referred to in Chapter 4.)

1. *Survey questions should be clear and unambiguous.* All words and phrases should have precise and easily understood meanings. The question "Do you read news magazines regularly?" is exceedingly ambiguous. Exactly what constitutes "news magazines" is subject to varying interpretations. Moreover, it is not clear whether the question refers to one magazine or several. Likewise, the word "regularly" is indefinite, capable of meaning anything from daily readings to one or two readings a month. Similarly, does "read" refer to an entire magazine or only parts of it? A less ambiguous question might be "Do you read one or more news reports in *Newsweek*, *Time*, *U.S. News and World Report*, or some other comparable news magazine every week?"
2. *A survey question should be simple and brief.* Words should be chosen for simplicity and ease of understanding. The open-ended question "What is your predisposition toward commercial advertising?" will be better understood if a more common term like "attitude" or "opinion" is substituted for "predisposition." If possible, sentence structure should be simple, containing a single subject-verb-object linkage, not compound-complex. Short and simple questions are usually clearer, and they can be responded to more quickly than long and complicated ones.
3. *Survey questions should not be leading.* **Leading questions** contain emotionally loaded language that encourages biased responses. A question like "Do you agree with the generally accepted view that television programs contain too much explicit violence?" is likely to encourage a positive response, whereas the substitution of "generally rejected" for "accepted" will probably encourage more negative reactions. Researchers can encourage unbiased responses by asking for respondents' opinions on an issue without appending emotionally loaded labels.
4. *Survey questions should not be double-barreled.* A **double-barreled question** asks for a single response to several questions. The question "Do you find the CBS program 'Sixty Minutes' informative and entertaining?" raises two different issues. A respondent might have one position on the program's informational value, yet hold quite a different view of its entertaining qualities. Double-barreled questions produce uninterpretable responses, and they have no place in well-constructed questionnaires.
5. *Survey questions should be as nonthreatening as possible.* Questions that ask respondents about personally or socially sensitive issues like their sexual behavior or drug habits are potentially threatening. People will sometimes refuse to respond or they may report "socially acceptable" responses differing from their private beliefs and behaviors.

**228**

PART III
Contemporary
Research
Designs in
Communi-
cation

When a researcher requires sensitive information, several practices can reduce a question's threatening qualities. If respondents are assured that their answers will remain confidential, they are more likely to respond openly and honestly. Additionally, questions can be worded so that the target attitudes or behaviors appear socially neutral. For example, a relatively nonthreatening form of the question "Do you approve of a homosexual life style?" might be, "Some people object to a homosexual life style, yet others do not. What is your view?[8]

## Ordering Questions in Survey Questionnaires

The order of presenting questions can affect people's responses. For instance, Belson found that opinion questions appearing early in a list of questions are more likely to be agreed to than ones appearing later.[9] Additionally, the wording of early questions can bias responses to subsequent related questions. Suppose respondents are asked first to rank various news media in terms of believability and then are presented with specific questions about individual news sources. Responses to later questions are likely to be biased by earlier general rankings. The following four guidelines are useful for achieving a satisfactory ordering of survey questions.

1. *Adopt a general organizational pattern that complements a survey's research objectives.* Two general patterns are available: the funnel sequence and the inverted funnel sequence. A **funnel pattern** begins with broad questions followed by progressively narrower or more specific ones. With this approach, questions about motion pictures in general would be followed by items asking about specific movies. In an **inverted funnel pattern**, narrowly focused questions are followed by more general ones.

Proponents of the funnel approach claim that respondents are more comfortable with general questions and that placing them first increases incentives to complete questionnaires. Inverted funnel advocates argue that specific questions are easier to answer and therefore more motivating for respondents. Moreover, they suggest that general questions followed by specific related ones may set up the biasing effect described earlier. Thus, the inverted funnel approach is preferred by many researchers who believe it is less vulnerable to question sequence biases. However, the funnel pattern should be chosen if the information a researcher requires lends itself to that organizational format.

2. *Topically related questions should be grouped together.* Questions that follow a logical sequence are always easier to answer than questions having no coherent order. Thus, researchers should group all questions pertinent to a single topic and then move to the next topical set, rather than mixing questions on multiple topics throughout a survey questionnaire.

3. *Easy-to-answer questions should be placed first.* Easy questions motivate respondents to continue a questionnaire, whereas difficult or time-consuming ones may be discouraging or frustrating. Among other things, this criterion implies that closed questions should precede open-ended ones and potentially threatening questions should be placed toward the end.

4. *Questions should be ordered to avoid establishing a response bias.* As described in Chapter 4, **response bias** is a tendency of some respondents to react to all closed questions the same way regardless of content. For example, a respondent may repeatedly check either "agreement" or "disagreement" on a sequence of Likert scales. Or, the middle position may be marked consistently on a set of semantic differentials. This response bias tendency might be countered by mixing

questions of different lengths and types, with Likert scales interspersed with ranking questions, open-ended ones, and so forth. Similarly, the positive and negative poles of semantic differential scales should be alternated. Importantly, structurally different questions may be mixed, but not the topics that questions address. Topically related questions should be grouped, as the second guideline suggested.

## Preparing Instructions for Respondents

Two kinds of response instructions are required: an introductory statement explaining the nature of the questionnaire and directions for responding to individual questions. Introductory materials take the form of an oral statement for personally administered questionnaires, either face-to-face instruments or telephone surveys. For mailed questionnaires, a cover letter contains the introductory materials. Introductory statements should be persuasive documents that stress the importance of a survey and its brevity. ("It will take only a few minutes of your time to provide this valuable data," for example.) Additionally, the introductory statement should include the following information: (1) the sponsor or person conducting the survey, (2) the nature and purposes of the survey, along with the uses to which the information will be put, (3) assurances that the information will be held in confidence, and (4) general directions for responding to the survey.

In addition to these introductory instructions, the researcher must provide clear directions for answering specific questions. The nature of all questions (for example, Likert rating scales, semantic differentials, ranking questions, inventory questions, and open-ended questions) should be clarified along with procedures for responding to them. Presenting re-spondents with a sample question or two before they actually begin the questionnaire is often an excellent way to ensure that instructions are understood.

## Designing a Layout

**Layout**, the physical features of a written questionnaire, should be attractive and inviting. The questionnaire should be neatly typed and all copies should be clear and legible. To avoid a cluttered appearance, the typist should leave plenty of space between questions.

# ADMINISTERING THE SURVEY QUESTIONNAIRE

Many of the design issues we have already discussed, including preparing introductory statements and providing clear response instructions, bear on procedures for administering questionnaires. Two additional administrative matters remain to be considered: selecting a method of data collection (either written or oral) and managing response rate problems.

## Written Versus Oral Data Collection

Survey data may be collected from written questionnaires and through oral interviews. The former ask respondents to report in writing their responses to survey questions, either by checking structured scales or composing free-response narratives. Questionnaires may be administered by mail or personally delivered to respondents. Mailed questionnaires are often required with very large sample sizes, whereas personal delivery is feasible with smaller samples.

In oral interviews, participants are asked to report their responses to survey questions directly to the researcher. The interview method

**230**

PART III
Contemporary
Research
Designs in
Communi-
cation

is often useful for questionnaires that contain mostly open-ended questions or when important follow-up questions based on one or more closed questions are included. Interviews can be conducted on a face-to-face basis or administered by telephone. Interpersonal interviews are often preferred for relatively small samples. However, a large sample may necessitate the use of telephone interviews.

## Response Rate Problems

Whether survey researchers use written questionnaires or oral interviews, they must strive to gather all the required information. To the extent that they are unable to collect any of the required data from each sample element, they have a response rate problem. The **response rate** is the ratio of the number of elements about which the researcher successfully secures data to the total number of elements in the selected sample.[10] "Nonresponse" refers to the elements about which it proved impossible to collect data.

Longitudinal surveys often present more response rate difficulties than cross-sectional ones, since longitudinal researchers must return on several occasions to collect data from respondents. Moreover, response problems are usually more prevalent with mailed questionnaires than with oral interviews. Researchers can alleviate the problem with follow-up mailings to nonrespondents. The first follow-up should usually come around two weeks after initial mailings, and any additional follow-ups are made roughly at two-week intervals.

There are two varieties of nonresponse, each of which diminishes a researcher's response rate: total nonresponse, referring to the absence of any information about a given element or elements, and item nonresponse, which indicates that the researcher got some but not all of the information required from certain elements.[11] Four factors variously contribute to

**total nonresponse**, usually the more serious of the problems: (1) the researcher is unable to locate an element for questioning, (2) located elements are unwilling to respond to questions, (3) certain elements are incapable of responding due to factors such as illness and communication deficits (for example, deafness or the inability to speak English), and (4) the researcher misplaces or otherwise loses one or more pieces of collected information.

A large nonresponse rate jeopardizes a selected sample's representativeness, especially when missing elements are not spread evenly across the parent population. If, for example, whites have a greater nonresponse rate than blacks, or if urban dwellers respond less frequently than rural residents, the resulting nonresponse bias reduces sample representativeness. Researchers can often reduce participation refusals by assuring respondents of the confidentiality of their responses. Many writers argue that nonresponse bias is unlikely to become a serious problem if a researcher's response rate is 70% or above.[12] Other experts have suggested that a 60% response rate is generally adequate and that response rates as low as 50% may retain sufficient representativeness to warrant valid inferences to population characteristics.[13]

**Item nonresponse** problems, or the inability to elicit responses to all the questions put to each sample element, often result from two factors: a respondent's unwillingness to answer personally sensitive questions like requests for information about personal income or sexual preference, and a respondent's inability to answer questions because they are poorly constructed, being obscure or uninterpretable. As with total nonresponse refusals, the assurance of confidentiality diminishes the first problem. Both problems can be alleviated by drafting research questions that are non-threatening and easily understood. All the guidelines for questionnaire design discussed earlier should be followed, including using clear and unambiguous language, phrasing questions in a nonthreatening way, and avoiding leading and double-barreled questions.

## ANALYZING SURVEY RESULTS

After survey data have been collected, the researcher must select appropriate statistical procedures for analyzing results. Statistical analysis tests the reliability of sample-to-population inferences. Two factors determine one's choice of statistical tools: the nature of the research problem and the data's measurement levels.

If one's research problem requires relationship assessment, bivariate or multivariate correlation is in order. However, significance of difference tests are required for assessing population discrepancies. As a general rule, single-sample surveys make extensive use of relationship analysis, whereas multiple-sample designs often employ population difference tests. Within these two broad categories, the measurement levels assumed by one's sample data will dictate specific statistical methods. We learned in Chapters 7 and 8 that categorical and continuous data require different tools for assessing statistical significance.

## INTERFACE: CHAPTERS 11 AND 12

This chapter has described the nature and functions of survey research. Detailed instructions for conducting surveys were presented. I examined methods of selecting representative survey samples and outlined practical guidelines for designing survey questionnaires. The chapter concluded with a discussion of techniques for administering surveys and analyzing survey results.

Chapter 12 will explore methods of studying interactive discourse, including communication forms like ordinary conversations, interviews, discussions, and debates. A research design called conversational analysis is described. Unlike survey research, which takes a scientific approach to communication inquiry, conversational analysis is a hybrid methodology partaking of both scientific and humanistic research assumptions.

## MAIN POINTS

**1.** Survey research examines samples for the purpose of inferring conclusions about the populations from which samples were drawn. Since its utility depends on sample representativeness, survey research uses probability sampling methods.

**2.** Survey research serves two principal functions: description and explanation. Description produces a profile of pertinent population characteristics, whereas explanation explores the reasons for descriptive data.

**3.** Surveys may be cross-sectional or longitudinal. A cross-sectional survey collects information from a sample at a single point in time. Longitudinal surveys collect several samples at different points in time. Longitudinal surveys may be trend or panel studies. A trend study selects different samples from a population at different times, whereas a panel survey follows the same sample across time.

**4.** Single-sample surveys examine one population, whereas multiple sample surveys study relationships and differences among two or more populations.

**5.** Four procedures are required to conduct survey research: select a representative survey sample, design a survey questionnaire, administer the survey questionnaire, and analyze the survey results.

**232**

PART III
Contemporary
Research
Designs in
Communi-
cation

**6.** Five tasks are necessary to select a representative survey sample: define the population, specify sampling elements, secure a sampling frame, select a probability sampling method, and determine the required sample size.

**7.** Three sampling frame deficiencies can threaten the validity of survey findings: missing elements, foreign elements, and duplicate elements.

**8.** The minimum sample size required for representing a population can be calculated; it depends on the homogeneity of the population as well as the size of the population relative to the sample.

**9.** Designing a survey questionnaire entails five tasks: (a) determine the types of questions required for responding to the research question or hypothesis; (b) construct questions that will elicit the desired information; (c) organize questions into effective patterns; (d) develop appropriate instructions for responding to questions; and (e) design an attractive layout.

**10.** Survey questions may be classified as: factual and opinion questions, closed and open-ended questions, and contingency and filter questions. Factual questions solicit information about a respondent's background and behaviors, whereas opinion questions ask about beliefs and attitudes. Closed questions require respondents to choose from a fixed set of response options. Open-ended ones encourage free and unstructured responses. Contingency questions apply to a subset of respondents, and filter questions identify that subset.

**11.** Commonly used closed questions are rating questions such as Likert scales and semantic differentials, ranking questions, and inventory or checklist questions.

**12.** Survey questions should be constructed to be clear and unambiguous, and simple and brief. Questions should avoid leading language and should not be double-barreled. Questions should be as nonthreatening as possible.

**13.** There are two general organizational

formats for questionnaires: a funnel pattern, which begins with broad questions followed by more specific ones, and an inverted funnel pattern, which begins with narrow questions followed by more general ones.

**14.** Criteria for ordering questions include: (a) the general organizational pattern should complement research objectives; (b) topically related questions should be grouped together; (c) easy-to-answer questions should be placed first; and (d) questions should be ordered to avoid establishing a response bias.

**15.** Two kinds of questionnaire instructions are needed: a persuasive introductory statement explaining the nature of a questionnaire and directions for responding to individual questions.

**16.** Survey data may be collected with written questionnaires or oral interviews. Written questionnaires can be mailed or delivered in person. Interviews may be conducted "live" or by telephone.

**17.** The two kinds of response rate problems are total nonresponse, referring to the inability to collect any information about a given element or elements, and item nonresponse, which occurs when the researcher obtains some but not all of the required information from each element.

**18.** The statistical tools required to analyze survey data are determined by the nature of the research problem and the data's measurement level.

## REVIEW EXERCISES

**1.** Suppose you wish to conduct a six-month survey of the reactions of viewers in your hometown to a television network talk show called "Firestorm." Describe a trend and a panel study that could address this research problem. Which of the two approaches is likely to provide the most valid information? Why?

**2.** Suppose you have been employed by the mayor of Keezletown, U.S.A. to survey local residents' attitudes toward a proposed new municipal recreation center. Keezletown has a population of 5000. Local newspaper accounts suggest that most residents (perhaps as many as 80%) favor the plan. Calculate the minimum sample size you will require for your survey, assuming you desire a confidence level of .95 and a confidence interval of $\pm.03$. Then, describe the probability sampling method you will use for selecting a representative sample. Why did you choose the method you did?

[Answer: Assuming the value of $p$ is estimated conservatively at .70 rather than .80, the initial sample size estimate is 896; the final sample size estimate adjusted for population size is 760.]

**3.** Suppose you have been hired by a local radio station to survey listeners' reactions to its three-hour nightly classical music program called "A Classy Evening." Write a questionnaire containing at least 10 questions that will address the matter you have been employed to investigate. Include at least one question of each of the following types: a factual question, an opinion question, a closed rating question, a closed ranking question, a closed inventory question, a contingency question preceded by an appropriate filter question, and an open-ended question. How well do your questions conform to each of the criteria outlined in this chapter for constructing questions? How well does the organization of the questionnaire conform to the criteria for ordering questions? Redraft your questionnaire until it meets all pertinent criteria.

## NOTES

**1.** For a sketch of the history of survey research, see Earl R. Babbie, *Survey Research Methods* (Belmont, CA: Wadsworth, 1973), pp. 41–45.

**2.** See Paul F. Lazarsfeld, Bernard Berelson, and Hazel Gaudet, *The People's Choice*, 2nd ed. (New York: Columbia University Press, 1948); Paul F. Lazarsfeld and Robert K. Merton, *The Communication of Ideas* (New York: Institute for Religious and Social Studies, 1948); and Joseph R. Klapper, *The Effects of Mass Communication* (New York: Free Press, 1960).

**3.** See George Gerbner, Larry Gross, Michael Morgan, and Nancy Signorielli, "The 'Mainstreaming' of America: Violence Profile No. 11," *Journal of Communication*, 30, No. 3 (1980): 10–29; and James D. Culley and Rex Bennett, "Selling Women, Selling Blacks," *Journal of Communication*, 26, No. 4 (1976): 160–74.

**4.** Babbie, p. 59.

**5.** Graham Kalton, *Introduction to Survey Sampling* (Beverly Hills, CA: Sage, 1983), p. 56.

**6.** Leslie Kish, *Survey Sampling* (New York: John Wiley, 1965), pp. 53–59.

**7.** Kalton, p. 61.

**8.** For example, see Bernard S. Phillips, *Social Research: Strategy and Tactics*, 2nd ed. (New York: Macmillan, 1971). The "randomized response" procedure is a relatively new approach to designing sensitive survey inquiries. For a discussion of this useful method, see James Alan Fox and Paul E. Tracy, *Randomized Response: A Method for Sensitive Surveys* (Beverly Hills, CA: Sage, 1987).

**9.** William A. Belson, "The Effects of Reversing the Presentation Order on Verbal Rating Scales," *Journal of Advertising*, 6, No. 4 (1966): 30–37.

**10.** Kalton, p. 66.

**11.** Kalton, p. 64.

**12.** Kalton, p. 66.

**13.** Earl Babbie, *The Practice of Social Research*, 3rd ed. (Belmont, CA: Wadsworth, 1983), p. 226.

# CHAPTER
# 12

# ANALYSIS OF INTERACTIVE DISCOURSE

This chapter presents methods for studying interactive discourse. Interactive discourse is characterized by alternating speaker-listener roles and includes ordinary conversations, interviews, discussions, and debates. The chapter focuses on a naturalistic research method called conversational analysis. Conversational analysis aims to describe, explain, and evaluate the structure and function of conversations. Conversational data bases are discussed, as are the requirements for supporting research claims about conversations. Step-by-step procedures for conducting a conversational analysis are described.

# CHAPTER OUTLINE

Over the past decade, communication researchers have increasingly employed a number of hybrid research designs that blend traditional science with analytical and critical methods of the arts and humanities.[1] Addressing this contemporary trend, Geertz observed metaphorically that "many social scientists are looking less for the sort of thing that connects planets and pendulums and more for the sort that connects chrysanthemums and swords." It has finally dawned on social scientists, said Geertz, that they are not required to be either "mimic physicists or closet humanists" to pursue the subject matter of their discipline. Instead, "social scientists have become free to shape their work in terms of its necessities" rather than traditional notions about "what they ought or ought not to be doing. Something," he concluded, "is happening to the way we think about the way we think."[2]

The last two chapters in Part III will explore several hybrid research designs—methods we might call **humanistic science**. By combining procedures that previously were thought incompatible, researchers can explore theoretical relationships that are not easily studied with scientific or humanistic methods alone. All the designs share two interrelated attributes. First, they are inherently communicative; they focus on the structure and functions of human talk—what people say to one another and how they go about saying it. The designs described in the two preceding chapters are general scientific methods that scholars have adapted to communication; they are not distinctively communicative. However, the designs that remain to be explored have few functions save the analysis of communicative actions and interactions.

Second, the remaining designs are "interpretive" research methods, which focus "on the study of meanings, that is, the way individuals make sense of their world through their communicative behaviors."[3] The research models discussed earlier—experimentation and survey research—are so-called functional methods that often treat meanings as baseline data for inferring conclusions about related behaviors and effects. By contrast, interpretive research treats people's individual and shared meanings as the end product, not the starting point of research. Taken together, these two characteristics render the balance of our research designs inherently communicative in form as well as substance.

Two broad sets of meaning-based models are covered in the remaining chapters of Part III. In this chapter, methods of exploring communicative *interactions* between two or more individuals are examined. To that end, I will focus on a naturalistic research tool called conversational analysis, which often partakes of both scientific and humanistic assumptions. In Chapter 13, I discuss methodological approaches to *narrative* discourse. Narrative forms include public speeches and mass media presentations that involve relatively few spontaneous interactions.

# THE NATURE OF INTERACTIVE DISCOURSE

**Interactive discourse** is characterized by alternating source and receiver roles, so that "during the course of interaction the roles of speaker and hearer are frequently exchanged."[4] Ordinary conversations, both face-to-face and telephonic, are prototypes of interactive discourse. However, other discourse forms are interactive as well: structured interviews, formal debates, legal proceedings, public hearings, small group discussions, and certain types of computer-mediated information exchange are examples.

Conversation is often distinguished from other interactive communications in that conversationalists may take as many turns-at-talk (that is, may make as many separate contribu-

**238**

PART III
Contemporary
Research
Designs in
Communi-
cation

tions) as they wish, their contributions can be of any length, and the order of the speakers' talking turns is highly flexible.[5] By contrast, interviews often implicitly give interviewers more turns-at-talk than applicants; legal adversaries and debaters usually have a fixed allocation of turns, and their speaking order is predetermined; finally, the number and length of conversational turns is often regulated in structured conferences and hearings. In short, in all forms of interactive discourse except ordinary conversation some constraints are placed on either the nature or the order of each party's contributions.

# CONVERSATIONAL ANALYSIS

**Conversational analysis** is a systematic method for describing, explaining, and evaluating the structure and function of rules governing conversations.[6] Although the methodology is applied most often to ordinary conversations, it is easily adapted to more structured interactive discourse like interviews, group deliberations, and formal and informal debates.

To fully understand conversational analysis, it will be useful to explore the meanings of the four key terms comprising its definition: conversation, rules, structure, and function. **Conversation**, as we have defined it, is at first blush an amazingly ordinary creature, something we enact on a regular basis and with little apparent effort. However, deeper reflection suggests that even the simplest of conversations is a highly complex negotiation requiring vast knowledge about when to say what to whom in a given interactional context. At a minimum, the ability to enact a reasonably satisfactory conversation requires a thorough grasp of the implicit and explicit rules that govern the timing and appropriateness of particular kinds of talk in specified social settings.

# The Nature of Conversational Rules

A conversational **rule** is an "if-then" assumption or goal-action linkage that defines the communication behaviors required to achieve desired objectives in specified social contexts. Some common conversational rules include expressions like "Speak only when spoken to" and "When in Rome, do as the Romans do." These cultural clichés inform us that if we wish to be liked or admired (goal) when we are interacting in particular social settings (context), then we should adopt certain specified communication behaviors (action). The general structure of a conversational rule is: *If* X (goal) in situation Z (context), *then* behavior Y (action).

Rules of two general types govern conversations: interpretative rules, also called constitutive rules, and behavioral rules, sometimes referred to as regulative rules. **Interpretative rules** are networks of situational, semantic, and syntactic knowledge that allow conversationalists to attach meaning to each other's utterances. They take the form: If X (utterance) in situation Z (context), then Y (meaning). To illustrate interpretative rules with a rather transparent example, consider the declarative statement "I am sick." Spoken by a student after seeing a disappointing final examination grade and uttered by a patient in a hospital bed, the statement means something quite different. Through years of experience, we learn to quickly process all situational, semantic, and syntactic cues associated with a given utterance and thereby impart meaning to it. "Communication breakdowns" often occur because people apply inappropriate interpretative rules and therefore misconstrue others' utterances. The frequency of misunderstandings among humans is powerful if depressing evidence that applying interpretative rules in conversations is not as effortless as it first appears.

The second type of conversational rule, a **behavioral rule**, represents anticipatory assumptions about the kinds of utterances that are appropriate in specified social contexts. Simple behavioral rules include such assumptions as "When somebody says hello, you must respond with a similar greeting if you wish to be considered polite" and "If someone asks you a question, you should answer." Some rules are more complex: "When somebody in authority issues a command, either obey it or explain your noncompliance" and "When another person falsely accuses you, you may become angry and refuse to respond or you may deny the accusation." These examples indicate that behavioral rules stipulate *required* behaviors, *preferred* behaviors, *prohibited* behaviors, or a range of *permissible* behavior in specified contexts. Thus, behavioral rules take the general form: If X (goal) in situation Z (context), then Y (required, preferred, prohibited, or permissible utterances).

# Conversational Structure and Function

Recall that the purpose of conversational analysis is to describe, explain, and evaluate a conversation's structure and function. Interpretative and behavioral rules lend both structure and function to conversations; thus to describe, explain, and evaluate a conversation, one must search for the interpretative and behavioral rules responsible for its structure and function.

**Conversational structure** refers to the way people organize meaning by producing interrelated utterances. Structure focuses on the organization of a conversation's constituent parts and is analyzed at two levels: *local structure* refers to meanings derived from relationships between individual utterances, and *global structure* concerns the meanings created by the relationship between utterances as a group and a conversation's overall purpose. A principal objective of conversational analysis is to evaluate the **structural coherence** of a conversation,

that is, the extent to which the meanings created by utterances coincide with the general goal or reason for the conversation in question.[7]

The function of a conversation describes how people organize their actions by talking with one another. More particularly, **conversational functions** refer to what people "do to" one another when they talk. To understand this notion, consider the following sequence:

Person A: Your blue suit is attractive.
Person B: Thank you. I'm flattered.

From a semantic perspective, person A's assertion means only that a suit belonging to person B has the attributes of blueness and attractiveness. However, the two utterances taken together suggest that in functional terms, person A has performed an action called "complimenting" person B, who has, in turn, acknowledged the action and indicated what it has "done to" him or her ("I'm flattered"). Like conversational structure, a conversation's functions are analyzed at both the *local* or utterance-by-utterance level and the *global* level. Global functionality refers to the coordinated actions accomplished by a conversation as a whole. A primary objective of conversational analysis is to assess a conversation's **functional coherence**, or the extent to which a sequence of utterances produces the actions desired by conversationalists.

A complete conversational analysis entails both a structural and a functional analysis. I shall now describe each analysis, indicating how the two can accomplish the three principal tasks of conversational analysis: description, explanation, and evaluation of interactive discourse.

## The structural analysis of conversation

Structurally, a conversation is said to have three basic components: the conversational utterance, the conversational turn, and the conversational topic. An **utterance** is a verbal

**240**

PART III
Contemporary
Research
Designs in
Communi-
cation

assertion and includes any comment with a stated or implied subject and predicate. In addition to complete declarative sentences and questions, elliptical statements such as "What?" and "Fantastic!" along with affirmations and negations like "Uh huh" and "No" qualify as utterances. A **turn** is akin to the notion of "taking the floor" and it "begins the instant one conversational participant starts talking alone and ends immediately prior to the instant another participant starts talking alone."[8] Finally, a conversational **topic** is the subject matter of a sequence of utterances, in short, what the conversation is about.

A structural analysis focuses on a conversation's *microstructure*, or the local organizational features that create meaning, and on its *macrostructure*, the global meanings that emerge from sequential talk. At the micro or local level, conversational analysts examine the relationships between utterances. Research indicates that relationships between sequential utterances may include the following types: *elaboration*, whereby an utterance extends or expands on the topic of a preceding utterance; *exemplification*, in which a second utterance provides an example deduced from the first; *generalization*, in which a second utterance represents a broad inference from a more specific prior one; *digression*, in which a second utterance departs from or interrupts the thought expressed in the first; and *causation*, whereby an utterance expresses an effect of some cause mentioned in a previous utterance.[9] In addition to relationship types, conversational analysts study the meanings of conversational lapses and pauses, simultaneous or overlapping talk, side comments, and so-called back-channel utterances like "Uh huh" and "Uhmm."

At the macro or global level, conversational analysts examine interpretative and behavioral rules that link utterances to a conversation's overall purpose. The management of conversational topics and turn-taking behaviors are often central macrostructural issues. For instance, some researchers study the strategies that interactants use to signal topic changes, including linguistic cues like "Incidentally," "By the way," and "So." Verbal and nonverbal cues indicating that one interactant wishes to take or relinquish the floor are also important macrostructural concerns.

Taken together, a structural analysis at the local and global levels yields a systematic description of the recurring utterances that people use to make sense of their discussions. Moreover, structural analysis allows the researcher to discover the interpretative and behavioral rules that explain observed utterance patterns. Finally, structural analysis provides the data required for evaluating whether the meanings created by interrelated utterances coincide with the general goals of conversationalists.

## The functional analysis of conversation

A functional analysis explores the actions people perform toward one another when they talk. (Notice that the meaning of the term "functional" as used here differs remarkably from its earlier usage in differentiating "functional" and "interpretive" research designs.) The central elements of a functional analysis are said to be the illocutionary act and the perlocutionary response. An **illocutionary act**, also called a speech act and a performative, represents something that one communicator "does to" another with an utterance or sequence of utterances.[10] For example, the utterance "You are a slob" usually "does an insult" to another, just as the comment "You have beautiful eyes" counts as a "compliment." Utterances that acknowledge the impact of another's illocutionary acts are called **perlocutionary responses**. Comments admitting hurt or anger in response to insults and positive reactions to compliments are perlocutionary responses.

Researchers analyze interactive discourse at the *microfunctional* or local level as well as the *macrofunctional* or global level. Local or utterance-by-utterance analysis often focuses on the actions inherent in adjacency pairs. An **adjacency pair**, also called a couplet, a minimal dialogue unit, and an action-reaction pair, is defined as two sequential utterances, each produced by a different speaker.[11] The first utterance in an adjacency pair is an illocutionary act whereas the second is a perlocutionary response.[12] Adjacency pairs that researchers have identified include: question-answer; request-comply/refuse; accuse-confess/deny; apology-accept/refuse; greeting-greeting; goodbye-goodbye; insult-response; summons-answer; assertion-assent/dissent; challenge-response; threat-response; boast-appreciate/deride; and compliment-accept/reject. Some researchers have proposed that all these adjacency pairs can be collapsed into one of two general categories: *solicit-give* and *give-acknowledge*.[13] Microfunctional analysts often search for the interpretative and behavioral rules that account for these consistently recurring adjacency pairs.

At the macrofunctional or global level, researchers study how the actions implicit in utterances relate to the conversationalists' overall goal or plan. Bach and Harnish have identified four types of actions that utterances contribute to a conversation's plan.[14] *Constatives* are utterances expressing a speaker's beliefs together with his or her intent that the conversational partner adopt similar beliefs. Constatives include such speech acts as informing, suggesting, asserting, predicting, and describing. *Directives* express a desire that another person perform some action and are exemplified by illocutionary acts such as requests, questions, advice, and admonitions. *Commissives* express a speaker's willingness to perform an action together with an implicit request that the conversational partner(s) recognize the action commitment. Promises, threats, and offers are prototypical commissives. *Acknowledgments*, which are expressions of a speaker's feelings toward others, include illocutionary acts such as apologies, congratulations, thank-yous, acceptances, and rejections. As with local analysis, the global researcher is looking for the interpretative and behavioral rules that account for the relationship between action clusters like directives and acknowledgments and a conversation's overall plan.

Taken together, a functional analysis at the local and global levels yields a systematic description of recurring clusters of actions that conversationalists "do to" one another. Moreover, functional analysis enables researchers to uncover rule-structures that explain action sequences. Finally, functional analysis provides data for evaluating a conversation's coherence, that is, determining whether the combined actions performed in a conversation accomplish the conversation's goals, including the reasons prompting people to engage in a given conversation in the first place.

# CONVERSATIONAL RESEARCH METHODOLOGIES

A combined structural-functional analysis seeks to: (1) *describe* recurring patterns of communicative interaction, (2) *explain* observed conversation patterns by referring to interpretative and behavioral rules, and (3) *evaluate* or *critique* the extent to which an interaction has attained **conversational coherence**, defined as the coordination of meaning and actions to accomplish communicative objectives.

The achievement of these aims requires three parallel sorts of information. First, the researcher needs an adequate **conversational data base**, defined by McLaughlin as "a corpus of conversations or conversation excerpts held to be representative of the domain of interest."[15] Second, a methodological perspective and its associated research protocols are required to

**242**

PART III
Contemporary
Research
Designs in
Communi-
cation

discover rule-structures that explain observed conversational patterns. Finally, a researcher needs a set of judgmental standards or criteria to evaluate the target conversation's structural and functional coherence, that is, its relative success in achieving interactional goals. Let us examine these research requirements, first describing sources of conversational data, then discussing alternative methodologies for describing, explaining, and evaluating data-based conversations.

# The Conversational Data Base

Recall that a data base consists of a body of conversations or conversational excerpts that represent well the domain of talk that interests a researcher. Domains of interest include what we have called ordinary conversations as well as interview conversations, structured group interactions like administrative deliberations and public hearings, and formal debates such as legal adversary proceedings. Conversational samples may be chosen to represent pertinent characteristics of well-defined populations of utterances or they may be selected purposively, depending on the research problem. Representative samples are required if a researcher wishes to infer conclusions to parent populations. However, if one is concerned with a specialized subset of utterances, a purposive or case study approach may be useful.

Grimshaw and McLaughlin discuss five different sources of conversational data: (1) conversations appearing in literary materials, (2) hypothetical conversations contrived by a researcher, (3) conversations recalled or contrived by research participants at the researcher's request, (4) "natural" conversations enacted by research participants in controlled laboratory settings, and (5) naturalistic conversations enacted in settings that are a part of people's normal life activity.[16]

## Literary conversation

**Literary conversation** consists of samples of interactive discourse found in novels and plays; it is contrived by authors and playwrights to service the development of a plot. Conversation drawn from pertinent fiction is a natural data source for a researcher who is interested in literary phenomena—writers themselves, plots or characters appearing in a specific work or genre of works, or some other aspect of literary analysis and criticism.

However, if one is interested in ordinary conversation, including interviews, discussions, debates, and unstructured talk, literary data are usually inappropriate. Literary discourse often differs in structure and content from actual conversation. For example, dialogue may be compressed or elongated to facilitate character and plot development. Furthermore, literary conversations typically involve more conflict than natural ones. In short, literary data are objects for the study of literature, not useful sources of information about naturalistic conversation.

## Researcher-contrived conversation

**Researcher-contrived conversation** consists of hypothetical examples of discourse made up by a researcher to illustrate particular kinds of conversational strategies. Some writers have argued that researcher-contrived discourse may be useful for testing theoretical claims about conversational phenomena.[17] Conversational events that might be studied using a researcher-contrived data base include strategies that are theoretically interesting but relatively rare in natural interactions, for example, conversational devices like "transparent questions" ("Is the pope Catholic?") and other infrequently occurring utterances.[18] Even in these special circumstances, researchers should be sure that contrived data conform faithfully to people's actual usages.

Aside from these specialized uses, researcher-contrived conversation is usually not an acceptable substitute for "real" human talk. In addition to being artificial, researcher-generated conversation may be susceptible to inadvertent distortion toward confirming a preferred hypothesis. Because of its make-believe qualities and its vulnerability to accidental misuse, I recommend that self-contrived data be used only to illustrate and supplement actual conversations.

## Elicited conversation

**Elicited conversation** consists of talk that research participants recall or create at a researcher's request. For example, researchers may ask people to recall specific conversations they recently participated in and to record their recollections in writing or on tape. Alternately, researchers may construct conversational scenarios or some other hypothetical stimulus and ask research participants to role-play conversations relevant to the supplied stimuli. For instance, a researcher might elicit compliance-gaining data by presenting research participants with a hypothetical scenario ("Imagine you got an unfair grade on an examination and wish to persuade the instructor to alter it") and ask them what conversational strategies they would use if the imaginary situation actually occurred.

Elicited conversations are usually superior to researcher-contrived data for two reasons. First, recalled conversations may be more realistic than researcher-generated talk. If hypothetical stimuli are carefully chosen to approximate "real-life" situations, the resulting contrivances can be a reasonable facsimile of natural conversation. Second, subject-generated conversations are less susceptible than researcher-constructed data to hypothesis-confirming distortions.

Despite these advantages, elicited data fall short of capturing the richness and fidelity of naturally occurring talk. Recall is not always accurate. Moreover, recalled and contrived conversations are usually more compressed

and elliptical than "real" ones, and nonverbal cues are likely to be missing. If the researcher chooses the recall method, each of these problems can be alleviated by using Jackson and Jacobs's method of *collective recall* in which two or more persons, rather than a single individual, are asked to jointly reconstruct a past conversation.[19] Collaborative recall should generate more detailed and accurate recollections than individual recall.

## "Natural" laboratory conversation

A researcher who uses **"natural" laboratory conversation** simply records research participants' unprompted conversation in a laboratory setting. Unstructured laboratory talk is usually generated in one of two ways. First, the researcher may unobtrusively record conversations while people are ostensibly waiting to participate in a nonexistent study. (The ethical implications of surreptitious data gathering are discussed in Chapter 14.) Second, research participants may be told that their conversations will be recorded, whereupon they are instructed to talk about anything they wish.

Unlike conversations elicited by researcher-supplied stimuli, these two approaches generate conversations that are independent of the researcher's hypotheses. However, the methods have potential validity problems. When participants know that their talk is being recorded, they may behave nonnaturally. On the other hand, if hidden recording methods are used, the researcher risks generating conversational data that are at best trivial and at worst nonexistent. Because of these difficulties, "natural" laboratory data are sometimes less informative and less reliable than elicited conversations.

## Naturalistic conversation

**Naturalistic conversation** is gathered in noncontrived social settings that are a part of people's normal environment—homes, places of work and leisure, and so on. Naturalistic

**244**

PART III
Contemporary
Research
Designs in
Communi-
cation

conversation is probably the most desirable of all data bases. It is a realistic and reasonably complete representation of normal talk.

Despite these positive features, naturalistic conversation is not without validity problems. Its internal validity is threatened by reactivity, since researchers must tape the conversations. Reactivity sometimes may be greater in naturalistic than in laboratory settings because recording devices are remarkably obvious and so clearly out of place in the home, the office, and leisure settings. Researchers can reduce these validity problems by allowing recording devices to remain at a research site over a period of time, thereby desensitizing people to their presence. Similarly, selecting conversational samples from later rather than earlier stages of a lengthy interaction takes advantage of the desensitization effects of time passage.

Naturalistic data may also present external validity problems. Naturalistic talk is often gathered from "convenience" samples who volunteer their services. Since volunteers may be different from the general population—for example, they are likely to be more outgoing and better educated—the external validity of naturalistic findings may be compromised. This presents a problem only if research objectives require a representative sample of some conversational population. Despite these difficulties, the "realism" of naturalistic conversation is a major advantage over other sources of data. If the research problem requires a descriptive analysis of how people actually talk with one another, naturalistic conversation is usually the preferred data base.

## Evidentiary Materials for Supporting Research Claims

The describing, explaining, and evaluating of conversational data is largely a process of searching for the interpretative and behavioral rules that govern people's talk. Assuming that the researcher has gathered an adequate data base, McLaughlin suggests that four types of evidence derived from such data can credibly support claims about the conversational rules.[20]

The first type of evidence, labeled conversational regularity, is a researcher's observation that a particular pattern of utterances recurs on a persistent basis. The existence of adjacency pair rules like "Answers should follow questions" and "A compliment should be properly acknowledged" has been confirmed by observations that such sequential utterances occur regularly. Second, the researcher may show that communicators have a knowledge of conversational rules. If a communicator can articulate (either verbally or nonverbally) a rule he or she is following, the researcher has evidence to support claims about conversational rules. Even when communicators are not consciously aware of their rule-following behaviors and therefore cannot directly confirm them, they often exhibit rule knowledge behaviorally, especially when others violate shared rules. If a person's conversational partner is consistently rude or unresponsive, the person toward whom these rule-breaking behaviors are directed will often show signs of annoyance, embarrassment, or hurt—all clear indications that he or she is implicitly aware of accepted rules of politeness and responsiveness.

Third, a researcher can confirm the existence of conversational rules by showing that people's conversational behaviors change with changing contexts. Rules are context-specific; they are appropriate in certain social situations but not in others. For instance, certain language that is acceptable in one's home may be considered inappropriate in a religious service. And, rules of politeness that usually are operative when one is talking with strangers are sometimes ignored among friends. A researcher who can show that particular conversational behaviors are specific to one context but not another has found support for the existence of rule-governed behavior. Fourth, a rule can be demonstrated by showing that a communicator's behavior is critiqueable; that is, breaking commonly accepted rules of conversation is sanctioned negatively, whereas conformity is rewarded.

## Alternative Methodologies for Supporting Research Claims

A methodological perspective answers such questions as the following. What type of proof is required to support descriptive, explanatory, and evaluative claims derived from the four evidentiary sources just discussed? How much proof must be presented to adequately support a claim? Two general methodologies are available: science and humanism.

### Science

**Science**, a methodology that emphasizes the counting and measuring of data, has many proof requirements, but four are especially important:

1. *External validity requirement.* A researcher's conversational data base should be a representative sample selected from a well-defined population of utterances. This requirement implies that one's descriptive, explanatory, and evaluative conclusions are generalizable to a parent population, not confined to sample data. Importantly, conversational analysts usually cannot generate purely "random" conversational samples, since it is difficult to acquire adequate sampling frames of all population elements. However, Shimanoff has argued that researchers must select "sample conversations [that] reflect a wide enough range of conversations that the researchers are justified in concluding that their rules apply to all conversations."[21] This suggestion implies that a conversational analyst might compensate for a lack of randomness by augmenting

sample size, thereby increasing the chances of capturing a diverse cross-section of the population of interest.

2. *Internal validity requirement.* Internal validity implies that one is measuring what he or she intends to measure. In the case of conversational analysis, scientists are attempting to "measure" rules that account for interaction patterns. Thus, the empirical data supporting claims about rules must be authentic, realistic, and reasonably free from any confounding effects that may be produced by variables other than the claimed rule-structure.

3. *Data analysis requirement.* The two preceding requirements imply that conversational data are usually quantitative and therefore amenable to statistical analysis. For example, we might check to see whether the frequency with which a certain rule pattern is used differs significantly from one context to another. Moreover, we might assess the statistical relationship between a given pattern of illocutionary actions and the actors' conversational goals.

4. *Replicability requirement.* Only if scientific research can be replicated can it be confirmed or disconfirmed by other scientists. Among other things, this requirement compels the researcher to articulate explicitly all research protocols so that others can faithfully duplicate the research.

### Humanism

**Humanism**, a perspective emphasizing analytical and critical methods, adheres to the following parallel proof requirements:

1. *External validity requirement.* The data yielding descriptive, explanatory, and evaluative conclusions may, but need not be representative of a well-defined population of utterances. As I indicated earlier, a conversational analyst may use either purposive or representative samples depending on the research

**246**

PART III
Contemporary
Research
Designs in
Communi-
cation

problem. When a humanist's samples are purposive, claims are not necessarily generalizable beyond the examined conversation.

2. *Internal validity requirement.* Like scientists, humanists require that research be internally valid. Descriptive, explanatory, and evaluative conclusions must be logically inferred from available data. However, humanistic proof requirements may differ somewhat from those employed by science. Whereas scientists usually infer conclusions about populations based on representative data, humanists sometimes support claims by citing prototypes or examples that illustrate the reasonableness of their conclusions. Moreover, humanists attempt to show that no outstanding counterexamples contradict conclusions. Jackson's method of analytic induction is a rigorous humanistic methodology for establishing internally valid claims using examples and counterexamples.[22]

3. *Data analysis requirement.* As the two preceding requirements imply, humanistic data are often qualitative, consisting of narrative claims reasoned from carefully selected data, including examples and counterexamples.

4. *Replicability requirement.* Although much humanistic research is replicable, it need not be. Indeed, if a given analysis concerns some unique and therefore nonrecurring conversational event—for example, summit negotiations between two world leaders—precise replicability may be impossible.

Contemporary conversational analysis varies markedly in methodological perspective. For instance, McLaughlin's compliance-gaining studies have a scientific orientation,[23] whereas Goldberg's interpersonal research and Putnam's interpretive work on organizational communication take humanistic viewpoints.[24] Finally, Jackson and Jacobs's research on argument and persuasion nicely integrates science and humanism into a hybrid approach to conversational analysis.[25]

The nature of a research problem will determine which approach is most appropriate. If the researcher is interested in describing entire populations of utterances, scientific methods are usually preferred. However, case studies of particularized conversations require the purposive sampling that characterizes much humanistic research. Other research purposes will lend themselves to a judicious blend of the two perspectives. In all cases, the communication researcher should select the methodological posture that promises to illuminate most clearly the richness and subtlety of human talk.

# PROCEDURES FOR DOING CONVERSATIONAL ANALYSIS

Before conducting a conversational analysis, the researcher must make informed decisions about four methodological issues: general perspectives, observational roles, interpretation methods, and research design linearity.

## Preresearch Issues

First, the researcher must settle on a global methodological perspective, either scientific, humanistic, or a healthy blend of these approaches. This decision affects profoundly a researcher's methods of gathering and processing conversational data. Second, the researcher must decide on an appropriate personal *observational role*, that is, participatory or nonparticipatory roles. In addition, as explained in Chapter 9, data can be gathered overtly or unobtrusively.

Combining the participatory and overtness dimensions, the researcher can adopt one of the four observational roles shown in Table 12.1.

RESEARCHER OBSERVATIONAL ROLES

|  | Participant | Nonparticipant |
|---|---|---|
| Overt | Role 1 | Role 2 |
| Unobtrusive | Role 3 | Role 4 |

Each of the four roles has advantages and drawbacks. Unobtrusive observations by participant or nonparticipant observers (roles 3 and 4) produce few reactivity problems because communicators don't know they are being observed. However, both roles raise serious ethical concerns, including privacy invasion and deception, which researchers should try to avoid. (See Chapter 14 for a discussion of these ethical issues.) Although both overt roles (roles 1 and 2) engender reactivity, overt participant observation (role 1) may produce fewer reactive effects because the researcher has assumed the role of a "natural" group member. However, researchers who are participants in group conversation are forced to partially create what they wish to study, and this may have the unintended consequence of distorting results toward confirming research hypotheses. Because the overt nonparticipatory role (role 2) prevents researchers from partially creating the object of their study, it may be an appropriate choice if reactivity is not expected to be a major validity problem. However, if the researcher expects serious reactivity effects, a participatory stance (role 1) might be a wiser option.

Third, the researcher must choose an appropriate means of interpreting or assigning meaning to observed utterances. Two general interpretive approaches are available: researcher meanings and communicator meanings. As the name implies, *researcher meanings* are those

imposed by the investigator on research participants' utterances. By contrast, the *communicator meaning* perspective involves questioning participants to ascertain their explanations of their meanings. The researcher-based approach is more objective, since interpretations are not influenced by participants' natural inclinations to project socially acceptable meanings to outsiders. However, the researcher perspective may promote inaccuracy because an investigator can never truly know what another person's utterances mean. Moreover, researcher meanings are subject to inadvertent distortion in the direction of confirming preconceived ideas and hypotheses. A judicious decision is to combine the two approaches, so that both researchers and communicators assign meanings to the same utterances. If the interpretations are similar, the researcher has strong support for the authenticity of meanings.

Fourth and finally, the researcher must resolve an issue that Philipsen has called the *linearity of research design problem.*[26] Philipsen uses the term "linearity" to address the question of how one should build theoretical explanations for conversational phenomena. Two approaches discussed in Chapter 1 are available: the data-to-theory and the theory-to-data perspectives. A data-to-theory researcher observes conversations with few if any preconceptions about observations; in short, the researcher has no explicit hypothesis to test. By contrast, the

**248**

PART III
Contemporary
Research
Designs in
Communi-
cation

theory-to-data researcher has preformulated notions about the nature of observed conversation and the rules governing it. Such researchers observe conversational data for the purpose of confirming or disconfirming hypotheses.

Many conversational analysts today prefer a data-to-theory emphasis. However, each researcher's decision will ultimately turn on whether he or she in fact has preconceived hypotheses. Conversational hypotheses include not only explanatory generalizations but also descriptive frameworks or taxonomies. Taxonomies are the categories of utterances that one expects either to discover or to confirm by observing conversations. For example, a theory-to-data researcher might analyze a series of conversations for the purpose of classifying illocutionary acts into Bach and Harnish's four-category taxonomy discussed earlier ("constatives," "directives," "commissives," and "acknowledgments"). Alternately, adjacency pairs might be categorized according to a two-part "solicit-give" or "give-acknowledge" descriptive framework. Contrasted with this approach, data-to-theory researchers observe conversations without predetermined utterance categories and allow groups of utterances to emerge naturally from the data. Indeed, a principal objective of data-to-theory research is to generate taxonomies rather than to classify utterances according to preconceived descriptive frameworks.

# Conducting Conversational Research

Once researchers have resolved these four issues, five steps are required to conduct a conversational analysis: identify the relevant population or domain of conversation; specify pertinent elements and observational units; select a sample of conversations; observe, record, and code the conversational sample; and analyze the results.

## Identifying the population

In the scientific approach, population identification methods are similar to those described in Chapter 5, which treated sampling methods. First, an idealized target population is conceptualized; then a concrete population from which to select samples is identified.

Depending on individual research aims and the nature of available conversational data, the humanistic researcher takes one of two approaches to population identification. A humanist who wishes to generalize findings to a sample's parent population follows the same general procedures as the scientist. However, if a particularized conversation is the research focus, or alternately, if the sample conversation of interest is unique and not conducive to meaningful population inferences, the researcher may omit the population identification stage.

## Specifying elements and observational units

Scientists and humanists alike rigorously specify their primary elements, the "things" they wish to study. Three different elements are commonly used in conversational studies: the utterance, defined as a single assertion; the turn, referring to a stretch of uninterrupted talk by a single conversationalist; and the adjacency pair, that is, two sequential utterances consisting of one party's illocutionary act followed by a second person's perlocutionary response.

In addition to specifying elements, researchers must stipulate their observational unit, the person or persons from whom they will get information about the elements. Given the interactive nature of conversations, the theoretically smallest possible observational unit is the dyad, but a larger unit of three or more interactants may be used. As a matter of practice, researchers sometimes ask a single person to report on his or her recalled interactions with one or more other persons.

## Selecting a conversational sample

Whether humanist or scientist, the researcher must obtain a conversational sample from one of the five sources described earlier. Assuming that the researcher is interested in studying actual conversations, one of three data sources should be tapped in the following order of preference: naturalistic talk in uncontrolled settings, elicited recall or role-playing data, and "natural" laboratory conversations. The researcher may employ literary data and researcher-contrived conversations in the specialized circumstances described earlier.

The scientist and the humanist sometimes part company regarding methods of selecting conversational samples from a chosen data source. Scientists often employ a variant of probability sampling to generate representative samples. In contrast, the humanist may use purposive sampling, selecting from a body of data the examples of conversation that pertain most directly to the research problem. Thus, if humanistic researchers were interested in analyzing an ongoing debate between proponents and opponents of abortion, they might purposely select one or two prototypical debates that best illustrate the argumentative tension between the antagonists.

## Observing, recording, and coding data

If no record of sample conversations is available, the researcher must construct one. Although audiotaping is acceptable, videotaped records are preferred because they display not only verbal interchanges but also pertinent nonverbal cues that variously extend, replace, or contradict the spoken word. When tapes have been assembled, the researcher should reduce them to written transcripts for in-depth analysis.

Transcription is a tedious process having important practical as well as theoretical implications. The transcriber inevitably selects certain aspects of a conversation and excludes others. Many nonverbal cues like pitch, intonation, dialect, and loudness may be lost because of the difficulty of retaining them in written form. To generate as complete and accurate a transcription as possible, researchers often adopt **coding schemes**, which are systems of symbols used for the consistent classification of verbal and nonverbal cues. The researcher's primary elements (for example, the utterance or the turn) usually are numbered sequentially throughout a transcript.[27]

Once a consistent coding scheme has been adopted, the researcher typically asks several individuals (usually three to five) to do the coding task. If two or more people agree on the classification of conversational units, a researcher can have more confidence in the transcript's authenticity than would be possible if a single person had made all pertinent coding decisions.

## Analyzing results

Conversational findings are often measured nominally. Observed elements and inferred rules are grouped by structure or function into interrelated categories. The frequency with which elements fall into each category is often computed. Thus, the data yielded by many conversational analyses consist of lists or taxonomies representing either observed conversational elements (a descriptive taxonomy) or interpretative and behavioral rules that people follow in conversations (an explanatory taxonomy).

Taxonomies are generated in one of two ways. First, researchers taking a theory-to-data perspective analyze data to determine their

**250**

PART III
Contemporary
Research
Designs in
Communi-
cation

goodness-of-fit with a preformulated descriptive or explanatory taxonomy. For example, a study of verbal conflict might begin with a taxonomy that classifies all conflict resolution strategies as "conciliation," "confrontation," or "avoidance." This three-part descriptive framework is applied to observed conflict situations to assess how well it matches the strategies people actually use. Second, data-to-theory researchers generate descriptive and explanatory taxonomies during observation. Observed conversational units and inferred rule-structures that appear to be related are grouped into clusters and given appropriate labels. Thus, data-to-theory analysis is exploratory, whereas theory-to-data research is confirmatory, testing the usefulness of preexisting taxonomies.

Whether one's research is exploratory or confirmatory, the conversational analyst often uses multiple raters (usually three to five people) to group or classify related elements. As with transcript coding, the researcher can have greater confidence in a taxonomy's validity if several people agree that a given array of utterances or rules is in fact an interrelated set. Researchers sometimes assess rater agreement by computing an **interrater reliability coefficient**, a statistical index ranging from 0 to 1 that registers the extent to which raters' judgments converge. The closer a coefficient is to 1, the greater the interrater agreement.

Once reasonably reliable taxonomies have been generated or verified, the researcher must decide how to analyze the resulting data. Scientists apply statistical tests for significance of relationships and differences to the frequencies with which conversational units fall into various taxonomic categories. To illustrate, suppose a conversational analyst has classified the illocutionary acts of a sample of people participating in employment interviews. The data might be analyzed by assessing differences in the frequency with which interviewers versus applicants use one or more strategy types.

Alternately, different strategies might be correlated to determine their relationship. Contrasted with this statistical approach, humanists might present examples to illustrate the nature of taxonomic categories and their interrelationships.[28]

# INTERFACE:
# CHAPTERS 12 AND 13

In this chapter, I have presented methods for analyzing interactive discourse, focusing on a naturalistic research design called conversational analysis. Conversational data bases were discussed, along with requirements for supporting research claims about the structure and functions of conversation. Step-by-step procedures for conducting a conversational analysis were described.

Chapter 13 will conclude our survey of contemporary research designs by examining methods of analyzing narrative discourse. Two general approaches to narrative discourse analysis are discussed: a scientific methodology called content analysis and a pair of humanistic methods of rhetorical criticism—neo-Aristotelian criticism and fantasy theme analysis.

# MAIN POINTS

**1.** Interactive discourse is characterized by alternating source-receiver roles. Ordinary conversations are prototypes of interactive discourse, but interviews, discussions, and debates, and other more structured forms of discourse are interactive as well.

**2.** Conversational analysis is a method for describing, explaining, and evaluating the structure and function of rules governing conversations.

**3.** A conversational rule is an "if-then" assumption that defines the communication behaviors required to achieve desired objectives in specified social contexts. Conversational rules can be interpretative or behavioral. An interpretative rule is an anticipatory assumption about the meaning of utterances, whereas a behavioral rule is an anticipatory assumption about the kinds of utterances that are appropriate in certain contexts.

**4.** A structural analysis of conversation focuses on meanings, including a conversation's microstructural or local organization of meanings and a conversation's macrostructure or the global meanings that emerge from sequential talk.

**5.** Central units of a structural analysis are the utterance (a verbal assertion), the turn (an uninterrupted stretch of talk by one person), and the topic (the subject matter of a conversation).

**6.** A functional analysis of conversation explores the actions people perform toward one another when they talk. The functions of a conversation are analyzed at both the local or microfunctional level and the global or macrofunctional level. Local analysis is an utterance-by-utterance examination of communicative actions, whereas a macrofunctional analysis explores the coordinated actions accomplished by a conversation as a whole.

**7.** The central elements of functional analysis are the illocutionary act and the perlocutionary response. An illocutionary act represents something one communicator "does to" another with an utterance, whereas a perlocutionary response is an utterance that acknowledges the impact of an illocutionary act. An adjacency pair is an illocutionary act followed by a perlocutionary response.

**8.** A combined structural-functional analysis seeks to accomplish three tasks: to describe recurring patterns of communicative interaction, to explain observed patterns by referring to interpretative and behavioral rules, and to evaluate the extent to which a conversation attains coherence—that is, the coordination of meanings and actions to achieve conversational goals.

**9.** A conversational data base consists of a body of conversations or conversational excerpts. Five sources of data are: conversations appearing in literary materials, hypothetical conversations contrived by a researcher, elicited conversations recalled or created by research participants at the researcher's request, "natural" conversations enacted by research participants in controlled laboratory settings, and naturalistic conversations enacted in settings that are part of people's normal life activity.

**10.** Four types of evidence can support claims about the existence of conversational rules: observations that a pattern of utterances recurs on a regular basis, observations that communicators can articulate the rules they are following, observations that people's conversational behaviors change with changing contexts, and observations that people's communication behaviors are critiqueable.

**11.** Two general methodological perspectives are adopted by conversational analysts: science and humanism. These approaches are distinguished on the basis of their requirements for proving claims about conversational rules.

**12.** Scientific and humanistic perspectives can be compared on four proof requirement dimensions: internal validity, external validity, replicability, and data analysis. Scientists and humanists alike require that their findings display internal validity. However, they often differ regarding external validity. Scientists typically select representative samples whose

**252**

PART III
Contemporary
Research
Designs in
Communi-
cation

characteristics can be generalized to parent populations. Humanists may use either representative or purposive samples. Thus, humanistic findings are not necessarily generalizable to parent populations. Scientific studies can be duplicated by other scientists, whereas humanistic research may or may not be replicable in the strict sense of the word. Finally, scientific data are often quantitative, whereas humanistic data are usually qualitative.

**13.** Before conducting a conversational analysis, a researcher must make informed decisions about four methodological issues: (a) a general methodological perspective, either scientific, humanistic, or a judicious blend of the two; (b) approaches to interpreting utterances, either the imposition of researcher meanings, communicator meanings, or both; (c) the observational role that a researcher will assume, whether participatory or nonparticipatory, overt or unobtrusive; and (d) approaches to theory construction, either a data-to-theory perspective or a theory-to-data approach.

**14.** Five steps are required to conduct a conversational analysis:

**a.** identify the relevant population or domain of conversation;

**b.** specify pertinent elements and observational units;

**c.** select a sample of conversations;

**d.** observe, record, and code the conversational sample; and

**e.** analyze the results.

# REVIEW EXERCISES

**1.** Indicate what conversational data base would be most appropriate for selecting a sample of each of the following types of communication. Explain the reasons for your choices.

**a.** Persuasive strategies that students use to try to influence their course instructors.

**b.** Conversations between married couples.

**c.** "First encounter" conversations between strangers.

**d.** Uses of the "royal we" as a self-reference by individual speakers and writers.

**2.** Suppose you wish to study conversations among assembly line employees in a group of large manufacturing plants. Explain how you would resolve the following preresearch methodological issues:

**a.** What general methodological perspective would you assume? Scientific? Humanistic? A blend of the two?

**b.** What observational role would you adopt? Participatory or nonparticipatory? Overt or unobtrusive?

**c.** What approach would you take to assigning meanings to utterances? Researcher meanings? Communicator meanings? Both?

**d.** How would you go about building explanations for observations? Data-to-theory perspective? Theory-to-data approach?

Explain the reasons for your various decisions.

**3.** Suppose you wish to analyze conversations among dormitory or apartment roommates. Adopt a general methodological stance, either scientific or humanistic, and then do the following: identify the relevant population of conversations; specify your elements and observational units; explain how you would select a sample of conversations; describe how you might observe, record, and code conversations; and discuss generally how you might analyze your results.

# NOTES

**1.** See Elihu Katz, "The Return of the Humanities and Sociology," *Journal of Communication*, 33, No. 3 (1983): 51–52.

**2.** Clifford Geertz, "Blurred Genres: The Refiguration of Social Thought," *American Scholar*, 39 (1979–1980): 165–67. This quotation was called to my attention by Charles Conrad, "Chrysanthemums and Swords: A Reading of Contemporary Organizational Communication Theory and Research," *Southern Journal of Speech Communication*, 50 (1985): 189–200.

**3.** Linda L. Putnam, "The Interpretive Perspective: An Alternative to Functionalism," in *Communication and Organizations: An Interpretive Approach*, eds. Linda L. Putnam and Michael E. Pacanowsky (Beverly Hills, CA: Sage, 1983), p. 31.

**4.** Margaret L. McLaughlin, *Conversation: How Talk Is Organized* (Beverly Hills, CA: Sage, 1984), p. 91.

**5.** These distinctions are extrapolated from McLaughlin.

**6.** This conception of conversational analysis follows McLaughlin's treatment of the subject.

**7.** See Scott Jacobs and Sally Jackson, "Conversational Argument: A Discourse Analytic Approach," in *Recent Advances in Argumentation Theory and Research*, eds. J. Robert Cox and Charles A. Willard (Carbondale and Edwardsville: Southern Illinois University Press, 1982).

**8.** Stanley Feldstein and J. Welkowitz, "A Chronology of Conversation: In Defense of an Objective Approach," in *Nonverbal Behavior and Communication*, eds. A. W. Siegman and Stanley Feldstein (Hillsdale, NJ: Lawrence Erlbaum, 1978), p. 335.

**9.** See J. R. Hobbes, *Why Is Discourse Coherent?* Technical Note 176 (Menlo Park, CA: SRI International, 1978).

**10.** John L. Austin, *How to Do Things with Words* (Oxford: Oxford University Press, 1962); and John R. Searle, *Speech Acts* (Cambridge: Cambridge University Press, 1969).

**11.** See Emanuel A. Schegloff, "Notes on a Conversational Practice: Formulating Place," in *Studies in Social Interaction*, ed. David Sudnow (New York: Free Press, 1972). Goffman uses the terms "couplets" and "minimal dialogue units" and van Dijk calls adjacent utterances "action-reaction pairs." See Erving Goffman, "Replies and Responses," *Language in Society*, 5 (1976): 257–313; and Teun A. van Dijk, *Text and Context: Explorations in the Semantics and Pragmatics of Discourse* (New York: Longmans, Green, 1977).

**12.** See Scott Jacobs and Sally Jackson, Collaborative Aspects of Argument Production, paper presented at the meeting of the Speech Communication Association, San Antonio, 1979; and P. Benoit, Structural Coherence Production in the Conversations of Preschool Children, paper presented at the meeting of the Speech Communication Association, New York, 1980.

**13.** G. Wells, M. MacClure, and M. Montgomery, "Some Strategies for Sustaining Conversation," in *Conversation and Discourse: Structure and Interpretation*, ed. P. Werth (New York: St. Martin's Press, 1981).

**14.** Kent Bach and Robert M. Harnish, *Linguistic Communication and Speech Acts* (Cambridge, MA: MIT Press, 1979).

**15.** McLaughlin, p. 236.

**16.** See A. D. Grimshaw, "Data and Data Use in an Analysis of Communicative Events," in *Explorations in the Ethnography of Speaking*, eds. R. Bauman and J. Sherzer (London: Cambridge University Press, 1974); and McLaughlin, pp. 237–44.

**17.** See McLaughlin, pp. 237–40.

**18.** McLaughlin, p. 238.

**19.** Sally Jackson and Scott Jacobs, "The Collective Production of Proposals in Conversational Argument and Persuasion: A Study of Disagreement Regulation," *Journal of the American Forensic Association*, 18 (1981): 77–90.

**20.** McLaughlin, pp. 247–59.

**21.** Susan B. Shimanoff, *Communication Rules: Theory and Research* (Beverly Hills, CA: Sage, 1980), p. 163.

**22.** See Sally Jackson, Building a Case for Claims About Discourse Structure, paper presented at the Michigan State University Summer Conference on Language and Discourse Processes, East Lansing, 1982.

**23.** See McLaughlin.

**24.** See Julia A. Goldberg, "A Move Toward Describing Conversational Coherence," in *Conversational Coherence: Form, Structure, and Strategy*, eds. Robert T. Craig and Karen Tracy (Beverly Hills, CA: Sage, 1983), pp. 25–45; and Putnam.

**254**

PART III
Contemporary
Research
Designs in
Communi-
cation

· **25.** See Scott Jacobs and Sally Jackson, "Strategy and Structure in Conversational Influence Attempts," *Communication Monographs*, 50 (1983): 285–304.

**26.** Gerry Philipsen, "Linearity of Research Design in Ethnographic Studies of Speaking," *Communication Quarterly*, 25 (1977): 42–50.

**27.** For an example of a typical coding scheme and a sample transcript, see Robert T. Craig and Karen Tracy, eds. *Conversational Coherence: Form, Structure, and Function* (Beverly Hills, CA: Sage, 1983), pp. 299–320.

**28.** Because conversational analysis is a relatively new research method, analysts differ remarkably in their approaches to the analysis of results. The procedure I have presented is relatively easy to execute and it reflects the practice of many conversational researchers.

# CHAPTER

# 13

# ANALYSIS OF NARRATIVE DISCOURSE

This chapter describes methods of analyzing narrative discourse. Narrative discourse is construed as a story-telling genre of speech in which speaker-listener roles are relatively fixed. Public speeches and mass communicated messages are narrative. Two general methods of narrative discourse analysis are presented. First, a scientific methodology called content analysis is discussed, including step-by-step procedures for conducting such investigations. Second, two humanistic methods of rhetorical criticism are examined: neo-Aristotelian criticism and fantasy theme analysis. Throughout, the chapter emphasizes the complementary nature of science and humanism as approaches to narrative discourse analysis.

CHAPTER
OUTLINE

W hereas conversational analysis is a relatively recent methodology, scholars have studied narrative discourse for over 2000 years. Somewhere between the fifth and fourth centuries B.C., the Greeks formalized the study of speech into an academic discipline called **rhetoric**. The need for a rhetorical education arose from the nature of Greek democracy: citizens were required to defend themselves personally and to prosecute others in courts of law. Moreover, they participated directly in the formulation of public policy, engaging in public debates and other deliberative oratory.[1]

The Athenian philosopher Aristotle was largely responsible for systematizing the principles of rhetoric, which he defined as "the faculty of observing in a given case the available means of persuasion."[2] In his classic treatise called *Rhetoric*, Aristotle divided the means of persuasion into three classes: ethos, pathos, and logos. According to Aristotle, **ethos** "depends on the personal character of the speaker"; **pathos** consists of emotional appeals and depends "on putting the audience into a certain frame of mind"; and **logos** represents the argumentative content of a message, its effectiveness hinging "on the proof, or apparent proof, provided by the words of the speech itself."[3]

Since Aristotle's time, the contours of communication's world have changed dramatically. The invention of the printing press, the advent of radio, television, and film, and the use of computer-transmitted messages are among the technological innovations that have extended the forms and functions of narrative discourse. In this chapter, I will examine methods of analyzing narrative discourse, including the public forms of speech that interested Aristotle along with mass-communicated discourse that even the most perceptive Greek visionaries could never have foreseen.

I begin by discussing the nature of narrative discourse, then describe methodological issues associated with narrative discourse analysis, paying particular attention to similarities and differences between scientific and humanistic methods. Next, the scientific methodology called content analysis is examined, followed by a treatment of some humanistic perspectives broadly labeled rhetorical criticism. Throughout the chapter, I emphasize the complementary nature of science and humanism, illustrating how the two approaches can produce a richer understanding of narrative discourse than either alone.

## THE NATURE OF NARRATIVE DISCOURSE

Narrative discourse has been defined in numerous ways. Many classical rhetoricians construed narration as the persuasive statement of a case, yet others identified it with a speaker's use of illustrative myths and anecdotes.[4] Contemporary definitions are equally diverse,[5] although most equate narrative discourse with the telling of stories. For example, Fisher views narration as a story-telling paradigm that synthesizes the persuasive and literary themes in rhetorical history.[6] Similarly, I regard narrative discourse as a story-telling genre that may serve either rhetorical or artistic functions.

For our purposes, **narrative discourse** is characterized by relatively fixed source-receiver roles, leaving little room for spontaneous role reversals. Narrative discourse includes formal public speeches, technical reports, and messages transmitted by television, radio, film, videotape, computer, and the print media. Novels and plays, letters and diaries, live and recorded music, and theatrical performances are narrative as well. Although audiences feed back responses to narrative messages, their reactions are usually receiver-based, not source-oriented, as in conversations.

**258**

PART III
Contemporary
Research
Designs in
Communi-
cation

Common receiver-based feedback forms are applause for "live" presentations and, for mediated messages, responses like letters to the editor, approval ratings, and purchases of printed material. Narrative discourse is interactive to the extent that exchanges take place between speaker and audience. However, the messages transmitted by each are typically peculiar to their *roles* as source and receiver.

Narrative discourse can be differentiated in two ways: by transmission medium and by use or function.

## Narrative Discourse and Media Form

When classified by medium, narrative discourse falls broadly into the categories of face-to-face communication and mediated communication. Face-to-face discourse is "live," so that source and receiver are physically conjoined. All five channels of communication—sight, sound, touch, taste, and smell—are available for message transmission, although sight and sound are dominant modes. Being "live," audience feedback is rapid, taking forms like applause, laughter, questions, and heckling. Public speeches including political rhetoric, social commentary, and sermons typify face-to-face narratives, but the genre also encompasses technical reports and other types of interpersonal information exchange.

In addition to traditional rhetorical narratives, "live" narration includes artistic forms like musical and theatrical performances. Popular music and theatre are often rhetorical as well as artistic, transmitting political and social commentary. For example, "protest" songs performed in the 1960s by artists like Bob Dylan, Joan Baez, and Peter, Paul, and Mary spoke of the injustices associated with racial prejudice and war.[7] Similarly, the public performances of folk artists like Woody Guthrie in the 1930s exposed the economic and social conditions of a depression-ridden America. More generally, music and group singing in churches and synagogues have always transmitted messages of unity, renewal, and hope to the worshipers.

Because of the widespread availability of television, radio, film, and print media, mass-mediated messages are often more influential than "live" rhetoric. Mass communication is limited to sight and/or sound channels and, because source and receiver are physically separated, audience feedback is typically delayed. Four types of mass communication can be differentiated by medium: television, radio, print (both traditional and electronic), and film and videotape.

Television, perhaps the most pervasive of all mass media, transmits an exceedingly broad spectrum of narrative discourse including news, documentaries, drama and comedy programs, political and social commentary, advertisements, music, and religious broadcasting. Radio likewise presents news, commentary, and advertisements, but it often specializes in musical recordings.

The print medium offers a range of narrative discourse as varied as television, encompassing public message forms like newspapers, magazines, billboards, plays, and books, along with private writings in the form of letters, diaries, and other personal documents. In addition to traditional printed artifacts, electronic "print" is rapidly becoming a major communication source. Transmitted by computerized communication modems, electronic "mail" is gaining popularity. Moreover, one can now receive the "news" on home and office microcomputers. Computer owners can buy access to several prominent news sources including Associated Press and United Press International.[8] Undoubtedly, we are only beginning to see the vast potential of microcomputers as media for transmitting electronically "printed" narratives.

Finally, films and videotapes are major sources of narrative discourse, especially entertainment programs. Motion pictures, available on film in movie theatres and in videotaped or televised form for home viewing, not only serve an entertainment function but are important sources of social and political commentary. Post-Vietnam movies such as *The Deer Hunter*, *Apocalypse Now*, *Platoon*, and the documentary *Hearts and Minds*, spoke of the senselessness and devastation of war.[9] Much earlier, the filmed version of *All Quiet on the Western Front*, a book about German soldiers in World War I, addressed with equal intensity the psychological ravages of war. The filmed version of John Steinbeck's book *The Grapes of Wrath* and Edward R. Murrow's televised documentary "Harvest of Shame" graphically depicted domestic social and economic injustices in America. Motion pictures and documentaries, then, are potent forms of artistic as well as persuasive discourse.

Filmed and videotaped musical performances likewise exert an important influence on fashion, social attitudes, and political beliefs. The televised and commercial "videos" of many contemporary performers send messages that transcend the music itself, including changing views about gender roles and other social rules and customs. Thus, popular music, which has always carried profound political and social overtones, is more influential than ever because of novel mass dissemination systems.

## The Functions of Narrative Discourse

Narrative discourse can be classified not only by transmission medium but also by the uses people make of narratives. Whether "live" or mediated, narrative discourse serves a persuasive function, an informational function, and an entertainment function.

**Persuasive discourse** influences audiences by creating, reinforcing, or changing their modes of thinking, feeling, or acting. Persuaders include "live" public speakers, television and radio commentators, newspaper editors, songwriters and performers, authors of fiction and nonfiction, commercial advertisers in the print and electronic media, "electronic" ministers, and the writers and directors of "entertainment" programs for television and motion pictures. For example, television often paints influential portraits of the "proper" roles of various groups in American society. Television dramas and advertisements sometimes portray a world in which men are doctors but not nurses and women are rarely plumbers or lumberjacks. Thus, television often "persuades" by its presentation of diverse social groups in fictional dramatic roles.

**Informational discourse** disseminates "facts" about the physical, social, and political world. Informational sources include television and print reporters, writers of technical documents, authors of many nonfiction books, and the writers and producers of television documentaries. Moreover, the writers of private letters and diaries often become, sometimes unwittingly, the purveyors of important social and historical information. For example, the letters and other private papers of prominent statesmen like George Washington, literary figures such as Virginia Woolf, and ordinary citizens like the Nazi Holocaust victim Anne Frank provide important information about the times as well as the character and temperament of the individual writer.

Informational discourse such as news reports and technical documents often persuades as well as informs. Information is not a neutral phenomenon; people sometimes change their opinions simply because they learn new things. Moreover, information sources often reveal their viewpoints by the kinds of information they select and the ways they present the information. Thus, we usually classify narrative discourse as "informational" when the acquisition of "facts" appears to be its principal effect.

**260**

PART III
Contemporary
Research
Designs in
Communi-
cation

Finally, **entertainment discourse** amuses, delights, or otherwise diverts listeners from the drudgery of the work-a-day world. Television situation comedies or "sitcoms," fantasy works like cartoons and science fiction, humorous public addresses (often called "after-dinner speeches"), musical performances, and dramatic television programs are examples of entertaining discourse. In addition to their artistic functions, certain entertainment forms have persuasive overtones as well. Television sitcoms, although highly amusing, can be remarkably persuasive. For example, the syndicated series "M\*A\*S\*H" satirized war and Norman Lear's "All in the Family," a long-running show starring Carroll O'Connor as Archie Bunker, ridiculed ethnic and sexual bigotry.

# NARRATIVE DISCOURSE ANALYSIS

**Narrative discourse analysis** is an unobtrusive methodology that explores the meaning, structure, and function of narrative messages. It aims to achieve one or more of the following four purposes: description, inference, interpretation, and criticism or evaluation. Descriptive analysis is expository, spelling out the meanings, organizational features, and functions of narrative messages. Inferential analysis draws conclusions about phenomena external to a message based on salient message characteristics. For example, an analysis of 1950s television programming that allows us to draw conclusions about the social norms or political attitudes of that era is inferential. Inferential analysis uses descriptive information to project conclusions about phenomena that correlate with message content.

Interpretation goes beyond inference and speculates about the intrinsic content of a message and its relation to extrinsic phenomena.

For example, an analysis construing a narrative genre like American Western movies as a series of allegorical confrontations between good and evil captures the flavor of interpretative research. Finally, criticism involves an explicit discussion of the meanings, structure, and functions of narrative discourse based on a set of evaluative criteria. **Rhetorical criticism** focuses on artistic and pragmatic issues such as evaluating a speaker's language uses and his or her skill in adapting a message to audiences and to situational constraints.

# Issues in Narrative Discourse Analysis

The extent to which researchers engage in description, inference, interpretation, and criticism/evaluation depends on methodological perspective, specifically whether they embrace the tenets of science or humanism. Scientists focus on description and inference, observing communication data and inferring conclusions with regard to other empirically based phenomena. By contrast, the humanistic perspective emphasizes interpretation and criticism. Although humanists generate descriptions and inferences about narrative artifacts, descriptive and inferential data usually serve as starting points for interpreting and evaluating discourse.

All narrative discourse analysts must resolve five methodological issues: (1) quantitative versus qualitative data analysis, (2) manifest versus latent message content, (3) probability versus purposive sampling, (4) intrinsic versus extrinsic data bases, and (5) analytical versus critical research. When fashioning a comprehensive research plan, the researcher puts together a "package" design combining in a consistent way one of the two alternatives posed by each of these contrasting approaches. Thus, the final research design can be classified on all five dimensions. The choice of one alternative over its opposing perspective often turns on whether a research project is undertaken from a scientific or a humanistic posture.

## Quantitative versus qualitative data analysis

Quantitative data are numerals representing the salient features of narrative content. Quantitative data usually consist of the frequencies with which certain words, themes, episodes, and so forth appear in a given narrative. For example, a researcher examining the portrayal of women on prime time television might count the number of female characters appearing in roles as two-dimensional sex objects, as full-time housewives and mothers, and as working professionals. Quantitative data may also represent a tabulation of the presence or absence of some characteristic in a sample of narratives. A researcher might categorize entire television programs as either violent or nonviolent and count the number falling into each set. After making frequency counts, the researcher typically performs statistical tests to determine whether the frequencies differ or are related significantly.

Qualitative data are often described as "narrative" information consisting of verbal summaries of observations. Being linguistic, such data are not amenable to standard statistical analysis. To illustrate, a researcher might analyze the thematic structure of Bob Dylan's early "protest" lyrics and conclude that they repeatedly stress themes like economic oppression, racial injustice, the absurdity of war, and the transitory nature of interpersonal relationships.

Notice the similarities between this "qualitative" analysis and a "quantitative" perspective. Both characterize samples of discourse by explicitly or implicitly noting the presence or absence of certain attributes of interest—for example, lyrical themes, televised violence, or female dramatic roles. Certain differences appear to turn on the fact that "quantitative" analysts actually count recurring analytical units, whereas "qualitative" researchers present their informed judgments of the magnitude and intensity of repetitive themes. The latter perspective precludes statistical analysis, whereas the former invites it. Despite apparent similarities, many researchers regard the two approaches as remarkably different. Regardless of the view one takes, researchers who consider themselves scientists usually take a quantitative perspective and apply statistical methods, whereas self-identified humanists often prefer to leave data in linguistic form.

## Manifest versus latent content analysis

The **manifest content** of narrative discourse consists of surface meanings that are intrinsic to a text or script, including its apparent themes, its linguistic usages, and its stylistic and structural features. By contrast, **latent content** refers to deeper layers of meaning that must be inferred by "reading between the lines." Latent meanings often consist of inferences about the personality traits, intentions, and values of a message source. Alternately, latent meanings include inferrable information about target audiences and message contexts, that is, the social, economic, and political conditions prevailing at the time the discourse was presented.

During the early years of narrative discourse analysis, scientists emphasized manifest content, whereas humanists focused on deep or latent meanings.[10] However, later investigators have argued that such a distinction is no longer tenable.[11] Scientists and humanists alike study both manifest and latent content. Indeed, a major goal of contemporary scientific researchers is to logically infer latent content from surface data. On the manifest versus latent content issue, then, there are few if any differences between scientific and humanistic analysts.

**262**

PART III
Contemporary
Research
Designs in
Communi-
cation

## Probability versus purposive sampling

Scientific researchers usually employ probability methods to select representative samples of narrative discourse. Probability methods (discussed fully in Chapter 5) include simple random sampling, systematic sampling with a random start, stratified sampling, and multi-stage cluster sampling. Probability sampling allows researchers to infer conclusions with respect to the populations from which the samples were selected. Humanistic researchers are not bound by a probability sampling requirement and therefore are free to study purposive samples having important historical or artistic value. As we learned in Chapter 5, purposively selected data are not necessarily generalizable to parent populations.

## Intrinsic versus extrinsic data analysis

**Intrinsic data analysis** is limited to the content—both manifest and latent—of the discourse to be studied. In **extrinsic data analysis**, however, researchers use information about the context, including the personal, social, economic, and political milieus in which a discourse was presented. The question raised by these data sources concerns the proper subject matter of narrative discourse analysis: Must one's analysis be restricted to the data yielded by the discourse alone, or should the researcher base an analysis on the discourse-in-context, implying that all relevant situational information is an integral component of narrative data?

Many scientific researchers argue that a discourse and its context are inseparable and that both are legitimate evidence for narrative discourse analysis.[12] Humanistic researchers sometimes disagree regarding the appropriate subject matter of discourse analysis. Rhetorical critics often make a distinction between "history" and "criticism," and certain of them contend that a communication researcher's role is to apply critical standards to discourse, leaving historical-situational data to the devices of historians.[13] Others argue that situational and historical data are essential ingredients of rhetorical studies.[14] Despite these theoretical differences, most humanists as a matter of practice utilize both intrinsic and extrinsic data when analyzing and criticizing narrative discourse.

## Analytical versus critical research

Analysis variously combines description, inference, and interpretation, whereas criticism applies evaluative standards to assess the pragmatic and artistic quality of narrative discourse. This issue sharply differentiates scientists from humanists. Science, said to be a value-free methodology, relies principally on descriptive and explanatory analysis. However, evaluative criteria are essential components of much humanistic research. Humanists assess the pragmatic effects of narrative discourse as well as the appropriateness and artistry of the methods sources use to persuade, inform, and entertain.

# Selecting a Method of Analysis

Our discussion of the five issues in narrative discourse analysis has clarified some critical differences and similarities between scientific and humanistic methods. Both are useful ways to understand human discourse. When appropriately applied, they should complement one another in the pursuit of meaningful descriptive, explanatory, and evaluative information.

When deciding which method to use, the researcher should be guided by the nature of the problem to be resolved. For example, a humanistic approach is appropriate for purposive studies of particular discourse types, whereas the study of populations of discourse lends itself to a scientific stance. Descriptive and inferential analyses are amenable to the methods of science. However, evaluative criticism is the proper domain of humanistic methodologies. Narrative discourse analysis as a general methodology can benefit from both scientific and humanistic insights. As George Gerbner has observed, the scholarly debate between the scientist and the humanist is not primarily methodological, since "both are needed for different purposes"; rather, the dialogue "is, as it should be, about how to make research most productive in illuminating the dynamics . . . of communications in society." [15]

Given this prologue to narrative discourse analysis, we are now ready to examine several specific methodologies. I will begin by exploring a dominant scientific approach called content analysis, then two humanistic methods will be examined: a traditional neo-Aristotelian perspective and a dramatistic methodology called fantasy theme analysis.

## CONTENT ANALYSIS

**Content analysis** as a scientific method dates to eighteenth-century Sweden when a group of scholars and clergy analyzed a collection of 90 nonorthodox hymns called the *Songs of Zion*. To determine whether the songs blasphemed the doctrines of the Swedish state church, one group of researchers compared the religious symbols found in the *Songs of Zion* with those contained in the established hymnbook. Finding no differences, they concluded that the songs were an acceptable alternative to orthodox church music. [16] Content analysis began in the United States in the late nineteenth century with a series of "quantitative newspaper analyses." A typical study published in 1893 analyzed the content of leading New York newspapers over time and found that between 1881 and 1893 reports on religious, scientific, and literary topics declined dramatically in favor of gossip, sporting events, and political scandals. [17]

Modern content analysis came of age during World War II when the United States government enlisted specialists to study the content of German radio transmissions. All Nazi broadcasts, including commentary and music, along with the public speeches of political leaders, were analyzed for manifest and latent meanings. Based on these studies, the researchers were able to correctly predict several major German military campaigns, the development of new weaponry, changes in public morale, and shifts in political relationships both within the Nazi elite and between the Axis countries. [18] After the war, content analysis became a major tool for assessing the nature, functions, and effects of mass communication. Its popularity and general usefulness are undiminished today.

## The Nature and Purposes of Content Analysis

According to Ole Holsti, content analysis is "any technique for making inferences by objectively and systematically identifying specified characteristics of messages," [19] and Klaus Krippendorff defined it as "a research technique for making replicable and valid inferences" from narrative "data to their context." [20] Taken together, these definitions clarify two critical functions of content analysis: to provide a systematic and verifiable description of the manifest and latent content of narrative discourse, and to produce logically valid and replicable inferences about a narrative's context based on its descriptive content. The context of discourse refers to its "empirical environment," [21] including characteristics of the message source, the audience, the historical-situational milieu in which the discourse was presented, and the nature and magnitude of its effects.

Irving Janis captured these descriptive and inferential functions by differentiating two varieties of content analysis: *semantical content*

**264**

PART III
Contemporary
Research
Designs in
Communi-
cation

*analysis*, which he defined as exploration of narrative discourse to ascertain its meaning, and *pragmatical content analysis*, characterized as the use of meaningful content to infer external causes and effects.[22] Holsti elaborated on Janis's distinction by arguing that content analysis has three principal functions: (1) to describe the characteristics of communication, asking what, how, and to whom something is said; (2) to make inferences as to the antecedents of communication, asking why something is said; and (3) to make inferences about the consequences of communication, asking with what effects something is said.[23]

Descriptive functions served by content analysis include the identification of recurring thematic and structural patterns in messages, and the comparison of the content of messages delivered by different communicators, or alternately, messages presented by the same communicator in different contexts. Critical inferential tasks include drawing conclusions about the probable characteristics of message sources, audiences, and contexts; inferring conclusions about the likely effects of messages; and inferring the cultural norms and social behaviors that a message appears to reflect.

Certain of these descriptive and inferential functions can be accomplished with a **cross-sectional survey**. For example, a sample of public speeches or newspaper reports pertaining to a significant historical event, say, the resignation of former President Richard Nixon, might be analyzed for purposes of inferring the event's consequences, say, its effects on American attitudes toward government. Alternately, a sample of movies or books that represent some genre—for instance, science fiction—might be studied to isolate its defining characteristics. Other descriptive and inferential tasks require **longitudinal** studies, which analyze samples of discourse over time to ascertain trends in content and effects. For instance, we might select samples of prime time television programs shown over a 10-year period to study shifts in

portrayals of minorities or the elderly. Or, the works of a single author or musician could be examined over the course of his or her career to track evolving thematic or structural developments.

As with all methodological decisions, the choice of cross-sectional versus longitudinal studies depends on the nature of the research problem. Moreover, the extent to which a content analyst emphasizes description versus inference or gives the two functions equal weight is likewise dependent on research objectives.

## Scientific Requirements and Content Analysis

As a scientific method, content analysis must satisfy certain fundamental requirements. Three of these requirements are especially important. First, content analysis produces generalizable conclusions about classes of discourse. Content analysts use probability sampling methods to generate representative samples of discourse that reflect well the characteristics of parent populations. Second, content analysis is predominantly quantitative in that researchers typically group the characteristics of discourse into related categories, determine the frequency with which pertinent characteristics fall into categories, and apply statistical tests for significance of differences or relationships to these frequency data.

Third, content analysis is objective in two related respects. First, content analysis is said to be objective because of its intersubjectivity or replicability. Assuming that researchers have fully described their research methods (including decision rules and evidentiary materials), other independent researchers can duplicate the research and confirm or disconfirm it. Second, researchers restrict their descriptions and inferences to directly and indirectly observable phenomena. Directly observable data include manifest message content and documentable information about message sources, audiences, and situational conditions. Indirectly observable data refer to latent message content and to the empirical correlates of a message, including its causes and effects. For example, by examining early mass communications involving black Americans—for example, defunct radio and television shows such as "Amos 'n Andy"—we can infer that blacks of the time were portrayed in demeaning roles. Moreover, historical evidence supports this indirectly observable conclusion. Content analysis, then, is objective in the sense that researchers limited themselves to empirically based conclusions that can be confirmed by others.

## Conducting Content Analysis

Six steps are required to conduct content analysis: (1) identify the research problem, (2) determine a suitable data base, (3) select a representative sample, (4) collect contextual information, (5) develop a measurement scheme, and (6) analyze data.

### Identifying the research problem

This first step entails deciding exactly what one wants to know, including whether the desired information is predominantly descriptive, inferential, or both. Once general aims have been identified, the researcher must clarify specific objectives. For example, one might want to describe persuasive strategies used in prime time television advertising or, alternately, to infer conclusions about the social effects of the roles blacks play in movies today. Notice that these hypothetical objectives not only specify the problems of interest (persuasive strategies and social effects), but they also clarify the narrative data base that is suitable for studying the problems (prime time television and contemporary motion pictures). The second inquiry stage

elaborates on the critical question of finding appropriate data bases.

### Determining a suitable data base

As I indicated earlier, a problem statement should define appropriate data bases. Indeed, a well-framed problem statement clarifies not only the problem of interest, but also the data base that is most suitable for exploring the problem.

Narrative data are often conceptualized as "physical traces" that the problem of interest has left behind or as "actuarial records" that were created and maintained for reasons other than a researcher's interest in them.[24] When searching for suitable narrative data, the researcher must select communication artifacts that are directly pertinent to the research problem. If one wishes to learn about American attitudes toward personal and household fashion, popular television programs will surely be a more suitable data base than public speeches. However, public statements are likely to be excellent data for establishing inferences about a nation's political and social attitudes.

### Selecting a representative sample

Once the research problem and its associated data base have been clarified, the analyst must select a representative sample of data. There are two preliminary steps. First, the researcher must operationalize the population of interest. Suppose, for example, that I am interested in studying how racial minorities are portrayed on television. To concretize the narrative population, I must say exactly what "television" consists of for this study. Commercial television only? If so, what aspects of commercial television? Prime time programming only? If so, are advertisements included? What programming time period is used for defining the population? The past six months? The past week?

When population boundaries have been precisely defined, the researcher must specify

**266**

PART III
Contemporary
Research
Designs in
Communi-
cation

the smallest entities within a population that are of interest—the elements. For example, in a study of television portrayals of women, elements might be all female characters who appear in drama or comedy shows on prime time commercial television. Alternately, we might decide to limit our study to female characters who have speaking roles. To become even more restrictive, we could define our elements as female characters having major or "starring" roles.

When the elements of a well-defined population have been specified, the researcher is ready to select a representative sample. Two sample selection approaches are often used. First, the researcher can construct a sampling frame that lists every element in a population, then select a representative sample using simple random, systematic, or stratified probability methods. Since this approach can be quite time-consuming especially with large populations, a multistage cluster procedure is often used. With the latter approach, a representative sample of subsets is selected from the population, whereupon either a representative sample is analyzed, or all the elements appearing in the selected subsets are studied.

To illustrate these two sampling methods, suppose I am interested in television portrayals of minorities. Suppose further that my population consists of "all prime time commercial television programs excluding advertisements that were broadcast over the past six months," and that my elements are "minority characters with speaking roles." Using the single-stage sampling approach, I need to identify every minority character with a speaking role in six months' worth of prime time programming, a rather formidable task. Once a list (sampling frame) has been compiled, I will apply a method like simple random sampling or systematic sampling with a random start. The systematic approach involves choosing every $k$th (perhaps every 50th or every 75th) element for the sample, picking the first element at random.

Using the multistage cluster approach, I

might begin by selecting at random a collection of weeks (a primary sampling unit) from the six-month period, then randomly select a series of days (a secondary sampling unit) from within each selected week. I could then select at random a group of minority characters from within each programming day as my final sample. Or, I could create an additional sampling unit before selecting the final sample. A randomly selected group of programs from within each selected day might be useful as an added sampling unit. My final sampling units or elements, minority speaking roles, would then be drawn from the sample of television programs. If a multistage cluster method includes three or more stages, researchers often analyze the entire array of elements appearing in the last selected clusters. Taking this approach, I would study every minority speaking character that appears in the final set of randomly selected programs. (To refresh your understanding of the sampling methods described in this section, refer back to Chapter 5.)

## Collecting contextual information

Upon collecting a representative discourse sample, the researcher must search for relevant **contextual information**—data about phenomena extrinsic to a given discourse, including information about the message source, the audience, the message's historical-situational background, and documentable message effects. As Krippendorff has noted, "some empirical evidence about the connections" between narrative data and "what is to be inferred from them" is required in order "to justify inferences."[25]

Common sources of contextual data include audience surveys seeking opinions about the nature and effects of a given narrative; interviews with message sources exploring their intentions and motivations; contemporaneous and historical documents detailing discourse-related situational information; and relevant theories postulating relationships between antecedent conditions, messages, and their consequent effects. Such information is useful for assigning meaning to a given narrative and for inferring conclusions both about its motivational basis and its short- and long-range effects.

## Developing a measurement system

By the fifth or measurement stage of content analysis, both the sample data and pertinent contextual information have been collected. The researcher is now ready to perform one of the most important tasks in content analysis: devising a scheme for measuring data. (Measurement schemes were discussed at length in Chapters 3 and 4.) Like conversational data, narrative data are usually measured nominally by grouping related information into categories. For example, a researcher analyzing television portrayals of women might measure elements (for example, female characters with speaking roles) by sorting them into the categories developed by Suzanne Pingree and her associates: (1) decorative sex objects, (2) full-time housewives and mothers, (3) housewives and mothers who have culturally insignificant outside work, (4) working professional women, and (5) women having no explicit or implicit gender-based roles.[26]

Whether researchers begin with preformulated categories or generate their categories during observation depends on whether they take a theory-to-data or a data-to-theory research perspective. Theory-to-data researchers develop categories in advance (perhaps based on contextual information) that they believe will adequately characterize a given narrative. The measurement process then serves as a means of testing the predetermined category system. In a data-to-theory analysis there are no preconceived categories; rather, these emerge naturally from narrative content. The preferred approach depends on whether appropriate category systems are available and on the research objectives—principally, whether a researcher wishes to develop or to test theoretical categories.

Regardless of perspective, all content analysts employ raters or judges (usually three or more persons) to independently sort narrative data into related categories, a process called **coding**. As discussed in Chapter 12, researchers often compute **interrater reliability coefficients** ranging from 0 to 1 to index the level of agreement among raters. The closer a coefficient is to 1, the greater the magnitude of intersubjective agreement.

## Analyzing the results

The results of a content analysis typically represent the frequency with which elements are placed into each category associated with the chosen nominal scale. To illustrate, recall the five-category scale of female roles referred to earlier. Pingree and her colleagues applied this scale to a random sample of 447 advertisements that appeared during one year in *Playboy*, *Time*, *Newsweek*, and *Ms.* magazines. The resulting data showed that, across all four magazines, 27% of the ads fell into the "decorative sex object" category, 48% portrayed women as full-time housewives and mothers, 4% were coded as working housewives and mothers, 19% depicted women as independent professionals, and 2% of the ads evidenced no sexual stereotyping whatsoever. Pingree and her associates used a chi-square statistic to analyze these frequencies for significance differences.[27] This research illustrates a typical analysis of categorical content data. Results are displayed as numerals, usually frequencies, which are then statistically tested for significant population differences or relationships.

## Contemporary Content Analysis: A Prototype

From 1967 to date, Gerbner and his colleagues have conducted longitudinal studies of televised violence using a two-stage research protocol called the cultural indicators approach.[28] The first stage is a content analysis which

**268**

PART III
Contemporary
Research
Designs in
Communi-
cation

Gerbner calls a "message system analysis." Each year, the researchers select a large random sample of prime time adult dramas along with a random sample of children's dramatic programs shown on weekend mornings. Based on these samples, they classify violent episodes into a three-category "Violence Index" that includes the "prevalence," the "rate," and the "role" of all dramatized "expression[s] of physical force."[29] The second method, called "cultivation analysis," is a survey procedure designed to collect contextual information about the impact of televised violence on perceptions of social reality. More generally, cultivation analysis attempts to determine whether television fosters in viewers certain unrealistic assumptions about "the facts, norms, and values of society."[30]

Based on a content analysis of nearly 1000 programs aired between 1967 and 1975, including almost 3000 leading characters appearing in more than 600 hours of viewing time, Gerbner and his associates found that 79.8% of the programs contained explicit violence. Moreover, 83.6% of all leading characters were involved in some kind of violence, with 10.2% involved in a killing. Finally, the researchers found that an average of 7.4 violent episodes occurred during each hour of viewing time. Based on this profile, Gerbner and Gross concluded that television presents "a symbolic world ruled largely by violence."[31]

Gerbner and his colleagues periodically gather contextual information to determine whether viewers' perceptions of the "real world" are affected by what they see on television. They ask both "heavy" and "light" viewers about their perceptions of the nature and magnitude of violence in their own lives. These findings show that people's perceptions of violence reflect "television reality" more accurately than "actual" environmental occurrences. For example, one longitudinal study showed that 52% of "heavy" television viewers expressed strong fears of being victimized by violence, whereas only 39% of "light" viewers reported

similar fears. In response to the question "Can most people be trusted?", 65% of the "heavy" viewers expressed little trust in people, compared to 48% of "light" viewers. Finally, 59% of "heavy" viewers reported an exaggerated impression of the number of people employed in law enforcement in the United States compared to 50% of "light" viewers.[32] Based on this evidence, Gerbner and his associates concluded that "TV appears to cultivate assumptions [in viewers] that fit its socially functional myths," including an exaggerated belief in the legitimacy of force, a diminished trust in other people, a heavy emotional dependence on established authority, and a heightened sense of risk, insecurity, and fear of victimization.[33]

This research illustrates the contributions that content analysis can make to our understanding of communication's role in contemporary culture. The descriptive function of content analysis is exemplified well by Gerbner's "Violence Index" methods. The inferential role, relying heavily on contextual information, is nicely chronicled by the survey techniques used in cultivation analysis. Finally, Gerbner's program of research illustrates well how a scientific analysis can yield "humanistically" meaningful conclusions about the world of human communication.[34]

# HUMANISTIC ANALYSIS AND RHETORICAL CRITICISM

The humanistic approach to narrative discourse analysis generates descriptive and inferential information, but its principal contributions consist of interpretations and criticisms of communication artifacts. Criticisms are based on evaluative criteria that set forth artistic and pragmatic standards for judging a given discourse. Although the reasonableness of critiques can be checked by independent analysts who share a common set of evaluative standards, criticism cannot be replicated in the scientific sense of the word.

From a humanistic perspective, any narrative discourse can be interpreted and critiqued at two different levels of meaning.[35] The first, called the level of **discursive logic**, pertains to the rational progression of ideas in a message. Thus, a discursive analysis focuses on the arguments developed in a message, language usages, a message's organizational features, and modes of message presentation. The second level of meaning, called the level of **creative imagination** or **nondiscursive logic**, concerns the myths, fantasies, and dramatic characterizations that emerge from messages. Mythic stories of "good against evil," which often appear in movies and books, along with emotionally charged symbols that capture the public imagination (for example, Franklin Roosevelt's "New Deal" and John Kennedy's "New Frontier") are examples of creative imagery in discourse. In this section, I will examine two methods of rhetorical analysis and criticism: neo-Aristotelian criticism, which focuses on the rational or discursive level of analysis, and fantasy theme analysis, which interprets and criticizes narrative discourse as a creative myth-making activity.

## Neo-Aristotelian Criticism

The rhetorical tradition originated by Aristotle was elaborated by several Roman scholars writing around the time of the birth of Christ. The Roman rhetoricians, among them Cicero and Quintilian, are credited with dividing the study of rhetoric into five major topics, the classical canons of rhetoric, namely: invention, disposition, elocution, delivery, and memory. **Invention** involves the gathering of materials to support the arguments in a message and the methods selected for adapting these materials to the audience. Traditional inventive materials include evidence and logic (Aristotle's logos), emotional appeals (pathos), and appeals based on a speaker's credibility (ethos). **Disposition** is the organization and arrangement of the materials in a message, whereas **elocution** concerns a message's language and style. **Delivery**, of course, consists of message presentation, including all the vocal and physical elements of speaking. Finally, **memory** comprises devices for recalling materials for message presentation.[36]

All the canons of rhetoric, save memory (often called the "lost" canon), form the basis of **neo-Aristotelian criticism**. This mode of criticism focuses on the rational or discursive logic of narrative discourse, seeking to analyze and critique: (1) the materials used to develop ideas and adapt them to an audience, (2) the structure of a message, (3) the stylistic features of a message, including the clarity and artistry of language use, and (4) techniques of delivery or message presentation. Neo-Aristotelian criticism usually proceeds in two stages: a descriptive analysis and interpretation of a rhetorical artifact, followed by an evaluative criticism of the pragmatic and artistic quality of a message.[37]

### Analysis and interpretation

Whether the narrative discourse is a speech, an essay, a book, a television program, a piece of lyrical music, or a motion picture, the rhetorical critic begins by describing and interpreting the various components of the discourse. The analysis usually covers four issues: theme, structure, style, and presentation.

A *thematic analysis* describes and synthesizes the ideational content of a message. What are its major themes? What materials, including informational, persuasive, and artistic devices, are used to develop ideas and adapt them to the audience? What motivational materials are used to appeal to the audience? What kind of image does the message source project to the audience? These questions address Aristotle's three rhetorical methods: *logos* (argumentative and ideational content), *pathos* (emotional appeals), and *ethos* (message source credibility).

**270**

PART III
Contemporary
Research
Designs in
Communi-
cation

A *structural analysis* describes the aspects of a message that give it *unity*, or singleness of purpose, *order*, or the sequencing of ideas, and *coherence*, which refers first to the way ideas are linked transitionally and second to the manner in which the ideas-as-a-unit are related to the overall purpose of a message.[38] Thus, coherence captures the salient features of both unity and order.

A *stylistic analysis* describes a speaker's or writer's use of language, including such linguistic features as vocabulary, syntax, and embellishments (often called "figures of speech"). Is the source's language simple or complex? Is it "conversational" or embellished with "poetic" usages? In general, stylistic analysts look for evidence of *clarity* and *interestingness* in the language of a message.

*Presentational analysis* focuses on the means of delivering a message. If the discourse is "live" speaking, the vocal and gestural qualities of a speaker's delivery are analyzed. With mass communications such as motion pictures or television programs, the rhetorical critic must consider additional factors. For example, variables such as camera angle and editing decisions are important presentational features of filmed and videotaped materials. The researcher must analyze these factors along with verbal and nonverbal delivery cues. When the discourse to be analyzed is printed material, presentational strategies take on a quite different character, since structure and style are integral to presentation. Indeed, visual presentations are accomplished principally through an author's choice of structural and stylistic devices. For this reason, a separate presentational analysis of printed documents is usually unnecessary.

## Evaluation and criticism

Rhetorical critics typically employ one or more of the following three forms of criticism: pragmatic, artistic, and historical. **Pragmatic criticism** assesses the immediate and long-range effects of a message on the audience and the society toward which the message was directed. Pragmatic critics estimate how well a source adapted his or her message to the target audience and to contemporary issues. Long-term effects are also evaluated, including the impact, if any, of a given discourse—whether speech, book, motion picture, or musical form—on the customs, values, and habits of society.

**Artistic criticism** addresses the literary beauty or aesthetic value of narrative discourse. Thus, the elegance and durability of the style, structure, and ideational content of narrative discourse are important issues for the artistic critic. Finally, **historical criticism** focuses on the "historical truth" of the ideas in a message. Historical critics "ask whether or not history bears out the truth of what the speaker said [and] evaluate the extent to which the speaker reflects, leads, or trails behind the society in what he believes and says."[39]

As one might expect, it is possible to place radically different evaluations on a given narrative discourse depending on which of the three approaches is embraced. Narrative forms that have little pragmatic effect can possess great artistic beauty and may in addition carry profound historical truths. On the other hand, historically "empty" rhetoric is often exceedingly effective both on immediate audiences and on the general culture. For example, Adolf Hitler's anti-Semitic rhetoric had a powerful impact on listeners, and indeed on all the world, yet the ideational content of such speeches was contrary to every value that one might remotely call "human." As with other discourse analysis decisions, researchers are guided in the choice of critical mode by the nature of the problem they wish to illuminate.

As a matter of disciplinary preference, some rhetorical critics emphasize pragmatic and historical criticisms, leaving the critique of artistry to literary critics. Others focus exclusively on pragmatic issues, arguing that the criticism of effects is the only legitimate domain of rhetorical scholarship.[40] Regardless of academic perspective, all three critical perspectives are practical, useful tools for studying discourse. Therefore, I recommend that researchers let the research problem at hand rather than academic territorial issues govern their choice of methods.

# Fantasy Theme Analysis and Dramatistic Criticism

Whereas neo-Aristotelian criticism emphasizes discursive logic, that is, the rational development of a discourse, fantasy theme analysis is a genre of **dramatistic criticism** focusing on the level of meaning we referred to earlier as "creative imagination." More particularly, **fantasy theme analysis** construes narrative discourse as a story-telling or myth-making activity akin to theatrical presentations. As such, all discourse forms, including public speeches, motion pictures, telecasts, and printed materials, are believed to present powerful symbolic characterizations capable of moving their audiences into "a new realm of reality—a world of heroes, villains, saints, and enemies." When an audience is caught up emotionally in narrative dramatizations, it is "transported to a world which seems somehow even more real than the everyday world. One may feel exalted, fascinated, perhaps horrified or threatened, or powerfully impelled to action, but in any case, involved." In short, an audience "is psychologically taken into a psychodramatic fantasy world" and its members become attached to one another because they share the same dramatized symbolic reality.[41]

## Components of fantasy theme analysis

Developed by Ernest Bormann,[42] fantasy theme analysis owes a great intellectual debt to Kenneth Burke's original work on dramatistic criticism and to Robert Bales's treatment of fantasizing processes in small interacting groups.[43] According to Bormann, narrative discourse as psychodrama entails four related components: fantasy themes, fantasy types, rhetorical visions, and rhetorical communities. A **fantasy theme** is a story or dramatic reference in a message that presents characters, principally heroes and villains, performing action sequences somewhere other than the "here and now." The principal characters may be living persons, historical figures, or envisioned future personalities. Moreover, they may be ordinary mortals or superhuman figures. The fantasy theme is essentially a **myth**, a "story about a particular incident which is put forward as containing or suggesting some general truth."[44] Fantasy themes present heroes and villains not as literal creatures but rather as *symbols* of a more general message the speaker or writer wishes to convey.

To illustrate the fantasy theme, consider the American Western film. Western movies almost always depict a gunfight in which some "hero," perhaps the town marshal or the local sheriff, defeats a "villain," usually a gang of misfits who precipitate a fight through acts of lawlessness. As Peter Homans has noted, such a dramatic portrayal is a symbolic confrontation between good and evil; it is "a myth in which evil appears as a series of temptations to be resisted by the hero . . . through inner control." When faced with an evil villain, the hero "destroys the threat," yet "the story is so structured that the responsibility for this act [of destruction] falls upon the adversary, permitting the hero to destroy while appearing to save."[45] This analysis of the Western genre fits many science fiction works and other narrative forms as well.

Fantasy themes such as these appear not only in intrinsically dramatic forms like movies, novels, and plays, but also in public rhetoric. For example, black orators in the 1960s mobilized the nation to break the grip of racial discrimination by creating a series of villains in

272

PART III
Contemporary
Research
Designs in
Communi-
cation

the form of the "white racist" and the "redneck bigot." Individuals like Alabama's governor George Wallace, Birmingham's police commissioner Eugene "Bull" Connor, and Georgia's ax-wielding governor Lester Maddox were presented as embodiments of racial oppression. Prominent black rhetorical heroes included "god" (the ultimate source of redemption, salvation, and freedom) and revered black leaders such as Martin Luther King, Jr., and Malcolm X. The symbolic confrontation in which good ultimately triumphs over evil was dramatically played out over and over again with the singing of "We Shall Overcome." As these examples suggest, fantasy themes are mythic stories inhabited by heroes and villains who articulate general truths that transcend the literal aspects of the story.

The second component, the **fantasy type**, is a general category of recurring fantasy themes appearing in a series of related messages. Parables of "good versus evil" constitute a prominent fantasy type in much narrative discourse. Indeed, other fantasy types are often subsets of "good," "evil," or the conflict between the two. For example, a recurring fantasy associated with certain feminist rhetoric is "the powerful versus the powerless," with speakers and writers attributing power to the male establishment (the evil villain) and powerlessness to women (the good victim). "Oppression" of various sorts is a common fantasy type in minority rhetoric, including gay and lesbian communication and Hispanic rhetoric. The "oppressor" is imbued with evil, often "sinful" characteristics, whereas the "oppressed" are presented as long-suffering victims who ultimately will be released because it is morally "right." Along this line, the notion of "redemption," whether in this life or a life hereafter, is a prominent fantasy type, both in secular and religious speaking. In sum, a fantasy type is a group of fantasy themes so closely related that they constitute a general thematic class.

A third construct in fantasy theme analysis, the **rhetorical vision**, is defined from an audience's perspective. It consists of shared fantasies or composite dramas that capture the imagination and allegiance of sizable groups of people, creating for them a unique but common symbolic reality. The followers of Martin Luther King, Jr., shared his "dream" of a time when the sons of former slaves and the sons of former slaveowners would sit down together at the table of brotherhood. Similarly, social activists on both sides of the abortion controversy are caught up in rhetorical visions that include fantasy themes such as "murder" and "life" on the one hand and "personal choice" and "control" on the other.

Fourth and finally, a **rhetorical community** consists of the people who share rhetorical visions. As such, they are active participants in a rhetorically inspired drama, which has created for them an involving social reality. Thus, rhetorical visions are shared dreams and rhetorical communities are unified dreamers acting out the reality of their special vision.

## Doing fantasy theme analysis

Like neo-Aristotelian criticism, fantasy theme analysis involves two tasks: a descriptive analysis and interpretation of the myth-making activity embodied in a body of narrative discourse, and an evaluation and critique of the pragmatic, artistic, and historical merits of the dramatizations developed in a discourse.[46]

The analysis phase entails a full description of the social reality that is dramatized in discourse. Thus, the researcher identifies pertinent fantasy themes, fantasy types, rhetorical visions, and the participating members of the rhetorical community. Major dramatic characters, principally "heroes" and "villains," are described along with the dramatic scenario (the "plot"), and the dramatic motive or purpose the speaker or writer is seeking to accomplish. Finally, researchers describe the effects of the discourse, principally by sketching the nature and implications of the social reality that is contained in a given rhetorical vision.

The criticism stage of fantasy theme analysis focuses on the artistic value, the pragmatic consequences, and the "historical truths" inherent in mythic discourse. Artistic criticism explores how skillfully fantasy themes are developed and how artfully the source uses ideas, language, structure, and presentational devices to spin the web of a complete rhetorical vision. Pragmatic evaluation assesses the fidelity and practical consequences of a given rhetorical vision. Pertinent questions include: "What are the immediate and long-range effects of the rhetorical vision?" and "What impact does the rhetorical vision have on the general society from which it sprang?"

Finally, historical criticism evaluates whether history bears out the "truth" or normative utility of a rhetorical vision. The overriding historical question is: Did the rhetorical vision emancipate and enrich human experience or, alternately, did it enslave and degrade the people affected by it? Rhetorical visions like those created by Gandhi, Churchill, and Lincoln uplifted the spirits of nations and enriched whole peoples. In contrast, history documents that figures like Hitler and Stalin mocked the values of the civilized world.

## INTERFACE:
## CHAPTER 13 AND PART IV

This chapter has presented methods of analyzing narrative discourse. Two general types of analysis were explored: a scientific methodology called content analysis and two humanistic approaches to rhetorical criticism, namely, neo-Aristotelian criticism and fantasy theme analysis. The chapter emphasized the comple-

mentarity of science and humanism as perspectives on narrative discourse analysis.

With this chapter's end, we conclude our treatment of communication research designs. Part IV contains two chapters that highlight several contemporary issues in communication research. Chapter 14 describes ethical and pragmatic constraints on the research process, and Chapter 15 examines some current conceptual directions in the communication discipline.

## MAIN POINTS

**1.** Narrative discourse is a story-telling genre that is characterized by relatively fixed source-receiver roles. Narrative discourse may be face-to-face communication or mediated communication. It may serve persuasive, informational, or entertaining functions.

**2.** Narrative discourse analysis is an unobtrusive methodology for exploring the meaning, structure, and function of messages. Narrative discourse analysis variously entails four types of analysis: description, inference, interpretation, and criticism. Scientists emphasize description and inference, whereas humanists focus on interpretation and criticism.

**3.** Five methodological issues must be resolved by discourse analysts: quantitative versus qualitative data analysis, manifest versus latent message content, probability versus purposive sampling, intrinsic versus extrinsic data bases, and analytical versus critical research. Scientists and humanists alike examine both manifest and latent content and utilize intrinsic and extrinsic data. However, they often differ on the other three issues. Scientists employ quantitative data, use probability sampling methods, and engage in analytical research. Humanists typically employ qualitative data,

**274**

PART III
Contemporary
Research
Designs in
Communi-
cation

they often use purposive samples, and they engage in critical research.

**4.** Content analysis is a scientific method for describing and inferring conclusions about the content of messages. Three characteristics distinguish content analysis as a scientific methodology: it yields generalizable conclusions about representative samples of discourse, it is predominantly a quantitative method, and it is said to be an objective method of studying message content.

**5.** Six steps are required to conduct a content analysis: identify the research problem, determine a suitable data base, select a representative sample, collect contextual information, develop a measurement scheme, and analyze data.

**6.** A well-framed problem statement for a content analysis not only clarifies the problem of interest but also points out the data base that is most suitable for exploring the problem.

**7.** To select a representative sample of message content, the content analyst must define the population of interest, specify the elements to be studied within the population, and use a probability sampling method to select a representative sample of population elements.

**8.** Contextual information is situational data relevant to a message, including information about the message source, the audience, the setting, and message effects. Contextual information, derived from surveys, interviews, and printed documents, is a useful adjunct to content analysis.

**9.** The data derived from content analysis are usually measured nominally by grouping pieces of related information into categories. Content analysts typically employ several raters or judges to sort narrative data into categories. The frequency with which data fall into various nominal categories is statistically analyzed for relationships and differences.

**10.** From a humanistic perspective, any nar-

rative discourse can be interpreted and critiqued at two levels of meaning: at the discursive logic level, which pertains to the rational progression of ideas in a message, and at the level of creative imagination (or nondiscursive logic), which concerns the myths, fantasies, and dramatic characterizations contained in messages.

**11.** Neo-Aristotelian criticism focuses on the rational or discursive logic of a message; it involves both analysis and interpretation, and evaluation and criticism.

**12.** The neo-Aristotelian researcher analyzes and interprets messages at four levels: (a) a thematic analysis, which describes the ideas in a message and the methods used to adapt messages to audiences; (b) a structural analysis, describing the organizational aspects of a message that give it unity, order, and coherence; (c) a stylistic analysis, which describes a speaker's language uses; and (d) a presentational analysis, focusing on the means of delivering a message.

**13.** Neo-Aristotelian researchers typically employ three forms of criticism: pragmatic, artistic, and historical, assessing message effects, the aesthetic qualities of narrative discourse, and its "truth" or normative utility, respectively.

**14.** Fantasy theme analysis focuses on the level of meaning in a message called creative imagination or nondiscursive logic. It analyzes messages as story-telling or myth-making activities akin to dramatic theatre presentations.

**15.** Fantasy theme analysis considers that narrative discourse contains four related components: (a) fantasy themes defined as myths that symbolize some general "truth," (b) fantasy types or general categories of recurring fantasy themes, (c) rhetorical visions referring to shared fantasies, and (d) rhetorical communities, or people who share rhetorical visions.

**16.** Fantasy theme analysis involves analyzing and interpreting the myth-making activity in a message and evaluating and criticizing the pragmatic, artistic, and historical merits of a message's dramatizations.

## REVIEW EXERCISES

**1.** Suppose you wish to conduct a content analysis of the newspaper commentaries of a particular syndicated political columnist. Frame a problem statement and then describe procedures for selecting a representative sample. In particular, do the following: (a) define the population of interest, being sure to indicate a time frame (for example, all commentaries appearing in the past year or in a single month of some year); (b) specify the precise element to be sampled (a word, a theme, a topic, a stylistic device, and so on); and (c) describe a probability sampling method for selecting a representative sample of your chosen elements from the population as you have defined it.

**2.** Select a notable public speech, either current or historical, and obtain a copy of it. (The publication *Vital Speeches of the Day* is a useful source of recent speeches.) Describe how you would do a neo-Aristotelian analysis and criticism of the speech. Your analysis should address themes, structure, style, and presentation. Criticism should focus on pragmatic, artistic, and historical values.

**3.** Select either a popular lyrical musician or musicians or a popular movie or set of movies. The material may be past or current. Listen to a sample of the music or view the film(s). Now describe how you might conduct a fantasy theme analysis of the lyrics/dialogue in the chosen works. Discuss major fantasy themes, fantasy types, rhetorical visions, and relevant rhetorical communities. Who are the major heroes and villains? Evaluate the work on its pragmatic, artistic, and historical merits.

## NOTES

**1.** See George Kennedy, *The Art of Persuasion in Greece* (Princeton, NJ: Princeton University Press, 1963), pp. 3–25; and Phillip K. Tompkins, *Communication as Action: An Introduction to Rhetoric and Communication* (Belmont, CA: Wadsworth, 1982), pp. 28–29.

**2.** Aristotle, *Rhetoric*, trans. W. Rhys Roberts (New York: Random House, 1954), p. 24.

**3.** Aristotle, pp. 24–25.

**4.** Donald Lemen Clark, *Rhetoric in Greco-Roman Education* (New York: Columbia University Press, 1957), p. 115.

**5.** Six different perspectives are presented in "Homo Narrans: Story-Telling in Mass Culture and Everyday Life," *Journal of Communication*, 35, No. 4 (1985): 73–171.

**6.** See Walter R. Fisher, "Narration as a Human Communication Paradigm: The Case of Public Moral Argument," *Communication Monographs*, 51 (1984): 1–22; "The Narrative Paradigm: An Elaboration," *Communication Monographs*, 52 (1985): 347–67; and "The Narrative Paradigm: In the Beginning," *Journal of Communication*, 35, No. 4 (1985): 74–89.

**7.** For a communications analysis of some of Bob Dylan's more recent music, see Alberto Gonzalez and John J. Makay, "Rhetorical Ascription and the Gospel According to Dylan," *Quarterly Journal of Speech*, 69 (1983): 1–14.

**8.** Daniel A. Beucke, "News Offered on Home Computers," *Denver Post*, May 3, 1985, p. 1-C.

**9.** For a communications analysis of *The Deer Hunter*, see Janice Hocker Rushing and Thomas S. Frentz, "'The Deer Hunter': Rhetoric of the Warrior," *Quarterly Journal of Speech*, 66 (1980): 392–406. For communications analyses of films as a genre, see Garth Jowett and James M. Linton, *Movies as Mass Communication* (Beverly Hills, CA: Sage, 1980).

**10.** See Bernard Berelson, *Content Analysis in Communication Research* (New York: Free Press, 1952).

**11.** Ole R. Holsti, "Content Analysis: An Introduction," in *Reader in Public Opinion and Mass Communication*, 3rd ed., eds. Morris Janowitz and Paul Hirsch (New York: Free Press, 1981), p. 227; and Klaus Krippendorff, *Content Analysis: An Introduction to its Methodology* (Beverly Hills, CA: Sage, 1980), pp. 21–23.

**276**

PART III
Contemporary
Research
Designs in
Communi-
cation

**12.** See Irving L. Janis, "The Problem of Validating Content Analysis," in *Language of Politics*, eds. Harold D. Lasswell, et al. (Cambridge, MA: MIT Press, 1965); and Krippendorff, p. 23.

**13.** See Barnett Baskerville, "Must We All Be 'Rhetorical Critics'?" *Quarterly Journal of Speech*, 63 (1977): 107–16.

**14.** See Ernest J. Wrage, "Public Address: A Study in Social and Intellectual History," *Quarterly Journal of Speech*, 33 (1947): 451–57.

**15.** George Gerbner, "The Importance of Being Critical—In One's Own Fashion," *Journal of Communication*, 33, No. 3 (1983): 356.

**16.** Krippendorff, p. 13.

**17.** See Krippendorff; and G. J. Speed, "Do Newspapers Now Give the News?" *Forum*, 15 (1983): 705–11.

**18.** A. L. George, *Propaganda Analysis: A Study of Inferences Made from Nazi Propaganda in World War II* (Evanston, IL: Row, Peterson, 1959).

**19.** Holsti, p. 227.

**20.** Krippendorff, p. 21.

**21.** Krippendorff, p. 23.

**22.** Janis, pp. 55–82.

**23.** Ole R. Holsti, *Content Analysis for the Social Sciences and Humanities* (Reading, MA: Addison-Wesley, 1969).

**24.** See Krippendorff, p. 171; and Eugene J. Webb, Donald T. Campbell, Richard D. Schwartz, and Lee Sechrest, *Unobtrusive Measures: Nonreactive Research in the Social Sciences* (Chicago: Rand McNally, 1966).

**25.** Krippendorff, p. 172.

**26.** Suzanne Pingree, Robert Parker Hawkins, Matilda Butler, and William Paisley, "A Scale for Sexism," *Journal of Communication*, 26, No. 4 (1976): 193–200.

**27.** Pingree, et al., 197.

**28.** See George Gerbner, Larry Gross, Michael Morgan, and Nancy Signorielli, "The 'Mainstreaming' of America: Violence Profile No. 11," *Journal of Communication*, 30, No. 3 (1980): 10–29. Also see George Gerbner and Larry Gross, "Living with Television: The Violence Profile," *Journal of Communication*, 26, No. 2 (1976): 173–99. For a cultural indicators analysis of the portrayal on television of older persons, see George Gerbner, Larry Gross, Nancy Signorielli, and Michael Morgan, "Aging with Television: Images on Television Drama and Concep-tions of Social Reality," *Journal of Communication*, 30, No. 1 (1980): 37–47.

**29.** Gerbner, Gross, Morgan, and Signorielli, 11.

**30.** Gerbner and Gross, 182.

**31.** Gerbner and Gross, 178.

**32.** Gerbner and Gross, 191–94.

**33.** Gerbner and Gross, 194.

**34.** For an analysis and criticism of cultural indicators research arguing that the approach combines scientific and humanistic methodologies, see Horace Newcomb, "Assessing the Violence Profile Studies of Gerbner and Gross: A Humanistic Critique and Suggestion," *Communication Research*, 5 (1978): 264–82.

**35.** See Ernst Cassirer, *Language and Myth*, trans. Susanne K. Langer (New York: Harper & Row, 1946), pp. viii–ix.

**36.** See Kennedy, pp. 10–12; Clark, pp. 71–113; Thomas M. Scheidel, *Persuasive Speaking* (Glenview, IL: Scott, Foresman, 1967), pp. 12–16; and Tompkins, pp. 35–40. For a more detailed treatment of the Roman rhetorical tradition, see George Kennedy, *The Art of Rhetoric in the Roman World: 300 B.C.— A.D. 300* (Princeton, NJ: Princeton University Press, 1972).

**37.** The following discussion of the mechanics of neo-Aristotelian criticism draws heavily on Charles S. Mudd and Malcolm O. Sillars, *Speech: Content and Communication*, 3rd ed. (New York: Thomas Y. Crowell, 1975), pp. 421–34. Also see Robert L. Scott and Bernard L. Brock, *Methods of Rhetorical Criticism: A Twentieth-Century Perspective* (New York: Harper & Row, 1972), pp. 25–100.

**38.** Mudd and Sillars, p. 427.

**39.** Mudd and Sillars, p. 431.

**40.** Herbert Wichelns, "The Literary Criticism of Oratory," in *Studies in Rhetoric and Public Speaking in Honor of James Albert Winans*, ed. A. M. Drummond (New York: Century, 1925).

**41.** Robert F. Bales, *Interaction Process Analysis: A Method for the Study of Small Groups* (Reading, MA: Addison-Wesley, 1950), p. 152.

**42.** See Ernest G. Bormann, "Fantasy and Rhetorical Vision: The Rhetorical Criticism of Social Reality," *Quarterly Journal of Speech*, 58 (1972): 396–407; "Colloquy I. Fantasy and Rhetorical Vision: Ten Years Later," *Quarterly Journal of Speech*, 68 (1982): 288–305; and "Symbolic Convergence: Organizational Communication and Culture," in *Communication and Organizations: An Interpretive Approach*, eds. Linda L. Putnam and Michael E. Pacanowsky (Beverly Hills, CA: Sage, 1983), pp. 99–122.

**43.** See Kenneth Burke, *A Grammar of Motives* (Englewood Cliffs, NJ: Prentice-Hall, 1946); and *A Rhetoric of Motives* (Englewood Cliffs, NJ: Prentice-Hall, 1950); and Bales.

**44.** A.J.M. Sykes, "Myth in Communication," *Journal of Communication*, 20 (1970): p. 17.

**45.** Peter Homans, "Puritanism Revisited: An Analysis of the Contemporary Screen-Image West-

ern," in *Reader in Public Opinion and Mass Communication*, 3rd ed., eds. Morris Janowitz and Paul Hirsch (New York: Free Press, 1981), p. 239.

**46.** For some examples of fantasy theme analyses of discourse, see James W. Chesebro, "Paradoxical Views of 'Homosexuality' in the Rhetoric of Social Scientists: A Fantasy Theme Analysis," *Quarterly Journal of Speech*, 66 (1980): 127–39; and Ernest G. Bormann, "The Eagleton Affair: A Fantasy Theme Analysis," *Quarterly Journal of Speech*, 59 (1973): 143–59.

# CONTEMPORARY ISSUES IN COMMUNICATION RESEARCH

# THE ETHICS AND PRAGMATICS OF RESEARCH

This chapter describes ethical and pragmatic constraints on the research process. Ethics are behavioral norms reflecting the "goodness or badness" of research practices, whereas pragmatics are political and personal concerns that affect the means, ends, motives, and consequences of research. Ethical principles require researchers to protect research participants' right to informed and voluntary participation, their right to freedom from harm, their right to anonymity or confidentiality, and their right to privacy of thought and action. Pragmatic considerations include both political and personal constraints on research. This chapter discusses the possible effects of a researcher's political biases on scholarship, along with the potential impact of available intellectual and material resources on the research process.

CHAPTER
OUTLINE

**283**

CHAPTER 14
The Ethics
and Prag-
matics of
Research

S aul Alinsky, the well-known political and social activist, argued that ethical judgments reflect both people's political persuasion and their personal stake in the matter to be decided. When our interest in a decision's outcome is minimal, we can afford the luxury of rendering "impartial" moral judgments. However, when strong personal and political allegiances are involved, we often regard our own position as "ethical" and opposing views as "immoral," suggesting that in intellectual warfare there are no "rules of fair play." Alinsky concluded that ethical systems must be tempered by pragmatic considerations if they are to be "workable in the world as it is and not unrealistically aimed toward the world as we would like it to be."[1]

Alinsky's views highlight the issues this chapter addresses. In discussing practices that intrude on the research process and threaten its **intellectual integrity**, I begin by describing major ethical considerations in scholarly research. Then, two sets of pragmatic issues are examined. The first, political constraints on the research process, include the effects a researcher's political biases may have on scholarship. Next, personal influences are discussed, among them the ways a researcher's economic and professional interests can affect research. Throughout the chapter, I emphasize the inseparable nature of ethical and pragmatic concerns in communication inquiry.

# ETHICAL ISSUES IN COMMUNICATION RESEARCH

The integrity of research, whether scientific or humanistic, refers to the faithfulness with which researchers adhere to the standards or rules of the **research game**, an intellectual and social process of accumulating and disseminating information to interested publics. The stan-dards for conducting research include appropriate methods of collecting and analyzing data and generally agreed upon ethical guidelines for collecting, analyzing, and publicizing research.

I have spent the better part of this book elaborating the methodology of the research game, including conceptual and operational issues, sampling techniques, statistical procedures, and principles of designing scientific and humanistic research. It is now time to consider the ethical criteria for conducting research and disseminating the results. As a general concept, ethics refers to "value judgments concerning degrees of rightness and wrongness, goodness and badness, in human conduct."[2] Beyond a consensus that ethics are standards of "value," scholars differ considerably in their views of the nature and source of ethics. One well-worn argument concerns the absolute versus relative nature of ethical criteria: Are ethics cross-situational or do they vary from one social setting to another? For the purpose of discussing research, I take **ethics** to be a relative and therefore evolutionary system of behavioral norms created by agreement among members of a social grouping, in this case, a community of scholars.

According to Fletcher, four situational factors are pertinent to making judgments about the "ethics" of a given practice or behavior: (1) the means or methods used to enact the practice or behavior, (2) the end or goal of the behavior, (3) the motive or intentions of the individual enacting the behavior, and (4) the consequences or effects of the behavior in question.[3] Applied to research, the "means" refer to methods of collecting, analyzing, and reporting data and the "end" is the general purpose of the research. For example, research may be conducted to increase our theoretical understanding of human communication, or in the case of applied research, to solve pressing social problems. "Motives," referring to a researcher's reasons for conducting research, may or may not

**284**

PART IV
Contemporary
Issues in
Communi-
cation
Research

coincide with ends. For instance, individuals often engage in research to advance their careers, to fulfill a course requirement, to become well known, to make money, and for other pragmatic reasons. In such cases, the *end* of advancing knowledge or solving problems may be unrelated to the researcher's personal *motives*. Finally, the "consequences" of research include its effects on research participants, on researchers themselves, and on the larger scholarly and social communities.

Based on this four-part taxonomy, the ethics of a given item of research can be judged by critically evaluating its means, ends, motives, and consequences. To critique something implies the existence of a set of agreed upon standards of "goodness and badness" to apply to these four research components. Let us examine some of the standards the scholarly community uses for evaluating its products.

## Ethical Principles of Research

Contemporary research activities are regulated by the following general behavioral norms: universalism, communality, disinterestedness, organized skepticism, honesty, and respect. The first four ethical principles were advanced by Robert Merton in his treatment of the "scientific ethos,"[4] and the last two are suggested by several codes of professional ethics, including those of the American Psychological Association,[5] the American Association for Public Opinion Research,[6] and by the regulations of the U.S. Department of Health and Human Services (HHS) for protecting human research participants.[7]

### Universalism
The norm of **universalism** has been honored for a given project when all research, including its means, ends, motives, and consequences, can be evaluated according to predetermined standards set by a scholarly community. These standards are impersonal and therefore not peculiar to any one researcher. Rather, they are derived from empirical data and previously accepted knowledge.

The principle of universalism, then, requires that one's research pass the muster of peer review that asks: Is the research to be judged consonant with prior thinking and knowledge on the subject it addresses? Universalism militates against unorthodox methods or unusual findings unless the researcher can produce powerful evidence supporting his or her novel findings and methodologies.

### Communality
The principle of **communality** compels all researchers to share their research findings, including means, ends, motives, and consequences, freely and honestly with all other members of the research community. Thus, researchers are required to report fully and accurately their methods and results, including all shortcomings of a given piece of research. Findings that disconfirm one's hypothesis must be reported as fully and honestly as those confirming it.

### Disinterestedness
The principle of **disinterestedness** speaks primarily to a researcher's motives for conducting inquiry, and it states that scholars should seek knowledge for its own sake rather than for personal gain. "Personal gain" includes financial reward, professional recognition, job security, and career advancement. Although personal gain in any of these forms is an acceptable consequence of research activity, it should not be the researcher's principal motive or scholarly end.

### Organized skepticism
Following the principle of **organized skepticism**, researchers must be critical of their own research as well as the research of others. Thus,

**285**

CHAPTER 14
The Ethics
and Prag-
matics of
Research

the means, ends, motives, and consequences of all scholarship including one's own must be scrutinized for errors, omissions, and biases—both deliberate and inadvertent. Thus, the best scholar is a dedicated skeptic who takes nothing for granted, but rather questions all intellectual inquiry, both the conventional and the controversial, with equal intensity and vigor.

## Honesty

The principle of **honesty** cuts in three directions, involving the self, the scholarly community, and the participants in one's research activity. Honesty implies that the truth is reported as the reporter understands it, and the practice of being honest begins, as the adage suggests, "at home." Thus, researchers must take care to "see" things in the empirical world as they are, not as they would like them to be. Often our pet theories, our formal hypotheses, and our political persuasions act as conceptual blinders, directing us to "see" things that confirm personal beliefs and suspicions. The most important step researchers can take to keep themselves reasonably "honest" is to develop a full awareness of the biases they bring to a given research endeavor. Self-awareness enables a researcher to report personal biases so that readers can judge for themselves their potential impact on research findings.

In addition to self-honesty, researchers are compelled to be honest with other members of the research community. As I noted in connection with the communality principle, researchers must report fully and accurately all aspects of their methodologies and their findings, whether they confirm or fail to confirm favored theories and hypotheses. Moreover, research limitations should be admitted candidly and recommendations advanced for methodological improvements.

Finally, the honesty principle extends to all who agree to participate in a research project, perhaps as experimental subjects or as actors in a naturalistic study. Researchers are obligated to minimize deception, either by stating their research aims and revealing their true identities at the outset, or alternately, by fully debriefing participants who were initially mislead about the research or the researcher's identity. I will elaborate on these honesty issues in the next section, which addresses ethical rules peculiar to communication research.

## Respect

According to the principle of **respect**, which is applied primarily to the participants in a research project, researchers must protect all the basic human and civil rights of those who serve as research subjects. These rights, which are elaborated below, include the right to informed and voluntary participation, the right to freedom from physical, social, and psychological harm, and the right to privacy of thought and action.

Twenty years ago, Herbert Kelman captured the essence of the respect principle when he observed that in our everyday relationships with others, "most of us would never think of doing the kinds of things we do to our subjects," such as deliberately misinforming them of our intentions or surreptitiously observing their behavior without their knowledge and permission. "We would view such behavior," said Kelman, "as a violation of the respect to which all fellow humans are entitled." In this regard, Kelman concluded that "we seem to forget that [the researcher-subject partnership] is a *real* interhuman relationship, in which we have responsibility toward the subject as another human being whose dignity we must preserve."[8]

# Ethical Rules for Communication Research

In this section, I examine several specific ethical guidelines for communication inquiry derived from the six general criteria just

**286**

PART IV
Contemporary
Issues in
Communi-
cation
Research

summarized.[9] The rules are partitioned into two general categories: obligations to communication research participants and obligations to the research community.

## Obligations to research participants

The rights of research participants fall into five categories: (1) voluntary participation and informed consent rights, (2) the right to freedom from harm, (3) rights of anonymity and confidentiality, (4) the right to complete and accurate information about a research project, and (5) the right to privacy of thought and action.

1. *Voluntary participation and informed consent.* It is fundamental to all research that subjects' participation should be informed and voluntary. **Informed consent** means voluntary agreement to participate in research after having been given full and accurate information about the nature of the research project, including all potential physical, social, and psychological risks. Informed consent is obtained in writing from adult participants; for children, written consent is required from all individuals acting **in loco parentis** (for example, parents, legal guardians, teachers, principals, superintendents). Coerced participation is forbidden not only by professional ethics, but also by federal regulations that are legally binding on all universities and other institutions receiving government financial support.

2. *Freedom from harm.* Research must not expose participants to physical, social, or psychological harm. Unlike many medical and psychological studies, communication research typically involves no physical risks and little potential for social and psychological harm. There are, however, risk factors of two principal kinds in communication studies. First, experimental manipulations have the capacity to "create" behaviors that are socially questionable. For example, exposing people, especially impressionable children, to stimuli like televised violence or to graphic fear appeals in persuasive messages may either exacerbate preexisting aggressive tendencies or activate latent anxieties. Although these effects are usually temporary, they can have long-range negative consequences.[10] If any experiment risks potentially serious short- or long-term harm, it should be abandoned.

Second, certain types of communication research, including survey studies and naturalistic observations, may uncover socially or psychologically sensitive materials—for example, information about drug and alcohol use or sexual habits and preferences—that could, if disclosed, place participants in legal or social jeopardy. Joseph Hayes's study of common conversational ploys used by homosexuals in "secret," "social," and "radical-activist" settings is an example of communication research involving socially sensitive issues.[11] The deliberate or accidental disclosure of certain discovered information could put participants in risk of personal embarrassment, loss of employment and financial security, or civil or criminal liability. Researchers contemplating studies involving socially sensitive matters must be able to guarantee the anonymity or confidentiality of results; if this is impossible, plans for such research must be abandoned.

Beyond these two areas, other communication studies fall into categories that HHS regards either as "no-risk" or "minimal-risk" research.[12] Projects involving no risks include confidential surveys and interviews whose results, if accidentally disclosed, would not be likely to result in social, economic, or legal sanctions; naturalistic observations of public behavior such as people's everyday conversations; and unobtrusive research using existing data (public speeches, motion pictures, televised materials, printed documents, and so on). "Minimal-risk" research, according to HHS regulations, en-

**287**

CHAPTER 14
The Ethics
and Prag-
matics of
Research

tails risks no greater than those encountered in daily life. Most nonmanipulative communication research conducted either in the laboratory or the field falls into this classification.

3. *Anonymity and confidentiality.* According to Babbie, a research participant is considered "anonymous" when the researcher cannot pair a given response with a given respondent, whereas **confidentiality** means that "the researcher is able to identify a given person's responses but essentially promises not to do so publicly."[13] Thus, **anonymity** implies confidentiality, but the reverse is not the case. Participants have the right to confidentiality in all communication research. When researchers cannot guarantee nondisclosure, anonymity must be granted if participants desire it. Anonymity is usually assured by assigning participants a code that carries no self-identifying data.

4. *Honesty and the practice of deception.* Deception is practiced in communication research in two primary circumstances. First, we learned in Chapter 9 that experimenters often develop cover stories to mislead subjects about experimental hypotheses. This practice, especially prevalent in laboratory studies, is designed to minimize the biasing effects that can result when participants learn a study's true purpose. Second, naturalistic researchers who adopt participatory roles sometimes surreptitiously observe and record ongoing communication without revealing their true identities. The aim, of course, is to avoid reactivity effects, that is, behavioral alterations resulting when people know they are being observed.

Obviously, however, such practices have the effect of suspending temporarily people's right to full and accurate information about the studies in which they participate. Researchers traditionally have minimized the consequences of deception by providing complete debriefings at a study's conclusion, informing participants of the researcher's true identity and the study's actual purposes and, where appropriate, obtaining after-the-fact permissions to use surreptitious observations. Aside from ethical questions, the usefulness of deceptive practices has been called into question by research showing them to be only partially successful. For instance, some studies indicate that only about half of all experimental subjects are fooled by a researcher's deceptions in the first place.[14] The relative ineffectiveness of deceptions coupled with their unfavorable ethical implications have prompted some researchers to abandon them altogether. In certain cases where deception might be scientifically useful, researchers have adopted alternative practices such as asking participants to role-play hypothetical scenarios.[15] If alternatives like these can satisfy one's research objectives, deception is unnecessary. Where deceptive practices are required, the researcher should fully and carefully debrief participants.

5. *Privacy of thought and action.* Privacy invasions occur in communication research in two principal circumstances. First, naturalistic researchers may sometimes surreptitiously record communications without the subjects' knowledge and consent. For example, conversational analysts seeking to gather "natural" talk in laboratory settings may use hidden recording devices to collect data. Second, privacy invasions occur when researchers either deliberately or inadvertently disclose information about research participants that they have promised to keep in confidence. Both practices are ethically unacceptable, since they plainly open participants to the risk of embarrassment and, at worst, expose them to potential social, economic, or legal sanctions. For these reasons, researchers are obligated both morally and legally to respect people's rights to privacy in matters of thought as well as action.

**288**

PART IV
Contemporary
Issues in
Communi-
cation
Research

## Obligations to the research community

In addition to the obligations to research participants just described, the communication researcher has three principal responsibilities to those who read and use research findings. First, researchers are obliged to provide a complete and accurate account of the methods employed in a given research endeavor. Without such information, readers cannot evaluate the validity of reported research and independent researchers are unable to replicate it. Thus, inadequate methodological reporting renders scientific research incapable of verification. Moreover, when humanistic methods are not fully and accurately detailed, the reasonableness of such research cannot be evaluated.

Second, researchers are obligated to provide a complete and honest report of all the findings of a given research project. Negative results, that is, those that do not confirm the hypotheses, should be discussed along with confirmatory findings. Third, researchers are ethically compelled to keep their personal biases out of the research process to the extent possible. Whenever personal ideologies are reflected in a piece of research, the researcher is obliged to inform readers, thereby allowing them to evaluate methodological choices and findings in the context of these biases. As we shall see in the next section, some humanistic studies entailing evaluative judgments are vulnerable to personal and ideological influences. Scientific research is subject to distorting influences as well, despite its claim to "objectivity." This is especially the case for research that has potent political or social implications, for example, studies of media portrayals of minorities, women, and various "establishment" groups.

In sum, researchers are obliged to accord the research community the same honesty and respect due research participants. Such behavior is manifested in the full and accurate reporting of methods and results. Moreover, an honest and respectful attitude compels one to separate ideological biases from "facts," eliminating the former wherever possible, but in any case, making certain that the two are never confused either in the researcher's mind or in the minds of readers. (Appendices A and B present detailed instructions for writing research proposals and final research reports, including guidelines specifying the kind and quantity of information about a research project that writers should provide for readers.)

## Ethics and Intellectual Integrity

As our discussion of general research norms and their derivative rules has indicated, ethical standards are terribly useful creatures. They are valuable not because of their laudable "moral" qualities, but because they spell out concrete behavioral rules to protect the integrity of intellectual inquiry. Ethical systems, then, are the research game's "rules of fair play." Because of them, research as a *collective* activity is possible. Shared norms admonish researchers to cast aside personal differences and work as a community to advance knowledge. Of course, ethical principles are idealized standards, and practicing researchers sometimes fall short of achieving a perfect match between what ought to be done and what actually is done in research. In the next section, I will examine several pragmatic constraints that often intrude on the research game, compromising researchers' adherence to the rules of fair play in communication inquiry.

## PRAGMATIC ISSUES IN COMMUNICATION RESEARCH

By **pragmatics**, I mean practical constraints that intrude on the research game and have the capacity to compromise adherence to the ethical principles just elaborated. Two related cate-

**289**

CHAPTER 14
The Ethics
and Prag-
matics of
Research

gories of pragmatic issues are relevant to communication research: political constraints and personal constraints.

# Political Constraints on Research

**Political constraints** refer to the impact of prevailing political ideologies and exigencies on the means, ends, motives, and consequences of research. Sources of political constraint that can affect the research process include the political attitudes of the governing elite and the political ideologies of researchers themselves.

By the "governing elite," I refer to federal and state agencies as well as university and corporate boards that fund and regulate research activities. Governmental, corporate, and academic attitudes influence scholarly research principally by funding research projects of specified types and not others. Some national and state administrations have generously supported basic research in the humanities and social sciences. Others have favored "hard" scientific research, especially projects with military and industrial applications. Although universities vary considerably in their institutional research priorities, well-established and therefore politically powerful disciplines often get the lion's share of internal research grants. Corporations, of course, typically fund research efforts that promise to advance their shareholders' interests. Since large-scale research programs require financial support, funding decisions may affect research activities by defining those subject matters or research "ends" that are deemed worthy of investigation. This influence can compromise intellectual inquiry insofar as factors other than disinterested scholarly concerns are allowed to determine any part of the problems the research community addresses.

Whereas the effects of government, private, and university funding decisions are indirect and often diffuse, the impact on scholarly activity of a researcher's own political ideology is more direct and profound. Let us examine the nature and effects of ideological intrusions into the research game in scientific communication studies and in humanistic inquiry.

## The politics of scientific research

Two general areas of research have been vulnerable to personal political ideology in recent years: the first I shall call "activist" research; and the second is conventionally referred to as applied research. **Activist research** is topical or issue-oriented, with researchers focusing on topics of concern to identifiable groups like women and minorities such as blacks, Hispanics, and gays.

The topical interests of an activist research agenda have clear political and social overtones. Moreover, issue-oriented researchers, being ordinary mortals and not scientific automatons, have ideological preferences that may affect their research activities. For example, a number of researchers are interested in media portrayals of women, and their published findings often report that females are depicted in "demeaning" and "subservient" roles.[16] I am not suggesting that such results are inaccurate or misleading (quite to the contrary, the reports generally confirm my own impressions of most commercial media fare!). However, I am arguing that research reports like these, whether the findings are favorable or unfavorable to particular causes, carry potent political messages. Furthermore, it is difficult to imagine that a researcher's political leanings can be divorced completely from the observation process. The political ideologies of all of us probably affect, at least inadvertently, what we "see" when we conduct observations.

A second area of inquiry, called **applied research**, is sometimes vulnerable to political influence. Applied communication research is often put to such practical uses as gathering demographic and opinion data, which allow political candidates to appeal effectively to the needs of the voting public; assembling

**290**

PART IV
Contemporary
Issues in
Communi-
cation
Research

information on the characteristics of television audiences, which are used to maximize a network's share of the advertising dollar; and collecting social data on the personal and cultural effects of media violence or eroticism.

Some applied research is financed by individuals and groups whose special interests help define the nature of the research problem. Beyond influencing the "ends" of research, the political persuasions of financial benefactors may affect a researcher's perceptual processes, sometimes influencing the choice of methodologies, occasionally affecting what the researcher "sees" during the observation process. For example, it is not uncommon for paid political pollsters to find more support for the candidates employing them than is found by polling agencies engaged by the opposition.

I am not suggesting that applied research consultants rig their research or doctor their findings to confirm the expectations of the individuals and groups who employ them. There is little or no support for such a conclusion. I am simply pointing out that different researchers can be led to draw divergent conclusions from a given data set if the research aims are defined by people who stand to gain politically and financially from the fruits of their scholarship.

## The politics of humanistic research

Recall that humanistic research focuses on interpretations and critiques of communication artifacts: public speeches, television programs, motion pictures, and the like. Certain forms of humanistic research explicitly incorporate political ideologies into their critical and interpretative judgments. Indeed, a few rhetorical critics equate critical research with political and social activism. For instance, Deetz and Kersten argue that "the principal goal of critical research [in communication] is social change." Moreover, they observe that "social change or reconstruction involves the identification and removal of illegitimate constraints on communication," concluding that "critical theory

[aims] to emancipate and to enlighten, [to] make people aware of the conditions under which they exist and through awareness and action [and to] "free them from these conditions."[17]

Although most humanists shun an explicitly political approach to scholarship, the act of critically evaluating discourse, especially from a "historical truth" perspective, often entails ideological judgments. For example, a positive evaluation of the rhetoric of Abraham Lincoln or Martin Luther King, Jr., can be construed to impute to the critic a belief that the issues for which these men fought were politically legitimate and historically justified. Similarly, a critical condemnation of former Alabama governor George Wallace's segregationist rhetoric of the 1960s or the "red-baiting" tactics of McCarthyism in the 1950s carries potent political as well as rhetorical judgments.

## Ethics, politics, and intellectual integrity

Political influences in both scientific and humanistic research have the capacity to compromise and to enrich communication scholarship. When political ideologies affect substantially one's choice of investigative means or ends, but the researcher fails to recognize and report this circumstance, intellectual integrity is jeopardized. This is so because readers are unable to evaluate the reported research in the context of the political influences that shaped it. However, if researchers fully and accurately detail their ideological biases, no ethical imperative is compromised. In such cases, readers have the opportunity to evaluate reported findings within the context of the political philosophy giving rise to them.

Yet in other cases, an explicitly political analysis of discourse might provide insights that would be obscured by more "objective" studies. For example, a Marxist-like criticism of organizational communication similar to that proposed by Deetz[18] might be useful insofar as

**291**
CHAPTER 14
The Ethics
and Prag-
matics of
Research

it identifies organizational constraints on free speech and points to ways for members to emancipate themselves from so-called rhetorical domination. So long as one's ideological leanings are clearly labeled, communication scholarship might benefit rather than suffer from such politically oriented research.

# Personal Constraints on Research

**Personal constraints** refer to the impact a researcher's motivations and capabilities can exert on the research process. Personal constraints fall into two general categories: self-interests and professional aspirations, and intellectual and material resources. The first category addresses the researcher's "motives" for engaging in intellectual inquiry, whereas the second involves the "means" available to a researcher for conducting scholarly research.

### Personal and professional aspirations

Although many dedicated scholars pursue knowledge for its own sake, considerable evidence suggests that the desire for personal gain in the form of professional recognition and economic security can be a powerful motive for scholarly activity. Such self-serving motivations can affect the nature of the problems researchers choose to study and the methodologies they employ. Based on a study that included interviews with a number of academic researchers, Hagstrom concluded that the desire for professional recognition not only prompts the scholar to submit papers for publication, but "it also influences his selection of problems and methods. He will tend to select problems the solution of which will result in greater recognition and he will tend to select methods that will make his work acceptable to his colleagues."[19] Similar motivations undoubtedly affect the work of researchers employed in nonacademic settings.

Beyond the choice of problems and methods, considerable temptation exists for researchers to selectively report findings that confirm hypotheses and to gloss over disconfirming data. For instance, the editors of the journals of many professional societies are reluctant to publish articles reporting insignificant or mixed findings. Similarly, researchers working for business organizations may be tempted to report results that present their company or its products in a favorable light. In certain cases, the desire for professional recognition has led some researchers to report fraudulent as well as plagiarized materials. Perhaps the most famous case of fraudulent academic scholarship occurred outside the communication discipline. More than a decade ago, Kamin discovered that the British psychologist Sir Cyril Burt had concocted "data" to support his views regarding the importance of genetic influences on human intelligence.[20]

The achievement mentality is alive and well in both academic and nonacademic circles. Researchers, like all humans, desire professional respect and financial advancement. As long as people seek after "specialness," the scholar's motivation for personal acclaim is unlikely to diminish. The pertinent issue, then, concerns the impact of personal and professional aspirations on scholarly integrity. Fraudulent research, including the selective reporting of hypothesis-confirming results, clearly jeopardizes the fidelity of scholarship. Moreover, when professional aspirations dictate the choice of problems and methods, intellectual integrity may be compromised as well. In both cases, the guiding principles of honesty, respect, and disinterestedness are cast aside in favor of personal aggrandizement. In the final analysis, the health of scholarship, like most other human endeavors, depends on the integrity of individual researchers coupled with a research community's willingness to exact swift and severe sanctions on all who violate intellectual bonds of trust.

292

PART IV
Contemporary
Issues in
Communi-
cation
Research

## Intellectual and material resources

Intellectual and material **resources** refer to the assets and liabilities of a researcher that may influence the research process. **Intellectual resources** include the researcher's skills and knowledge along with his or her special interests in particular problems and methodologies. **Material resources** refer to the availability or unavailability of such support factors as adequate financial backing, specialized research equipment, appropriate samples of research participants, adequate research facilities, and sufficient time to devote to research activity.

A researcher's intellectual and material assets may sometimes influence the "ends" of research, referring to the problems one chooses to investigate, as well as the "means" or methods one selects to study a problem. Indeed, some writers contend that a researcher's resources are primary determinants of the means and ends of scholarly research. This view runs counter to the traditional rational mode of inquiry, holding that research problems dictate the choice of methods and that methods in turn determine the allocation of intellectual and material resources.

Elaborating a resource-based perspective called the **garbage can research model**, Joanne Martin has argued that the availability of intellectual and material resources drives much research activity.[21] According to Martin, the **rational research model**, which holds that problems determine methods and methods dictate resources, is a "normative approach to the research process, [indicating] how research ought to be conducted," whereas the so-called garbage can perspective is "a realistic descriptive model [detailing] the process whereby research decisions are actually made."[22]

As the name implies, Martin's model conceptualizes the research process as a garbage can with four circulating components or "streams":

1. *Theoretical problems*, corresponding directly to the "ends" or goals of scholarly research.
2. *Resources*, which include intangible items (a

researcher's abilities, special interests and methodological skills, and so forth) as well as a host of tangible items (for example, the availability of time and money for conducting research, the accessibility of appropriate samples of research participants, and the availability of needed facilities and equipment).
3. *Methods*, referring to research designs, measurement tools, and procedures for data analysis.
4. *Solutions*, meaning research results providing answers to scholarly problems.

Based on this model, Martin contends that actual research practices conflict with the rational model in three primary ways. First, she argues that resources, including a researcher's abilities and interests and the availability of research materials, can indeed affect research decisions. According to Martin, resource availability often determines "the selection of a theoretical problem, the choice of a method, and even the interpretation of a solution."[23] For instance, the availability of research monies can encourage researchers to develop a theoretical interest in the funded issue. Additionally, Martin notes that a researcher's choice of problems and methods may be influenced by his or her knowledge and capabilities. Furthermore, the availability of special equipment or a pool of research subjects required for a particular kind of research can prompt researchers to choose these avenues over others.

Second, Martin argues that a researcher's methodological preferences sometimes dictate the choice of a research problem, rather than the problem always determining the appropriate methodology, in accordance with the rational model. Thus, special expertise or interest may prompt researchers to choose a theoretical problem that can be studied using the preferred methodology. On the other hand, some important theoretical problems "are seldom addressed because of methodological difficulties," including the unavailability of an appropriate

**293**

CHAPTER 14
The Ethics
and Prag-
matics of
Research

method or the researcher's lack of competency in the use of an available method.[24]

Finally, the garbage can model assumes that solutions or research findings may be a starting point rather than the end product of research. The rational model regards the final step in the research process as "a feedback loop, whereby the empirical results of a study are interpreted in light of the theoretical problem they were designed to address."[25] By contrast, the garbage can model suggests that researchers do not always return to the theoretical problem that prompted a study, especially when results appear irrelevant to the original hypothesis or contradict it. In such situations, researchers may devise a new theory or hypothesis to explain the unexpected results. Thus, the garbage can model suggests that researchers with a set of results often go in search of a theory to explain them instead of interpreting obtained results in relation to a predetermined theoretical posture.

The garbage can model, then, "does not assume that the content of the solution is always "unknown until the end of the research."[26] Instead, Martin argues that researchers often have firm expectations about the results that particular studies should produce and that this knowledge may encourage them either deliberately or inadvertently to choose a methodology "because it is most likely to yield the expected solution."[27] This practice, she concludes, may reflect a researcher's desire to produce data that confirm preferred hypotheses and theories.

### Personal constraints and intellectual integrity

The garbage can model is a useful adjunct to the rational model of research. The rational model is, as Martin admits, a valuable guide detailing how intellectually sound scholarship *ought* to be conducted.[28] However, actual practices may be influenced by resource availability as well as a researcher's personal and professional self-interests. For that reason, research practices may sometimes diverge from ideal standards of scholarly integrity. Martin's analysis nicely pinpoints the areas in which divergent practices are likely to occur.

Whether personal constraints compromise the intellectual integrity of research depends on the exact nature of their effects. As I noted earlier, personal and professional aspirations can lead to unacceptable behavior, including deception and fraud. Although one's resources may dictate both the ends and means of research, the ethical implications in such cases are usually less serious than those stemming from decisions prompted by self-serving motives. If we lived in an ideal world, resources would be limitless and scarcity could not compromise scholarly integrity. However, we live in a world of limited means and researchers must accept the effects of these unwanted limitations as facts of life. We can maintain our intellectual integrity, even as we accommodate the impact of limited resources, as long as we report to interested readers any effects that scarcity has exerted on our research decisions.

## INTERFACE: CHAPTERS 14 AND 15

This chapter has explored ethical and pragmatic constraints on the research process. We examined the researcher's ethical obligations to research participants and to the research community. Pragmatic research considerations, both political and personal, were described. Throughout its development, the chapter emphasized the impact of ethical and pragmatic considerations on the intellectual integrity of communication research.

In the next and final chapter, I will survey contemporary trends in communication research. The chapter's purpose is to evaluate current research practices in light of the conceptual frameworks or paradigms that shaped their forms and determined their functions.

**294**

PART IV
Contemporary
Issues in
Communi-
cation
Research

# MAIN POINTS

**1.** "Ethics" refers to an evolving system of behavioral norms or value judgments about the goodness or badness of research practices. Four situational factors affect ethical judgments about a given practice: the means used to enact the practice, the end or goal of the practice, the motive of the practitioner, and the consequences of the practice.

**2.** Contemporary research activities are regulated by six general ethical principles: universalism, communality, disinterestedness, organized skepticism, honesty, and respect.

**3.** Researchers are obligated to respect five categories of rights of research participants: voluntary participation and informed consent, freedom from harm, anonymity and confidentiality, freedom from deception, and privacy of thought and action.

**4.** Cover stories mislead research participants about the nature of research hypotheses, whereas debriefings correctly inform them of a study's true nature.

**5.** Researchers have three obligations to the research community: to completely and accurately describe research methods, to honestly and fully report all findings, and to keep personal biases out of research to the extent possible.

**6.** "Pragmatics" refers to practical constraints having the capacity to compromise a researcher's adherence to ethical principles of research. Two categories of pragmatic issues are political constraints and personal constraints.

**7.** Two sources of political constraint can affect the research process: the political attitudes of the governing elite and the political ideologies of researchers themselves. Three forms of research are particularly vulnerable to the influence of political ideology: activist research, applied research, and historical "truth" criticism.

**8.** "Personal constraints" refers to the impact a researcher's motivations and capabilities can exert on the research process. Personal constraints fall into two general categories: self-interests and professional aspirations, and the intellectual and material resources of the individual researcher.

**9.** The desires for professional recognition and economic security can be powerful motives for scholarly activity, affecting choices of research problems and methodologies.

**10.** "Resources" refers to a researcher's intellectual and material assets and liabilities that may influence the research process. "Intellectual resources" includes a researcher's knowledge and skills along with special research interests. "Material resources" refers to the availability of support factors like financial backing, research equipment, research participants, and adequate research facilities.

**11.** The rational model of research describes research as it ought to be conducted, whereas the garbage can model purports to describe research as it is actually done in some cases. Among other things, the garbage can model suggests that the scope of a researcher's intellectual and material resources affects profoundly the process of scholarly activity.

# REVIEW EXERCISES

**1.** Suppose you wish to conduct a conversational analysis of the communication of homosexual couples. Suppose further that you have located an appropriate sample for study but have not yet approached these individuals about participating in your research. Describe precisely how you might design and conduct your study so as to protect the following participant rights: the right to voluntary participation and informed consent; the right to freedom from physical, social, or psychological harm;

**295**

CHAPTER 14
The Ethics
and Prag-
matics of
Research

the right to anonymity or confidentiality; the right to freedom from deception; and the right to privacy of thought and action.

**2.** Suppose that you have designed an experiment to test the research hypothesis that male and female listeners exhibit different attitudinal responses to persuasive messages containing obscene language. Assume that you need to initially mislead subjects about the nature of your hypothesis. Construct a cover story to disguise your research aims. Then, describe the debriefing procedures you would use.

**3.** Suggest a communication problem you believe is worthy of study. Discuss how your own personal resources are likely to affect the means, ends, motives, and consequences of your research. Personal resources include intellectual resources (general knowledge, research skills, special interests, and so on) and material resources (the availability or unavailability of appropriate samples of subjects, specialized equipment, adequate research facilities, and so on). Will the intellectual integrity of your research be compromised in any substantial ways by resource availability problems?

# NOTES

**1.** Saul D. Alinsky, *Reveille for Radicals* (New York: Vintage Books, 1969), pp. 132–33, 207. Also see Saul D. Alinsky, *Rules for Radicals: A Practical Primer for Realistic Radicals* (New York: Random House, 1971).

**2.** Richard L. Johannesen, *Ethics in Human Communication* (Prospect Heights, IL: Waveland Press, 1978), p. 11.

**3.** Joseph Fletcher, *Situation Ethics: The New Morality* (Philadelphia: Westminster Press, 1966), pp. 127–28.

**4.** Robert K. Merton, *Social Theory and Social Structure* (New York: Free Press, 1949).

**5.** American Psychological Association, *Ethical Principles in the Conduct of Research with Human Par-*

*ticipants* (Washington, DC: American Psychological Association, 1983).

**6.** American Association for Public Opinion Research, *By-Laws* (New York: American Association for Public Opinion Research, 1977).

**7.** U.S. Department of Health and Human Services, "Final Regulations Amending Basic HHS Policy for the Protection of Human Subjects," *Federal Register*, 16 (1981): 8366–92.

**8.** Herbert C. Kelman, "Human Use of Human Subjects: The Problem of Deception in Social Psychological Experiments," *Psychological Bulletin*, 67 (1967): 1–11.

**9.** Like the general ethical criteria, the specific rules discussed in this section draw on Merton and the professional standards of the American Psychological Association, the American Association for Public Opinion Research, and the HHS regulations for the protection of human subjects. See the citations in notes 4 through 7.

**10.** For a communication study documenting the persistence of experimentally induced beliefs in adult subjects even after a complete debriefing, see Mary John Smith, "Cognitive Schema Theory and the Perseverance and Attenuation of Unwarranted Empirical Beliefs," *Communication Monographs*, 49 (1982): 115–26.

**11.** Joseph J. Hayes, "Gayspeak," *Quarterly Journal of Speech*, 62 (1976): 256–65.

**12.** U.S. Department of Health and Human Services, 8866–92.

**13.** Earl Babbie, *The Practice of Social Research*, 3rd ed. (Belmont, CA: Wadsworth, 1983), p. 455.

**14.** See Samuel Fillenbaum, "Prior Deception and Subsequent Experimental Performance: The 'Faithful Subject,'" *Journal of Personality and Social Psychology*, 24 (1966): 532–37; and Barry Spinner, John G. Adair, and Gordon E. Barnes, "A Reexamination of the Faithful Subject Role," *Journal of Experimental Social Psychology*, 13 (1977): 543–51.

**15.** For a discussion of alternatives to deception, including the "honest" experiment, see Paul C. Cozby, *Methods in Behavioral Research*, 3rd ed. (Palo Alto, CA: Mayfield, 1985), pp. 193–95.

**16.** See Pingree, et al., "A Scale for Sexism," *Journal of Communication*, 26, No. 4 (1976): 193–200; and James D. Culley and Rex Bennett, "Selling Women, Selling Blacks," *Journal of Communication*, 26, No. 4 (1976): 160–74.

**296**

PART IV
Contemporary
Issues in
Communi-
cation
Research

**17.** Stanley A. Deetz and Astrid Kersten, "Critical Models of Interpretive Research," in *Communication and Organizations: An Interpretive Approach*, eds. Linda L. Putnam and Michael E. Pacanowsky (Beverly Hills, CA: Sage, 1983), pp. 148, 155.

**18.** Deetz and Kersten, pp. 150–51.

**19.** W. O. Hagstrom, *The Scientific Community* (New York: Basic Books, 1965), p. 17.

**20.** L. G. Kamin, *The Science and Politics of IQ* (New York: John Wiley, 1974).

**21.** Joanne Martin, "A Garbage Can Model of the Psychological Research Process," *American Behavioral Scientist*, 25 (1981): 131–51.

**22.** Martin, 132–33.

**23.** Martin, 139.

**24.** Martin, 142.

**25.** Martin, 144.

**26.** Martin, 145.

**27.** Ibid.

**28.** Martin, 132.

# CHAPTER
# 15

# CONTEMPORARY RESEARCH PARADIGMS

This chapter examines contemporary research paradigms in the communication discipline. A paradigm is a world view or conceptual model that defines how scholarly inquiry should be conducted. Several paradigms or world views that have influenced communication researchers in recent decades are discussed. The chapter presents contemporary ontological assumptions about the nature of human communication, epistemological beliefs about appropriate ways of studying communication, metatheoretical assumptions about explanations that are suitable to human communication, and methodological views about research techniques that are most applicable to communication inquiry. The chapter concludes by reviewing recent paradigmatic changes in the communication discipline.

uring the early Renaissance, scholars were divided into two schools of thought concerning the nature of the universe. Proponents of Ptolemy's geocentric view believed the earth to be a fixed base around which the sun revolved, whereas supporters of the heliocentric paradigm of Nicolaus Copernicus regarded the earth as a spherical planet revolving around an unmoving sun. Norwood Russel Hanson illustrated the influence of these contrasting world views by imagining that the Copernican astronomer Johannes Kepler and Tycho Brahe, who was a geocentrist, got together early one sixteenth-century morning to watch the sun rise. Given their strikingly different views of the universe, Hanson wondered whether the two astronomers would have "seen" the same thing at the breaking of dawn.

In one sense they should have, since both would have perceived identical sense impressions of a yellow-white disk appearing on the horizon. However, a retinal image is not the same as a visual experience, reasoned Hanson, and in this respect the astronomers probably would have "seen" remarkably different things. Brahe would have "seen" the sun move to illuminate a fixed-in-place earth, whereas Kepler would have "seen" the earth rotate to expose a fixed-in-place sun.[1]

This imaginary incident illustrates the profound impact that world views or disciplinary *paradigms* exert on observation and explanation. Researchers inevitably "see" the world through lenses colored by their preconceptions of that world. In this chapter, I explore the nature of world views or paradigms, then examine the role of paradigms in the growth of knowledge. Next, several world views that have influenced communication researchers in recent decades are detailed. Then, I discuss contemporary paradigmatic assumptions about the nature of communication, the process of communication research, theoretical explanations, and research methodologies. Finally, recent paradigmatic changes in the communication discipline are summarized.

# THE NATURE OF PARADIGMS

Thomas Kuhn introduced the terms "**paradigm**" and its synonym "**disciplinary matrix**" to signify a perspective or *Weltanschauung* that structures research within a scholarly community.[2] More formally, a paradigm is a world view or conceptual model shared by members of a scholarly community that defines how inquiry within the community should be conducted. Paradigms determine what questions a discipline deems worthy of asking and what kind of data are required to provide acceptable answers to these questions.[3]

All disciplinary paradigms have four components or sets of assumptions. The first set consists of *ontological* assumptions, or beliefs about the nature of the subject matter to be studied. Applied to communication, ontological beliefs describe the nature of human communicators and the process of communication itself. Second, paradigms include *epistemological* assumptions about appropriate ways of studying the subject matter of a discipline. Third, paradigms entail *metatheoretical* assumptions about the kinds of explanations that are appropriate to a discipline's subject matter. Finally, paradigms contain *methodological* assumptions about the research techniques that are most applicable to disciplinary inquiry.

Two features of paradigms are critically important. First, a paradigm's four components are hierarchically and reciprocally interrelated, with ontological views at the hierarchy's apex and methodological beliefs at its base. As Figure 15.1 shows, ontological assumptions exert a downward influence on epistemological beliefs; ontological and epistemological assumptions in turn structure metatheoretical views; and finally one's choice of appropriate research

FIGURE 15.1
COMPONENTS OF PARADIGMS

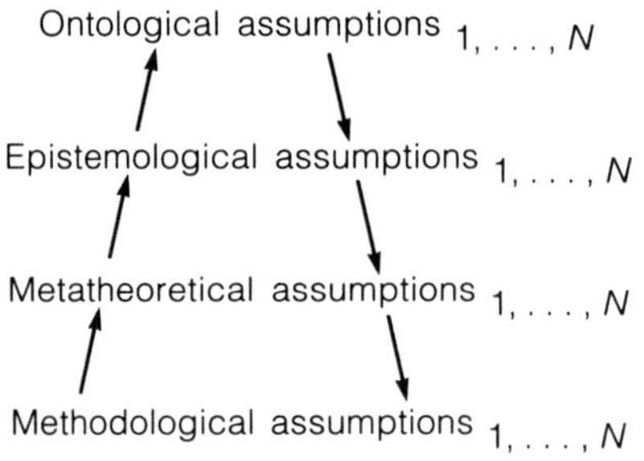

Ontological assumptions $_{1, \ldots, N}$

Epistemological assumptions $_{1, \ldots, N}$

Metatheoretical assumptions $_{1, \ldots, N}$

Methodological assumptions $_{1, \ldots, N}$

tools is constrained by all three prior hierarchical components. Importantly, the paradigmatic hierarchy turns back upon itself, so that research strategies exert an upward influence on theory construction; theoretical views and methodological choices structure epistemological perspectives; and together the three sets of assumptions affect one's ontological posture. Thus, the interrelationship among paradigmatic assumptions represents what Richard Hofstadler called a "strange loop," a phenomenon occurring "whenever, by moving upwards (or downwards) through the levels of some hierarchical system, we unexpectedly find ourselves right back where we started."[4]

Second, the four paradigmatic assumptions are just that—assumptions; they are beliefs shared by a scholarly community about the nature of its subject matter and appropriate modes of describing and explaining that material. As such, paradigmatic assumptions are unproved and unprovable, representing nothing more than a scholarly discipline's best judgment at any time about appropriate ways of conducting research. Paradigmatic assumptions, then, are neither true nor false, but rather their adequacy is determined by three standards: *internal consistency*, that is, the extent to which all assumptions are congruent with one another; *exhaustiveness*, referring to whether the assumptions cover all relevant aspects of a discipline's subject matter; and *usefulness*,

or the extent to which they produce meaningful information about disciplinary concerns.[5] Thus, an adequate paradigm is internally consistent, complete, and practically valuable to a scholarly community.

## Paradigms and Disciplinary Inquiry

The "acquisition of a paradigm," said Kuhn, "is a sign of maturity in the development of any given scientific field."[6] Without some common understanding of a discipline's subject matter and appropriate methodologies, research would proceed in a piecemeal fashion. Researchers would work independently, often at cross-purposes, and thereby produce noncomparable, perhaps even contradictory information about the same disciplinary phenomenon. Paradigms, then, are essential if scholarly research is to progress smoothly and coherently. Indeed, research as a collective activity is impossible if researchers do not share certain primary assumptions about how inquiry should be conducted.

Although essential to collective inquiry, paradigms have the quality of a double-edged sword. They can either stimulate or stifle the development of knowledge, depending on a scholarly community's paradigmatic perspective. Researchers may adopt one of two general perspectives: monism or pluralism. **Monism** is characterized by the belief that a single set of paradigmatic assumptions is appropriate to a discipline. Because it fosters a slavish reverence for one way of looking at the world, a monistic perspective can impede the advancement of knowledge. Paradigmatic beliefs can function as conceptual blinders, shielding researchers from new and more profitable modes of research. A monist often represents what Joseph Royce called "the encapsulated man," a person who confuses assumptions with truth and who accepts "*one* approach to reality as if it were *the* approach" to research.[7]

**Pluralism** fosters a healthy respect for alternative world views, holding that prevailing paradigms are always subject to intradisciplinary criticism. The pluralist adopts a particular paradigm, not because it is correct, but because it is the most useful approach to inquiry at a given time. Karl Popper described a pluralistic community as an open society in which no dominant paradigm is ever sacred. Criticism, he argued, is the touchstone of a scholarly enterprise.[8] The appreciation of paradigms differing from a preferred view gives one "the curious ability to look around the corners of one's own *Weltanschauung*, the ability to imagine oneself holding quite a different position."[9] Because pluralists understand their preferred paradigm relative to alternative views, they are acutely sensitive to its values and limitations. Unlike the monist, the pluralist is the master of his or her paradigm, not its prisoner.

## Paradigmatic Change and Knowledge Development

The history of scholarly inquiry is, in many respects, a chronicle of changing paradigms. As new ways of understanding the world emerge, old world views collapse in their wake. In the field of astronomy, the "Copernican revolution" with its heliocentric theory of planetary motion eclipsed Ptolemy's geocentric view. Develop-

ments in theoretical physics since Sir Isaac Newton's time have modified and expanded our conceptions of mass, energy, time, and space. In the discipline of communication, a transactional model of human talk long ago replaced the static, one-way-influence paradigm that held sway during the first half of the twentieth century.

Similarly, research methodologies continually change to reflect changing views of a discipline's subject matter. For instance, contemporary views of communication as a uniquely "human" phenomenon, entailing values as well as observable actions, have prompted researchers to adopt humanistic methods as a supplement to traditional science. Likewise, current interests in communication's evolutionary qualities have led to an increasing use of longitudinal research designs, rather than the once popular cross-sectional approach. Paradigmatic change, then, is a constant fact of disciplinary life. Indeed, a discipline's "working postulational system of today [will inevitably become its] "museum piece of tomorrow."[10]

Although scholars agree that paradigms are in constant flux, they disagree about the precise mechanisms underlying paradigmatic change. Contemporary thinkers typically adopt one of two perspectives on the nature of changing paradigms: either a revolutionary or an evolutionary view.

### A revolutionary model

According to Kuhn's revolutionary perspective,[11] paradigmatic changes are intellectual upheavals having qualities akin to political and social revolutions. Just as political revolutions replace the "old order" with a "new guard," a **scientific revolution** represents the substitution of one monistic paradigm for another. Prototypical "scientific revolutions" include the acknowledgment that the earth is a spherical rather than a flat-surfaced mass and a displacement of certain portions of Newtonian physics with quantum mechanics and Albert Einstein's

302

PART IV
Contemporary
Issues in
Communi-
cation
Research

theories of relativity. In our own field, paradigmatic revolutions include the adoption of
scientific methods in the 1940s and 1950s and
the more recent preference for humanistic science over "hard" scientific assumptions originally borrowed from disciplines like chemistry,
biology, and physics.

Basic to Kuhn's revolutionary model is a distinction between what he terms "normal science" and "revolutionary science." **Normal
science** is routine scholarly inquiry guided
by a dominant disciplinary matrix. There is
little disagreement among scholars about fundamental ontological, epistemological, metatheoretical, and methodological assumptions.
Normal scientists direct their research efforts to
problems and questions raised by the prevailing disciplinary paradigm.

In contrast, **revolutionary science** involves
the development of a new paradigm that ultimately replaces the old world view. The process
of rejecting a dominant paradigm commences
when researchers discover information that
is inconsistent with current paradigmatic assumptions. As these incongruities or "anomalies" accumulate, a rival paradigm is constructed to explain the anomalies. Once the
new paradigm has been introduced, conflict
rages between supporters of the old and the
new paradigms, culminating finally in acceptance of the new world view and a return to
normal science under its assumptions. According to Kuhn, the transition between the old and
a new order is characterized by aimless research efforts and accidental discoveries. Thus,
the revolutionary perspective assumes that coherent research programs are possible only
when a discipline is engaged in paradigm-
guided normal research activity.

### An evolutionary model

Advocated by Popper, Toulmin, Campbell, and
others,[12] the evolutionary perspective differs
from the revolutionary model in two principal
respects. First, the evolutionary view is plu-

ralistic rather than monistic, holding that
scholars should encourage as many paradigms
as possible in the course of routine scientific
activity. Popper argues that scholarly communities are not justified in maintaining one paradigm to the exclusion of others because no
single paradigm is ever the "true" or "correct"
approach.[13] From the evolutionary perspective,
the proliferation of paradigms is critical to the
growth of knowledge.

Second, the evolutionary model regards
paradigmatic change as a gradual process of
accumulating new perspectives that either are
incorporated into the old order or are substituted for segments of the dominant view.
Campbell described evolutionary change as a
three-stage sequence, beginning with the emer-
gence of "variations" or alterations in existing
paradigms. According to Campbell, this first
phase is exploratory, involving groping and
often haphazard research into questions not
suggested by the prevailing paradigm. Next,
scholars systematically select the most promis-
ing new ideas from among the discovered variations. Finally, the scholarly community retains
paradigmatic alterations principally through
publications that disseminate the new perspectives to the research community.[14]

## CONTEMPORARY
## COMMUNICATION
## PARADIGMS

To conduct meaningful research, a scholarly
discipline must have a unique set of interrelated
ontological, epistemological, metatheoretical,
and methodological assumptions. As F.S.C.
Northrop has argued, scholarly "inquiry in any
field must begin not with some method taken
over a priori from some other field, but with the
character of its own field and the analysis of
these problems." A discipline becomes legiti-
mized, said Northrop, "by beginning with the
peculiar character of its own particular prob-

lems."[15] As a relatively young scholarly discipline, communication floundered for many years without a clear consensus regarding the nature of its subject matter and methods. Even as recently as 1977, Charles Rossiter described communication as an "aparadigmatic discipline"[16] and Aubrey Fisher declared that "communication scholars have nothing approaching unanimity of opinion [regarding] the conducting of communication inquiry."[17]

Lacking their own paradigm, communication scholars liberally adopted the paradigmatic assumptions of other disciplines, principally social psychology and sociology. As a consequence, much early communication research was, according to Gerald Miller, derivative, "borrowing heavily from the theoretical and empirical contributions of scholars in other social and behavioral sciences."[18] Using a fragmentary paradigmatic base that fits imperfectly the subject matter of their discipline, communication researchers from the 1940s through the 1960s often were guided more by their pet interests than by the unique problems of human communication. As a result, much pre-1970s communication research has an incoherent, discontinuous quality.

In recent decades, the communication discipline has moved away from this fragmented stage of inquiry, developing a unique self-identity based on shared assumptions peculiar to human communication. Substantial agreement has developed regarding the nature of the discipline's subject matter, appropriate modes of studying it, useful approaches to theory construction, and meaningful strategies for conducting disciplinary research.[19] Although the field of communication maintains a healthy respect for scholarly disagreement and welcomes the clash of competing paradigms, a coherent set of disciplinary assumptions has emerged, dislodging the borrowed patchwork paradigm of two decades ago. It is to these contemporary paradigmatic assumptions that we now turn our attention.

# ONTOLOGY: THE NATURE OF COMMUNICATION

**Ontology** refers to the nature of reality or existence; thus ontological assumptions in communication represent beliefs about the nature of human communicators and the nature of communication itself. To fully understand contemporary ontological beliefs, we need to examine three ontological paradigms that have influenced communication scholars for many years: mechanism, actionalism, and actional realism.

All three paradigms address the centuries-old issue of determinism versus free will. Do people control their own destinies by the free choices they make, or are our lives determined by situational and social forces beyond our personal control? Applied to communication, the question asks whether communication behaviors are freely chosen or, alternately, whether they are governed by conditions imposed by the society, the culture, and the environment.

## Mechanism

**Mechanism**, also called **determinism**, is derived from the Latin root *machina*, meaning "machine" or "mechanical device." As the name implies, a mechanistic perspective construes humans as machine-like, having no capacity for choice and self-motivated behavior. First articulated by the Greek philosopher Democritus in the fifth century B.C.,[20] the mechanistic model of human behavior finds its fullest contemporary expression in Skinnerian psychology, often called "radical behaviorism."[21] According to B. F. Skinner, human behavior including communication processes can be fully explained within a stimulus-response (S-R) paradigm, with no reference to internal motivations. People are regarded as passive victims of environmental stimuli, which shape

**304**

PART IV
Contemporary
Issues in
Communi-
cation
Research

their communicative behaviors. The mechanistic model is, in many respects, an attempt to adapt the assumptions of the physical sciences to human social action.

Early communication perspectives embraced a mechanistic view of communicators and the communication process. One such perspective, the "hypodermic needle" or "bullet" theory, was popular from the end of World War I through the 1950s. This view regards communication as a unidirectional process whereby powerful sources influence relatively passive message recipients. The receiver was considered to be a reactive "victim" of others' communication strategies, not a full partner in the communication process.[22] A more contemporary perspective, Gregory Bateson's interactional theory, has a deterministic flavor, holding that people are easily victimized by others' paradoxical communication and can escape the "vicious circle" of dysfunctional talk only by "an outside intervention."[23]

## Actionalism

Grounded in the writings of Aristotle, **actionalism** as a model of human behavior was systematically developed by Immanuel Kant in the eighteenth century[24] and later elaborated by such contemporary philosophers as Romano Harré, Charles Taylor, and John Searle.[25] From this perspective, humans are active agents who possess goals and have the capacity to choose goal-maximizing actions. Communication behaviors are explained by referring to people's intentions, goals, and reasons for behaving, not to external factors forcing the behaviors upon the actors.

The actional model is an influential ontological paradigm among contemporary communication theorists, spawning such current perspectives as Jesse Delia's constructivism and Donald Cushman's rules theory of interpersonal communication.[26] Miller summarized the role of actionalism in contemporary communication research by noting that "an influential, vocal segment of the field has renounced the view of human communicators as marionettes dancing on deterministic threads and has replaced it with a vision of people as masters of their own communicative destinies."[27]

## Actional Realism

I call the third perspective **actional realism** because it embraces the basic tenets of actionalism, yet acknowledges that in "reality" situational and social forces interact with choice-making behavior to determine communicative actions. Addressing the need to integrate elements of determinism into the actional perspective, Barnett Pearce noted that an adequate communication "theory must include an account of how cultural forces are manifest in the perceptions of persons, but it must also represent persons as social actors—not mere puppets on the strings of social forces."[28]

Among other contemporary perspectives, Pearce's coordinated management of meaning theory and Mary John Smith's contingency rules theory adopt actional realist ontologies. Each holds that people's communicative choices take place within boundaries that expand and contract as a function of certain intractable situational, physiological, and psychological forces.[29]

## Contemporary Ontological Assumptions

Eight assumptions about the nature of human communication, all derived from the models I have just described, characterize the thinking of many contemporary scholars: (1) communication as social reality, (2) communication as a creative process, (3) communication as a developmental process, (4) communication as an interrelated system, (5) communication as a contextual phenomenon, (6) communication as a purposive activity, (7) communication as an interactive reality, and (8) communication as an orderly process. Most of these beliefs reflect the view that human communication differs radically from the subject matter of the natural sciences.

## Communication as social reality

All phenomena in the empirical world represent either physical (objective) reality or social (subjective) reality. Physical reality consists of atoms, biological systems, the planets, and other phenomena that have objective existence; their presence can be confirmed or denied by sight, sound, touch, and other sense processes. In contrast, social phenomena are created by consensus; they exist only because people collectively agree that they have existence. Agreement is reached, and social reality is thereby created, when people assign common meanings to the same phenomenon. Phenomena such as "freedom" and "love" are socially constructed. The state of "being free" exists only if people believe they are not in bondage, and "love" exists when individuals so interpret their feelings toward others.

Likewise, human communication phenomena are social realities. To understand the socially created nature of communication, consider the statement, "You're looking good, sweetheart." If uttered by one romantic partner to another, the comment will likely be interpreted as a "compliment" or some other "caring" gesture. However, if an employer makes the same statement to a newly hired employee, it probably will be interpreted as potential sexual harassment or an otherwise inappropriate come-on. As this illustration suggests, people create communication phenomena by the common meanings they assign to verbal and nonverbal behaviors.

## Communication as a creative process

Whereas communication is itself a socially constructed phenomenon, all instances of social reality, communication among them, are created by the process of communication. Communication, then, occupies the strange position of constructing itself as well as other noncommunicative social realities. To illustrate communication's self-creative role, consider an episode such as an "argument." An argument is itself a communication phenomenon, yet arguments are created by smaller communicative units called speech acts, which typically take the form of angry charges and countercharges.

In addition to being self-creating, communication plays a wider role in the construction of noncommunicative social realities. Social creations ranging from a person's "self-concept," through "relationships" we establish with others, to larger "social communities," including small groups, organizations, subcultures, and entire cultures, are created by the process of people talking with one another. For instance, our self perceptions, including feelings of self-worth, are functions of others' positive and negative communicative reactions. Similarly, we establish and maintain relationships, including friendships and romantic partnerships, by talking with others about our common interests. Likewise, groups ranging from small social clubs to nation-states are bound together by mutual needs identified through the process of communication. In this respect, all social contracts are created, maintained, and destroyed largely by talk.

## Communication as a developmental process

Consistent with its creative quality, human communication is a developmental process, implying that the content and character of communication and the social realities it creates evolve and change over time. As people talk with one another from first meetings through mature relational stages to relationship termination, their communication changes in depth and in breadth and with these changes, the nature of the relationship itself is modified. Thus, communication is a continually evolving

**306**

PART IV
Contemporary
Issues in
Communi-
cation
Research

process that changes us and our social world as we progress through time.

## Communication as a complex system

Contrary to early views of communication as a simple, one-way-influence process, most contemporary scholars believe that human communication is a complex, interrelated **system** of actions and meanings. People do not communicate in a vacuum; each person's actions and meanings can be understood only in relation to others' reciprocal messages as well as the settings in which messages are exchanged. Each part of a communication system affects every other part, and the whole of a communication episode is something more than the sum of the individual speech acts constituting it.

## Communication as a contextual phenomenon

Consistent with a systemic view of communication, contemporary researchers generally regard human communication as a context-dependent phenomenon. Some early scholars sought to draw universal conclusions about messages, making claims like "Physical attractiveness relates to increased persuasibility at all times and under all conditions." Most contemporary theorists reject this view, arguing that message effects vary as a function of physical, social, and psychological contexts. For example, a threatening message may elicit compliance when message recipients have little status relative to the communicator, yet the same message is likely to backfire in an equal-status context. Communication, then, cannot be decontextualized without destroying its original meaning for communicators and for researchers who seek to study it.[30]

## Communication as a purposive activity

"Among communication researchers," said Miller, "a respect for the role of human volition has replaced the law-governed, deterministic para-digm of communication behavior."[31] This statement reflects the belief of many scholars that human communicators are capable of choice and self-directed action. People communicate for reasons, to get the things they want for themselves, including meaningful relationships, favorable public images, and social and material assets. In seeking desired objects, people choose the communication strategies they believe are most likely to meet their needs. Communication, then, is often regarded as a purposive activity that people use to get what they want for themselves and important others.

## Communication as an interactive reality

As I noted earlier, contemporary theorists often temper an actional ontological posture with realism, believing that human communication behaviors are shaped by an interaction between individual choice-making behavior and the operation of forces that at the time are not under the communicator's personal control. Uncontrollable phenomena influencing communicative choices include physiological attributes such as age and intelligence and enduring personality syndromes like shyness and dogmatism. Summarizing this interactive perspective, Smith has argued that communication "choice-making behavior takes place within boundaries that expand and contract as a function of a relatively fixed potential context."[32]

## Communication as an orderly process

Finally, contemporary scholars generally maintain that human communication behaviors are patterned and orderly, not chaotic and unpredictable. Because people are regarded as choice-laden, several writers have suggested that human behavior is unstructured, unpredictable, and therefore not amenable to scientific study.[33] Most communication scholars reject this view, arguing that communicative behaviors are prestructured by the meanings that communicators assign to their utterances. Moreover, the assumption of free will does not necessarily imply that people's meanings and actions are chaotic and unpredictable. Rather, many researchers believe that human volition is exercised in an orderly fashion, with communicators consistently following established rules of meaning and action that promote individual and collective goals.

# EPISTEMOLOGY: THE NATURE OF COMMUNICATION INQUIRY

**Epistemology**, the science of knowledge, involves assumptions about how one "knows" the world. Thus, epistemological beliefs are shared opinions about appropriate ways to conduct scholarly inquiry. Six traditional epistemological paradigms have influenced communication scholars in recent decades: rationalism, rational empiricism, mechanistic empiricism, logical positivism, constructivism, and constructive realism.[34]

All six paradigms concern the interrelationship among the researcher (or "knower"), the subject matter to be studied (or "the known"), and a researcher's methods and procedures (or the "process of knowing"). Thus, the perspectives raise the central question: How can the communication scholar most fruitfully come to know and understand the world of human communication? In responding to this question, each paradigm variously addresses three interrelated issues: (1) "rationalism versus empiricism," or the comparative importance of human mental activity on the one hand and empirical observations on the other in developing reliable knowledge; (2) "objectivism versus subjectivism," referring to the relative influence of a researcher's interpretive processes on the process of observation;

and (3) "science versus humanism," or the comparative importance of description and inference on the one hand and interpretation and criticism on the other in understanding human communication.

## Rationalism

**Rationalism**, which originated with the Greek philosopher Plato, found its way into modern thought through the writings of René Descartes in the seventeenth century. According to Plato, Descartes, and such twentieth century rationalists as Ernst Cassirer and Einstein, creative human thought is the key to unlocking the secrets of the empirical world.[35] From a rationalist perspective, an understanding of the world is not pieced together from scattered observations, but rather is gained by rational contemplation of the logical structure of the world. Thus, Descartes believed that scholars who move systematically from one "clear idea" to another "can not only arrive . . . at some indubitable knowledge, but at the construction of a unified, all-embracing body of such knowledge."[36] Similarly, Einstein argued that theoretical explanations are "free creations of the mind . . . that cannot be fabricated out of the results of observation, but that can only be invented."[37]

Noam Chomsky's "generative" or "transformational" linguistics is a prototypical rationalist approach to communication inquiry, setting forth the rules of linguistic competence required for the ideal speaker-listener to produce and comprehend utterances. Chomsky's competence rules were not derived from observations of linguistic behaviors; rather, they represent a logical model defining the cognitive structure humans necessarily must possess if they are to use language effectively.[38] Similarly, many contemporary rhetorical models are rational in nature. For example, Kenneth Burke's dramatistic theory of rhetoric conceptualizes discourse as a theatrical performance entailing an act (the message), a scene (the situation), an agent (the speaker), an agency (the means of

**308**

PART IV
Contemporary
Issues in
Communi-
cation
Research

communication), and a purpose (the speaker's objective).[39] Like Chomsky's work, Burke's dramatistic analogy did not emerge from empirical inquiry—it represents, instead, a metaphorical model within which rhetorical actions can be understood.

## Rational Empiricism

First systematically developed by Aristotle, **rational empiricism** is a "theory-to-data" perspective holding that human understanding is best achieved by applying rational thought to observational data.[40] The approach embraces a rationalist philosophy, but additionally requires that logical systems be tested against empirical evidence. The rational empiricist Popper argues that knowledge is advanced most fruitfully by developing a system of ideas, called "conjectures" or "highly informed guesses about the world," then testing one's conjectures against empirical data, a process he refers to as "refutations."[41] Rational empiricism, then, aims to construct logical explanatory models that account for patterns of observed communication behaviors.

Rational empiricism is an influential epistemology among many researchers. Contemporary examples include Paul Grice's "logic of conversation," detailing a set of maxims that explain why conversations occur as they do; Harvey Sacks's work on rules accounting for observed systems of conversational turn-taking; and Pearce's "logic of interpersonal communication systems," setting forth a rules explanation for human talk.[42] Similarly, much contemporary rhetorical criticism has a rational empiricist flavor, applying well-reasoned analytical and critical standards to empirical communication events like public speeches, printed artifacts, and motion pictures. Both neo-Aristotelianism and fantasy theme analysis, explored in Chapter 13, advance conceptual frameworks that humanistic researchers test for goodness-of-fit against narrative discourse.

## Mechanistic Empiricism

Mechanistic empiricism is a special variety of the more general epistemology known as "empiricism." Developed extensively by Francis Bacon in the seventeenth century, **empiricism** is a counterpoint to rationalism, holding that knowledge is best derived from empirical observations with a minimal intrusion of rational thought.[43] As a "data-to-theory" approach, empiricists advocate an upward flow of explanations from observations.

Attributed principally to Newton, **mechanistic empiricism** embraces the basic tenets of a general empiricist philosophy, treating human reasoning as a potentially misleading ingredient in scholarly inquiry.[44] For Newton, the empirical world is ordered like a machine, consisting of sequences of cause-to-effect relationships, and the business of science is to discover "the causes of sensible events."[45] Through observations, Newton believed that researchers can discover the world's organizing principles and can express them as general cause-to-effect theories.

Much early communication research followed the mechanistic empirical epistemology, seeking to discover causal forces producing consequent communicative effects. Prominent among mechanistic research programs of the 1950s and 1960s were persuasion studies that treated influence strategies as causal forces leading to attitudinal and behavioral changes in message recipients.[46] Although its impact has waned over the past decade, the Newtonian tradition continues to inform a number of distinguished theorists. Prototypical theories include Joseph Woelfel's linear force aggregation model, which explains persuasive effects by referring to a message recipient's "inertial mass" or preexisting store of information, and

Michael Burgoon's theory of resistance to persuasion, detailing causal-like pretreatments that render people capable of effectively combating persuasive influence.[47]

## Logical Positivism

**Logical positivism**, a form of empiricism, was developed in the 1920s by a group of philosophers and mathematicians known as the Vienna Circle.[48] Members of the Vienna Circle, including Alfred North Whitehead and Bertrand Russell, sought to unify science with a general method of inquiry based on two fundamental premises: (1) that "a real, objective world" of empirical phenomena "exists independent of individual perceivers,"[49] meaning that a researcher's interpretations need not affect what he or she "sees" when observing the world, and (2) that an understanding of the objective world can be based on empirical inquiry, which implies that creative thought and rational speculation should be excluded from inquiry.[50]

For the logical positivist, knowledge consists of conclusions about recurring correlations among observed phenomena. Thus, scientific theories are abbreviated descriptions of observed regularities that take the form $Y = f(X)$, meaning $Y$ varies as a function of $X$. Put another way, if the phenomenon $X$ occurs, then we can expect that $Y$ will also occur. Importantly, logical positivists do not assume that $X$ causes $Y$, only that the two phenomena vary together. This assumption rejects Newton's view that science aims to discover the "causes of sensible events" and accepts instead the "skeptical empiricist" argument of David Hume that the nature of empirical relationships cannot be known.[51] From a positivist perspective, then, all we can ever know is that certain events in the world occur together; we can never know what caused the related events.

In developing correlational conclusions,

most logical positivists are committed to the principles of reductionism and operationalism. **Reductionism**, also called logical atomism, assumes that the smallest units of observation are the most meaningful objects of inquiry and that the whole of any process is equal to the sum of its parts. A reductionist studying small group communication would focus on individual group members and would equate the total group communication process with the sum of each member's utterances.

The principle of **operationalism** is also known as the "verification theory of meaning" and the "doctrine of cognitive significance." It assumes that all concepts in theoretical statements are defined "by specifying the operations that the scientist performs to observe them, and they have *no other* meaning or existence."[52] As Pearce described it, "[the concept] cake is operationally defined by a recipe; surplus meanings such as *sweet, birthday, company coming,* and so on, are both irrelevant and dysfunctional."[53] Similarly, communication constructs such as "shyness" or "dogmatism" are equivalent to people's scores on questionnaires designed to measure the two personality syndromes. These examples indicate that operationalists deny a meaningful distinction between abstract concepts and their empirical indicators. Indeed, for the logical positivist, the empirical indicators are the concepts.

From its inception through the 1960s, the communication discipline was heavily influenced by logical positivism. Following the lead of social psychologists like Carl Hovland, early persuasion researchers were especially enamored with the positivist tradition.[54] These researchers focused on such individual components of the persuasion process as "source credibility," "message organization," and "receiver attitude." The effects of persuasive messages were usually equated with recipients' scores on a variety of "attitude change" scales. Such research produced a body of observed regularities or statistical correlations between

**310**

PART IV
Contemporary
Issues in
Communi-
cation
Research

certain types of message strategies and receivers' reactions to them. Typical of these correlative conclusions are statements such as "High source credibility is associated with increased compliance with persuasive messages," and "Initial disagreement with a message is related to decreased message acceptance."

Over the past decade, logical positivism's influence in communication has declined, paralleling its decreasing impact in other academic disciplines. Frederick Suppe provided one view of the current status of positivism when he commented that "virtually all the positivistic program . . . has been repudiated by contemporary philosophy of science, [and this includes] its treatments of explanation and reduction. Positivism today truly belongs to the history of the philosophy of science, and its influence is that of a movement historically important in shaping the landscape of a much-changed philosophy of science."[55]

## Constructivism

First developed by Kant,[56] **constructivism** is a reaction to radical empiricist epistemologies. Contemporary constructivists such as Kuhn, Hanson, and Toulmin believe that scholarly inquiry is conducted from within a global perspective or world view that shapes the process of research.[57] This implies that "the mind of the observer has an inherent and active role in the process of knowing [the world]."[58]

Five assumptions underpin the constructivist epistemology. First, constructivism rejects the logical positivist view of an objectively real world, believing instead that the world is subjectively "constructed" by the meanings that people assign to observations. Second, constructivists assume that the empirical world is not independent of perceivers, but rather that a researcher's perceptions and interpretations affect what he or she "sees" when observing the

world. For the constructivist, then, the object of scholarly inquiry is the "world-as-perceived," not some raw reality untouched by human perception and interpretation.

Third, constructivism rejects the reductionist perspective, believing like Kant that "experience is not atomic but integrated."[59] From a constructivist view, the most useful units of observation are the systemic wholes of human communication, not isolated utterances. Fourth, constructivists disavow operationalism, arguing that theoretical concepts are fundamentally different from their empirical indicators. To follow Pearce's analogy mentioned earlier, constructivists believe that the meaning of a "cake" is more than its recipe. Indeed, "surplus meanings" like "sweet" and "birthday" are regarded as more central to the meaning of "cake" than is a list of its ingredients. Fifth and finally, constructivism assumes that communication theories are more than statistical correlations, believing instead that we can explain communicative behavior by referring to people's reasons for talking with one another.

In many respects, constructivism is a systematic compromise between scientific empiricism and humanism. It embraces traditional science, yet tempers scientific assumptions to accommodate the socially constructed nature of communication. As such, constructivism is an influential paradigm, lying at the heart of many hybrid methodologies that partake of both science and humanism. The interpretive models discussed in Chapters 12 and 13, including conversational analysis, content analysis, and rhetorical criticism, owe a considerable debt to constructivism. Other examples of contemporary constructivist work include Delia's developmental constructivism, focusing on the communicative impact of cognitive structures; and Pearce's coordinated management of meaning theory, which examines the ways people construct social reality with communication.[60]

## Constructive Realism

This sixth position, which I call **constructive realism**,[61] embraces the basic tenets of constructivism, such that a communicator's "meanings for a given situation [are believed to] constitute the primary data for communication researchers."[62] Moreover, researchers are thought to reconstruct a communicator's meanings by the interpretations they assign to them. Like constructivists, constructive realists repudiate the radical positivist vision of an objective world unaffected by human interpretations. However, constructive realists also reject a radical constructivist perspective, which taken to its logical extreme, renders scholarly inquiry a subjective enterprise, with each researcher applying idiosyncratic interpretations to the same phenomenon. From a realist perspective, radical constructivism makes collective scholarly inquiry impossible, yet radical positivism is contrary to the socially constructed nature of human communication.

To escape this dilemma, many contemporary communication researchers steer a middle ground between the two epistemological extremes, believing (1) that communication phenomena are prestructured by the meanings communicators assign to them, lending a measure of objectivity to communication's world, and (2) that scholars apply to observed phenomena a set of shared interpretations, rendering their inquiry an intersubjective rather than a subjective activity.

A realistic perspective characterizes much contemporary research. For example, Delia's constructivist work on cognitive structure and Pearce's research on the logic of conversations show a healthy respect for the interaction between communication's preexisting structure and a researcher's interpretive processes.[63] However, constructive realism is best exemplified in the work of contemporary conversational analysts like Jackson and Jacobs, whose rational model of conversational coherence reflects a constructive realist epistemology.[64]

# METATHEORY: THE NATURE OF EXPLANATION

The term **metatheory** refers to beliefs about the nature of theory. Thus, metatheoretical assumptions address the types of theoretical explanations that are appropriate to human communication. Consistent with the hierarchically interrelated nature of paradigms, a researcher's ontological and epistemological views will largely determine the sorts of theoretical explanations he or she deems suitable.

Two approaches to theory construction, paralleling two sets of ontological and epistemological perspectives, have influenced communication researchers in recent decades: the laws approach and the rules perspective.[65] Laws researchers often embrace a deterministic ontology. They may subscribe either to mechanistic empiricism or to logical positivist assumptions. By contrast, rules theorists usually adopt an actional or actional realist ontology and either a constructivist or a constructive realist epistemology.

## The Laws Approach

Laws theorists often explain communication behavior by referring to causes or antecedent conditions over which communicators have no control.[66] This explanatory perspective derives from an ontological view of humans as relatively passive objects whose behavior is determined by "a combination of the effects of external stimuli and prevailing organismic states."[67] The laws theoretical posture is also shaped by an empiricist epistemology that assumes the world to be a lawfully ordered and reasonably objective reality. Virginia McDermott argues

312

PART IV
Contemporary
Issues in
Communi-
cation
Research

that causal explanations deny that "the intentions and aims of human beings play . . . any role in generating . . . behavior."[68] Most laws approaches, then, assume that people's communication behaviors can be explained without knowing what motivated them.

## Types of laws

There are two general types of communication laws: natural necessity laws, derived from a mechanistic empiricist epistemology, and logical positivist laws.[69] A **natural necessity law** presumes that powerful environmental or organismic forces cause communication behaviors, and therefore it takes the simple form "X causes Y." Typical examples are "Physical attractiveness causes increased communicative effectiveness," and "Shyness causes conversational incoherence." A **logical positivist law** identifies correlations, not causal links, between empirical phenomena, taking the form "X covaries with Y." "The inclusion in messages of supporting evidence is correlated with increased message acceptance" and "Heavy viewing of televised violence covaries with aggressive behavior" are examples of logical positivist laws.

Laws of the two types just defined generate radically different explanations. Natural necessity laws answer the question "Why did communication behavior Y occur?" by referring to a causal force X that produced the behavior. In contrast, the logical positivist law assumes that the question "Why did communication behavior Y occur?" can be adequately answered with the response "Because X occurred previously." Suppe argues that this "positivistic treatment of explanation" is "fundamentally defective," since it confuses prediction, that is, the capacity to use one event (X) to anticipate another (Y), with a genuine account of why events covary.[70]

Most natural necessity and logical positivist laws are **inductive-statistical laws**, taking the following form: If X, then probably Y, under the conditions $Z_1, . . . ,Z_n$.[71] As the name implies, such laws are derived inductively from

observations, following a "data-to-theory" discovery pattern. Moreover, the relationship between X and Y can be expressed as a statistical probability, such that one may conclude there is a 95% chance that X will cause (or covary) with Y. Thus, the relationships specified in communication laws are probable, not certain. Furthermore, we can expect that X will probably imply (cause or covary with) Y only under certain specified boundary conditions $(Z_1, . . . ,Z_n)$. Some examples of communication laws are "Heavy viewing of media violence (X) is probably related to overt aggression (Y), among viewers who already have latent aggressive tendencies (Z)," and "Physical attractiveness (X) will usually increase communicative effectiveness (Y), but only among opposite-sex receivers (Z)."

## The current status of communication laws

Laws explanations dominated early communication research, paralleling the widespread popularity of a deterministic model of human behavior as well as mechanistic empiricist and logical positivist epistemologies. Over the past two decades, scholarly interest in the laws paradigm has declined somewhat, reflecting an increasing acceptance of actional and constructivist assumptions. Despite its waning influence, the laws perspective retains many distinguished advocates.[72] Moreover, several insightful laws theories inform current communication research, among them Woelfel's linear force aggregation theory, the deterministic model of attitude change proposed by Marshall Poole and John Hunter, and David Seibold's causal process theory of persuasion.[73]

# The Rules Perspective

Whereas laws account for human communication by referring to uncontrollable causes and covariates, rules explain communication behavior by referring to a communicator's goals, intentions, and reasons for communicating.[74] Recall that rules as explanations for conversational behavior were described in Chapter 12. The view that behavior can be explained by referring to people's reasons for acting is called **teleological explanation**. According to Harré and Secord, such "an explanation of action is intentional and purposive. Actions are explained in terms of the ends for which they are performed."[75]

Ontologically, the rules perspective typically is actional or actional realist. Communicators are usually seen as active agents possessing goals and the capacity to choose goal-maximizing communication strategies. Moreover, rules theorists often adopt either a constructivist or a constructive realist epistemology, believing that communication is a socially constructed system of meanings and actions. Teleological explanation, then, focuses on the things done by a person for goal-oriented reasons, whereas causal explanation emphasizes the things done to people by forces outside their control.[76]

Structurally, a rules theory links human goals with actions that are goal-satisfying, taking the form presented in Chapter 12: If $X$ (some goal), in the context $Z_1, \ldots, Z_n$, then probably $Y$ (some goal-satisfying communicative action). Thus, rules are goal-action linkages, stipulating what a person must or must not do in specified social settings to achieve desired objectives. Some examples of rules include "If a person wishes to project a favorable self-image ($X$) when interacting with strangers ($Z$), then he or she should probably engage in polite social conversation ($Y$)," and "If one wishes to maintain a satisfying relationship ($X$) when talking to a close friend ($Z$), then one should probably communicate openly and honestly ($Y$)."

These examples indicate that rules, like laws, express probable relationships between communication phenomena. Conversational strategies such as politeness and openness are likely to contribute to goal achievement, although they are not certain to do so. Moreover, rules are context-specific just as laws are; a communication behavior will probably lead to goal achievement only under certain specified boundary conditions. Thus, self-disclosing conversation is usually appropriate with close friends but not with strangers, just as "small talk" is likely to convey a positive social image at a party but not at a working business meeting. The context in which communicators interact, then, largely determines the types of rules that are likely to be appropriate and effective.

## Types of teleological explanations

Three types of reason-based explanations are used in communication rules: the intentional view, the teleonomic script or programmatic perspective, and the systems approach.[77] According to the **intentional rule**, people's intentions or goals are regarded as motivational forces responsible for communicative actions. From this view, "it is not the *goal* that brings about the action," but "rather the agent's *wanting* the goal together with his *belief* that the action would contribute to the realization of the goal, that does so."[78]

With its focus on cognitive activities like "wanting" and "believing," the intentional perspective emphasizes the deliberative nature of goal-seeking actions. Thus, an intentional explanation is appropriate only when people are aware of their inner motives for talking with others. Examples include novel situations such as first encounters, or contexts like employment interviews, which serve to focus communicative behaviors clearly on specific objectives.

Many everyday interactions, of course, do not involve a high level of motivational awareness. Rather, we often talk in a habitual, even "mindless" fashion, relying on a previously learned repertoire or script specifying appropriate ways to achieve our communication

314

PART IV
Contemporary
Issues in
Communi-
cation
Research

goals.[79] Although, if asked, we might be able to articulate the reasons for our utterances, we often do not actively monitor those reasons in ordinary social interactions. Casual conversations with friends and family are typical examples of scripted communication situations.

To explain communicative behaviors occurring at lower levels of awareness, rules theorists rely on a form of teleological explanation called the **teleonomic script rule** or *programmatic* perspective.[80] From a programmatic view, people's reasons for communicating are embedded in scripts, defined as "prearranged information that controls a process (or behavior) leading it toward a given end."[81] As Ernst Mayr described it, a teleonomic script contains programmed goals, instructions for achieving the goals, and prescriptions for dealing with internal and external disruptions of the process leading to the goals.[82] Thus, teleonomic scripts allow us to communicate purposively, yet avoid continuous deliberation about our reasons for communicating.

Whereas both the intentional and programmatic views address the motivations of individual communicators, the **systems rule** focuses on the interrelatedness of communicators belonging to "the social system *as a whole*."[83] A social system may consist of two individuals, a small group, an organization, or an entire culture. From the systems perspective, people's communicative behaviors are explained by referring to systemic goals, that is, the collective objectives shared by a group of communicators. A systems analysis explores how individual messages contribute to systemic goals and how a system's rule structure affects individual communication patterns.

### The current status of communication rules

The rules approach is an influential paradigm, paralleling the increasing acceptance of action-based ontologies and constructivist-oriented epistemologies. Thus, many current scholars believe that human communication phenomena are best explained by referring to people's personal and social reasons for communicating, rather than to uncontrollable forces that impose communication patterns on passive people.[84] Prominent examples of contemporary rules theories include Pearce's coordinated management of meaning theory, Cushman's interpersonal rules theory, Kathleen Reardon's rules approach to persuasion, and the structural-functional systems theory of Norman Fontes and his associates.[85]

# METHODOLOGY: CONTEMPORARY RESEARCH STRATEGIES

Over the past few decades, communication research methods have changed remarkably, paralleling our changing views of the nature of communication, the process of inquiry, and the nature of communication theory. From an almost exclusive reliance on the experimental paradigm in the 1950s and 1960s, contemporary communication researchers employ a rich and varied assortment of methods tailored to unravel the peculiarities of human communication.

Two interrelated methodological trends characterize contemporary communication research: (1) a shift from methodological monism to pluralism, implying that researchers no longer rely exclusively on the experiment but rather employ a variety of methods, including naturalistic designs and humanistic perspectives; and (2) the development of several distinctively communicative research methods like conversational analysis and rhetorical models, instead of continued reliance on general social scientific methodologies. Seven methodological trends derived from these general perspectives permeate contemporary research practices: (1) a blending of science and humanism, (2) the use of distinctively communicative research designs, (3) a preference for naturalistic methodologies, (4) an emphasis on longitudinal studies, (5) a multivariate methodological focus, (6) a communicator-centered research emphasis, and (7) a preference for theory-guided inquiry.[86]

## A Union of Science and Humanism

Before the 1970s, many communication researchers used methods derived from the natural sciences, making few systematic attempts to adapt them to the peculiarities of communication. Human talk was treated as an empirical artifact to be studied in much the same way as a physical object. Thus, atoms and utterances were regarded as equivalent for purposes of scientific observation and inference. That atoms have no intrinsic meaning whereas talk is inherently meaningful was often disregarded by researchers calling themselves communication "scientists." During this same period, another group of communication scholars identified as "rhetoricians" were studying meaningful human discourse, but often treating it as a "particularistic or idiosyncratic" phenomenon.[87] Stephen Wasby observed in 1971 that the rhetorician's preoccupation with discourse as a unique event produced rhetorical studies that were "difficult for anyone to integrate in order to develop general explanations or theories."[88]

Throughout the 1960s and the early 1970s, these two scholarly camps viewed one another with considerable suspicion. Scientists regarded rhetorical studies as unduly personalized and intuitive, having little generalizability beyond a single communication event studied by a single scholar. On the other hand, rhetoricians scoffed at the scientists' treatment of human discourse as a natural object whose meaning could be reduced to numbers and transformed into general theoretical propositions. The temper of these times was captured in Earnest Bormann's argument that "scientific

studies and rhetorical criticism . . . are incompatible in method and in the explanation and understanding they provide . . . and we ought not try to force them together."[89]

In the latter half of the 1970s, communication scientists and rhetoricians alike began to rethink these assumptions, suggesting that science and humanism are not only *not* incompatible, but that a blending of the two might be necessary to capture the richness of communication processes. In 1978, the rhetorician Herbert Simons proposed "a scientific approach to the study of rhetorical genres."[90] At about the same time the communication scientist Pearce advanced a theory of communication that "purports both to be scientific, complete with measuring apparati and statistical tests of hypotheses, *and* to be based on a humanistic conceptualization of social reality."[91] Since then, the reunification of science and humanism in the communication discipline has continued apace, so that contemporary researchers routinely employ hybrid methodologies that recognize the essentially "human" nature of communication yet apply the rigors of science to the study of meaningful discourse.[92]

## The Use of Distinctively Communicative Methods

Many of the methods employed by communication scholars before 1970 were general social scientific designs adapted to the study of communication. They were not distinctively communicative in either function or form. Experimental and survey methods are examples of these general research perspectives, which are often called "functional" designs. We learned in Chapter 9 that functional designs typically treat meanings as baseline data for inferring conclusions about related causes and effects.

Around the mid-1970s, communication researchers began to employ distinctively communicative methodologies, which focus on the

**316**

PART IV
Contemporary
Issues in
Communi-
cation
Research

meanings and actions inherent in communicative interactions—what we say to each other,
how we go about saying it, and what we "do to"
each other when we engage in communicative
exchanges. Such methods are often called "interpretive" models, and they treat people's individual and shared meanings as the end product,
not the starting point of research. Conversational analysis, content analysis, and a variety of
rhetorical methods exemplify contemporary
interpretive designs that have few functions
save the analysis of communicative actions and
interactions.

## A Preference for
## Naturalistic Research

As noted repeatedly, most pre-1970s communication research was experimental and was
conducted principally in laboratory settings.
However, the past decade and a half has seen a
burgeoning trend toward naturalistic studies as
a supplement to manipulated experimental designs, including a preference for field rather
than laboratory research environments. This
methodological direction reflects the ontological view that human communication is a
developmental process whereby people construct social reality, including interpersonal relationships, in the course of their everyday interactions. Although the laboratory experiment
continues to play an important role in communication research, it has lost its once dominant
position principally because its ability to capture people's normal communicative activities
is limited.

## An Emphasis on
## Longitudinal Research

Many contemporary researchers are employing
longitudinal designs rather than the "one-shot"
or cross-sectional methods that dominated

pre-1970s communication research. This trend
reflects the ontological perspective that human
communication is a highly developmental activity whose effects often are obscured or dis-
torted by time-locked research methods. Miller
captured the flavor of this paradigmatic change,
noting that "since relationships necessarily
evolve and develop over time, research snapshots that capture only a relational moment—
the cross-sectional, ahistorical generalizations
associated with most prior communication research—are, at best, oversimplified and, at
worst, scientifically counterproductive."[93]

## A Multivariate
## Methodological Focus

Reflecting the belief that communication is a
simple, one-way process of influence, much
early communication research was univariate
(called bivariate in Chapter 8). Researchers
often studied two communication variables at a
time and included only a few pairs of variables
in a single research design. Most contemporary
researchers supplement these univariate methods with multivariate designs capable of investigating the interrelationships among a very
large number of variables within a single research design. Moreover, researchers are increasingly using multidimensional measures of
human talk, thereby capturing more fully its
multifaceted character. (Multivariate methods
were discussed in Chapter 8 and multidimensional measurements were described in Chapter 4.)

This shift to multivariate methodologies reflects the current ontological view of human
communication as a marvelously complex *system*, involving multiple sets of interdependent
variables. Miller has noted that because "univariate statistics . . . have given way to multivariate techniques, it is now possible not only
to speculate about the many variables influencing symbolic transactions, but also to tease out

evidence of the impact of these variables. Such methodological advancements herald . . . the promise of a research future in which the complex mysteries of human communication will be bared to public understanding."[94]

## A Communicator-Centered Research Emphasis

Consistent with a positivist view of communication as an objective reality "out there" to be discovered, many early researchers imposed their own interpretations on the utterances they studied. In recent years, this researcher-based approach has been supplemented with a communicator-centered perspective; that is, researchers often seek people's meanings for their communicative actions rather than imposing meanings on observed or reported behaviors. This trend reflects the constructivist view that communication phenomena are social realities created by the meanings that communicators assign to their own utterances.

## A Preference for Theory-Guided Research

Much pre-1970s research was influenced by empiricist epistemologies, holding that human thought has a limited function in scholarly inquiry. Moreover, many researchers took a reductionist stance, believing that the most meaningful units of research were the individual parts of the communication process. These twin assumptions led to a *variable analytic* research orientation, an approach focusing on individual communication variables and characterized by few theoretical notions about relationships among variables.

The popularity of this atheoretical research perspective has declined in recent years, and most contemporary research is guided by underlying theoretical notions about how the

variables within a given communication system "ought to fit together." This *theory-guided* trend reflects a rational empiricist epistemology that regards human thought as an essential guide to observation. Additionally, the approach rejects the reductionist view that studying the parts of a communication process will generate meaningful information about the "whole" of human communication.

## COMMUNICATION AND PARADIGMATIC CHANGE: A HISTORICAL PERSPECTIVE

Over the past several decades, the communication discipline has undergone paradigmatic changes that amount to a Kuhnian "scientific revolution."[95] From the beginning of this century through the 1950s, the field was dominated by what some writers call a **functional paradigm**.[96] This world view is frequently associated with a mechanistic model of human behavior and an epistemological blend of mechanistic empiricism and logical positivism. Functional researchers typically have a laws theoretical perspective and often use methodological tools that treat meanings as a starting point for inferring conclusions about communication causes and effects.

Dissatisfaction with "normal science" under these paradigmatic assumptions surfaced in the 1950s and grew steadily during the decades of the 1960s and the 1970s. Increasingly, communication scholars questioned the adequacy of the prevailing paradigm for studying the unique properties of human talk. During this period of "revolutionary science," five scholarly works were particularly notable because they signaled the introduction of a competing paradigmatic view:[97]

1960    Berlo's book exploring the "process" qualities of human communication

**318**

PART IV
Contemporary
Issues in
Communi-
cation
Research

1972    Cushman and Whiting's monograph advocating a rules approach to communication theory

1975    O'Keefe's attack on logical positivism

1976    Pearce's meaning-based rules theory of communication

1977    Delia's advocacy of an alternative
constructivist epistemology, which promised to
reconcile many traditional scientific assumptions with the humanistic qualities of communication.

These works, along with numerous supplementary publications, introduced what some
writers call an **interpretive paradigm**.[98] The
interpretive perspective typically pairs an actional or actional realist ontology with rational
empiricist and constructivist-like epistemologies. It often takes a rules approach to theory
construction, and its methodological tools
are usually distinctively communicative, taking
meanings as the central focus of research. Furthermore, many interpretive research methods
partake of both scientific and humanistic assumptions.

The 1970s were intellectually volatile years,
characterized by acrimonious debate between
supporters of the so-called functional paradigm
and the new interpretive approach.[99] Following
Kuhn's analysis of the final stages of scientific
revolutions, the new paradigm gained increasing acceptance during the late 1970s and the
early 1980s, loosening traditional empiricism's
exclusive grip on communication research.
Miller's report on the status of the communication discipline, published in 1983, nicely
chronicles the fundamental assumptions of the
new order, including its ontological, epistemological, metatheoretical, and methodological
postures.[100]

Although the functional perspective retains
many distinguished advocates, the hybrid interpretive paradigm is exerting an important
influence on contemporary communication inquiry. Communication researchers are beginning to place considerable emphasis on the
structure and functions of meaning. Moreover,
researchers are increasingly adapting traditional scientific methods to the peculiarities
of communication phenomena. As a consequence, many are applying novel methodologies that signal a reunification of science and
humanism. Thus, the late 1980s and early
1990s could be characterized by a return to
"normal science" under a new set of paradigmatic assumptions about how we can best
know the world of human communication.

## A RECAPITULATION

This chapter has discussed contemporary research in the communication discipline, describing several general paradigms that have
influenced researchers in recent decades. We
examined current ontological views of the
nature of human communication, epistemological assumptions about appropriate ways to
study communication, metatheoretical beliefs
regarding suitable explanations for communication events, and methodological perspectives
on research strategies that are most applicable
to communication inquiry. We concluded by
reviewing recent paradigmatic changes in the
communication discipline.

In writing this final chapter, I have sought to
describe current research practices in the context of the intellectual milieu that gave rise to
them. I have tried to show that research methods are neither isolated nor time-locked but,
rather, they are embedded in a robust conceptual framework that changes with our changing
views of human communication. Given this
evolving quality of knowledge, certain of the
"contemporary" trends I have discussed may
well become tomorrow's historical curiosities.

But, as we move toward new and better ways of understanding our world, that is how it should be.

# MAIN POINTS

**1.** A paradigm is a world view or conceptual model that defines how scholarly inquiry should be conducted. Paradigms have four components: ontological assumptions about the nature of the subject matter to be studied, epistemological assumptions about appropriate ways of studying the subject matter, metatheoretical assumptions about suitable explanations, and methodological assumptions about applicable research strategies.

**2.** Researchers may adopt one of two general paradigmatic perspectives: monism or pluralism. A monistic view is characterized by the adoption of a single paradigm, whereas pluralism encourages the acceptance of alternative paradigmatic viewpoints.

**3.** Contemporary thinkers adopt one of two views of paradigmatic change: a revolutionary model or an evolutionary model. The revolutionary model assumes that change is abrupt, involving the replacement of one competing paradigm for another. The evolutionary perspective assumes that paradigmatic change is a gradual process whereby new ideas are assimilated into dominant world views.

**4.** Ontological assumptions refer to the nature of reality and represent beliefs about the nature of human communication. Three ontological paradigms have influenced communication researchers: mechanism (determinism), which assumes that people have no capacity for choice; actionalism, assuming that human behavior is self-motivated; and actional realism, which incorporates elements of mechanism into an actional model.

**5.** Eight ontological assumptions characterize the thinking of many contemporary communication scholars: communication is a social reality; communication is a creative process; communication is a developmental process; communication is an interrelated system; communication is a contextual phenomenon; communication is a purposive activity; communication is an interactive reality; and communication is an orderly process.

**6.** Epistemology, the science of knowledge, refers to assumptions about the nature of scholarly inquiry. Six epistemological paradigms have influenced communication scholars: rationalism, which assumes that thought is the key to inquiry; rational empiricism, which tests thought against observations; mechanistic empiricism, which focuses on observations of cause-to-effect relationships; logical positivism, which focuses on observations of correlative relationships; constructivism, which assumes that reality is subjectively created by people's meanings; and constructive realism, which blends some elements of empiricism into constructivism.

**7.** Logical positivists embrace the concepts of reductionism and operationalism. Reductionists assume that the smallest units of observation are preferred and that the whole of a process is the sum of its parts. Operationalism assumes that theoretical concepts are defined by the activities required to measure them. Logical positivism assumes that the world is an objective reality "out there" to be discovered by observers.

**8.** Constructivism rejects both reductionism and operationalism, believing that the whole of communication is greater than its parts and that theoretical concepts are more than measures of their empirical indicators. Constructivists assume that the world is a subjective reality that is affected by observers' perceptions and interpretations.

**320**

PART IV
Contemporary
Issues in
Communi-
cation
Research

9. Metatheory refers to beliefs about the nature of theory. Two metatheoretical perspectives have influenced communication researchers: the laws approach and the rules perspective. Laws may be either natural necessity (causal) or logical positivist (correlational) in nature, and they explain communication behavior by referring to causes and covariates over which people have no control. Rules, which may be intentional, programmatic, or systemic, explain communication behavior by referring to people's reasons for behaving. Such an explanation is called teleological.

10. Methodology refers to the choice of research strategies for studying communication. Seven methodological trends characterize contemporary communication research: a blending of science and humanism, the use of distinctively communicative research designs, a preference for naturalistic methods, an emphasis on longitudinal studies, a multivariate research focus, a communicator-centered emphasis, and a preference for theory-guided research.

11. Over the past three decades, the communication discipline has shifted from a functional paradigmatic perspective to an interpretive one. Interpretists focus on communicative meanings, and functionalists emphasize communicative antecedents and consequences.

12. A functional paradigm typically is mechanistic, positivist, and laws-oriented, whereas an interpretive world view is more actional, constructivist, and rules-based.

## REVIEW EXERCISES

1. Discuss the relative merits of mechanistic, actional, and actional realistic ontological perspectives on human communication. Which perspective makes the most sense to you? Why?

2. Suppose you want to conduct a conversational analysis of the communication between romantic partners. What effects might each of the following epistemological perspectives have on your research design decisions and your analysis of results: rationalism, rational empiricism, mechanistic empiricism, logical positivism, constructivism, and constructive realism?

3. Frame an example of each of the following types of theories: a natural necessity law, a logical positivist law, and a rule. In what ways do the three types of explanations differ? How are they similar?

4. Seven contemporary methodological trends are discussed in the chapter. Make up examples of studies that illustrate each of the dominant methodologies: a study that blends science and humanism, a distinctively communicative research design, a naturalistic study, a longitudinal study, a multivariate research design, a communicator-centered study, and a theory-guided research project.

## NOTES

1. Norwood Russel Hanson, *Patterns of Discovery* (Cambridge: Cambridge University Press, 1958).
2. Thomas S. Kuhn, "Second Thoughts on Paradigms," in *The Structure of Scientific Theories*, 2nd ed., ed. Frederick Suppe (Urbana: University of Illinois Press, 1977), pp. 469–82; *The Structure of Scientific Revolutions*, enlarged ed. (Chicago: University of Chicago Press, 1970); and *The Structure of Scientific Revolutions* (Chicago: University of Chicago Press, 1962).
3. Kuhn, 1962, pp. 4–5.
4. Richard Hofstadler, *Gödel, Escher, Bach: An Eternal Golden Braid* (New York: Basic Books, 1979), p. 10.
5. Gary Cronkhite and Jo Liska, "Symposium: What Criteria Should Be Used to Judge the Admissibility of Evidence to Support Theoretical Propositions in Communication Research: Introduc-

tion," *Western Journal of Speech Communication*, 41 (1977): 6.

**6.** Kuhn, 1970, p. 11.

**7.** Joseph R. Royce, *The Encapsulated Man* (New York: Van Nostrand Reinhold, 1964), p. 6.

**8.** Karl R. Popper, "Normal Science and Its Dangers," in *Criticism and the Growth of Knowledge*, eds. Irme Lakatos and Alan Musgrave (Cambridge: Cambridge University Press, 1970); and *Conjectures and Refutations: The Growth of Scientific Knowledge*, 2nd ed. (New York: Basic Books, 1965).

**9.** Peter L. Berger, *The Precarious Vision* (Garden City, NY: Doubleday, 1961), p. 7.

**10.** See Edwin A. Burtt, *In Search of Philosophic Understanding* (Indianapolis: Hackett, 1980), pp. 163–64.

**11.** Kuhn, 1970; 1962.

**12.** Popper, 1970; 1965; Stephen Toulmin, *Human Understanding*, Vol. I (Princeton, NJ: Princeton University Press, 1972); Donald T. Campbell, "Unjustified Variation and Selective Retention in Scientific Discovery," in *Studies in the Philosophy of Biology*, eds. Theodosius Dobzhansky and Francisco J. Ayala (London: Macmillan, 1970); and Paul K. Feyerabend, "How To Be a Good Empiricist—A Plea for Tolerance in Matters Epistemological," in *Philosophy of Science: The Delaware Seminar*, Vol. II (New York: Wiley-Interscience, 1963), pp. 3–40.

**13.** Popper, 1965.

**14.** Campbell.

**15.** Filmer S. C. Northrop, *The Logic of the Sciences and the Humanities* (New York: Meridian Books, 1959), p. 274.

**16.** Charles M. Rossiter, "Models of Paradigmatic Change," *Communication Quarterly*, 25 (1977): 69.

**17.** B. Aubrey Fisher, "Evidence Varies with Theoretical Perspective," *Western Journal of Speech Communication*, 41 (1977): 12.

**18.** Gerald R. Miller, "Taking Stock of a Discipline," *Journal of Communication*, 33, No. 3 (1983): 40.

**19.** Miller, 31–41.

**20.** Albert E. Avey, *Handbook in the History of Philosophy*, 2nd ed. (New York: Barnes & Noble, 1961), p. 22.

**21.** B. F. Skinner, *Verbal Behavior* (New York: Appleton-Century-Crofts, 1957); and *Science and Human Behavior* (New York: Free Press, 1953).

**22.** See Mary John Smith, *Persuasion and Human Action: A Review and Critique of Social Influence Theories* (Belmont, CA: Wadsworth, 1982a), pp. 4–5; and Wilbur Schramm, "The Nature of Communication Between Humans," in *The Process and Effects of Mass Communication*, eds. Wilbur Schramm and Donald F. Roberts (Urbana: University of Illinois Press, 1971), pp. 8–9.

**23.** Carol Wilder, "The Palo Alto Group: Difficulties and Directions of the Interactional View for Human Communication Research," *Human Communication Research*, 5 (1979): 176–77.

**24.** Immanuel Kant, *Critique of Pure Reason*, trans. N. Kemp Smith (London: Macmillan, 1929); and *Critique of Practical Reason and Other Works*, trans. T. K. Abbott (New York: Longmans Green, 1909).

**25.** See Romano Harré and Paul F. Secord, *The Explanation of Social Behavior* (Oxford: Basil Blackwell, 1972); Charles Taylor, *The Explanation of Behaviour* (London: Routledge & Kegan Paul, 1964); and John R. Searle, *Intentionality: An Essay in the Philosophy of Mind* (Cambridge: Cambridge University Press, 1983).

**26.** See Jesse G. Delia, "Constructivism and the Study of Human Communication," *Quarterly Journal of Speech*, 63 (1977): 66–83; and Donald P. Cushman, Barry Valentinsen, and David Dietrich, "A Rules Theory of Interpersonal Relationships," in *Human Communication Theory: Comparative Essays*, ed. Frank E. X. Dance (New York: Harper & Row, 1982), pp. 90–119.

**27.** Miller, 32.

**28.** Vernon E. Cronen, W. Barnett Pearce, and Linda M. Harris, "The Coordinated Management of Meaning: A Theory of Communication," in *Human Communication Theory: Comparative Essays*, ed. Frank E. X. Dance (New York: Harper & Row, 1982), p. 66.

**29.** See W. Barnett Pearce and Vernon E. Cronen, *Communication, Action, and Meaning: The Creation of Social Realities* (New York: Praeger, 1980); Mary John Smith, "Contingency Rules Theory, Context, and Compliance Behaviors," *Human Communication Research*, 10 (1984): 489–512; "The Contingency Rules Theory of Persuasion: An Empirical Test," *Communication Quarterly*, 30 (1982b): 359–67; and "Cognitive Schemata and Persuasive Communication: Toward a Contingency Rules Theory," in

**322**

PART IV
Contemporary
Issues in
Communi-
cation
Research

*Communication Yearbook 6*, ed. Michael Burgoon (Beverly Hills, CA: Sage, 1982c), pp. 330–62.

**30.** See Ragnar Rommetveit, *On Message Structure: A Framework for the Study of Language and Communication* (New York: John Wiley, 1974).

**31.** Miller, 31.

**32.** Smith, 1982c, p. 341.

**33.** See for example Adolf Grünbaum, "Causality and the Science of Human Behavior," *American Scientist*, 40 (1952): 667.

**34.** My discussion of these paradigms draws heavily on W. Barnett Pearce, Vernon E. Cronen, and Linda M. Harris, "Methodological Considerations in Building Human Communication Theory," in *Human Communication Theory: Comparative Essays*, ed. Frank E. X. Dance (New York: Harper & Row, 1982), pp. 1–41.

**35.** See Edwin Arthur Burtt, *The Metaphysical Foundations of Modern Physical Science* (New York: Harcourt Brace Jovanovich, 1927); Marjorie Grene, *The Knower and the Known* (Berkeley: University of California Press, 1974); Gerald Holton, "Mach, Einstein, and the Search for Reality," in *The Twentieth-Century Sciences: Studies in the Biography of Ideas*, ed. Gerald Holton (New York: W. W. Norton, 1972), pp. 344–81; Ernst Cassirer, *Substance and Function and Einstein's Theory of Relativity* (Chicago: Open Court, 1923); and Avey, pp. 23–28, 129–32.

**36.** See Grene, p. 66.

**37.** See Ernest Nagel, *Technology Revisited and Other Essays in the History and Philosophy of Science* (New York: Columbia University Press, 1979), p. 15; and Karl R. Popper, *The Logic of Scientific Discovery* (New York: Science Editions, 1961), p. 458.

**38.** See Noam Chomsky, *Cartesian Linguistics: A Chapter in the History of Rationalist Thought* (New York: Harper & Row, 1966); and Frederick Williams, *Language and Speech: Introductory Perspectives* (Englewood Cliffs, NJ: Prentice-Hall, 1972), p. 90.

**39.** See Kenneth Burke, *A Grammar of Motives* (Englewood Cliffs, NJ: Prentice-Hall, 1946); and *A Rhetoric of Motives* (Englewood Cliffs, NJ: Prentice-Hall, 1950).

**40.** See Burtt, 1980; 1927; Grene; and Avey, pp. 30–36.

**41.** Popper, 1965, p. 115; and Popper, 1961.

**42.** See H. Paul Grice, "The Logic of Conversation," in *Syntax and Semantics Volume 3: Speech Acts*, eds. Peter Cole and Jerry L. Morgan (New York: Academic

Press, 1975), pp. 41–58; Harvey Sacks, Emanuel A. Schegloff, and Gail Johnson, "A Simplest Systematics for the Organization of Turn-Taking in Conversation," *Language*, 50 (1974): 696–735; and Pearce and Cronen.

**43.** See C. West Churchman and Russell L. Ackoff, *Methods of Inquiry* (St. Louis: Educational Publishers, 1950); and Avey, pp. 126–27.

**44.** W. Barnett Pearce, Vernon E. Cronen, and Linda M. Harris, pp. 17–19.

**45.** See Burtt, 1927, p. 208.

**46.** See Smith, 1982a.

**47.** See Joseph Woelfel, "Foundations of Cognitive Theory: A Multidimensional Model of the Message-Attitude-Behavior Relationship," in *Message-Attitude-Behavior Relationship: Theory, Methodology, and Application*, eds. Donald P. Cushman and Robert D. McPhee (New York: Academic Press, 1980), pp. 89–116; John Saltiel and Joseph Woelfel, "Inertia in Cognitive Processes: The Role of Accumulated Information in Attitude Change," *Human Communication Research*, 1 (1975): 333–44; and Michael Burgoon, Marshall Cohen, Michael D. Miller, and Charles L. Montgomery, "An Empirical Test of a Model of Resistance to Persuasion," *Human Communication Research*, 4 (1978): 27–39.

**48.** See A. J. Ayer, ed. *Logical Positivism* (New York: Free Press, 1959); and Frederick Suppe, ed. *The Structure of Scientific Theories*, 2nd ed. (Urbana: University of Illinois Press, 1977), pp. 6–118.

**49.** Frederick Suppe, "Historical Background to the Received View," in *The Structure of Scientific Theories*, 2nd ed., ed. Frederick Suppe (Urbana: University of Illinois Press, 1977), p. 8.

**50.** Ayer, pp. 10–17.

**51.** Pearce, Cronen, and Harris, pp. 19–20.

**52.** Pearce, Cronen, and Harris, p. 21.

**53.** Pearce, Cronen, and Harris.

**54.** See Smith, 1982a, pp. 213–40.

**55.** Frederick Suppe, "Swan Song for Positivism," in *The Structure of Scientific Theories*, 2nd ed., ed. Frederick Suppe (Urbana: University of Illinois Press, 1977), p. 632.

**56.** Kant, 1929; 1909.

**57.** Kuhn, 1970; Hanson; and Toulmin.

**58.** Pearce, Cronen, and Harris, p. 22.

**59.** See Grene, p. 135.

**60.** See Delia; and Pearce and Cronen.

**61.** Suppe refers to this epistemological position as

"historical realism." See Frederick Suppe, "Historical Realism," in *The Structure of Scientific Theories*, 2nd ed., ed. Frederick Suppe (Urbana: University of Illinois Press, 1977), pp. 650–720.

**62.** Miller, 32.

**63.** See Delia; and Pearce and Cronen.

**64.** Scott Jacobs and Sally Jackson, "Speech Act Structure in Conversation: Rational Aspects of Pragmatic Coherence," in *Conversational Coherence: Form, Structure, and Strategy*, eds. Robert T. Craig and Karen Tracy (Beverly Hills, CA: Sage, 1983), pp. 47–66.

**65.** The systems perspective is often discussed as a third approach to communication theory. Following Monge's analysis, I have taken the position that a systems view is a general epistemological stance, not a specific variety of theory. As such, the systems epistemology is central to one variety of rules analysis discussed later in this chapter. See Peter R. Monge, "The Systems Perspective as a Theoretical Basis for the Study of Human Communication," *Communication Quarterly*, 25 (1977): 19–29.

**66.** See Charles R. Berger, "The Covering Law Perspective as a Theoretical Basis for the Study of Human Communication," *Communication Quarterly*, 25 (1977): 7–18.

**67.** Harré and Secord, p. 30.

**68.** Virginia McDermott, "The Literature on Classical Theory Construction," *Human Communication Research*, 2 (1975): 83–84.

**69.** See Donald P. Cushman and W. Barnett Pearce, "Generality and Necessity in Three Types of Theory About Human Communication, with Special Attention to Rules Theory," *Human Communication Research*, 3 (1977): 345.

**70.** Suppe, "Swan Song for Positivism," p. 623.

**71.** Carl G. Hempel, *Aspects of Scientific Explanation and Other Essays in the Philosophy of Science* (New York: Free Press, 1965), pp. 381–412.

**72.** See Gerald R. Miller and Charles R. Berger, "On Keeping the Faith in Matters Scientific," *Western Journal of Speech Communication*, 42 (1978): 44–57; and Miller, 32.

**73.** See Woelfel, 1980; Saltiel and Woelfel, 1975; Marshall Scott Poole and John E. Hunter, "Behavior and Hierarchies of Attitudes: A Deterministic Model," in *Message-Attitude-Behavior Relationship: Theory, Methodology, and Application*, eds. Donald P. Cushman and Robert D. McPhee (New York: Academic Press, 1980), pp. 245–71; and David R. Seibold, "Attitude-Verbal Report-Behavior Relationships as Causal Processes: Formalization, Test, and Communication Implications," in *Message-Attitude-Behavior Relationship: Theory, Methodology, and Application*, eds. Donald P. Cushman and Robert D. McPhee (New York: Academic Press, 1980), pp. 195–244.

**74.** See Donald P. Cushman, "The Rules Perspective as a Theoretical Basis for the Study of Human Communication," *Communication Quarterly*, 25 (1977): 30–45; and Smith, 1982a, pp. 61–70.

**75.** Harré and Secord, p. 40.

**76.** See Harré and Secord, p. 148.

**77.** For a full discussion of these three perspectives, see Nagel, pp. 275–316.

**78.** Nagel, p. 278.

**79.** See Ellen J. Langer, "Rethinking the Role of Thought in Social Interaction," in *New Directions in Attribution Research*, eds. John H. Harvey and Robert F. Kidd (Hillsdale, NJ: Lawrence Erlbaum, 1978), pp. 35–58.

**80.** See Ernst Mayr, "Teleological and Teleonomic, a New Analysis," in *Methodological and Historical Essays in the Natural and Social Sciences, Vol. XIV, Boston Studies in the Philosophy of Science*, eds. R. S. Cohen and M. W. Wartofsky (Boston: D. Reidel, 1974).

**81.** Mayr, p. 102.

**82.** Mayr, p. 99.

**83.** B. Aubrey Fisher, "The Pragmatic Perspective of Human Communication: A View from System Theory," in *Human Communication Theory: Comparative Essays*, ed. Frank E. X. Dance (New York: Harper & Row, 1983), p. 202.

**84.** Miller, 31.

**85.** See Pearce and Cronen; Cronen, Pearce, and Harris; Cushman, Valentinsen, and Dietrich; Kathleen Kelley Reardon, *Persuasion: Theory and Context* (Beverly Hills, CA: Sage, 1981); Smith, 1984; 1982b; 1982c; and Norman E. Fontes, Jennifer L. Shelby, and Barbara O'Connor, "A Structural-Functional Model of the Message-Attitude-Behavior Relationship," in *Message-Attitude-Behavior Relationship: Theory, Methodology, and Application*, eds. Donald P. Cushman and Robert D. McPhee (New York: Academic Press, 1980), pp. 303–17.

**86.** Most of these trends are discussed in *Ferment in the Field*, Special Issue No. 3, *Journal of Communication*, 33 (1983).

**324**

PART IV
Contemporary
Issues in
Communi-
cation
Research

**87.** Stephen L. Wasby, "Rhetoricians and Political Scientists: Some Lines of Converging Interest," *Southern Speech Journal*, 36 (1971), 237.

**88.** Wasby, 237.

**89.** Ernest G. Bormann, "Generalizing About Significant Form: Science and Humanism Compared and Contrasted," in *Form and Genre: Shaping Rhetorical Action*, eds. Karlyn Kohrs Campbell and Kathleen Hall Jamieson (Falls Church, VA: Speech Communication Association, 1978), pp. 51, 67.

**90.** Herbert W. Simons, "'Genre-alizing' About Rhetoric: A Scientific Approach," in *Form and Genre: Shaping Rhetorical Action*, eds. Karlyn Kohrs Campbell and Kathleen Hall Jamieson (Falls Church, VA: Speech Communication Association, 1978), p. 44. Also see Herbert W. Simons, "The Rhetoric of Science and the Science of Rhetoric," *Western Journal of Speech Communication*, 42 (1978): 37–43.

**91.** W. Barnett Pearce, Linda M. Harris, and Vernon E. Cronen, *The Coordinated Management of Meaning: Human Communication Theory in a New Key*, unpublished ms, University of Massachusetts, Amherst, undated. (Based on personal correspondence with Barnett Pearce, I estimate the manuscript date to be around 1977–1978.)

**92.** See Elihu Katz, "The Return of the Humanities and Sociology," *Journal of Communication*, 33, No. 3 (1983): 51–52.

**93.** Miller, 34–35.

**94.** Miller, 33–34.

**95.** See Kuhn, 1977; 1970.

**96.** For a discussion of functionalism, see Linda L. Putnam, "The Interpretive Perspective: An Alternative to Functionalism," in *Communication and Organizations: An Interpretive Approach*, eds. Linda L. Putnam and Michael E. Pacanowsky (Beverly Hills, CA: Sage, 1983), pp. 31–54.

**97.** See David K. Berlo, *The Process of Communication* (New York: Holt, Rinehart & Winston, 1960); Donald Cushman and Gordon C. Whiting, "An Approach to Communication Theory: Toward Consensus on Rules," *Journal of Communication*, 22 (1972): 217–38; Daniel J. O'Keefe, "Logical Empiricism and the Study of Human Communication," *Speech Monographs*, 42 (1975): 169–83; W. Barnett Pearce, "The Coordinated Management of Meaning: A Rules-Based Theory of Interpersonal Communication," in *Explorations in Interpersonal Communication*, ed. Gerald R. Miller (Beverly Hills, CA: Sage, 1976), pp. 17–35; and Delia.

**98.** See Putnam.

**99.** See Miller and Berger; and Thomas W. Benson and W. Barnett Pearce, eds., "Alternative Theoretical Bases for the Study of Human Communication: A Symposium," *Communication Quarterly*, 25 (1977): 3–73.

**100.** Miller, 31–41.

# APPENDICES

# APPENDIX A
# PROPOSING RESEARCH: THE PROSPECTUS

The work involved in any research project can be facilitated greatly by constructing a detailed research proposal, often called a **prospectus**. A prospectus isolates the problem for research, describes its theoretical and empirical bases, and discusses the procedures required to resolve the problem. This appendix describes the materials included in a typical research proposal. Since the guidelines I will elaborate are "generic," they are flexible enough to accommodate the peculiarities of most communication research projects.

A research proposal or prospectus normally contains three major sections:

I.  Problem
II. Method
III. References

Each of these sections is discussed below.

## I. Problem

The problem section of a research proposal contains two subsections: the theoretical and empirical rationale for conducting the research, and a statement of the research problem.

A. *Rationale*. The rationale sets forth the reasons for conducting a given research project. One's "reasons" normally grow out of relevant theory underlying the research problem and research findings bearing directly on the proposed research. Thus, the rationale section is a theoretical and empirical discussion. It should read like a good argument leading unequivocally to the problem to be investigated.

B. *The problem statement*. The research problem is framed either as a hypothesis, a research question, or a purpose statement. Assuming that one's rationale leads unequivocally to predictions, the problem should be stated as a hypothesis, or more usually, a series of hypotheses. Common hypothesis formulation difficulties include a rationale that does not lead to clear predictions and hypotheses that are ambiguously worded.

A research question is appropriate when one's rationale does not lead directly to predictions. Researchers usually require a series of questions to capture all the implications of their research problem. Like hypotheses, questions should be stated as precisely and completely as possible.

The weakest problem statement discusses the purpose or aims of proposed research. Purpose-type statements are general and prone to ambiguity, often failing to pinpoint the precise information sought in an investigation.

## II. Method

The section on method describes the researcher's strategies for gathering data, along with all required supporting materials and measuring instruments. Moreover, it specifies the analytical method, either statistical or argumentative, that is suitable for testing the hypotheses and questions selected. The following five kinds of information typically appear in a proposal's method section.

A. *Research design*. This subsection describes in detail the nature of the chosen research plan, whether an experiment, a survey, a conversational analysis, a content analysis, or a rhetorical criticism. The researcher should specify why the chosen design is an appropriate mechanism for testing the research hypotheses.

B. *Variable specification*. This subsection details the conceptual and operational definitions of all pertinent variables, including any independent and dependent variables. Additionally, the researcher should discuss procedures for certifying the validity and reliability of all variables. Finally, the means for controlling any potentially confounding effects should be described.

C. *Elements and sampling method.* The number and pertinent characteristics of the proposed study's elements or units of analysis are identified next. Elements include any individuals who will serve as research participants in the proposed project as well as communication artifacts (television programs, films, public speeches, conversational episodes, and so on) that are targeted for study. Additionally, the sampling method used to secure a sample (typically, a representative sample) of the elements must be specified and its appropriateness defended.

D. *Procedure.* This subsection describes the researcher's plan for conducting the proposed research, including any cover story and debriefing materials to be used, instructions to be given to research participants, and the setting and time frame for the research. In general, it is a step-by-step narrative detailing how the researcher will administer the proposed research from initiation to completion.

E. *Data analysis.* This final subsection describes any statistical procedures the researcher will use to analyze results, including the specific statistical tests to be performed. If one's data are narrative rather than numerical, all descriptive, inferential, interpretive, and critical tools should be detailed. The subsection concludes with a statement indicating why the chosen data analytical methods will provide an adequate test of one's hypotheses, research questions, or general research aims.

## III. References

The final part of the prospectus lists all reference materials the researcher has consulted or expects to consult during the course of the research. The style of the reference list should conform to the stylistic format the researcher will employ in the final research report. Typical stylistic forms used in communication research include those suggested by the American Psychological Association (APA)[1] and the Modern Language Association (MLA).[2] Consult the style manual of your choice for details regarding acceptable reference formats.

## Notes

1. *Publication Manual of the American Psychological Association*, 3rd ed. (Washington, DC: American Psychological Association, 1983).
2. *MLA Handbook for Writers of Research Papers*, 2nd ed. (New York: Modern Language Association, 1984).

# APPENDIX B
## WRITING THE RESEARCH REPORT

Writing a report of completed research is relatively straightforward because all such reports share a common structure. This general organizational format is:

I.   Title page
II.  Abstract
III. Text of report
IV.  Tables and figures
V.   Footnotes and references

The text, representing the actual report of one's completed research, contains four major parts:

I.   Problem
II.  Method
III. Results
IV.  Discussion

Although these parts vary in organization and content depending on the nature of the research being reported, each section ordinarily contains the materials discussed below.

## I. Problem
The introductory section addresses two major issues: the rationale for the reported research and the problem investigated.

A. *Rationale.* The rationale contains the reasons justifying the worth and general usefulness of the research being reported. Thus, the section normally includes a discussion of relevant theory underlying the research problem and a review of pertinent research findings. This theoretical and empirical discussion should lead unequivocally to the research problem. In summary, the rationale is a concise but convincing argument telling why the reported problem merited study.

B. *Statement of the problem.* The research problem is usually stated either as hypotheses or as research questions. If the rationale origi-

nally prompting the research led to clear predictions, the problem is framed as a hypothesis or more usually, a series of hypotheses. However, research questions are appropriate when no predictions were tested in the reported research.

## II. Method
The section on method describes the research design and details the procedures the researcher used to gather data. Depending on the nature of the research design, the following four issues are variously addressed:

A. *Research design overview.* This subpart identifies the research design, whether an experiment, survey research, conversational analysis, content analysis, or humanistic (rhetorical) study. Moreover, the section briefly summarizes the major variables included in the chosen design.

B. *Elements and sampling method.* This section describes the study's elements or units of analysis, including any research subjects who participated in the study as well as any communication artifacts (television programs, films, public speeches, conversational episodes, and so on) that were analyzed. Pertinent characteristics of the elements such as research participants' age and gender and all relevant features of analyzed artifacts are noted. Finally, the researcher should specify the total size of the analytical sample and describe the sampling method used to select it.

C. *Procedure.* The part contains a step-by-step narrative detailing how the researcher administered the study. The researcher should describe the setting in which the research was conducted, the instructions given to research participants, and any cover story and debriefing materials that were used. In short, the researcher must detail all the activities required to conduct the project from initiation to completion.

**D.** *Description of variables.* The section details the conceptual and operational definitions of all major variables included in the study. If the research was experimental, independent manipulations should be described fully, including any materials (for example, written or oral messages) that were used as experimental treatments. The researcher likewise should discuss the conceptual and operational definitions of all dependent variables. Representative written questionnaire items and questions used in oral interviews are typically cited. Finally, the researcher should describe all procedures used to certify the validity and reliability of both independent and dependent variables.

## III. Results

Next comes a description of all research findings pertinent to the original hypotheses and research questions, focusing on the extent to which the hypotheses were confirmed and the questions were satisfactorily answered. Moreover, the results of validity checks on variables included in the design are normally reported. Statistical analyses, if any, are described fully and their significance levels cited. Tables and figures, which are often used to display results parsimoniously, can be incorporated into the text proper or recorded on separate pages at the text's conclusion. With the latter approach, which typically is used if a study is to be published, the researcher simply refers readers to the displayed information by table or figure number, for example "Table 1" or "Figure 3," and indicates with notations like "Table 1 about here" where the tables and figures should appear in a final printing of the text.

## IV. Discussion

This final section of the text ordinarily includes the following three types of information: (1) a concise summary of major findings in relation to the original research problem, focusing on the extent to which hypotheses were confirmed or disconfirmed; (2) a full explanation justifying the reasonableness of obtained results in light of relevant theory and past research findings; and (3) a complete discussion of the theoretical, methodological, and practical significance of the research results. Pertinent questions to be answered here include:

In what way does the research extend our theoretical understanding of the problem of interest?

Does the research have any methodological implications for future studies?

What follow-up research is needed?

What were the major methodological weaknesses in the research, and how might these be corrected in future studies?

Are there significant practical implications of the research?

As these guidelines suggest, the discussion section should explain obtained results in relation to relevant theory and research, clearly indicating the significance of the results for scholars and practitioners of human communication.

## Pretext and posttext sections of the research report

The pretext and posttext sections of the research report, usually assembled after the text has been written, include the following four items: title page, abstract, tables and figures, and footnotes and references.

The *title page* contains the full title of the report, the author's full name and affiliation, and sometimes an abbreviated running title of the report. If used, the running title normally appears in the upper right-hand corner of each page of the research report beginning with page 2 of the text and continuing through the footnotes and references.

The *abstract* consists of a 100–200 word summary of the reported research, including a concise description of the study's rationale, a short discussion of the research design, and a brief synopsis of major research results and their implications. The abstract appears on a separate (usually unnumbered) page immediately following the title page.

Although *tables and figures* can be put in the section on results, they may also appear at the conclusion of all text material. If the latter approach is used, each item should be placed on a separate (usually unnumbered) page and identified with numerical labels such as "Table 1" and "Figure 2," along with brief descriptive titles.

*Footnotes and references* are the last sections of the research report following the text. Their form varies depending on the stylistic format the researcher selects. If the American Psychological Association (APA) style is used, all works cited in the text appear in a single alphabetized list called "References."[1] However, the Modern Language Association (MLA) format requires that text references be cited in sequential footnote form and then alphabetized in a second list called a "Bibliography," which follows footnote citations.[2] Consult the style manual of your choice for details regarding the form of the footnotes and references section of the research report.

## The length of research reports

Research report texts are ordinarily no longer than 20 double-spaced typewritten pages and in many cases are considerably shorter. Tables and figures are held to the minimum necessary for displaying essential research results. In general, the research report should be concise and to the point, consuming no more space than is absolutely essential for a reader to grasp the nature and implications of the reported work.

### Notes

**1.** *Publication Manual of the American Psychological Association*, 3rd ed. (Washington, DC: American Psychological Association, 1983).

**2.** *MLA Handbook for Writers of Research Papers*, 2nd ed. (New York: Modern Language Association, 1984).

# APPENDIX C
## TABLE OF RANDOM NUMBERS

| | | | | | | | | | |
|---|---|---|---|---|---|---|---|---|---|
| 18232 | 92132 | 66537 | 70141 | 42854 | 25120 | 39581 | 28249 | 14215 | 34810 |
| 19767 | 03409 | 11807 | 06566 | 66138 | 42997 | 41999 | 67504 | 87117 | 28961 |
| 05000 | 29673 | 77726 | 73225 | 54753 | 69712 | 71576 | 92337 | 17713 | 63185 |
| 87923 | 91889 | 68351 | 17712 | 75532 | 93849 | 48280 | 62219 | 00317 | 25290 |
| 29209 | 90927 | 92929 | 92762 | 60413 | 02018 | 31793 | 76290 | 73373 | 80777 |
| 60819 | 77375 | 57886 | 47291 | 99670 | 32605 | 29064 | 99476 | 80999 | 31217 |
| 00035 | 91300 | 14892 | 73653 | 26593 | 25305 | 56797 | 12837 | 39560 | 27582 |
| 37253 | 38531 | 76489 | 49946 | 69108 | 58687 | 43092 | 73807 | 96282 | 06648 |
| 67431 | 87124 | 57694 | 21660 | 64002 | 00006 | 33600 | 30245 | 60636 | 80164 |
| 09285 | 61426 | 04658 | 54130 | 14710 | 76553 | 01904 | 93668 | 63110 | 98618 |
| 05601 | 32199 | 74923 | 98049 | 49717 | 55539 | 35940 | 58545 | 43295 | 35810 |
| 45451 | 38735 | 42065 | 66769 | 69825 | 45461 | 83881 | 67372 | 67351 | 90612 |
| 79502 | 69460 | 23108 | 74421 | 82990 | 46821 | 40683 | 71603 | 55267 | 48192 |
| 50242 | 79738 | 96417 | 06664 | 19929 | 23644 | 41116 | 51056 | 00219 | 45086 |
| 32747 | 49492 | 15399 | 24874 | 80825 | 95928 | 61457 | 45813 | 59037 | 16136 |
| 03953 | 83583 | 05910 | 12654 | 53630 | 92997 | 22168 | 93491 | 71897 | 74579 |
| 24022 | 06278 | 24049 | 71670 | 43044 | 08474 | 38572 | 77402 | 35800 | 07455 |
| 96177 | 41653 | 74493 | 20802 | 65843 | 73050 | 73349 | 02638 | 65813 | 96209 |
| 49196 | 45007 | 32207 | 14097 | 66059 | 46681 | 07534 | 71263 | 20582 | 10171 |
| 51514 | 52142 | 60961 | 57951 | 25637 | 37860 | 21683 | 86190 | 90434 | 94481 |
| 85697 | 95344 | 02606 | 74095 | 61133 | 07472 | 64777 | 94050 | 41482 | 00975 |
| 23471 | 76052 | 82021 | 87676 | 91345 | 20196 | 02612 | 86299 | 44996 | 40312 |
| 65712 | 46079 | 88514 | 08610 | 03685 | 63197 | 09073 | 53105 | 86824 | 28112 |
| 99306 | 40706 | 66840 | 83003 | 51590 | 52755 | 32285 | 68454 | 85058 | 13645 |
| 23073 | 24724 | 52989 | 71880 | 21952 | 44144 | 74975 | 76715 | 07844 | 46447 |
| 86643 | 75579 | 29276 | 10864 | 83179 | 36721 | 19300 | 35066 | 29383 | 47478 |
| 56644 | 33354 | 31414 | 17643 | 92374 | 85085 | 88458 | 87191 | 85248 | 34963 |
| 76278 | 53230 | 13953 | 76985 | 70959 | 36663 | 05293 | 32658 | 56767 | 56997 |
| 76736 | 06558 | 64248 | 11907 | 29123 | 78458 | 17678 | 63805 | 89973 | 05076 |
| 39263 | 54404 | 04355 | 64957 | 74407 | 99838 | 18836 | 78098 | 06490 | 74888 |
| 73719 | 80675 | 86178 | 56283 | 33591 | 96957 | 38382 | 18772 | 74773 | 71229 |
| 02603 | 52673 | 44609 | 14843 | 58418 | 18060 | 95459 | 00626 | 30914 | 13550 |
| 42195 | 44863 | 08871 | 89182 | 64446 | 78422 | 41140 | 15312 | 98274 | 48168 |
| 95651 | 35562 | 85386 | 56252 | 72136 | 85088 | 68761 | 78434 | 98143 | 61330 |
| 02446 | 64409 | 49406 | 99127 | 98626 | 55095 | 44808 | 13594 | 87370 | 89472 |
| 12833 | 98932 | 68064 | 58193 | 20225 | 05192 | 28425 | 23978 | 24542 | 80845 |
| 55858 | 04015 | 21454 | 37346 | 51007 | 17202 | 10242 | 12682 | 55933 | 96922 |
| 22280 | 75597 | 50227 | 70712 | 44236 | 20470 | 36320 | 49339 | 60536 | 80083 |
| 38880 | 93327 | 49522 | 93585 | 09918 | 55268 | 04671 | 57526 | 11457 | 48424 |
| 54610 | 07211 | 78610 | 09473 | 72923 | 27347 | 30057 | 76968 | 26177 | 59367 |
| 46172 | 88951 | 40229 | 34921 | 60405 | 88959 | 16779 | 29547 | 92231 | 61997 |
| 36002 | 21080 | 39795 | 77221 | 10012 | 49748 | 76900 | 15964 | 03803 | 40260 |
| 92351 | 92844 | 10288 | 57483 | 10881 | 70408 | 75688 | 16610 | 01638 | 93082 |
| 44282 | 66849 | 75702 | 69428 | 34047 | 84968 | 71281 | 72328 | 73143 | 88672 |
| 49802 | 50639 | 18129 | 93659 | 58389 | 49095 | 45971 | 34196 | 84609 | 59222 |
| 19332 | 17777 | 41004 | 47057 | 30688 | 16039 | 20906 | 41477 | 42915 | 60877 |
| 33864 | 75195 | 62294 | 03371 | 11672 | 01370 | 02486 | 35553 | 17907 | 90621 |
| 45136 | 09722 | 67635 | 12114 | 63055 | 16004 | 21625 | 24321 | 20491 | 26881 |
| 66259 | 94287 | 54751 | 36242 | 36557 | 05842 | 30687 | 65418 | 94608 | 24741 |
| 45887 | 78800 | 86912 | 42076 | 50287 | 09284 | 68891 | 76368 | 83094 | 96302 |

| 35997 | 30761 | 97081 | 09501 | 68887 | 32876 | 01705 | 34260 | 95065 | 45528 |
| 88241 | 30402 | 12318 | 52430 | 40139 | 96986 | 84900 | 72408 | 42027 | 31676 |
| 54382 | 73370 | 26184 | 14024 | 57444 | 57660 | 52173 | 30274 | 93448 | 63273 |
| 77681 | 74946 | 02099 | 69091 | 19372 | 66961 | 14595 | 58642 | 75760 | 52253 |
| 53148 | 26074 | 52293 | 65359 | 63971 | 04833 | 86492 | 01227 | 54505 | 19515 |
| 89889 | 46933 | 13364 | 33883 | 83389 | 36952 | 52505 | 67513 | 40071 | 31001 |
| 03105 | 87912 | 29610 | 75108 | 37363 | 28479 | 43546 | 89992 | 19550 | 54863 |
| 82633 | 19209 | 21548 | 35022 | 21960 | 57961 | 11815 | 95867 | 00559 | 26428 |
| 69386 | 57453 | 70147 | 73538 | 49562 | 46806 | 64550 | 36653 | 25718 | 68792 |
| 31113 | 07607 | 48037 | 71020 | 22666 | 65957 | 11141 | 39227 | 07990 | 19849 |
| 65972 | 74528 | 40888 | 55386 | 95918 | 92088 | 91125 | 53648 | 66122 | 00138 |
| 79933 | 71058 | 34826 | 97725 | 69513 | 22915 | 18246 | 52244 | 91161 | 40861 |
| 40374 | 13239 | 56162 | 04703 | 95851 | 22824 | 41271 | 28202 | 62852 | 84238 |
| 46625 | 20031 | 08524 | 20077 | 65817 | 21174 | 29279 | 57712 | 22401 | 67500 |
| 30980 | 74485 | 26480 | 21343 | 30031 | 61921 | 35744 | 57308 | 71196 | 01865 |
| 49234 | 62616 | 54021 | 29008 | 83672 | 85839 | 96836 | 45077 | 80900 | 66906 |
| 63526 | 93824 | 71820 | 11033 | 20183 | 85704 | 04683 | 63512 | 39144 | 56880 |
| 64424 | 95979 | 17709 | 94849 | 31771 | 05737 | 84286 | 16757 | 46256 | 24478 |
| 73180 | 59978 | 08254 | 78963 | 95437 | 86351 | 33824 | 32540 | 18357 | 02668 |
| 99260 | 21284 | 81351 | 70961 | 10255 | 06911 | 47394 | 72408 | 23827 | 59865 |
| 96395 | 30665 | 43699 | 03593 | 29165 | 23388 | 26628 | 92402 | 16731 | 86740 |
| 29493 | 09069 | 78653 | 90094 | 42735 | 33682 | 95041 | 89887 | 92369 | 57949 |
| 81585 | 50593 | 14698 | 04737 | 72551 | 57271 | 59433 | 00156 | 33966 | 58773 |
| 59108 | 49578 | 18100 | 59836 | 73221 | 21110 | 01650 | 11058 | 47770 | 66141 |
| 84576 | 58388 | 40915 | 94507 | 32209 | 17272 | 65674 | 95552 | 25685 | 05345 |
| 36995 | 36302 | 07971 | 67001 | 62062 | 75939 | 36005 | 26739 | 56484 | 46885 |
| 66348 | 87666 | 78055 | 44485 | 82955 | 85936 | 09219 | 01847 | 92687 | 72579 |
| 45457 | 78252 | 98239 | 40000 | 75563 | 92408 | 17175 | 78845 | 32638 | 26959 |
| 35406 | 59553 | 57852 | 07506 | 00009 | 93172 | 77713 | 93880 | 40981 | 27924 |
| 09678 | 24538 | 52426 | 84852 | 83781 | 23712 | 82490 | 77890 | 22482 | 66668 |
| 55850 | 25644 | 44972 | 62275 | 78089 | 28894 | 98685 | 32998 | 98766 | 89119 |
| 34355 | 75127 | 69797 | 71419 | 62067 | 57990 | 96514 | 50603 | 79807 | 26135 |
| 29207 | 43632 | 32905 | 38513 | 18924 | 88872 | 20758 | 70232 | 60425 | 01116 |
| 24077 | 21369 | 93541 | 75329 | 78656 | 44251 | 42014 | 98154 | 42552 | 14575 |
| 30765 | 00348 | 01134 | 71581 | 68420 | 78141 | 21105 | 63305 | 09718 | 54851 |
| 65867 | 08595 | 47390 | 39182 | 51174 | 41478 | 64433 | 59628 | 31945 | 87322 |
| 78667 | 95282 | 05622 | 26224 | 19972 | 97269 | 98376 | 14779 | 51138 | 49658 |
| 45345 | 04972 | 52794 | 15737 | 00496 | 48939 | 63485 | 42780 | 16061 | 59631 |
| 37171 | 13483 | 56058 | 51093 | 62290 | 88227 | 17400 | 88433 | 67363 | 89507 |
| 26482 | 85964 | 71336 | 67799 | 28342 | 37747 | 61722 | 27180 | 78755 | 18603 |
| 42953 | 06606 | 23875 | 56766 | 01932 | 36113 | 62807 | 84012 | 21103 | 09685 |
| 69662 | 76755 | 13701 | 95168 | 13169 | 44726 | 15284 | 16702 | 89617 | 54397 |
| 52052 | 12835 | 37741 | 86434 | 22400 | 37947 | 95763 | 86337 | 35189 | 22756 |
| 47473 | 16618 | 42479 | 47405 | 14055 | 64262 | 66670 | 89692 | 54032 | 94591 |
| 44149 | 29854 | 76691 | 33263 | 62048 | 25116 | 88598 | 16119 | 62116 | 54517 |
| 31883 | 86707 | 18895 | 81790 | 71294 | 02684 | 15292 | 48107 | 14341 | 91416 |
| 75609 | 92564 | 39987 | 02283 | 89970 | 95855 | 80970 | 05432 | 89860 | 90293 |
| 99851 | 94648 | 05598 | 32171 | 28793 | 92305 | 64244 | 08277 | 93391 | 96717 |
| 34464 | 29838 | 10664 | 28050 | 60122 | 77934 | 10758 | 84922 | 92220 | 45071 |
| 97697 | 36368 | 17792 | 84792 | 76594 | 67319 | 51886 | 05665 | 45201 | 11348 |

D. B. Owen, *Handbook of Statistical Tables,* © 1962, Addison-Wesley, Reading, Massachusetts. Pgs. 14 & 15. Reprinted with permission.

# APPENDIX D
# CRITICAL VALUES FOR STUDENT'S $t$ DISTRIBUTION

| | **Significance levels for a one-tailed t test** | | | | | |
|---|---|---|---|---|---|---|
| | .25 | .10 | .05 | .025 | .01 | .005 |
| | **Significance levels for a two-tailed t test** | | | | | |
| df | .50 | .20 | .10 | .05 | .02 | .01 |
| 1 | 1.0000 | 3.0777 | 6.3138 | 12.7062 | 31.8207 | 63.6574 |
| 2 | 0.8165 | 1.8856 | 2.9200 | 4.3027 | 6.9646 | 9.9248 |
| 3 | 0.7649 | 1.6377 | 2.3534 | 3.1824 | 4.5407 | 5.8409 |
| 4 | 0.7407 | 1.5332 | 2.1318 | 2.7764 | 3.7469 | 4.6041 |
| 5 | 0.7267 | 1.4759 | 2.0150 | 2.5706 | 3.3649 | 4.0322 |
| 6 | 0.7176 | 1.4398 | 1.9432 | 2.4469 | 3.1427 | 3.7074 |
| 7 | 0.7111 | 1.4149 | 1.8946 | 2.3646 | 2.9980 | 3.4995 |
| 8 | 0.7064 | 1.3968 | 1.8595 | 2.3060 | 2.8965 | 3.3554 |
| 9 | 0.7027 | 1.3830 | 1.8331 | 2.2622 | 2.8214 | 3.2498 |
| 10 | 0.6998 | 1.3722 | 1.8125 | 2.2281 | 2.7638 | 3.1693 |
| 11 | 0.6974 | 1.3634 | 1.7959 | 2.2010 | 2.7181 | 3.1058 |
| 12 | 0.6955 | 1.3562 | 1.7823 | 2.1788 | 2.6810 | 3.0545 |
| 13 | 0.6938 | 1.3502 | 1.7709 | 2.1604 | 2.6503 | 3.0123 |
| 14 | 0.6924 | 1.3450 | 1.7613 | 2.1448 | 2.6245 | 2.9768 |
| 15 | 0.6912 | 1.3406 | 1.7531 | 2.1315 | 2.6025 | 2.9467 |
| 16 | 0.6901 | 1.3368 | 1.7459 | 2.1199 | 2.5835 | 2.9208 |
| 17 | 0.6892 | 1.3334 | 1.7396 | 2.1098 | 2.5669 | 2.8982 |
| 18 | 0.6884 | 1.3304 | 1.7341 | 2.1009 | 2.5524 | 2.8784 |
| 19 | 0.6876 | 1.3277 | 1.7291 | 2.0930 | 2.5395 | 2.8609 |
| 20 | 0.6870 | 1.3253 | 1.7247 | 2.0860 | 2.5280 | 2.8453 |
| 21 | 0.6864 | 1.3232 | 1.7207 | 2.0796 | 2.5177 | 2.8314 |
| 22 | 0.6858 | 1.3212 | 1.7171 | 2.0739 | 2.5083 | 2.8188 |
| 23 | 0.6853 | 1.3195 | 1.7139 | 2.0687 | 2.4999 | 2.8073 |
| 24 | 0.6848 | 1.3178 | 1.7109 | 2.0639 | 2.4922 | 2.7969 |
| 25 | 0.6844 | 1.3163 | 1.7081 | 2.0595 | 2.4851 | 2.7874 |
| 26 | 0.6840 | 1.3150 | 1.7056 | 2.0555 | 2.4786 | 2.7787 |
| 27 | 0.6837 | 1.3137 | 1.7033 | 2.0518 | 2.4727 | 2.7707 |
| 28 | 0.6834 | 1.3125 | 1.7011 | 2.0484 | 2.4671 | 2.7633 |
| 29 | 0.6830 | 1.3114 | 1.6991 | 2.0452 | 2.4620 | 2.7564 |
| 30 | 0.6828 | 1.3104 | 1.6973 | 2.0423 | 2.4573 | 2.7500 |
| 31 | 0.6825 | 1.3095 | 1.6955 | 2.0395 | 2.4528 | 2.7440 |
| 32 | 0.6822 | 1.3086 | 1.6939 | 2.0369 | 2.4487 | 2.7385 |
| 33 | 0.6820 | 1.3077 | 1.6924 | 2.0345 | 2.4448 | 2.7333 |
| 34 | 0.6818 | 1.3070 | 1.6909 | 2.0322 | 2.4411 | 2.7284 |
| 35 | 0.6816 | 1.3062 | 1.6896 | 2.0301 | 2.4377 | 2.7238 |
| 36 | 0.6814 | 1.3055 | 1.6883 | 2.0281 | 2.4345 | 2.7195 |
| 37 | 0.6812 | 1.3049 | 1.6871 | 2.0262 | 2.4314 | 2.7154 |
| 38 | 0.6810 | 1.3042 | 1.6860 | 2.0244 | 2.4286 | 2.7116 |
| 39 | 0.6808 | 1.3036 | 1.6849 | 2.0227 | 2.4258 | 2.7079 |
| 40 | 0.6807 | 1.3031 | 1.6839 | 2.0211 | 2.4233 | 2.7045 |
| 41 | 0.6805 | 1.3025 | 1.6829 | 2.0195 | 2.4208 | 2.7012 |
| 42 | 0.6804 | 1.3020 | 1.6820 | 2.0181 | 2.4185 | 2.6981 |
| 43 | 0.6802 | 1.3016 | 1.6811 | 2.0167 | 2.4163 | 2.6951 |
| 44 | 0.6801 | 1.3011 | 1.6802 | 2.0154 | 2.4141 | 2.6923 |
| 45 | 0.6800 | 1.3006 | 1.6794 | 2.0141 | 2.4121 | 2.6896 |

| | Significance levels for a one-tailed t test | | | | | |
|---|---|---|---|---|---|---|
| | .25 | .10 | .05 | .025 | .01 | .005 |
| | Significance levels for a two-tailed t test | | | | | |
| df | .50 | .20 | .10 | .05 | .02 | .01 |
| 46 | 0.6799 | 1.3002 | 1.6787 | 2.0129 | 2.4102 | 2.6870 |
| 47 | 0.6797 | 1.2998 | 1.6779 | 2.0117 | 2.4083 | 2.6846 |
| 48 | 0.6796 | 1.2994 | 1.6772 | 2.0106 | 2.4066 | 2.6822 |
| 49 | 0.6795 | 1.2991 | 1.6766 | 2.0096 | 2.4049 | 2.6800 |
| 50 | 0.6794 | 1.2987 | 1.6759 | 2.0086 | 2.4033 | 2.6778 |
| 51 | 0.6793 | 1.2984 | 1.6753 | 2.0076 | 2.4017 | 2.6757 |
| 52 | 0.6792 | 1.2980 | 1.6747 | 2.0066 | 2.4002 | 2.6737 |
| 53 | 0.6791 | 1.2977 | 1.6741 | 2.0057 | 2.3988 | 2.6718 |
| 54 | 0.6791 | 1.2974 | 1.6736 | 2.0049 | 2.3974 | 2.6700 |
| 55 | 0.6790 | 1.2971 | 1.6730 | 2.0040 | 2.3961 | 2.6682 |
| 56 | 0.6789 | 1.2969 | 1.6725 | 2.0032 | 2.3948 | 2.6665 |
| 57 | 0.6788 | 1.2966 | 1.6720 | 2.0025 | 2.3936 | 2.6649 |
| 58 | 0.6787 | 1.2963 | 1.6716 | 2.0017 | 2.3924 | 2.6633 |
| 59 | 0.6787 | 1.2961 | 1.6711 | 2.0010 | 2.3912 | 2.6618 |
| 60 | 0.6786 | 1.2958 | 1.6706 | 2.0003 | 2.3901 | 2.6603 |
| 61 | 0.6785 | 1.2956 | 1.6702 | 1.9996 | 2.3890 | 2.6589 |
| 62 | 0.6785 | 1.2954 | 1.6698 | 1.9990 | 2.3880 | 2.6575 |
| 63 | 0.6784 | 1.2951 | 1.6694 | 1.9983 | 2.3870 | 2.6561 |
| 64 | 0.6783 | 1.2949 | 1.6690 | 1.9977 | 2.3860 | 2.6549 |
| 65 | 0.6783 | 1.2947 | 1.6686 | 1.9971 | 2.3851 | 2.6536 |
| 66 | 0.6782 | 1.2945 | 1.6683 | 1.9966 | 2.3842 | 2.6524 |
| 67 | 0.6782 | 1.2943 | 1.6679 | 1.9960 | 2.3833 | 2.6512 |
| 68 | 0.6781 | 1.2941 | 1.6676 | 1.9955 | 2.3824 | 2.6501 |
| 69 | 0.6781 | 1.2939 | 1.6672 | 1.9949 | 2.3816 | 2.6490 |
| 70 | 0.6780 | 1.2938 | 1.6669 | 1.9944 | 2.3808 | 2.6479 |
| 71 | 0.6780 | 1.2936 | 1.6666 | 1.9939 | 2.3800 | 2.6469 |
| 72 | 0.6779 | 1.2934 | 1.6663 | 1.9935 | 2.3793 | 2.6459 |
| 73 | 0.6779 | 1.2933 | 1.6660 | 1.9930 | 2.3785 | 2.6449 |
| 74 | 0.6778 | 1.2931 | 1.6657 | 1.9925 | 2.3778 | 2.6439 |
| 75 | 0.6778 | 1.2929 | 1.6654 | 1.9921 | 2.3771 | 2.6430 |
| 76 | 0.6777 | 1.2928 | 1.6652 | 1.9917 | 2.3764 | 2.6421 |
| 77 | 0.6777 | 1.2926 | 1.6649 | 1.9913 | 2.3758 | 2.6412 |
| 78 | 0.6776 | 1.2925 | 1.6646 | 1.9908 | 2.3751 | 2.6403 |
| 79 | 0.6776 | 1.2924 | 1.6644 | 1.9905 | 2.3745 | 2.6395 |
| 80 | 0.6776 | 1.2922 | 1.6641 | 1.9901 | 2.3739 | 2.6387 |
| 81 | 0.6775 | 1.2921 | 1.6639 | 1.9897 | 2.3733 | 2.6379 |
| 82 | 0.6775 | 1.2920 | 1.6636 | 1.9893 | 2.3727 | 2.6371 |
| 83 | 0.6775 | 1.2918 | 1.6634 | 1.9890 | 2.3721 | 2.6364 |
| 84 | 0.6774 | 1.2917 | 1.6632 | 1.9886 | 2.3716 | 2.6356 |
| 85 | 0.6774 | 1.2916 | 1.6630 | 1.9883 | 2.3710 | 2.6349 |
| 86 | 0.6774 | 1.2915 | 1.6628 | 1.9879 | 2.3705 | 2.6342 |
| 87 | 0.6773 | 1.2914 | 1.6626 | 1.9876 | 2.3700 | 2.6335 |
| 88 | 0.6773 | 1.2912 | 1.6624 | 1.9873 | 2.3695 | 2.6329 |
| 89 | 0.6773 | 1.2911 | 1.6622 | 1.9870 | 2.3690 | 2.6322 |
| 90 | 0.6772 | 1.2910 | 1.6620 | 1.9867 | 2.3685 | 2.6316 |

| | Significance levels for a one-tailed t test | | | | | |
|---|---|---|---|---|---|---|
| | .25 | .10 | .05 | .025 | .01 | .005 |
| | Significance levels for a two-tailed t test | | | | | |
| df | .50 | .20 | .10 | .05 | .02 | .01 |
| 91 | 0.6772 | 1.2909 | 1.6618 | 1.9864 | 2.3680 | 2.6309 |
| 92 | 0.6772 | 1.2908 | 1.6616 | 1.9861 | 2.3676 | 2.6303 |
| 93 | 0.6771 | 1.2907 | 1.6614 | 1.9858 | 2.3671 | 2.6297 |
| 94 | 0.6771 | 1.2906 | 1.6612 | 1.9855 | 2.3667 | 2.6291 |
| 95 | 0.6771 | 1.2905 | 1.6611 | 1.9853 | 2.3662 | 2.6286 |
| 96 | 0.6771 | 1.2904 | 1.6609 | 1.9850 | 2.3658 | 2.6280 |
| 97 | 0.6770 | 1.2903 | 1.6607 | 1.9847 | 2.3654 | 2.6275 |
| 98 | 0.6770 | 1.2902 | 1.6606 | 1.9845 | 2.3650 | 2.6269 |
| 99 | 0.6770 | 1.2902 | 1.6604 | 1.9842 | 2.3646 | 2.6264 |
| 100 | 0.6770 | 1.2901 | 1.6602 | 1.9840 | 2.3642 | 2.6259 |
| 102 | 0.6769 | 1.2899 | 1.6599 | 1.9835 | 2.3635 | 2.6249 |
| 104 | 0.6769 | 1.2897 | 1.6596 | 1.9830 | 2.3627 | 2.6239 |
| 106 | 0.6768 | 1.2896 | 1.6594 | 1.9826 | 2.3620 | 2.6230 |
| 108 | 0.6768 | 1.2894 | 1.6591 | 1.9822 | 2.3614 | 2.6221 |
| 110 | 0.6767 | 1.2893 | 1.6588 | 1.9818 | 2.3607 | 2.6213 |
| 112 | 0.6767 | 1.2892 | 1.6586 | 1.9814 | 2.3601 | 2.6204 |
| 114 | 0.6766 | 1.2890 | 1.6583 | 1.9810 | 2.3595 | 2.6196 |
| 116 | 0.6766 | 1.2889 | 1.6581 | 1.9806 | 2.3589 | 2.6189 |
| 118 | 0.6766 | 1.2888 | 1.6579 | 1.9803 | 2.3584 | 2.6181 |
| 120 | 0.6765 | 1.2886 | 1.6577 | 1.9799 | 2.3578 | 2.6174 |
| 122 | 0.6765 | 1.2885 | 1.6574 | 1.9796 | 2.3573 | 2.6167 |
| 124 | 0.6765 | 1.2884 | 1.6572 | 1.9793 | 2.3568 | 2.6161 |
| 126 | 0.6764 | 1.2883 | 1.6570 | 1.9790 | 2.3563 | 2.6154 |
| 128 | 0.6764 | 1.2882 | 1.6568 | 1.9787 | 2.3558 | 2.6148 |
| 130 | 0.6764 | 1.2881 | 1.6567 | 1.9784 | 2.3554 | 2.6142 |
| 132 | 0.6764 | 1.2880 | 1.6565 | 1.9781 | 2.3549 | 2.6136 |
| 134 | 0.6763 | 1.2879 | 1.6563 | 1.9778 | 2.3545 | 2.6130 |
| 136 | 0.6763 | 1.2878 | 1.6561 | 1.9776 | 2.3541 | 2.6125 |
| 138 | 0.6763 | 1.2877 | 1.6560 | 1.9773 | 2.3537 | 2.6119 |
| 140 | 0.6762 | 1.2876 | 1.6558 | 1.9771 | 2.3533 | 2.6114 |
| 142 | 0.6762 | 1.2875 | 1.6557 | 1.9768 | 2.3529 | 2.6109 |
| 144 | 0.6762 | 1.2875 | 1.6555 | 1.9766 | 2.3525 | 2.6104 |
| 146 | 0.6762 | 1.2874 | 1.6554 | 1.9763 | 2.3522 | 2.6099 |
| 148 | 0.6762 | 1.2873 | 1.6552 | 1.9761 | 2.3518 | 2.6095 |
| 150 | 0.6761 | 1.2872 | 1.6551 | 1.9759 | 2.3515 | 2.6090 |
| 200 | 0.6757 | 1.2858 | 1.6525 | 1.9719 | 2.3451 | 2.6006 |
| 300 | 0.6753 | 1.2844 | 1.6499 | 1.9679 | 2.3388 | 2.5923 |
| 400 | 0.6751 | 1.2837 | 1.6487 | 1.9659 | 2.3357 | 2.5882 |
| 500 | 0.6750 | 1.2832 | 1.6479 | 1.9647 | 2.3338 | 2.5857 |
| 600 | 0.6749 | 1.2830 | 1.6474 | 1.9639 | 2.3326 | 2.5840 |
| 700 | 0.6748 | 1.2828 | 1.6470 | 1.9634 | 2.3317 | 2.5829 |
| 800 | 0.6748 | 1.2826 | 1.6468 | 1.9629 | 2.3310 | 2.5820 |
| 900 | 0.6748 | 1.2825 | 1.6465 | 1.9626 | 2.3305 | 2.5813 |
| 1000 | 0.6747 | 1.2824 | 1.6464 | 1.9623 | 2.3301 | 2.5808 |
| ∞ | 0.6745 | 1.2816 | 1.6449 | 1.9600 | 2.3263 | 2.5758 |

D. B. Owen, *Handbook of Statistical Tables*, © 1962, Addison-Wesley, Reading, Massachusetts. Pgs. 28–30 (Table 2.1). Reprinted with permission.

# APPENDIX E
## CRITICAL VALUES FOR THE *F* DISTRIBUTION

**NOTE: The .05 significance level appears in lightface type and the .01 level is printed in boldface type.**

### Numerator degrees of freedom

| | | 1 | 2 | 3 | 4 | 5 | 6 | 7 | 8 | 9 | 10 | 11 | 12 |
|---|---|---|---|---|---|---|---|---|---|---|---|---|---|
| | 1 | 161.45 | 199.50 | 215.71 | 224.58 | 230.16 | 233.99 | 236.77 | 238.88 | 240.54 | 241.88 | 242.99 | 243.91 |
| | | **4052.2** | **4999.5** | **5403.3** | **5624.6** | **5763.7** | **5859.0** | **5928.3** | **5981.1** | **6022.5** | **6055.8** | **6083.3** | **6106.3** |
| | 2 | 18.513 | 19.000 | 19.164 | 19.247 | 19.296 | 19.330 | 19.353 | 19.371 | 19.385 | 19.396 | 19.405 | 19.413 |
| | | **98.503** | **99.000** | **99.166** | **99.249** | **99.299** | **99.332** | **99.356** | **99.374** | **99.388** | **99.399** | **99.408** | **99.416** |
| | 3 | 10.128 | 9.5521 | 9.2766 | 9.1172 | 9.0135 | 8.9406 | 8.8868 | 8.8452 | 8.8123 | 8.7855 | 8.7632 | 8.7446 |
| | | **34.116** | **30.817** | **29.457** | **28.710** | **28.237** | **27.911** | **27.672** | **27.489** | **27.345** | **27.229** | **27.132** | **27.052** |
| | 4 | 7.7086 | 6.9443 | 6.5914 | 6.3883 | 6.2560 | 6.1631 | 6.0942 | 6.0410 | 5.9988 | 5.9644 | 5.9357 | 5.9117 |
| | | **21.198** | **18.000** | **16.694** | **15.977** | **15.522** | **15.207** | **14.976** | **14.799** | **14.659** | **14.546** | **14.452** | **14.374** |
| | 5 | 6.6079 | 5.7861 | 5.4095 | 5.1922 | 5.0503 | 4.9503 | 4.8759 | 4.8183 | 4.7725 | 4.7351 | 4.7038 | 4.6777 |
| | | **16.258** | **13.274** | **12.060** | **11.392** | **10.967** | **10.672** | **10.456** | **10.289** | **10.158** | **10.051** | **9.9623** | **9.8883** |
| | 6 | 5.9874 | 5.1433 | 4.7571 | 4.5337 | 4.3874 | 4.2839 | 4.2066 | 4.1468 | 4.0990 | 4.0600 | 4.0272 | 3.9999 |
| | | **13.745** | **10.925** | **9.7795** | **9.1483** | **8.7459** | **8.4661** | **8.2600** | **8.1016** | **7.9761** | **7.8741** | **7.7891** | **7.7183** |
| | 7 | 5.5914 | 4.7374 | 4.3468 | 4.1203 | 3.9715 | 3.8660 | 3.7870 | 3.7257 | 3.6767 | 3.6365 | 3.6028 | 3.5747 |
| | | **12.246** | **9.5466** | **8.4513** | **7.8467** | **7.4604** | **7.1914** | **6.9928** | **6.8401** | **6.7188** | **6.6201** | **6.5377** | **6.4691** |
| | 8 | 5.3177 | 4.4590 | 4.0662 | 3.8378 | 3.6875 | 3.5806 | 3.5005 | 3.4381 | 3.3881 | 3.3472 | 3.3127 | 3.2840 |
| | | **11.259** | **8.6491** | **7.5910** | **7.0060** | **6.6318** | **6.3707** | **6.1776** | **6.0289** | **5.9106** | **5.8143** | **5.7338** | **5.6668** |
| | 9 | 5.1174 | 4.2565 | 3.8626 | 3.6331 | 3.4817 | 3.3738 | 3.2927 | 3.2296 | 3.1789 | 3.1373 | 3.1022 | 3.0729 |
| | | **10.561** | **8.0215** | **6.9919** | **6.4221** | **6.0569** | **5.8018** | **5.6129** | **5.4671** | **5.3511** | **5.2565** | **5.1774** | **5.1114** |
| | 10 | 4.9646 | 4.1028 | 3.7083 | 3.4780 | 3.3258 | 3.2172 | 3.1355 | 3.0717 | 3.0204 | 2.9782 | 2.9426 | 2.9130 |
| | | **10.044** | **7.5594** | **6.5523** | **5.9943** | **5.6363** | **5.3858** | **5.2001** | **5.0567** | **4.9424** | **4.8492** | **4.7710** | **4.7059** |
| | 11 | 4.8443 | 3.9823 | 3.5874 | 3.3567 | 3.2039 | 3.0946 | 3.0123 | 2.9480 | 2.8962 | 2.8536 | 2.8176 | 2.7876 |
| | | **9.6460** | **7.2057** | **6.2167** | **5.6683** | **5.3160** | **5.0692** | **4.8861** | **4.7445** | **4.6315** | **4.5393** | **4.4619** | **4.3974** |
| | 12 | 4.7472 | 3.8853 | 3.4903 | 3.2592 | 3.1059 | 2.9961 | 2.9134 | 2.8486 | 2.7964 | 2.7534 | 2.7170 | 2.6866 |
| | | **9.3302** | **6.9266** | **5.9526** | **5.4119** | **5.0643** | **4.8206** | **4.6395** | **4.4994** | **4.3875** | **4.2961** | **4.2193** | **4.1553** |
| | 13 | 4.6672 | 3.8056 | 3.4105 | 3.1791 | 3.0254 | 2.9153 | 2.8321 | 2.7669 | 2.7144 | 2.6710 | 2.6343 | 2.6037 |
| | | **9.0738** | **6.7010** | **5.7394** | **5.2053** | **4.8616** | **4.6204** | **4.4410** | **4.3021** | **4.1911** | **4.1003** | **4.0239** | **3.9603** |
| | 14 | 4.6001 | 3.7389 | 3.3439 | 3.1122 | 2.9582 | 2.8477 | 2.7642 | 2.6987 | 2.6458 | 2.6021 | 2.5651 | 2.5342 |
| | | **8.8616** | **6.5149** | **5.5639** | **5.0354** | **4.6950** | **4.4558** | **4.2779** | **4.1399** | **4.0297** | **3.9394** | **3.8634** | **3.8001** |
| | 15 | 4.5431 | 3.6823 | 3.2874 | 3.0556 | 2.9013 | 2.7905 | 2.7066 | 2.6408 | 2.5876 | 2.5437 | 2.5064 | 2.4753 |
| | | **8.6831** | **6.3589** | **5.4170** | **4.8932** | **4.5556** | **4.3183** | **4.1415** | **4.0045** | **3.8948** | **3.8049** | **3.7292** | **3.6662** |
| | 16 | 4.4940 | 3.6337 | 3.2389 | 3.0069 | 2.8524 | 2.7413 | 2.6572 | 2.5911 | 2.5377 | 2.4935 | 2.4560 | 2.4247 |
| | | **8.5310** | **6.2262** | **5.2922** | **4.7726** | **4.4374** | **4.2016** | **4.0259** | **3.8896** | **3.7804** | **3.6909** | **3.6155** | **3.5527** |
| | 17 | 4.4513 | 3.5915 | 3.1968 | 2.9647 | 2.8100 | 2.6987 | 2.6143 | 2.5480 | 2.4943 | 2.4499 | 2.4122 | 2.3807 |
| | | **8.3997** | **6.1121** | **5.1850** | **4.6690** | **4.3359** | **4.1015** | **3.9267** | **3.7910** | **3.6822** | **3.5931** | **3.5179** | **3.4552** |
| | 18 | 4.4139 | 3.5546 | 3.1599 | 2.9277 | 2.7729 | 2.6613 | 2.5767 | 2.5102 | 2.4563 | 2.4117 | 2.3737 | 2.3421 |
| | | **8.2854** | **6.0129** | **5.0919** | **4.5790** | **4.2479** | **4.0146** | **3.8406** | **3.7054** | **3.5971** | **3.5082** | **3.4331** | **3.3706** |

Denominator degrees of freedom

**Numerator degrees of freedom**

| 13 | 14 | 15 | 18 | 20 | 24 | 30 | 40 | 48 | 60 | 120 | ∞ |
|---|---|---|---|---|---|---|---|---|---|---|---|
| 244.69 | 245.37 | 245.95 | 247.32 | 248.01 | 249.05 | 250.09 | 251.14 | 251.67 | 252.20 | 253.25 | 254.32 |
| **6125.9** | **6142.7** | **6157.3** | **6191.6** | **6208.7** | **6234.6** | **6260.7** | **6286.8** | **6299.9** | **6313.0** | **6339.4** | **6366.0** |
| 19.419 | 19.424 | 19.429 | 19.440 | 19.446 | 19.454 | 19.462 | 19.471 | 19.475 | 19.479 | 19.487 | 19.496 |
| **99.422** | **99.427** | **99.432** | **99.443** | **99.449** | **99.458** | **99.466** | **99.474** | **99.478** | **99.483** | **99.491** | **99.499** |
| 8.7286 | 8.7148 | 8.7029 | 8.6744 | 8.6602 | 8.6385 | 8.6166 | 8.5944 | 8.5832 | 8.5720 | 8.5494 | 8.5265 |
| **26.983** | **26.923** | **26.872** | **26.751** | **26.690** | **26.598** | **26.505** | **26.411** | **26.364** | **26.316** | **26.221** | **26.125** |
| 5.8910 | 5.8732 | 5.8578 | 5.8209 | 5.8025 | 5.7744 | 5.7459 | 5.7170 | 5.7024 | 5.6878 | 5.6581 | 5.6281 |
| **14.306** | **14.248** | **14.198** | **14.079** | **14.020** | **13.929** | **13.838** | **13.745** | **13.699** | **13.652** | **13.558** | **13.463** |
| 4.6550 | 4.6356 | 4.6188 | 4.5783 | 4.5581 | 4.5272 | 4.4957 | 4.4638 | 4.4476 | 4.4314 | 4.3984 | 4.3650 |
| **9.8244** | **9.7697** | **9.7222** | **9.6092** | **9.5527** | **9.4665** | **9.3793** | **9.2912** | **9.2466** | **9.2020** | **9.1118** | **9.0204** |
| 3.9761 | 3.9558 | 3.9381 | 3.8955 | 3.8742 | 3.8415 | 3.8082 | 3.7743 | 3.7571 | 3.7398 | 3.7047 | 3.6688 |
| **7.6570** | **7.6045** | **7.5590** | **7.4502** | **7.3958** | **7.3127** | **7.2285** | **7.1432** | **7.1000** | **7.0568** | **6.9690** | **6.8801** |
| 3.5501 | 3.5291 | 3.5108 | 3.4666 | 3.4445 | 3.4105 | 3.3758 | 3.3404 | 3.3224 | 3.3043 | 3.2674 | 3.2298 |
| **6.4096** | **6.3585** | **6.3143** | **6.2084** | **6.1554** | **6.0743** | **5.9921** | **5.9084** | **5.8660** | **5.8236** | **5.7372** | **5.6495** |
| 3.2588 | 3.2371 | 3.2184 | 3.1730 | 3.1503 | 3.1152 | 3.0794 | 3.0428 | 3.0241 | 3.0053 | 2.9669 | 2.9276 |
| **5.6085** | **5.5584** | **5.5151** | **5.4111** | **5.3591** | **5.2793** | **5.1981** | **5.1156** | **5.0736** | **5.0316** | **4.9460** | **4.8588** |
| 3.0472 | 3.0252 | 3.0061 | 2.9597 | 2.9365 | 2.9005 | 2.8637 | 2.8259 | 2.8066 | 2.7872 | 2.7475 | 2.7067 |
| **5.0540** | **5.0048** | **4.9621** | **4.8594** | **4.8080** | **4.7290** | **4.6486** | **4.5667** | **4.5249** | **4.4831** | **4.3978** | **4.3105** |
| 2.8868 | 2.8644 | 2.8450 | 2.7977 | 2.7740 | 2.7372 | 2.6996 | 2.6609 | 2.6410 | 2.6211 | 2.5801 | 2.5379 |
| **4.6491** | **4.6004** | **4.5582** | **4.4563** | **4.4054** | **4.3269** | **4.2469** | **4.1653** | **4.1236** | **4.0819** | **3.9965** | **3.9090** |
| 2.7611 | 2.7383 | 2.7186 | 2.6705 | 2.6464 | 2.6090 | 2.5705 | 2.5309 | 2.5105 | 2.4901 | 2.4480 | 2.4045 |
| **4.3411** | **4.2928** | **4.2509** | **4.1496** | **4.0990** | **4.0209** | **3.9411** | **3.8596** | **3.8179** | **3.7761** | **3.6904** | **3.6025** |
| 2.6598 | 2.6368 | 2.6169 | 2.5680 | 2.5436 | 2.5055 | 2.4663 | 2.4259 | 2.4051 | 2.3842 | 2.3410 | 2.2962 |
| **4.0993** | **4.0512** | **4.0096** | **3.9088** | **3.8584** | **3.7805** | **3.7008** | **3.6192** | **3.5774** | **3.5355** | **3.4494** | **3.3608** |
| 2.5765 | 2.5533 | 2.5331 | 2.4836 | 2.4589 | 2.4202 | 2.3803 | 2.3392 | 2.3179 | 2.2966 | 2.2524 | 2.2064 |
| **3.9046** | **3.8568** | **3.8154** | **3.7149** | **3.6646** | **3.5868** | **3.5070** | **3.4253** | **3.3833** | **3.3413** | **3.2548** | **3.1654** |
| 2.5068 | 2.4833 | 2.4630 | 2.4129 | 2.3879 | 2.3487 | 2.3082 | 2.2664 | 2.2447 | 2.2230 | 2.1778 | 2.1307 |
| **3.7446** | **3.6970** | **3.6557** | **3.5554** | **3.5052** | **3.4274** | **3.3476** | **3.2656** | **3.2235** | **3.1813** | **3.0942** | **3.0040** |
| 2.4477 | 2.4240 | 2.4035 | 2.3528 | 2.3275 | 2.2878 | 2.2468 | 2.2043 | 2.1822 | 2.1601 | 2.1141 | 2.0658 |
| **3.6108** | **3.5633** | **3.5222** | **3.4220** | **3.3719** | **3.2940** | **3.2141** | **3.1319** | **3.0895** | **3.0471** | **2.9595** | **2.8684** |
| 2.3968 | 2.3729 | 2.3522 | 2.3011 | 2.2756 | 2.2354 | 2.1938 | 2.1507 | 2.1283 | 2.1058 | 2.0589 | 2.0096 |
| **3.4974** | **3.4500** | **3.4089** | **3.3088** | **3.2588** | **3.1808** | **3.1007** | **3.0182** | **2.9756** | **2.9330** | **2.8447** | **2.7528** |
| 2.3526 | 2.3286 | 2.3077 | 2.2562 | 2.2304 | 2.1898 | 2.1477 | 2.1040 | 2.0812 | 2.0584 | 2.0107 | 1.9604 |
| **3.4000** | **3.3527** | **3.3117** | **3.2116** | **3.1615** | **3.0835** | **3.0032** | **2.9205** | **2.8777** | **2.8348** | **2.7459** | **2.6530** |
| 2.3138 | 2.2896 | 2.2686 | 2.2166 | 2.1906 | 2.1497 | 2.1071 | 2.0629 | 2.0398 | 2.0166 | 1.9681 | 1.9168 |
| **3.3155** | **3.2682** | **3.2273** | **3.1272** | **3.0771** | **2.9990** | **2.9185** | **2.8354** | **2.7924** | **2.7493** | **2.6597** | **2.5660** |

2/27 ⟵ interaction point

| | **1** | **2** | **3** | **4** | **5** | **6** | **7** | **8** | **9** | **10** | **11** | **12** |
|---|---|---|---|---|---|---|---|---|---|---|---|---|
| **19** | 4.3808 | 3.5219 | 3.1274 | 2.8951 | 2.7401 | 2.6283 | 2.5435 | 2.4768 | 2.4227 | 2.3779 | 2.3398 | 2.3080 |
| | **8.1850** | **5.9259** | **5.0103** | **4.5003** | **4.1708** | **3.9386** | **3.7653** | **3.6305** | **3.5225** | **3.4338** | **3.3589** | **3.2965** |
| **20** | 4.3513 | 3.4928 | 3.0984 | 2.8661 | 2.7109 | 2.5990 | 2.5140 | 2.4471 | 2.3928 | 2.3479 | 2.3096 | 2.2776 |
| | **8.0960** | **5.8489** | **4.9382** | **4.4307** | **4.1027** | **3.8714** | **3.6987** | **3.5644** | **3.4567** | **3.3682** | **3.2934** | **3.2311** |
| **21** | 4.3248 | 3.4668 | 3.0725 | 2.8401 | 2.6848 | 2.5727 | 2.4876 | 2.4205 | 2.3661 | 2.3210 | 2.2825 | 2.2504 |
| | **8.0166** | **5.7804** | **4.8740** | **4.3688** | **4.0421** | **3.8117** | **3.6396** | **3.5056** | **3.3981** | **3.3098** | **3.2351** | **3.1729** |
| **22** | 4.3009 | 3.4434 | 3.0491 | 2.8167 | 2.6613 | 2.5491 | 2.4638 | 2.3965 | 2.3419 | 2.2967 | 2.2580 | 2.2258 |
| | **7.9454** | **5.7190** | **4.8166** | **4.3134** | **3.9880** | **3.7583** | **3.5867** | **3.4530** | **3.3458** | **3.2576** | **3.1830** | **3.1209** |
| **23** | 4.2793 | 3.4221 | 3.0280 | 2.7955 | 2.6400 | 2.5277 | 2.4422 | 2.3748 | 2.3201 | 2.2747 | 2.2359 | 2.2036 |
| | **7.8811** | **5.6637** | **4.7649** | **4.2635** | **3.9392** | **3.7102** | **3.5390** | **3.4057** | **3.2986** | **3.2106** | **3.1361** | **3.0740** |
| **24** | 4.2597 | 3.4028 | 3.0088 | 2.7763 | 2.6207 | 2.5082 | 2.4226 | 2.3551 | 2.3002 | 2.2547 | 2.2158 | 2.1834 |
| | **7.8229** | **5.6136** | **4.7181** | **4.2184** | **3.8951** | **3.6667** | **3.4959** | **3.3629** | **3.2560** | **3.1681** | **3.0936** | **3.0316** |
| **25** | 4.2417 | 3.3852 | 2.9912 | 2.7587 | 2.6030 | 2.4904 | 2.4047 | 2.3371 | 2.2821 | 2.2365 | 2.1974 | 2.1649 |
| | **7.7698** | **5.5680** | **4.6755** | **4.1774** | **3.8550** | **3.6272** | **3.4568** | **3.3239** | **3.2172** | **3.1294** | **3.0551** | **2.9931** |
| **26** | 4.2252 | 3.3690 | 2.9751 | 2.7426 | 2.5868 | 2.4741 | 2.3883 | 2.3205 | 2.2655 | 2.2197 | 2.1805 | 2.1479 |
| | **7.7213** | **5.5263** | **4.6366** | **4.1400** | **3.8183** | **3.5911** | **3.4210** | **3.2884** | **3.1818** | **3.0941** | **3.0198** | **2.9579** |
| **27** | 4.2100 | 3.3541 | 2.9604 | 2.7278 | 2.5719 | 2.4591 | 2.3732 | 2.3053 | 2.2501 | 2.2043 | 2.1650 | 2.1323 |
| | **7.6767** | **5.4881** | **4.6009** | **4.1056** | **3.7848** | **3.5580** | **3.3882** | **3.2558** | **3.1494** | **3.0618** | **2.9875** | **2.9256** |
| **28** | 4.1960 | 3.3404 | 2.9467 | 2.7141 | 2.5581 | 2.4453 | 2.3593 | 2.2913 | 2.2360 | 2.1900 | 2.1507 | 2.1179 |
| | **7.6356** | **5.4529** | **4.5681** | **4.0740** | **3.7539** | **3.5276** | **3.3581** | **3.2259** | **3.1195** | **3.0320** | **2.9578** | **2.8959** |
| **29** | 4.1830 | 3.3277 | 2.9340 | 2.7014 | 2.5454 | 2.4324 | 2.3463 | 2.2782 | 2.2229 | 2.1768 | 2.1374 | 2.1045 |
| | **7.5976** | **5.4205** | **4.5378** | **4.0449** | **3.7254** | **3.4995** | **3.3302** | **3.1982** | **3.0920** | **3.0045** | **2.9303** | **2.8685** |
| **30** | 4.1709 | 3.3158 | 2.9223 | 2.6896 | 2.5336 | 2.4205 | 2.3343 | 2.2662 | 2.2107 | 2.1646 | 2.1251 | 2.0921 |
| | **7.5625** | **5.3903** | **4.5097** | **4.0179** | **3.6990** | **3.4735** | **3.3045** | **3.1726** | **3.0665** | **2.9791** | **2.9049** | **2.8431** |
| **40** | 4.0848 | 3.2317 | 2.8387 | 2.6060 | 2.4495 | 2.3359 | 2.2490 | 2.1802 | 2.1240 | 2.0772 | 2.0370 | 2.0035 |
| | **7.3141** | **5.1785** | **4.3126** | **3.8283** | **3.5138** | **3.2910** | **3.1238** | **2.9930** | **2.8876** | **2.8005** | **2.7265** | **2.6648** |
| **48** | 4.0430 | 3.1911 | 2.7984 | 2.5656 | 2.4089 | 2.2950 | 2.2078 | 2.1386 | 2.0821 | 2.0349 | 1.9943 | 1.9605 |
| | **7.1956** | **5.0780** | **4.2193** | **3.7387** | **3.4264** | **3.2049** | **3.0384** | **2.9082** | **2.8031** | **2.7162** | **2.6421** | **2.5805** |
| **60** | 4.0012 | 3.1504 | 2.7581 | 2.5252 | 2.3683 | 2.2540 | 2.1665 | 2.0970 | 2.0401 | 1.9926 | 1.9516 | 1.9174 |
| | **7.0771** | **4.9774** | **4.1259** | **3.6491** | **3.3389** | **3.1187** | **2.9530** | **2.8233** | **2.7185** | **2.6318** | **2.5578** | **2.4961** |
| **80** | 3.9607 | 3.1111 | 2.7192 | 2.4862 | 2.3292 | 2.2145 | 2.1266 | 2.0567 | 1.9995 | 1.9516 | 1.9101 | 1.8756 |
| | **6.9641** | **4.8820** | **4.0375** | **3.5644** | **3.2562** | **3.0373** | **2.8724** | **2.7431** | **2.6386** | **2.5520** | **2.4779** | **2.4162** |
| **120** | 3.9201 | 3.0718 | 2.6802 | 2.4472 | 2.2900 | 2.1750 | 2.0867 | 2.0164 | 1.9588 | 1.9105 | 1.8686 | 1.8337 |
| | **6.8510** | **4.7865** | **3.9491** | **3.4796** | **3.1735** | **2.9559** | **2.7918** | **2.6629** | **2.5586** | **2.4721** | **2.3980** | **2.3363** |
| **∞** | 3.8415 | 2.9957 | 2.6049 | 2.3719 | 2.2141 | 2.0986 | 2.0096 | 1.9384 | 1.8799 | 1.8307 | 1.7879 | 1.7522 |
| | **6.6349** | **4.6052** | **3.7816** | **3.3192** | **3.0173** | **2.8020** | **2.6393** | **2.5113** | **2.4073** | **2.3209** | **2.2467** | **2.1848** |

**Denominator degrees of freedom**

D. B. Owen, *Handbook of Statistical Tables*, © 1962, Addison-Wesley, Reading,
Massachusetts. Pgs. 64–87 (adapted material). Reprinted with permission.

**Numerator degrees of freedom**

| 13 | 14 | 15 | 18 | 20 | 24 | 30 | 40 | 48 | 60 | 120 | ∞ |
|---|---|---|---|---|---|---|---|---|---|---|---|
| 2.2796 | 2.2552 | 2.2341 | 2.1817 | 2.1555 | 2.1141 | 2.0712 | 2.0264 | 2.0030 | 1.9796 | 1.9302 | 1.8780 |
| **3.2414** | **3.1942** | **3.1533** | **3.0532** | **3.0031** | **2.9249** | **2.8442** | **2.7608** | **2.7175** | **2.6742** | **2.5839** | **2.4893** |
| 2.2490 | 2.2245 | 2.2033 | 2.1506 | 2.1242 | 2.0825 | 2.0391 | 1.9938 | 1.9701 | 1.9464 | 1.8963 | 1.8432 |
| **3.1761** | **3.1289** | **3.0880** | **2.9878** | **2.9377** | **2.8594** | **2.7785** | **2.6947** | **2.6512** | **2.6077** | **2.5168** | **2.4212** |
| 2.2217 | 2.1970 | 2.1757 | 2.1226 | 2.0960 | 2.0540 | 2.0102 | 1.9645 | 1.9405 | 1.9165 | 1.8657 | 1.8117 |
| **3.1179** | **3.0708** | **3.0299** | **2.9297** | **2.8796** | **2.8011** | **2.7200** | **2.6359** | **2.5922** | **2.5484** | **2.4568** | **2.3603** |
| 2.1970 | 2.1722 | 2.1508 | 2.0974 | 2.0707 | 2.0283 | 1.9842 | 1.9380 | 1.9138 | 1.8895 | 1.8380 | 1.7831 |
| **3.0659** | **3.0188** | **2.9780** | **2.8776** | **2.8274** | **2.7488** | **2.6675** | **2.5831** | **2.5391** | **2.4951** | **2.4029** | **2.3055** |
| 2.1746 | 2.1497 | 2.1282 | 2.0745 | 2.0476 | 2.0050 | 1.9605 | 1.9139 | 1.8894 | 1.8649 | 1.8128 | 1.7570 |
| **3.0190** | **2.9719** | **2.9311** | **2.8307** | **2.7805** | **2.7017** | **2.6202** | **2.5355** | **2.4913** | **2.4471** | **2.3542** | **2.2559** |
| 2.1543 | 2.1293 | 2.1077 | 2.0537 | 2.0267 | 1.9838 | 1.9390 | 1.8920 | 1.8672 | 1.8424 | 1.7897 | 1.7331 |
| **2.9766** | **2.9295** | **2.8887** | **2.7882** | **2.7380** | **2.6591** | **2.5773** | **2.4923** | **2.4479** | **2.4035** | **2.3099** | **2.2107** |
| 2.1357 | 2.1106 | 2.0889 | 2.0346 | 2.0075 | 1.9643 | 1.9192 | 1.8718 | 1.8468 | 1.8217 | 1.7684 | 1.7110 |
| **2.9381** | **2.8910** | **2.8502** | **2.7496** | **2.6993** | **2.6203** | **2.5383** | **2.4530** | **2.4084** | **2.3637** | **2.2695** | **2.1694** |
| 2.1186 | 2.0934 | 2.0716 | 2.0171 | 1.9898 | 1.9464 | 1.9010 | 1.8533 | 1.8280 | 1.8027 | 1.7488 | 1.6906 |
| **2.9029** | **2.8558** | **2.8150** | **2.7143** | **2.6640** | **2.5848** | **2.5026** | **2.4170** | **2.3722** | **2.3273** | **2.2325** | **2.1315** |
| 2.1029 | 2.0777 | 2.0558 | 2.0010 | 1.9736 | 1.9299 | 1.8842 | 1.8361 | 1.8106 | 1.7851 | 1.7307 | 1.6717 |
| **2.8706** | **2.8235** | **2.7827** | **2.6820** | **2.6316** | **2.5522** | **2.4699** | **2.3840** | **2.3389** | **2.2938** | **2.1984** | **2.0965** |
| 2.0884 | 2.0630 | 2.0411 | 1.9861 | 1.9586 | 1.9147 | 1.8687 | 1.8203 | 1.7946 | 1.7689 | 1.7138 | 1.6541 |
| **2.8409** | **2.7938** | **2.7530** | **2.6521** | **2.6017** | **2.5223** | **2.4397** | **2.3535** | **2.3082** | **2.2629** | **2.1670** | **2.0642** |
| 2.0749 | 2.0495 | 2.0275 | 1.9722 | 1.9446 | 1.9005 | 1.8543 | 1.8055 | 1.7796 | 1.7537 | 1.6981 | 1.6377 |
| **2.8135** | **2.7664** | **2.7256** | **2.6247** | **2.5742** | **2.4946** | **2.4118** | **2.3253** | **2.2799** | **2.2344** | **2.1378** | **2.0342** |
| 2.0624 | 2.0369 | 2.0148 | 1.9594 | 1.9317 | 1.8874 | 1.8409 | 1.7918 | 1.7657 | 1.7396 | 1.6835 | 1.6223 |
| **2.7881** | **2.7410** | **2.7002** | **2.5992** | **2.5487** | **2.4689** | **2.3860** | **2.2992** | **2.2536** | **2.2079** | **2.1107** | **2.0062** |
| 1.9731 | 1.9471 | 1.9245 | 1.8674 | 1.8389 | 1.7929 | 1.7444 | 1.6928 | 1.6651 | 1.6373 | 1.5766 | 1.5089 |
| **2.6097** | **2.5625** | **2.5216** | **2.4198** | **2.3689** | **2.2880** | **2.2034** | **2.1142** | **2.0668** | **2.0194** | **1.9172** | **1.8047** |
| 1.9297 | 1.9033 | 1.8805 | 1.8225 | 1.7935 | 1.7465 | 1.6968 | 1.6436 | 1.6147 | 1.5858 | 1.5220 | 1.4491 |
| **2.5253** | **2.4780** | **2.4370** | **2.3346** | **2.2834** | **2.2017** | **2.1160** | **2.0251** | **1.9765** | **1.9279** | **1.8218** | **1.7027** |
| 1.8862 | 1.8595 | 1.8364 | 1.7775 | 1.7480 | 1.7001 | 1.6491 | 1.5943 | 1.5643 | 1.5343 | 1.4673 | 1.3893 |
| **2.4408** | **2.3934** | **2.3523** | **2.2493** | **2.1978** | **2.1154** | **2.0285** | **1.9360** | **1.8862** | **1.8363** | **1.7263** | **1.6006** |
| 1.8440 | 1.8169 | 1.7935 | 1.7334 | 1.7034 | 1.6543 | 1.6017 | 1.5448 | 1.5132 | 1.4817 | 1.4096 | 1.3216 |
| **2.3607** | **2.3131** | **2.2719** | **2.1681** | **2.1162** | **2.0327** | **1.9443** | **1.8494** | **1.7977** | **1.7460** | **1.6297** | **1.4906** |
| 1.8017 | 1.7743 | 1.7505 | 1.6893 | 1.6587 | 1.6084 | 1.5543 | 1.4952 | 1.4621 | 1.4290 | 1.3519 | 1.2539 |
| **2.2806** | **2.2329** | **2.1915** | **2.0869** | **2.0346** | **1.9500** | **1.8600** | **1.7628** | **1.7093** | **1.6557** | **1.5330** | **1.3805** |
| 1.7192 | 1.6909 | 1.6664 | 1.6025 | 1.5705 | 1.5173 | 1.4591 | 1.3940 | 1.3560 | 1.3180 | 1.2214 | 1.0000 |
| **2.1285** | **2.0803** | **2.0385** | **1.9317** | **1.8783** | **1.7908** | **1.6964** | **1.5923** | **1.5327** | **1.4730** | **1.3246** | **1.0000** |

# APPENDIX F
## CRITICAL VALUES FOR THE CHI-SQUARE ($\chi^2$) DISTRIBUTION

| df | Significance levels for upper tail test | | | | | |
|---|---|---|---|---|---|---|
| | .25 | .10 | .05 | .025 | .01 | .005 |
| 1 | 1.323 | 2.706 | 3.841 | 5.024 | 6.635 | 7.879 |
| 2 | 2.773 | 4.605 | 5.991 | 7.378 | 9.210 | 10.597 |
| 3 | 4.108 | 6.251 | 7.815 | 9.348 | 11.345 | 12.838 |
| 4 | 5.385 | 7.779 | 9.488 | 11.143 | 13.277 | 14.860 |
| 5 | 6.626 | 9.236 | 11.071 | 12.833 | 15.086 | 16.750 |
| 6 | 7.841 | 10.645 | 12.592 | 14.449 | 16.812 | 18.548 |
| 7 | 9.037 | 12.017 | 14.067 | 16.013 | 18.475 | 20.278 |
| 8 | 10.219 | 13.362 | 15.507 | 17.535 | 20.090 | 21.955 |
| 9 | 11.389 | 14.684 | 16.919 | 19.023 | 21.666 | 23.589 |
| 10 | 12.549 | 15.987 | 18.307 | 20.483 | 23.209 | 25.188 |
| 11 | 13.701 | 17.275 | 19.675 | 21.920 | 24.725 | 26.757 |
| 12 | 14.845 | 18.549 | 21.026 | 23.337 | 26.217 | 28.299 |
| 13 | 15.984 | 19.812 | 22.362 | 24.736 | 27.688 | 29.819 |
| 14 | 17.117 | 21.064 | 23.685 | 26.119 | 29.141 | 31.319 |
| 15 | 18.245 | 22.307 | 24.996 | 27.488 | 30.578 | 32.801 |
| 16 | 19.369 | 23.542 | 26.296 | 28.845 | 32.000 | 34.267 |
| 17 | 20.489 | 24.769 | 27.587 | 30.191 | 33.409 | 35.718 |
| 18 | 21.605 | 25.989 | 28.869 | 31.526 | 34.805 | 37.156 |
| 19 | 22.718 | 27.204 | 30.144 | 32.852 | 36.191 | 38.582 |
| 20 | 23.828 | 28.412 | 31.410 | 34.170 | 37.566 | 39.997 |
| 21 | 24.935 | 29.615 | 32.671 | 35.479 | 38.932 | 41.401 |
| 22 | 26.039 | 30.813 | 33.924 | 36.781 | 40.289 | 42.796 |
| 23 | 27.141 | 32.007 | 35.172 | 38.076 | 41.638 | 44.181 |
| 24 | 28.241 | 33.196 | 36.415 | 39.364 | 42.980 | 45.559 |
| 25 | 29.339 | 34.382 | 37.652 | 40.646 | 44.314 | 46.928 |
| 26 | 30.435 | 35.563 | 38.885 | 41.923 | 45.642 | 48.290 |
| 27 | 31.528 | 36.741 | 40.113 | 43.194 | 46.963 | 49.645 |
| 28 | 32.620 | 37.916 | 41.337 | 44.461 | 48.278 | 50.993 |
| 29 | 33.711 | 39.087 | 42.557 | 45.722 | 49.588 | 52.336 |
| 30 | 34.800 | 40.256 | 43.773 | 46.979 | 50.892 | 53.672 |
| 31 | 35.887 | 41.422 | 44.985 | 48.232 | 52.191 | 55.003 |
| 32 | 36.973 | 42.585 | 46.194 | 49.480 | 53.486 | 56.328 |
| 33 | 38.058 | 43.745 | 47.400 | 50.725 | 54.776 | 57.648 |
| 34 | 39.141 | 44.903 | 48.602 | 51.966 | 56.061 | 58.964 |
| 35 | 40.223 | 46.059 | 49.802 | 53.203 | 57.342 | 60.275 |
| 36 | 41.304 | 47.212 | 50.998 | 54.437 | 58.619 | 61.581 |
| 37 | 42.383 | 48.363 | 52.192 | 55.668 | 59.892 | 62.883 |
| 38 | 43.462 | 49.513 | 53.384 | 56.896 | 61.162 | 64.181 |
| 39 | 44.539 | 50.660 | 54.572 | 58.120 | 62.428 | 65.476 |
| 40 | 45.616 | 51.805 | 55.758 | 59.342 | 63.691 | 66.766 |
| 41 | 46.692 | 52.949 | 56.942 | 60.561 | 64.950 | 68.053 |
| 42 | 47.766 | 54.090 | 58.124 | 61.777 | 66.206 | 69.336 |
| 43 | 48.840 | 55.230 | 59.304 | 62.990 | 67.459 | 70.616 |
| 44 | 49.913 | 56.369 | 60.481 | 64.201 | 68.710 | 77.893 |
| 45 | 50.985 | 57.505 | 61.656 | 65.410 | 69.957 | 73.166 |

**341**

APPENDIX F
Critical Values
for the Chi-
Square ($\chi^2$)
Distribution

**Significance levels for upper tail test**

| df | .25 | .10 | .05 | .025 | .01 | .005 |
|----|-----|-----|-----|------|-----|------|
| 46 | 52.056 | 58.641 | 62.830 | 66.617 | 71.201 | 74.437 |
| 47 | 53.127 | 59.774 | 64.001 | 67.821 | 72.443 | 75.704 |
| 48 | 54.196 | 60.907 | 65.171 | 69.023 | 73.683 | 76.969 |
| 49 | 55.265 | 62.038 | 66.339 | 70.222 | 74.919 | 78.231 |
| 50 | 56.334 | 63.167 | 67.505 | 71.420 | 76.154 | 79.490 |
| 51 | 57.401 | 64.295 | 68.669 | 72.616 | 77.386 | 80.747 |
| 52 | 58.468 | 65.422 | 69.832 | 73.810 | 78.616 | 82.001 |
| 53 | 59.534 | 66.548 | 70.993 | 75.002 | 79.843 | 83.253 |
| 54 | 60.600 | 67.673 | 72.153 | 76.192 | 81.069 | 84.502 |
| 55 | 61.665 | 68.796 | 73.311 | 77.380 | 82.292 | 85.749 |
| 56 | 62.729 | 69.919 | 74.468 | 78.567 | 83.513 | 86.994 |
| 57 | 63.793 | 71.040 | 75.624 | 76.752 | 84.733 | 88.236 |
| 58 | 64.857 | 72.160 | 76.778 | 80.936 | 85.950 | 89.477 |
| 59 | 65.919 | 73.279 | 77.931 | 82.117 | 87.166 | 90.715 |
| 60 | 66.981 | 74.397 | 79.082 | 83.298 | 88.379 | 91.952 |
| 61 | 68.043 | 75.514 | 80.232 | 84.476 | 89.591 | 93.186 |
| 62 | 69.104 | 76.630 | 81.381 | 85.654 | 90.802 | 94.419 |
| 63 | 70.165 | 77.745 | 82.529 | 86.830 | 92.010 | 95.649 |
| 64 | 71.225 | 78.860 | 83.675 | 88.004 | 93.217 | 96.878 |
| 65 | 72.285 | 79.973 | 84.821 | 89.177 | 94.422 | 98.105 |
| 66 | 73.344 | 81.085 | 85.965 | 90.349 | 95.626 | 99.330 |
| 67 | 74.403 | 82.197 | 87.108 | 91.519 | 96.828 | 100.554 |
| 68 | 75.461 | 83.308 | 88.250 | 92.689 | 98.028 | 101.776 |
| 69 | 76.519 | 84.418 | 89.391 | 93.856 | 99.228 | 102.996 |
| 70 | 77.577 | 85.527 | 90.531 | 95.023 | 100.425 | 104.215 |
| 71 | 78.634 | 86.635 | 91.670 | 96.189 | 101.621 | 105.432 |
| 72 | 79.690 | 87.743 | 92.808 | 97.353 | 102.816 | 106.648 |
| 73 | 80.747 | 88.850 | 93.945 | 98.516 | 104.010 | 107.862 |
| 74 | 81.803 | 89.956 | 95.081 | 99.678 | 105.202 | 109.074 |
| 75 | 82.858 | 91.061 | 96.217 | 100.839 | 106.393 | 110.286 |
| 76 | 83.913 | 92.166 | 97.351 | 101.999 | 107.583 | 111.495 |
| 77 | 84.968 | 93.270 | 98.484 | 103.158 | 108.771 | 112.704 |
| 78 | 86.022 | 94.374 | 99.617 | 104.316 | 109.958 | 113.911 |
| 79 | 87.077 | 95.476 | 100.749 | 105.473 | 111.144 | 115.117 |
| 80 | 88.130 | 96.578 | 101.879 | 106.629 | 112.329 | 116.321 |
| 81 | 89.184 | 97.680 | 103.010 | 107.783 | 113.512 | 117.524 |
| 82 | 90.237 | 98.780 | 104.139 | 108.937 | 114.695 | 118.726 |
| 83 | 91.289 | 99.880 | 105.267 | 110.090 | 115.876 | 119.927 |
| 84 | 92.342 | 100.980 | 106.395 | 111.242 | 117.057 | 121.126 |
| 85 | 93.394 | 102.079 | 107.522 | 112.393 | 118.236 | 122.325 |
| 86 | 94.446 | 103.177 | 108.648 | 113.544 | 119.414 | 123.522 |
| 87 | 95.497 | 104.275 | 109.773 | 114.693 | 120.591 | 124.718 |
| 88 | 96.548 | 105.372 | 110.898 | 115.841 | 121.767 | 125.913 |
| 89 | 97.599 | 106.469 | 112.022 | 116.989 | 122.942 | 127.106 |
| 90 | 98.650 | 107.565 | 113.145 | 118.136 | 124.116 | 128.299 |

**342**

APPENDIX F
Critical Values
for the Chi-
Square ($\chi^2$)
Distribution

### Significance levels for upper tail test

| df | .25 | .10 | .05 | .025 | .01 | .005 |
|---|---|---|---|---|---|---|
| 91 | 99.700 | 108.661 | 114.268 | 119.282 | 125.289 | 129.491 |
| 92 | 100.750 | 109.756 | 115.390 | 120.427 | 126.462 | 130.681 |
| 93 | 101.800 | 110.850 | 116.511 | 121.571 | 127.633 | 131.871 |
| 94 | 102.850 | 111.944 | 117.632 | 122.715 | 128.803 | 133.059 |
| 95 | 103.899 | 113.038 | 118.752 | 123.858 | 129.973 | 134.247 |
| 96 | 104.948 | 114.131 | 119.871 | 125.000 | 131.141 | 135.433 |
| 97 | 105.997 | 115.223 | 120.990 | 126.141 | 132.309 | 136.619 |
| 98 | 107.045 | 116.315 | 122.108 | 127.282 | 133.476 | 137.803 |
| 99 | 108.093 | 117.407 | 123.225 | 128.422 | 134.642 | 138.987 |
| 100 | 109.141 | 118.498 | 124.342 | 129.561 | 135.807 | 140.169 |
| 102 | 111.236 | 120.679 | 126.574 | 131.838 | 138.134 | 142.532 |
| 104 | 113.331 | 122.858 | 128.804 | 134.111 | 140.459 | 144.891 |
| 106 | 115.424 | 125.035 | 131.031 | 136.382 | 142.780 | 147.247 |
| 108 | 117.517 | 127.211 | 133.257 | 138.651 | 145.099 | 149.599 |
| 110 | 119.608 | 129.385 | 135.480 | 140.917 | 147.414 | 151.948 |
| 112 | 121.699 | 131.558 | 137.701 | 143.180 | 149.727 | 154.294 |
| 114 | 123.789 | 133.729 | 139.921 | 145.441 | 152.037 | 156.637 |
| 116 | 125.878 | 135.898 | 142.138 | 147.700 | 154.344 | 158.977 |
| 118 | 127.967 | 138.066 | 144.354 | 149.957 | 156.648 | 161.314 |
| 120 | 130.055 | 140.233 | 146.567 | 152.211 | 158.950 | 163.648 |
| 122 | 132.142 | 142.398 | 148.779 | 154.464 | 161.250 | 165.980 |
| 124 | 134.228 | 144.562 | 150.989 | 156.714 | 163.546 | 168.308 |
| 126 | 136.313 | 146.724 | 153.198 | 158.962 | 165.841 | 170.634 |
| 128 | 138.398 | 148.885 | 155.405 | 161.209 | 168.133 | 172.957 |
| 130 | 140.482 | 151.045 | 157.610 | 163.453 | 170.423 | 175.278 |
| 132 | 142.566 | 153.204 | 159.814 | 165.696 | 172.711 | 177.597 |
| 134 | 144.649 | 155.361 | 162.016 | 167.936 | 174.996 | 179.913 |
| 136 | 146.731 | 157.518 | 164.216 | 170.175 | 177.280 | 182.226 |
| 138 | 148.813 | 159.673 | 166.415 | 172.412 | 179.561 | 184.538 |
| 140 | 150.894 | 161.827 | 168.613 | 174.648 | 181.840 | 186.847 |
| 142 | 152.975 | 163.980 | 170.809 | 176.882 | 184.118 | 189.154 |
| 144 | 155.055 | 166.132 | 173.004 | 179.114 | 186.393 | 191.458 |
| 146 | 157.134 | 168.283 | 175.198 | 181.344 | 188.666 | 193.761 |
| 148 | 159.213 | 170.432 | 177.390 | 183.573 | 190.938 | 196.062 |
| 150 | 161.291 | 172.581 | 179.581 | 185.800 | 193.208 | 198.360 |
| 200 | 213.102 | 226.021 | 233.994 | 241.058 | 249.445 | 255.264 |
| 250 | 264.697 | 279.050 | 287.882 | 295.689 | 304.940 | 311.346 |
| 300 | 316.138 | 331.789 | 341.395 | 349.874 | 359.906 | 366.844 |
| 400 | 418.697 | 436.649 | 447.632 | 457.305 | 468.724 | 476.606 |
| 500 | 520.950 | 540.930 | 553.127 | 563.852 | 576.493 | 585.207 |
| 600 | 622.988 | 644.800 | 658.094 | 669.769 | 683.516 | 692.982 |
| 700 | 724.861 | 748.359 | 762.661 | 775.211 | 789.974 | 800.131 |
| 800 | 826.604 | 851.671 | 866.911 | 880.275 | 895.984 | 906.786 |
| 900 | 928.241 | 954.782 | 970.904 | 985.032 | 1001.630 | 1013.036 |
| 1000 | 1029.790 | 1057.724 | 1074.679 | 1089.531 | 1106.969 | 1118.948 |

D. B. Owen, *Handbook of Statistical Tables*, © 1962, Addison-Wesley, Reading, Massachusetts. Pgs. 51–55 (Table). Reprinted with permission.

# GLOSSARY OF SYMBOLS

$d$ — deviation of a sample score from the sample mean

$D$ — deviation of a subgroup mean from the grand mean; also, deviation of a sample score from the population mean

$df$ — degrees of freedom

$E$ — expected frequency

$F$ — F distribution statistic

$H_0$ — null hypothesis

$H_1, \ldots, H_n$ — research (or alternative) hypothesis

$k$ — number of categories or cells in a sample

$MS$ — mean square

$n$ — sample size

$N$ — population size; also, grand sum

$O$ — observed frequency

$p$ — probability; also population proportion

$\bar{p}$ — sample proportion

$\bar{p}_e$ — estimate of a population proportion

$q$ — $1 - p$

$\bar{q}$ — $1 - \bar{p}$

$\bar{q}_e$ — $1 - \bar{p}_e$

$r$ — a linear correlation coefficient

$r^2$ — a linear coefficient of determination

$R$ — a multiple linear correlation coefficient

$R^2$ — a multiple linear coefficient of determination

$s$ — sample standard deviation

$s^2$ — sample variance

$s_e$ — standard error of estimate

$s_{\bar{p}}$ — standard error of proportions estimated from sample data

$s_{\bar{p}_1 - \bar{p}_2}$ — standard error of difference between proportions estimated from sample data

$s_{\bar{x}}$ — standard error of the mean estimated from sample data

$s_{\bar{x}_1 - \bar{x}_2}$ — standard error of difference between means estimated from sample data

$SS$ — sum of squares

$t$ — Student's $t$ distribution statistic

$x$ — sample score

$\bar{x}$ — sample mean

$\bar{X}$ — grand mean

$z$ — normal distribution statistic; a standard score

$\alpha$ (alpha) — probability of a Type I error

$\beta$ (beta) — probability of a Type II error

$1 - \beta$ — power of a statistical test

$\eta$ (eta) — a nonlinear correlation coefficient

$\mu$ (mu) — population mean

$\rho$ (rho) — population linear correlation coefficient

$\sigma$ (lowercase sigma) — population standard deviation

$\sigma^2$ — population variance

$\sigma_{\bar{p}}$ — population standard error of proportions

$\sigma_{\bar{p}_1 - \bar{p}_2}$ — population standard error of difference between proportions

$\sigma_{\bar{x}}$ — population standard error of the mean

343

| | | | |
|---|---|---|---|
| $\sigma_{\bar{x} - \bar{x}}$ | population standard error of difference between means | $\neq$ | not equal to |
| $\Sigma$ (uppercase sigma) | summation notation | $<$ | less than |
| | | $\leq$ | less than or equal to |
| $\phi$ (phi) | a linear correlation coefficient | $>$ | greater than |
| $\chi^2$ (chi-square) | chi-square statistic | $\geq$ | greater than or equal to |
| $=$ | equal to | $\approx$ | approximately equal to |
| | | $\sqrt{\phantom{x}}$ | square root |

# GLOSSARY OF TERMS

**Actional realism.**  An ontological perspective that incorporates some elements of determinism into the choice-oriented model of human behavior, actionalism.

**Actionalism.**  An ontological perspective that assumes people are active agents who possess the capacity for choice and self-motivated behavior.

**Activist research.**  Topical or issue-oriented research.

**Adjacency pair.**  Two sequential utterances, each produced by a different speaker.

**All-organismic paradigm.**  An experiment that employs only independent variables representing internal characteristics of subjects.

**All-stimulus paradigm.**  An experiment employing only externally manipulated independent variables.

**Alpha.**  The probability of committing a Type I error.

**Alternative hypothesis.**  See **Research hypothesis.**

**Analysis of variance (ANOVA).**  A set of methods for assessing significance of differences among two or more population means based on data derived from independent or related samples.

**Anonymity.**  A quality describing a researcher's inability to identify a given response or behavior with a given research participant.

**Applied research.**  An analysis of theoretical relationships for the purpose of understanding and solving practical problems.

**Artistic criticism.**  An assessment of the aesthetic qualities of messages.

**Bar graph.**  A presentation used to summarize data, especially nominal data, in which the display consists of rectangles or bars, each having a height equal to the frequency of the score or group it represents.

**Basic research.**  An analysis of theoretical relationships with no immediate concern for their practical implications.

**Behavioral data.**  Information collected by observing people's overt communicative activities.

**Behavioral rule.**  An anticipatory assumption about appropriate utterances in specified social contexts.

**Beta.**  The probability of committing a Type II error.

**Between-groups variance.**  Systematic differences between samples. See **Systematic variance.**

**Bivariate correlation.**  A relationship between two and only two variables.

**Causal explanation.**  A theory that accounts for a pattern of effects by referring to uncontrollable antecedents. See **Law.**

**Cause.**  An antecedent condition that produces a consequent effect over which individuals have no control.

**Cell.**  An experimental treatment group.

**Chi-square ($\chi^2$).**  A test statistic for assessing significance of difference between two or more independent samples of frequencies.

**Closed question.** A forced-choice statement that asks respondents to select responses from a set of fixed options supplied by the researcher.

**Cluster analysis.** A procedure for grouping a large set of measurements into related classes.

**Coding.** A process of sorting data into categories.

**Coding scheme.** A consistent system for classifying verbal and nonverbal cues.

**Coefficient of correlation.** A measure of the strength of relationship between two variables.

**Coefficient of determination.** A measure of the percentage of combined variability that is common to two variables.

**Coefficient of multiple correlation.** A measure of the strength of relationship among three or more variables.

**Coefficient of multiple determination.** A measure of the percentage of variability in a criterion variable that is explained by its predictor variables.

**Communality.** The ethical principle according to which researchers must freely and candidly share their research findings with others. (The statistical concept of "communality" is not discussed in this book.)

**Conceptual definition.** A statement defining a construct by relating it to other constructs.

**Conceptualization.** The process of formulating and defining a problem in communication research.

**Confidence interval.** The set of values around a sample statistic within which a population parameter is "believed" to reside.

**Confidence level.** The probability that a confidence interval contains the appropriate population parameter.

**Confidentiality.** A quality describing a researcher's promise not to publicly identify a given response or behavior with a given research participant.

**Confounded effects.** Research results that may be contaminated by the presence of one or more systematic, but uncontrolled variables.

**Construct.** An abstract class of objects bound together by the possession of some common characteristic.

**Constructive realism.** The epistemological perspective that incorporates some elements of empiricism into a constructivist viewpoint.

**Constructivism.** The epistemological perspective according to which the world is subjectively created by the meanings people assign to observations.

**Content analysis.** A methodology for describing and inferring characteristics of messages.

**Contextual information.** Situational data relevant to messages.

**Contingency question.** An information-seeking statement that is applicable to a subset of a sample of respondents.

**Contingency table analysis.** An analysis of differences among categories of frequencies associated with two or more samples. See **Multiple-sample chi-square.**

**Continuous variable.** A variable that takes on an ordered set of values ranging from low to high.

**Control group.** A sample of subjects that is not exposed to an experimental treatment or manipulation.

**Convenience sampling.** A nonrandom selection of elements that are readily accessible to a researcher.

**Conversation.** An interactive discourse form characterized by flexible rules of turn-taking.

**Conversational analysis.** A methodology for exploring the structure and functions of rules governing conversations.

**Conversational coherence.** A quality describing the relationship between conversational meanings and actions and conversational goals.

**Conversational data base.** A body of conversations or conversational excerpts that represents a domain of interest.

**Conversational function.** The organization of communicative actions.

**Conversational structure.** The organization of communicative meanings.

**Covariance.** Variance that is common to two or more variables.

**Cover story.** An instruction intended to mislead research participants regarding the nature of a research hypothesis.

**Cramer's V coefficient.** A coefficient that registers the strength of association between two nominal variables having two or more frequency categories each.

**Creative imagination.** A level of meaning concerned with the dramatic characterizations in messages. (Also called the level of nondiscursive logic.)

**Criterion variable.** A dependent variable.

**Critical region.** The set of values of a test statistic for which we will reject the null hypothesis. (When the value of a test statistic falls within the critical region, we are justified in rejecting the null hypothesis.)

**Critical value.** A "cutoff" number or a numerical "dividing line" that defines a critical region.

**Cross-sectional research.** Observations at a single point in time.

**Cross-sectional survey.** A survey of a sample at a single point in time.

**Curvilinear correlation.** A relationship between two variables that does not follow a straight-line pattern.

**Data.** Reports of observations.

**Data-to-theory.** An inductive approach to the discovery of theory, which assumes that explanations are derived principally from observations.

**Debriefing.** An instruction that informs research participants of a study's true nature.

**Deduction.** The reasoning process that begins with a general premise assumed to be true and derives a conclusion about particular instances within the initial generalization.

**Degrees of freedom.** Indices of sample size.

**Delivery.** The presentation of a message.

**Demand characteristics.** Situational cues that implicitly convey a research hypothesis to research participants.

**Dependence correlation.** An association between independent and dependent variables.

**Dependent variable.** An outcome or output variable that represents a set of measurable effects.

**Derived term.** A term that must be defined by the use of primitive terms. See **Primitive term.**

**Descriptive statistics** (singular). The science of summarizing the characteristics of sample data.

**Descriptive term.** A term designating classes of communication phenomena or constructs.

**Determinism.** See **Mechanism.**

**Direct correlation.** A linear relationship occurring when two variables rise and fall together.

**Disciplinary matrix.** See **Paradigm.**

**Discovery.** The process of constructing theoretical explanations.

**Discrete variable.** A variable whose values change by distinct steps or categories.

**Discriminative power.** A scale's ability to measure the construct under investigation and no other construct.

**Discursive logic.** A level of meaning pertaining to the rational progression of ideas in a message.

**Disinterestedness.** The ethical principle according to which researchers are to pursue knowledge for its own sake.

**Disordinal interaction.** An effect occurring when an independent variable exhibits significant differences at each of a second independent variable's treatment levels.

**Disposition.** The organization of materials in a message.

**Distribution.** See **Frequency distribution; Theoretical probability distribution;** and **Normal distribution.**

**Double-barreled question.** A interrogatory statement that calls for a single response applying to two (or more) different issues.

**Double-blind paradigm.** A research design in which neither researchers nor research subjects are aware of the hypothesis being tested.

**Dramatistic criticism.** Evaluation of speech as a theatrical presentation.

**Duplicate elements.** Population members listed more than once in a sampling frame.

**Ecological validity.** A quality indicating that the results obtained in a research environment are generalizable to more natural social settings.

**Eigenvalue.** The sum of the squared factor loadings associated with a single hypothetical factor.

**Element.** The basic unit or "thing" about which information is collected.

**Elementary linkage analysis.** A simple cluster analysis that creates clusters by grouping variables that correlate strongly with one another and weakly with other variables.

**Elicited conversation.** Talk recalled or constructed by research participants at a researcher's request.

**Elocution.** The use of language and style in a message.

**Empirical indicators.** The properties of a construct or variable that can be observed and measured.

**Empiricism.** The epistemological perspective according to which knowledge is best derived from observations, with minimal intrusion of thought processes.

**Entertainment discourse.** Discourse designed to amuse and delight.

**Epistemology.** The science of knowledge.

**Error variance.** Fluctuations in scores that are attributable to random or chance factors. See **Within-groups variance.**

**Eta coefficient.** An index of nonlinear correlation between two variables.

**Ethics.** An evolutionary system of value judgments about the goodness or badness of research practices.

**Ethos.** The credibility of a message source.

**Evaluation apprehension.** Concern over whether one will present a positive self-image when participating in research.

**Evolutionary model.** The perspective on paradigmatic change according to which alternative world views can coexist and genuine paradigmatic change is gradual rather than abrupt.

**Experimental group.** A sample of subjects exposed to some treatment or manipulation.

**Experimental research.** The type of research design whose purpose is to assess the relationship between independent and dependent variables.

**External validity.** A quality indicating that sample results can be inferred to relevant parent populations.

**Extrinsic data analysis.** The analysis of the context of a discourse.

**Factor.** An independent variable.

**Factor analysis.** A method for assessing the interrelationships among a large set of variables for purposes of reducing the large set to a smaller set of hypothetical factors.

**Factor loading.** A coefficient that registers the magnitude and direction of the relationship between an observed variable and a hypothetical factor.

**Factorial design.** A complex experiment having two or more independent variables, each with two or more treatment levels.

**Factual question.** A statement soliciting information about a respondent's background, behaviors, and habits.

**Fantasy theme.** A myth-making story or a dramatic reference in a message that conveys some general "truth."

**Fantasy theme analysis.** A method of analyzing and criticizing narrative discourse as a myth-making activity akin to dramatic theatre presentations.

**Fantasy type.** A general category of recurring fantasy themes.

**Field research.** Observations in a natural social setting.

**Filter question.** A question that identifies a subset in a sample of respondents.

**Foreign elements.** Elements listed in a sampling frame that are not legitimate population members.

**F ratio.** The ratio of between-groups variance to within-groups variance. See **Analysis of variance.**

**Free-response scaling.** A measurement procedure that asks individuals to respond in an open-ended fashion to some communication stimulus.

**Frequency distribution.** An empirically derived description or summary of data that lists the scores or values together with their frequencies. Each score may be listed alone or scores may be categorized or grouped.

**Frequency polygon.** A graphic presentation used to summarize data, characterized by a series of broken lines joining points on a graph. Each point has a horizontal coordinate that references a score or group of scores and a vertical coordinate that equals the frequency of that score (or group).

**F test.** See **Analysis of variance; F ratio.**

**Functional coherence.** A quality describing the

relationship between conversational actions and conversational goals.

**Functional paradigm.** A world view that treats communicative antecedents and consequences as central to an understanding of human communication.

**Functional research.** An analysis that focuses on communicative antecedents and consequences rather than communicative meanings.

**Funnel pattern.** An organizational sequence for presenting questions that begins with broad questions followed by progressively narrower ones.

**Garbage can research model.** A descriptive conceptualization positing that the intellectual and material resources available to researchers profoundly affect how research is conducted.

**Histogram.** A graphic presentation used to summarize data; similar to a bar graph except that the horizontal scale is a continuous one.

**Historical criticism.** An evaluation of the historical "truth" or normative utility of a message.

**History.** Incidental environmental changes occurring during data collection.

**Honesty.** The ethical principle according to which researchers must be truthful with themselves, the scholarly community, and research participants.

**Humanism.** A research perspective that utilizes analytical and critical methodologies to support claims about narrative data. See **Rhetorical criticism.**

**Humanistic science.** A genre of hybrid research methods partaking of both scientific and humanistic assumptions. See **Scientific inquiry; Humanism.**

**Hypothesis.** A "prediction" about a population.

**Illocutionary act.** The action that one communicator "does to" another with an utterance or sequence of utterances.

**Independent groups.** Two or more samples whose members are unrelated to one another.

**Independent groups design.** An experiment characterized by the random assignment of different samples of subjects to each experimental cell.

**Independent variable.** An input variable that consists of either a manipulation or a natural characteristic of subjects.

**Induction.** The reasoning process that begins with observations of particular instances of a phenomenon and infers a general conclusion about the probable properties of the phenomenon.

**Inductive–statistical theory.** A probabilistic generalization derived from observations.

**Inferential statistics (singular).** The science of drawing conclusions about population characteristics based on sample descriptions.

**Informational discourse.** Messages whose function is to educate receivers about events in the physical and social world.

**Informed consent.** Voluntary participation in a research project based on full and accurate knowledge of the nature of the research.

**In loco parentis.** Acting in the place of parents.

**Intact groups (sample) assignment.** A non-probability method of assigning matched aggregate groups to experimental conditions.

**Intellectual integrity.** The faithfulness with which researchers follow ethical norms of research.

**Intellectual resources.** A researcher's knowledge, skills, and special research interests.

**Intentional rule.** A reason-based explanation that emphasizes the deliberative nature of individual goal-seeking actions.

**Interaction effect.** The joint impact of two or more independent variables on a dependent measure.

**Interactive discourse.** A communication form characterized by alternating source–receiver roles.

**Interdependence correlation.** An association among three or more variables without regard to independent–dependent connections.

**Internal validity.** A quality indicating that a research design measures the sample effects of interest to a researcher and no other effects. Applied to an experiment, internal validity exists when dependent measures are attributable to the independent variables.

**Interpretative rule.** An anticipatory assumption about the meaning of utterances in specified contexts.

**Interpretive paradigm.** A world view that treats communicative meanings as central to an understanding of human communication.

**Interpretive research.** An analysis of communicative meanings.

**Interrater reliability coefficient.** A statistical index that registers the extent to which several judgments converge.

**Intersubjectivity.** A collective agreement or consensus that some phenomenon or characteristic of a phenomenon has "real" existence.

**Interval measurement.** The assignment of numbers to represent a series of values that have an arbitrary zero point and equal distances between the values.

**Intervening variable.** A variable other than a designated independent variable that has the capacity to influence dependent measures.

**Intrinsic data analysis.** An analysis of the manifest and latent meanings of message content.

**Invention.** The gathering and adaptation to audiences of the materials in a message.

**Inventory question.** A closed interrogatory statement consisting of a checklist of response options that are not mutually exclusive.

**Inverse correlation.** A linear relationship occurring when one of two variables increases as the other systematically declines.

**Inverted funnel pattern.** An organizational sequence for presenting questions that begins with narrowly focused questions followed by more general ones.

**Inverted-U correlation.** A curvilinear relationship between two variables occurring when both initially increase together, whereupon one continues to increase as the other systematically declines.

**Item nonresponse.** The inability to collect all required information from each element in a sample.

**Justification.** The process of verifying theoretical explanations.

**Laboratory research.** Observations in a controlled environment.

**Latent content.** Deep layers of meaning that must be inferred from a text or script.

**Latent variable.** A variable that cannot be directly observed.

**Law.** A theory that explains behavior by referring to uncontrollable causes and covariates.

**Layout.** The physical features of a written measuring instrument.

**Leading question.** An interrogatory statement that encourages a biased response.

**Likert scales.** A series of positive and negative opinion statements, each of which is usually accompanied by a five-point or seven-point response scale.

**Linear correlation.** A straight-line relationship between two variables.

**Literary conversation.** Samples of interactive discourse in novels or plays.

**Logical positivism.** The epistemological perspective according to which observations (with a minimal intrusion of thought) can generate correlative knowledge about the objective world.

**Logical positivist law.** A theory that explains behavior by referring to empirical correlations.

**Logos.** The argumentative content of a message.

**Longitudinal research.** Observations of changes over time.

**Main effect.** The unique impact of a single independent variable on a dependent measure.

**Manifest content.** Surface meanings that are apparent in a text or script.

**Manifest variable.** A variable that can be directly observed.

**Mapping.** The systematic matching of a set of substantive concepts (the empirical indicators of variables) with a corresponding set of structural values (numerals).

**Matched subject assignment.** A nonprobability method of assigning paired individual subjects to experimental groups.

**Material resources.** Research support factors including finances, equipment, subjects, and facilities.

**Maturation.** Physiological and psychological changes occurring in research participants during data collection.

**Mean.** The sum of all the scores in a distribution divided by the total number of distribution scores.

**Mean square.** A sum of squares divided by the appropriate degrees of freedom; a variance. See **Variance.**

**Measurement.** The process of assigning numerals to objects or events according to rules.

**Measuring instrument.** A set of scales for assigning numerals to a construct's empirical indicators.

**Mechanism.** An ontological perspective that regards humans as machine-like, having no capacity for choice and self-motivated behavior.

**Mechanistic empiricism.** The epistemological perspective according to which observations (with a minimal intrusion of thought) can generate cause-to-effect knowledge about the world.

**Median.** The midpoint of a distribution above and below which half the distribution's scores fall.

**Memory.** Techniques for recalling message materials.

**Metatheory.** Assumptions about the nature of theoretical explanations.

**Methodology.** Assumptions about research strategies.

**Missing elements.** Legitimate members of a population that are not listed in a sampling frame.

**Mixed independent groups/repeated measures design.** An experiment characterized by the random assignment of different groups of subjects to one independent variable's treatment cells, although the same subjects are assigned to a second independent variable's treatment cells.

**Mixed model paradigm.** An experiment that employs at least one stimulus-independent variable and at least one organismic-independent variable.

**Mode.** The most frequently occurring score(s) in a distribution.

**Model.** A verbal or visual representation of the structure or functions of some object or process.

**Monism.** A perspective characterized by the belief that a single paradigm is appropriate for scholarly inquiry.

**Mortality.** The loss of research participants during a data collection process.

**Multidimensional measuring instrument.** A set of measurement scales that, as a group, measure more than one dimension associated with a construct.

**Multiple correlation.** A statistical procedure for measuring the strength of association between a set of independent (predictor) variables and a single dependent (criterion) variable.

**Multiple-factor analysis of variance.** A test statistic for assessing group differences that are attributable to more than one independent variable.

**Multiple regression.** A statistical procedure for predicting the probable values of a single dependent (criterion) variable based on the values of a set of independent (predictor) variables. See **Regression analysis.**

**Multiple-sample chi-square.** A test statistic for assessing differences among the categories of frequencies associated with two or more independent samples.

**Multiple-sample survey.** A survey that examines two or more samples for purposes of describing and explaining population relationships and differences.

**Multistage cluster sampling.** The systematic or simple random selection of clusters from a large population followed by a systematic or simple random selection of elements within each cluster.

**Multivariate correlation.** A correlation among three or more variables.

**Myth.** A story that symbolizes a general "truth."

**Narrative data.** Physical traces or actuarial records of messages.

**Narrative discourse.** A story-telling class of speech characterized by relatively fixed source-receiver roles.

**Narrative discourse analysis.** An unobtrusive methodology for exploring the meaning, structure, and functions of narrative discourse.

**"Natural" laboratory conversation.** An unprompted talk in a researcher-controlled social setting.

**Natural necessity law.** A theory that explains behavior by referring to causes.

**Naturalistic conversation.** An unprompted talk in an uncontrolled social setting.

**Naturalistic research.** A field study of behaviors that are a part of normal life activity.

**Negative correlation.** See **Inverse correlation.**

**Neo-Aristotelian criticism.** A method of rhetorical criticism that focuses on the rational level of meaning in messages.

**Nominal measurement.** The use of qualitative numerals as labels for classifying a variable's empirical indicators.

**Nondiscursive logic.** See **Creative imagination.**

**Nonparametric test statistics.** Statistical procedures that make no assumptions about either population parameters or sampling distribution shapes.

**Nonparticipant research.** The method of data collection in which the researcher assumes the role of an outside spectator of the collection process.

**Nonprobability sampling.** A nonrandom sampling method that does not ensure the representativeness of selected samples.

**Nonsymmetrical interaction.** An effect occurring when one independent variable's treatment levels do not exhibit opposing results at a second independent variable's treatment levels.

**Nontraditional experiment.** An experiment that accommodates both discrete and continuous independent variables.

**Normal distribution.** A theoretical probability distribution that is symmetrical and bell-shaped; also called a "normal curve."

**Normal science.** Routine scholarly inquiry informed by a single dominant paradigm.

**Null hypothesis.** A conjecture that no relationship exists between population parameters of interest; antithesis of a research hypothesis.

**Numbers.** Quantitative numerals for representing phenomena that take on an ordered set of mathematical values.

**Numerals.** Symbols used to represent the values of a variable's empirical indicators.

**Oblique.** Correlated or dependent.

**Observation unit.** The person or persons from whom one collects information about elements.

**One-tailed test.** A statistical test that takes the probability level required to reject the null hypothesis from the area under only one tail of a sampling distribution.

**Ontology.** Assumptions about the nature of reality or existence.

**Open-ended question.** A statement asking for free and unstructured narrative responses.

**Operational definition.** A statement describing the activities necessary to measure constructs.

**Operationalism.** The tenet of logical positivism according to which theoretical concepts are equivalent to the activities required to measure them.

**Operationalization.** The process of transforming abstract constructs into a set of concrete indicators that can be observed and measured.

**Operative term.** A term designating the nature of the relationship between constructs or variables.

**Opinion question.** A statement soliciting a verbal expression of a respondent's internal inclinations and attitudes.

**Ordinal interaction.** An effect occurring when one independent variable exhibits significant differences at one treatment level of a second independent but not at another level of the second variable.

**Ordinal measurement.** The assignment of numbers to represent the rank order of a series of values.

**Organismic variable.** An internal characteristic of research subjects.

**Organized skepticism.** The ethical principal according to which researchers must be critical of their own research and the research of others.

**Orthogonal.** Uncorrelated or independent.

**Overt research.** The method of data collection in which the individuals being observed are aware of the researcher's presence in the research environment.

**Pairwise comparisons.** Modified $t$-test procedures for systematically assessing differences between every unique pair of groups in a set containing more than two groups.

**Panel study.** A longitudinal survey that follows the same sample across time.

**Paradigm.** A world view or conceptual model that defines how scholarly inquiry should be conducted within a discipline.

**Parameter.** A numerical characteristic of a population.

**Parametric test statistics.** Statistical procedures that incorporate assumptions about either a sample's parent population or the associated sampling distribution.

**Participant research.** The method of data collection in which the researcher contributes a portion of the collected data.

**Pathos.** The emotional content of a message.

**Pearson's phi ($\phi$) coefficient.** A coefficient that

registers the strength of association between two nominal variables having two frequency categories each.

**Pearson's *r* coefficient.** A correlation coefficient that indexes the linear relationship between two variables measured at interval or ratio levels.

**Perlocutionary response.** An utterance that acknowledges the impact of another communicator's illocutionary act.

**Personal constraints.** A researcher's motivations and capabilities.

**Persuasive discourse.** Discourse designed to influence audiences by creating, reinforcing, or changing their attitudes or behaviors.

**Physiological data.** Information derived from physical responses that are not subject to the respondent's conscious control.

**Pluralism.** The belief that multiple alternative paradigms are appropriate for scholarly inquiry.

**Political constraints.** Political ideologies and exigencies.

**Population.** A well-defined, universal set of elements.

**Positive correlation.** See **Direct correlation.**

**Positivism.** See **Logical positivism.**

**Posttest-only control group design.** A simple experiment characterized by the random assignment of subjects to one experimental group and one control group, both of which are posttested but not pretested.

**Power.** The probability of not committing a Type II error; the probability of correctly rejecting a false null hypothesis.

**Pragmatic criticism.** An evaluation of the immediate and long-range effects of a message.

**Pragmatics.** Practical constraints on the means, ends, motives, and consequences of research.

**Predictor variable.** An independent variable.

**Pretest-posttest control group design.** A simple experiment characterized by the random assignment of subjects to one experimental group and one control group, both of which are pretested and posttested.

**Primitive term.** A concept with an agreed-upon meaning.

**Probability distribution.** See **Theoretical probability distribution.**

**Probability sampling.** A scientific method that uses random selection to generate representative samples from populations.

**Problem statement.** An interrogatory or declarative sentence that addresses the relationship between two or more communication variables.

**Programmatic rule.** See Teleonomic script rule.

**Prospectus.** A detailed proposal for research.

**Purposive sampling.** A nonrandom selection of samples that are of particular interest to researchers.

**Qualitative research.** An analysis of narrative data.

**Qualitative scale.** A nominal measure used for differentiating the subclasses associated with constructs.

**Quantitative research.** An analysis of numerical data.

**Quantitative scale.** An ordinal, interval, or ratio scale for measuring variables whose empirical properties have an ordered mathematical relationship among them.

**Questionnaire.** An instrument for collecting survey data.

**Quota sampling.** A nonrandom method of selecting samples from a comprehensive population matrix.

**Random sample.** A sample of fixed size *n* selected in such a way that every other sample of size *n* in the parent population has an equal chance of selection.

**Random (sample) assignment.** A probability method of assigning a sample of subjects to experimental groups.

**Range.** The difference between the highest and lowest scores in a distribution.

**Ranking question.** A closed interrogatory statement employing a series of ordinally scaled response options.

**Rating question.** A closed interrogatory statement employing response options scaled by intervals.

**Ratio measurement.** The assignment of numbers to represent a series of values that have a natural zero point and equal distances between the values.

**Rational empiricism.** The epistemological perspective according to which human understanding is best achieved by applying thought to observational data.

**Rationalism.** The epistemological perspective according to which human thought is the key to understanding the world.

**Rational research model.** A normative conceptualization positing that research problems dictate both the selection of research methods and the allocation of personal and material research resources.

**Reactivity.** The effect whereby people alter their behaviors because of awareness of being observed.

**Reality isomorphism principle.** The rule stating that one's measurement schemes should be similar in structure to the structure of the objects or events being measured.

**Reason.** An intention, purpose, or goal.

**Reductionism.** The tenet of logical positivism according to which the smallest units of observation are preferred and the whole is equal to the sum of its parts.

**Regression analysis.** A statistical procedure for predicting the probable values of a criterion variable based on known values of its predictor variables. See **Multiple regression.**

**Related groups.** Two or more samples that are correlated or associated in some fashion.

**Reliability.** The consistency or stability of a measurement; an index that registers the extent to which measured data are free from random errors of measurement.

**Repeated measures design.** The type of experiment in which the same sample is assigned to each experimental cell.

**Representative sample.** A subset of a population that reflects well the population's important characteristics.

**Research design.** A comprehensive data collection plan whose purpose is to answer research questions and test hypotheses.

**Research game.** The process of accumulating and disseminating information.

**Research hypothesis.** A conjecture that a relationship exists between population parameters.

**Research progression effects.** Changes occurring during a data collection process that can jeopardize research design validity.

**Research question.** An interrogatory statement that asks what kind of relationship, or whether a specified relationship, exists between two or more communication variables.

**Researcher-contrived conversation.** Hypothetical talk constructed by a researcher.

**Researcher effects.** Biosocial and psychosocial characteristics of researchers that can affect research participants' responses.

**Resources.** A researcher's intellectual and material assets and liabilities.

**Respect.** The ethical principle according to which researchers must protect the human rights of research participants.

**Response bias.** A tendency to respond in the same way to a series of measurement scales. Also called a "response set."

**Response rate.** The ratio of the number of elements about which a researcher secures information relative to the total number of elements in a selected sample.

**Revolutionary model.** The perspective on paradigmatic change according to which competing paradigms cannot coexist and paradigmatic change is characterized by the substitution of one rival paradigm for another.

**Revolutionary science.** An unstable period of scholarly inquiry that is informed by competing alternative paradigms.

**Rhetoric.** The faculty of observing in a given case the available means of persuasion.

**Rhetorical community.** Persons who share rhetorical visions or common fantasies.

**Rhetorical criticism.** A humanistic methodology for interpreting and evaluating discourse.

**Rhetorical vision.** An audience's shared fantasy.

**Rule.** A theory that explains a pattern of effects by referring to human intentions, reasons, or goals.

**Sample.** A subset of a population; a group of elements selected from a larger, well-defined pool of elements.

**Sampling deficiency effects.** Sample selection and sample assignment procedures that can affect a research design's validity.

**Sampling distribution.** A distribution of values for a particular sample statistic, obtained from all possible random samples of a given size $n$ selected from a well-defined population.

**Sampling error.** The standard deviation of a sampling distribution; a description of the probable deviations of a population parameter from a given sample statistic at some level of confidence.

**Sampling frame.** A list of the elements in a population.

**Sampling interval.** The constant distance ($k$) between elements systematically selected from a sampling frame.

**Sampling ratio.** The proportion of elements in a desired sample relative to the total number of elements in a sampling frame.

**Sampling unit.** An element or set of elements considered for selection at some stage of sampling.

**Scale.** A scheme for assigning numerals to designate the empirical properties of constructs.

**Scientific inquiry (science).** A systematic investigation of the relationships among and explanations for the empirical phenomena with which a discipline is concerned.

**Scientific revolution.** The replacement of one paradigm with a competing world view.

**Self-report data.** Information gathered by asking people to report on their communicative beliefs and behaviors.

**Semantic differential scales.** A series of seven-point scales whose end points consist of bipolar adjective pairs.

**Significance level.** The probability of committing a Type I (alpha) error; the probability threshold set for rejecting a null hypothesis, conventionally less than .05 or .01.

**Simple experiment.** An experiment employing only one independent variable.

**Simple random sample.** A representative sample that is generated by selecting from a sampling frame all elements with assigned numbers that correspond to a set of randomly derived numbers.

**Single-factor analysis of variance.** A test statistic for assessing mean differences that are attributable to a single independent variable or factor.

**Single-sample chi-square.** A test statistic for assessing differences between or among categories of frequencies associated with a single sample.

**Skewed distribution.** A frequency distribution in which data cluster or "pile up" at one of the end points of a measurement scale.

**Solomon four-group design.** A simple experiment characterized by the random assignment of subjects to four groups, including one experimental and control group pair that is both pretested and posttested and a second experimental and control group pair exposed to posttesting only.

**Standard deviation.** The square root of a distribution's variance.

**Standard error.** The standard deviation of a sampling distribution. See **Sampling error.**

**Standard error of difference between proportions.** The standard deviation of a sampling distribution of proportional (percentage) differences.

**Standard error of difference between means.** The standard deviation of a sampling distribution of mean differences.

**Standard error of estimate.** The standard deviation of a regression line; the margin of error associated with prediction; the common standard deviation of sampling distributions of a criterion value ($Y$) for given values of a predictor ($X$).

**Standard error of proportions.** The standard deviation of a sampling distribution of proportions (percentages).

**Standard error of the mean.** The standard deviation of a sampling distribution of means.

**Statistic.** A numerical characteristic of a sample.

**Statistical regression.** An effect describing the tendency of high and low initial measures in a data set to move toward the mean of the set upon subsequent measurement.

**Statistics** (singular). The science of describing and reasoning from numerical data.

**Stimulus variable.** A variable that is external to research subjects.

**Stratified sample.** A sample that is randomly or systematically selected from elements within certain homogeneous subsets of a population.

**Stratified sampling.** A sampling method in which a sample is randomly or systematically selected from elements within certain homogeneous subsets of a population.

**Structural coherence.** A quality describing the relationship between conversational meanings and conversational goals.

**Sum of squares** (sample). The sum of the squared deviations of all sample scores from the sample mean.

**Survey population.** The actual set of elements from which a sample will be selected.

**Survey research.** The examination of samples for purposes of inferring descriptive and explanatory conclusions about parent populations.

**Symmetrical interaction.** An effect occurring when one independent variable's treatment levels exhibit opposing results at a second independent variable's treatment levels.

**System.** An integrated whole greater than the sum of its interdependent parts.

**Systematic sample.** A sample generated by selecting every *k*th element in a sampling frame, with the first element being selected at random.

**Systematic sampling.** A sampling method in which a sample is generated by selecting every *k*th element in a sampling frame, with the first element being selected at random.

**Systematic variance.** Variations among scores that are attributable to an influence that "pushes" scores in one direction or another. See **Between-groups variance.**

**Systems rule.** A reason-based explanation which assumes that the reasons for behavior inhere in collective or group objectives.

**_t_ test.** A test statistic for assessing the significance of difference between two population means based on data derived from small samples.

**Target population.** An idealized aggregation of all the elements in a population.

**Taxonomy.** A descriptive list of the subclasses associated with constructs; a classification. See **Qualitative scale; Nominal measurement.**

**Teleological explanation.** A theory that accounts for a pattern of effects by referring to subjective reasons for the effects. See **Rule.**

**Teleonomic script rule.** A reason-based explanation that assumes the reasons for behavior to be embedded in individual scripts or programmed repertoires of goal–action linkages.

**Test sensitization.** A heightened awareness level in research participants induced by measurement procedures.

**Test statistic.** A statistic, based on a sampling distribution, used in hypothesis testing.

**Theoretical probability distribution.** A description of data containing all possible scores or values in a theoretical population, together with the probabilities associated with each.

**Theory.** A generalization that stipulates an explanatory relationship between two or more classes of communication phenomena.

**Theory-to-data.** A deductive approach to the discovery of theory, which begins with the formulation of an explanation that is then tested against observations.

**Topic.** The subject matter of a conversation.

**Total nonresponse.** The inability to collect any information about a selected element or elements.

**Total variance.** The sum of systematic or between-groups variance and error or within-groups variance.

**Traditional experiment.** An experiment characterized by the use of discrete independent variables.

**Treatment levels.** Variations or divisions of an independent variable.

**Trend study.** A longitudinal survey that selects different representative samples for analysis at different points in time.

**Turn.** A stretch of uninterrupted talk by a single person.

**Two-tailed test.** A statistical test that takes the probability level required to reject a null hypothesis from the areas under both tails of a sampling distribution.

**Type I error.** The rejection of a true null hypothesis. See **Alpha.**

**Type II error.** The failure to reject (or acceptance of) a false null hypothesis. See **Beta.**

**Typology.** See **Taxonomy.**

**Unidimensional measuring instrument.** A set of measurement scales that, as a group, measure a single dimension associated with a construct.

**Universalism.** The ethical principle according to which all research is subject to evaluation by members of the scholarly community.

**Unobtrusive research.** A method of data collection that removes the researcher from the process of observation.

**U-shaped correlation.** A curvilinear relationship between two variables occurring when one variable initially increases as the other declines, after which the two increase together.

**Utterance.** A verbal assertion.

**Validity.** A quality indicating that a measuring instrument accurately measures the construct it purports to measure.

**Variable.** Any class of communication behaviors that can take on different values.

**Variance.** The sum of the squared deviations of all scores in a distribution about the distribution's mean, divided by one less than the total number of scores, if a sample, and divided by the total number of scores, if a population. See **Mean square.**

**Verification.** The process of testing the validity of a theory. See **Justification.**

**Weltanschauung.** A perspective or viewpoint.

**Within-groups variance.** Differences between samples that are attributable to random error variations. See **Error variance.**

**$z$ test for mean differences.** A test statistic for assessing the significance of difference between two population means based on data drawn from two large independent samples.

**$z$ test for proportional differences.** A test statistic for assessing significance of difference between two large independent samples of frequencies.

# BIBLIOGRAPHY

ACHEN, CHRISTOPHER H. *Interpreting and Using Regression.* Beverly Hills, CA: Sage, 1982.

ADAIR, JOHN G., and SCHACHTER, BRENDA S. "To Cooperate or To Look Good?" The Subjects' and Experimenters' Perceptions of Each Other's Intentions." *Journal of Experimental Social Psychology* 8 (1972): 75–85.

ADORNO, THEODORE W., FRENKEL-BRUNSWICK, ELSE, LENINSON, D. J., and SANFORD, R. N. *The Authoritarian Personality.* New York: Harper & Row, 1950.

ALDENDERFER, MARK S., and BLASHFIELD, ROGER K. *Cluster Analysis.* Beverly Hills, CA: Sage, 1984.

ALINSKY, SAUL D. *Reveille for Radicals.* New York: Vintage Books, 1969.

——————.*Rules for Radicals: A Practical Primer for Realistic Radicals.* New York: Random House, 1971.

AMERICAN ASSOCIATION FOR PUBLIC OPINION RESEARCH. *By-Laws.* New York: American Association for Public Opinion Research, 1977.

AMERICAN PSYCHOLOGICAL ASSOCIATION. *Ethical Principles in the Conduct of Research with Human Subjects.* Washington, DC: American Psychological Association, 1983.

——————. *Publication Manual of the American Psychological Association,* 3rd ed. Washington, DC: American Psychological Association, 1983.

APPLBAUM, RONALD L., and ANATOL, KARL W. E. "Dimensions of Source Credibility: A Test for Reproducibility." *Speech Monographs* 40 (1973): 231–37.

ARISTOTLE. *Rhetoric.* Translated by W. Rhys Roberts. New York: Random House, 1954.

ASHER, HERBERT B. *Causal Modeling,* 2nd ed. Beverly Hills, CA: Sage, 1983.

AUSTIN, JOHN L. *How to Do Things with Words.* Cambridge, MA: Harvard University Press, 1962.

AVEY, ALBERT. *Handbook in the History of Philosophy,* 2nd ed. New York: Barnes & Noble, 1961.

AYER, A. J., ed. *Logical Positivism.* New York: Free Press, 1959.

BABBIE, EARL R. *Survey Research Methods.* Belmont, CA: Wadsworth, 1973.

——————. *The Practice of Social Research,* 3rd ed. Belmont, CA: Wadsworth, 1983.

——————. *The Practice of Social Research,* 4th ed. Belmont, CA: Wadsworth, 1986.

BACH, KENT, and HARNISH, ROBERT M. *Linguistic Communication and Speech Acts.* Cambridge, MA: MIT Press, 1979.

BADIA, PIETRO, and RUNYON, RICHARD P. *Fundamentals of Behavioral Research.* Reading, MA: Addison-Wesley, 1982.

BAILEY, KENNETH D. *Methods of Social Research,* 2nd ed. New York: Free Press, 1982.

BALES, ROBERT F. *Interaction Process Analysis: A Method for the Study of Small Groups.* Reading, MA: Addison-Wesley, 1950.

BASKERVILLE, BARNETT. "Must We All Be 'Rhetorical Critics'?" *Quarterly Journal of Speech* 63 (1977): 107–116.

BELSON, WILLIAM A. "The Effect of Reversing the Presentation Order on Verbal Rating Scales." *Journal of Advertising Research* 6, No. 4 (1966), 30–37.

BEM, DARYL J. "Self-Perception Theory." In *Advances in Experimental Social Psychology,* edited by Leonard Berkowitz. New York: Academic Press, 1972.

BEM, SANDRA L. "On the Utility of Alternative Procedures of Assessing Psychological Androgyny." *Journal of Consulting and Clinical Psychology* 45 (1977): 196–205.

BENOIT, PAMELA. "Structural Coherence Production in the Conversation of Preschool Children." Paper presented at the meeting of the Speech Communication Association, New York, 1980.

BENSON, THOMAS W., and PEARCE, W. BARNETT. "Alternative Theoretical Basis for the Study of Human Communication: A Symposium." *Communication Quarterly* 25 (1977): 3–73.

BERELSON, BERNARD. *Content Analysis in Communication Research.* Glencoe, IL: Free Press, 1952.

BERGER, CHARLES R. "The Covering Law Perspective as a Theoretical Basis for the Study of Human Communication." *Communication Quarterly* 25 (1977): 7–18.

BERGER, CHARLES R., and BRADAC, JAMES J. *Language*

358

and Social Knowledge: Uncertainty in Interpersonal Relations. London: Edward Arnold, 1982.

BERGER, PETER L. The Precarious Vision. Garden City, NY: Doubleday, 1961.

BERLO, DAVID K. The Process of Communication. New York: Holt, Rinehart & Winston, 1960.

BEUCKE, DANIEL A. "News Offered on Home Computers." The Denver Post, May 3, 1985, p. 1-C.

BORMANN, ERNEST G. "Fantasy and Rhetorical Vision: The Rhetorical Criticism of Social Reality." Quarterly Journal of Speech 58 (1972): 396–407.

————. "The Eagleton Affair: A Fantasy Theme Analysis." Quarterly Journal of Speech 59 (1973): 143–59.

————. "Generalizing About Significant Form: Science and Humanism Compared and Contrasted." In Form and Genre: Shaping Rhetorical Action, edited by Karlyn Kohrs Campbell and Kathleen Hall Jamieson. Falls Church, VA: Speech Communication Association, 1978.

————. "Colloquy I. Fantasy and Rhetorical Vision: Ten Years Later." Quarterly Journal of Speech 68 (1982): 288–305.

————. "Symbolic Convergence: Organizational Communication and Culture." In Communication and Organizations: An Interpretive Approach, edited by Linda L. Putnam and Michael E. Pacanowsky. Beverly Hills, CA: Sage, 1983.

BROCKETT, PATRICK, and LEVINE, ARNOLD. Statistics and Probability and Their Applications. Philadelphia: Saunders, 1984.

BRONOWSKI, J. Science and Human Values. New York: Harper & Row, 1965.

BURGOON, MICHAEL; COHEN, MARSHALL; MILLER, MICHAEL D.; and MONTGOMERY, CHARLES L. "An Empirical Test of a Model of Resistance to Persuasion." Human Communication Research 4 (1978): 27–39.

BURKE, KENNETH. A Grammar of Motives. Englewood Cliffs, NJ: Prentice-Hall, 1946.

————. A Rhetoric of Motives. Englewood Cliffs, NJ: Prentice-Hall, 1950.

BURTT, EDWIN ARTHUR. The Metaphysical Foundations of Modern Physical Science. New York: Harcourt Brace Jovanovich, 1927.

————. In Search of Philosophic Understanding. Indianapolis: Hackett, 1980.

BUSBY, LINDA J. "Sex-Role Research on the Mass Media." Journal of Communication 25, No. 4 (1975): 107–131.

CACIOPPO, JOHN T., and PETTY, RICHARD E. "Attitudes and Cognitive Responses: An Electrophysiological Approach." Journal of Personality and Social Psychology 37 (1979): 2181–99.

CAMPBELL, DONALD T. "Reforms as Experiments." American Psychologist 24 (1969): 409–29.

————. "Unjustified Variation and Selective Retention in Scientific Discovery." In Studies in the Philosophy of Biology, edited by Theodosius Dobzhansky and Francisco J. Ayala. London: Macmillan, 1970.

CAMPBELL, DONALD T., and FISKE, DONALD W. "Convergent and Discriminant Validation by the Multitrait–Multimethod Matrix." Psychological Bulletin 56 (1959): 81–105.

CAMPBELL, DONALD T., and STANLEY, JULIAN C. Experimental and Quasi-Experimental Designs for Research. Chicago: Rand McNally, 1963.

CARMINES, EDWARD G., and ZELLER, RICHARD A. Reliability and Validity Assessment. Beverly Hills, CA: Sage, 1979.

CASSIRER, ERNST. Substance and Function and Einstein's Theory of Relativity. Chicago: Open Court, 1923.

————. Language and Myth, translated by Susanne K. Langer. New York: Harper & Row, 1946.

CHESEBRO, JAMES W. "Paradoxical Views of 'Homosexuality' in the Rhetoric of Social Scientists: A Fantasy Theme Analysis." Quarterly Journal of Speech 66 (1980): 127–39.

CHOMSKY, NOAM. Cartesian Linguistics: A Chapter in the History of Rationalist Thought. New York: Harper & Row, 1966.

CHURCHMAN, C. WEST, and ACKOFF, RUSSELL L. Methods of Inquiry. St. Louis: Educational Publishers, 1950.

CLARK, DONALD LEMEN. Rhetoric in Greco-Roman Education. New York: Columbia University Press, 1957.

CODY, MICHAEL J., McLAUGHLIN, MARGARET L., and JORDAN, WILLIAM J. "A Multidimensional Scaling of Three Sets of Compliance-Gaining Strategies." Communication Quarterly 28 (1980): 34–46.

CONRAD, CHARLES. "Chrysanthemums and Swords: A Reading of Contemporary Organizational Communication Theory and Research." Southern Journal of Speech Communication 50 (1985): 189–200.

COOK, THOMAS D., and REICHARDT, CHARLES S. Qualitative and Quantitative Methods in Evaluation Research. Beverly Hills, CA: Sage, 1979.

COPI, IRVING M. Introduction to Logic, 3rd ed. New York: Macmillan, 1968.

COZBY, PAUL C. Methods in Behavioral Research, 3rd ed. Palo Alto, CA: Mayfield, 1985.

CRAIG, ROBERT T., and TRACY, KAREN, eds. Conversational Coherence: Form, Structure and Function. Beverly Hills, CA: Sage, 1983.

CRONBACH, LEE J. "Coefficient Alpha and the Internal Structure of Tests." Psychometrika 16 (1951): 279–334.

————. "Test Validation." In Educational Measurement, 2nd ed., edited by R. Thorndike. Washington, DC: American Council on Education, 1971, pp. 443–507.

CRONEN, VERNON E.; PEARCE, W. BARNETT; and HARRIS, LINDA M. "The Coordinated Management of Meaning: A Theory of Communication." In Human Communication Theory: Comparative Essays, edited by Frank E. X. Dance. New York: Harper & Row, 1982, pp. 73–74.

CRONKHITE, GARY, and LISKA, JO. "Symposium: What Criteria Should Be Used to Judge the Admissibility of Evidence to Support Theoretical Propositions in Communication Research: Introduction." Western Journal of Speech Communication 41 (1977), 6.

CULLEY, JAMES D., and BENNETT, REX. "Selling Women, Selling Blacks," Journal of Communication 26, No. 4 (1976): 160–74.

CUSHMAN, DONALD P. "The Rules Perspective as a Theoretical Basis for the Study of Human Communication." Communication Quarterly 25 (1977): 30–45.

CUSHMAN, DONALD P., and PEARCE, W. BARNETT.

"Generality and Necessity in Three Types of Theory About Human Communication, with Special Attention to Rules Theory." *Human Communication Research* 3 (1977): 345.

CUSHMAN, DONALD P., and WHITING, GORDON C. "An Approach to Communication Theory: Toward a Consensus on Rules." *Journal of Communication* 22 (1972): 217–38.

CUSHMAN, DONALD P.; VALENTINSEN, BARRY; and DIETRICH, DAVID. "A Rules Theory of Interpersonal Relationships." In *Human Communication Theory: Comparative Essays,* edited by Frank E. X. Dance. New York: Harper & Row, 1982.

DAMPIER, SIR WILLIAM CECIL. *A History of Science and Its Relations with Philosophy and Religion,* 4th ed. Cambridge: Cambridge University Press, 1966.

DAYTON, C. MITCHELL. *The Design of Educational Experiments.* New York: McGraw-Hill, 1970.

DEETZ, STANLEY A., and KERSTEN, ASTRID. "Critical Models of Interpretive Research." In *Communication and Organizations: An Interpretive Approach,* edited by Linda L. Putnam and Michael E. Pacanowsky. Beverly Hills, CA: Sage, 1983.

de KRUIF, PAUL. *Microbe Hunters.* New York: Harcourt, Brace and Company, 1926.

DELIA, JESSE G. "Constructivism and the Study of Human Communication." *Quarterly Journal of Speech* 63 (1977): 66–83.

*DENVER POST,* November 5, 1984, 3a.

—————. November 11, 1984, 6I.

DEUTSCH, MORTON, and KRAUSS, ROBERT M. *Theories in Social Psychology.* New York: Basic Books, 1965.

DICK, WALTER, and HAGERTY, NANCY. *Topics in Measurement: Reliability and Validity.* New York: McGraw-Hill, 1971.

DIXON, W. J., ed. *BMDP Statistical Software.* Berkeley, CA: University of California Press, 1983.

DONAHUE, WILLIAM A.; DIEZ, MARY E.; and HAMILTON, MARK. "Coding Naturalistic Negotiation Interaction." *Human Communication Research* 10 (1984): 403–23.

DUPEE, F. W. "General Introduction." In *Selected Writings of Gertrude Stein,* edited by Carl van Vechten. New York: Modern Library, 1962.

ERICKSEN, GERALD L. *Scientific Inquiry in the Behavioral Sciences: An Introduction to Statistics.* Glenview, IL: Scott, Foresman, 1970.

FELDSTEIN, STANLEY, and WELKOWITZ, J. "A Chronology of Conversation: In Defense of an Objective Approach." In *Nonverbal Behavior and Communication,* edited by A. W. Siegman and Stanley Feldstein. Hillsdale, NJ: Lawrence Erlbaum, 1978.

FERMENT IN THE FIELD, Special Issue No. 3, *Journal of Communication* 33 (1983).

FESTINGER, LEON. *A Theory of Cognitive Dissonance.* Stanford, CA: Stanford University Press, 1957.

FESTINGER, LEON, and CARLSMITH, JAMES M. "Cognitive Consequences of Forced Compliance." *Journal of Abnormal and Social Psychology* 58 (1959): 203–210.

FESTINGER, LEON; RIECKEN, HENRY; and SCHACTER, STANLEY. *When Prophecy Fails.* Minneapolis: University of Minnesota Press, 1956.

FEYERBEND, PAUL K. "How To Be a Good Empiricist—A Plea for Tolerance in Matters Epistemological." In *Philosophy of Science: The Delaware Seminar.* Vol. II. New York: Wiley-Interscience, 1963.

FILLENBAUM, SAMUEL. "Prior Deception and Subsequent Experimental Performance: The 'Faithful' Subject." *Journal of Personality and Social Psychology* 4 (1966): 532–37.

FILLENBAUM, SAMUEL, and FREY, ROBERT. "More on the 'Faithful' Behavior of Suspicious Subjects." *Journal of Personality* 38 (1970): 43–51.

FISHER, B. AUBREY. "Evidence Varies with Theoretical Perspective." *Western Journal of Speech Communication* 41 (1977): 12.

—————. "The Pragmatic Perspective of Human Communication: A View from System Theory." *Human Communication Theory: Comparative Essays,* edited by Frank E. X. Dance. New York: Harper & Row, 1982, pp. 192–219.

FISHER, WALTER R. "Narration as a Human Communication Paradigm: The Case of Public Moral Argument." *Communication Monographs* 51 (1984): 1–22.

—————. "The Narrative Paradigm: An Elaboration." *Communication Monographs* 52 (1985): 347–67.

—————. "The Narrative Paradigm: In the Beginning." *Journal of Communication* 35, No. 4 (1985): 74–89.

FLETCHER, JOSEPH. *Situation Ethics: The New Morality.* Philadelphia: Westminster Press, 1966.

FONTES, NORMAN E.; SHELBY, JENNIFER L.; and O'CONNOR, BARBARA. "A Structure–Functional Model of the Message–Attitude–Behavior Relationship." In *Message–Attitude–Behavior Relationship: Theory, Methodology, and Application,* edited by Donald P. Cushman and Robert D. McPhee. New York: Academic Press, 1980, pp. 303–17.

FOX, JAMES ALAN, and TRACY, PAUL E. *Randomized Response: A Method for Sensitive Surveys.* Beverly Hills, CA: Sage, 1987.

FREUND, JOHN E. *Modern Elementary Statistics,* 6th ed. Englewood Cliffs, NJ: Prentice-Hall, 1984.

GABBARD-ALLEY, ANNE S. "A Study of the Influence Strategies and Communication Style of Physicians." Paper presented at Speech Communication Association, Denver, 1985.

GAES, GERALD G.; KALLE, ROBERT J.; and TEDESCHI, JAMES T. "Impression Management in the Forced-Compliance Situation: Two Studies Using the Bogus Pipeline." *Journal of Experimental Social Psychology* 14 (1978): 493–510.

GANZ, JOAN SAFRON. *Rules: A Systematic Study.* Paris: Mouton, 1971.

GEERTZ, CLIFFORD. "Blurred Genres: The Refiguration of Social Thought." *American Scholar* 49 (1979–1980): 165–67.

GERBNER, GEORGE. "The Importance of Being Critical—In One's Own Fashion." *Journal of Communication* 33, No. 3 (1983): 356.

GERBNER, GEORGE, and GROSS, LARRY. "Living with Television: The Violence Profile." *Journal of Communication* 26, No. 2 (1976): 173–99.

GERBNER, GEORGE; GROSS, LARRY; SIGNORIELLI, NANCY; and MORGAN, MICHAEL. "Aging with Television: Images on Television Drama and Conceptions of Social Reality." *Journal of Communication* 30, No. 1 (1980): 37–47.

GERBNER, GEORGE; GROSS, LARRY; MORGAN, MICHAEL; and SIGNORIELLI, NANCY. "The 'Mainstreaming' of America: Violence Profile No. 11." *Journal of Communication* 30, No. 3 (1980): 10–29.

GEORGE, A. L. *Propaganda Analysis: A Study of Inferences Made from Nazi Propaganda in World War II.* Evanston, IL: Row, Peterson, 1959.

GLASS, GENE V, and STANLEY, JULIAN C. *Statistical Methods in Psychology and Education.* Englewood Cliffs, NJ: Prentice-Hall, 1970.

GOFFMAN, ERVING. "Replies and Responses." *Language in Society* 5 (1976): 257–313.

GOLD, RAYMOND L. "Roles in Sociological Field Observation." In *Issues in Participant Observation,* edited by George J. McCall and J. L. Simmons. Reading, MA: Addison-Wesley, 1969, pp. 30–39.

GOLDBERG, JULIA A. "A Move Toward Describing Conversational Coherence." In *Conversational Coherence: Form, Structure, and Stategy,* edited by Robert T. Craig and Karen Tracy. Beverly Hills, CA: Sage, 1983.

GONZALEZ, ALBERTO, and MAKAY, JOHN J., "Rhetorical Ascription and the Gospel According to Dylan." *Quarterly Journal of Speech* 69 (1983): 1–14.

GRENE, MARJORIE. *The Knower and the Known.* Berkeley: University of California Press, 1974.

GRICE, H. PAUL. "The Logic Conversation." In *Syntax and Semantics, Vol. 3, Speech Arts,* edited by Peter Cole and Jerry L. Morgan. New York: Academic Press, 1975.

GRIMSHAW, A. D. "Data and Data Use in an Analysis of Communication Events." In *Explorations in the Ethnography of Speaking,* edited by R. Bauman and J. Sherzer. Cambridge: Cambridge University Press, 1974.

GRÜNBAUM, ADOLF. "Causality and the Science of Human Behavior." *American Scientist* 40 (1952): 667.

GUILFORD, J. P., and FRUCHTER, BENJAMIN. *Fundamental Statistics in Psychology and Education,* 5th ed. New York: McGraw-Hill, 1973.

GUTTMAN, LOUIS. "A Basis for Scaling Qualitative Data." *American Sociological Review* 9 (1944): 139–50.

HAGSTROM, W. O. *The Scientific Community.* New York: Basic Books, 1965.

HANSON, NORWOOD RUSSEL. *Patterns of Discovery.* Cambridge: Cambridge University Press, 1958.

HARRÉ, ROMANO, and SECORD, PAUL F. *The Explanation of Social Behavior.* Oxford: Basil Blackwell, 1972.

HAWES, LEONARD C. *Pragmatics of Analoguing: Theory and Model Construction in Communication.* Reading, MA: Addison-Wesley, 1975.

HAYES, JOSEPH J. "Gayspeak." *Quarterly Journal of Speech* 62 (1976): 256–65.

HEIDER, FRITZ. *The Psychology of Interpersonal Relations.* New York: John Wiley, 1958.

HEISE, DAVID R. "The Semantic Differential and Attitude Research." In *Attitude Measurement,* edited by Gene F. Summers. Chicago: Rand McNally, 1970.

HEMPEL, CARL G. *Aspects of Scientific Explanation and Other Essays in the Philosophy of Science.* New York: Free Press, 1965.

HOBBES, J. R. *Why is Discourse Coherent?* Technical Note 176. Menlo Park, CA: SRI International, 1978.

HOFSTADLER, RICHARD. *Gödel, Escher, Bach: An Eternal Golden Braid.* New York: Basic Books, 1979.

HOLSTI, OLE R. *Content Analysis for the Social Sciences and Humanities.* Reading, MA: Addison-Wesley, 1969.

————. "Content Analysis: An Introduction." In *Reader in Public Opinion and Mass Communication,* 3rd. ed., edited by Morris Janowitz and Paul Hirsch. New York: Free Press, 1981.

HOLTON, GERALD. "Mach, Einstein, and the Search for Reality." In *The Twentieth-Century Science: Studies in the Biography of Ideas,* edited by Gerald Holton. New York: W. W. Norton, 1972, pp. 344–81.

"Homo Narrans: Story-Telling in Mass Culture and Everyday Life," *Journal of Communication* 35, No. 4 (1985): 73–171.

HOMANS, PETER. "Puritanism Revisited: An Analysis of the Contemporary Screen-Image Western." In *Reader in Public Opinion and Mass Communication,* 3rd ed., edited by Morris Janowitz and Paul Hirsch. New York: Free Press, 1981, pp. 230–40.

HUNTER, JOHN E. "Factor Analysis." In *Multivariate Techniques in Human Communication Research,* edited by Peter R. Monge and Joseph N. Cappella. New York: Academic Press, 1980, pp. 229–57.

JACKSON, SALLY. "Building a Case for Claims About Discourse Structure." Paper presented at the Michigan State University Summer Conference on Language and Discourse Processes, East Lansing, 1982.

JACKSON, SALLY, and JACOBS, SCOTT. "The Collective Production of Proposals in Conversational Argument and Persuasion: A Study of Disagreement Regulation." *Journal of the American Forensic Association* 18 (1981): 77–90.

————. "Conversational Argument: A Discourse Analysis Approach." In *Recent Advances in Argumentation Theory and Research,* edited by J. Robert Cox and Charles A. Willard. Carbondale and Edwardsville, IL: Southern Illinois University Press, 1982.

————. "Speech Act Structure in Conversation: Rational Aspects of Pragmatic Coherence." In *Conversational Coherence: Form, Structure, and Strategy,* edited by Robert T. Craig and Karen Tracy. Beverly Hills, CA: Sage, 1983, pp. 47–66.

————. "Strategy and Structure in Conversational Influence Attempts." *Communication Monographs* 50 (1983): 285–304.

JACOBS, SCOTT, and JACKSON, SALLY. "Collaboration Aspects of Argument Production." Paper presented at the meeting of the Speech Communication Association, San Antonio, 1979.

JANIS, IRVING. "The Problems of Validating Content Analysis." In *Language of Politics,* edited by Harold D. Lasswell, et al. Cambridge, MA: MIT Press, 1965, pp. 55–82.

JANOWITZ, MORRIS, and HIRSCH, PAUL, eds. *Reader in*

*Public Opinion and Mass Communication,* 3rd ed. New York: Free Press, 1981.

JOHANNESEN, RICHARD L. *Ethics in Human Communication.* Prospect Heights, IL: Waveland Press, 1978.

JOHNSON, ROBERT. *Elementary Statistics,* 4th ed. Boston: Duxbury Press, 1984.

JOWETT, GARTH, and LINTON, JAMES M. *Movies as Mass Communication.* Beverly Hills, CA: Sage, 1980.

KALTON, GRAHAM. *Introduction to Survey Sampling.* Beverly Hills, CA: Sage, 1983.

KAMIN, L. G. *The Science and Politics of IQ.* New York: John Wiley, 1974.

KANT, IMMANUEL. *Critique of Practical Reason and Other Works,* translated by T. K. Abbott. New York: Longmans, Green, 1909.

——————. *Critique of Pure Reason,* translated by N. Kemp Smith. London: Macmillan, 1929.

KAPLAN, ABRAHAM. *The Conduct of Inquiry.* San Francisco: Chandler, 1964.

KATZ, ELIHU. "The Return of the Humanities and Sociology." *Journal of Communication* 33, No. 3 (1983): 51–52.

KELLEY, HAROLD H. "The Process of Causal Attribution." *American Psychologist* 28 (1973): 107–28.

KELMAN, HERBERT C. "Human Use of Human Subjects: The Problems of Deception in Social Psychological Experiments." *Psychological Bulletin* 67 (1967): 1–11.

KENNEDY, GEORGE. *The Art of Persuasion in Greece.* Princeton, NJ: Princeton University Press, 1963.

——————. *The Act of Rhetoric in the Roman World: 300 B.C.–A.D. 300.* Princeton, NJ: Princeton University Press, 1972.

KENNEDY, JOHN J. *Analyzing Qualitative Data: Introductory Log–Linear Analysis for Behavioral Research.* New York: Praeger, 1983.

KERLINGER, FRED N. *Foundations of Behavioral Research.* New York: Holt, Rinehart & Winston, 1964.

——————. *Foundations of Behavioral Research,* 2nd ed. New York: Holt, Rinehart & Winston, 1973.

KIM, JAE-ON, and MUELLER, CHARLES W. *Factor Analysis: Statistical Methods and Practical Issues.* Beverly Hills, CA: Sage, 1978.

——————. *Introduction to Factor Analysis: What It Is and How To Do It.* Beverly Hills, CA: Sage, 1978.

KISH, LESLIE. *Survey Sampling.* New York: John Wiley, 1965.

KLAPPER, JOSEPH R. *The Effects of Mass Communication.* New York: Free Press, 1960.

KNOKE, DAVID, and BURKE, PETER J. *Log–Linear Models.* Beverly Hills, CA: Sage, 1980.

KRIPPENDORFF, KLAUS. *Content Analysis: An Introduction to Its Methodology.* Beverly Hills, CA: Sage, 1980.

——————. "Clustering." In *Multivariate Techniques in Communication Research,* edited by Peter R. Monge and Joseph N. Cappella. New York: Academic Press, 1980, pp. 259–308.

KRUGLANSKI, ARIE W. "Much Ado About the 'Volunteer Artifacts.'" *Journal of Personality and Social Psychology* 28 (1973): 350.

KUHN, THOMAS S. *The Structure of Scientific Revolutions.* Chicago: University of Chicago Press, 1962.

——————. *The Structure of Scientific Revolutions,* enlarged ed. Chicago: University of Chicago Press, 1970.

——————. "Second Thoughts on Paradigms." In *The Structure of Scientific Theories,* edited by Frederick Suppe. Urbana, IL: University of Illinois Press, 1977.

——————. *The Essential Tension.* Chicago: University of Chicago Press, 1977.

LANGER, ELLEN J. "Rethinking the Role of Thought in Social Interaction." In *New Directions in Attribution Research,* edited by John H. Harvey and Robert F. Kidd. Hillsdale, NJ: Lawrence Erlbaum, 1978, pp. 35–58.

LAZARSFELD, PAUL F.; BERELSON, BERNARD; and GAUDET, HAZEL. *The People's Choice,* 2nd ed. New York: Columbia University Press, 1948.

LAZARSFELD, PAUL F., and MERTON, ROBERT K. *The Communication of Ideas.* New York: Institute for Religious and Social Studies, 1948.

LEVINE, MARK S. *Canonical Analysis and Factor Comparisons.* Beverly Hills, CA: Sage, 1977.

LEWIS-BECK, MICHAEL S. *Applied Regression: An Introduction.* Beverly Hills, CA: Sage, 1980.

LIKERT, RENSIS. "A Technique for the Measurement of Attitudes." *Archives of Psychology,* No. 140. New York: Columbia University Press, 1932.

LINTON, JAMES M. *Movies as Mass Communication.* Beverly Hills, CA: Sage, 1980.

LODGE, MILTON. *Magnitude Scaling: Quantitative Measurement of Opinions.* Beverly Hills, CA: Sage, 1981.

LONG, J. SCOTT. *Confirmatory Factor Analysis.* Beverly Hills, CA: Sage, 1983.

LUTZ, GENE M. *Understanding Social Statistics.* New York: Macmillan, 1983.

MALINOWSKI, BRONISLAW. "The Problem of Meaning in Primitive Languages." In C. K. Ogden and I. A. Richards, *The Meaning of Meaning.* New York: Harcourt, Brace, 1923.

MARTIN, JOANNE. "A Garbage Can Model of the Psychological Research Process." *American Behavioral Scientist* 25 (1981): 131–51.

MASLING, JOSEPH. "Role-Related Behavior of the Subject and Psychologist and Its Effects Upon Psychological Data." In *Nebraska Symposium on Motivation,* edited by David Levine. Lincoln: University of Nebraska Press, 1966.

MAYR, ERNST. "Teleological and Teleonomic: A New Analysis." In *Methodological and Historical Essays in the Natural and Social Sciences, Vol. XIV. Boston Studies in the Philosophy of Science,* edited by R. S. Cohen and M. W. Wartofsky. Boston: D. Reidel, 1974.

McDERMOTT, VIRGINIA. "The Literature on Classical Theory Construction." *Human Communication Research* 2 (1975): 83–84.

McIVER, JOHN P., and CARMINES, EDWARD G. *Unidimensional Scaling.* Beverly Hills, CA: Sage, 1981.

McLAUGHLIN, MARGARET L. *Conversation: How Talk Is Organized.* Beverly Hills, CA: Sage, 1984.

McNEMAR, QUINN. "Opinion–Attitude Methodology." *Psychological Bulletin* 43 (1946): 333.

MEAD, GEORGE HERBERT. *Mind, Self, and Society.* Chicago: University of Chicago Press, 1953.

MERTON, ROBERT K. *Social Theory and Social Structure.* New York: Free Press, 1949.

MILES, MATTHEW B., and HUBERMAN, A. MICHAEL. *Qualitative Data Analysis: A Sourcebook of New Methods.* Beverly Hills, CA: Sage, 1984.

MILGRAM, STANLEY. *Obedience to Authority: An Experimental View.* New York: Harper & Row, 1974.

MILLER, GERALD R. "Research Setting: Laboratory Studies." In *Methods of Research in Communication,* edited by Philip Emmert and William D. Brooks. Boston: Houghton Mifflin, 1970.

————————. "Taking Stock of a Discipline." *Journal of Communication* 33, No. 3 (1983): 40.

MILLER, GERALD R., and BERGER, CHARLES R. "On Keeping the Faith in Matters Scientific." *Western Journal of Speech Communication* 42 (1978): 44–57.

MODERN LANGUAGE ASSOCIATION, *MLA Handbook for Writers of Research Papers,* 2nd ed. New York: Modern Language Association, 1984.

MONGE, PETER R. "The Systems Perspective as a Theoretical Basis for the Study of Human Communication." *Communication Quarterly* 25 (1977): 19–29.

————————. "Multivariate Multiple Regression." In *Multivariate Techniques in Human Communication Research,* edited by Peter R. Monge and Joseph N. Cappella. New York: Academic Press, 1980.

MONGE, PETER R., and CAPPELLA, JOSEPH N. "Introduction." In *Multivariate Techniques in Human Communication Research,* edited by Peter R. Monge and Joseph N. Cappella. New York: Academic Press, 1980, pp. 1–2.

MONGE, PETER R., and DAY, PATRICK D. "Multivariate Analysis in Communication Research." *Human Communication Research* 2 (1976): 207–20.

MUDD, CHARLES S., and SILLARS, MALCOLM O. *Speech: Content and Communication,* 3rd ed. New York: Thomas Y. Crowell, 1975.

MURPHY, G., and LIKERT, RENSIS. *Public Opinion and the Individual.* New York: Harper & Row, 1937.

NACHMIAS, DAVID, and NACHMIAS, CHAVA. *Research Methods in the Social Sciences.* New York: St. Martin's Press, 1981.

NAGEL, ERNEST. *Technology Revisited and Other Essays in the History and Philosophy of Science.* New York: Columbia University Press, 1979.

NEWCOMB, HORACE. "Assessing the Violence Profile Studies of Gerbner and Gross: A Humanistic Critique and Suggestion." *Communication Research* 5 (1978): 264–82.

NEWTON-SMITH, W. H. *The Rationality of Science.* Boston: Routledge & Kegan Paul, 1981.

NEWTSON, DARREN A. "Attribution and the Unit of Perception of Ongoing Behavior." *Journal of Personality and Social Psychology* 28 (1973): 28–38.

————————. "Foundations of Attribution: The Perception of Ongoing Behavior." In *New Directions in Attribution Research,* edited by John H. Harvey, William J. Ickes, and Robert F. Kidd. Hillsdale, NJ: Lawrence Erlbaum, 1976.

NORTHROP, FILMER S. C. *The Logic of the Sciences and the Humanities.* New York: Meridian Books, 1959.

NORTON, ROBERT W. "Nonmetric Multidimensional Scaling in Communication Research: Smallest Space Analysis." In *Multivariate Techniques in Human Communication Research,* edited by Peter R. Monge and Joseph N. Cappella. New York: Academic Press, 1980.

NUNNALLY, JIM C. *Educational Measurement and Evaluation.* New York: McGraw-Hill, 1964.

————————. *Psychometric Theory.* New York: McGraw-Hill, 1978.

OGDEN, C. K., and RICHARDS, I. A. *The Meaning of Meaning.* New York: Harcourt, Brace, 1923.

O'KEEFE, DANIEL J. "Logical Empiricism and the Study of Human Communication." *Speech Monographs* 42 (1975): 169–83.

ORNE, MARTIN T. "On the Social Psychology of the Psychological Experiment: With Particular Reference to Demand Characteristics and Their Implications." *American Psychologist* 17 (1962): 776–83.

OSGOOD, CHARLES E.; SUCI, GEORGE J.; and TANNENBAUM, PERCY H. *The Measurement of Meaning.* Urbana: University of Illinois Press, 1957.

OWEN, D. B. *Handbook of Statistical Tables.* Reading, MA: Addison-Wesley, 1962.

PEARCE, W. BARNETT. "The Coordinated Management of Meaning: A Rules-Based Theory of Interpersonal Communication." In *Explorations in Interpersonal Communication,* edited by Gerald R. Miller. Beverly Hills, CA: Sage, 1976, pp. 17–35.

PEARCE, W. BARNETT, and CRONEN, VERNON E. *Communication, Action, and Meaning: The Creation of Social Realities.* New York: Praeger, 1980.

PEARCE, BARNETT W.; CRONEN, VERNON E.; and HARRIS, LINDA M. "Methodological Considerations in Building Human Communication Theory." In *Human Communication Theory: Comparative Essays,* edited by Frank E. X. Dance. New York: Harper & Row, 1982, pp. 1–41.

PEARCE, W. BARNETT; HARRIS, LINDA M.; and CRONEN, VERNON. *The Coordinated Management of Meaning: Human Communication Theory in a New Key.* Unpublished MS, University of Massachusetts, Amherst, undated.

PEIRCE, CHARLES S. *Essays in the Philosophy of Science.* Edited by Vincent Tomas. Indianapolis: Bobbs-Merrill, 1957.

PHILIPSEN, GERRY. "Linearity of Research Design in Ethnographic Studies of Speaking." *Communication Quarterly* 25 (1977): 42–50.

PHILLIPS, BERNARD S. *Social Research: Strategy and Tactics,* 2nd ed. New York: Macmillan, 1971.

PINGREE, SUZANNE; HAWKINS, ROBERT PARKER; BUTLER, MATILDA; and PAISLEY, WILLIAM. "A Scale for Sexism." *Journal of Communication* 26, No. 4 (1976): 193–200.

POOLE, MARSHALL SCOTT, and HUNTER, JOHN E. "Behavior and Hierarchies of Attitudes: A Deterministic Model." In *Message–Attitude–Behavior Relationship: Theory, Methodology, and Application,* edited by Donald P. Cushman and Robert D. McPhee. New York: Academic Press, 1980, pp. 245–71.

POPPER, KARL R. *The Logic of Scientific Discovery.* New York: Science Editions, 1961.

————————. *Conjectures and Refutations: The Growth of Scientific Knowledge,* 2nd ed. New York: Basic Books, 1965.

_____. "Normal Science and Its Dangers." In *Criticism and the Growth of Knowledge,* edited by Irme Lakatos and Alan Musgrave. Cambridge: Cambridge University Press, 1970.

PUTNAM, LINDA L. "The Interpretive Perspective: An Alternative to Functionalism." In *Communication and Organizations: An Interpretive Approach,* edited by Linda L. Putnam and Michael E. Pacanowsky. Beverly Hills, CA: Sage, 1983, pp. 31–54.

RAGAN, SANDRA L. "Alignment and Conversational Coherence." In *Conversational Coherence: Form, Structure, and Strategy,* edited by Robert T. Craig and Karen Tracy. Beverly Hills, CA: Sage, 1983.

REARDON, KATHLEEN KELLEY. *Persuasion: Theory and Context.* Beverly Hills, CA: Sage, 1981.

REICHENBACH, HANS. *Experience and Prediction.* Chicago: University of Chicago Press, 1938.

REYNOLDS, H. T. *Analysis of Nominal Data.* Beverly Hills, CA: Sage, 1977.

RICHARDS, I. A. *The Philosophy of Rhetoric.* London: Oxford University Press, 1936.

ROKEACH, MILTON. *The Open and the Closed Mind.* New York: Basic Books, 1960.

ROMMETVEIT, RAGNAR. *On Message Structure: A Framework for the Study of Language and Communication.* New York: John Wiley, 1974.

ROSENBERG, MILTON J. *Society and the Adolescent Self-Image.* Princeton, NJ: Princeton University Press, 1965.

_____. "The Conditions and Consequences of Evaluation Apprehension." In *Artifact in Behavioral Research,* edited by Robert Rosenthal and Ralph L. Rosnow. New York: Academic Press, 1969, p. 281.

ROSENTHAL, ROBERT. "Interpersonal Expectations: Effects of the Experimenter's Hypothesis." In *Artifact in Behavioral Research,* edited by Robert Rosenthal and Ralph L. Rosnow. New York: Academic Press, 1969, pp. 181–277.

ROSENTHAL, ROBERT, and ROSNOW, RALPH L. "The Volunteer Subject." In *Artifact in Behavioral Research,* edited by Robert Rosenthal and Ralph L. Rosnow. New York: Academic Press, 1969, pp. 59–118.

ROSSITER, CHARLES M. "Models of Paradigmatic Change." *Communication Quarterly* 25 (1977): 69.

ROYCE, JOSEPH R. *The Encapsulated Man.* New York: Van Nostrand Reinhold, 1964.

RUBIN, REBECCA B.; RUBIN, ALAN M.; and PIELE, LINDA J. *Communication Research: Strategies and Sources.* Belmont, CA: Wadsworth, 1986.

RUSHING, JANICE HOCKER, and FRENTZ, THOMAS S. "'The Deer Hunter': Rhetoric of the Warrior." *Quarterly Journal of Speech* 66 (1980): 392–406.

SACKS, HARVEY; SCHEGLOFF, EMANUEL A.; and JOHNSON, GAIL. "A Simplest Systematics for the Organization of Turn-Taking in Conversation." *Language* 50 (1974): 696–735.

SALTIEL, JOHN, and WOELFEL, JOSEPH. "Inertia in Cognitive Processes: The Role of Accumulated Information in Attitude Change." *Human Communication Research* 1 (1975): 333–44.

SCHEGLOFF, EMANUEL A. "Notes on a Conversational Practice: Formulating Place." In *Studies in Social Interaction,* edited by David Sudnow. New York: Free Press, 1972.

SCHEIDEL, THOMAS M. *Persuasive Speaking.* Glenview, IL: Scott, Foresman, 1967.

SCHRAMM, WILBUR. "The Nature of Communication Between Humans." In *The Process and Effects of Mass Communication,* edited by Wilbur Schramm and Donald F. Roberts. Urbana: University of Illinois Press, 1971, pp. 3–53.

SCOTT, ROBERT L., and BROCK, BERNARD L. *Methods of Rhetorical Criticism: A Twentieth-Century Perspective.* New York: Harper & Row, 1972.

SEARLE, JOHN R. *Speech Acts: An Essay in the Philosophy of Language.* Cambridge: Cambridge University Press, 1969.

_____. *Intentionality: An Essay in the Philosophy of Mind.* Cambridge: Cambridge University Press, 1983.

SEIBOLD, DAVID R. "Attitude–Verbal Report–Behavior Relationships as Causal Processes: Formalization, Test, and Communication Implications." In *Message–Attitude–Behavior Relationship: Theory, Methodology, and Application,* edited by Donald P. Cushman and Robert D. McPhee. New York: Academic Press, 1980, pp. 195–244.

SHIMANOFF, SUSAN B. *Communication Rules: Theory and Research.* Beverly Hills, CA: Sage, 1980.

SILLARS, ALAN. "Attributions and Communication in Roommate Conflicts." *Communication Monographs* 47 (1980): 180–200.

SIMONS, HERBERT W. "The Rhetoric of Science and the Science of Rhetoric." *Western Journal of Speech Communication* 42 (1978): 37–43.

_____. "'Genre-alizing' About Rhetoric: A Scientific Approach." In *Form and Genre: Shaping Rhetorical Action,* edited by Karlyn Kohrs Campbell and Kathleen Hall Jamieson. Falls Church, VA: Speech Communication Association, 1978.

SKINNER, B. F. *Science and Human Behavior.* New York: Free Press, 1953.

_____. *Verbal Behavior.* New York: Appleton-Century-Crofts, 1957.

SMITH, MARY JOHN. *Persuasion and Human Action: A Review and Critique of Social Influence Theories.* Belmont, CA: Wadsworth, 1982.

_____. "Cognitive Schemata and Persuasive Communication: Toward a Contingency Rules Theory." In *Communication Yearbook 6,* edited by Michael Burgoon. Beverly Hills, CA: Sage, 1982.

_____. "Contingency Rules Theory, Context, and Compliance Behaviors." *Human Communication Research* 10 (1984): 489–512.

_____. "The Contingency Rules Theory of Persuasion: An Empirical Test." *Communication Quarterly* 30 (1982): 359–67.

_____. Unpublished data. University of Wyoming, Laramie, 1985.

SMYTH, KILEEN T. "Toward Discourse Categorization of Compliance-Gaining Strategies in Lieu of Influential Context Variables." Unpublished master's thesis, University of Wyoming, Laramie, 1986.

SPECTOR, PAUL E. *Research Designs.* Beverly Hills, CA: Sage, 1981.

SPEED, G. J. "Do Newspapers Now Give the News?" *Forum* 15 (1983): 705–11.

SPINNER, BARRY; ADAIR, JOHN G.; and BARNES, GORDON E. "A Reexamination of the Faithful Subject Role."

*Journal of Experimental Social Psychology* 13 (1977): 543–51.

*SPSS$^X$ USER'S GUIDE.* New York: McGraw-Hill, 1983.

STEVENS, S. S. "Mathematics, Measurement and Psychophysics." In *Handbook of Experimental Psychology,* edited by S. S. Stevens. New York: John Wiley, 1951.

SUPPE, FREDERICK, ed. *The Structure of Scientific Theories,* 2nd ed. Urbana: University of Illinois Press, 1977.

——————. "Historical Realism." In *The Structure of Scientific Theories,* 2nd ed., edited by Frederick Suppe. Urbana: University of Illinois Press, 1977, pp. 650–728.

——————. "Historical Background to the Received View." In *The Structure of Scientific Theories,* 2nd ed., edited by Frederick Suppe. Urbana: University of Illinois Press, 1977, pp. 6–15.

——————. "Swan Song for Positivism." In *The Structure of Scientific Theories,* 2nd ed., edited by Frederick Suppe. Urbana: University of Illinois Press, 1977, pp. 619–32.

SYKES, A. J. M. "Myth in Communication." *Journal of Communication* 20 (1970): 17–31.

TATE, PETER. "Doctors' Style." In *Doctor–Patient Communication,* edited by David Pendleton and John Hasler. London: Academic Press, 1983.

TAYLOR, CHARLES. *The Explanation of Behaviour.* London: Routledge & Kegan Paul, 1964.

TEDESCHI, JAMES T.; SCHLENKER, BARRY R.; and BONOMA, THOMAS V. "Cognitive Dissonance: Private Ratinocination or Public Spectacle?" *American Psychologist* 26 (1971): 685–95.

THURSTONE, LOUIS L. "Attitudes Can Be Measured." *American Journal of Sociology* 33 (1928): 529–54.

TOMPKINS, PHILLIP K. *Communication as Action: An Introduction to Rhetoric and Communication.* Belmont, CA: Wadsworth, 1982.

TOULMIN, STEPHEN. *Human Understanding,* Vol. I. Princeton, NJ: Princeton University Press, 1972.

TRACY, KAREN; CRAIG, ROBERT T.; SMITH, MARTIN; and SPISAK, FRANCES. "The Discourse of Requests: Assessment of a Compliance-Gaining Approach." *Human Communication Research* 10 (1984): 513–38.

TUCKER, RAYMOND K., and CHASE, LAWRENCE J. "Canonical Correlation." In *Multivariate Techniques in Human Communication Research,* edited by Peter R. Monge and Joseph N. Cappella. New York: Academic Press, 1980, pp. 205–28.

U.S. DEPARTMENT OF HEALTH AND HUMAN SERVICES, "Final Regulations Amending Basic HHS Policy for the Protection of Human Subjects." *Federal Register* 16 (1981), 8366–92.

van DIJK, TEUN A. *Text and Context: Explorations in the Semantics and Pragmatics of Discourse.* New York: Longmans, Green, 1977.

VIDMAR, NEIL, and ROKEACH, MILTON. "Archie

Bunker's Bigotry: A Study in Selective Perception and Exposure." *Journal of Communication* 24, No. 1 (1974): 36–47.

WASBY, STEPHEN L. "Rhetoricians and Political Scientists: Some Lines of Converging Interest." *Southern Speech Journal* 36 (1971): 237.

*WASHINGTON POST.* November 4, 1984, A16.

WEAVER, WARREN. "Imperfections of Science." In *Science: Method and Meaning,* edited by S. Rapport and H. Wright. New York: Washington Square Press, 1964.

WEBB, EUGENE J.; CAMPBELL, DONALD T.; SCHWARTZ, RICHARD D.; and SECHREST, LEE. *Unobtrusive Measures: Nonreactive Research in the Social Sciences.* Chicago: Rand McNally, 1966.

WEBER, MAX. *The Theory of Social and Economic Organization,* translated by A. M. Henderson and Talcott Parsons, edited by Talcott Parsons. New York: Free Press, 1964.

WEBER, STEPHEN J., and COOK, THOMAS D. "Subject Effects in Laboratory Research: An Examination of Subject Roles, Demand Characteristics, and Valid Inference." *Psychological Bulletin* 77 (1972): 273–95.

WELLS, G.; MacCLURE, M.; and MONTGOMERY, M. "Some Strategies for Sustaining Conversation." In *Conversation and Discourse: Structure and Interpretation,* edited by P. Werth. New York: St. Martin's Press, 1981.

WELLS, W. D., and SMITH, GEORGIANNA. "Four Semantic Rating Scales Compared." *Journal of Applied Psychology* 44 (1960): 393–97.

WICHELNS, HERBERT. The Literary Criticism of Oratory." In *Studies in Rhetoric and Public Speaking in Honor of James Albert Winans,* edited by A. M. Drummond. New York: Century, 1925.

WILDER, CAROL. "The Palo Alto Group: Difficulties and Directions of the Interactional View for Human Communication Research." *Human Communication Research* 5 (1979): 176–77.

WILLIAMS, FREDERICK. *Language and Speech: Introductory Perspectives.* Englewood Cliffs, NJ: Prentice-Hall, 1972.

——————. *Reasoning with Statistics,* 2nd ed. New York: Holt, Rinehart & Winston, 1979.

WOELFEL, JOSEPH. "Foundations of Cognitive Theory: A Multidimensional Model of the Message–Attitude–Behavior Relationship." In *Message–Attitude–Behavior Relationship: Theory, Methodology, and Application,* edited by Donald P. Cushman and Robert D. McPhee. New York: Academic Press, 1980.

WOELFEL, JOSEPH, and DANES, JEFFREY E. "Multidimensional Scaling Models for Communication Research." In *Multivariate Techniques in Human Communication Research,* edited by Peter R. Monge and Joseph N. Cappella. New York: Academic Press, 1980, pp. 333–64.

WRAGE, ERNEST J. "Public Address: A Study in Social and Intellectual History." *Quarterly Journal of Speech* 33 (1947): 451–57.

# NAME INDEX

# SUBJECT INDEX

## A

Action theory, 5, 18, 304, 312–314

Actional realism, 304, 345

Actionalism, 304, 345

Activist research, 289, 345
  defined, 289, 345
  and ethics, 289

Adjacency pair, 241, 248, 345

"After dinner" speech, 260

All-organismic experiment, 200–201, 212, 345

*All Quiet on the Western Front,* 259

All-stimulus experiment, 200, 212, 345

Alpha coefficient, 47

Alpha error. See Type I error.

Alpha level. See Significance level.

Alternative hypothesis. See Research hypothesis.

*Amos 'n Andy,* 265

Analysis of variance, 130–137, 210, 345
  defined, 130–131, 345
  multiple-factor, 132–137
  single-factor, 131–132

Analytical research, 262

Anonymity, 287, 345

ANOVA. See Analysis of variance.

*Apocalypse Now,* 259

Applied research, 182, 219, 289–290, 345
  defined, 182
  and ethics, 289–290
  and surveys, 219

"Archie Bunker," 260

Artistic criticism, 270, 273, 345

Attrition. See Mortality.

Availability sampling. See Convenience sampling.

## B

Bar graph, 94, 345

Basic research, 182, 345

Behavioral data, 55, 345

Behavioral rules, 238–239, 345

Bell-shaped distribution. See Normal distribution.

Beta error. See Type II error.
Between-groups variance, 125, 345

Bimodal distribution, 99, 101

Binomial sampling distribution, 121

Bivariate correlation, 153, 155–160, 345
  and Cramer's $V$, 158–160
  and curvilinearity, 157–158
  defined, 153, 345
  and frequency data, 158–160
  and interval/ratio data, 155–157
  and Pearson's phi, 158–160
  and Pearson's $r$, 155–157

Black rhetoric, 271–272, 290

BMDP statistical software, 147, 172

Boundary condition, 11, 26–27, 312–313

Brute facts, 9

## C

Canonical correlation, 161, 172

Case study, 85, 242

Categorical data. See Frequency data.

Causal explanation (Also see Laws), 11, 308–309, 311–312, 345

Causal modeling (Path analysis), 161, 172

Cause, 11, 308–309, 312, 345

CBS News-*New York Times* poll, 75

Cell, 197, 345

Central tendency, 99–102
  defined, 99
  indices of, 99–102

Chi-square distribution, 340–342

Chi-square test, 140–144, 158–160, 345
  and contingency table analysis, 142–144
  and correlation, 158–160
  multiple-sample, 142–144, 351
  single-sample, 140–142, 355

Chi-square values, 140–143, 158–160, 340–342
  expected, 140, 143
  maximum, 158–159
  observed, 140, 143, 158

Civil rights, 271–272, 285, 287, 290
  and ethics, 285, 287
  rhetoric of, 271–272, 290

Classical canons of rhetoric. See Rhetoric.

Closed question, 27, 68, 226, 346

# GLOSSARY OF SYMBOLS

| | |
|---|---|
| $d$ | deviation of a sample score from the sample mean |
| $D$ | deviation of a subgroup mean from the grand mean; also, deviation of a sample score from the population mean |
| df | degrees of freedom |
| $E$ | expected frequency |
| $F$ | F distribution statistic |
| $H_0$ | null hypothesis |
| $H_1, \ldots, H_n$ | research (or alternative) hypothesis |
| $k$ | number of categories or cells in a sample |
| MS | mean square |
| $n$ | sample size |
| $N$ | population size; also, grand sum |
| $O$ | observed frequency |
| $p$ | probability; also population proportion |
| $\bar{p}$ | sample proportion |
| $\bar{p}_e$ | estimate of a population proportion |
| $q$ | $1 - p$ |
| $\bar{q}$ | $1 - \bar{p}$ |
| $\bar{q}_e$ | $1 - \bar{p}_e$ |
| $r$ | a linear correlation coefficient |
| $r^2$ | a linear coefficient of determination |
| $R$ | a multiple linear correlation coefficient |
| $R^2$ | a multiple linear coefficient of determination |
| $s$ | sample standard deviation |
| $s^2$ | sample variance |